Management Science

J. C. Hsiao
Chairman, Department of Economics
Southern Connecticut State College

David S. Cleaver
Coordinator, Management Information Systems
Connecticut State Department of Education

Houghton Mifflin Company Boston
Dallas Geneva, Illinois Hopewell, New Jersey Palo Alto London

Printed in the U.S.A.

Library of Congress Catalog Card Number: 80-80960

ISBN: 0-395-29488-6

To Jean, Eugene, and Huey Hsiao
and William G. Cleaver

CONTENTS

PREFACE

Readers of this book—students, faculty, and practitioners—will find it to be a comprehensive introduction to management science. The treatment of the quantitative techniques used in management science begins at ground zero with logical development of elementary terms and concepts. Topics are developed to the point where the reader who is confronted with a practical application will have gained sufficient knowledge to tackle the situation and properly interpret the results. Since courses in operations research techniques for managerial decision making have become a standard part of the business curriculum, we have designed this text for upper-level undergraduate or beginning graduate courses offered in business or public administration and in economics.

A unique feature of our presentation is the way in which we have tried to explain their use of quantitative methods. Insofar as the development of management science has benefited from basic economic theory, we often present underlying economic concepts to fully clarify why a particular method works as it does. This means that we treat basic trade-off concepts, in particular marginal analysis and opportunity costs. This approach, we believe, leads toward a better understanding of the methods involved. It also allows us to offer reasonable explanations of difficult topics, such as integer programming and quadratic programming. Furthermore, our goal is to inspire interest in using management science's tools of analysis. We avoid rigorous mathematical proofs; rather, we stress the application and illustration of techniques. The reader, by using this approach of economic reasoning and motivation, will be able to master the techniques rather than be enslaved by them. Techniques may soon be forgotten, but the concepts behind the techniques should remain with students after they complete their tour of this book.

Organization of the Text

The text is organized in two general divisions. The first of these treats deterministic, programming models including, of course, linear programming and duality concepts, the transportation model, and the assignment problem. Also featured in this first section are comprehensive introductions to integer programming, goal programming, and quadratic programming. The second major division presents probability methods and stochastic decision-making models. Included here are Bayesian models, inventory models, queuing models, simulation techniques, game theory, and Markov processes. Refer to the organization chart for an overview of these topics in the textbook. Notice also that dynamic programming, PERT, and forecasting techniques are presented at appropriate points. Relating to all of these, a short introduction to methods of solving complex quantitative decision problems using computer routines is given.

The introduction of linear programming in Chapter 2 provides a beginning for the subsequent discussion of quantitative optimization methods. Three elementary examples in this chapter are carried through in later chapters as illustrations of linear programming and goal programming models. This approach will enable students, we believe, to apply new ideas and techniques to familiar problems, an approach that will reduce "new material shock." Underlying assumptions are carefully presented and discussed to help students in mastering the tools of analysis.

In Chapter 3, we incorporate the economic and logical explanations of procedural operations to be used in applying the simplex method. We believe this is pertinent because it enables students to acquire both mechanical orientation and theoretical understanding without being bogged down in sophisticated mathematical details.

We consider duality to be the central underlying concept of linear programming and essential for a complete understanding of linear programming, transportation problems, quadratic programming, and game theory. Presenting the simplex tableau with the objective function in the last row—see Chapters 3 and 4—eases conversion to the study of dual problems by providing a convenient symmetry to the simplex tableaus of the primal and dual problems. Furthermore, this device not only makes the subsequent primal-dual formulation for quadratic programming more straightforward, but also simplifies the presentation of the simplex tableau for goal programming models. We consider this to be a pedagogical innovation.

Transportation problems and the closely related assignment problems are presented in Chapter 5. Heavily influenced by Koopmans' original contribution, the transportation algorithm is fully explained using duality and economic interpretation—considerations that are seldom presented in other management science or operations research textbooks.

Following a logical arrangement, with appropriate development from elementary to more complex operations, we introduce the chapters on integer programming, goal programming, quadratic programming and dynamic programming. Naturally, as in other management science or quantitative textbooks, the procedural operations and techniques of these topics require much calculation. Consequently, carefully formulated, step-by-step instructional sequences have been prepared to assist readers in grasping these basics. Here again, the underlying logic using economic reasoning is given. The broad scope of programming methods is completed by covering dynamic programming. This is followed by Chapter 10 where PERT techniques are introduced.

In Chapter 11, Bayesian decision theory and the basic concepts of probability theory lead into the treatment of decision-making models in Chapters 12 through 16. Chapter 11 offers careful treatment of Bayes' Theorem and of differences between the Bayesian and classical approaches. In Chapters 12 and 13, the inventory and queuing models demonstrate fundamental trade-off concepts. By placing these chapters in sequence, the textbook emphasizes the similarity of underlying economic concepts even in seemingly different operational problems. Basic simulation techniques are begun in Chapter 13 on queuing, and are then expanded in Chapter 14, which shifts away from queuing examples and provides a unique business decision-making model involving competing firms and sequential periods of decision making. The model can either be operated by hand calculations or be computerized. It is suitable for teams of students to use in competition with one another. This broad section of the textbook dealing with stochastic models is completed with chapters on game theory and Markov chains.

Among the indispensable tools of management science for business decision making, we feel that one must include forecasting techniques and an appropriate orientation to computer methodology. There is no doubt that realistic business situations require knowledge of these methods as part of the decision-making process, and treatment of these topics therefore has been presented in Chapters 17 and 18, respectively. These chapters, together with the chapters on goal programming and quadratic programming, offer a most comprehensive coverage of quantitative decision-making techniques.

As a final perspective, insights are presented in Chapter 19 into the future opportunities and potentials in the field of management science for business decision making. Above all, an attempt has been made throughout all chapters to conform to a fundamental goal of this text—that it should be readable and teachable.

With regard to mathematical prerequisites, no calculus or matrix algebra is needed for using this text. Extensive exercises are presented at the end of each chapter. The overall purpose of these exercises is to reinforce the reader's understanding of the basic concepts of quantitative methods and to provide the reader with a *working* knowledge of the application of quantitative techniques. To achieve this purpose, all exercises were selected so that the need to do computations by hand should not intimidate students. Each chapter is also followed by a list of suggested readings.

Many persons have given us help in the preparation of this book. Our chief acknowledgment must go to our colleagues who have reviewed the entire manuscript and made helpful suggestions and comments that have led to substantial improvement. They are: Professor Nesa L. J. Wu of Eastern Michigan University, Professor Donald S. Miller of Emporia State University, Professor Stanley R. Schultz of Cleveland State University, and Professor Whewon Cho of Tennessee Technological University. We also extend our thanks to both Professors Howard A. Plotkin and Andrew J. Thacker, Jr., of the University of Houston, who evaluated several preliminary chapters of our manuscript in its early stages. Others who have provided valuable assistance are Dr. Andrew Hook of the New York Federal Reserve Bank, Professor T. C. Lee of the University of Connecticut, and Professors Yu-Chu Hsu and Frank E. Whelan of Southern Connecticut State College. To them we are indebted.

The unedited version of the manuscript has been used several times in both undergraduate and graduate classes at Southern Connecticut State College. Needless to say, we are extremely grateful to all students who have used these materials and helped improve them by their reactions.

J. C. H.
D. S. C.

1

Introduction

Everyone must make decisions. How well these decisions are made affects the success of individuals, the performance of organizations, and ultimately the well-being of society. Many decision problems are deeply rooted in the economic problem of allocating scarce resources.

In recent years, the industrialized world has witnessed the rapid development of quantitative tools for solving increasingly complex management problems. The primary purpose of this book is to present and illustrate these quantitative analyses.

1.1 Economizing Resources and Decision Making

The fundamental problem of economics and business is the need to choose among alternative uses of scarce resources in order to achieve the greatest return from them. The key words are ***scarce***, ***alternative***, and ***greatest***.

Scarcity means that resources are not free; any scarce resource has a price attached to it. If resources were free, there would be no economic problem—everyone would be able to obtain enough of everything to satisfy all wants. Although air may still be a free resource in such places as Alaska and Wyoming, it can no longer be considered free (at least not to society, which must pay for keeping it fit to breathe) in such cities as Pittsburgh and New York. The supply of all resources (including land, labor, capital, and managerial ability) is limited; we must use them efficiently to receive the optimal return from them.

Choosing among alternative uses implies cost considerations. Allocating more of a resource for one use means that there will be less available for other uses. Suppose a company produces both machines and related antipollution equipment but has limited production capacity. If the company decides to produce large amounts of machinery, production of the antipollution equipment may have to be forgone. On the other hand, if large amounts of antipollution equipment are to be produced, contracts for machinery may have to be forgone. Scarcity forces the company to choose and to forgo an alternative. The cost of this forgone alternative is called an ***opportunity cost.*** Opportunity costs always are measured in terms of forgone alternatives.

Allocation implies action and decision making. Given a limited amount of resources, people must make decisions that yield the greatest possible return for the given situation. Each individual, business firm, and organization—and even each society—must make its own choices among options and among actions. People make decisions routinely in their everyday lives. What food to eat? What clothing to wear? What music to listen to? What TV program to watch? What course to take in college? These simple decisions involve intuition and common sense. However, an opportunity cost is always attached to any decision that involves scarcity.

People often make wrong decisions in their daily lives without disastrous consequences. For example, a person may choose to eat a piece of apple pie for dessert and may later regret not eating strawberries instead. Even though there was opportunity cost in the form of regret, this kind of wrong decision can hardly cause serious trouble. One chooses between strawberries and apple pie on the basis of snap judgment. Any application of sophisticated techniques and/or analysis to a decision of this sort is obviously unnecessary—and might even encourage making no decision at all.

Most important personal and business decisions, however, cannot be made simply on the basis of common sense or snap judgment. Common sense may be misleading or incorrect, and snap decisions may cause varying degrees of discomfort in our lives. For very large business firms (like General Motors, IBM, or U.S. Steel), a wrong decision may not only lead to serious misfortune, such as loss of profit or possible bankruptcy, but it could also affect national or even international economies. Because of the complex nature of the modern business, management must make sound decisions on the basis of scientific knowledge. Business managers must often invoke the scientific method to help them make the proper choices. Therefore, decision makers in the realm of business must understand scientific methodology.

1.2 Scientific Methodology

Scientific methodology consists of logical steps by which researchers seek the real nature of a problem on the basis of objective and explicit criteria rather than subjective opinions. The steps involved in the scientific method are essentially the same as those in the field of management science for business decision making. Briefly, these are enumerated and explained in the following paragraphs.

Step 1 ***Identify the Problem*** Identifying or formulating the problem for investigation is a basic step in any scientific inquiry. The simple logic is that one can hardly get the ***right*** answer by solving the ***wrong*** problem! If the problem is identified incorrectly, the solution derived from it is apt to be useless, and efforts devoted to answering it have been wasted. Research is not undertaken solely for its own sake, but in order to realistically solve a particular problem. Furthermore, determining pertinent goals or objectives is a very important aspect of problem formulation. Consequently, one should exercise considerable care in the first step of problem formulation. In practice, it is important to reexamine this formulation continually in the light of new evidence or observations obtained during later steps of inquiry.

Step 2 ***Formulate a Hypothesis or Construct a Model*** A hypothesis is a premise or proposition advanced to describe or explain some observed phenomenon. It can be stated merely as a provisional conjecture to direct investigation, or it can be accepted as highly probable in the light of accumulated evidence. A hypothesis often takes the form of a ***model***—that is, a theoretical abstraction of the actual problem. By specifying relevant variables and assumptions, one reduces complex problems to manageable proportions. Through analysis and manipulation of the model, the researcher arrives at logical solutions that can be applied in turn to the actual problem. In modern business operations research, the concepts of models and model building constitute the very heart of the analysis. Various basic forms of decision-making models and their usefulness will be the subject of Section 1.3 of this chapter.

Step 3 ***Collect Relevant Data*** Having identified the problem and formulated a hypothesis about it, the next step is to gather relevant data. This step may require substantial effort, and assembling irrelevant data would be time-consuming and economically wasteful. For this reason, ***the scientific researcher does not collect data prior to the completion of steps***

1 and 2, because one may not know what information is pertinent until the problem is formulated properly and until the purpose and relationships of important variables in the model are postulated.

Step 4 *Analyze Data and Test the Hypothesis* Experiments with the observed data must be designed and performed to test the hypothesis and to work out results that may be expected to flow from the hypothesis. In this way, the empirical results can be checked for consistency with the hypothesis. Only after the hypothesis has been tested rigorously by well-designed experiments can it be accepted as valid.

Step 5 *Verification and Conclusion* Testing the hypothesis implies its confirmation or verification, thus enabling the investigator to draw conclusions. If the empirical results do not support the hypothesis, that hypothesis must be rejected. In either case—acceptance or rejection of the hypothesis—the conclusion should be interpreted in view of the defined problem and the stated assumptions.

The steps of the scientific method are not a rigidly defined set of rules or procedures. In practice, the scientific method involves continual feedback and reexamination in the light of new evidence and insights generated by the ongoing study of the problem.

1.3 Management Science and Quantitative Methods

Meaning of Management Science The early application of management science to business and organizations can be traced back many decades, even centuries. But modern management science was born during World War II when the British military management called a group of scientists together to study the strategies and tactics of various military operations. The goal was efficient allocation of scarce resources for the war effort. The name ***operations research*** came directly from the context in which it was used and developed: research on (military) operations.

British scientists spurred the American military management to similar research activities. The success of the new technique in England and the United States interested the private sector in using operations research to assist in managerial decision making. In this realm, the term ***management science*** has become synonymous with ***operations research.*** In fact, professional organizations such as the Institute of Management Science and the Operations Research Society have often held joint meetings and their membership overlaps to a large extent. Many colleges and universities that offer programs in business, economics, public administration, industrial engineering, and the like include management science or operations research courses as part of their required curriculum. Today management science is widely used, not only in the military and in business and industry, but also in such governmental pursuits as mass transit, regional planning, and even crime investigation and prevention.

Investigation of a management science problem should follow the scientific methodology that was presented in Section 1.2. Typically, management science seeks to find the best decision for achieving a given objective. Hence, in simplified form, management science involves at least the following steps:

1. Identify the problem area wherein the decision is needed and choose the right objective of the firm or organization.
2. Construct the relevant models.
3. Find the best way to achieve the objective.

From a business point of view, management science must attempt to resolve any conflicts that may exist within an organization by selecting the objective(s) that best fit the organization as a whole. Therefore, a distinguishing feature of management science is its wholistic approach to management's decision making and problem solving.

Decision-Making Models

The concepts of models and model building are at the very heart of modern management science. We will now examine models and their classification (Figure 1.1) and usefulness in some detail.

Physical Models A physical or schematic representation of a real object is generally called a ***physical model.*** There are two types of physical models, analog models and iconic models. An ***analog model*** looks and works like the object or system it represents. Many children's toys, for example, a model railroad, are all analog models. Whereas the real objects are complex and might not allow direct handling or manipulation, the analog models that portray these objects or systems usually are simple and easy to see and understand. They are especially useful for demonstration.

A photographic or schematic representation of an object is called an ***iconic model.*** Technical drawings of airplanes or houses, blueprints, city maps, and engineers' drawings of construction projects are all iconic models. Iconic models might also be flow charts or organization charts.

Figure 1.1
A Diagrammatic Classification of Models

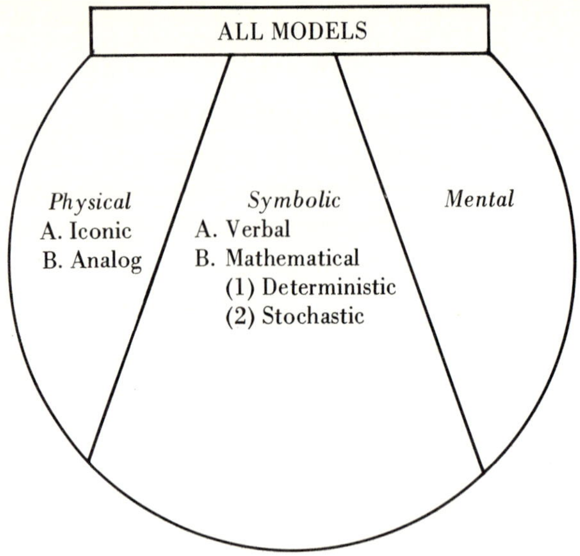

Very often flow charts are useful in showing or summarizing certain routinized procedures or steps. Some of the methods presented in this book have been summarized in this way, using ordinary flow charts.

Mental Models A mental image or conceptual representation of some phenomenon or object is a ***mental model.*** An example is a manager's concept of the firm's market. Even though mental models may not be cast in a precise, concrete, or visible form, they are commonly used by management in decision making. Often, other types of models evolve from mental models.

Symbolic Models Many actual problems can be described with ***symbolic models,*** in either verbal or mathematical form. ***A verbal model*** describes a situation in spoken language or written words. For example, a book is a verbal model. Very often one uses verbal models to explain other types of models.

Mathematical models are generally the most abstract and sophisticated models of all. Unlike verbal models, they use mathematical notation to represent, in a precise way, the variables of real situations. Such models are indispensable for abstracting the essence of a problem under study, for showing the interrelationships among all decision variables, and for facilitating analysis of the overall structure of the problem. In particular, mathematical models help the decision maker to evaluate cause-and-effect relationships and to predict the relative effects of alternative courses of action with measurable accuracy.

Modern management science approaches may use various types of mathematical models, the two broad categories of which are deterministic and probabilistic models. In a ***deterministic model,*** all the coefficients or parameters in the mathematical formulation are fixed at predetermined values. Errors and uncertainty are excluded from the model. In a ***probabilistic model***, some or all of the basic characteristics may be ***random variables—variables that can assume a number of values with given probabilities.*** Uncertainty, or the chance for error, must be explicitly included in probabilistic models. A random variable is sometimes called a ***stochastic*** or chance variable, and probabilistic models are called ***stochastic models.***

It is important to recognize the limitations of the various types of models. For example, some physical models (iconic or analog) may be too simple to be useful in managerial decision making. On the other hand, mathematical models may be too idealized to give a valid representation of an actual problem. Furthermore, mathematical models are conditioned by quantifiable data. Because many imponderables and qualitative factors affect outcomes, management should apply mathematical models cautiously. The proper criterion for judging the validity of any model is whether it helps us understand and analyze real problems.

Quantitative Methods and Management Science

Determining the best way to achieve an objective is another essential aspect of management science. After we construct an appropriate mathematical model for the problem under investigation, our next step is to manipulate the model and to obtain the optimal problem solution. To ***optimize*** may mean to maximize output, profit, or market share, or to minimize cost. Here the need for special quantitative techniques inevitably arises, because various mathematical models contain many variables and sophisticated structures. Consequently, management-science models have generated a number of quantitative methods or techniques suitable for dealing with these mathematical structures. Management-science models depend heavily on the use of quantitative methods.

During the past several decades, a parallel development in computer science has reinforced the usefulness and adaptability of quantitative methods for managerial decision making. The computer's capacity to perform high-speed computation, data storage, and retrieval has made it possible for decision makers to use quantitative analysis to help solve highly complex and detailed problems.

1.4 The Quantitative Approach and Business Applications: Illustrative Examples

Breakeven Analysis

In this section, a simple quantitative technique used by many business decision makers—breakeven analysis—will be discussed. We present this technique here to demonstrate the mathematical formulation of a business problem in quantitative terms. Breakeven analysis assumes that total revenue and total cost are directly proportional to volume of output and that only one product is under consideration. A ***breakeven point*** is defined to be that level of output at which total revenue and total cost are equal. In a ***breakeven chart*** (Figure 1.2) the breakeven point indicates the least volume of output that the firm can sell or produce without incurring a loss. Any output in excess of the breakeven volume is profitable.

To formulate this mathematical model, let us first identify the set of variables involved. Let

$$Q = \text{output volume}$$
$$R = \text{total revenue}$$
$$C = \text{total cost}$$

The last two variables are measured in dollars. The following assumptions apply: First, total revenue R depends on the quantity of output

Figure 1.2
Breakeven Chart Indicating the Breakeven Quantity at Point B

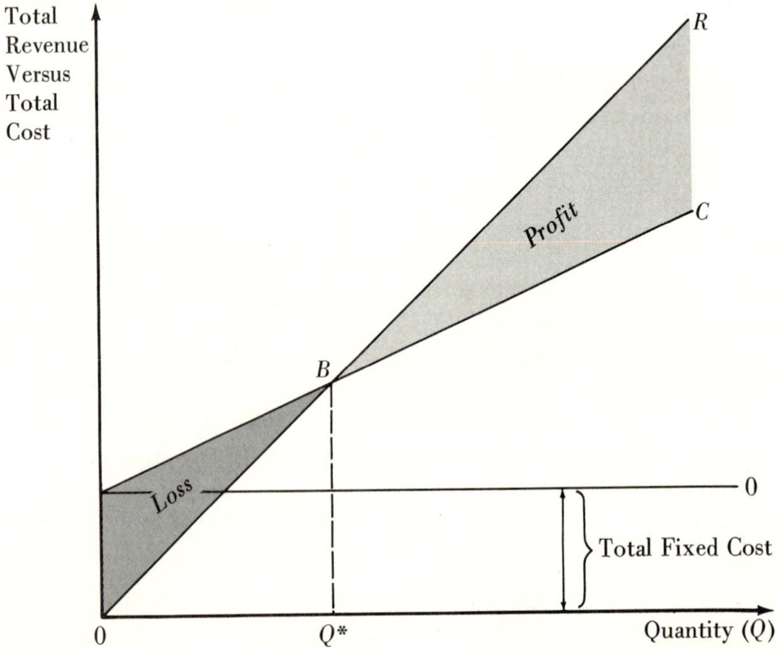

sold and its selling price per unit, p. For a given price p, total revenue R is assumed to be an increasing linear function of volume Q. That is, Q and R are directly (or positively) related. Second, total cost C is the sum of total fixed cost F and total variable cost vQ, where v represents the variable cost ***per unit.*** The total fixed cost F does not vary with the number of units of output sold. Therefore, total cost C is also an increasing linear function of volume.

The preceding paragraph can be translated into the following mathematical model:

$$R = pQ \qquad (p > 0) \tag{1.1}$$

$$C = F + vQ \qquad (F > 0,\ v > 0) \tag{1.2}$$

Note that the variables R, C, and Q in the model are subject to the control of the decision maker; that is, they are ***endogenous variables.*** Fixed costs, on the other hand, affect the controllable variables but are not subject to the control of the decision maker in the short run. Consequently, the total fixed cost F is referred to as an ***exogenous variable*** (constant in the short run). The constants p and v are ***parameters*** of the model. The values of exogenous variables are generally determined by forces external to the model. The values of endogenous variables are determined by the model. Of course, this distinction is meaningful only in the context of a given model. A term that is endogenous in one model may well be exogenous in another.

By definition, the breakeven output Q^* is derived by equating total revenue and total cost:

$$R = C \quad \text{or} \quad pQ = F + vQ \tag{1.3}$$

Rearranging and factoring (1.3) results in

$$(p - v)\,Q = F \tag{1.4}$$

$$\therefore\ Q^* = \frac{F}{p - v} \qquad \text{for } p > v \tag{1.5}$$

In equation (1.5) we compute the breakeven quantity by dividing fixed cost by price minus average variable cost. Why do we impose the restriction that price be greater than variable cost? The meaning of this restriction is illustrated in the breakeven chart shown in Figure 1.2. Graphically, the breakeven quantity (solution) is indicated by the breakeven point B where the two lines R and C intersect. For a meaningful solution, the selling price per unit must be greater than the variable cost per unit; otherwise, a negative breakeven output would result. This might be mathematically correct, but it makes no sense economically! We emphasize this point to remind the decision maker that mathematical models are only tools based on certain assumptions and restrictions. The user of the tool must always be its master, not its slave.

The position of the breakeven point is important to management. Other things being equal, a firm obviously strives for a lower breakeven point so that it can begin to realize profit at a lower sales volume. The effect of manipulating variables in order to do this will now be discussed.

Example An industrial manufacturing company makes a product, the selling price of which is \$10. The firm's fixed costs—full-time employees' salaries, rent, insurance fees, and other expenses—are \$6,000 per month. If the variable costs are \$5 for each unit produced, what is the breakeven volume? We have given

$$p = 10 \qquad F = 6{,}000 \qquad v = 5$$

Substituting these values into (1.5), we have

$$Q^* = \frac{6{,}000}{10 - 5} = 1{,}200 \text{ units}$$

The firm now knows that any sales beyond 1,200 units will earn a profit.

The Effect of Changes in Price and Cost

The breakeven model can also be used by the decision maker to help determine the impact of changes in fixed cost F, selling price p, and variable cost v. For example, a decrease in p means that the slope of the new revenue line (R') will become flatter. This, in turn, will raise the breakeven point from B to B' (Figure 1.3). The economic effect of decreasing price, therefore, is to make profit begin at a higher sales volume. On the other hand, if the selling price increases, the breakeven point will move to the left of B in Figure 1.3, because the total-revenue line becomes steeper. This is more desirable for the firm, of course, because it makes profits begin at a lower sales volume.

A rise in cost, either fixed or variable, will move the breakeven point to the right. An increase in fixed cost F, for instance, shifts the total-cost line upward vertically by the amount of the increment. If the variable cost per unit goes up, the slope of the total-cost line becomes steeper. A decrease in cost, either fixed or variable, has the opposite result. (You should verify this hypothesis to test your understanding.)

Figure 1.3
Effect of Changes in Price

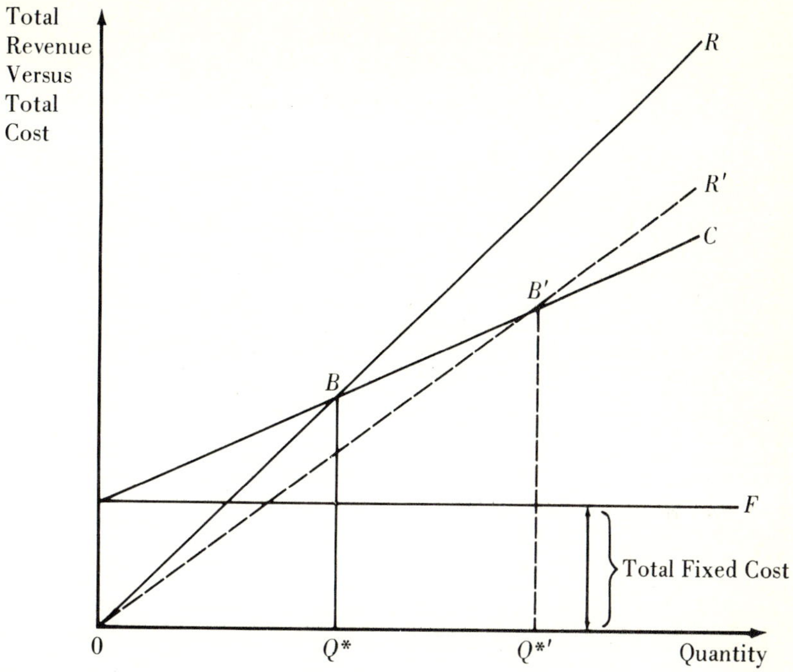

Other Applications of Breakeven Analysis

Breakeven analysis can also be used to facilitate decision making in leasing options, make-or-buy decisions, and decisions involving plant expansion and equipment replacement. Two examples of modified breakeven analysis for these purposes follow.

A Buy-or-Rent Decision Business managers often face the problem of whether to buy or to rent a machine. A decision to buy means incurring an inescapable fixed cost but relatively low operating costs. If the decision is to rent, there are no fixed rental costs, but the variable cost will probably be higher. This problem can be analyzed by using the breakeven chart with a slight modification. The following example is a simplified illustration.

The administrative officer of the School of Business Administration at a major university has the option of either buying a duplicating machine or renting one. According to the vendor's proposal, the lump-sum payment for purchasing the machine is $50,000. The alternative plan is a leasing option under which the company charges 5 cents for each copy the machine produces.[1]

[1]In order to simplify, fixed cost is assumed to be zero. In reality, some fixed cost is typically associated with the rental arrangement. However, this is easy to incorporate in the model. See equations (1.11)–(1.13).

If the purchase price of equipment is amortized over 10 years, the annual fixed cost is $5,000 per year. The school estimates the operating cost to be 3 cents per copy. Let

Q = number of copies (decision variable)
C_b = total cost of buying
C_r = total cost of renting
F = $5,000 (annual fixed cost)
v = $.03 (variable cost ***per copy***)
r = $.05 (rental cost ***per copy***)

The mathematical model is

$$C_b = F + vQ \tag{1.6}$$

$$C_r = rQ \tag{1.7}$$

The breakeven point here is defined at a volume of copies where the total cost of buying (C_b) and the total cost of renting (C_r) are the same. If so, we have

$$rQ = F + vQ \tag{1.8}$$

$$\therefore Q^* = \frac{F}{r - v} \qquad \text{for } r > v \tag{1.9}$$

Substituting our example values into (1.9), we get

$$Q^* = \frac{5{,}000}{0.05 - 0.03} = 250{,}000 \tag{1.10}$$

Consequently, as seen in Figure 1.4, if the school uses the equipment for 250,000 copies annually, buying and renting cost the same. If the machine will be used for more than 250,000 copies per year, it will be more economical to buy. If the school estimates that it will need less than 250,000 copies, it will be cheaper to rent. At any volume of copies, the vertical distance between C_r and C_b in Figure 1.4 indicates the difference in cost between buying and renting.

Figure 1.4
Buying or Renting Decision

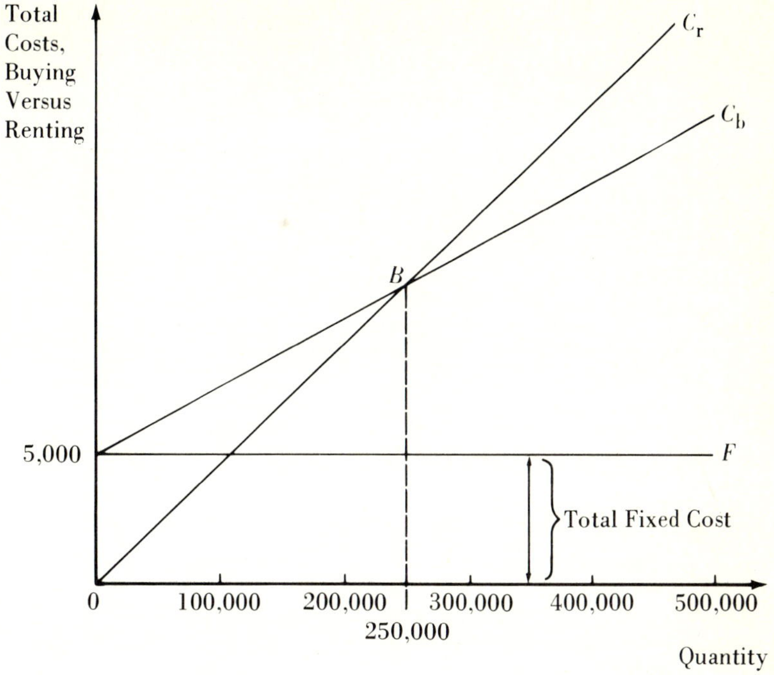

Note that, if some fixed cost is involved in the renting method, the term F_r should be added to total renting cost in (1.7), which becomes $C_r = F_r + rQ$. The more general form of (1.8) then becomes:

$$F_r + rQ = F + vQ \tag{1.11}$$

By rearranging and factoring, we obtain

$$(r - v)\,Q = F - F_r \tag{1.12}$$

or

$$\therefore Q^* = \frac{F - F_r}{r - v} \quad \text{for } F > F_r \text{ and } r > v \tag{1.13}$$

$$\text{or for } F < F_r \text{ and } r < v$$

(Why? See problem 1.6 in the exercise section.)

Buying or Making Decision: A Clinical Microbiology Laboratory Problem Organizations must often face the problem of determining whether to manufacture or to purchase certain components. Here we present a decision problem faced by the clinical microbiology laboratory of a large university hospital. The laboratory has been preparing its own culture medium, but the lab director is now considering purchasing pretubed and preplated medium from commercial firms. Although these firms have been producing medium for the past decade, there has been no analysis of whether the laboratory, given its present size, should continue preparing the medium. Furthermore, the optimal number of units of culture to be prepared during a given time has yet to be determined.

It is possible to apply a breakeven analysis to this problem in a straightforward manner. Assume that there is only one culture, DXA (desoxycholate agar), and that there is no fixed cost involved when the culture is purchased from commercial firms. Let

$$C_m = \text{total cost of manufacturing}$$
$$F = \text{total fixed cost}$$
$$v = \text{variable cost per unit}$$
$$p = \text{unit price of purchasing}$$
$$Q = \text{number of units of DXA}$$
$$C_b = \text{total cost of buying}$$

The mathematical equations for producing and buying are

$$C_m = F + vQ \tag{1.14}$$
$$C_b = pQ \tag{1.15}$$

The breakeven quantity, at which the total cost of buying and the total cost of making are equal, can be calculated by

$$Q^* = \frac{F}{p - v} \qquad \text{for } p > v \tag{1.16}$$

The breakeven chart (Figure 1.5) has been drawn using (1.14) and (1.15). Clearly the breakeven chart suggests that, if the clinical microbiology laboratory needs fewer than Q^* units of DXA for the given time, it is more economical to purchase than to manufacture.

Extensions of the Breakeven Model

We pointed out earlier that the breakeven model is based on a set of assumptions: linear revenue and cost functions, a single product, and the deterministic nature of the exogenous variables. In an attempt to relax these assumptions, we offer the following extensions of the basic breakeven model.

Figure 1.5
Buying or Making Decision

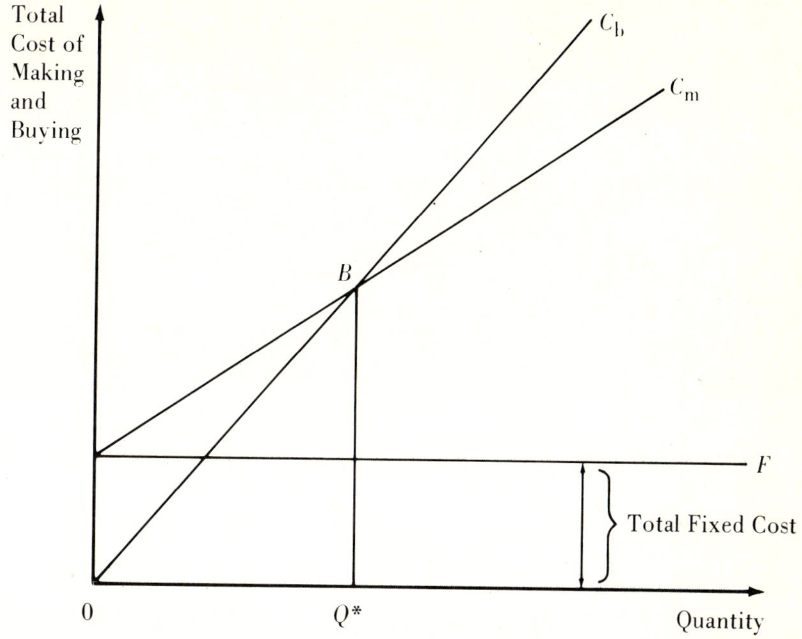

Nonlinear Revenue Function The assumption of a linear revenue function implies that the selling price is constant, no matter how much volume the firm produces or sells. This would be true only if the individual firm's supply constituted a tiny fraction of the whole industry's output. In such a case, the individual firm's supply cannot influence the industry price; so the assumption of constant price may be justified. On the other hand, a firm can often influence its own market by charging different prices for different quantities supplied. In such a case, the assumption of a linear total-revenue function may no longer be valid.

Suppose that the price charged by a company is not constant and that there is a linear demand function in which price is inversely related to quantity sold. That is,

$$p = a - bQ \quad a > 0, b > 0 \tag{1.17}$$

Total revenue R, by definition, is:

$$R = p \times Q \tag{1.18}$$

or

$$\begin{aligned} R &= (a - bQ)Q \\ &= aQ - bQ^2 \end{aligned} \tag{1.18'}$$

Figure 1.6
Profit Maximization in a Generalized Breakeven Model

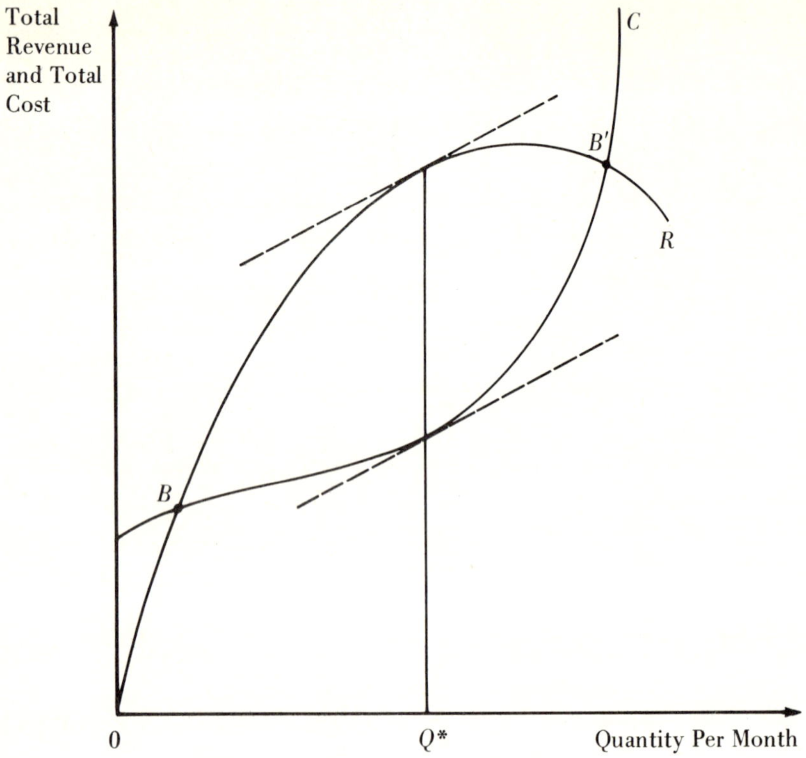

Clearly, instead of being linear, the total-revenue function R is a quadratic function, as shown in Figure 1.6.

Nonlinear Cost Function The assumption of constant average variable cost, regardless of volume produced or sales, implies that (1) the unit cost of input material is constant and (2) the production is carried out in such a way that output is proportional to input. If, however, the unit input cost declines because of quantity discounts or other economic reasons when sales increase, then the cost function is no longer linear. Also, by the law of diminishing returns,[2] large-volume production may eventually cause an increasing average variable cost. Thus the breakeven model must be modified on the cost side to take into account a nonlinear relationship between total cost C and volume (Figure 1.6).

Optimization and Nonlinear Breakeven Models The major criticism of the linear breakeven model is that it does not provide the decision

[2]If a business keeps expanding its volume of output from a set of fixed inputs (such as a factory) by adding more variables (such as labor or raw materials), there comes a point at which the return from each additional variable becomes smaller and smaller. Correspondingly, the cost for each additional unit of output gets larger and larger. This basic concept is what economists call the ***law of diminishing returns.***

maker with a unique optimal solution. If the manager's motivation is based on profit maximization, the problem is to determine the volume that will yield maximum profits. However, because of its infinite production possibilities in the profit area, the linear breakeven chart does not yield a unique optimal solution. This is because both revenue and cost functions are straight lines and go on into infinity without bounds.[3]

In a more general model, both revenue and cost functions are nonlinear, as shown in Figure 1.6. This model provides not only the location of the two breakeven points (B and B') but also the unique optimal-solution position at which the firm's profit is maximized. The reader who has studied elementary economic analysis will recall that the maximum-profit solution occurs at the output Q^* where the slopes of the revenue and cost functions are equal—that is, where marginal cost equals marginal revenue.

Multiple Products and Stochastic Features The number of products included in the simple breakeven chart is usually limited to one. In the case of the clinical microbiology laboratory, however, numerous culture media are involved. Analysis based on the assumption of only one culture, which does help us understand the nature of the problem, is an obvious oversimplification of the practical operation of the laboratory's problem. To incorporate all products and additional activities, we have to construct more powerful mathematical models—techniques that are discussed later in this book.

Finally, to obtain a solution for the basic breakeven model, one must have predetermined values for the exogenous variables, such as fixed cost F, selling price p, and unit variable cost v. However, the availability and quality of information on F, p, and v are not likely to be so certain. Consider the fixed cost, which we have defined as the cost that does not vary with volume. Such a definition is sometimes valid only in the short run or for a certain range of output volume. In the long run or beyond their range, the "fixed" facilities (land or machine, for instance) might change, affecting the corresponding fixed costs.

Furthermore, fixed costs are difficult to deal with when there are multiple products because the amount of those costs attributable to any individual product is difficult to assign. For example, consider the case of a clinical laboratory for which there are many products. How does one assign a fixed cost for a particular product? How much of the laboratory director's fixed annual salary, for instance, should be assigned to the culture medium DXA? Obviously, it is difficult to determine the

[3]In mathematical terms, this means that the profit area (Figure 1.2) is an open convex space. Thus the value of the profit function is mathematically unbounded.

exact amount of fixed cost for a particular culture medium with absolute accuracy, even if the laboratory in question has a good cost accounting system.

It is unlikely that a manager will know the precise values of v and p. For example, in the case of the duplicating machine problem, the unit variable cost v is affected by many factors, such as the quality of the paper, labor hours of operation, and electricity rate hikes, to name a few. Generally, because of the chance of error or risk, the uncontrollable or exogenous variables v and p are likely to be random variables, and the decision maker will know only their probability distributions. Random variables and probability distributions will be discussed more fully later.

To summarize, businesspeople often use breakeven analysis as a helpful tool to estimate the breakeven volume, to compare different alternatives, and to predict the profitability of a firm or of particular products. The purposes of discussing the extension of the breakeven model are: (1) to recognize the shortcomings inherent in the linear breakeven model and point out a way to overcome them, and (2) to direct the reader toward new levels of quantitative analysis. The managerial techniques of programming methods, used to optimize resource allocation, and probability models, used to optimize decision making, are the central topics of this book.

1.5 Overview and Approach of This Book

Overview Briefly, this book attempts to treat managerial decision problems on two fronts: optimizing resource allocation through programming methods, and optimizing decision making through probability models. Studying linear, deterministic optimization models is the best way to begin learning about modern quantitative methods. Therefore, linear programming techniques are the subject of the first part of this book. Chapter 2 presents a problem-oriented introduction to linear programming. Three elementary examples in this chapter are extended through later chapters as illustrations of linear programming techniques. In Chapter 3 the well-known simplex method is presented. Whenever possible, economic reasoning is applied to motivate discussion of the underlying principles. In Chapter 4 duality theory is explained as the central concept of linear programming. The economic interpretation of duality will facilitate the reader's understanding of linear programming.

The transportation algorithm is discussed in Chapter 5, the quadratic programming formulation in Chapter 8, and game theory in Chapter 15. Extensions of linear programming (integer programming, goal programming, and quadratic programming) appear in Chapters 6, 7, and 8, respectively. Whereas these techniques relate to determining a single optimal decision, Chapter 9, which treats dynamic programming methods, considers the overall optimization of a series of interrelated decisions.

The second part of the book focuses on stochastic models for optimum decision making. Chapter 10 shifts the emphasis away from programming techniques to the common scheduling techniques of PERT. The Bayesian approach, which permits decision makers to make use of additional knowledge about certain chance events by altering the probability values attached to those events, is discussed in Chapter 11.

Chapters 12 and 13 present inventory and queuing models. Broadly defined, a queuing model is a waiting-line problem in which a decision maker has to decide on an optimal level of service facilities by balancing two opposing costs—the costs of making people wait due to inadequate facilities and the costs of maintaining adequate facilities. Similarly, the inventory problem involves finding the optimal level of inventory that balances the opposing costs of stocking and ordering. Since simulation methods are widely used in queuing models, as well as in other areas of business management, Chapter 14 shows how simulation techniques are used in research and managerial decision making. Decision making in competitive situations is examined in Chapter 15, using the concepts of game theory.

In Chapter 16, elementary Markov chains are introduced as a method of analyzing the outcome of one experiment that depends only on the outcome of an immediately preceding experiment, assuming that the experiment changes from one state to another with known probabilities. The most important basic forecasting techniques are presented in Chapter 17. Since electronic computers are indispensable in modern operations research, Chapter 18 presents applications using a digital computer to solve typical decision problems. Finally, Chapter 19 presents some reflections on quantitative techniques in the field of management science and its future prospects.

The Economic Approach

An Illustration of Environmental Issues and Management Science An understanding of economic concepts and behavior is the foundation of management-decision–directed analysis. Throughout this book, fundamental economic concepts (such as trade-offs, marginal analysis, and opportunity costs) are combined with quantitative business methods to enhance the understanding of topics. Economic reasoning both deepens and stimulates the reader's appreciation of the underlying quantitative techniques.

As an example, in a typical pollution problem, two types of costs are involved. One is the direct cost of pollution to society, C_d, in the form of damage to life or property. Clearly C_d is a declining function graphed against the probability of safety; that is, the higher the probability of safety, the less the direct cost (Figure 1.7).

The other cost, C_t, arises from measures taken to control pollution, such as the manufacture of emission-reduction equipment. As the probability of safety increases, the cost of control C_t rises rapidly (Figure 1.7). The total cost TC for the society is the sum of the direct cost C_d and the cost of control C_t. The economist does not ask how safe is safe, but rather at what level of safety the total cost is minimized. (Total cost equals the sum of the two opposing costs.) As shown in Figure 1.7, the minimum total cost is at point m, where the direct cost C_d and the cost of control C_t are equal.[4]

Through economic reasoning, we can examine various problems (even very controversial problems) in a rational way. Interestingly, the general economic notion demonstrated in pollution control can also be used to illustrate the basic economic and business concepts of queuing and inventory models,[5] where it is necessary to minimize the total of similarly opposing costs.

1.6 Summary

All business managerial decisions are rooted in the need to allocate scarce resources for optimal return. Because of the scarcity of those resources, the decision maker must choose among alternatives, and an opportunity cost is attached to every decision.

Management must make sound decisions on the basis of scientifically acquired knowledge. The five major steps in any scientific inquiry are (1) identify the problem, (2) formulate a hypothesis or construct a model, (3) collect relevant data, (4) analyze data and test the hypothesis, and (5) verify the hypothesis and draw a conclusion.

[4]For a detailed explanation of this statement, see Section 12.2.

[5]The same notion of economic reasoning can be applied to many other decision problems. For more examples (such as crime control, personnel training, and spare-part supply problems), see Exercise 1.14 at the end of this chapter.

Figure 1.7
Minimizing the Total
Cost of Pollution

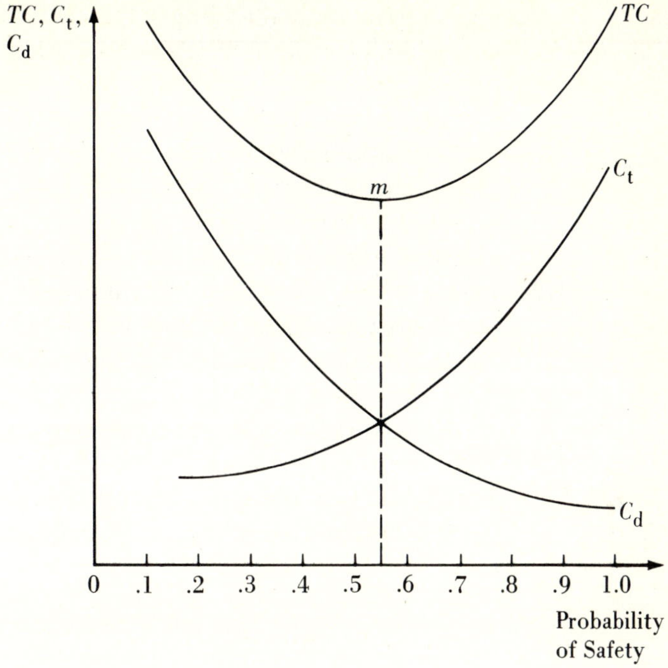

Mathematical models that show interrelationships among decision variables are indispensable to management science. In particular, mathematical models facilitate analysis of the overall structure of the problem and help the decision maker predict the relative effects of alternative courses of action. Quantitative methods or techniques are vital to the solution of management science problems. For practical purposes, then, we may designate quantitative methods used for managerial decision making as management science.

Breakeven analysis is a simple quantitative technique used by many business analysts. Other things being equal, a firm prefers to have a lower breakeven point in order to enhance profit potential. By varying a particular factor—price, fixed cost, or variable cost—a decision maker can dictate the direction and the amount of change in the breakeven quantity. Breakeven analysis, however, is valid only when it is based on a set of assumptions, including linear revenue and cost functions, a single product, and predetermined exogenous variables.

This book treats decision problems from two perspectives: optimization of resource allocation through programming models, and optimization in decision making through probability models. Fundamental economic concepts are brought in wherever they are needed to elucidate the discussion of quantitative methods.

Exercises

1.1 Define or explain the following terms:
a. Operations research
b. Opportunity cost
c. Mathematical model
d. Breakeven point

1.2 How are the following terms different?
a. Analog model and iconic model
b. Endogenous variable and exogenous variable
c. Deterministic model and stochastic model
d. Total variable cost and total fixed cost

1.3 What are the logical steps of the scientific method?

1.4 The D. R. G. Publishing Company is selling a textbook at $10.50 per copy; total fixed costs are estimated to be $20,000. Unit variable costs are

Paper and other materials	$1.25
Labor	2.50
Royalty fee	1.00
Salesperson's commission	3.75

a. Find the breakeven volume.
b. Predict the amount of profit if the sales volume for the academic year is estimated to be 20,000 copies.
c. If the fixed cost is reduced to $15,000, what will the new breakeven volume be?
d. Calculate the breakeven volume, assuming that the selling price is raised by 10% and at the same time the unit variable cost also goes up by 10%.

1.5 The following information is provided by the manager of the American Motor Inns, Inc.

Average price charged per room per day	$18.00
Salaries and wages (fixed by labor contract) and other fixed portions of expenses	520.00
Average utilities, supplies, and maintenance expenses per day per room	15.00

a. Draw a breakeven chart.
b. Compute and show the breakeven occupancy of the motel per day.

c. If the average room price drops to \$15, what will happen? Can you determine the breakeven occupancy? If not, why not?
d. Calculate the breakeven level of occupancy if the average room price goes up to \$20.

1.6 Why do we impose the restriction $F > F_r$ and $r > v$, or $F < F_r$ and $r < v$ in equation (1.13)? (*Hint:* Draw breakeven charts for two cases and think of the economic meaning of slopes.)

1.7 Mini-Computer, Inc., has been quite successful with the sale of its W307 calculator. Recently its engineers in the R&D department have developed a new model that can also make the multiple xerographic copies and works even more efficiently than the successful W307. However, the company estimates that the initial investment for developing the new production plan will be \$1.5 million. Once the production plan is completed, the unit cost for producing each machine is expected to be \$5,500. It has been the company's traditional policy to sell its products only to wholesalers. The marketing department has received inquiries about the new machine from its wholesalers indicating that they would buy at least 550 machines, if the machine is developed, at a quoted wholesale price of \$8,500 per unit.
a. How many units of this machine must the company sell to reach the breakeven point? Should the company develop the new machine or not?
b. Given the current order indicated by its distributors, is there profit to be realized or not? If yes, how much profit would the company make?

1.8 The general price policy for Mr. Spencer's retail store is to mark wholesale cost up by 50% to arrive at the retail price for merchandise. The fixed expenditures incurred by the store are \$5,000 a month.
a. Draw a breakeven chart. (*Hint:* View 50% mark-up as the slope of the revenue line.)
b. Determine the breakeven volume by the formula

$$\frac{\text{Fixed cost}}{\text{Percent mark-up}}$$

1.9 A total-revenue model is

$$R = a + bQ$$

where
R = total sales
Q = volume of output
a = constant term
b = coefficient of output

a. Give an economic interpretation of the terms a and b.
b. Indicate the essential assumption(s) that must hold for us to predict total revenue with a given output.

1.10 Let

Total revenue function $R = pQ$

Total cost function $C = F + vQ$

where

p = selling price per unit of output

F = total fixed cost

v = variable cost per unit

Discuss the effect of each of the following on the breakeven position.
a. An increase in total fixed cost
b. A decrease in variable cost per unit
c. A decrease in total fixed cost
d. An increase in variable cost per unit
e. An increase in selling price
f. An increase in selling price and a decrease in total fixed cost

1.11 a. A manufacturer of lawn mower motors currently buys exhaust valves for \$2.50 each. An estimate of what it would cost the company to manufacture these valves itself reveals that the fixed costs would be \$4,800 per year and that the variable costs per valve would be \$1.22. Each motor requires one exhaust valve, and annual production at full capacity is 6,000 lawn mowers. At what level of production would it pay the company to manufacture its own valves? Express your answer as a percentage of full-capacity production.
b. Starting from the most basic condition of breakeven, give an algebraic derivation that results in an expression for breakeven as a percentage of full-capacity production. Apply this breakeven formula to part (a) to check your results.

1.12 A manufacturer sells bearing assemblies at \$10 each. Cost analysis of the firm's operations shows fixed costs of \$40,000 for the manufacturing process and variable costs of \$3.75 per assembly unit. Maximum productive capacity is 16,000 units. Find the breakeven point for this process both in units and as a percentage of full-capacity production.

1.13 Consider a firm that has the following costs:

Depreciation	$45,000
Direct Labor	10,000
Materials Used	2,300
Advertising	800
Taxes	500

a. The price of this firm's product is $17.30 per unit and 1,000 units are sold annually. Find total fixed cost, total variable cost, variable cost per unit, and profits.
b. What is the breakeven point for the firm expressed in units and in dollar sales volume?
c. How would increasing the price of the product to $18.10 affect the breakeven point? How would it affect current profits?
d. If, in addition to the change indicated in part (c), variable cost per unit is reduced by $.22, how would the breakeven point be affected? How would current profits be affected?

1.14 Apply the basic economic concepts underlying environmental issues (Section 1.5) to the following problems. Construct models like Figure 1.7, and indicate the different concepts of costs involved.
a. ***Crime Prevention*** The economic dilemma of crime is that it involves two opposite costs—the direct cost of crime (damage to the victims) and the cost of controlling criminal activities. The direct cost of crime is inversely related to the probability that a criminal will be apprehended and convicted. What is the relationship between the cost of control (police officers, prosecutors, judges, wardens, jail facilities and the like) and the probability of apprehending and convicting criminals? What is the total cost of crime to society? What proportion of criminals should society try to apprehend and convict? Should all criminals be caught and convicted? If yes, what is the economic cost of fighting crime that a society must pay? If no, why not? Is there an *optimal* level of crime? If so, show it in your diagram.
b. ***Personnel Training*** A giant multinational corporation is considering training employees on a group-by-group basis. The question the decision maker faces is: What class size should the company establish to minimize total cost? If class size is too large, the cor-

poration may train people it does not immediately need. But if class size is too small, the company will have to repeat the courses, which obviously results in higher costs. Using economic reasoning to formulate a model like Figure 1.7, show the probable relationship between the various costs and class size.

c. ***Spare-Parts Supply*** A local supplier of electrical appliances has the following decision problem: What is the optimal level of spare parts that the firm should have on hand? Can you determine two types of opposing costs in this case?

d. These problems and the three problems discussed in the text (pollution control, queuing, and inventory) may seem dissimilar in form, and they arise in completely different areas. Do you see, however, that they are similar in terms of the basic economic reasoning required? If so, think of one or two problems of your own that are dominated by this fundamental economic notion.

1.15 Referring to the preceding problem, which part is most likely to require a value judgment? How can we best cope with it rationally?

1.16 Explain the relationship between managerial decision making and the fundamental concept of economics.

Suggested Readings

Ackoff, Russell L., and Maurice W. Sasieni. *Fundamentals of Operations Research.* New York: Wiley, 1968.

Alman, A. J., and D. G. Parisi. *Quantitative Methods for Decision Making.* Morristown, N.J.: General Learning Press, 1974. Chapter 1.

Baumol, William J. *Economic Theory and Operations Analysis.* 3rd ed. Englewood Cliffs, N.J.: Prentice-Hall, 1972. Chapter 1.

Hillier, Frederick S., and Gerald J. Lieberman. *Introduction to Operations Research.* San Francisco, Calif.: Holden-Day, 1967.

Horngren, C. T. *Accounting for Management Control: An Introduction.* Englewood Cliffs, N.J.: Prentice-Hall, 1970.

Johnson, Ross H., and Paul R. Winn. *Quantitative Methods for Management.* Boston, Mass.: Houghton Mifflin, 1975.

Kim, Chaiho. *Quantitative Analysis for Managerial Decisions.* Reading, Mass.: Addison-Wesley, 1975. Chapters 5 and 6.

Patrick, A. W. "Some Observations on the Break-Even Chart." *The Accounting Review,* October 1958, 573–580.

Simon, Herbert A. "Theories of Decision-Making in Economics and Behavioral Science." *The American Economic Review,* June 1959.

Tucker, S. P. *The Breakeven System: A Tool for Profit Planning.* Englewood Cliffs, N.J.: Prentice-Hall, 1975. Chapter 1.

Ulmer, Melville J. *Economics: Theory and Practice*. Boston, Mass.: Houghton Mifflin, 1965.

Williamson, Oliver E. "Managerial Discretion and Business Behavior." *The American Economic Review*, December 1963.

2

Linear Programming and Specific Types of Problems

To achieve the basic operational goals of maximum profits or minimum costs, effective business management must be concerned with how to allocate scarce resources most efficiently. Indeed, it is characteristic of the business environment that resources can be substituted for one another, and business decisions must be aimed at determining optimal levels of business activity affecting these resources. A modern, mathematical technique for planning and obtaining such optimization is known as linear programming. When this technique is used, the overall objective must be quantified as a linear function. Likewise, resource limitations are also specified as linear relationships. Thus, given a set of decision variables, ***linear programming either maximizes or minimizes a linear objective function subject to a set of linear constraints.***

Mathematicians have made this method a powerful tool for attacking optimization problems. It has been widely applied not only in industrial analysis and business management, but also in economic analysis. In terms of fundamental mathematical structure, linear programming, input-output analysis, and game theory are closely related, and linear programming is the core of all three.[1] In fact, before the name ***linear programming*** was devised by T. C. Koopmans, this part of mathematical theory was known as ***programming in a linear structure.***[2]

[1]R. Dorfman, P. A. Samuelson, and R. M. Solow, *Linear Programming and Economic Analysis* (New York: McGraw-Hill, 1958), pp. 4–5.

[2]*Activity Analysis of Production and Allocation*, ed. Tjalling C. Koopmans, Cowles Commission for Research in Economics, Monograph No. 13 (New York: Wiley, 1951), p. 5.

This chapter offers concrete examples of linear programming problems and gives a detailed explanation of graphical methods that can be used to solve problems involving two variables. The two-variables case will provide some geometrical insight into, and economic logic about, the nature of linear programming problems in general. The assumptions that must be made for a given linear problem are then evaluated. Next we state the general formulation of the linear programming problem and finally manipulate the structure of the models algebraically.

2.1 Maximization: A Potato–Tomato Problem

Consider a farmer who has the option of producing potatoes, tomatoes, or any combination of the two crops on a small farm of approximately 30 acres. In addition to the limitation of land as a resource, the farmer's production is restricted by two other factors: labor and storage space. Only 60 hours of labor and 24 square yards of storage space are available for any given period of production. Technical data indicate that producing 1 unit of potatoes requires 1 acre of land and 3 hours of labor, and that producing 1 unit of tomatoes requires 2 acres of land, 2 hours of labor, and 2 square yards of storage space. Market information reveals that any amounts of potatoes and tomatoes can be sold at fixed prices that, after subtracting the cost of transportation and other variable expenses, would yield the farmer an average net profit—or "contribution"—of \$40 per unit of potatoes and \$50 per unit of tomatoes.

Assuming that the farmer's goal is profit maximization, which crop or combination of the two crops should the farmer produce, and in what amounts? Table 2.1 summarizes the farmer's problem.

Let X_1 be the amount of potatoes and X_2 be the amount of tomatoes that the farmer plans to produce, and let Z represent the farmer's cash return. Then the formal linear problem can be stated as follows:

$$\text{Maximize}^3 \quad Z = 40X_1 + 50X_2 \tag{2.1a}$$

$$\text{subject to} \quad \begin{aligned} X_1 + 2X_2 &\leq 30 \quad &\text{(land)} \\ 3X_1 + 2X_2 &\leq 60 \quad &\text{(labor)} \\ 2X_2 &\leq 24 \quad &\text{(storage space)} \end{aligned} \tag{2.1b}$$

$$\text{and} \quad X_1 \geq 0,\ X_2 \geq 0 \tag{2.1c}$$

[3]Hereafter, "Max" will be used instead of "Maximize" and "Min" instead of "Minimize."

Table 2.1
Amount of Resources Required Per Unit of Output

Resources	Potato	Tomato	Total Availability
Land (acres)	1	2	30
Labor (hours)	3	2	60
Storage Space (square yards)	0	2	24
Unit Contribution to Profit	\$40	\$50	

Equation (2.1a) is the objective function. This function indicates that the farmer should try to find a combination of X_1 and X_2 that will make the total profit Z as large as possible. The first inequality in (2.1b) is a land-resource constraint, which states that the sum of the amount of land used for production of potatoes and the amount of land used for production of tomatoes must not exceed the total amount of the land resource available, which is 30 acres. Diagrammatically, this first constraint may be interpreted as follows:

$$\begin{bmatrix}\text{1 acre per}\\ \text{unit of}\\ \text{potatoes}\end{bmatrix} \times \begin{bmatrix}X_1\text{ units}\\ \text{produced}\end{bmatrix} + \begin{bmatrix}\text{2 acres per}\\ \text{unit of}\\ \text{tomatoes}\end{bmatrix} \times \begin{bmatrix}X_2\text{ units}\\ \text{produced}\end{bmatrix} \leq \begin{matrix}30\\ \text{acres}\end{matrix}$$

Similarly, the limitations of 60 hours of labor and 24 square yards of storage space, at most, are expressed by the second and third inequalities. Since both X_1 and X_2 represent units of output, there is no physical or economic meaning to a negative output level; therefore, production levels are not allowed to be negative. The inequalities in (2.1c) state that all variables must be either zero or positive; these are generally called nonnegativity constraints. The statement of all linear programming problems has these three important parts: an objective function, constraints, and nonnegativity requirements.

Graphical Solution and Its Economic Meaning How are we to solve this problem? Since there are only two variables in this simple problem, we can use a two-dimensional graph to portray the problem and to obtain the solution.

Equality Versus Inequality Relationships

Consider the nonnegativity constraints in (2.1c): $X_1 \geq 0$ and $X_2 \geq 0$. According to these constraints, the problem must be confined to points within, or on the boundary of, the first quadrant. In Figure 2.1, which is a graphical representation of the linear programming problem, small

Figure 2.1
All Constraints Portrayed Simultaneously

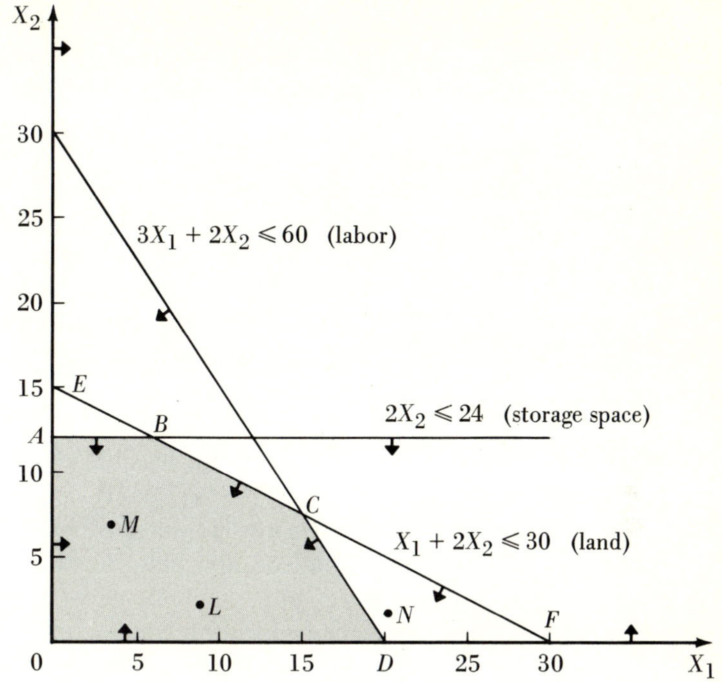

arrows are drawn pointing upward and to the right, indicating that the two axes act as constraints on values of the production variables.

The first constraint, which involves the land resource, can be separated into two parts—one representing the equality relationship and the other representing the strict inequality:

$$X_1 + 2X_2 = 30 \quad \text{and} \quad X_1 + 2X_2 < 30$$

The equality is readily graphed as a straight line, which is shown in Figure 2.1 as EF. Any point, such as point B, whose coordinates (6, 12) satisfy the equality relationship must lie on the line. Point B represents a production combination of 6 units of potatoes and 12 units of tomatoes, which is technically feasible and utilizes all available land resources (6 acres for potatoes and 24 acres for tomatoes).

The strict inequality that we have just stated represents all points on the graph that are found below and to the left of the line EF. Any such point is also technically feasible, but the production activity will not utilize the given resource fully. Geometrically, combining all feasible points, the first constraint ($X_1 + 2X_2 \leq 30$) must therefore represent the ***half-plane*** consisting of all points on or below the line $X_1 + 2X_2 = 30$.

The Feasible Region and Feasible Solutions The remaining two constraints have also been drawn in Figure 2.1, and additional half-planes are determined. Of course, variables X_1 and X_2 must satisfy all constraints simultaneously. Any such combination of the two variables is called a ***feasible point*** or a feasible solution to the problem, and all constraints together determine a closed set or geometrical region of feasible solutions. Thus the ***feasible region*** for the farmer's linear programming problem is identified by the corner points 0*ABCD* in Figure 2.1. For example, the points *B*, *L*, and *M*, which are either on the boundary of or within the feasible region, are all feasible solutions. Note, however, that point *N*, which is feasible in relation to the land constraint, does not represent a feasible solution because it lies outside the labor constraint.

The Optimal Solution Although all points in the feasible region represent a set of feasible solutions that satisfy the inequality constraints as well as the nonnegativity conditions, some points result in higher profit than others. The particular feasible solution that yields the highest profit is the ***optimal solution.*** Fortunately, it is not necessary to examine all points in the feasible region (of which there are an infinite number) to find the optimal point or points. For reasons to be explained shortly, the optimal point must occur at one of the corner points of the feasible region. In Figure 2.2 the feasible region of Figure 2.1 is enlarged. The coordinates of each corner point and the corresponding profit values are listed in Table 2.2.

Substituting the coordinates of each corner point into the objective function, we obtain values for the total contribution to profits. It is apparent from Table 2.2 that the optimal solution occurs at the corner point *C*. This solution to the farmer's linear programming problem—15 units of potatoes and 7.5 units of tomatoes—is better than any other feasible production combination. It maximizes the farmer's total contribution to profits at a value of \$975 per production period.

In order to illustrate why the optimal solution is at point *C*, rewrite the objective function in the following form:

$$X_2 = \frac{Z}{50} - \frac{40}{50}X_1$$

Where the profit symbol Z can be identified as a parameter having indefinite values and the ratio of Z to 50 is assigned various representative values—for example, Z_1 = \$600, Z_2 = \$800, Z_3 = \$975, and Z_4 = \$1,200—a mapping of straight lines results. This is shown superimposed on the feasible region of Figure 2.2. Since the slope does not change with different values of Z, the lines in the mapping are

Figure 2.2
The Feasible Region and Mapping of the Objective Function

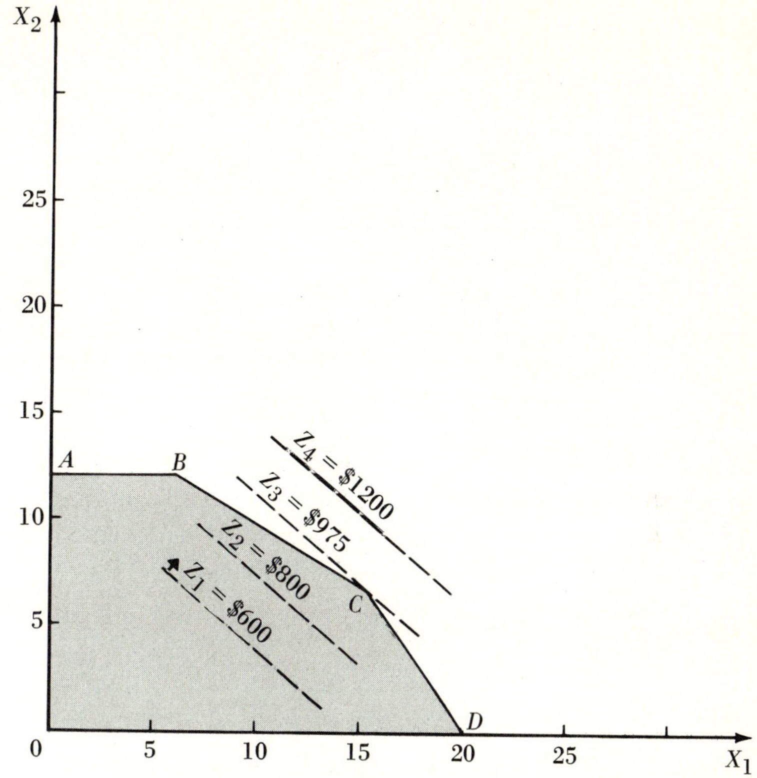

Table 2.2
The Evaluation of Corner Points

Corner Point	Coordinates, (X_1,X_2)	Values of the Objective Function, $Z = 40X_1 + 50X_2$
0	(0,0)	$ 0 = 40(0) + 50(0)
A	(0,12)	600 = 40(0) + 50(12)
B	(6,12)	840 = 40(6) + 50(12)
C	(15,7.5)	975 = 40(15) + 50(7.5)
D	(20,0)	800 = 40(20) + 50(0)

parallel to each other. Each line represents a locus of points, or combinations of X_1 and X_2, that yield the same level of profit. For this reason, the objective function describes a set of ***isoprofit lines.***

As the production of potatoes and tomatoes increases, the value of the objective function also increases, so that the profit line is farther from the origin and moving in the northeast direction. The line that is farthest from the origin but has at least one point still touching the feasible region is the line of maximum profit. In this problem, the point of contact between the isoprofit line and the feasible region is the corner point C. It is the optimal solution yielding a total contribution of $975. Any higher value would be unobtainable, because the isoprofit line would lie entirely outside the feasible region.

It is now clear that the way to find the optimal solution in a two-variable linear programming problem is simply to map the objective function on the feasible region formed by the constraints. In this map of the objective function, the profit line that lies farthest from the origin but has at least ***one*** point in common with the feasible region determines the maximum profit value of the objective function. The coordinates of the appropriate corner point of the feasible region identify the optimal production levels of the two variables.

We can identify the optimal production combination not only graphically but also mathematically, by solving simultaneously the ***effective constraints*** that constitute the corner point. For example, remembering that C is the optimal corner point in Figure 2.1, solve simultaneously the following two equations:

$$X_1 + 2X_2 = 30 \qquad \text{(land)}$$

$$3X_1 + 2X_2 = 60 \qquad \text{(labor)}$$

Again, we find $X_1 = 15$ and $X_2 = 7.5$ to be the optimal solution. Only land and labor are effective constraints, because both resources are fully utilized. The third constraint, storage space, does not impose a limitation at the optimal level of production. In fact, at optimal production levels this third constraint reveals that the farmer should have nine square yards of storage space left unused. (Why?)

Multiple Optimal Solutions

We have learned by delineating the feasible region that an optimal solution is obtained at one of the corner points. Two questions remain. How will a change in per-unit profit contribution values affect the optimal solution? And will such a change affect the feasible region?

The answer to the second question is simple. The profit contribution values are merely the coefficients of the objective function, which plays no part in determining the feasible region. Therefore, any change in the objective function will not affect the feasible region. The answer to the first question depends on the relative proportion of the change. If simultaneous changes occur in the profit ratio such that the slope of the isoprofit line remains the same, the optimal solution will not be affected. Likewise, relatively small changes in the profit ratio may not be sufficient to cause a change in the optimal solution. In this case, the range of slopes that the objective function can assume without affecting the optimal solution is determined by the slope values of adjacent segments of the feasible region. In effect, the objective function can sway back and forth on the optimal corner point without initiating a new optimal solution. If the slope of the objective function is altered beyond this range, the corresponding adjacent corner point will become optimal.

An interesting case arises when the profit ratio is altered in such a way that it becomes the same as the slope of the land constraint. For example, suppose that the average profit contribution for tomatoes increases, other things being equal, from \$50 to \$80 per unit. The new objective function will have a slope of $-40/80$, which equals $-1/2$, and we can verify that this is the same as the slope of the land constraint, $X_1 + 2X_2 \leq 30$. The feasible region and three representative isoprofit lines are shown in Figure 2.3. This diagram makes it immediately apparent that, over the entire line segment BC, the highest attainable isoprofit line coincides exactly with the land constraint. Thus each point on this line segment, including the two corner points B and C, satisfies the criterion for an optimal solution. In this case there is no unique

Figure 2.3
Multiple Optimal Solutions

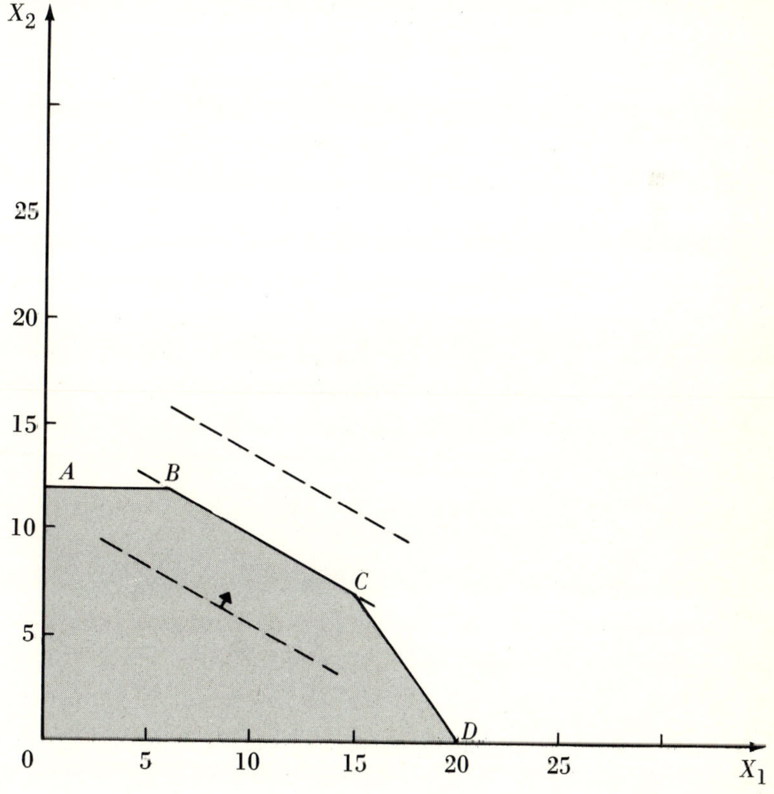

optimal solution. Instead, we have found ***multiple optimal solutions*** that all yield the same level of profit—$1200. The reader is invited to check the five corner points (0, A, B, C, and D) to verify that, in this case, both B and C are optimal solutions.

In the case of multiple optimal solutions, it is interesting to note that the normal profit incentive does not provide a unique, optimal production combination, and the decision maker may now apply other criteria in making a choice. For example, the farmer may wish to produce as many potatoes and as few tomatoes as possible, because potatoes can be stored for a long time whereas tomatoes are perishable. In this case, perishability may become a secondary criterion for determining the product mix.

2.2 Minimization: A Presidential Election Problem

Most American campaign managers feel that the mass media offer the best way of reaching the voter. Candidates now hire experts to conduct television and radio campaign programs much as corporations employ advertising agencies to market their products. For simplicity, suppose that a presidential candidate campaigns by using only television and radio. Suppose also that this person is confident of winning if no less than two-thirds of each of the constituent voting groups is reached with radio and television ads. Statistics on voter registration show that there are 36 million Democrats, 27 million Republicans, and 18 million Independents. Table 2.3 provides information about costs and advertising effectiveness.

What is the least-cost combination of television and radio ads that will meet the minimum requirement for audience size in each group? Let

Table 2.3
Costs and Number of Voters Reached Per Unit of Advertising (millions population)

Group of Voters	Television	Radio	Minimum Number of Voters to be Reached
Democrats	6	2	24 ($= \frac{2}{3} \times 36$)
Republicans	3	2	18 ($= \frac{2}{3} \times 27$)
Independents	1	3	12 ($= \frac{2}{3} \times 18$)
Cost Per Ad (millions of $)	1	0.5	

X_1 and X_2 represent the number of television ads and radio ads, respectively. Using this notation, the candidate's financial adviser forms the following linear programming model to solve the problem:

$$\text{Min} \quad C = X_1 + 0.5X_2 \tag{2.2a}$$

subject to

$$\begin{aligned} 6X_1 + 2X_2 &\geq 24 \\ 3X_1 + 2X_2 &\geq 18 \\ X_1 + 3X_2 &\geq 12 \end{aligned} \tag{2.2b}$$

and

$$X_1 \geq 0, X_2 \geq 0 \tag{2.2c}$$

Equation (2.2a), the objective function, indicates that the total advertising cost for the campaign should be minimized. Note that the inequality signs in the constraints (2.2b) are ***greater-than-or-equal-to*** signs. The first constraint indicates that each ad can be expected to reach 2 million Democrats by radio and 6 million by television. Furthermore, the total Democratic audience reached by both radio and television ads must not be less than 24 million. We interpret the other constraints similarly.

The Graphical Solution As in the maximization problem, the nonnegativity conditions again confine the feasible region to the first quadrant of a two-dimensional Cartesian graph. Figure 2.4 is a graph of the three constraints. Because of the greater-than-or-equal-to conditions, all feasible solutions lie either ***on*** or to the ***right*** of the constraint lines in the graph. (This contrasts with the maximization problem, wherein the set of all feasible solutions was bounded from above by ***less-than-or-equal-to*** constraints.) The feasible region in Figure 2.4 is determined by the line segments *AB*, *BD*, *DE*, and the ***outer*** portions of the two axes.

Once again, the optimal solution will occur at one of the corner points of the feasible region. By rewriting the objective function as

$$X_2 = \frac{C}{0.5} - \frac{1}{0.5} - X_1$$

we can see that, just as in the previous problem, the objective function is a mapping of straight lines for various values of cost. Three representative lines of the mapping are shown in Figure 2.4. Each indicates combinations of X_1 and X_2 that give equal levels of cost. For this reason they are also called ***isocost*** lines.

Figure 2.4
The Feasible Region for Minimization

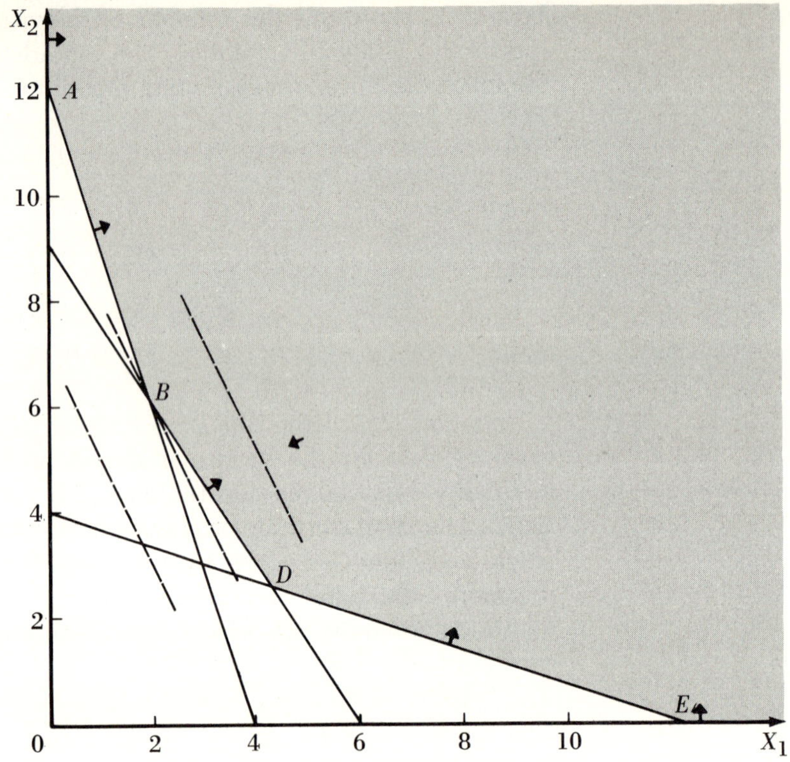

In order to minimize total cost, one must select the lowest isocost line that still has at least one point in common with the feasible region. In this case point *B* is the optimal solution, and its coordinates can best be found by solving simultaneously the equations of the two effective constraints:

$$6X_1 + 2X_2 = 24$$

$$3X_1 + 2X_2 = 18$$

The minimum cost is achieved by combining 2 television and 6 radio advertising units for a total cost of \$5 million. In terms of the budget, the financial adviser should allocate \$2 million for television and \$3 million for radio ads during the campaign. If the adviser's assumptions were correct, and this amount of money may be spent, then the candidate should soon be in the White House.

The reader may already have perceived, however, that there may be problems with the assumptions of this model. In particular, the coefficients associated with the constraints might not be constant. What does this mean? One would expect, for example, that a television ad that is repeated a number of times will reach a decreasing number of new viewers each time. This represents diminishing returns, so the model must have a nonlinear objective function. In such a situation, the candidate's financial adviser might choose to employ quadratic programming methods, which are discussed in Chapter 8. One should also consider the competitive effect of the opponent's campaign. An optimal strategy for such a situation can best be found using the tools of game theory, which are presented in Chapter 15.

2.3 A Transportation Problem

Consider a commodity being produced by a company that owns two factories, F_1 and F_2, which are located in two distant cities. Suppose that the outputs of the two factories are 18 and 15 units respectively, and that the number of units required by 3 markets (or warehouses), M_1, M_2, and M_3, are 16, 10, and 7, respectively. Figure 2.5 gives the cost of shipping from either factory to any market. For example, it may cost \$1 per unit to ship from factory 1 to market 3, or it may cost \$4 per unit to ship from factory 2 to market 3, and so on.

The problem this company faces is to find a shipping schedule that will minimize total shipping costs according to the following restrictions:

1. The amount of commodity shipped from each factory must be no greater than its production capacity.
2. The amount of commodity received by each market must be no less than its demand requirement.
3. The amount of any shipment must not be negative.

Figure 2.5 Graphic Representation of the Transportation Network

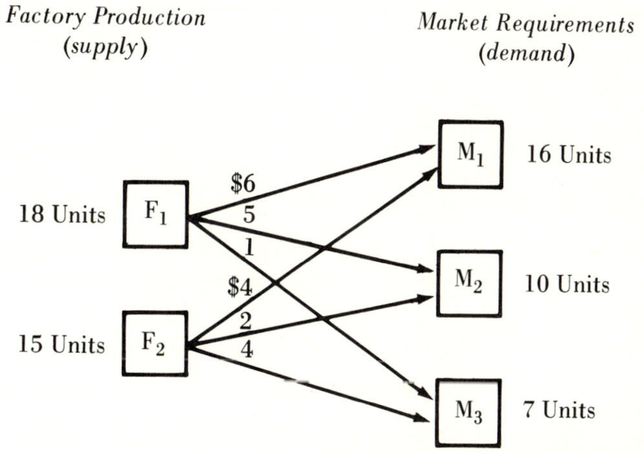

Let the variable X_{ij} represent the amount of shipment from factory i to market j (the subscript i will be 1 or 2, and the subscript j will be 1, 2, or 3). Then the total cost for all shipments must be

$$C = 6X_{11} + 5X_{12} + 1X_{13} + 4X_{21} + 2X_{22} + 4X_{23} \tag{2.3a}$$

The first and second restrictions can be expressed in the following mathematical form:

$$\begin{aligned} X_{11} + X_{12} + X_{13} &\leq 18 \\ X_{21} + X_{22} + X_{23} &\leq 15 \end{aligned} \tag{2.3b}$$

and

$$\begin{aligned} X_{11} + X_{21} &\geq 16 \\ X_{12} + X_{22} &\geq 10 \\ X_{13} + X_{23} &\geq 7 \end{aligned} \tag{2.3c}$$

The third restriction also must be included in the statement of the model:

$$X_{ij} \geq 0 \quad \text{for all } i, j \tag{2.3d}$$

The company must attempt to arrange a minimum-cost shipping schedule that will satisfy all of the constraint conditions, (2.3b), (2.3c), and (2.3d). Note that this problem has the same structure—an objective function, resource restrictions, and nonnegativity requirements—as the previous two problems. In the earlier problems, which had two variables, we could obtain solutions using a two-dimensional graph. A three-variable problem may sometimes be solved graphically by a person skilled in three-dimensional drafting. But there are six variables in the statement of this problem, so the graphical method is not available. The solution, though involved, is not overly difficult. The appropriate techniques will be developed in Chapters 3 and 5.

2.4 The Basic Assumptions and Economic Reasoning of Linear Programming

Proportionality The flow of resources into an activity is proportional to the level of the activity. For example, each unit of potatoes produced—activity X_1—

required 1 acre of land and 3 hours of labor. Thus 2 units of potatoes require 2 acres of land and 6 hours of labor. This property of ***proportionality*** arises from the assumptions of linearity, and it is known in conventional production economics as ***constant returns to scale.***

Additivity

The total amount of resources used by all activities must equal the sum of the resources used by the individual activities. In the potato–tomato example, the optimal level for potatoes is 15 units, which requires 15 acres of land and 45 hours of labor. The optimal level for tomatoes is 7.5 units, which requires 15 acres of land, 15 hours of labor, and 15 square yards of storage space. Thus the total amount of resources required for a firm to conduct both activities at the optimal level is 30 acres of land, 60 hours of labor, and 15 square yards of storage space.

The property of ***additivity*** implies that there is no interaction between activities in the production process. When, on the other hand, a producer obtains a by-product from one of the firm's primary products, the total resources required are less than the sum of the resources required to produce the three products—two primary products and one by-product—individually.

Divisibility

The ***divisibility*** assumption requires that each activity be allowed to take any fractional value in the production process. Some activity levels, such as the number of potatoes or tomatoes produced, have practical meaning only if they are integer values. But there is no guarantee that the linear programming solution will always be an integer solution. If the divisibility of activities is not realistic in application, integer programming methods that will yield the optimal integer solution can be employed.

A Linear Objective Function

The proportionality and additivity properties hold for the objective function as well as for the constraints. All coefficients in both the objective function and the constraints of a linear programming model are assumed to be constant. Because of this property, the linear programming approach is especially well suited to purely competitive market situations wherein the prices of both outputs and inputs are assumed to be unaffected by the actions of any single individual or activity.

In an imperfect market, the selling price a firm faces may be a random variable, in which case the objective function is not linear. One special case of nonlinear programming problems, known as quadratic programming, can be approached using a modification of standard linear programming techniques. All constraints remain linear, but the objective function is a quadratic formula. Such problems are discussed in Chapter 8.

Nonnegativity We have already explained (see Section 2.1) that activity levels must be nonnegative. Nonnegativity is necessary to guarantee the real economic interpretability of activity levels. Most advanced analysis is based on this assumption.

2.5 The General Formulation of Linear Programming Models

In this section we will formulate the general linear programming model in which there are n activities and m constraints. We will see how a linear programming problem can be presented in different forms, and we will study the manipulation and connections among them.

The Sigma Notation First, however, we should recall the simple and convenient mathematical shorthand notation for expressing sums. The Greek letter sigma, Σ, is used in mathematics with the meaning ***to take the sum of.*** For instance, one may write

$$X_1 + X_2 + X_3 + X_4 = \sum_{j=1}^{4} X_j$$

The subscript j is usually called the ***summation index,*** and it takes only a finite number of integer values. In this example, j assumes the values of 1, 2, 3, and 4. The number 4, written ***above*** the Σ, is the terminal value of j. The expression $j = 1$, written ***below*** the Σ, indicates the initial value of j. More generally, one may write

$$X_1 + X_2 + X_3 + \ldots + X_n = \sum_{j=1}^{n} X_j$$

In other words, the right-hand-side expression can be read: ***take the sum of X_j as j increases from 1 to n.*** By induction, this formula can also be expressed as

$$\begin{aligned}
&(X_1 + X_2 + \ldots + X_k) + (X_{k+1} + X_{k+2} + \ldots + X_n) \\
&= \sum_{j=1}^{k} X_j + \sum_{k+1}^{n} X_j \\
&= \sum_{j=1}^{n} X_j
\end{aligned}$$

The application of the Σ (sigma) notation can be expanded to cases in which the term X_j is associated with a profit coefficient.

Example An expression of total profit of a multiproduct firm is

$$C_1X_1 + C_2X_2 + \ldots . + C_nX_n = \sum_{j=1}^{n} C_jX_j$$

where the coefficient C_j is the profit rate per unit of the jth product, and X_j is the number of units produced or sold. If all coefficients are the same constant, we may write

$$\begin{aligned} &CX_1 + CX_2 + CX_3 \\ &= C(X_1 + X_2 + X_3) \\ &= C \sum_{j=1}^{3} X_j \end{aligned}$$

For simplicity, the Σ notation can be used without a summation index, as long as the range of the summation is clear in the context of the notation. Accordingly, the expression

$$\sum_{j=1}^{n} X_j$$

can be written either

$$\sum_{j} X_j \quad \text{or} \quad \sum X_j$$

When the problem requires double subscripts, the sigma notation may be further extended to represent a finite ***double*** sum. That is, the double Σ notation

$$\sum_{i=1}^{m} \sum_{j=1}^{n} C_{ij}X_{ij}$$

represents

$$\begin{aligned} &C_{11}X_{11} + C_{12}X_{12} + \ldots + C_{1n}X_{1n} \\ &+ C_{21}X_{21} + C_{22}X_{22} + \ldots + C_{2n}X_{2n} \\ &\quad \cdot \\ &\quad \cdot \\ &\quad \cdot \\ &+ C_{m1}X_{m1} + C_{m2}X_{m2} + \ldots + C_{mn}X_{mn} \end{aligned}$$

Example An expression of total transportation costs for the company shipping its product from two factories to three markets is

$$C = C_{11}X_{11} + C_{12}X_{12} + C_{13}X_{13} + C_{21}X_{21} + C_{22}X_{22} + C_{23}X_{23}$$

More simply,

$$C = \sum \sum C_{ij}X_{ij} \qquad \text{for } i = 1, 2 \text{ and } j = 1, 2, 3$$

The coefficient C_{ij} represents per-unit shipping costs from the ith factory to the jth market. The variable X_{ij} is the amount of the shipment from the ith factory to the jth market.

An important special application is the use of the sigma notation to designate a system of simultaneous equations or inequalities:

$$\begin{aligned} A_{11}X_1 + A_{12}X_2 + \cdots + A_{1n}X_n &\le b_1 \\ A_{21}X_1 + A_{22}X_2 + \cdots + A_{2n}X_n &\le b_2 \\ &\vdots \\ A_{m1}X_1 + A_{m2}X_2 + \cdots + A_{mn}X_n &\le b_m \end{aligned}$$

We need only one summation sign to add all columns for each row. For example, for $i=1$, the first row is

$$\sum_{j=1}^{n} A_{1j}X_j \le b_1$$

For $i=2$, the second row is

$$\sum_{j=1}^{n} A_{2j}X_j \le b_2$$

For $i = m$, the mth row is

$$\sum_{j=1}^{n} A_{mj}X_j \le b_m$$

Consequently, we can write the preceding set of inequalities more compactly by using one summation sign:

$$\sum_{j=1}^{n} A_{ij}X_j \le b_i \qquad \text{for } i = 1, 2, \ldots, m$$

The General Form of Linear Programming Models

We can now apply the sigma notation to the general formulation of linear programming models.

Let X_j represent the level of the jth activity ($j = 1, 2, \ldots, n$), and let b_i represent the ***right-hand-side*** constraint restrictions ($i = 1, 2, \ldots, m$). The coefficients of the objective function are represented by C_j (where $j = 1, 2, \ldots, n$), and the symbol Z represents the total value of the objective function. Then the general form for a maximization linear programming problem is as follows:

$$
\begin{aligned}
&\text{Max} \quad Z = C_1X_1 + C_2X_2 + \cdots + C_nX_n \\
&\text{subject to} \quad A_{11}X_1 + A_{12}X_2 + \cdots + A_{1n}X_n \leq b_1 \\
&\qquad A_{21}X_1 + A_{22}X_2 + \cdots + A_{2n}X_n \leq b_2 \\
&\qquad \vdots \\
&\qquad A_{m1}X_1 + A_{m2}X_2 + \cdots + A_{mn}X_n \leq b_m \\
&\text{and} \quad X_j \geq 0; j = 1, 2, \ldots, n
\end{aligned}
\tag{2.4}
$$

By applying sigma notation, we can express this general form in a more compact manner.

$$
\begin{aligned}
&\text{Max} \quad Z = \sum_j C_jX_j \\
&\text{subject to} \quad \sum_j A_{ij}X_j \leq b_i \\
&\text{and} \quad X_j \geq 0 \\
&\text{where} \quad i = 1, 2, \ldots, m; \text{ and } j = 1, 2, \ldots, n
\end{aligned}
\tag{2.5}
$$

Deriving the general form of minimization linear programming is analogous; we leave it as an exercise for the reader.

Converting an Inequality into an Equality

A set of less-than-or-equal-to constraints in general form can be converted into equality relationships by adding a nonnegative variable called a ***slack variable.*** Specifically, given

$$\sum_j A_{ij}X_j \leq b_i; i = 1, 2, \ldots, m \tag{2.6}$$

the corresponding equality relationships must be:

$$\sum_j A_{ij}X_j + S_i = b_i \tag{2.7}$$

where $i = 1, 2, \ldots, m$; and $S_i \geq 0$

It is evident that a slack variable accounts for the amount of a resource that is left idle or unused in a given production plan. Analogously, greater-than-or-equal-to constraints can be converted into equality relationships by subtracting nonnegative ***surplus variables.*** Thus

$$\sum_j A_{ij}X_j \geq b_i; i = 1, 2, \ldots, m \tag{2.8}$$

becomes an equality relationship in the following form:

$$\sum_j A_{ij}X_j - S_i = b_i \tag{2.9}$$

where $i = 1, 2, \ldots, m$; and $S_i \geq 0$

Note that S_i now stands for surplus instead of slack.

Consider, for example, the constraints (2.1b) in the potato-tomato problem. We can convert them into equality relationships by adding slack variables, as follows:

$$\begin{aligned} X_1 + 2X_2 + S_1 \qquad\qquad &= 30 \\ 3X_1 + 2X_2 \qquad + S_2 \qquad &= 60 \\ 2X_2 \qquad\qquad + S_3 &= 24 \end{aligned} \tag{2.10}$$

where $S_i \geq 0$ for all i

The slack variables are interpreted as unused land resources, idle labor hours, and unused storage space.

Analogously, we can convert the constraints of the presidential election problem into equality relationships by introducing surplus variables, as follows:

$$\begin{aligned} 6X_1 + 2X_2 - S_1 \qquad\qquad &= 24 \\ 3X_1 + 2X_2 \qquad - S_2 \qquad &= 18 \\ X_1 + 3X_2 \qquad\qquad - S_3 &= 12 \end{aligned} \tag{2.11}$$

where $S_i \geq 0$ for all i

In this case, the first surplus variable must be interpreted as overfulfillment of the minimum required audience of Democrats. Similar interpretations can be extended to the other two surplus variables.

The Standard Form and the Mixed Form

When the statement of a linear programming model expresses all constraints in the form of equalities, the model is said to be in ***standard form.*** Of course, in their original form the constraints are generally inequalities, so the standard form must usually be developed using slack and/or surplus variables.

Occasionally, a linear programming model may be written in ***mixed form,*** in which some constraints are inequalities and others are equalities.

Algebraic Manipulation of the Objective Function

Any linear programming maximization problem can be converted into an equivalent minimization problem, and vice versa.

$$\text{Max} \quad Z = \sum_j C_j X_j$$

is equivalent to (2.12)

$$\text{Min} \quad -Z = \sum_j (-C_j) X_j$$

The conversion is made by changing the sign of every coefficient in the objective function. No changes should be made to the constraints. Thus, for example, maximizing the function

$$Z = 2X_1 + 3X_2$$

is equivalent to minimizing its negative counterpart,

$$-Z = -2X_1 - 3X_2$$

A Note on Unrestricted Variables

As we mentioned earlier, variables in linear programming models are generally confined to nonnegative values. Nevertheless, it is possible to incorporate variables that may be unrestricted in sign. To do so, we use a simple device that treats the unrestricted variable as the difference between two nonnegative variables. Consider, for example, the variable X_j, which in a particular application may be positive, zero, or negative. Then define X_j to be an unrestricted variable in the following way:

$$X_j \equiv X_j' - X_j''$$

where $X_j' \geq 0, X_j'' \geq 0$

Accordingly, one should substitute the two-variable difference for the unrestricted variable wherever it appears in the linear programming model. Suppose that the variable X_3 must be unrestricted in the system

$$3X_1 + 2X_2 + 3X_3 = 5$$
$$X_1 + X_2 - X_3 = 1$$

where $X_1 \geq 0,\ X_2 \geq 0$

Define the unrestricted variable as

$$X_3 \equiv X_3' - X_3''$$

such that $X_3' \geq 0,\ X_3'' \geq 0$

Replacing the unrestricted variable with the difference of nonnegative variables in the original system of equations yields a new, equivalent system in which all variables assume nonnegative values:

$$3X_1 + 2X_2 + 3X_3' - 3X_3'' = 5$$
$$X_1 + X_2 - X_3' + X_3'' = 1$$

where $X_1 \geq 0,\ X_2 \geq 0,\ X_3' \geq 0,\ X_3'' \geq 0$

When a solution is obtained, calculating the appropriate difference will determine the solution of the unrestricted variable.

2.6 Summary

Linear programming is the optimization (maximization or minimization) of a linear objective function relating to a set of specific decision variables subject to a given set of linear constraints.

In the case of two-decision variables, the following essential points have been demonstrated.

1. The nonnegativity requirements, $X_1 \geq 0$ and $X_2 \geq 0$, confine the feasible solution to the first quadrant.

2. Equality constraints are represented by lines; inequality constraints are represented by regions.
3. The feasible region satisfies all constraints and nonnegativity requirements simultaneously.
4. A feasible solution is any combination of variables X_1 and X_2 in the feasible region.
5. An optimal solution is that particular feasible solution on the boundary of the feasible region which optimizes the objective function.
6. An optimal solution to any linear programming problem can be found at one of the corner points of the feasible region.

The basic assumptions of linear programming are proportionality, additivity, divisibility, linearity of the objective function, and nonnegativity.

Having examined the formulation of linear programming problems in the two-variable case, and having investigated the general algebraic form of linear programming problems, we will turn in the next chapter to the ***simplex method***—a general computational device for solving linear programming problems.

Exercises

2.1 Define or explain the following terms:

a. Linear programming
b. Feasible region
c. Feasible solution
d. Optimal solution
e. Multiple optimal solutions
f. Nonnegativity

2.2 Solve the following problems graphically:

a. $$\text{Max } Z = 10X_1 + 5X_2$$

subject to
$$X_1 + 3X_2 \leq 5$$
$$5X_1 + 4X_2 \leq 60$$

and
$$X_1 \geq 0, X_2 \geq 0$$

b.

$$\text{Min} \quad C = 3X_1 + 5X_2$$

subject to

$$3X_1 + X_2 \geq 9$$

$$X_1 + 2X_2 \geq 8$$

$$X_1 + 5X_2 \geq 10$$

and

$$X_1 \geq 0, X_2 \geq 0$$

2.3 Solve the following linear programming problem graphically:

$$\text{Max} \quad Z = 2X_1 + 3X_2$$

subject to

$$4X_1 + 2X_2 \leq 20$$

$$X_1 + 3X_2 \leq 18$$

$$X_1 \leq 4$$

and

$$X_1 \geq 0, X_2 \geq 0$$

2.4 Add the constraint $2X_1 + 3X_2 \leq 30$ to problem 2.3. Add this new constraint to the graph you drew for problem 2.3. Would the new constraint affect the solution? If not, why not?

2.5 Give an example of a problem in which a redundant constraint occurs and show it graphically.

2.6 Why, normally, is the optimal solution always at one of the corner points or vertices of the feasibility region?

2.7 Explain briefly the basic assumptions of linear programming.

2.8 Two colors of raw marble are used by a manufacturing firm that produces products made of marble. White raw marble costs \$4 per unit and gray raw marble costs \$2 per unit. Each unit of white marble weighs 2 pounds and each unit of gray marble weighs 3 pounds. The firm has received an order from a retailer with the following specifications: (1) Total weight of the final marble combined must be 18 pounds. (2) At least 6 units of white raw marble must be used in the final product. (3) No more than 4 units of gray raw marble may be used. Formulate a minimum-cost linear programming model for the firm, and draw a graph that shows the feasible region and the optimal solution.

2.9 A local machine shop produces products 1 and 2, which require two technical operations—stamping and assembly. The stamping equipment has a 140-hour monthly capacity. A total of 200 labor hours is available monthly for assembly. Each unit of product 1 requires 7 hours of stamping and 5 hours of assembly. Product 2 requires 2 hours of stamping and 4 hours of assembly per unit. The net profit for product 1 is \$40;

for product 2, it is \$30. A market survey estimates that the maximum sales volume of product 1 is 8 units per month. The management feels that there will be no limitations on sales of product 2, at least in the next few months. The owner of the shop is anxious to know the product mix that will yield the maximum profit.

a. Formulate this problem in a linear programming model.
b. Find the optimum monthly production schedule by the graphical method.
c. Which will be the limiting constraint if the production schedule you obtained in part (b) is adopted?

2.10 Consider a commercial bank with the following balance sheet:[4]

Assets	Liabilities
Loans	Demand deposit
Securities	Time deposit
	Capital accounts

The total amount of funds available is \$100 million. The liability accounts show \$45 million in demand deposits, \$45 million in time deposits, and the remaining \$10 million in capital accounts. The rates of return on loans and securities are 10% and 5%, respectively, during the given period. For simplicity, assume that no loans will mature and that the securities can be liquidated at any time during the period without risk of capital loss. Furthermore, assume that there are no costs involved in attracting and maintaining deposits.

However, in making the portfolio choice, the management of the bank must consider three conditions:

1. The sum of loans and securities cannot be greater than \$100 million (the total availability of funds).
2. Because the loans cannot be liquidated during the given time period, the bank always holds a securities balance equal to at least 25% of total assets in order to meet unanticipated deposit withdrawals.
3. To foster relations with important customers, the bank deems it advisable to maintain \$30 million in loans outstanding.

The bank's goal is to select a feasible asset portfolio that will maximize total return.

[4]Exercises 2.10 and 2.11 are based on Alfred Broaddus, "Linear Programming: A New Approach to Bank Portfolio Management," *Monthly Review*, Federal Reserve Bank of Richmond, November 1972, 3–11. Used by permission.

a. Formulate a linear programming model for the bank's portfolio selection, defining all variables used.
b. Find the optimal portfolio graphically.
c. Presumably, the bank's liquidity ratio varies inversely with the ratio of time deposits to total deposits, because time deposits are generally more stable than demand deposits. If the liquidity ratio increases, what happens to the feasible region of the portfolio?

2.11 Referring to exercise 2.10, suppose that the bank gains an additional \$10 million in time deposits (hence the availability of total funds is now \$10 million). With \$55 million in time deposits, management decides that the liquidity constraint should now be 20% of total assets. The management's policy for its loan balance remains unchanged. Using the graphical method, find the optimal portfolio combination that will maximize gross income during the given time for the bank.

2.12 A medical scientist claims to have found a cure for the common cold that consists of three drugs called K, S, and H. His results indicate that the minimum daily adult dosage for effective treatment is 10 mg of drug K, 6 mg of drug S, and 8 mg of drug H. Two substances are readily available for preparing pills for distribution to cold sufferers. Both substances contain all three of the required drugs. Each unit of substance A contains 6 mg, 1 mg, and 2 mg of drugs K, S, and H, respectively, and each unit of substance B contains 2 mg, 3 mg, and 2 mg of the same drugs. Substance A costs \$3 per unit and substance B costs \$5 per unit.

a. Find the least-cost combination of the two substances that will yield a pill designed to contain the minimum daily recommended adult dosage.
b. Suppose that the costs of the two substances are interchanged so that substance A costs \$5 per unit and substance B costs \$3 per unit. Find the new optimal solution.

2.13 The Jesse James Silver Mining Company is operating mines A and B, which are geographically separated. Silver from the mines is separated into high, medium, and low grades. In a particular week, the company can mine at least 0.6 tons of high-grade, 0.4 tons of medium-grade, and 1.2 tons of low-grade silver. Each day mine A produces 0.1, 0.1, and 0.6 tons of the high, medium, and low grades, respectively. Mine B's daily capacity is 0.3, 0.1, and 0.2 tons of the same grades. Mine A costs \$200 per day to operate; mine B costs \$400 per day.

The company has received an offer from a major silverware manufacturing company to buy as many tons (of all grades) as can be produced during the life of the contract. Using the linear programming technique, determine how many days per week each mine should be operated to minimize the total cost the mine company incurs. Solve the problem graphically.

2.14 An advertising agency wishes to reach two types of audiences: (1) customers with annual incomes greater than \$15,000 and (2) customers with annual incomes of less than \$15,000. The total advertising budget is \$200,000. One program of TV advertising costs \$50,000; one program of radio advertising costs \$20,000. For contract reasons, at least 3 programs ought to be on TV, and the number of radio programs must be limited to 5. Surveys indicate that a single TV program reaches 450,000 customers in the high-income group and 50,000 in the low-income group. One radio program reaches 20,000 in the high-income group and 80,000 in the low-income group.

a. Formulate a linear programming model.
b. Solve it graphically.
c. Will eliminating the radio constraint from the model affect the optimal solution? If not, why not?

2.15 In blending cheese, a food company must satisfy certain butterfat requirements at least cost. There are two raw materials—sweet cream and cheese—that both contain butterfat. Chemical analysis reveals that sweet cream contains 4 pounds of butterfat and curd cheese contains 1 pound of butterfat. The law stipulates that the total amount of butterfat from sweet cream and curd cheese should be at least 56 pounds and that the curd cheese should be at least 51 pounds. For technical reasons, the sweet cream is limited to 5 pounds at most. The raw-material costs for sweet cream and curd cheese are \$40 and \$30, respectively. The company's problem is to find the cheapest combination of sweet cream and curd cheese subject to these technical and legal requirements.[5]

a. Formulate a linear programming model.
b. Using the graphical method, find the optimal combination of sweet cream and curd cheese.

2.16 The Nature Food Company has peach canning plants in Hialeah, Florida, and in San Diego, California. The production capacities of these plants are 3 and 6 million cans, respectively. The company generally serves 3 market centers in the United States: Chicago, Philadelphia, and New York City. The demands corresponding to each market center are 3, 2, and 4 million cans, respectively. The shipping rates per can are as follows:

[5]This exercise is largely based on I. Katzman, "Solving Feed Problems Through Linear Programming," *Journal of Farm Economics*, 38, No. 2 (May 1956), 420–429. Used by permission.

To \ From	Hialeah	San Diego
Chicago	\$.05	\$.08
Philadelphia	.06	.07
New York City	.11	.10

Formulate this transportation problem as a linear programming model for the Nature Food Company with the goal of minimizing total transportation cost. Do not solve it until you have finished Chapter 5.

2.17 The Orlando Steel Company produces three products, A (rods), B (bars), and C (wire). Each product must pass through three manufacturing processes, P_1, P_2, and P_3. The technological information and running costs for each unit of product are shown in the following table:

Product \ Process	P_1	P_2	P_3
A	50	10	20
B	40	40	15
C	25	20	15
Running Cost	\$300	\$250	\$180

For example, the table indicates that the hourly production rates of the process P_1 for products A, B, and C are 50, 40, and 25, respectively. We can interpret the technological information contained in the second and third columns of the table similarly. The material costs and selling prices for each product are as follows:

Product	Material Cost	Selling Price
A	\$100	\$150
B	130	170
C	90	145

a. Find the profit margin for each unit of product.

b. The company's goal is to find a production schedule that maximizes the total hourly profit. Formulate the linear programming model for this decision problem. Do not solve it. (***Hint***: From the table of technological coefficients, we can figure out that a unit of A, B, and C will require 3%, 2.5%, and 4% of the hourly capacity of processes P_1, P_2, and P_3, respectively. Thus, for example, the technological constraint for process P_1 may be expressed as $0.02A + 0.025B + 0.04C \leq 1$.)

2.18 P & T Manufacturing has three plants producing widgets. The company has to decide how to distribute its products among four wholesale distribution centers. The following table presents the shipping cost per unit from each plant to each center.

Distribution Center \ Plant	A	B	C	Demand
1	$.20	$.40	$.15	140,000
2	.15	.40	.20	200,000
3	.10	.25	.25	160,000
4	.20	.45	.15	100,000
Production Capacity	250,000	150,000	300,000	

The management of the company also provides the following production cost and price information:

Plant	Production Cost	Distribution Center	Selling Price Per Unit
A	$1.00	1	$2.00
B	1.20	2	1.50
C	1.05	3	2.00
		4	1.90

a. In this situation, it is likely that demand from a particular distribution center will not be met if there is no profit contribution. Formulate a linear programming model that will help management maximize profits. Do not try to solve it until you have read Chapter 5.

b. Suppose that the demand by each distribution center stands for the ***least*** amount of requirement and that the company's goal is to minimize the total cost (production cost plus transportation cost) subject to production capacity and the demand constraints. Reformulate the problem, but do not attempt to solve it yet.

2.19 The Young Brothers Radio Company produces three models of radios, which are identified by their model numbers: A1600, A1601, and A1602. The per-unit contributions of these models to company profits are \$40, \$20, and \$20, respectively. The company has three production departments—one for manufacturing component parts, one for assembling, and one for packaging. In each production period, 200 labor hours are available for packaging and 300 labor hours are available for both manufacturing and assembling. Each unit of the A1600 radio requires 1 hour of manufacturing time, 3 hours of assembly time, and 1 hour of packaging time. The corresponding labor hours required by each unit of the A1601 radio are 2, 1, and 1; likewise, the A1602 radio requires 3, 1, and 3 labor hours. On the basis of this information, formulate the production scheduling problem as a linear programming model, but do not try to find an optimal production solution until you have learned the simplex method, which is presented in Chapter 3.

2.20 Using the following model, rewrite the model so that all variables are nonnegative. (***Hint***: Let $X_2 = X_2' - X_2''$.)

$$\text{Max} \quad Z = C_1X_1 + C_2X_2$$

subject to

$$A_{11}X_1 + A_{12}X_2 \leq b_1$$

$$A_{21}X_1 + A_{22}X_2 \leq b_2$$

where

$$X_1 \geq 0,\ X_2 \text{ is unrestricted}$$

2.21 Verify the following:

a. $$\sum_{j=0}^{n} kA_jX_j = k\sum_{j=0}^{n} A_jX_j$$

b. $$\sum_{j=1}^{n} AX_j = A\sum_{j=1}^{n} X_j$$

c. $$\sum_{i=1}^{k} (X_i + Y_i + Z_i) = \sum_{i=1}^{k} X_i + \sum_{i=1}^{k} Y_i + \sum_{i=1}^{k} Z_i$$

d. $$\sum_{j=1}^{n} Y_jX_j = \sum_{j=1}^{n} X_jY_j$$

2.22 Write out these expressions in detail:

a. $$\sum_{i=0}^{5} k_iY_i$$

b. $$\sum_{k=1}^{n} A_{jk}X_{kj}$$

2.23 Write out these expressions in full:

a. $\sum_{j=1}^{n} A_{ij}X_j \leq b_i \qquad \text{for } i = 1, 2, \ldots, m$

b. $\sum_{i=1}^{m} A_{ij}Y_i \geq C_j \qquad \text{for } j = 1, 2, \ldots, n$

2.24 Formulate the general statement of a minimization linear programming problem. Use both the regular algebraic notation and the sigma notation.

2.25 Formulate the general statement of a maximization linear programming problem. Use both the regular algebraic notation and the sigma notation.

2.26 An enterprise has m factories and supplies n markets. Transportation costs from factory i to market j are denoted by C_{ij} ($i = 1, 2, \ldots, m$; and $j = 1, 2, \ldots, n$).

a. Formulate the statement of this general transportation problem as a linear programming model.

b. Write it out in Σ notation.

2.27 Given the following linear programming problem:

$$\text{Min} \quad C = 2X_1 + 4X_2$$

subject to

$$2X_1 + 3X_2 \leq 18$$
$$X_1 + 2X_2 \geq 10$$

where

$$X_1 \geq 0, X_2 \text{ is unrestricted}$$

rewrite the model so that all variables are nonnegative. Then transform the rewritten model into the standard form of a minimization problem.

Suggested Readings

Anderson, D. "Models for Determining Least-Cost Investments in Electricity Supply." *The Bell Journal of Economics,* 3, No. 1 (Spring 1972), 267–299.

Averill, Richard F., and J. Lloyd Suttle. "A Model for University Enrollment Planning." *Socio-Economics Planning Sciences,* 9 (1975), 257–261.

Baumol, William J. *Economic Theory and Operations Analysis.* 3rd ed. Englewood Cliffs, N.J.: Prentice-Hall, 1972. Chapter 5.

Bowles, S. "The Efficient Allocation of Resources in Education." *Quarterly Journal of Economics* (May 1967), 189–219.

Broaddus, Alfred. "A New Approach to Bank Portfolio Management." *Monthly Review.* Federal Reserve Bank of Richmond (November 1972), 3–11.

Chappell, A. E. "Linear Programming Cuts Cost in Production of Animal Feeds." *Operational Research Quarterly,* 25, No. 1 (March 1974), 19–26.

Charnes, A., C. Colantoni, W. W. Cooper, and K. O. Kortanek. "Economic, Social and Enterprise Accounting and Mathematical Models." *The Accounting Review* (January 1972), 85–108.

Dantzig, George B. *Linear Programming and Extensions*. Princeton, N.J.: Princeton University Press, 1963.

Demski, Joel S. "An Accounting System Structured on a Linear Programming Model." *The Accounting Review* (October 1967), 701–712.

Dorfman, Robert, Paul A. Samuelson, and Robert M. Solow. *Linear Programming and Economic Analysis*. New York: McGraw-Hill, 1958.

Feldstein, M., and H. Luft. "Distributional Constraints in Public Expenditure Planning." *Management Science* (August 1973), 1414–1422.

Gale, David. *The Theory of Linear Economic Models*. New York: McGraw-Hill, 1960.

Garvin, W. W. *Introduction to Linear Programming*. New York: McGraw-Hill, 1960.

Gensch, D. H. "Computer Models in Advertising Media Selection." *Journal of Marketing Research* (November 1968), 414–424.

Hadley, G. *Linear Programming*. Reading, Mass.: Addison-Wesley, 1962.

Johnson, Ross H., and Paul R. Winn. *Quantitative Methods for Management*. Boston, Mass.: Houghton Mifflin, 1976.

Naylor, T. H., E. T. Byrne, and J. M. Vernon. *Introduction to Linear Programming: Methods and Cases*. Belmont, Calif.: Wadsworth Publishing, 1971.

Stimson, David H., and Ronald P. Thompson. "Linear Programming, Busing and Educational Administration." *Socio-Economics Planning Sciences*, vol. 8, 1974, 195–206.

Wagner, Harvey M. *Principles of Operations Research*. Englewood Cliffs, N.J.: Prentice-Hall, 1969.

3

Linear Programming: The Simplex Method

In Chapter 2 we looked at the graphical solution of linear programming problems involving only two products. For more complicated problems, such as the transportation problem, we need general computational procedures. The ***simplex*** method, developed by George Dantzig, is the algorithm (that is, a systematic and efficient computational procedure) commonly used for solving well-defined linear programming problems.

We begin this chapter with a preview of the simplex method by using the same potato–tomato problem that was solved earlier, using graphical methods. First, we will demonstrate the underlying logic of the simplex method. Next, we will present precise steps that make up the computational procedure for solving linear programming problems. Once the techniques for maximization problems are mastered fully, we will examine some complications and methods of resolving them. Finally, we will extend the application of the simplex method to a minimization problem. Whenever appropriate, economic reasons or interpretations associated with the computational operations are considered.

3.1 The Simplex Method: A Preview

Corner Points, Slack Variables, and Basic Variables

In Chapter 2, we demonstrated graphically that, if an optimal solution exists for any linear programming problem, it is located at one of the corner points of the feasible region. We also noted that by adding slack variables, which generally represent idle resources, we can convert an inequality constraint into an equality. Thus, the potato–tomato problem with slack variables takes the following form:

$$
\begin{aligned}
&\text{Max} \quad Z = 40X_1 + 50X_2 + 0S_1 + 0S_2 + 0S_3 \\
&\text{subject to} \\
&\left.\begin{aligned}
X_1 + 2X_2 + S_1 + 0 + 0 &= 30 \quad (3.1a) \\
3X_1 + 2X_2 + 0 + S_2 + 0 &= 60 \quad (3.1b) \\
0 + 2X_2 + 0 + 0 + S_3 &= 24 \quad (3.1c)
\end{aligned}\right\} \quad (3.1) \\
&\text{and} \quad X_1 \geq 0,\ X_2 \geq 0,\ S_1 \geq 0,\ S_2 \geq 0,\ S_3 \geq 0
\end{aligned}
$$

where the nonnegative slack variables S_1, S_2, and S_3 represent unused land, labor, and storage space, respectively. Since each column represents an activity or a process, the addition of three slack variables is equivalent to the addition of three extra activities, each representing the idle amount of productive resource. A slack activity does nothing to contribute to the value of production, so each slack variable is assigned a zero coefficient in the objective function. To distinguish the original production variables X_1 and X_2 from the slack variables, we also refer to the former as ordinary or real variables.

The coordinates of the corner points A, B, C, and D, which were determined in Chapter 2, are reproduced in the first three columns of Table 3.1.

Since all the corner points are derived from a two-dimensional diagram (Figure 2.2), the corner coordinates clearly produce only the two ordinary variables X_1 and X_2. Given the corner coordinates of X_1 and X_2, however, we can easily determine the values of the corresponding slack variables from the programming model we have derived. At the origin, for example, both X_1 and X_2 are zeros, and the values of the slack

Table 3.1 Corner Points and Values of Ordinary and Slack Variables

Corner Point (from Table 2.2)	**Coordinates of Ordinary Variables (from Table 2.2)**		**Slack Variables**			**Value of Objective Function (from Table 2.2)**
			[from (3.1a)]	**[from (3.1b)]**	**[from (3.1c)]**	
	X_1	X_2	S_1	S_2	S_3	Z
0	0	0	30	60	24	0
A	0	12	6	36	0	600
B	6	12	0	18	0	840
C	15	7.5	0	0	9	975
D	20	0	10	0	24	800

variables S_1, S_2, and S_3 are determined from the constraints (3.1a), (3.1b), and (3.1c) as 30, 60, and 24, respectively. Similarly, given any other point, we can determine the corresponding value(s) of its slack variable(s). The values of both ordinary and slack variables corresponding to each corner point are listed in Table 3.1. Since the slack variables are profitless activities, as shown in the Z column of Table 3.1, they do not affect values of the objective function.

We will now introduce a set of important definitions.

Basic Variables The variables that normally take nonzero values at any solution are defined as ***basic variables,***[1] often shortened to ***the basis.***

Nonbasic Variables The variables that assume zero values are said to be nonbasic variables.

Basic Solution Any set of values of the variables is said to be a basic solution if the number of nonzero-valued variables (either ordinary or slack) is equal to the number of constraints.

Basic Feasible Solution A basic solution is said to be a basic feasible solution (BFS) if all the original constraints hold.

With these definitions in mind, we can make a very important observation about Table 3.1: Every corner point that represents a BFS has three basic variables and two nonbasic variables. Note that a variable may be basic at one corner and nonbasic at another. Furthermore, the number of nonzero-valued variables is exactly equal to the number of constraints. This is always true if the constraints are not redundant and if a basic feasible solution exists. In general terms, with m constraints and n variables (ordinary and slack), any BFS will have m basic variables, and $(n - m)$ nonbasic variables. Since there are three constraints and five variables in the potato–tomato example, each feasible solution must contain three basic variables, which equals the number of constraints. The remaining two variables are nonbasic.

Interestingly, when we add slack variables to the model, the optimal solution at point C (see Table 3.1) not only yields the solution of ordinary variables, $X_1 = 15$ and $X_2 = 7.5$, but also gives the value of a slack variable, $S_3 = 9$, which was not explicitly or directly shown in the graphical solution. The value of the slack variable in the optimal solution indicates which of the firm's resources should be fully utilized (no slack) and to what extent a given resource should remain idle (positive slack).

[1]This definition does not hold in a "degenerate" case, which will be discussed later. In a degenerate solution, there is at least one basic variable with zero value.

With slack variables there is an initial set of basic variables (the ***basis***), which occurs at the origin (see Table 3.1). This initial basic feasible solution facilitates the operation of the simplex method. The general idea of the simplex algorithm is to determine which variable must be basic (that is, in the basis) and which variable must be nonbasic (not in the basis). Once the set of initial basic feasible variables (or initial basis) is formulated through the introduction of slack variables, the simplex process can start.

We will see that the ***simplex procedure is essentially a set of systematic rules for interchanging a nonbasic and a basic variable in order to obtain an improved basis.*** Repetition of this process leads to the optimal solution. In terms of the graphical approach shown in Figure 2.2, the simplex procedure starts from the origin and moves in steps to an adjacent corner point until the optimal corner is reached. In terms of Table 3.1, the simplex process starts with the initial basic feasible solution (slack variables) and moves progressively to another basic solution until the optimal basic solution is determined.

Pivoting—Formulating a New Basis

First, let us rewrite the system (3.1) with all basic variables (S_1, S_2, and S_3) on the left and the constants and nonbasic variables (X_1 and X_2) on the right. This gives us

$$\begin{aligned} Z &= 0 + 40X_1 + 50X_2 \\ S_1 &= 30 - X_1 - 2X_2 \\ S_2 &= 60 - 3X_1 - 2X_2 \\ S_3 &= 24 - 0 - 2X_2 \end{aligned} \qquad (3.1')$$

By definition, all nonbasic variables are equal to zero; therefore, the initial basic solution that contains all slack variables is

$$S_1 = 30 \qquad S_2 = 60 \qquad S_3 = 24$$

With all idle activities in this basis, the value of the objective function is $Z = 0$. Although this initial solution with all slack variables may seem trivial, it is a basic feasible solution—a basis—from which we can find improved solutions.

A question arises. Which nonbasic variable should be brought into the basis to become one of the basic variables in the next solution? Examining the objective function of the potato–tomato problem in system (3.1′), we see that 1 unit of X_2 will contribute the most profit ($50) to the value of the objective function. Directed by this simple economic reasoning, we decide to produce X_2—that is, to convert X_2 from a nonbasic to a basic variable.

Indeed, there are two additional important questions. (1) How large can X_2 become? (2) Given that the number of basic variables for this problem can be only three (Do you see why?), which basic variable must be removed to make a place for the new member, X_2?

Looking at the potato–tomato problem as expressed in system (3.1′), we clearly see that every unit of the production of X_2 (tomatoes) causes a decline in each of S_1, S_2, and S_3 (land, labor, and storage space) by 2 units. The production of X_2 cannot increase beyond 12 units, because slack variable S_3 becomes zero at that level. This means that S_3 has changed from a basic to a nonbasic variable. As shown in Figure 2.2, we can increase X_2 only to the corner point A, where the storage space constraint becomes binding. At this point, the objective function has a value of \$600.

In short, we know now which nonbasic variable should be brought into the ***new*** basis as a basic variable and by how much it should be increased. We also know which basic variable in the ***old*** basis will become nonbasic. However, an alert reader might ask how this interchange of a basic and a nonbasic variable would affect the values of the other two basic values (S_1 and S_2). Intuitively, we suspect that this interchange of variables will have repercussions throughout the system. We are, after all, working with a set of simultaneous equations. To show this, we return to the ***old*** basis (3.1) at the origin. This time, for reasons to be explained shortly, we move the objective function to the last row and arrange all variable terms on the left hand side:

$$\left.\begin{array}{lr} 0 + X_1 + 2X_2 + S_1 + 0 + 0 = 30 & \text{(3.2a)} \\ 0 + 3X_1 + 2X_2 + 0 + S_2 + 0 = 60 & \text{(3.2b)} \\ 0 + 0 + 2X_2 + 0 + 0 + S_3 = 24 & \text{(3.2c)} \\ Z - 40X_1 - 50X_2 + 0 + 0 + 0 = 0 & \text{(3.2d)} \end{array}\right\} \quad (3.2)$$

A distinguishing feature of the column of a basic variable (in this case, the slack variables) is that there is one occurrence of the coefficient 1; all other entries in the column are zeros.[2] Also, since X_1 and X_2 are nonbasic, we can immediately spot the basic solution.

[2]One could include the variable Z in the objective function (3.2d), but we normally refer only to those basic variables that occur in the constraints.

Having decided to enter X_2 as a basic variable, we must manipulate the system such that the X_2 column has a coefficient of 1 in the third constraint and zeros elsewhere. To do this, we ***normalize the coefficient*** of X_2 in constraint (3.2c) by dividing all its terms by 2, yielding

$$0 + 0 + X_2 + 0 + 0 + \tfrac{1}{2}S_3 = 12 \tag{3.3c}$$

Equation (3.3c) with the coefficient 1 in the X_2 position is referred to as the ***replacing equation.***

Our next task is to convert other coefficients in the X_2 column of the system into zeros. We accomplish this by manipulating the system through the usual elimination method for solving a set of simultaneous linear equations in elementary algebra. We can now perform this operation by multiplying the replacing equation (3.3c) by certain constants and then adding the results to other equations in system (3.2).

To eliminate $-50X_2$ from equation (3.2d), for example, we multiply the replacing equation (3.3c) by 50 and then add the result (3.2d):

$$Z - 40X_1 + 0 + 0 + 0 + 25S_3 = 600 \tag{3.3d}$$

To eliminate $2X_2$ from equation (3.2a), we multiply all terms on both sides of the replacing equation (3.3c) by (-2) and then add the result to equation (3.2a). The resulting equation is

$$0 + X_1 + 0 + S_1 + 0 - S_3 = 6 \tag{3.3a}$$

Similarly, we can eliminate $2X_2$ from (3.2b) by multiplying all terms in the replacing equation (3.3c) by (-2) and adding the result to (3.2b), yielding

$$0 + 3X_1 + 0 + 0 + S_2 - S_3 = 36 \tag{3.3b}$$

Normalizing a coefficient and eliminating a variable are called ***pivoting*** which brings about a ***change of basis.*** The purpose of pivoting is to change from one solution basis to another—to interchange a nonbasic and a basic variable. When a pivoting operation is finished, one ***iteration*** has been completed, and a new basis is formulated. Grouping the new basis equations (3.3a)–(3.3d) together, we get

$$\left.\begin{array}{lr} 0 + X_1 + 0 + S_1 + 0 - \phantom{\tfrac{1}{2}}S_3 = 6 & (3.3a) \\ 0 + 3X_1 + 0 + 0 + S_2 - \phantom{\tfrac{1}{2}}S_3 = 36 & (3.3b) \\ 0 + 0 + X_2 + 0 + 0 + \tfrac{1}{2}S_3 = 12 & (3.3c) \\ Z - 40X_1 + 0 + 0 + 0 + 25S_3 = 600 & (3.3d) \end{array}\right\} \quad (3.3)$$

Thus the *new* basic variables (columns with the coefficient 1 for the particular basic variable and zeros elsewhere) are $X_2 = 12$, $S_1 = 6$, and $S_2 = 36$. The nonbasic variables are $X_1 = S_3 = 0$. The value of the objective function, as we predicted earlier, is $Z = \$600$. In terms of Figure 2.2 or Table 3.1, we have, through pivoting, moved from corner 0 to corner A, or from one basic function to another. And we have enhanced the value of the objective function.

3.2 The Simplex Method

The logic of the simplex method, illustrated in Section 3.1, is to work toward the optimal BFS by using a set of general rules. We now distill those rules and study the simplex algorithm in detail, again using the potato–tomato example.

Step 1 ***Finding an Initial Basic Feasible Solution*** Begin with the form of the system of equations expressed in (3.2). First, write all constraint coefficients in a table known as the ***simplex tableau*** (see Table 3.2). The right-hand-side—RHS—column of the tableau contains the resource availability levels. Row 0 stands for the objective function, which we separate from the constraint functions with a broken line. (Placing row 0 in the last row of the simplex tableau confers a most convenient symmetry on the simplex tableau of the duality theory, to be discussed in the next chapter. Furthermore, this device makes the primal–dual formulation for quadratic programming, discussed in Chapter 8, more straightforward.)

In this form, activities X_1 and X_2 must be identified as nonbasic variables, and the initial basic feasible solution (IBFS) falls out as

$$S_1 = 30 \quad S_2 = 60 \quad S_3 = 24 \quad X_1 = X_2 = 0$$

Table 3.2
The Initial Simplex Tableau: The Potato–Tomato Problem

Row	Z	X_1	X_2	S_1	S_2	S_3	RHS
1	0	1	2	1	0	0	30
2	0	3	2	0	1	0	60
3	0	0	(2)	0	0	1	24
0	1	−40	−50	0	0	0	0

With all resources idle, the value of the objective function is zero. All coefficients in the RHS column must be nonnegative because of their interpretation as levels of resource availability. Note also that these RHS values become the activity levels of the slack variables in the IBFS, which further necessitates their nonnegativity.

Step 2 ***Choosing the Pivot Column*** Next, examine the objective function to see whether there is a nonbasic variable that, if increased, will improve the value of Z. If so, select the one that will contribute most to the value of the objective function and proceed to step 3. If not, the iteration process is complete and you have reached an optimal solution. In the problem we are considering, the optimal solution has not been reached, because we can increase the objective function by increasing either activity X_1 or activity X_2 from zero to a positive level. Only one variable at a time may come into a succeeding BFS. We choose activity X_2 because it contributes \$50 per unit to the value of Z, whereas activity X_1 contributes only \$40 per unit.

In row 0 of the simplex tableau, the ***most negative coefficient identifies the nonbasic variable that should enter the next solution.*** The column of the tableau that corresponds to this activity becomes the ***pivot column*** in the iteration procedure. If no negative values appear in row 0, improvement is not possible, an optimal solution is indicated, and further iteration is unnecessary.

Step 3 ***Choosing the Pivot Row*** A few simple arithmetical calculations will determine the ***pivot row*** of the simplex tableau for the iteration procedure. First, divide all elements in the RHS column by the corresponding elements in the pivot column. Ignore zero or negative pivot column elements if you encounter them. Second, locate the smallest ratio, which identifies the pivot row—that is, the ***limiting constraint.*** The element that lies at the intersection of the pivot column and the pivot row is the ***pivot element,*** which is often circled for computational convenience.

In the illustrative problem (see Table 3.2), step 3 requires formation of the following ratios:

Row 1: RHS_1/(first pivot column element) $= 30/2 = 15$

Row 2: RHS_2/(second pivot column element) $= 60/2 = 30$

Row 3: RHS_3/(third pivot column element) $= 24/2 = 12$ (min. ratio)

The minimum ratio, $24/2 = 12$, designates the third row as the pivot row. Thus, in the succeeding solution, activity X_2 equals 12 and slack

S_3 equals zero. The pivot element is 2, located at the intersection of the pivot row and the pivot column.

Step 4 ***Forming a New Tableau—Pivoting***

a. Convert all entries in the pivot column of the current tableau to zeros in a new tableau—except the pivot element, which is normalized to a value of 1.
b. Then replace the present pivot row by dividing all elements in the old pivot row by the pivot element. This new row of the next tableau is called the ***replacing row.***
c. Create the remaining rows in the new tableau one at a time by adding to each old row a constant times the replacing row.

This set of pivot rules is no more than an application of standard algebraic procedures for manipulating a system of simultaneous equations. In step 4b, we divide the equation corresponding to the pivot row by a constant—the pivot element. This establishes the replacing row in the next tableau (see row 3 of Table 3.3). In step 4c, we form the remaining rows of the new tableau by adding to each old row a constant times the replacing row. Step 4a is always consistent with these operations and can be done routinely. The more algebraic interpretation of pivoting was presented in the previous section. Applied to this example, the operations would be performed as follows:

$$\begin{bmatrix}\text{Row 1}\\\text{Table 3.3}\end{bmatrix} = \begin{bmatrix}\text{Row 3}\\\text{Table 3.3}\end{bmatrix} \times (-2) + \begin{bmatrix}\text{Row 1}\\\text{Table 3.2}\end{bmatrix}$$

$$\begin{bmatrix}\text{Row 2}\\\text{Table 3.3}\end{bmatrix} = \begin{bmatrix}\text{Row 3}\\\text{Table 3.3}\end{bmatrix} \times (-2) + \begin{bmatrix}\text{Row 2}\\\text{Table 3.2}\end{bmatrix}$$

and

$$\begin{bmatrix}\text{Row 0}\\\text{Table 3.3}\end{bmatrix} = \begin{bmatrix}\text{Row 3}\\\text{Table 3.3}\end{bmatrix} \times (50) + \begin{bmatrix}\text{Row 0}\\\text{Table 3.2}\end{bmatrix}$$

Table 3.3
First Iteration

Row	Z	X_1	X_2	S_1	S_2	S_3	RHS
1	0	(1)	0	1	0	−1	6
2	0	3	0	0	1	−1	36
3	0	0	1	0	0	$\frac{1}{2}$	12
0	1	−40	0	0	0	25	600

Note: As we expect, the coefficients we obtain in Table 3.3 are exactly the same as the system of equations we obtained in (3.3).

By ignoring the nonbasic variables X_1 and S_3 in Table 3.3 (their values are zero anyway), we can immediately read the basic feasible solution as

$$S_1 = 6 \qquad S_2 = 36 \qquad X_2 = 12$$

In this second BFS, the value of the objective function is \$600. Since a negative coefficient appears in row 0, another iteration will further improve the value of the objective function. We can easily see this by writing Table 3.3 in the equivalent system of simultaneous equations:

$$\begin{aligned} Z &= 600 + 40X_1 - 25S_3 \\ S_1 &= 6 - X_1 + S_3 \\ S_2 &= 36 - 3X_1 + S_3 \\ X_2 &= 12 - \tfrac{1}{2}S_3 \end{aligned} \tag{3.4}$$

Clearly, the value of Z will increase further if activity X_1 becomes basic.

Second Iteration To start the next iteration, return to step 2. The most negative coefficient, −40, occurs at the X_1 column in row 0. Thus the nonbasic variable X_1 is identified as the pivot column that should be converted into a basic variable in the next basis. In step 3, we choose the pivot row by selecting the minimum ratio from the following calculations:

Row 1: RHS_1/(first pivot column element) = 6/1 = 6 (min. ratio)

Row 2: RHS_2/(second pivot column element) = 36/3 = 12

Row 3: ignored (because the third pivot column element is zero)

It is interesting to note the economic interpretations of the RHS ratios in rows 1 and 3. System (3.4) shows that we can increase the production of X_1 ***only*** up to 6 units where S_1 (land resources) is equal to zero. Any further increase of X_1 would require a negative value of S_1, which is impossible. Choosing the smallest-ratio row as the pivot row is really the reflection of an economic necessity. Production of X_1 in this case is limited by the row 1 constraint, land. In row 3, not only is division by zero mathematically undefined, but storage capacity is not an ***effective*** constraint on the production of potatoes (X_1). The negative ratio that we will encounter later can likewise be disregarded.

We now proceed to the second iteration. The minimum ratio, 6, determines several things: first, that the first row is to be the pivot row;

Table 3.4
Second Iteration

Row	Z	X_1	X_2	S_1	S_2	S_3	RHS
1	0	1	0	1	0	−1	6
2	0	0	0	−3	1	(2)	18
3	0	0	1	0	0	$\frac{1}{2}$	12
0	1	0	0	40	0	−15	840

second, that in the succeeding solution, the largest value of X_1 will be 6, at which the slack variable S_1 (basic in the ***current*** basis) will become zero (nonbasic in the next basis); third, that the pivot element is 1, circled at the intersection of the first row and the pivot column in the current tableau (Table 3.3). We now perform the pivoting procedure of step 4 to formulate a new tableau. The normalization (step 4b) is omitted in the present case, because the pivot element is already equal to 1. Consequently, the ***replacing row*** in the next tableau (row 0 in Table 3.4) is the same as the row in the previous tableau. Then we complete step 4c by creating zeros for the X_1 column in rows 2, 3, and 0 as follows:

$$\begin{bmatrix}\text{Row 2}\\ \text{Table 3.4}\end{bmatrix} = \begin{bmatrix}\text{Row 1}\\ \text{Table 3.4}\end{bmatrix} \times (-3) + \begin{bmatrix}\text{Row 2}\\ \text{Table 3.3}\end{bmatrix}$$

$$\begin{bmatrix}\text{Row 3}\\ \text{Table 3.4}\end{bmatrix} : \text{(Nothing needs to be done, because row 3 in the } X_1 \text{ column is already equal to zero.)}$$

and

$$\begin{bmatrix}\text{Row 0}\\ \text{Table 3.4}\end{bmatrix} = \begin{bmatrix}\text{Row 1}\\ \text{Table 3.4}\end{bmatrix} \times (40) + \begin{bmatrix}\text{Row 0}\\ \text{Table 3.3}\end{bmatrix}$$

In this solution, activities S_1 and S_3 are nonbasic; X_1, X_2, and S_2 are all basic at levels of 6, 12, and 18, respectively; and the value of the objective function has been improved to $840.

Third Iteration In the second simplex iteration, the coefficients of row 0 are not all nonnegative, so the value of the objective function should increase when we bring slack S_3 into the next BFS. Once the pivot column is determined, the pivot row will be identified by the minimum ratio among the following:

Row 1: ignored (because it is negative)

Row 2: $18/2 = 9$ (min. ratio)

Row 3: $12/\frac{1}{2} = 24$

We now leave the reader to explain why the negative ratio in row 1 is ignored. [***Hint:*** Rewriting Table 3.4 in the form of system (3.4), we can apply the same economic reasoning used in the second iteration.[3]]

The pivot element, 2, is located at the intersection of the S_3 column and row 2 of Table 3.4.

As with the preceding pivoting procedure, normalize a coefficient of 1 for the entering variable S_3 in row 2 by dividing row 2 by 2. This yields the ***replacing row*** shown in the next tableau (see row 2 in Table 3.5). All zero coefficients for S_3 in the remaining rows are created as follows:

$$\begin{bmatrix}\text{Row 1}\\ \text{Table 3.5}\end{bmatrix} = \begin{bmatrix}\text{Row 2}\\ \text{Table 3.5}\end{bmatrix} \times 1 + \begin{bmatrix}\text{Row 1}\\ \text{Table 3.4}\end{bmatrix}$$

$$\begin{bmatrix}\text{Row 3}\\ \text{Table 3.5}\end{bmatrix} = \begin{bmatrix}\text{Row 2}\\ \text{Table 3.5}\end{bmatrix} \times -\tfrac{1}{2} + \begin{bmatrix}\text{Row 3}\\ \text{Table 3.4}\end{bmatrix}$$

and

$$\begin{bmatrix}\text{Row 0}\\ \text{Table 3.5}\end{bmatrix} = \begin{bmatrix}\text{Row 2}\\ \text{Table 3.5}\end{bmatrix} \times 15 + \begin{bmatrix}\text{Row 0}\\ \text{Table 3.4}\end{bmatrix}$$

All coefficients in row 0 are nonnegative, so the optimal solution has been reached and the series of iterations has been terminated. The optimal solution is

$$X_1 = 15 \qquad X_2 = 7.5 \qquad S_3 = 9 \qquad S_1 = S_2 = 0$$

Note that, in the third iteration, we have increased the value of the objective function from \$840 to \$975 by bringing ***slack*** S_3 into the BFS. It may seem peculiar that introducing more of a slack activity increases the objective function, but examination of the constraints makes it apparent that the second slack variable, S_2, is thereby reduced to zero, making it possible for activity X_1 to increase to 15 units. Activity X_2 decreases to 7.5 units at the same time, but the net gain in profit is

Table 3.5
The Optimal Solution

Row	Z	X_1	X_2	S_1	S_2	S_3	RHS
1	0	1	0	$-\frac{1}{2}$	$\frac{1}{2}$	0	15
2	0	0	0	$-\frac{3}{2}$	$\frac{1}{2}$	1	9
3	0	0	1	$\frac{3}{4}$	$-\frac{1}{4}$	0	7.5
0	1	0	0	$\frac{35}{2}$	$\frac{15}{2}$	0	975

[3]For further explanation, see Section 3.3.

\$135. Therefore, the condition in step 2 of the simplex method is valid whether an ordinary or a slack variable is introduced into the next basis.

Of course, the simplex method gives the same optimal solution as Chapter 2's graphical method. Graphically, the simplex method starts at the origin (IBFS) and moves from there to points *A*, *B*, and *C* (see Figure 2.2). The simplex method is a set of systematic calculations for moving from one corner point to an adjacent corner point until the optimal solution is reached. It is certainly more powerful than the graphical method, because it makes possible the solution of large problems. And, thanks to electronic data processing, the simplex algorithm can be conveniently and accurately implemented. Powerful computer programs are available for this purpose.

Figure 3.1 summarizes diagramatically the iterative procedure of the simplex method for maximizing a linear programming model.

Figure 3.1
Basic Elements of the Simplex Procedure (Maximization Problem)

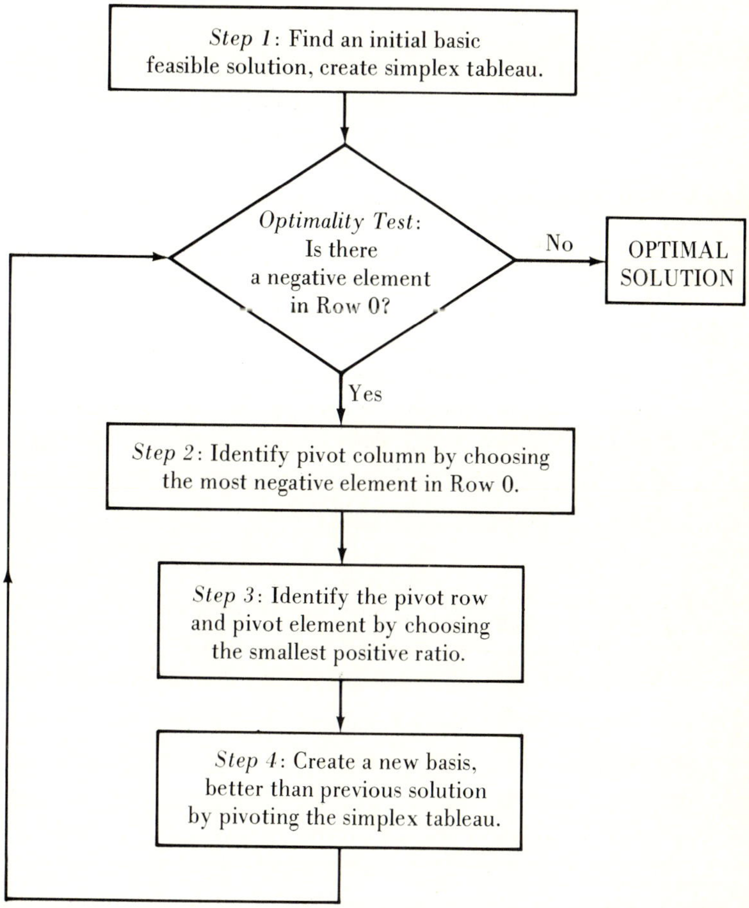

3.3 Complications and Their Resolution

Equal Contribution to Profit If, either in the initial solution or after some number of iterations, the most negative profit-contribution coefficient is the same for two or more nonbasic activities, it may not be clear which of the variables should enter the next BFS. This "tie" indicates computational indifference, and we may make our selection arbitrarily.

Degeneracy If in step 2 two or more of the calculated ratios should be equal and minimum, there will invariably be a complication after we pivot into the next BFS. In particular, one variable in this next BFS will assume a zero level of activity, and this contradicts the definition of a basic variable—a variable that assumes a positive solution value.

Suppose, for example, that the second constraint in the potato–tomato problem had been

$$3X_1 + 5X_2 \leq 60$$

Referring to Table 3.2, we see that this change would cause the row 2 coefficient corresponding to variable X_2 to be 5, rather than 2, and the subsequent ratios in rows 2 and 3 would be minimum and identical. One practical if arbitrary way to break the tie is simply to start with the tied variable on the left-hand side of the simplex tableau. In our example, suppose that row 3 is chosen to be the pivot row. After the pivot operation is complete, the next BFS becomes

$$X_2 = 12 \qquad S_1 = 6 \qquad S_2 = 0 \qquad X_1 = S_3 = 0$$

(The reader should verify this.) Note first that slack S_2 is now in the basis at a level of zero. Therefore, the number of nonzero variables in the current basis is smaller than, rather than equal to, the number of constraints. Whenever one or more of the basic solutions has a value of zero, a condition called ***degeneracy*** exists.

The complication presented by degeneracy is that later pivoting may fail to make any improvement in the value of the objective function. It is also possible to encounter again a basis that has already been calculated in a previous iteration. It may take several pivoting steps to break out of the zero-improvement deadlock.[4]

[4]This is known as ***cycling,*** and it sometimes is impossible to break out of the cycle of solutions using standard simplex procedures. A special technique called ***lexicographic ordering*** has been developed to handle the problems of cycling. Fortunately, we rarely encounter the cycling phenomenon in practice.

Unbounded Optimal Solutions

As indicated in the previous section, we ignore zero or negative coefficients in the pivot column when we calculate ratios. As a result, the minimum positive ratio maintains feasibility in the new BFS. However, cases can arise in which there is no positive coefficient in the pivot column. This is an indication that the feasible region is unbounded—a condition that allows the value of the objective function to increase indefinitely without exceeding the constraints of the model.

Furthermore, in all situations we interpret the sign of the technical constraint coefficients as follows:

1. ***Positive:*** Increasing activity levels will require more of a given resource.
2. ***Zero:*** Increasing activity levels will require no more of a given resource.
3. ***Negative:*** Increasing activity levels will generate more of a given resource.

Finally, by choosing only the positive ratios, we give consideration to those resources that will limit the level of a new activity. If no such limitations exist (that is, if all coefficients in the pivot column are either zero or negative), the activity level of the next variable to enter the basis will be unlimited. Likewise, the value of the objective function can become arbitrarily large, and the optimal solution is unbounded.

Let's take an example of this type of problem. Consider a government economist who makes policy decisions that affect the output of the economy in such broad categories as consumer goods (X_1) and capital goods (X_2). According to the economist's philosophy and the political objectives of the party in power, an objective is formulated that emphasizes the production of capital goods. This policy is oriented toward providing a long-run increase in the nation's standard of living. Over a typical 4-year term of office, numerical indices of the nation's standard of living are estimated to increase 0.05 points for each unit of consumer goods produced and 0.2 points for each unit of capital goods produced.

In formulating a linear programming model for the economy, this economist recognizes that two primary constraints affect the output of the economy: labor and productive capacity. It is also evident that the production of capital goods not only increases productive capacity, but also has a net labor-saving effect. Therefore, giving careful consideration to the technical coefficients of production, the economist assembles the following model:

$$\begin{aligned}
&\text{Max} \quad \Delta\text{SOL} = 0.05X_1 + 0.2X_2 \\
&\text{subject to} \qquad 4X_1 - X_2 \leq 100 \qquad \text{(labor)} \\
&\qquad\qquad\quad 1.6X_1 - X_2 \leq 10 \qquad \text{(productive capacity)} \\
&\text{and} \qquad X_1 \geq 0,\ X_2 \geq 0
\end{aligned} \tag{3.5}$$

where ΔSOL is the change in the current level of the standard-of-living index. The corresponding simplex tableau is given in Table 3.6.

Activity X_2 is clearly the most profitable variable to introduce into the next basis. However, both coefficients in the pivot column are negative, and there is evidently no restriction on the level of activity X_2 in the next BFS. Such an unbounded solution would seem to indicate that the standard of living could be raised to infinity by producing unlimited amounts of capital goods. This situation is represented graphically in Figure 3.2. The feasible region is obviously unbounded. Needless to say, such a solution is neither intuitively nor economically correct. There must surely be some constraint on the amount of capital goods that can be produced—and indeed there is. But it is a constraint that was not considered in the original specification of the problem. There are typically three constraints on the production of an economy: land, labor, and capital resources. The land, or natural resources, constraint was neglected.

Assume that the missing constraint is as follows:

$$2X_1 + 10X_2 \leq 700 \qquad \text{(land)}$$

This indicates that both consumer goods and capital goods require natural resources in the production process. Adding the land constraint to

Table 3.6
Illustration of an Unbounded Solution

Row	Z	X_1	X_2	S_1	S_2	RHS
1	0	4	−1	1	0	100
2	0	1.6	−1	0	1	10
0	1	−0.05	−0.2	0	0	0

Figure 3.2
An Unbounded
Feasible Region

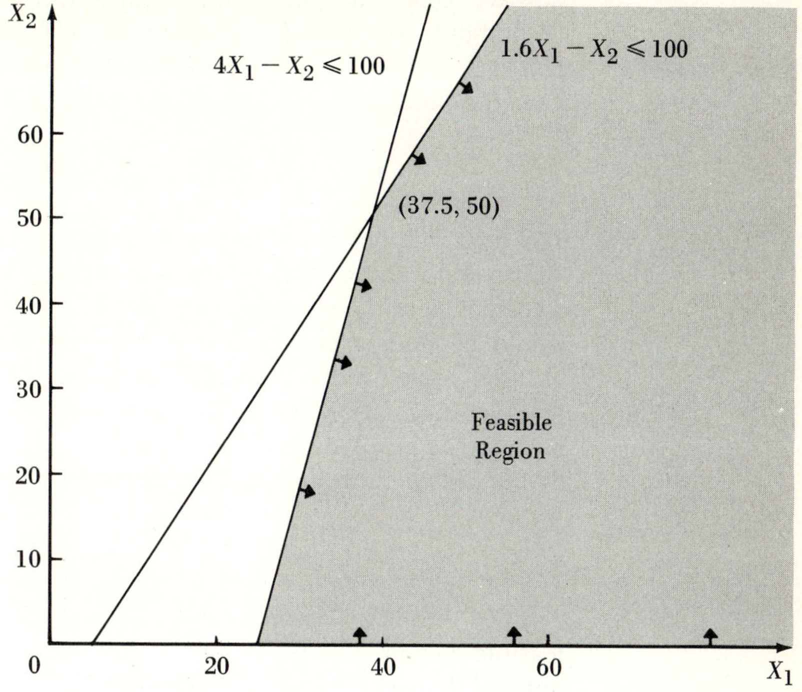

the model provides a closed feasible region with the usual corner points to be investigated in finding the optimal solution. The simplex tableau will contain an additional row, and pivoting can be performed normally. The optimal solution, found at 66⅔ units of capital goods and 41⅔ units of consumer goods (see Figure 3.2), will increase the standard of living index by 15.4 points in a 4-year period (about 4% per year). The reader should verify these calculations.

This problem is typical of problems yielding unbounded solutions. The cause is usually incomplete specification of the model—that is, the omission of one or more important constraints.

Multiple Optimal Solutions

Returning to the potato–tomato problem, suppose that the objective function is modified to become

$$Z = 40X_1 + 80X_2$$

subject to the same set of constraints. As we demonstrated when we used the graphical method in Section 2.1, the problem has more than one optimal solution. However, iteration stops with the simplex method as soon as one of the optimal solutions is reached. How does the final simplex tableau inform us of the existence of other optimal solutions? To find out, we can apply the simplex method to the revised problem. This is done in Table 3.7, where the optimal solution can be determined from the third tableau. The optimal solution is

$$X_1 = 6 \qquad X_2 = 12 \qquad S_2 = 18 \qquad S_1 = S_3 = 0$$

The total value of the objective function is \$1,200.

The important consideration here is that, in the last tableau, the row 0 coefficient of the nonbasic variable, S_3, is zero. This implies that there would be no net change in the objective function if slack S_3 should become basic. Indeed, by performing another iteration, we quickly discover that slack S_3 can be increased from zero to 9, causing the second resource to be binding ($S_2 = 0$), and the objective function remains at \$1,200. In this way, we find an alternative optimal solution:

$$X_1 = 15 \qquad X_2 = 7.5 \qquad S_3 = 9 \qquad S_1 = S_2 = 0$$

Since these two optimal solutions correspond to corner points of the feasible region, any point on the line segment between them is also optimal. It can be shown (see exercises 3.3–3.13) that a weighted average of two optimal solutions is also an optimal solution. Consequently, if

Table 3.7 Illustration of Multiple Optimal Solutions

Tableau	Row	Z	X_1	X_2	S_1	S_2	S_3	RHS
I	1	0	1	2	1	0	0	30
	2	0	3	2	0	1	0	60
	3	0	0	(2)	0	0	1	24
	0	1	−40	−80	0	0	0	0
II	1	0	(1)	0	1	0	−1	6
	2	0	3	0	0	1	−1	36
	3	0	0	1	0	0	$\frac{1}{2}$	12
	0	1	−40	0	0	0	40	960
III	1	0	1	0	1	0	−1	6
	2	0	0	0	−3	1	2	18
	3	0	0	1	0	0	$\frac{1}{2}$	12
	0	1	0	0	40	0	0	1200

more than one optimal solution exists, an infinite number of optimal solutions must exist.

Briefly, if a zero coefficient is found in row 0 of the final simplex tableau, and if this coefficient is in the column of a nonbasic variable, then the model has multiple optimal solutions. If two zero coefficients appear in row 0 corresponding to nonbasic variables, then the objective function is parallel to the ***face*** of a multidimensional feasible region, and all points on the face are optimal.

3.4 Minimization and Artificial Variables

So far, our treatment of the simplex method has been limited to maximization problems for which all constraints are of the less-than-or-equal-to type. In this case we find an initial basic feasible solution at the point of origin by setting the variables of the original model equal to zero. Programming problems that require minimization of the objective function (a cost function, for instance) often employ constraints of the greater-than-or-equal-to type, and the addition of ***surplus*** variables does not automatically provide a feasible initial solution.

Let us consider the presidential election problem in more detail. The following is a statement of the original problem, modified so that a surplus variable appears in each constraint.

$$\text{Min} \quad C = X_1 + 0.5X_2$$

subject to

$$\begin{aligned} 6X_1 + 2X_2 - S_1 \qquad\qquad &= 24 \\ 3X_1 + 2X_2 \qquad - S_2 \qquad &= 18 \qquad (3.6) \\ X_1 + 3X_2 \qquad\qquad - S_3 &= 12 \end{aligned}$$

and

$$X_1, X_2, S_1, S_2, S_3 \geq 0$$

As before, the variables X_1 and X_2 denote television and radio advertising, respectively.

If, in constructing an IBFS, we set activities X_1 and X_2 equal to zero and use the three surplus variables as basic variables, the initial solution becomes

$$S_1 = -24 \qquad S_2 = -18 \qquad S_3 = -12 \qquad X_1 = X_2 = 0$$

Note that this solution is not feasible, and the previous method of taking the origin as a starting point for the simplex procedure will not work for the typical minimization problem. The point of origin lies outside the feasible region (see Figure 2.4) in this case. Economically, this simply means that one cannot reach the prescribed minimum number of voters in each group with zero advertising.

The Big M Method—Elimination of Artificial Variables

We overcome this difficulty by introducing in each greater-than-or-equal-to constraint an ***artificial variable***[5] that must also be nonnegative. Thus the statement of the problem becomes

$$\begin{aligned}
\text{Min} \quad C = {} & X_1 + 0.5X_2 + 0S_1 + 0S_2 + 0S_3 + MT_1 + MT_2 + MT_3 \\
\text{subject to} \quad & 6X_1 + 2X_2 - S_1 + T_1 = 24 \\
& 3X_1 + 2X_2 - S_2 + T_2 = 18 \\
& X_1 + 3X_2 - S_3 + T_3 = 12 \\
\text{and} \quad & X_1, X_2, S_1, S_2, S_3, T_1, T_2, T_3 \geq 0
\end{aligned} \qquad (3.7)$$

where T_1, T_2, and T_3 are artificial variables with coefficients of $+1$, and M is an arbitrarily large number as the coefficient of the artificial variable T.

A procedure for assuring elimination of all artificial variables from the optimal solution is known as the ***big M method.*** Representing the coefficients of the artificial variables in the objective function—see equations (3.7)—the big M values can be interpreted as penalty-money coefficients. For example, if one chooses a value of \$100 million for the M coefficients in the presidential election problem, then the artificially created advertising activities are very expensive relative to either television or radio in minimizing the objective function. These expensive artificial variables will be rapidly eliminated. The value of the objective function can hardly be optimal if a solution contains a positive artificial variable, because the coefficient M is, by design, excessively expensive.

[5]Note that use of an artificial variable is not limited to minimization problems. An artificial variable may be used in maximization problems as well. In general, as long as at least one greater-than-or-equal-to constraint is involved, regardless of minimizations or maximizations, artificial variables are used. In actual computer applications, for the user's convenience, most of the linear programming computer routines are written in such a way that artificial variables are supplied automatically in the programming.

Thus, for economic reasons, when the simplex procedure is applied, each of the expensive artificial variables is forced out of the basis in each iteration until all become nonbasic.

By assuming 100 as the coefficient of each artificial variable in the objective function in (3.7), the system becomes:

$$\begin{aligned}
\text{Min} \quad C &= X_1 + 0.5X_2 + 0S_1 + 0S_2 + 0S_3 + 100T_1 + 100T_2 + 100T_3 \\
\text{subject to} \quad & 6X_1 + 2X_2 - S_1 + T_1 = 24 \\
& 3X_1 + 2X_2 - S_2 + T_2 = 18 \\
& X_1 + 3X_2 - S_3 + T_3 = 12 \\
\text{and} \quad & X_1, X_2, S_1, S_2, S_3, T_1, T_2, T_3 \geq 0
\end{aligned} \tag{3.8}$$

To obtain a basis that consists of all artificial variables, we need to manipulate the objective function so that the coefficients of all basic variables (T_1, T_2, and T_3) are zero instead of 100. To do this, we can first rewrite the three constraints in (3.8) as

$$\begin{aligned}
&\text{(a)}\ T_1 = 24 - 6X_1 - 2X_2 + S_1 \\
&\text{(b)}\ T_2 = 18 - 3X_1 - 2X_2 + S_2 \\
&\text{(c)}\ T_3 = 12 - X_1 - 3X_2 + S_3
\end{aligned}$$

Next, substituting (a), (b), and (c) into the objective function of (3.8), we have

$$\begin{aligned}
\text{Min} \quad C = X_1 + 0.5X_2 &+ 100(24 - 6X_1 - 2X_2 + S_1) \\
&+ 100(18 - 3X_1 - 2X_2 + S_2) \\
&+ 100(12 - X_1 - 3X_2 + S_3)
\end{aligned}$$

Rearranging the terms, we can express the model of (3.8) as

$$\begin{aligned}
\text{Min} \quad C &= -999X_1 - 699.5X_2 + 100S_1 + 100S_2 + 100S_3 + 5400 \\
\text{subject to} \quad & 6X_1 + 2X_2 - S_1 + T_1 = 24 \\
& 3X_1 + 2X_2 - S_2 + T_2 = 18 \\
& X_1 + 3X_2 - S_3 + T_3 = 12 \\
\text{and} \quad & X_1, X_2, S_1, S_2, S_3, T_1, T_2, T_3 \geq 0
\end{aligned} \tag{3.9}$$

Table 3.8 The Simplex Procedure—Minimization

Tableau	Row	C	X_1	X_2	S_1	S_2	S_3	T_1	T_2	T_3	RHS
I	1	0	(6)	2	−1	0	0	1	0	0	24
	2	0	3	2	0	−1	0	0	1	0	18
	3	0	1	3	0	0	−1	0	0	1	12
	0	1	999	699.5	−100	−100	−100	0	0	0	5400
II	1	0	1	$\frac{1}{3}$	$-\frac{1}{6}$	0	0	$\frac{1}{6}$	0	0	4
	2	0	0	1	$\frac{1}{2}$	−1	0	$-\frac{1}{2}$	1	0	6
	3	0	0	($\frac{8}{3}$)	$\frac{1}{6}$	0	−1	$-\frac{1}{6}$	0	1	8
	0	1	0	$\frac{733}{2}$	$\frac{133}{2}$	−100	−100	$-\frac{333}{2}$	0	0	1404
III	1	0	1	0	$-\frac{3}{16}$	0	$\frac{1}{8}$	$\frac{3}{16}$	0	$-\frac{1}{8}$	3
	2	0	0	0	($\frac{7}{16}$)	−1	$\frac{3}{8}$	$-\frac{7}{16}$	1	$-\frac{3}{8}$	3
	3	0	0	1	$\frac{1}{16}$	0	$-\frac{3}{8}$	$-\frac{1}{16}$	0	$\frac{3}{8}$	3
	0	1	0	0	$\frac{1395}{32}$	−100	$\frac{599}{16}$	$-\frac{4595}{32}$	0	$-\frac{2199}{16}$	$\frac{609}{2}$
IV	1	0	1	0	0	$-\frac{3}{7}$	$\frac{2}{7}$	0	$\frac{3}{7}$	$-\frac{2}{7}$	$\frac{30}{7}$
	2	0	0	0	1	$-\frac{16}{7}$	($\frac{6}{7}$)	−1	$\frac{16}{7}$	$-\frac{6}{7}$	$\frac{48}{7}$
	3	0	0	1	0	$\frac{1}{7}$	$-\frac{3}{7}$	0	$-\frac{1}{7}$	$\frac{3}{7}$	$\frac{18}{7}$
	0	1	0	0	0	$-\frac{5}{14}$	$\frac{1}{14}$	−100	$-\frac{1395}{14}$	$-\frac{1401}{14}$	$\frac{39}{7}$
V	1	0	1	0	$-\frac{1}{3}$	$\frac{1}{3}$	0	$\frac{1}{3}$	$-\frac{1}{3}$	0	2
	2	0	0	0	$\frac{7}{6}$	$-\frac{8}{3}$	1	$-\frac{7}{6}$	$\frac{8}{3}$	−1	8
	3	0	0	1	$\frac{1}{2}$	−1	0	$-\frac{1}{2}$	1	0	6
	0	1	0	0	$-\frac{1}{12}$	$-\frac{1}{6}$	0	−100	−100	−100	5

This model, in turn, is transferred to the regular simplex tableau format (Table 3.8). Now, in the initial solution, the artificial variables are made basic and all other variables equal zero. The IBFS is formulated:

$$T_1 = 24, T_2 = 18, T_3 = 12 \qquad \text{where } X_j = S_i = 0 \text{ for all } i, j$$

The sole purpose of the artificial variables is to make this possible.

The Simplex Method Again Once the IBFS is formulated, we apply the simplex method to minimization problems with only minor revision of the standard maximization techniques. For a minimization problem, each successive iteration should ***reduce*** the objective function. Therefore, after scanning the elements of row 0, we should select the ***largest*** positive element corresponding to a nonbasic variable. For example, the first tableau in Table 3.8 shows that activity X_1 will contribute most to cost reduction if it is changed from a nonbasic to a basic variable. Iterations should be performed until there is no positive element in row 0.

In the fifth tableau, the objective function reaches its optimal value of $5 million. With negative coefficients in row 0 for all nonbasic variables, the value of the objective function cannot be reduced further. Consequently, the optimal solution is

$$X_1 = 2 \qquad X_2 = 6 \qquad S_3 = 8$$

All other variables equal zero. This solution is the same as the one we found graphically in Section 2.2, and there are no artificial variables in the optimal basis.

The Two-Phase Method[6] So far, in discussing the minimization problem and the elimination of artificial variables, we have assumed that a solution to the problem exists. One occasionally encounters linear programs in which the set of constraints may be either redundant or inconsistent. The so-called ***two-phase method***, which is a somewhat different way of eliminating artificial variables, enables one to handle these complications. Artificial variables are used as needed in the constraints just as before, but, as its name implies, ***this method separates the solution procedure into two phases.***

In phase I, all artificial variables are eliminated from the basis. If a feasible solution with no artificial variables in the basis is found in the final tableau of phase I, then phase II proceeds to an optimal basis. But

[6]This section is optional. The student can skip it, if the instructor wishes, without losing continuity in the study of this book.

if there are redundant or inconsistent constraints in the original system of equations, the final tableau of phase I explicitly reveals this information before further effort is wasted. Let's look at a few examples.

Recognition of a Redundant System in Phase I One constraint of a linear program might be no more than a restatement of another constraint. Consider, for example, the following problem:

$$\text{Min} \quad C = 2X_1 + 2X_2$$

subject to

$$X_1 + 2X_2 = 6$$

$$2X_1 + 4X_2 = 12 \qquad \text{(P)}$$

and

$$X_1 \geq 0, X_2 \geq 0$$

In this system of equations, the second constraint is simply twice the first constraint, so one of the two is redundant. This means that one can be eliminated without our losing any necessary information. Redundancy in a complicated system of equations might not be so obvious as it is in this case, and the analyst might proceed to seek a solution. Nevertheless, the condition becomes evident once the final tableau of phase I has been determined. We will use the foregoing simple example to illustrate this procedure.

In this simple example, there is no need for surplus or slack variables because the constraints are equations. Begin by assigning zero coefficients to activities X_1 and X_2 and unit coefficients to the artificial variables in the objective function. Clearly, the penalty-money values assigned to the artificial variables are much more "expensive" than those assigned to the original variables. The two-phase method here uses the same concept as the big M method. The following ***auxiliary program*** (AP) is formed:

$$\text{Min} \quad W = 0X_1 + 0X_2 + T_1 + T_2$$

subject to

$$X_1 + 2X_2 + T_1 \qquad = 6$$

$$2X_1 + 4X_2 \qquad + T_2 = 12 \qquad \text{(AP)}$$

and

$$X_1, X_2, T_1, T_2 \geq 0$$

The original function (P) has now been replaced by the sum of the artificial variables in the auxiliary program. Substituting the constraints into the objective functions so that every artificial variable is eliminated, we can express the system (AP) in standard form (AP′) with respect to the initially basic variables T_1, T_2, and W. That is,

$$\text{Min} \quad W = 18 - 3X_1 - 6X_2$$

subject to

$$X_1 + 2X_2 + T_1 = 6$$

$$2X_1 + 4X_2 + T_2 = 12 \qquad \text{(AP}')$$

and

$$X_1, X_2, T_1, T_2 \geq 0$$

The corresponding simplex tableau is presented in Table 3.9. Degeneracy is indicated by identical minimum ratios. Arbitrarily choosing row 1 to be the pivot row, we force the variable T_1 out of the current basis, and phase I terminates in the second tableau.

In the second tableau, the basic feasible solution is

$$X_2 = 3 \qquad T_2 = 0 \qquad W = 0$$

However, the artificial variable T_2 has not been eliminated from the basis, so the second row is redundant and may be removed completely from the original system.

Removing row 2 permits us to transform the final tableau of phase I into the first tableau of phase II (Table 3.10). Formally, it is stated as follows:

$$\text{Min} \quad C = 2X_1 + 2X_2 \qquad \text{(original objective function)}$$

subject to

$$X_2 = 3 - \tfrac{1}{2}X_1 \qquad \text{(from final tableau of phase I)}$$

Hence

$$\text{Min} \quad C = 6 + X_1 \qquad \text{(by substitution)}$$

Table 3.9
Phase I

Tableau	Row	W	X_1	X_2	T_1	T_2	RHS
I	1	0	1	(2)	1	0	6
	2	0	2	4	0	1	12
	0	1	3	6	0	0	18
II	1	0	$\frac{1}{2}$	1	$\frac{1}{2}$	0	3
	2	0	0	0	−2	1	0
	0	1	0	0	−3	0	0

Table 3.10
Phase II

Row	C	X_1	X_2	RHS
1	0	$\frac{1}{2}$	1	3
0	1	−1	0	6

Since the coefficient in row 0 of the only nonbasic variable—X_1—is negative, phase II is terminated. Thus the BFS that we found at the end of phase I ($X_2 = 3$) is also the optimal solution, and the optimal value of the objective function is $C = 6$.

No Feasible Solution Exists Consider the following problem, which has contradictory, or inconsistent, constraints.

$$\text{Min} \quad C = X_1 + 2X_2$$

$$\begin{aligned} \text{subject to} \quad & X_1 + 3X_2 = 6 \\ & X_1 + 3X_2 = 9 \\ \text{and} \quad & X_1 \geq 0, X_2 \geq 0 \end{aligned} \qquad \text{(P)}$$

Phase I of the problem is formulated as follows:

$$\text{Min} \quad W = T_1 + T_2$$

$$\begin{aligned} \text{subject to} \quad & X_1 + 3X_2 + T_1 = 6 \\ & X_1 + 3X_2 + T_2 = 9 \\ \text{and} \quad & X_1, X_2, T_1, T_2 \geq 0 \end{aligned} \qquad \text{(AP)}$$

This, after elimination of T_1 and T_2 from the objective function, is transformed into the form, (AP′):

$$\text{Min} \quad W = 15 - 2X_1 - 6X_2$$

$$\begin{aligned} \text{subject to} \quad & X_1 + 3X_2 + T_1 = 6 \\ & X_1 + 3X_2 + T_2 = 9 \\ \text{and} \quad & X_1, X_2, T_1, T_2 \geq 0 \end{aligned} \qquad \text{(AP′)}$$

Phase I terminates in the second tableau of the simplex method, given in Table 3.11. In this case, the objective function equals 3, and the artificial variable remains in the basis at a positive level ($T_2 = 3$). Hence we know that no feasible solution exists for the original problem.

Table 3.11
Phase I—
Inconsistent System

Tableau	Row	W	X_1	X_2	T_1	T_2	RHS
I	1	0	1	(3)	1	0	6
	2	0	1	3	0	1	9
	0	1	2	6	0	0	15
II	1	0	$\frac{1}{3}$	1	$\frac{1}{3}$	0	2
	2	0	0	0	−1	1	3
	0	1	0	0	−2	0	3

An Optimal Solution Exists There is an optimal solution in cases wherein phase I terminates with the objective function W equal to zero and no artificial variable appears in the final basis. We then start phase II by using the solution from phase I as the IBFS and use the simplex method to find an optimal solution. For example, this technique can be applied to the presidential election problem just as well as the big M method was in the last section. The underlying logic for the two methods is really the same, so there is little justification for choosing one method over the other. Programming routines for a digital computer can easily use either method. The significance of the two-phase method is that the final tableau of the first phase explicitly reveals information about redundancy, inconsistency, or the existence of a unique optimal solution in the original system.

The Generalized Two-Phase Model[7]

To summarize, consider a general linear program (P) in a regular minimization form.

$$\text{Min} \quad C = \sum_j C_j X_j$$

subject to

$$\sum_j a_{ij} X_j \geq b_i \qquad i = 1, 2, \ldots, m \qquad \text{(P)}$$

and

$$X_j \geq 0 \qquad j = 1, 2, \ldots, n$$

By subtracting a surplus variable S_1 and adding an artificial variable to each constraint, we can make the constraints equality relationships. In the objective function, zero coefficients are assigned to ordinary variables X_j and to surplus variables S_i. Unit coefficients are assigned to the

[7]This section is optional. The student can skip it, if the instructor wishes, without losing continuity in the study of this book.

artificial variables T_i in the objective function. This yields the following auxiliary program (AP).

$$\text{Min} \quad W = \sum_j 0X_j + \sum_i 0S_i + \sum_i 1T_i \qquad \text{or} \qquad \text{Min} \quad W = \sum T_i$$

$$\text{subject to} \qquad \sum_j a_{ij}X_j - S_i + T_i = b_i \qquad i = 1, 2, \ldots, m \qquad \text{(AP)}$$

$$\text{and} \qquad X_j, S_i, T_i \geq 0 \quad \text{for all } i \text{ and } j$$

Again, this means that the original objective function in the general program has been replaced by the sum of the artificial variables in the auxiliary program. By substituting the constraint into the objective function so that every artificial variable is eliminated, we can express the system (AP) in standard form (AP′) with respect to the initially basic variables T_i and W. That is,

$$\text{Min} \quad W = \sum_i b_i - \sum_i \sum_j a_{ij}X_j + \sum_i S_i$$

$$\text{subject to} \qquad \sum_j a_{ij}X_j - S_i + T_i = b_i \qquad i = 1, 2, \ldots, m \qquad \text{(AP')}$$

$$\text{and} \qquad X_j, S_i, T_i \geq 0 \quad \text{for all } i \text{ and } j$$

Phase I is then the application of the simplex algorithm to the system of equations (AP′). It is important to note that the value W of the objective function in phase I is bounded from below by zero. This is because the phase I objective function is the sum of all artificial variables with positive unit coefficients. Thus the auxiliary program cannot have an unbounded solution, and it should terminate after a finite number of iterations.

During phase I, the simplex method removes the artificial variables from the basis one by one. At the end of this first phase, all coefficients for the minimization problem in row 0 are either negative or zero. The final simplex tableau will exhibit one of the following three characteristics:

Case 1 $W = 0$, and one or more artificial variables remain in the basis, but at the zero level. The original program (P) has at least one feasible solution. This is the redundant system, such as the one in our first example. The artificial variable remains in the final basis at a level of zero. This means that there is also degeneracy at the end of phase I.

Case 2 $W > 0$, and one or more of the artificial variables remain in the basis at a positive level. The original program (P) has no feasible solution. In this case, the constraints in the original program are inconsistent. A positively valued objective function means that the original system has no feasible solution, as in our second example. There is no need to start phase II.

Case 3 $W = 0$, and no artificial variables remain in the basis. That is, $T_i = 0$ for all i—and the original program (P) has a feasible solution. In this case, we start phase II by using the solution in phase I as the IBFS and subsequently use the simplex method to find the optimal solution.

3.5 Summary

The simplex method is a systematic and efficient computational procedure for solving linear programming problems. Basic variables are those that take nonzero values to obtain a solution, and nonbasic variables take zero values. If all the solution values for basic variables are nonnegative, they are called basic feasible solutions (BFS). Assuming that the constraints are not redundant and that a BFS exists, the number of basic variables must equal the number of constraints. The steps for preparing a simplex tableau are as follows:

1. Convert each less-than constraint into an equality by adding a slack variable. (Subtract a surplus variable and add an artificial variable with a big coefficient to each greater-than constraint).
2. Rearrange the terms in the objective function with the constant term on the right-hand side (RHS).
3. Construct a simplex tableau with appropriate column headings. (Note: Each variable occupies one column.)
4. Write down all constraint coefficients and RHS constants in their appropriate slots in the tableau.
5. Identify the initial basic feasible solution (IBFS).

The iterative procedures of the simplex method are as follows:

Step 1 Find an IBFS by creating a simplex tableau.

Step 2 Identify the pivot column by choosing the most negative coefficient in row 0 (the most positive coefficient in a minimization problem).

Step 3 Identify the pivot row (and therefore the pivot element) by choosing the smallest positive ratio.

Step 4 Create a new basis, better than the previous solution, by pivoting the simplex tableau.

The optimality test is whether all the coefficients in row 0 are nonnegative (nonpositive for minimization problems). If so, the optimal solution has been reached; if not, reiterate from step 2.

The purpose of adding an artificial variable to a greater-than inequality constraint is to form an IBFS base for the simplex procedure. The big M method consists of assigning very large values to the coefficients of the artificial variables to assure their elimination from the optimal solution.

The two-phase method—another way of eliminating artificial variables—approaches the solution procedure in two phases. The final simplex tableau in phase I generally reveals further information about the original program (that is, whether it is redundant, inconsistent, or supports a feasible solution) before phase II is initiated.

Exercises

3.1 Differentiate between basic variables and nonbasic variables.

3.2 Define or explain the following terms:
a. Slack and surplus variables
b. Artificial variable
c. Degenerate basic solution
d. Unbounded solution

3.3 Review the following concepts:
a. Simplex method
b. Big M method
c. Iteration
d. Pivoting

3.4 Consider the following linear programming problem.

$$\text{Max } 35X_1 + 45X_2$$

subject to

$$3X_1 + 2X_2 \leq 60$$

$$2X_1 + 5X_2 \leq 90$$

and

$$X_1 \geq 0, X_2 \geq 0$$

a. Find the maximum number of basic variables in the solution.
b. List all corner solutions and their corresponding values of objective function.
c. Identify the optimal basic feasible solution.

3.5 Solve the following linear programming problem (a) by inspection and (b) by the simplex method.

$$\text{Max} \quad Z = 10X_1 + 16X_2$$

subject to $\quad X_1 + 2X_2 \leq 50$

and $\quad X_1 \geq 0, X_2 \geq 0$

3.6 Consider the following linear programming problem.

$$\text{Max} \quad Z = 2X_1 + 2X_2 + 4X_3$$

subject to

$$X_1 + X_2 + X_3 \leq 10$$
$$5X_1 + X_3 \leq 20$$
$$2X_2 + 3X_3 \leq 15$$

and $\quad X_1 \geq 0, X_2 \geq 0, X_3 \geq 0$

The simplex tableau is presented in the following table:

Row	Z	X_1	X_2	X_3	S_1	S_2	S_3	RHS
1	0	1	1	1	1			10
2	0	5	0	1		1		20
3	0	0	2	3			1	15
0	1	−2	−3	−4	0	0	0	0

a. Identify the IBFS.
b. What is the incoming or entering variable? Why? Answer in terms of economic reasoning.
c. What is the outgoing or replaced variable? Why? Answer in terms of economic reasoning.
d. The simplex tableau after one iteration is as follows:

Row	Z	X_1	X_2	X_3	S_1	S_2	S_3	RHS
1	0	1	$\frac{1}{3}$	0	1	0	$-\frac{1}{3}$	5
2	0	5	$-\frac{2}{3}$	0	0	1	$-\frac{1}{3}$	15
3	0	0	$\frac{2}{3}$	1	0	0	$\frac{1}{3}$	5
0	1	-2	$-\frac{1}{3}$	0	0	0	$\frac{4}{3}$	20

What is the best BFS shown by this tableau? Is it an optimal solution? If not, why not?

e. What is the incoming or entering variable? What is the outgoing or replaced variable?

f. After two more iterations, the simplex tableau becomes

Row	Z	X_1	X_2	X_3	S_1	S_2	S_3	RHS
1	0	0	1	0	$\frac{15}{7}$	$-\frac{3}{7}$	$-\frac{4}{7}$	$\frac{30}{7}$
2	0	1	0	0	$\frac{2}{7}$	$\frac{1}{7}$	$-\frac{1}{7}$	$\frac{25}{7}$
3	0	0	0	1	$-\frac{10}{7}$	$\frac{2}{7}$	$\frac{5}{7}$	$\frac{15}{7}$
0	1	0	0	0	$\frac{9}{7}$	$\frac{1}{7}$	$\frac{6}{7}$	$\frac{200}{7}$

g. What is the BFS shown by this tableau? Is it an optimal solution? If so, why?

h. Is the optimal solution unique? If so, why?

3.7 The Magic Toy Company produces two children's toys, goldfish and talking birds. The firm has just received a Christmas order from a wholesaler for as many as the company can supply before the beginning of December. Profit per dozen goldfish is \$50; profit per dozen talking birds is \$150. The company wants to determine the level of toys produced that will maximize profit. The level of production activity is limited by skilled labor, availability of raw materials, and machine time. The technological coefficients for each dozen toys and the corresponding profit are as follows:

	Toys		
Resource	**Goldfish**	**Talking Birds**	**Availability of Resource**
Labor	1	1.6	240
Raw Materials	1	3	300
Machine Time	0	1	60
Profit	\$50	\$150	

a. Formulate a linear programming model for the Magic Toy Company, and set up the corresponding simplex tableau.
b. What is the IBFS shown in this tableau? What is the entering variable? What is the outgoing variable? Give an economic interpretation for each of your answers.
c. After two iterations, the simplex tableau becomes

Row	Z	X_1	X_2	S_1	S_2	S_3	RHS
1	0	0	0	1	−1	1.4	24
2	0	1	0	0	1	−3	120
3	0	0	1	0	0	1	60
0	1	0	0	0	50	0	15,000

What is the BFS shown in this tableau? Is it the optimal solution? If not, how do you know?
d. If there are multiple optimal solutions in this problem, give at least one of them.
e. Using the graphical method discussed in Chapter 2, verify the existence of the multiple optimal solutions in this problem.

3.8 For the following three problems, first stop and think about solutions, then find them using the simplex method.

a.
$$\text{Max } Z = 3X_1 - 2X_2$$
subject to
$$2X_1 + X_2 \leq 8$$
and
$$X_1 \geq 0,\ X_2 \geq 0$$

b.
$$\text{Min } -C = -3X_1 + 2X_2$$
subject to
$$2X_1 + X_2 \leq 8$$
and
$$X_1 \geq 0,\ X_2 \geq 0$$

c.
$$\text{Min } C = 3X_1 - 2X_2$$
subject to
$$2X_1 + X_2 \geq 8$$
and
$$X_1 \geq 0,\ X_2 \geq 0$$

3.9 Apply the simplex method to the following problem.

$$\text{Max} \quad Z = 3X_1 + 4X_2 + 5X_3$$

subject to

$$X_1 + 2X_2 + 2X_3 \leq 10$$

$$3X_1 + X_2 + 5X_3 \leq 15$$

and

$$X_j \geq 0 \quad \text{for } j = 1, 2, 3$$

3.10 Using the simplex method, find the optimal solution to exercise 2.8 at the end of Chapter 2.

3.11 Consider the following production problem, for which there are three constraints (representing productive resources) and three variables (representing products: soybeans, lima beans, and peas).

$$\text{Max} \quad Z = 3X_1 + X_2 + 2X_3$$

subject to

$$-2X_1 + X_2 + X_3 \leq 8 \qquad \text{(nitrogen)}$$

$$X_1 - X_2 + 2X_3 \leq 10 \qquad \text{(phosphoric acid)}$$

$$X_1 + X_2 \leq 14 \qquad \text{(soluble potash)}$$

and

$$X_j \geq 0 \quad j = 1, 2, 3$$

a. Interpret the economic meaning of the negative coefficients that appear in the constraints.

b. Using the simplex method, find an optimal solution. Then interpret your results in terms of the objective function and the magnitudes of all basic variables. Finally, describe the overall utilization of resources, and show that the original constraints have been satisfied.

3.12 Is the optimal solution you found in exercise 3.11 unique? If not, why not?

3.13 Refer again to exercise 3.11. By further iteration, find another solution that also optimizes the objective function. It can be shown that weighted averages of two optimal solutions must also be optimal. For example,

$$(\lambda)12 + (1 - \lambda)4.5 = X_1^*$$

$$(\lambda)2 + (1 - \lambda)9.5 = X_2^*$$

$$(\lambda)0 + (1 - \lambda)7.5 = X_3^*$$

where

$$0 \leq \lambda \leq 1$$

Pick any two values of λ between zero and 1.

a. Show that each value can be applied to the equations shown to obtain another optimal solution.
b. How many values of λ can be chosen?
c. How many optimal solutions are there to this problem?

3.14 In the first constraint of exercise 3.11, change the sign of the coefficient of variable X_3 to minus. Likewise in the second constraint, reverse the signs of the coefficients of variables X_2 and X_3. Leave the third constraint unchanged. Now find the optimal solution to this revised linear programming model, and interpret your results.

3.15 In the potato–tomato problem, the equivalent system of equations corresponding to Table 3.4 is

$$\begin{aligned} Z &= 840 - 40S_1 + 15S_3 \\ X_1 &= 6 - S_1 + S_3 \\ S_2 &= 18 + 3S_1 - 2S_3 \\ X_2 &= 12 - 0S_1 - \tfrac{1}{2}S_3 \end{aligned}$$

Explain why the increase in the slack variable S_3 improves the value of the objective function, and also give an economic account of why the ***net*** contributions of bringing S_3 into the basis is \$135.

3.16 Consider the following problem:

$$\text{Max} \quad Z = 25X_1 + 30X_2$$

subject to

$$\begin{aligned} 3X_1 + 2X_2 &\leq 18 \\ 3X_1 + 4X_2 &\leq 24 \\ X_2 &\leq 3 \end{aligned}$$

and

$$X_1 \geq 0, X_2 \geq 0$$

a. Find a graphical solution and explain why this is a case of degeneracy.
b. Solve the problem using the simplex method, and indicate the degenerate basic solution.

3.17 By applying the simplex method, show that the following problem has no feasible solution by the graphical or the simplex method.

$$\text{Max} \quad Z_x = 3X_1 + 2X_2$$

subject to

$$\begin{aligned} X_1 + X_2 &\geq 10 \\ X_1 + X_2 &\leq 5 \end{aligned}$$

and

$$X_1 \geq 0, X_2 \geq 0$$

3.18 Consider the following problem.

$$\text{Max} \quad Z = X_1 + 2X_2$$

subject to

$$3X_1 + 2X_2 \leq 12$$

$$X_1 \geq 5$$

and

$$X_1 \geq 0,\ X_2 \geq 0$$

Is there a feasible solution? If not, why not?

3.19 Given the following production problem, offer an economic interpretation for the sign of the technical constraint coefficients.

$$\text{Max} \quad Z = C_1X_1 + C_2X_2$$

subject to

$$-A_{11}X_1 + A_{12}X_2 \leq b_1 \qquad \text{(capital)}$$

$$A_{21}X_1 + 0X_2 \leq b_2 \qquad \text{(raw materials)}$$

$$A_{31}X_1 - A_{32}X_2 \leq b_3 \qquad \text{(labor)}$$

and

$$X_1 \geq 0,\ X_2 \geq 0$$

3.20 Show by both the graphical and the simplex method that the following problem has no feasible solution.

$$\text{Max} \quad Z = 4X_1 + 2X_2$$

subject to

$$3X_1 + X_2 \geq 9$$

$$2X_1 + X_2 \leq 4$$

and

$$X_1 \geq 0,\ X_2 \geq 0$$

3.21 Consider the following problem.

$$\text{Max} \quad Z = 4X_1 + 2X_2$$

subject to

$$3X_1 - X_2 \leq 9$$

$$2X_1 - X_2 \leq 4$$

and

$$X_1 \geq 0,\ X_2 \geq 0$$

Show the unboundedness of the optimal solution by means of (a) the graphical method, (b) the simplex method, and (c) economic reasoning.

3.22 Solve the advertising agency's minimization problem presented in exercise 2.14 by the simplex method, and compare your optimal solution with the one obtained graphically.

3.23 Solve the food company's problem presented in exercise 2.15 by the simplex method, and compare your optimal solution with the one obtained graphically.

3.24 Solve the Young Brothers Radio Company's problem presented in exercise 2.19 by the simplex method, and indicate the optimal production decision.

3.25 The manager of Bishop Farm wants to determine the least-cost feed mixture for his dairy cows. Studies indicate that each dairy cow must be fed at least 40 units of nutrient A and 30 units of nutrient B per day. Two commercial feeds are available. Each pound of feed 1 contains 2 units of nutrient A and 1 unit of nutrient B. Each pound of feed 2 contains 1 unit of nutrient A and 1 unit of nutrient B. Feed 1 costs \$.05 per pound; feed 2 costs \$.03 per pound.

a. Formulate a linear programming model.
b. Determine the proportions of feeds 1 and 2 in an optimal feed mix and find the total minimum cost of feeding a cow.

Suggested Readings

Aarvik, O., and P. Randolph. "The Application of Linear Programming to the Determination of Transmission Fees in an Electrical Power Network," *Tims-ORSA Interfaces*, 6, No. 1 (November 1975), 47–49.

Barkan, Joel D., and James E. Bruno. "Operations Research in Planning Political Campaign Strategies." *Operations Research*, 20, No. 5 (September–October 1972), 925–941.

Carleton, W. T. "An Analytical Model for Long-Range Financial Planning." *The Journal of Finance* (May 1970), 291–315.

Chiang, Alpha C. *Fundamental Methods of Mathematical Economics.* 2nd ed. New York: McGraw-Hill, 1974. Chapter 18.

Dantzig, George B. *Linear Programming and Extensions.* Princeton, N.J.: Princeton University Press, 1963. Chapters 5, 10, and 11.

Drayer, Wayne, and Steve Seabury. "Facilities Expansion Model." *Interfaces*, 5, No. 2, pt. 2 (February 1975), 104–109.

Dyson, R. G., and A. S. Gregory. "The Cutting Stock Problem in the Flat Glass Industry." *Operational Research Quarterly*, 25, No. 1 (March 1974), 41–45.

Garvin, W. W. *Introduction to Linear Programming.* New York: McGraw-Hill, 1960.

Gass, Saul I. *An Illustrative Guide to Linear Programming.* New York: McGraw-Hill, 1970.

Glassey, C. R., and V. K. Gupta. "A Linear Programming Analysis of Paper Recycling." *Management Science* (December 1974), 392–408.

Hadley, G. *Linear Programming.* Reading, Mass.: Addison-Wesley, 1962.

Masse, P., and R. Gibrat. "Application of Linear Programming to Investments in the Electric Power Industry." Translated by George B. Dantzig. *Management Science* (January 1957), 149–166.

Reddy, James M. "A Model to Schedule Sales Optimally Blended from Scarce Resources." *Interfaces*, 6, No. 1, pt. 2 (November 1975), 97–107.

Richmond, Samuel B. *Operations Research for Management Decisions*. New York: Ronald Press, 1968. Chapter 11.

Simith, V. E. "A Diet Model With Protein Quality Variable." *Management Science* (February 1974), 971–980.

Wagner, Harvey M. *Principles of Operations Research*. Englewood Cliffs, N.J.: Prentice-Hall, 1969. Chapter 4.

4

Duality Theory: Resource Allocation and Its Valuation

In this chapter we will show that every linear programming problem is really two problems. A given linear programming maximization problem is closely associated with a minimization problem known as the ***dual problem,*** and vice versa. Studying duality theory gives us insight into linear programming theory and its economic interpretation.

First we will examine the mechanical relationship between the dual problem and the original problem, or ***primal problem.*** Then we will give some duality theorems and examine their implications and properties. After exploring the economic interpretation of the duality concept, we will conclude the chapter with sensitivity analysis—analysis of the effects of changes in various coefficients on the optimal solution.

4.1 The Primal Problem and the Dual Problem

Consider the original, primal linear programming problem (P) in the general standard form:

$$\text{Max} \quad Z_X = C_1X_1 + C_2X_2 + \ldots + C_nX_n$$

$$\text{subject to} \quad a_{11}X_1 + a_{12}X_2 + \ldots + a_{1n}X_n \leq b_1$$

$$a_{21}X_1 + a_{22}X_2 + \ldots + a_{2n}X_n \leq b_2$$

$$\vdots \qquad \text{(P)}$$

$$a_{m1}X_1 + a_{m2}X_2 + \ldots + a_{mn}X_n \leq b_m$$

and $\quad X_j \geq 0 \quad \text{for all } j$

In this chapter, the profit symbol Z for maximization is modified to be Z_X. Conversely, the value of the dual objective function is represented by the symbol Z_Y. For minimization problems, the notation will be C_X for the primal and C_Y for the dual.

The dual problem (D), derived from the general model is

$$\text{Min} \quad Z_Y = b_1Y_1 + b_2Y_2 + \ldots + b_mY_m$$

subject to

$$a_{11}Y_1 + a_{21}Y_2 + \ldots + a_{m1}Y_m \geq C_1$$

$$a_{12}Y_1 + a_{22}Y_2 + \ldots + a_{m2}Y_m \geq C_2$$

$$\vdots \qquad \text{(D)}$$

$$a_{1n}Y_1 + a_{2n}Y_2 + \ldots + a_{mn}Y_m \geq C_n$$

and $\quad Y_i \geq 0 \quad \text{for all } i$

In terms of sigma notation, the primal model is

$$\text{Max} \quad Z_X = \sum_j C_j X_j$$

subject to $\quad \sum_j a_{ij} X_j \leq b_i \qquad \text{for } i = 1, 2, \ldots, m \qquad \text{(P)}$

and $\quad X_j \geq 0 \qquad \text{for } j = 1, 2, \ldots, n$

Its corresponding dual model is

$$\text{Min} \quad Z_Y = \sum_i b_i Y_i$$

subject to $\quad \sum_i a_{ij} Y_i \geq C_j \qquad \text{for } j = 1, 2, \ldots, n \qquad \text{(D)}$

and $\quad Y_i \geq 0 \qquad \text{for } i = 1, 2, \ldots, m$

Generally, when the inequality signs of a linear programming model are all in the same direction, the mechanical aspects of transformation from primal to dual, or vice versa, are as follows:[1]

1. If the objective function in the primal is to be maximized, the dual objective function is to be minimized, and vice versa.
2. If a primal inequality is of the less-than-or-equal-to type, the dual inequality is of the greater-than-or-equal-to type. Thus the inequality sign is reversed in all constraints except the nonnegativity requirements.
3. Rows are interchanged with their respective columns. That is, the row coefficients in the constraints of the primal become the column coefficients in the constraints of the dual.
4. Each dual variable corresponds to one constraint in the primal. Therefore, if the primal problem has m constraints and n variables, the dual problem has n constraints and m variables.
5. The positions for coefficients C_j and b_i are interchanged.
6. The equations of the dual problem are functions of the dual variables Y_i, and all equations of the primal problem are expressed in terms of the primal variables X_j.

These rules are illustrated in the following two problems.

Example 1 If the primal is

$$\text{Max} \quad Z_X = 3X_1 + 2X_2 + 4X_3$$

subject to

$$\begin{aligned} 4X_1 + X_2 + 2X_3 &\leq 8 \\ 3X_2 + 5X_3 &\leq 12 \qquad \text{(P)} \end{aligned}$$

and

$$X_1 \geq 0,\ X_2 \geq 0,\ X_3 \geq 0$$

then its corresponding dual is

$$\text{Min} \quad Z_Y = 8Y_1 + 12Y_2$$

subject to

$$\begin{aligned} 4Y_1 \qquad &\geq 3 \\ Y_1 + 3Y_2 &\geq 2 \qquad \text{(D)} \\ 2Y_1 + 5Y_2 &\geq 4 \end{aligned}$$

and

$$Y_1 \geq 0,\ Y_2 \geq 0$$

[1]For the mixed form containing possibly unrestricted variables and equality constraints, two additional rules (which will be presented shortly) must be added.

Example 2 If the primal is

$$\text{Min} \quad C_X = X_1 + 2X_2$$

subject to

$$2X_1 + X_2 \geq 6$$
$$5X_1 + 4X_2 \geq 20 \qquad \text{(P)}$$

and

$$X_1 \geq 0, \; X_2 \geq 0$$

then its associated dual is

$$\text{Max} \quad C_Y = 6Y_1 + 20Y_2$$

subject to

$$2Y_1 + 5Y_2 \leq 1$$
$$Y_1 + 4Y_2 \leq 2 \qquad \text{(D)}$$

and

$$Y_1 \geq 0, \; Y_2 \geq 0$$

Following these rules, one can easily transform any given linear programming problem from the primal to the dual, and vice versa. The primal problem may be of either the maximization or the minimization type. Actually, it does not matter which statement of the problem is called the primal and which is called the dual. Customarily, however, the original problem is designated as the primal. The reader should verify that the dual statement of a dual problem is the primal problem itself—that is, the original linear program.

The transformation process reveals a remarkable property: a pair of primal and dual programs are completely symmetrical. First, the coefficients in the objective function of the primal are the RHS constants in the dual, and vice versa. Second, each constraint in the primal is assigned a variable Y_i in the dual, and each constraint of the dual is associated with a variable X_j in the primal. Third, each variable X_j in the primal corresponds to a constraint in the dual, and each variable Y_i in the dual corresponds to a constraint in the primal.

How is the dual problem formulated if the primal problem is in mixed form, containing possibly unrestricted variables and equality constraints? We resolve complications such as these by using the following additional duality rules:

1. If the primal constraint is in the form of an equality, the associated dual variable is unrestricted (positive, negative, or zero). Conversely, if a dual variable is unrestricted, the corresponding constraint in the primal is in the form of an equality.

2. If the variable in the primal is unrestricted, the corresponding constraint in the dual is in the form of an equality. Conversely, if the constraint in the dual is an equality, the corresponding primal variable is unrestricted.

Let's look at an example to demonstrate these rules.

$$\text{Max } Z_X = C_1X_1 + C_2X_2$$

subject to

$$\begin{aligned} a_{11}X_1 + a_{12}X_2 &\leq b_1 \\ a_{21}X_1 + a_{22}X_2 &= b_2 \qquad \text{(P)} \end{aligned}$$

and

$$X_1 \geq 0,\ X_2 \text{ is unrestricted}$$

As explained in Chapter 2, the value of the unrestricted variable can be derived from the difference between two ***nonnegative*** variables. That is,

$$X_2 \equiv X_2' - X_2'' \qquad \text{where } X_2' \geq 0 \text{ and } X_2'' \geq 0$$

Then the second, equality, constraint may be written as two inequality constraints. As a result the expanded model (P′) is stated as follows:

$$\text{Max } Z_X = C_1X_1 + C_2X_2' - C_2X_2''$$

subject to

$$\begin{aligned} a_{11}X_1 + a_{12}X_2' - a_{12}X_2'' &\leq b_1 \\ a_{21}X_1 + a_{22}X_2' - a_{22}X_2'' &\leq b_2 \qquad \text{(P')} \\ -a_{21}X_1 - a_{22}X_2' + a_{22}X_2'' &\leq -b_2 \end{aligned}$$

and

$$X_1 \geq 0,\ X_2' \geq 0,\ X_2'' \geq 0$$

The model is now in the standard form, in which all inequalities are in the same direction. In forming the dual, let the variable Y_1 represent the dual variable associated with the first constraint. Likewise, set the variables Y' and Y'' in correspondence with the second and third constraints, respectively. Then the dual model corresponding to equations (P′) is stated as follows:

$$\text{Min } Z_Y = b_1Y_1 + b_2Y' - b_2Y''$$

subject to

$$\begin{aligned} a_{11}Y_1 + a_{21}Y' - a_{21}Y'' &\geq C_1 \\ a_{12}Y_1 + a_{22}Y' - a_{22}Y'' &\geq C_2 \qquad \text{(D')} \\ -a_{12}Y_1 - a_{22}Y' + a_{22}Y'' &\geq -C_2 \end{aligned}$$

and

$$Y_1 \geq 0,\ Y' \geq 0,\ Y'' \geq 0$$

Note that the second and third inequalities can be combined in one equality constraint. Also the coefficients, b_2, a_{21}, and a_{22}, can be isolated by simple factoring. Hence the model (D′) becomes the model (D″):

$$\begin{aligned} \text{Min} \quad & Z_Y = b_1Y_1 + b_2(Y' - Y'') \\ \text{subject to} \quad & a_{11}Y_1 + a_{21}(Y' - Y'') \geq C_1 \\ & a_{12}Y_1 + a_{22}(Y' - Y'') = C_2 \qquad \text{(D'')} \\ \text{and} \quad & Y_1 \geq 0,\ Y' \geq 0,\ Y'' \geq 0 \end{aligned}$$

Subsequently, define

$$Y_2 \equiv Y' - Y''$$

and the dual model becomes

$$\begin{aligned} \text{Min} \quad & Z_Y = b_1Y_1 + b_2Y_2 \\ \text{subject to} \quad & a_{11}Y_1 + a_{21}Y_2 \geq C_1 \\ & a_{12}Y_1 + a_{22}Y_2 = C_2 \qquad \text{(D)} \\ \text{and} \quad & Y_1 \geq 0,\ Y_2 \text{ is unrestricted} \end{aligned}$$

As we examine the pairs of programs, (P) and (P′), and (D′) and (D″), it becomes evident that we create the statement of a dual model for a primal model in mixed form by applying directly the two additional rules given on pages 100 and 101.

Analogously, if the primal problem is of the minimization type and in mixed form, its dual is a corresponding maximization problem. The reader should now be able to formulate the general primal and dual problems in this case (see exercises 4.5 and 4.6).

4.2 Duality Theorems

Up to this point, we have performed the transformation between primal and dual statements of models in a purely mechanical fashion without considering the reasons for, meaning of, or usefulness of the dual formulation. These transformations are among the most important and interesting discoveries in the theory of linear programming. One would expect the dual formulation to yield the same optimal solution as its associated primal problem—that is, we would expect Max Z_X to equal Min Z_Y—but is this necessarily true? Also, it is important to determine how to derive a primal optimal solution in terms of the primal variables X_j from a given dual optimal solution expressed in terms of the dual variables Y_i. We shall investigate these possibilities now. Two powerful theorems are first introduced without proof[2] and then their usefulness is illustrated by some simple examples.

Duality Theorem 1 ***The Fundamental Duality Theorem*** To facilitate this discussion, refer to the primal and dual linear programs given in Section 4.1. The ***fundamental duality theorem*** is stated as follows:

a. If X_j and Y_i represent any feasible solution to the primal and dual problems, then

$$\text{Max} \quad Z_X \leq \text{Min} \quad Z_Y \qquad \text{or} \qquad \text{Max} \ \sum_j C_j X_j \leq \text{Min} \ \sum b_i Y_i$$

b. If both the primal and dual problems have feasible solutions, then both the dual and the primal have an optimal solution for which the optimal values of the primal and dual objective functions are identical. These optimal solutions are Y_i^* $(i = 1, 2, \ldots, m)$, for the dual, and X_j^* $(j = 1, 2, \ldots, n)$, for the primal. Therefore,

$$\text{Max} \quad Z_X = \text{Min} \quad Z_Y \qquad \text{or} \qquad \sum_j C_j X_j^* = \sum_i b_i Y_i^*$$

c. If either program has a feasible solution with an optimal value, then the other program has a feasible, optimal solution at the same value of the objective function.

Duality Theorem 2 ***The Equilibrium Theorem (Theorem of Complementary Slackness)*** The primal and dual problems may be stated to include slack variables as follows:

$$\text{Max} \quad Z_X = \sum_j C_j X_j$$

subject to $$\sum_j a_{ij} X_j + S_i = b_i \quad \text{for all } i \qquad \text{(PS)}$$

and $$X_j \geq 0, \ S_i \geq 0 \quad \text{for all } i \text{ and } j$$

[2]For rigorous mathematical proofs, see D. Gale, *The Theory of Linear Economic Models* (New York: McGraw-Hill, 1960), pp. 78–83.

Likewise,

$$\text{Min} \quad Z_Y = \sum_i b_i Y_i$$

subject to
$$\sum_i a_{ij} Y_i - V_j = C_j \quad \text{for all } j \qquad \text{(DV)}$$

and
$$Y_i \geq 0, V_j \geq 0 \quad \text{for all } i \text{ and } j$$

Now duality theorem 2, the equilibrium theorem, may be stated. Given any pair of feasible solutions, X_j for (PS) and Y_i for (DV), that yield the condition Max Z_X = Min Z_Y, the following conditions must hold:

(i)
$$Y_i\left[b_i - \sum_j a_{ij} X_j\right] = 0 \quad \text{for all } i$$

(ii)
$$X_j\left[\sum_i a_{ij} Y_i - C_j\right] = 0 \quad \text{for all } j$$

The expressions enclosed in brackets are nothing more than representations of the slack variables S_i and V_j in the primal and dual problems, respectively. Therefore, these conditions are equivalent to

(i′)
$$Y_i S_i = 0 \quad \text{for all } i$$

(ii′)
$$X_j V_j = 0 \quad \text{for all } j$$

To illustrate these two theorems, consider the potato–tomato problem, for which the primal problem is

$$\text{Max} \quad Z_X = 40X_1 + 50X_2$$

subject to
$$X_1 + 2X_2 \leq 30$$
$$3X_1 + 2X_2 \leq 60$$
$$2X_2 \leq 24$$

and
$$X_1 \geq 0, X_2 \geq 0$$

Accordingly, the dual is

$$\text{Min} \quad Z_Y = 30Y_1 + 60Y_2 + 24Y_3$$

subject to
$$Y_1 + 3Y_2 \geq 40$$
$$2Y_1 + 2Y_2 + 2Y_3 \geq 50$$

and
$$Y_1 \geq 0, Y_2 \geq 0, Y_3 \geq 0$$

The solution

$$X_1 = 6 \quad \text{and} \quad X_2 = 12$$

is a feasible solution for the primal; likewise, the solution

$$Y_1 = 10 \qquad Y_2 = 10 \qquad Y_3 = 10$$

is a feasible solution for the dual. Then, the value of the primal objective function is \$840, which is less than the value of the dual objective function—\$1140. Considering any feasible primal and dual solutions to this problem, it is true that

$$40X_1 + 50X_2 \leq 30Y_1 + 60Y_2 + 24Y_3$$

or that, in general, Max $Z_X \leq$ Min Z_Y.

For any feasible solution, the range of possible values of the objective function in the primal is upper-bounded by the value of the objective function in the dual. Conversely, for any feasible solution, the value of the objective function of the dual is lower-bounded by the value of the objective function of the primal. In this illustration, both the value of the primal and that of the dual objective functions lie in the range of \$840 to \$1140. This optimal value of the primal objective function, calculated earlier, is \$975.

What, then, is the optimal value of the dual? Applying simplex procedures to the minimization problem (the reader should verify this), we find that the optimal value of the dual objective function is also \$975. Thus the optimal value of the primal and that of the dual lie within the range of \$840 to \$1140. In addition, the optimal solution provides the upper bound for the primal problem and the lower bound for the dual problem. These concepts are illustrated schematically in Figure 4.1.

Figure 4.1 Schematic Representation of Duality Theorem 1

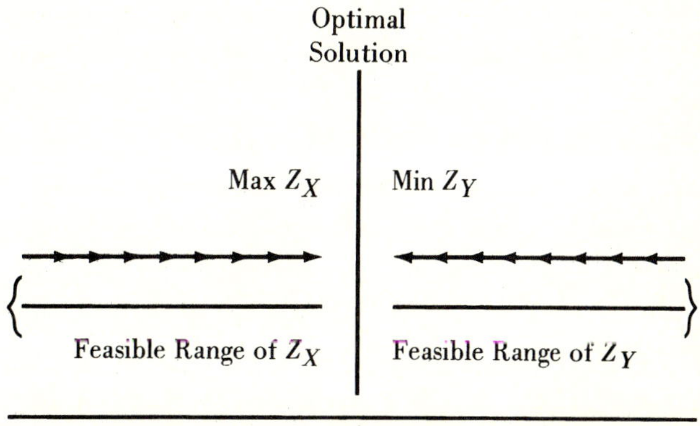

Clearly, the optimal value is the same for both the primal and the dual. Moving away from this value causes one or more of the primal and dual variables to become nonfeasible. This demonstrates that, if a solution to the linear program is feasible to both the primal and the dual problems, then the solution is optimal. Furthermore, it indicates that, if a feasible solution to either the dual or the primal exists such that the condition Max Z_X = Min Z_Y is true, then that solution is optimal. When the optimal solution to one of the two problems has been found, the solution to its dual has been found simultaneously. In fact, the optimal solutions for both the primal and the dual can be found from the same final optimal simplex tableau.

Finding the Dual Optimal Solution from the Primal Optimal Tableau

The primal optimal simplex tableau of the potato–tomato example is reconstructed in Table 4.1, with minor modifications. The optimal values of the dual variables can be read directly from the coefficients of row 0. Therefore, coefficients of the primal slack variables are the optimal values of the dual variables. That is, as indicated in Table 4.1,

$$Y_1 = \tfrac{35}{2} \qquad Y_2 = \tfrac{15}{2} \qquad Y_3 = 0$$

When we substitute the dual solution values into the constraints of the dual problem, it becomes evident both that the constraints are satisfied and that there is no slack in the constraints; the dual slack variables V_1 and V_2 equal zero. Indeed, zero values for the slack variables can be read directly from Table 4.1.

Complementary Slackness

To further investigate the primal–dual relationships, look at the optimal solutions to the potato–tomato problem given in Table 4.2. When we consider any pair of primal–dual optimal solution values—for example, $X_1 = 15$ and $V_1 = 0$—it becomes clear that the product of corresponding solution values must equal zero. It is also important to recognize the

Table 4.1
Optimal Simplex Tableau of the Potato–Tomato Problem

Row	Z_X	X_1	X_2	S_1	S_2	S_3	RHS	
1	0	1	0	$-\frac{1}{2}$	$\frac{1}{2}$	0	15	
2	0	0	0	$-\frac{3}{2}$	$\frac{1}{2}$	1	9	
3	0	0	1	$\frac{3}{4}$	$-\frac{1}{4}$	0	$\frac{15}{2}$	
0	1	0	0	$\frac{35}{2}$	$\frac{15}{2}$	0	975	$\leftarrow Z_X$
		↑ V_1	↑ V_2	↑ Y_1	↑ Y_2	↑ Y_3	↑ Z_Y	

Table 4.2
Optimal Solutions of Primal–Dual Relationships

Corresponding Solution Values from				
Primal		**Dual**		**Implication**
$X_1 = 15$	(ordinary)	$V_1 = 0$	(slack)	$X_1V_1 = 0$
$X_2 = 7.5$	(ordinary)	$V_2 = 0$	(slack)	$X_2V_2 = 0$
$S_1 = 0$	(slack)	$Y_1 = 17.5$	(ordinary)	$S_1Y_1 = 0$
$S_2 = 0$	(slack)	$Y_2 = 7.5$	(ordinary)	$S_2Y_2 = 0$
$S_3 = 0$	(slack)	$Y_3 = 0$	(ordinary)	$S_3Y_3 = 0$

Table 4.3
Symmetrical Relationships Between the Primal and Dual Problems

		Primal Ordinary Variables	Primal Slack Variables	
Row	Z_X	$X_1 \quad X_2 \quad \ldots \quad X_n$	$S_1 \quad S_2 \quad \ldots \quad S_m$	**RHS**
0				$Z_X = Z_Y$
	Z_Y	$V_1 \quad V_2 \quad \ldots \quad V_n$	$Y_1 \quad Y_2 \quad \ldots \quad Y_m$	
		Dual Slack Variables	**Dual Ordinary Variables**	

symmetry of these pairs of solution values in the optimal simplex tableau, as demonstrated in Table 4.3.

In general, having found the optimal primal solution, we can obtain the optimal dual solution directly by applying the following two rules:

1. The optimal values of the ordinary dual variables, Y_i ($i = 1, 2, \ldots, m$), are the coefficients of the primal slack variables S_1 in row 0 of the primal optimal tableau.
2. The optimal values of the dual slack variables, V_j ($j = 1, 2, \ldots, n$), are the coefficients of the primal ordinary variables X_j in row 0 of the primal optimal tableau.

Table 4.2 demonstrates duality theorem 2, the property of complementary slackness. Table 4.3 illustrates the advantage of placing the objective function last in the simplex tableau. Finally, it is clear by analogy that the same procedures and interpretations apply to finding the primal optimal solution from the dual optimal tableau. As an exercise, the reader should apply the simplex method to the dual and then interpret the final dual tableau.

Although the solutions of primal and dual problems are equivalent, one usually prefers to work with the formulation with fewer constraints. If there is no difference, it may then be easier to solve the maximization program—either primal or dual—because an initial basic feasible solution is found more conveniently and artificial variables are not required.

4.3 Economic Interpretation of the Dual

The concept of duality has a natural economic interpretation that is useful for economic analysis and managerial decision making.

Interpretation of the Dual Constraints

In general, finding an optimal linear programming solution amounts to allocating scarce resources among competing production activities in such a way as to maximize an objective function. Consider now the first constraint of a dual problem, which is associated with the first activity of the primal problem:

$$a_{11}Y_1 + a_{21}Y_2 + \ldots + a_{m1}Y_m \geq C_1$$

The constant C_1, expressed in dollar terms, is the per-unit contribution to profit of the first activity. Coefficients a_{11}, a_{21}, . . ., and a_{m1} indicate various physical amounts of resources consumed in the production of 1 unit of output in the first activity. So the dual variables Y_i must also be measured in dollar terms.

In economic analysis, the value of resources is ultimately derived from the value of the output produced. The per-unit contribution to profit should be distributed to the various production resources. Thus the contribution to profit of the first activity is assigned in an economic sense to all resources used in its production. As a result, the dual variables Y_i must be interpreted as values that are assigned, or imputed, to corresponding resources. Such a value is not an ordinary market price but a ***shadow price,*** or ***internal price,*** for the given resource. Consequently, the dual constraint inequality indicates that the total per-unit imputed value of resources used for production must not be less than the per-unit contribution to profit realized from this activity. In the potato–tomato problem, for example, the dual variables Y_1, Y_2, and Y_3

represent the per-unit imputed values of land, labor, and storage space, respectively, and each constraint specifies that the total value of resources used in producing 1 unit of output must be greater than or equal to the per-unit contribution that output makes to profit.

Interpretation of the Dual Objective Function

When the dual objective function is stated generally, as

$$\text{Min} \quad Z_Y = b_1Y_1 + b_2Y_2 + \ldots + b_mY_m$$

we can see that it is a representation of the total imputed value of all resources used in all activities by the firm. Remember that duality theorem 1 requires that the maximum contribution to profit in the primal be bounded from above by the total imputed value of the firm's scarce resources.

$$\text{Max} \quad Z_X \leq \text{Min} \quad Z_Y$$

But, because the total value of the resources is ultimately derived from the profit of their end products, the total imputed value of all resources should be equal to at least the total value of their output. The greater-than-or-equal-to inequality in a dual constraint means that the firm's unit profit may be ***overassigned*** to the resources in that activity. However, the optimal result, as given by duality theorem 1, is

$$\text{Max} \quad Z_X = \text{Min} \quad Z_Y$$

This means that, when production is brought to the optimal level, total contribution to profit is exactly equal to the total imputed value of the productive resources. It also means that the optimal imputed value of the resources is exactly equal to the total contribution to the firm's profit and that none of the profit contribution is left unassigned. The dual linear program minimizes the total imputed value of all resources subject to the appropriate constraints.

What is the value of each resource? Classical economic theory indicates that the value of each resource depends on its contribution to the production process—that is, its ***marginal value product,*** or ***the change in total profit produced by one additional unit of input.*** Algebraically,

$$\begin{array}{c}\text{Marginal value product}\\ \text{of the } i\text{th resource}\end{array} = \frac{\Delta Z_X^*}{\Delta b_i}$$

where Δ signifies the discrete amount of change in the associated variable.

A short algebraic derivation further clarifies the meaning of marginal value product in the context of primal and dual linear programming analysis. According to duality theorem 1,

$$\text{Max} \quad Z_X = \text{Min} \quad Z_Y \qquad \text{(at the optimal solution)}$$

Also, by definition,

$$\text{Min} \quad Z_Y \equiv b_1Y_1^* + b_2Y_2^* + \ldots + b_mY_m^*$$

Then it must also be true that

$$\text{Max} \quad Z_X = b_1Y_1^* + b_2Y_2^* + \ldots + b_mY_m^*$$

Other things being equal, a 1-unit change in the availability b_i of the ith resource causes total contribution to profit Z_X to change by Y_i dollars. This means simply that the marginal value product of the ith resource at the optimal solution is the value Y_i^*. That is,

$$\frac{\Delta Z_X^*}{\Delta b_i} = Y_i^* \quad \text{for all } i$$

In the potato–tomato example, optimal values of the dual variables were found to be

$$Y_1 = 17.5 \qquad Y_2 = 7.5 \qquad Y_3 = 0$$

Therefore, the marginal values of land and labor must be \$17.50 and \$7.50, respectively. Both land and labor are limiting resources, so their increased availability increases total contribution to profits. However, an increase in storage space does not yield additional profit, because, at the optimal solution, storage space is in excess supply. This is reflected in a marginal value product of storage space equal to zero.

Interpretation of the Dual Slack Variables

The economic interpretation of the dual slack variables V_j can best be understood by rearranging the dual constraint terms:

$$V_j = \underbrace{(a_{1j}Y_1 + a_{2j}Y_2 + \ldots + a_{mj}Y_m)}_{\substack{\text{total imputed value of all}\\\text{resources used up for the}\\j\text{th activity}}} - \underbrace{C_j}_{\substack{\text{per-unit}\\\text{contribution}\\\text{of the }j\text{th}\\\text{activity}}} \qquad \text{for all } j$$

The terms in the right-hand side of this equation are measured in dollar values that indicate the difference between the value of all resources used up in the jth activity and the value contributions of the jth activity at the unit level. Consequently, the dual slack variable in the left-hand side must be some monetary unit as well. If the dual slack variable is positive, the total value of resources used as inputs for the given activity is more than the per-unit contribution realized, and it is clear that resource allocation is not optimal. The level of the given activity should be reduced to release scarce resources for use by competing activities in the firm. In effect, the dual slack variables represent the opportunity costs of their respective activities. If the allocation of resources is optimal, the total imputed value equals the per-unit contribution to profit, ***and opportunity cost equals zero.*** Allocating resources to the given activity entails no sacrifice of an opportunity for greater gain via shifting those resources to other activities of the firm.

Whenever an opportunity cost is zero, the corresponding activity's use of resources is in balance with that of other competing activities. An opportunity cost that is greater than zero is a measure of the sacrifice, or forgone opportunity, incurred by using the excess resource in the given activity rather than in other activities. If such is the case in the optimal condition, then output of the corresponding activity must be zero. Finally, an opportunity cost that is less than zero indicates that the activity is more profitable than competing activities and that allocating more resources to it would increase overall profits. Such allocation leads to an optimal allocation of resources, in which the opportunity costs of all basic activities equal zero.

Interpretation of the Primal Slack Variables

Let us also examine the economic reasoning behind the primal slack variable and its dual counterpart. First, rearrange the general statement of a primal constraint:

$$S_i = b_i - (a_{i1}X_1 + a_{i2}X_2 + \ldots + a_{in}X_n) \quad \text{for all } i$$

Since the RHS value, b_i, represents the amount of the ith resource that is available, and the sum in parentheses indicates the production utilization of the given resource, the slack variable S_i must measure the amount of the resource that is unutilized. As previously explained, a resource that is in excess supply has an imputed value of zero. The positive value of the primal slack variable produces no profit, so its dual valuation is certainly zero. But if a given slack activity is equal to zero, the corresponding resource is fully utilized and the counterpart dual variable Y_i must be positive. In the potato–tomato problem, for example, both land and labor are completely utilized (so that $S_1 = S_2 = 0$) in the optimal solution. Consequently, positive imputed values are found for the counterpart dual variables: $Y_1 = \$17.50$ and $Y_2 = \$7.50$. On the other hand, storage space is in excess supply ($S_3 = 9$) and the corresponding valuation for these oversupplied goods is zero ($Y_3 = 0$). This interpretation of primal slack variables is consistent with the marginal analysis presented earlier.

Complementary Slackness and Its Economic Significance

The complementary slackness conditions stated in duality theorem 2 are necessary according to both mathematical and economic interpretations. The condition

$$X_jV_j = 0 \quad \text{for all } j$$

implies that either $X_j = 0$ or $V_j = 0$. When opportunity cost is zero ($V_j = 0$ in the optimal solution), the corresponding activity X_j is positive and the allocation of resources to the jth activity is optimal. We have also seen that, if the primal slack variable is positive in the optimal solution, the associated dual price must be zero and the condition

$$S_iY_i = 0 \quad \text{for all } i$$

is necessary, according to economic reasoning.

In general, ***the primal linear programming problem is one of resource allocation, and the dual linear programming problem is one of valuation or pricing of the allocated resources.*** The fundamental duality theorem requires that each of these problems yield the same optimal solution. The condition of complementary slackness is analogous to the equilibrium condition of many of the models of economics, so duality theorem 2 is also called the ***equilibrium theorem.*** A producing activity that yields a predetermined revenue and faces imputed costs of its various inputs can reach maximum profit level only when opportunity cost is zero. Forces of supply and demand operate through the price mechanism in such a way that the share of each resource employed in the production process is determined by its marginal value product.

Dual Interpretation of a Minimization Problem

In its most general, symbolic form, the presidential election problem we encountered in Chapter 2 is stated as follows:

$$\text{Min } Z_X = C_1X_1 + C_2X_2$$

subject to

$$a_{11}X_1 + a_{12}X_2 \geq b_1$$
$$a_{21}X_1 + a_{22}X_2 \geq b_2$$
$$a_{31}X_1 + a_{32}X_2 \geq b_3$$

and

$$X_1 \geq 0, X_2 \geq 0$$

As before, the variable X_j represents the number of campaign ads for either radio or television, C_j represents cost per ad, Z_X is the total cost of campaign advertising, b_i represents the minimum number of voters in each group who should be reached, and a_{ij} represents the number of voters in the ith group reached for each ad placed in the jth medium.

The corresponding dual problem must therefore be

$$\text{Max} \quad Z_Y = b_1Y_1 + b_2Y_2 + b_3Y_3$$

subject to

$$a_{11}Y_1 + a_{21}Y_2 + a_{31}Y_3 \leq C_1$$

$$a_{12}Y_1 + a_{22}Y_2 + a_{32}Y_3 \leq C_2$$

and

$$Y_1 \geq 0, \; Y_2 \geq 0, \; Y_3 \geq 0$$

Interpretation of the dual problem centers on the dual variables Y_i. Each such variable represents the imputed price (measured in monetary units) per campaign advertising program. The dual constraints require that the sum of imputed prices in each advertising medium not exceed the cost per unit of advertising. Otherwise, allocating scarce money to the given medium would not be worthwhile. In the optimal solution, money is allocated to advertising media such that the total imputed value of audience contact per ad is equal to the advertising cost. This reflects the requirements of duality theorem 2.

Whereas minimizing total cost is the objective of the primal problem, the goal of the dual problem is to maximize the total imputed value of group audiences subject to the requirement that advertising costs be imputed fully to the various audience groups. Accordingly, the requirements of duality theorem 1 are met.

4.4 Sensitivity Analysis

The optimal solution to a linear programming problem depends on the values of given coefficients—C_j, b_i, and a_{ij}. Not only may these values vary, but they are also seldom known with complete certainty. Therefore, in a practical application, one should be able to determine the economic impact of different values of any given coefficient. One way to do this would be to reconstruct the statement of the problem to reflect changes in the coefficients and then proceed from the beginning to solve the restated problem. Often, however, the same information can be obtained on the basis of data that are already available to the decision maker. The latter approach is called ***sensitivity analysis*** or

postoptimality analysis. It exploits the fact that information obtained from the simplex procedure can directly establish the sensitivity of a given solution to changes in any one of the coefficients.

A Change in Contribution Objective Function Coefficients

For convenience, we present a three-variable and two-constraint problem:

$$\text{Max} \quad Z = 3X_1 + 4X_2 + 5X_3$$

subject to

$$X_1 + 2X_2 + 2X_3 \leq 10$$

$$3X_1 + X_2 + 5X_3 \leq 15$$

and

$$X_1 \geq 0, X_2 \geq 0, X_3 \geq 0$$

We can easily solve this problem with the simplex method. The initial and final optimal simplex tableaux are given in Table 4.4.

Consider first the ***objective function coefficients.*** (1) Does an optimal solution remain optimal when a given coefficient changes? (2) What is the range of values of the coefficient for which a given solution remains optimal? We can answer these two questions by experimenting with coefficient values.

A Decrease in C_j When X_j Is Nonbasic In the optimal solution the variable X_3, for instance, is nonbasic. Economically, this means that it is not profitable enough relative to the other two activities to warrant including it in the product mix. Therefore, a decrease in the contribution coefficient C_3 makes this activity relatively even ***more*** unprofitable, and the optimal solution remains unchanged.

Table 4.4
The Three-Variable Problem

Row	Z_X	X_1	X_2	X_3	S_1	S_2	RHS	
1	0	1	2	2	1	0	10	**Initial Tableau**
2	0	3	1	5	0	1	15	
0	1	−3	−4	−5	0	0	0	
1	0	0	1	$\frac{1}{5}$	$\frac{3}{5}$	$-\frac{1}{5}$	3	**Final Tableau**
2	0	1	0	$\frac{8}{5}$	$-\frac{1}{5}$	$\frac{2}{5}$	4	
0	1	0	0	$\frac{3}{5}$	$\frac{9}{5}$	$\frac{2}{5}$	24	
		V_1	V_2	V_3	Y_1	Y_2		

An Increase in C_j When X_j Is Nonbasic A more interesting case involves an ***increase*** in the unit-profit coefficient of a nonbasic variable. For example, if the coefficient C_3 increases above \$5, it may become profitable (relative to the other activities) to produce activity X_3, resulting in a different optimal solution. The row 0 coefficient of any nonbasic variable in the final tableau represents the level to which a coefficient can be increased without affecting the original optimal solution. For example, the X_3 coefficient in row 0 of the final tableau shown in Table 4.4 is $\frac{3}{5}$. Hence, the nonbasic variable X_3 will remain nonbasic as long as the increase in the objective function coefficient C_3 does not exceed three-fifths of a dollar, or \$.60.

Let the increase in an objective function coefficient C_j be designated ΔC_j. Applying this change to the objective function of the initial tableau in Table 4.4 gives the following revised function:

$$Z_X - 3X_1 - 4X_2 - (5 + \Delta C_3)X_3 + 0S_1 + 0S_2 = 0$$

The simplex procedure adds multiples of the various rows to row 0 in each pivot operation so that, finally, the objective function for the optimal solution becomes

$$Z_X + 0X_1 + 0X_2 + (\tfrac{3}{5} - \Delta C_3)X_3 + \tfrac{9}{5}S_1 + \tfrac{2}{5}S_2 = 24$$

Thus it becomes apparent that, as long as the incremental change in the coefficient C_3 is less than $\frac{3}{5}$, the current optimal solution remains unchanged. If the coefficient were changed more than this, a negative row 0 coefficient would result, the simplex iteration process would not have ended, X_3 would enter the next basis, and a new optimal solution would be found.

Changing an objective function coefficient in the primal problem is the same as changing one of the RHS constants in the dual problem. For example, the change we have just considered causes the third dual constraint to change from

$$2Y_1 + 5Y_2 \geq 5 \quad \text{to} \quad 2Y_1 + 5Y_2 \geq (5 + \Delta C_3)$$

Since optimal values for the dual variables (see the final tableau of Table 4.4) are $\frac{9}{5}$ for Y_1 and $\frac{2}{5}$ for Y_2, the dual constraint can also be expressed as

$$2(\tfrac{9}{5}) + 5(\tfrac{2}{5}) \geq (5 + \Delta C_3) \quad \text{or} \quad \Delta C_3 \leq \tfrac{3}{5}$$

This result indicates that changing the coefficient less than $\frac{3}{5}$ leaves the dual constraint satisfied and that the dual solution remains feasible. If the coefficient were changed more than $\frac{3}{5}$, the dual solution would no longer be feasible, and iteration to obtain a new optimal solution would be necessary.

A Change in C_j When X_j Is Basic If a variable X_j is basic in the optimal solution, a change in its profit contribution may or may not affect the optimality of the original solution. The extent to which this parameter may vary without altering the original optimality condition is the subject of this section on sensitivity analysis.

Based upon the condition of complementary slackness, all row 0 coefficients associated with basic variables in the optimal solution (other than Z_X) are zero. A change in per-unit contribution of one of the basic variables therefore causes the corresponding row 0 coefficient in the original optimal solution to become nonzero, and further iteration may be necessary. For example, in our illustrative problem, if the per-unit contribution to profit of the basic variable X_2 becomes $(4 + \Delta C_2)$ rather than its original value of 4, then the objective function taken from row 0 of the final simplex tableau also changes, as follows:

$$Z_X - (0 + \Delta C_2)X_2 + \tfrac{3}{5}X_3 + \tfrac{9}{5}S_1 + \tfrac{2}{5}S_2 = 24$$

But the row 0 coefficient of the basic variable X_2 must equal zero. We multiply the first row of the final tableau by the value ΔC_2 and add it to the foregoing equation, yielding

$$Z_X + (\tfrac{3}{5} + \tfrac{1}{5}\Delta C_2)\,X_3 + (\tfrac{9}{5} + \tfrac{3}{5}\Delta C_2)S_1 + (\tfrac{2}{5} - \tfrac{1}{5}\Delta C_2)S_2 = 24 + 3\Delta C_2$$

Optimality conditions require that all row 0 coefficients be nonnegative, so

$$\left.\begin{aligned} \tfrac{3}{5} + \tfrac{1}{5}\Delta C_2 &\geq 0 \\ \tfrac{9}{5} + \tfrac{3}{5}\Delta C_2 &\geq 0 \\ \tfrac{2}{5} - \tfrac{1}{5}\Delta C_2 &\geq 0 \end{aligned}\right\} \begin{array}{c}\text{which} \\ \text{implies} \\ \text{that}\end{array} \left\{\begin{aligned} \Delta C_2 &\geq -3 \\ \Delta C_2 &\geq -3 \\ \Delta C_2 &\leq +2 \end{aligned}\right.$$

or

$$-3 \leq \Delta\, C_2 \leq 2$$

Therefore, a change in this contribution value within the range of -3 to $+\,2$ affects only total profits and not the optimality condition of the original solution. If the parameter change lies outside this range, the original solution does not remain optimal and further iteration is necessary to reach a new final tableau.

Changes in Technological Coefficients

So far we have assumed that all input–output coefficients a_{ij} are fixed. This assumption may well be true in the short run. However, these coefficients may change over longer periods of time because of changes in productivity or technology. Information concerning the effect of such changes may have important implications for the decision maker charged with shaping the firm's policy.

A Change in a_{ij} When X_j Is Nonbasic Consider again the example given in Table 4.4, in which activity X_3 is nonbasic in the optimal solution. A technical improvement in the production of this activity will decrease one or more of the corresponding technological coefficients and may affect the original optimality condition. Such a situation is best analyzed by interpreting the dual constraint of this activity,

$$\sum_i a_{ij} Y_i \geq C_j$$

According to duality concepts, an activity is properly undertaken only if all the imputed values of its resources equal its per-unit contribution to profit. To illustrate, suppose that the coefficient a_{23} decreases from 5 to $(5 - \Delta a_{23})$. The corresponding dual constraint becomes

$$2Y_1 + (5 - \Delta a_{23})Y_2 \geq 5$$

Substituting the original optimal solution ($Y_1 = \frac{9}{5}$ and $Y_2 = \frac{2}{5}$) into this inequality gives

$$2(\tfrac{9}{5}) + (5 - \Delta a_{23})\tfrac{2}{5} \geq 5$$

or

$$\Delta a_{23} \leq \tfrac{3}{2}$$

This means that a technological improvement resulting in a reduction of the coefficient value greater than $\frac{3}{2}$ will cause per-unit profit contribution to become greater than the sum of imputed values of the productive resources. Under these conditions, it would be profitable to introduce activity X_3 into the product mix. Any smaller change leaves this activity nonbasic.

A Change in a_{ij} When X_j Is Basic If activity X_j is basic, investigating the complex impact of a change in one of its technological coefficients is beyond the scope of this book. Readers with a background in matrix algebra may consult more advanced texts on linear programming.[3] Otherwise, we can more easily determine the effect by changing the initial simplex tableau accordingly and working in standard fashion to the optimal solution.

Changes in RHS Values Resource availability values b_i may change in either the short run or the long run, and the impact of such a change can be very important.

If, as shown in Table 3.5, the optimal simplex tableau indicates that a slack variable is in the final basis (such as $S_3 = 9$), then the resource of the corresponding constraint is not being utilized fully. An increase in resource availability does no more than increase the value of the corresponding slack activity. Likewise, any reduction that does not exceed the level of idle resources in the optimal solution has no effect on the optimal solution and only reduces the value of the basic slack variable. However, a greater reduction causes immediate violation of the corresponding constraint, and a new optimal solution necessarily results.

If the available amount of a given resource is fully utilized in the optimal solution, the corresponding slack variable S_i must be nonbasic. In this case, a change in resource availability must also change the value of the objective function and the levels of production activity. Using Table 3.5 once again as an illustration, we see that the slack resource S_1 is nonbasic in the final solution, indicating that all 30 acres of available land are fully utilized. Suppose that this resource is changed from 30 acres to $(30 + \Delta b_1)$. By applying the simplex algorithm to a restated problem, we see that the b_1 terms are carried in the RHS column for each row of the tableau with the same coefficient that appears in the same row of the S_1 column. The resulting final simplex tableau for this illustration is shown in Table 4.5.

Other things being equal, a change in a resource-availability coefficient affects only the RHS values; all other coefficients of the tableau remain unchanged. Therefore, each basic variable now has a solution

Table 4.5 Changes in RHS Values

Row	Z_X	X_1	X_2	S_1	S_2	S_3	RHS
1	0	1	0	$-\frac{1}{2}$	$\frac{1}{2}$	0	$15 - \frac{1}{2}\Delta b_1$
2	0	0	0	$-\frac{3}{2}$	$\frac{1}{2}$	1	$9 - \frac{3}{2}\Delta b_1$
3	0	0	1	$\frac{3}{4}$	$-\frac{1}{4}$	0	$\frac{15}{2} + \frac{3}{4}\Delta b_1$
0	1	0	0	$\frac{35}{2}$	$\frac{15}{2}$	0	$975 + \frac{35}{2}\Delta b_1$

[3]A good exposition is found in Chaiho Kim, *Introduction to Linear Programming* (New York: Holt, 1971), pp. 304–316.

value that is expressed in terms of the change in availability of the given resource. Of course, these RHS values must be nonnegative, which means that the following conditions must hold:

$$\left.\begin{aligned} 15 - \tfrac{1}{2}\Delta b_1 &\geq 0 \\ 9 - \tfrac{3}{2}\Delta b_1 &\geq 0 \\ \tfrac{15}{2} + \tfrac{3}{4}\Delta b_1 &\geq 0 \end{aligned}\right\} \quad \begin{matrix}\text{which} \\ \text{implies} \\ \text{that}\end{matrix} \quad \left\{\begin{aligned} \Delta b_1 &\leq 30 \\ \Delta b_1 &\leq 6 \\ \Delta b_1 &\geq -10 \end{aligned}\right.$$

or

$$-10 \leq \Delta b_1 \leq +6$$

Therefore, if the amount of land available varies up from its original value by no more than 6 acres or down by no more than 10 acres, the original optimal solution remains ***feasible.*** Any variation outside this range causes at least one of the constraints to become negative, in which case the composition of the optimal solution must change.

Extending the incremental analysis further, we find that an increase of 1 unit of the first resource increases the objective function by \$17.50 (see the RHS element of row 0 in Table 4.5). Since all functions are linear, each additional unit of this first resource changes the objective function by the same amount, within the limits we have derived.

The Addition of a New Activity

Continuing with the potato–tomato example, assume that the farmer receives an inquiry from a marketing dealer about producing as much as possible of a third product X_3 that requires, for each unit produced, 2 units of land, 3 units of labor, and 1.5 units of storage space. At what value of contribution to profits would the farmer be willing to add this third product to the product mix?

The new production activity has the following characteristics:

Contribution to Profit	C_3X_3
Land Utilization	$2X_3$
Labor Requirement	$3X_3$
Storage Space Requirement	$1.5X_3$

These characteristics contain all the information we need to revise the original linear programming problem. In its restated form, the model will contain these values in a new column that reflects the addition of a new activity. The dual problem must also expand by an additional constraint, which corresponds to the new column in the primal. That is,

$$2Y_1 + 3Y_2 + 1.5Y_3 \geq C_3$$

When we apply previously obtained optimal values for the dual variables—$Y_1 = 17.5$, $Y_2 = 7.5$, and $Y_3 = 0$—the new dual constraint provides the following information about the constant C_3:

$$2(17.5) + 3(7.5) + 1.5(0) \geq C_3$$

or

$$C_3 \leq 57.5$$

The value \$57.50 is the total imputed value of resources used in the production of the third product. Therefore, the third product should not be added to the product mix unless its contribution to profit C_3 is greater than \$57.50 per unit. If this value is exceeded, the new activity enters the optimal basis via the normal simplex iteration procedure. Otherwise, the original, primal solution remains optimal.

Additional Considerations So far, our sensitivity analysis has been confined to considering a change in a single coefficient only. In some cases, however, we may want to know the effect on optimality and feasibility of a simultaneous change in several of the coefficients. Such problems generally require restatement of the model and solution by standard methods. It should be noted that we could further extend the postoptimality analysis by considering the introduction of another constraint resource or another policy constraint imposed by the decision maker.

Also, instead of changing coefficients by discrete amounts, we may find it worthwhile to investigate continuous changes and determine optimal solutions as a function of a parameter λ. This sort of analysis is called ***parametric linear programming.*** Ordinary linear programming models can easily be shown to be a special case of parametric models where lambda equals zero. This analysis may be extended to the same coefficients—C_j, b_i, and a_{ij}—that we studied using sensitivity analysis. However, the procedures involved are beyond the scope of this book. Interested readers should consult other references.[4]

4.5 Summary

For every linear programming problem there is a closely associated dual problem. The primal and dual programs are completely symmetrical. Exploiting these symmetrical properties, we can easily transform any

[4]See Chaiho Kim, Chapter 9.

given linear programming problem from the primal to the dual, and vice versa. Sometimes one formulation is solvable at a lower computation cost than the other.

Duality theorem 1, the fundamental duality theorem, states that the dual program yields the same optimal solution as its associated primal or original problem. When the optimal solution to one of the two problems has been found, the solution to its dual has been found simultaneously. In fact, the optimal solutions for both the primal and the dual can be found from the final optimal simplex tableau.

Duality theorem 2, the equilibrium theorem, illustrates the complementary slackness between the primal–dual relationships; that is, the product of corresponding solution values must equal zero ($X_jV_j = 0$ and $S_iY_i = 0$).

When the primal linear programming problem is viewed as one of resource allocation, its corresponding dual problem can be interpreted as one of evaluation or pricing of the allocated resources. Each dual variable contains important economic information that can be interpreted as either the shadow price (shadow cost) or the unit marginal profit contribution of a particular resource.

The optimal solution to a linear programming problem depends on the values of the RHS and coefficients in both the objective function and the constraints. Sensitivity analysis reveals the effect of changes in these given values. Such analysis can also reveal the range over which the solution values for both the primal and dual variables are valid. In the following chapter, we will investigate the transportation problem further, using various computation-simplifying algorithms. However, even with the specialized computational methods, we will see that the essential economic interpretation will again emerge from duality theory.

Exercises

4.1 Given the following primal linear programming problem, formulate the dual problem.

$$\text{Max} \quad Z_X = C_1X_1 + C_2X_2 + C_3X_3$$

subject to

$$a_{11}X_1 + a_{12}X_2 + a_{13}X_3 \leq b_1$$
$$a_{21}X_1 + a_{22}X_2 + a_{23}X_3 \leq b_2$$
$$a_{31}X_1 + a_{32}X_2 + a_{33}X_3 \leq b_3$$

and

$$X_j \geq 0 \qquad \text{for } j = 1, 2, 3$$

4.2 Given the following primal linear programming problem, formulate the dual problem.

$$\text{Max} \quad Z_X = 2X_1 + 3X_2$$

subject to

$$2X_1 + 4X_2 \leq 20$$
$$3X_1 + X_2 \leq 12$$

and

$$X_1 \geq 0, X_2 \geq 0$$

4.3 Given the following dual linear programming problem, formulate the primal problem.

$$\text{Min} \quad Z_Y = 38Y_1 + 24Y_2 + 20Y_3$$

subject to

$$Y_2 + 2Y_3 \geq 2$$
$$2Y_1 + Y_3 \geq 1$$
$$Y_1 + 2Y_2 + Y_3 \geq 4$$
$$3Y_1 + Y_2 \geq 2$$

and

$$Y_i \geq 0 \quad \text{for } i = 1, 2, 3$$

4.4 Given the following primal linear programming problem, formulate the dual problem.

$$\text{Max} \quad Z_X = C_1X_1 + C_2X_2$$

subject to

$$a_{11}X_1 + a_{12}X_2 = b_1$$
$$a_{21}X_1 + a_{22}X_2 \leq b_2$$

and

$$X_2 \geq 0, X_1 \text{ is unrestricted}$$

4.5 Formulate the primal of the following dual linear programming problem.

$$\text{Min} \quad Z_Y = 40Y_1 + 30Y_2 + 20Y_3$$

subject to

$$Y_1 + 2Y_2 + Y_3 \geq 4$$
$$3Y_1 + Y_2 + 3Y_3 \geq 5$$

and

$$Y_1 \geq 0, Y_3 \geq 0, Y_2 \text{ is unrestricted}$$

4.6 Given the following primal linear programming problem, formulate the dual problem.

$$\text{Min} \quad Z_X = C_1X_1 + C_2X_2$$

subject to
$$a_{11}X_1 + a_{12}X_2 = b_1$$
$$a_{21}X_1 + a_{22}X_2 \geq b_2$$

and
$$X_2 \geq 0, X_1 \text{ is unrestricted}$$

4.7 For this exercise, let $j = 1, 2, \ldots, n$; let $i = 1, 2, \ldots, m$; and use sigma notation.
a. Write a pair of the primal (Max) and its dual problem.
b. Write a pair of the primal (Min) and its dual problem.

4.8 Be sure that you understand the following concepts:
a. Primal and dual programs
b. Equilibrium theorem
c. Complementary slackness
d. Marginal profitability of resource

4.9 Review the following terms:
a. Postoptimality analysis or sensitivity analysis
b. Parametric programming

4.10 Consider the following optimal simplex tableau:

Row	Z_X	X_1	X_2	X_3	S_1	S_2	S_3	RHS
1	0	0	0	4	1	$\frac{3}{2}$	$\frac{1}{2}$	30
2	0	1	0	1	0	$\frac{1}{2}$	$\frac{1}{2}$	12
3	0	0	1	-1	0	$-\frac{1}{2}$	$\frac{1}{2}$	2
0	1	0	0	0	0	1	2	38

a. Write the solutions of the primal variables.
b. Write the corresponding dual variables in their proper positions.
c. Write the solutions of the dual variables.
d. Are both solutions optimal? Why?
e. Are both solutions feasible? Why?
f. Is the optimal solution unique? If not, why not?

4.11 Referring to exercise 4.10, show that:
a. Duality theorem 1 is satisfied.
b. Duality theorem 2 is satisfied. (***Note:*** This is a case in which both a

primal variable and its corresponding dual variable equal zero simultaneously. Why?)

4.12 Suppose this is a production problem with the initial simplex tableau A and the final tableau B. The objective of the firm is to maximize profits subject to three resource constraints. The firm's outputs are X_1, X_2, and X_3. S_1, S_2, and S_3 are slack variables corresponding to three resources—raw materials, machine hours, and labor days, respectively.

Tableau A

Row	Z_X	X_1	X_2	X_3	S_1	S_2	S_3	RHS	Resource
1	0	2	3	4	1	0	0	60	Materials (pounds)
2	0	1	1	1	0	1	0	40	Machine time (hours)
3	0	2	3	0	0	0	1	50	Labor (worker-days)
0	1	−4	−5	−6	0	0	0	0	

Tableau B

Row	Z_X	X_1	X_2	X_3	S_1	S_2	S_3	RHS
1	0	0	0	1	$\frac{1}{4}$	0	$-\frac{1}{4}$	$\frac{5}{2}$
2	0	0	$-\frac{1}{2}$	0	$-\frac{1}{4}$	1	$-\frac{1}{4}$	$\frac{25}{2}$
3	0	1	$\frac{3}{2}$	0	0	0	$\frac{1}{2}$	25
0	1	0	1	0	$\frac{3}{2}$	0	$\frac{1}{2}$	115

a. What are the optimal values of the firm's output and the optimal value of the objective function?

b. Construct the associated dual program. Show the optimal values for the dual variables, and calculate the optimal value of the dual objective function.

4.13 For exercise 4.12, give:

a. An economic interpretation of any one of the primal constraints.

b. An economic interpretation of each dual variable, dual slack variable, objective function, and any one of the dual constraints.

4.14 Referring to exercise 4.12, answer the following questions.

a. What is the upper limit of the objective function coefficient of the nonbasic variable X_2 if the current solution remains optimal?

b. For basic variable X_1 (or X_3), give a range over which the objective function coefficient can vary and the current solution still remains optimal.

c. Give an interval for the materials resource over which the current solution remains optimal.
d. Give an interval for machine time over which the current solution remains optimal.

4.15 Refer to exercise 4.12. If the firm receives an inquiry about the possibility of producing a fourth output that requires 6 pounds of material resources, 2 hours of machine time, and 2 worker-days of labor per unit and would contribute a profit of $9 per unit, should the firm add the fourth output to their production line? If yes, why? And how much of the fourth output should the firm produce? If no, why not? And can we predict at what level of profit the firm ***would*** start to produce the fourth output?

4.16 After a number of iterations, the simplex tableau of a given linear program appears in the following form:

Row	Z_X	X_1	X_2	S_1	S_2	RHS
1	0	1	2	1	0	50
2	0	0	1	0	1	26
0	1	0	4	10	0	500

a. Is this an optimal tableau? Why?
b. Write out the optimal solution of the primal problem.
c. Write out the optimal solution of the dual problem.
d. Indicate the values of the primal and the dual objective functions.

4.17 Mr. Strange has two production activities, X_1 and X_2, and his production is restricted by a single resource, capital. Only 20 units of capital are currently available. Engineering data indicate that X_1 uses 2 units of capital per unit level and that X_2 uses 1 unit of capital per unit level. The profit activity of X_1 is $8 per unit, and the profit activity of X_2 is $5 per unit.

a. Formulate a linear programming problem for Mr. Strange, and give an economic interpretation of your constraint.
b. Specify the linear programming problem you formulated in part (a) as the primal problem, and formulate the corresponding dual problem.
c. Give an economic interpretation of your dual variable and dual constraint.
d. Solve your linear programming problem by the simplex method.
e. Write out the solution of the primal.
f. Write out the solution of the dual.

g. Are the answers from parts (e) and (f) both feasible? Why?
h. Are both solutions optimal? Why?
i. Show that duality theorem 1 is satisfied.
j. Show that duality theorem 2 is satisfied.
k. Of the two variables X_1 and X_2, which is the nonbasic variable (if there is one) in your optimal solution? To what extent can the objective function coefficient of the nonbasic variable increase while the current solution remains optimal?
l. Can you predict the marginal profitability of capital (within a certain range)? If so, what is it? Why is it?
m. Mr. Strange receives an inquiry about the possibility of adding a third production activity that requires 3 units of capital per unit output. At what level of profit would you suggest that Mr. Strange should consider including the third activity in his production plan?

4.18 Consider the following simplex tableau:

Row	Z_X	X_1	X_2	S_1	S_2	RHS
1	0	0	1	$\frac{1}{2}$	$-\frac{1}{4}$	10
2	0	1	0	$-\frac{1}{4}$	$\frac{3}{8}$	15
0	1	0	0	$\frac{9}{4}$	$\frac{1}{8}$	145

a. Write out the optimal solution of the primal problem.
b. Write out the optimal solution of the dual problem.
c. Show that duality theorem 1 is satisfied.
d. Show that duality theorem 2 is satisfied.

4.19 The National Lumber Company is producing for Racy's Department Store disc packs X_1, X_2, and X_3, for which the profit margins per unit are \$40, \$20, and \$20, respectively. Each product must pass through three production processes—cutting and clearing, grinding and coating, and assembly and testing. The following table gives the time required per unit of product in each process.

Process \ Product	X_1	X_2	X_3
Cutting and Clearing	1	3	1
Crinding and Coating	3	3	3
Assembly and Testing	2	1	1

There are 300 hours available for cutting and clearing, 300 hours for grinding and coating, and 240 hours for assembly and testing. The company has recently received a new order from Racy's to purchase as much of a fourth product as possible. The new product requires 1 hour each of cutting and clearing, grinding and coating, and assembly and testing per unit, and it carries a unit profit margin of $10. Should the company accept the order? If so, how much of the fourth product should the company produce? If not, what level of profit margin would be required for the company to accept the order?

4.20 Concord Manufacturing produces two products, model 1 and model 2, with three resources—labor, raw materials, and machine time. The following information is available for the solution of the firm's production problem:

	Technical Coefficients		Total
	Model 1	**Model 2**	**Availability**
Labor	2	$\frac{1}{2}$	162
Raw Materials	2	1	240
Machine Time	1	0	60
Profit Margin	45	15	

Let X_1 and X_2 represent model 1 and model 2, respectively, and let S_1, S_2, and S_3 be the slack variables corresponding to labor, raw materials, and machine time. The simplex tableau for the optimal solution is as follows:

Row	Z_X	X_1	X_2	S_1	S_2	S_3	RHS
1	0	0	0	1	$-\frac{1}{2}$	−1	42
2	0	0	1	0	1	−2	120
3	0	1	0	0	0	1	60
0	1	0	0	0	15	15	4500

a. What is the composition of the optimal production mix? How profitable is the optimal production mix?
b. What are the shadow prices for labor, raw materials, and machine time?

c. What is the marginal profit contribution for an additional unit of labor? For an additional unit of machine time? What is the shadow cost of machine time?
d. A competitor has just introduced a new model. If Concord Manufacturing is to make a similar model, it will require 1.5 units of labor, 2 units of raw materials, and 1 unit of machine time. At what level of profit margin should Concord Manufacturing introduce this new model?

4.21 Refer to exercise 4.20 and use the information provided by the optimal simplex tableau.
a. Establish the range of variation of raw materials over which the optimal solution remains optimal.
b. Determine the range over which the profit margin of model 1 can be varied without affecting the optimality condition of the original solution.
c. State whether total profit in part (b) will be affected.

4.22 Consider the following primal linear programming problem:

$$\text{Max } Z_X = X_1 + 2X_2$$

subject to

$$X_1 + X_2 \leq 8$$
$$X_1 + X_2 \geq 4$$

and

$$X_1 \geq 0, X_2 \geq 0$$

a. Write out its corresponding dual.
b. Solve the primal problem by the simplex method.
c. Substitute the primal variables (X_j, for $j = 1, 2$) and the dual variables (Y_i, for $i = 1, 2$) into the primal and dual objective functions, respectively, to verify that Max C_X = Min C_Y.

4.23 People's Cooperative is a hypothetical joint farming organization consisting of 3 farm members producing carrots, potatoes, and tomatoes. Their jointly owned facilities, operated by a professional management staff, are central electric power, 10 units; irrigation and drainage water, 15 units; and services, 8 units. Each member has only one activity at his or her disposal. The carrot-producing firm requires 1 unit of power, 3 units of water, and 2 units of services to produce 1 unit of carrots. The potato-producing activity requires 2 units of power, 3 units of water, and 1 unit of services to produce 1 unit of potatoes. The tomato-producing activity requires 3 units of power, 1 unit of water, and 2 units of services to produce 1 unit of tomatoes. The return values for each unit of carrots, potatoes, and tomatoes are $4, $5, and $6, respectively.

Because of limitations in the capacity of the individual farms, the carrot-producing activity cannot be run at a level greater than 3 units, and the potato- and tomato-producing activities cannot be run at a level greater than 2 units each. Assuming that the goal of the cooperative is to maximize the total value of output produced, formulate the problem the manager of the cooperative faces into a linear program model and write out the corresponding dual problem. (Hand calculation is not required, but computer solution is encouraged.)

Suggested Readings

Baumol, W. J. *Economic Theory and Operations Analysis.* 3rd ed. Englewood Cliffs, N.J.: Prentice-Hall, 1972. Chapter 6.

Baumol, W. J., and T. Fabian. "Decomposition, Pricing for Decentralization and External Economics." *Management Science,* 11, No. 1 (1964), 1–32.

Charnes, A., and W. W. Cooper. *Management Models and Industrial Applications of Linear Programming.* 2 vols. New York: Wiley, 1963.

Chiang, Alpha C. *Fundamental Methods of Mathematical Economics.* 2nd ed. New York: McGraw-Hill, 1974. Chapter 19.

Dantzig, G. B. *Linear Programming and Extensions.* Princeton, N.J.: Princeton University Press, 1963.

De Wet, G. L. "Comparative Costs, Linear Programming and the Decentralization of Industries." *South African Journal of Economics* (June 1972), 152–162.

Dorfman, Robert, Paul A. Samuelson, and Robert M. Solow. *Linear Programming and Economic Analysis.* New York: McGraw-Hill, 1958. Chapter 3.

Gale, David. *The Theory of Linear Economic Models.* New York: McGraw-Hill, 1960.

Hsiao, J. C. "An Economic Interpretation of the Transportation Algorithm." *American Journal of Agricultural Economics,* 53, No. 3 (August), 1971.

Kim, Chaiho. *Introduction to Linear Programming.* New York: Holt, 1971.

Lea, R. B. "A Note on the Definition of Cost Coefficients in a Linear Programming Model." *Accounting Review,* 47 (April 1972), 346–350.

Muller-Oehring, H. "Determining the Coal Wagon Requirements in Rhenish Lignite Mines." *Operational Research,* 20 (1972), 391–403.

Richmond, Samuel B. *Operations Research for Management Decisions.* New York: Ronald Press, 1968.

Samuels, J. M. "Opportunity Costing: An Application of Mathematical Programming." *Journal of Accounting Research,* 3 (Autumn 1965), 182–191.

Simmonard, Michel. *Linear Programming.* Translated by W. Jewell. Englewood Cliffs, N.J.: Prentice-Hall, 1966.

Wagner, H. *Principles of Operations Research.* Englewood Cliffs, N.J.: Prentice-Hall, 1969.

5

The Transportation Problem and Its Economic Interpretation

Within the realm of all linear programming problems, one finds applications with particular characteristics that recur often enough to warrant closer inspection. Two special linear programming problems will be investigated in depth in this chapter. The first—the ***transportation problem***—requires finding the most efficient routing of materials from alternative origins to alternative destinations within the designated constraints of supply and demand and based on the cost structure of the transportation routes. This problem was introduced in Chapter 2 as a type of linear programming problem, and a specific example, including its mathematical statement, was presented. The second special type of linear programming problem presented in this chapter is the ***assignment problem,*** which is the general type of problem faced when attempting to determine an optimal assignment of workers (productive abilities) to tasks (productive requirements). Typically, it is feasible to satisfy the constraints of both transportation problems and assignment problems in many ways; therefore, solution techniques focus on finding an optimal allocation of available resources. Both types of problems are true linear programming applications that we can solve using the principles already presented in preceding chapters (specifically, the simplex method), but investigation of the basic structures of these problems has led to techniques specifically applicable to each case. Using the algorithms so derived to determine optimal solutions is more efficient than using the simplex method.

5.1 The Characteristics of Transportation Problems

Fundamental Characteristics

Consider once again the simple transportation problem we discussed in Chapter 2, which is concerned with the transfer of goods from factories to markets according to a plan that will utilize transportation resources as efficiently as possible—that is, a plan that will minimize transportation costs. The objective function is

$$\text{Min} \quad C_X = 6X_{11} + 5X_{12} + 1X_{13} + 4X_{21} + 2X_{22} + 4X_{23}$$

The supply constraints (after reversing the direction of the inequalities by multiplying both sides of each inequality by -1) are

$$\begin{aligned} -X_{11} - X_{12} - X_{13} + 0 \quad + 0 \quad + 0 \quad &\geq -18 \\ 0 \quad + 0 \quad + 0 \quad - X_{21} - X_{22} - X_{23} &\geq -15 \end{aligned}$$

Finally, we add the demand constraints, taking care to keep each variable in its own separate column:

$$\begin{aligned} X_{11} + 0 \quad + 0 \quad + X_{21} + 0 \quad + 0 \quad &\geq 16 \\ 0 \quad + X_{12} + 0 \quad + 0 \quad + X_{22} + 0 \quad &\geq 10 \\ 0 \quad + 0 \quad + X_{13} + 0 \quad + 0 \quad + X_{23} &\geq 7 \end{aligned}$$

and $\quad X_{ij} \geq 0 \quad$ for all i and j

This entire system is a straightforward linear programming statement of the primal problem. Note that, in the column for each variable, there are only two nonzero coefficients, -1 and $+1$. Recognize also that the configuration of variables in the constraint inequalities is definite and is derived from the process of summing variables, first across rows and then down columns, and that each inequality represents one such summation.[1]

Before analyzing optimization methods other than the simplex method, let's consider the dual problem. For this two-factory, three-market problem, since the primal inequalities present summations of variables first according to factory supplies and then according to market

[1]The -1 and $+1$ in the column for each X_{ij} are necessary conditions for the so-called ***network problem.*** All transportation problems have a network problem structure.

demands, two subscripted variables will be adopted for presentation of the dual problem—one for factories, U_i, and one for markets, P_j. Then, following the rules presented in Chapter 4, we write the dual problem as

$$\text{Max}\quad C_{U,P} = \pi = -18U_1 - 15U_2 + 16P_1 + 10P_2 + 7P_3$$

subject to

$$\begin{aligned}
-U_1 + 0 + P_1 + 0 + 0 &\le 6\\
-U_1 + 0 + 0 + P_2 + 0 &\le 5\\
-U_1 + 0 + 0 + 0 + P_3 &\le 1\\
0 - U_2 + P_1 + 0 + 0 &\le 4\\
0 - U_2 + 0 + P_2 + 0 &\le 2\\
0 - U_2 + 0 + 0 + P_3 &\le 4
\end{aligned}$$

and $\quad P_j \ge 0, j = 1, 2, 3 \quad \text{and} \quad U_i \ge 0, i = 1, 2$

The General Case The general case for transportation problems is now apparent. Using sigma notation, we express the primal as

$$\text{Min}\quad C = \sum_i \sum_j C_{ij} X_{ij}$$

subject to

$$-\sum_j X_{ij} \ge -S_i \qquad \text{for } i = 1, \ldots, m \tag{5.1}$$

$$\sum_i X_{ij} \ge D_j \qquad \text{for } j = 1, \ldots, n$$

and $\quad X_{ij} \ge 0 \quad \text{for all } i \text{ and } j$

where S_i and D_j represent factory supplies and warehouse demands, respectively.

When we allow the variables P_j to precede, left to right, variable U_i, the corresponding dual is

$$\text{Max}\quad \pi = \sum_j P_j D_j - \sum_i U_i S_i$$

subject to

$$P_j - U_i \le C_{ij} \quad \text{for all } i \text{ and } j \tag{5.2}$$

and $\quad P_j \ge 0,\ U_i \ge 0 \quad \text{for all } i \text{ and } j$

Economic Interpretation Interpreting the meaning of the dual problem is particularly important. As we found in Chapter 4, the interpretation of linear programming problems where constraints are related to resources leads to dual variables that are imputed prices or shadow prices for the resources. In the transportation problem, the constraints relate either to the factory supply-of-product conditions or to the market demand-for-product conditions that exist for a given period of time. Therefore, the dual variables in the transportation problem represent the imputed prices of the product at the *j*th market, and the dual variable U_i is the imputed price or value of the product, free on board, at the *i*th factory. Alternatively, the value of each variable U_i measures the comparative location advantage of the *i*th factory, and thus we may call these values ***location rents***—a term used by Koopmans and Beckmann.[2]

From this perspective, the dual objective function and constraints take on added significance in the economic interpretation of the transportation problem. The objective is to maximize a difference between sums of products—between an imputed, market ***total revenue*** and an imputed, factory ***total location rent.*** The former is recognized to be $\Sigma P_j D_j$—the sum of the imputed market prices times the respective market demands—and the latter is, of course, $\Sigma U_i S_i$—the sum of the imputed location rents times the respective factory supplies. The dual constraints,

$$P_j - U_i \leq C_{ij} \quad \text{for all } i \text{ and } j \tag{5.3}$$

show that the advantage of shipping from any factory to any market is the difference between the corresponding imputed price and location rent ($P_j - U_i$). At most, this difference must be equal to the established, per-unit transportation cost. This becomes clearer when the dual constraint inequalities are rearranged, as follows:

$$P_j \leq U_i + C_{ij} \quad \text{for all } i \text{ and } j \tag{5.3'}$$

For a given transportation route, if the imputed market price is less than the sum of the factory location rent and the unit shipping cost along that route, then it would be economically inefficient to make a shipment over the given route. However, if the variable P_j just equals this sum (the constraint precludes its being greater), the transportation route can be used economically.

[2]Tjalling C. Koopmans and Martin Beckmann, "Assignment Problems and the Location of Economic Activities," *Econometrica*, January 1957, pp. 59–60. Also see J. C. Hsiao, "An Economic Interpretation of the Transportation Problem," *American Journal of Agricultural Economics*, 53, No. 3 (August 1971).

Interestingly, these concepts relate directly to the complementary slackness property of duality theorem 2, which in its application to the transportation problem requires that the following conditions hold true:

$$X_{ij}[P_j - (U_i + C_{ij})] = 0 \quad \text{for all } i \text{ and } j \tag{5.4}$$

Combining (5.4) with (5.3′) and the nonnegativity requirements for primal variables X_{ij}, we find that the following complementary slackness conditions must exist:

(i) If $P_j = U_i + C_{ij}$, then $X_{ij} > 0$.

(ii) If $P_j < U_i + C_{ij}$, then $X_{ij} = 0$.

Koopmans' original economic idea[3] has assumed central importance in the subsequent development of various transportation methods. In terms of Koopmans' original economic reasoning, we may state the two conditions as follows:

(i′) Each route in use ($X_{ij} > 0$) would yield a profit of zero.

(ii″) Routes not being used ($X_{ij} = 0$) would all yield a profit less than or equal to zero.

The presence of an optimal solution also requires that the conditions of duality theorem 1 be met. That is, Max π = Min C_X. Therefore, as with linear programming problems generally, an optimal solution to the transportation problem meets simultaneously the conditions of primal feasibility, complementary slackness, and dual feasibility. These conditions are as fundamental to the specialized iterative techniques presented in this chapter as they are to the more widely applicable simplex method.

5.2 Transportation Problem Algorithms

With a complete presentation of the linear programming model of the transportation problem in hand and the tools of previous chapters under

[3]Tjalling C. Koopmans, "Concepts of Optimality and Their Uses," *Cowles Foundation Discussion Paper*, No. 421, February 1, 1976 (copyright by the Nobel Foundation, 1976), p. 9.

our belts, we are poised to apply the simplex method and determine a minimum-cost solution. The number of identifiable constraints equals the number of factories plus the number of markets in the given problem. In other words, if there are m factories and n markets, there are $m + n$ constraints, or $2 + 3 = 5$ in our simple example. Parenthetically, one of these constraints will always be redundant in a transportation problem since, if all but one constraint in the system are specified, then the last constraint is determined. Therefore, if a total of $m + n$ constraints are identifiable, at most only $m + n - 1$ of these constraints are independent. As for the variables, there must be one for each possible transportation route $(m \times n)$ plus the necessary slack variable $(m + n)$ and artificial variables (n). Thus for our 2-by-3 problem there would be 14 variables; for a 3-by-4 problem there would be 23 variables; and so on. The sheer size of a simplex model for larger transportation problems makes the use of the simplex method cumbersome. Where computer processing is available, this factor need not be a disadvantage. But even specifying larger problems for computer input can be unwieldy.

Stemming from the early work of Hitchcock[4] and Koopmans,[5] algorithms more efficient than the simplex method have been developed for application to the transportation problem and to other problems that take the same form. As early as 1942, Leonid Kantorovich[6] developed the transportation model, but his work was not known in Western countries until the late 1950s. Koopmans and Kantorovich jointly received the Nobel Prize in economics (1975) for their work in determining the optimal allocation of resources growing out of activity analysis and transportation models. Differences are to be found in the algorithms that have been developed since these first studies. The variations are (1) alternative methods of finding an initial basic feasible solution and (2) alternative techniques for performing iteration. Using our familiar transportation problem, this section will present various methods in each category.

The Transportation Table

Although the manipulation of numbers varies according to the particular solution technique used with a transportation problem, all techniques utilize a transportation table. In its standard form, it records all of the

[4]F. L. Hitchcock, "The Distribution of a Product from Several Sources to Numerous Localities," *The Journal of Mathematics and Physics*, August 1941, pp. 224–230.

[5]Tjalling C. Koopmans, "Optimum Utilization of the Transportation System," *Econometrica*, July 1949 (supplement).

[6]Leonid Kantorovich, "On the Translocation of Masses," *Management Science*, 5, No. 1 (1958), pp. 1–4 (reprinted from the original article published in 1942).

Table 5.1 The Transportation Table

From \ To	Market 1	Market 2	Market 3	Supplies
Factory 1	6 X_{11}	5 X_{12}	1 X_{13}	18
Factory 2	4 X_{21}	2 X_{22}	4 X_{23}	15
Demands	16	10	7	33

essential elements of the given transportation problem: shipping costs and amounts shipped for all possible routes, points of origin and destination, and the specified supply and demand quantities. For example, consider Table 5.1.

This table is best conceived of as a matrix within a matrix. First, each cell contains one transportation variable—that is, one shipment value from the row-designated factory to the column-designated market. Each variable is expressed by X_{ij}, the amount shipped from factory i to market j, and all possible routes are represented. Second, the per-unit cost matrix with unit shipping costs for all possible transportation routes is superimposed so that the unit costs appear in the upper left-hand corner of each cell. Using this scheme, we can easily calculate total shipping cost as the sum of the products of unit costs times amounts shipped. We enter the positive numerical quantities that denote shipments in the appropriate matrix cells, often with a circle around the quantity to emphasize the presence of a basic variable. These are called ***filled cells.*** The matrix cells for routes not utilized by the transportation model are left blank, and called ***empty cells,*** and the corresponding variable of the transportation table is recognized to be nonbasic. Finally, we enter factory supplies and market demands in the right-hand and lower margins of the table, respectively. Note that, in this case, total supplies equal total demands. A case wherein total supplies do not equal total demands will be dealt with in a later section.

The Northwest Corner Rule and the Steppingstone Method

Although the number of constraints is $m + n$—the sum of the number of rows (factories) and columns (markets) in the transportation table—the number of variables required to form a basis is one less, or $m + n - 1$. We know intuitively that this is necessary, because there are only $m + n - 1$ ***independent*** variables in the solution basis. In other words, once the values of any $m + n - 1$ independent variables are given, the values of the remaining variables are determined; they depend on the given values of the other $m + n - 1$ variables. Considering also the conditions of feasibility and nonnegativity, the number of basic variables (representing utilized transportation routes) is $m + n - 1$, and all other variables must be nonbasic or zero (representing nonutilized routes).

The ***northwest corner rule*** is one method of finding an initial basic feasible solution (IBFS). Starting in the row 1, column 1 position of the transportation table (the ***northwest corner***), we form a basis by allocating shipments to routes, alternating in a way that exhausts factory supplies and satisfies market demands, in either order as the situation requires. By this procedure, we form an IBFS for the example shown in Table 5.1 by first letting variable X_{11} equal 16 units (the largest value possible according to the market 1 demand and the factory 1 supply). Then, in order to exhaust the remaining supply of factory 1, we assign 2 units to the factory 1, market 2 route. Now we need 8 units from factory 2 to meet total market 2 demand, after which 7 units can be applied to satisfy the remaining factory 2, market 3 requirements. The resulting basic feasible solution is given in Table 5.2.

The IBFS contains $m + n - 1$ (or $2 + 3 - 1 = 4$) basic variables. The total cost of this particular combination of transportation variables is

$$C_X = (\$6 \times 16) + (\$5 \times 2) + (\$2 \times 8) + (\$4 \times 7) = \$150$$

Table 5.2
IBFS, Using the Northwest Corner Rule

From \ To	Market 1	Market 2	Market 3	Supplies
Factory 1	6 → ↑ −6 (16) Stepping-stone	5 ↓ +5 (2) Stepping-stone	1 −$6 Empty-Cell Evaluation	18
Factory 2	4 +4 +$1 Empty-Cell Evaluation	2 ↙ −2 (8) Stepping-stone	4 (7) Stepping-stone	15
Demands	16	10	7	33

Now we must consider whether this particular solution is optimal. Both of the two empty cells represent nonbasic variables, and either one might conceivably lower cost when introduced into another solution basis. Particularly appealing from the standpoint of cost minimization is the factory 1, market 3 route for which the per-unit shipping cost is only \$1. But if no cost improvement can be found, the given solution is optimal.

Closer examination reveals that introducing a nonbasic variable must not be done arbitrarily. To do so, we must maintain the supply and demand conditions of all constraints and eliminate in the process one other basic variable, thereby preserving a set of $m + n - 1$ basic variables. The ***steppingstone method*** is a procedure for determining the potential for improvement of each nonbasic variable and for controlling the iteration from one solution basis to a better one, in terms of the objective function. Its name is derived from the idea that the filled cells of the transportation table act as steppingstones.

Let's assess the potential for improvement of the nonbasic variable X_{21}. The hypothetical shipment of 1 unit of product over this route would mean an additional cost of \$4, but it would also mean the necessary reduction of 1 unit of variable X_{11} and, therefore, \$6 of reduced cost. But to maintain feasibility, this requires in turn that variable X_{12} be increased by 1 unit and that variable X_{22} be decreased by 1 unit. This will increase cost in the former case by \$5 and reduce it in the latter by \$2.

This procedure is diagrammed in Table 5.2. Starting with an empty cell (for example, the route from factory 2 to market 1), we find that adding 1 unit of shipment to this cell affects other existing shipping routes also, because the supply and demand constraint conditions must be maintained. Consequently, Table 5.2 shows that a string of cost changes results when the hypothetical addition of 1 unit to variable X_{21} occurs. In particular, it causes:

1. A cost ***increase*** due to increasing X_{21} by 1 unit: \$4
2. A cost ***decrease*** due to decreasing X_{11} by 1 unit: \$6
3. A cost ***increase*** due to increasing X_{12} by 1 unit: \$5
4. A cost ***decrease*** due to decreasing X_{22} by 1 unit: \$2

The net cost effect of this evaluation is

$$\frac{\Delta C_X}{\Delta X_{21}} = \$4 - \$6 + \$5 - \$2 = +\$1$$

Considering the adjustments necessary to move from the current solution basis to another in which variable X_{21} becomes basic, we have just seen that the total cost of the shipping schedule will be \$1 more per unit of product shipped from factory 2 to market 1. Obviously, this effect is not desirable.

It is important to understand that the net cost effect we have just calculated is a hypothetical evaluation of the incremental (or per-unit) change in the objective function resulting from using a transportation route that is currently not used. The effect of such a change traces through the transportation table from one utilized route (steppingstone) to the next in a way that must preserve all supply and demand constraints. Due to the underlying dependence relationship, the string of changes progresses from the empty cell to a succession of steppingstones that finally lead back to the initial empty cell from which the evaluation originated. Since the string of changes always loops back via steppingstones to the original empty cell, the term ***closed loop*** is used to describe the pattern of calculations leading to the evaluation of an empty cell.

We must evaluate all empty cells in this fashion by finding closed loops and calculating an incremental cost change. For variable X_{13}, which is nonbasic, the calculation yields

1. A cost ***increase*** due to increasing X_{13} by 1 unit: \$1
2. A cost ***decrease*** due to decreasing X_{23} by 1 unit: \$4
3. A cost ***increase*** due to increasing X_{22} by 1 unit: \$2
4. A cost ***decrease*** due to decreasing X_{12} by 1 unit: \$5

As a result, this empty-cell evaluation is

$$\frac{\Delta C_X}{\Delta X_{13}} = \$1 - \$4 + \$2 - \$5 = -\$6$$

The incremental cost evaluations of empty cells should be recorded in the empty cells as they are calculated. They can be distinguished from shipping allocations, because the latter are circled and are not preceded by a plus or a minus and a dollar sign. The evaluations are not circled and are preceded by sign designations.

Now we have identified a nonbasic variable that, in becoming basic, has the net effect of lowering total cost by \$6 for each unit shipped over the designated route. Nevertheless, the allocation of product to this route cannot be made arbitrarily large if the constraints of the problem are to be met. Some shipping routes must dwindle at the expense of increasing the empty-cell route from zero, but none of those that dwindle must fall below zero. In becoming a basic variable, our variable X_{13} can accept at most 2 units of product, which causes variable X_{12} to become nonbasic. Corresponding shifts of 2 units must be applied to all cells in the selected closed loop so that we can perform iteration to an improved, feasible basis. This improved solution is shown in Table 5.3, and the evaluation of incremental costs for the empty cells has been included. As expected, the total transportation cost was reduced by \$12 (\$150 − \$138).

Once again, the number of basic variables meets the $m + n - 1$ requirement, because the iteration procedure brought into the solution one new variable, X_{13}, while eliminating from the solution variable X_{12}. The empty-cell evaluations in Table 5.3 indicate that further improvement is possible. The reader should verify these calculations by identifying the appropriate closed loops and applying the steppingstone method.

Perhaps more should now be said about closed loops. First, if there exists a basic solution with $m + n - 1$ positive variables, then there will be one and only one closed loop for each empty cell. This results fundamentally from the condition of independence existing in the basic solution. Second, closed loops often do not assume the configuration of a square or rectangle. In larger and more complex transportation tables, the loops necessary to evaluate empty cells may have peculiar configurations with many corners and even overlapping paths. Third, a closed loop is necessarily closed; it must emanate from and return to a given empty cell and can form corners only on filled cells. (The path of a closed loop may trace across other empty cells, but corners must utilize the filled cells.) And fourth, the direction of progression along the path of a closed loop is irrelevant; the corresponding calculations may proceed in either a clockwise or a counterclockwise direction without affecting the result.

From a review of Table 5.3, it should now be clear that another iteration will further decrease the transportation cost objective function. In fact, every unit that is allocated to the route from factory 2 to market 1 will reduce cost an additional \$5. Only 5 units can be shifted to this route, however, because the reallocation process that adds to variable X_{21} draws from variables X_{11} and X_{23}. Thus increasing variable X_{21} from zero to 5 units eliminates variable X_{23}, establishing a new set of $m + n - 1$ independent variables and a new feasible solution. As a result of this iteration to a new solution basis, total cost is lowered by \$25 (5 units times the −\$5 empty-cell evaluation), from \$138 to \$113 (see Table 5.4).

Table 5.3 After Iteration One, Using the Steppingstone Method

From \ To	Market 1	Market 2	Market 3	Supplies
Factory 1	6 (16)	5 +\$6	1 (2)	18
Factory 2	4 −\$5	2 (10)	4 (5)	15
Demands	16	10	7	33

Total cost:

$$C_X = (\$6 \times 16) + (\$1 \times 2) + (\$2 \times 10) + (\$4 \times 5) = \$138$$

Empty-cell evaluations:

$$\frac{\Delta C_X}{\Delta X_{12}} = +5 - 1 + 4 - 2 = +6$$

$$\frac{\Delta C_X}{\Delta X_{21}} = +4 - 6 + 1 - 4 = -5$$

Conclusion: An additional iteration that causes variable X_{21} to become basic reduces total cost by \$5 per unit of product shipped over the Factory 2, Market 1 route.

The important effect of this iteration was to increase allocation to the least-cost transportation route, variable X_{13}, while simultaneously reducing allocation to the highest-cost route, variable X_{11}. The net effect on total cost results from the overall cost changes of all variables in the given closed loop. This time, the empty-cell evaluations of Table 5.4 indicate that no further improvement is possible and that the optimal solution to this transportation problem has been determined:

Ship 11 units from factory 1 to market 1.
Ship 7 units from factory 1 to market 3.
Ship 5 units from factory 2 to market 1.
Ship 10 units from factory 2 to market 2.

This solution meets all constraints and minimizes total transportation cost at \$113.

Table 5.4
After Iteration Two, An Optimal Solution

From \ To	Market 1	Market 2	Market 3	Supplies
Factory 1	6 (11)	5 +$1	1 (7)	18
Factory 2	4 (5)	2 (10)	4 +$5	15
Demands	16	10	7	33

Total cost:

$$C_X = (\$6 \times 11) + (\$1 \times 7) + (\$4 \times 5) + (\$2 \times 10) = \$113$$

Empty-cell evaluations:

$$\frac{\Delta C_X}{\Delta X_{12}} = +5 - 2 + 4 - 6 = +1$$

$$\frac{\Delta C_X}{\Delta X_{23}} = +4 - 4 + 6 - 1 = +5$$

Conclusion: An additional iteration will not decrease total cost, because the empty-cell evaluations are all positive. This is an optimal solution.

The Minimum Cost Search Method

The northwest corner rule is a convenient and reliable technique for finding an initial basic feasible solution. Its primary drawback is its disregard for the costs in the cells receiving allocation. Whereas the structure of the simplex method required us to find a trivial IBFS just to get started, there are distinct advantages in finding an IBFS as close as possible to the optimal solution when using transportation problem algorithms. Indeed, some methods of determining an IBFS in transportation problems fall frequently on the optimal solution, and, although a check for optimality is required, iteration may be unnecessary. Several methods that are more efficient in this regard than the simple northwest corner rule are presented in the following sections.

An easy improvement on the northwest corner rule, called the ***minimum cost search method,*** follows the same basic technique of alternatively exhausting either factory supplies or market demands but modifies the requirement of working geographically from the upper left-hand corner. Instead, we make the initial allocation to ***the least-cost cell*** in the transportation table. If this allocation fulfills the demand requirement of a market, we proceed by finding the next lowest cost in the same row and exhausting, if possible, the supply of the given factory. The procedure exhausts factory supplies and market demands in like fashion, always inspecting costs to find the next cell for an allocation in the given row or column.

As an example of the minimum cost search method, consider now its application to the transportation problem we solved in the previous section. The first allocation would be made to the least-cost cell of the table: 7 units to variable X_{13}. Proceeding to exhaust the factory supply, we make the next allocation to the cell in the same row that has the next lowest cost: market 2, 10 units. The factory 1 supply of 18 units has still not been exhausted, so we allocate the remaining unit to market 1, whereupon market 1 demand is completed by drawing 15 units from factory 2. This IBFS is shown in Table 5.5. The evaluation of empty cells also is included.

This solution has a total cost that is $10 higher than the optimal solution, which is known from the previous section. The potential for improvement is $1 per unit for variable X_{22}, and 10 units can be shifted to achieve a lower-cost solution. Thus, it becomes clear that only one iteration is needed to reach the same optimal solution.

Creating Balance

Suppose that the same organization that has been shipping from its two factories to three markets responds to increased market demands of 19, 24, and 9 units by acquiring a third factory. Of course, the number of possible shipment routes increases correspondingly. For the sake of illustration, suppose that the unit shipping costs from the third factory

Table 5.5
An IBFS Using the Minimum Cost Search Method

From \ To	Market 1	Market 2	Market 3	Supplies
Factory 1	6 (1)	5 (10)	1 (7)	18
Factory 2	4 (15)	2 −$1	4 +$5	15
Demands	16	10	7	33

Total cost:

$$C_X = (\$6 \times 1) + (\$5 \times 10) + (\$1 \times 7) + (\$4 \times 15) = \$123$$

are \$7, \$3, and \$2 for markets 1, 2, and 3, respectively, and that the available factory supply is 26 units.

Whereas all previous examples were arranged so that total factory supplies equaled total market demands, factory supplies (59 units) now exceed total demand (52 units), and the problem is said to be out of ***balance.*** As a result, some of what is being produced will not be shipped to any market. On a period-by-period basis, growing inventories may require a subsequent decision to cut back production by operating the factories at less than capacity and/or by laying off workers. On the other hand, slack in the current period may be absorbed by fluctuating market demands in later periods. Such considerations are familiar to business managers.

Insofar as finding an optimal shipping plan for the current period is concerned, putting excess supply into inventory is assumed to cost nothing for shipping, and a new column of slack variables is added to the transportation table. This slack column can be regarded as a ***dummy market*** for which the transportation costs are zero. Next, the ***demand requirement*** of the dummy market is set equal to the excess of total factory supplies over real market demands, thereby restoring balance to the problem. The per-unit cost matrix of this revised example, including the margin specifications for supplies and demands, is given in Table 5.6.

The reverse situation can also arise; total market demands may exceed total factory supplies. In this case, we would add to the transportation table a slack row representing a dummy plant or, essentially, back-ordered goods. Again, the transportation costs are assumed to be zero

Table 5.6
The Per-Unit Cost Matrix with Another Factory

From \ To	Market 1	Market 2	Market 3	Slack	Supplies
Factory 1	6	5	1	0	18
Factory 2	4	2	4	0	15
Factory 3	7	3	2	0	26
Demands	19	24	9	7	59

in the slack row. In a practical situation, the possibility of nonzero slack variable costs should not be overlooked, however.

Our revised example affords us another chance to apply the northwest corner rule with cost inspection. Because there now is a dummy market, allocations to the slack variables are made last, even though the zero costs appear most attractive. Using this method, we should make the following allocations:

Allocation	Explanation
9 units to variable X_{13}	Least-cost cell.
9 units to variable X_{12}	Exhausting factory 1 supply in the cell with the next lowest cost.
15 units to variable X_{22}	Exhausting market 2 demand in the cell with the lowest remaining cost; this also exhausts factory 2 supply.
19 units to variable X_{31} and 7 units to variable X_{34}	Exhausting the remaining market 1 demand, and finally the slack column demand, with factory 3 supply.

The allocation procedure offers an IBFS for which there are not $m + n - 1$ basic variables. With 3 rows and 4 columns, there should be 6 variables in the derived basis, but only 5 have values greater than zero. One variable in the basis of $m + n - 1$ variables has fallen to zero. We recognize this condition from our work with the simplex method; it is called ***degeneracy.***

Coping with Degeneracy

The most direct way to deal with degeneracy is to avoid it. Indirectly, in cases where there is a potential for degeneracy in suboptimal solutions but not in the optimal solution, the choice of a very efficient method for finding an IBFS has the advantage of springing over the manipulations that might otherwise lead to complications. Two more such IBFS methods will be considered in the following sections.

Regardless of the IBFS method we use, it is often easy to recognize and avoid degeneracy directly as it occurs during the process of allocating product to transportation routes. For example, it is clear from our list of allocations and explanations that two cases arose in which factory supply and market demand were exhausted simultaneously. This is in contrast to the alternating pattern of exhausting first one and then the other. One case is the final allocation to variable X_{34}, which occurs naturally as a result of the structured demand–supply balance of the problem. The other case is the allocation of 15 units to X_{22}, and here a simultaneous match of row and column requirements has caused degeneracy. Had this simultaneous match not occurred, the pattern of allocation would have proceeded to variable X_{21}, variable X_{24}, or variable X_{32}, and one of these variables needs to be considered part of the solution basis even though its value is zero. Note, however, that had we recognized the complication, we would have avoided it by allocating the 15 units elsewhere (to variable X_{32} rather than to variable X_{22}) and could then have continued in normal fashion to complete the IBFS.

But what if the degenerate solution either is not or cannot be avoided? Without $m + n - 1$ variables that have values greater than zero in the solution basis, the steppingstone method is inoperative. Some empty cells cannot be evaluated for their improvement potentials because no closed loop will be found. Iteration, which also depends on the identification of a cost-advantageous closed loop, may likewise be impossible.

To overcome these difficulties, we give one variable an allocation of minute proportion in order to form a proper basis of $m + n - 1$ variables, and designate the amount of allocation by the Greek letter epsilon (ϵ). This symbol is often used in mathematics to represent a value very close to, but slightly greater than, zero. Note specifically that the ***epsilon allocation*** is considered insufficiently large to change either total cost or the satisfaction of margin requirements. The variable to receive the epsilon allocation must be one that preserves independence in the solution basis. If properly placed, the epsilon allocation ensures one and only one closed loop for each remaining empty cell. As a result, the steppingstone method is operative again, if only provisionally so.

In the preceding example, a proper epsilon allocation can be made by trial and error. However, as a consequence of having analyzed the point at which the degeneracy occurred, we have already determined that variable X_{21}, variable X_{24}, or variable X_{32} must be considered basic in this solution. In Table 5.7 the epsilon allocation is made to variable X_{24}, and the empty-cell evaluations then are derived in routine fashion.

Here, three empty cells show improvement potential. For each empty cell, the reader should identify the associated closed loop. The step-

Table 5.7
An Example
with Degeneracy

To / From	Market 1	Market 2	Market 3	Slack	Supplies
Factory 1	6 −$5	5 (9)	1 (9)	0 −$3	18
Factory 2	4 −$3	2 (15)	4 +$6	0 (ε)	15
Factory 3	7 (19)	3 +$1	2 +$4	0 (7)	26
Demands	19	24	9	7	59

Total cost:

$$C_X = (\$5 \times 9) + (\$1 \times 9) + (\$2 \times 15) + (\$0 \times \epsilon) + (\$7 \times 19) + (\$0 \times 7) = \$217$$

pingstone iteration that would result from using the route from factory 1 to market 1 would cause the following shifts:

1. Increase variable X_{11} by n units (present value, 0).
2. Decrease variable X_{12} by n units (present value, 9).
3. Increase variable X_{22} by n units (present value, 15).
4. Decrease variable X_{24} by n units (present value, ϵ).
5. Increase variable X_{34} by n units (present value, 7).
6. Decrease variable X_{14} by n units (present value, 19).

What number of units can be shifted? The answer is no more than the ***least*** present value from among the filled cells that must decrease. Unfortunately, the determining cell in this case is the epsilon cell, which by design has been given an allocation of approximately zero. Consequently, only epsilon units can be shifted; to shift any more would cause variable X_{24} to become negative and would violate the nonnegativity constraint.

Alternatively, we might try either of the other two empty cells that show potential for improvement, but inspection reveals that the same problem exists. This situation has led to a dead end.

We must now retrace our steps to see what other alternatives can be applied. The placement of epsilon was made arbitrarily in the preceding analysis; a different choice might spell different consequences. In the following attempt to find an optimal solution, the epsilon allocation is made to variable X_{32}. The corresponding transportation table (Table 5.8) includes all empty-cell evaluations.

In this case the factory 1, market 1 transportation route is attractive both because of its potential for cost improvement and because a shift in allocations is possible. The resulting iteration increases variable X_{11} and variable X_{32} to 9 units while reducing variable X_{12} and variable X_{31} to zero and 10 units, respectively. This case requires adding to the epsilon cell during the iteration procedure and does not violate any feasibility requirements. From this point on, the improvement procedure is routine. It requires three iterations before we reach an optimal solution (Table 5.9).

The optimal solution to this problem is unique. Reviewing the empty-cell evaluations shows that any other transportation network would require a greater shipping cost. In general, ***it is possible for an optimal solution not to be unique.*** Once the evaluation of empty cells in the optimal transportation table has been completed, if one or more proves to be zero, then another solution exists that will be no more or less costly. In such a case there are multiple optimal solutions, and all the

Table 5.8
Alternative Placement of Epsilon

From \ To	Market 1	Market 2	Market 3	Slack	Supplies
Factory 1	6 −$4	5 (9)	1 (9)	0 −$2	18
Factory 2	4 −$2	2 (15)	4 +$6	0 +$1	15
Factory 3	7 (19)	3 (ϵ)	2 +$3	0 (7)	26
Demands	19	24	9	7	59

Total cost:

$$C_X = (\$5 \times 9) + (\$1 \times 9) + (\$2 \times 15) + (\$7 \times 19) + (\$3 \times \epsilon)$$
$$+ (\$0 \times 7) = \$217$$

Table 5.9
Iterations One, Two, and Three, Yielding the Optimal Solution

First Iteration

From \ To	Market 1	Market 2	Market 3	Slack	Supplies
Factory 1	6 (9)	5 +$4	1 (9)	0 +$1	18
Factory 2	4 −$2	2 (15)	4 +$3	0 +$1	15
Factory 3	7 (10)	3 (9)	2 0	0 (7)	26
Demands	19	24	9	7	59

Total cost:

$$C_x = (\$6 \times 9) + (\$1 \times 9) + (\$2 \times 15) + (\$7 \times 10) + (\$3 \times 9) + (\$0 \times 7)$$
$$= \$190$$

Second Iteration

From \ To	Market 1	Market 2	Market 3	Slack	Supplies
Factory 1	6 (9)	5 +$1	1 (9)	0 −$1	18
Factory 2	4 (10)	2 (5)	4 +$5	0 +$1	15
Factory 3	7 +$2	3 (19)	2 +$2	0 (7)	26
Demands	19	24	9	7	59

Total cost:

$$C_x = (\$6 \times 9) + (\$1 \times 9) + (\$4 \times 10) + (\$2 \times 5) + (\$3 \times 19)$$
$$+ (\$0 \times 7) = \$170$$

Third Iteration

From \ To	Market 1	Market 2	Market 3	Slack	Supplies
Factory 1	6 (4)	5 +\$2	1 (9)	0 (5)	18
Factory 2	4 (15)	2 +\$1	4 +\$5	0 +\$2	15
Factory 3	7 +\$1	3 (24)	2 +\$1	0 (2)	26
Demands	19	24	9	7	59

Total cost:

$$C_x = (\$6 \times 4) + (\$1 \times 9) + (\$0 \times 5) + (\$4 \times 15) + (\$3 \times 24) + (\$0 \times 2) = \$165 \text{ (minimum)}$$

cost-equivalent alternatives should be considered. With more than one minimum-cost solution from which to choose, the decision maker can consider other decision criteria.

The Mutually Preferred Method

The allocation pattern of the northwest corner rule is simple and straightforward—across, down, across, down—always satisfying a market demand or depleting a factory supply. When we use the minimum cost search method, this pattern remains fundamentally the same. Depending on the next lowest cost after an allocation has been made, movement across a row may be either right or left and movement in a column either up or down. In both cases the procedure is logically appealing: always complete the requirement of a row (or column) once that row (or column) receives an initial allocation.

Nevertheless, completing a row or column once it has received a partial allocation may cause us to neglect cells with relatively low costs. Consequently, other cost-oriented IBFS methods of reaching the most advantageous initial solution have been devised. One effective approach applies shipping amounts to cells of the transportation table purely according to cost. This approach does not require us to complete a row or column immediately upon having established a partial allocation, and it often yields a lower-cost IBFS than the minimum cost search method. Cells may be chosen sequentially or in groups. Where the choice is

Table 5.10
Initial Allocations Using the Mutually Preferred Method

Unit Cost	That is Mutually Preferred in Row		Column	Allocation	Requirement Completed
$1	1	and	3	9 units	Market 3
2	2	and	2	15 units	Factory 2
0	3	and	4	7 units	Slack

made by ***groups***, each cell must be the lowest cost in the given row and column; that is, the costs are ***mutually preferred***. An example of this method is given in Table 5.10, which uses the problem presented in the preceding section. Again, allocation to zero-cost slack cells is held until last.

If the transportation table contains many more rows than columns, we make a second assessment of mutually preferred cells exclusive of the rows and columns whose requirements were met in the first round. In this case the remaining allocations fall out as follows:

9 units to X_{11} 10 units to X_{13} 9 units to X_{32}

The resulting IBFS is given in Table 5.11. The solution basis contains the required $m + n - 1$ basic variables. It is, in fact, the same trans-

Table 5.11
An IBFS Using the Mutually Preferred Method

From \ To	Market 1	Market 2	Market 3	Slack	Supplies
Factory 1	6 (9)	5 +$4	1 (9)	0 +$1	18
Factory 2	4 −$2	2 (15)	4 +$3	0 +$1	15
Factory 3	7 (10)	3 (9)	2 0	0 (7)	26
Demands	19	24	9	7	59

Total cost:

$$C_X = (\$6 \times 9) + (\$1 \times 9) + (\$2 \times 15) + (\$7 \times 10) + (\$3 \times 9) + (\$0 \times 7)$$
$$= \$190$$

portation table as is shown in Table 5.9, resulting from the first successful iteration after degeneracy was experienced. This IBFS will therefore require two iterations to reach the optimal solution.

The Vogel or Penalty Method A method that usually surpasses all others for finding an IBFS is called the ***Vogel approximation method*** or the ***penalty method.*** The term ***penalty*** is an indication of the method that is applied. For each row and column of the transportation table, there is a conceptual cost penalty that results from ***not*** choosing the lowest cell available during the allocation process. The penalties calculated are the ***differences for each row and column between the lowest-cost and the next-lowest-cost transportation routes.*** Therefore, allocations are made first to those cells where penalties are the ***greatest***, because this avoids the biggest cost increases arising from different allocations. Thus the penalty method emphasizes both the choice of low-cost transportation routes in an ab-

Table 5.12(a) An IBFS Found Using the Penalty Method

From \ To	Market 1	Market 2	Market 3	Slack	Supplies	Row Penalties
Factory 1	6 (4)	5 +\$2	1 (9)	0 (5)	~~18~~ ~~9~~ ~~5~~ 0	~~(4)~~ 1
Factory 2	4 (15)	2 +\$1	4 +\$5	0 +\$2	~~15~~ 0	~~2~~ 2
Factory 3	7 +\$1	3 (24)	2 +\$1	0 (2)	~~26~~ ~~2~~ 0	~~1~~ (4)
Demands	~~19~~ ~~4~~ 0	~~24~~ 0	~~9~~ 0	~~7~~ ~~2~~ 0	59	
Column Penalties	~~2~~ ~~2~~ (2)	~~1~~ 1	~~1~~			

Total cost:

$$C_X = (\$6 \times 4) + (\$1 \times 9) + (\$0 \times 5) + (\$4 \times 15) + (\$3 \times 24) + (\$0 \times 2) = \$165$$

solute sense and the choice of the low-cost routes that best avoid the relative cost penalties attached to the use of other alternatives.

This method requires simple row and column penalty calculations prior to each allocation. After an allocation is made, the row or column satisfied is eliminated from consideration, and all remaining row penalties are recalculated before another allocation is made. On the basis of the calculated penalties, a cell where the penalty is the ***largest*** is chosen, the largest possible allocation is made, the row or column satisfied is eliminated, the penalties are recalculated, and so on, until all row and column requirements have been satisfied and there is an IBFS.

Let us now apply this method to our example. First, all row and column penalties are calculated in the margins of the transportation table [see Table 5.12(a)]. Both penalties and margin requirements must be revised each time an allocation is made. Penalty calculations involving the slack column are saved until last. A more detailed explanation of the IBFS in Table 5.12(a) follows in Table 5.12(b).

Table 5.12(b) A Stepwise Explanation of the Penalty Method Calculations

Row or Column	Least Cost	Next Best	Penalty	Allocation to Cell
A. Start				
Factory 1	1	5	(4)	9 units to X_{13}
Factory 2	2	4	2	
Factory 3	2	3	1	
Market 1	4	6	2	
Market 2	2	3	1	
Market 3	1	2	1	
B. Eliminate market 3:				
Factory 1	5	6	1	
Factory 2	2	4	2	
Factory 3	3	7	(4)	24 units to X_{32}
Market 1	4	6	2	
Market 2	2	3	1	
C. Markets 2 and 3 eliminated:				
Market 1	4	6	(2)	15 units to X_{21}
D. With factory 2 and markets 2 and 3 eliminated, the following allocations are determined:				
(least cost to satisfy remainder of market 1 demand)				4 units to X_{11}
(slack to exhaust the remaining factory 1 supply)				5 units to X_{14}
(slack to exhaust the remaining factory 3 supply)				2 units to X_{34}

Comparing this solution with the earlier solution of this problem shown in Table 5.9 and scanning the evaluations of empty cells confirms this IBFS as the optimal solution. So, this time, no iteration is required.

This pattern of making allocations is interesting compared with that which we have seen in previous methods. Although the least-cost cell receives the first allocation, the succeeding two allocations by-pass the route from factory 2 to market 2, which has the next lowest cost. This is as a consequence of a relatively high penalty calculation associated with the factory 3, market 2 route. Insofar as the penalty calculations approximate the true opportunity costs of cells available for transportation allocation, the penalty method is more powerful than ordinary cost-oriented IBFS techniques.

The Modified Distribution Method (MODI)

At this point, a recurring emphasis on opportunity costs prompts a further look at the basic transportation problem. ***Evaluating*** the empty cells of a transportation table using the steppingstone method is nothing more than calculating the opportunity costs of nonutilized routes. Cost-advantageous opportunities point to an iterative process for finding improved solutions. Thus opportunity costs control the progress of transportation algorithms just as they do the simplex method. Even in the formation of an initial basic feasible solution (as with the Vogel approximation method), opportunity costs underlie the processes that are applied.

Recalling that the transportation table and its corresponding algorithms have been constructed in a way that requires factory supplies and market demands to be met exactly, we can specify a modified statement of the linear programming problem—one in which all constraints are equality relationships. This modified distribution model assures (by the practice of preserving balance by inserting the appropriate slack variables) that total supplies equal total demands. As we shall see, from the basic model with equality constraints, one can derive computationally advantageous methods for deriving opportunity costs.

The basic linear programming model is

$$\text{Min} \quad C_X = \sum_i \sum_j C_{ij} X_{ij}$$

subject to

$$\sum_j X_{ij} = S_i \qquad i = 1, \ldots, m$$
$$\sum_i X_{ij} = D_j \qquad j = 1, \ldots, n \tag{5.5}$$

and

$$X_{ij} \geq 0 \quad \text{for all } i, j$$

Its corresponding dual is

$$\text{Max} \quad C_Y = \sum_i S_i U_i + \sum_j D_j P_j \tag{5.6}$$

subject to $\quad U_i + P_j \leq C_{ij} \quad$ for all i, j

Also, since the primal constraints are equalities, the dual variables U_i and P_j must be unrestricted.[7]

The condition for complementary slackness is now

$$X_{ij}(U_i + P_j - C_{ij}) = 0 \quad \text{for all } i, j \tag{5.7}$$

Let $\Delta_{ij} = C_{ij} - (U_i + P_j)$ for all i, j. Then we have

$$X_{ij} \times \Delta_{ij} = 0 \quad \text{for all } i, j \tag{5.8}$$

Consequently, either the variable X_{ij} or the quantity $(U_i + P_j - C_{ij})$, or both, must equal zero.

Note that the relation $(U_i + P_j - C_{ij})$ is the dual constraint corresponding to the shipping route from factory i to market j. And this relation is forced once again to measure the dual variable U_i and P_j unit of money. In transportation problem literature, the difference Δ_{ij} is commonly defined as opportunity cost—an economic concept used to evaluate the corresponding route (X_{ij}). Therefore, in more basic terms, the complementary slackness condition requires that if variable X_{ij} is basic, its opportunity cost is zero. For nonbasic variables these opportunity costs are simply the standard "evaluations" of empty cells. In the optimal solution all Δ_{ij} must be either zero or positive; the opportunity costs of nonbasic variables in suboptimal solutions may be negative, zero, or positive.

The implications of this formula for calculating opportunity costs become clear. Whereas application of the steppingstone method for evaluating empty cells requires us to scan to find all closed loops and to calculate cost changes around the corners of the closed loops, the equation we have derived offers the same values directly. Often transportation problems are of a large size with many closed loops, some of which may be complex in their configurations. Thus, by allowing us to calculate each Δ_{ij} directly, the ***modified distribution method*** avoids extensive scanning, reduces the number of steps required to find evaluations of empty cells, and (not least important) presents a straightforward

[7]The economic interpretation for the case of unrestricted variables U_i and P_j is interesting, but it is quite involved and is beyond the scope of this text. For a lucid discussion, see J. C. Hsiao, "An Economic Interpretation of the Transportation Problem," *American Journal of Agricultural Economics*, 53, No. 3 (August 1971).

Table 5.13 Evaluating Empty Cells Using the Modified Distribution Method

To / From	Market 1	Market 2	Market 3	Slack	Supplies	Row numbers U_i
Factory 1	6 (9)	5	1 (9)	0	18	3
Factory 2	4 (10)	2 (5)	4	0	15	1
Factory 3	7	3 (19)	2	0 (7)	26	2
Demands	19	24	9	7	59	
Column numbers P_j	3	1	−2	−2		

computational scheme particularly suitable to the requirements of automated computer processing.

One question must still be answered. What are the values of variables U_i and P_j? After all, these are imputed values not directly available from the ordinary statement of transportation problems. We know that, for any basic variable X_{ij}, the sum of U_i and P_j must equal the corresponding unit transportation cost C_{ij}, because these opportunity costs Δ_{ij} are zero. Moreover, because there is normally an independent solution basis containing $m + n - 1$ basic variables, when one of the variables U_i or P_j is given, all of the remaining values are determined. Furthermore, the first, given value does not affect the calculation of Δ_{ij} values for the remaining nonbasic variables. Any number is sufficient to make the system of row numbers U_i and column numbers P_j consistent. Consider the example shown in Table 5.13, which is drawn from the next-to-last solution basis of Table 5.9.

The choice of row (U_i) and column (P_j) numbers in Table 5.13 is explained as follows:

A. For basic variables or filled cells

1. Pick any number; for example, let $U_1 = 3$
2. Then $P_1 = 3$ ($U_1 + P_1 = C_{11}$ or $3 + 3 = 6$: $\Delta_{11} = 0$)
3. Then $U_2 = 1$ ($U_2 + P_1 = C_{21}$ or $1 + 3 = 4$: $\Delta_{21} = 0$)

4. Then $P_2 = 1$ ($U_2 + P_2 = C_{22}$ or $1 + 1 = 2$: $\Delta_{22} = 0$)
5. Then $U_3 = 2$ ($U_3 + P_2 = C_{32}$ or $2 + 1 = 3$: $\Delta_{32} = 0$)
6. Then $P_4 = -2$ ($U_3 + P_4 = C_{34}$ or $2 + (-2) = 0$: $\Delta_{34} = 0$)
7. Also, $P_3 = -2$ ($U_1 + P_3 = C_{13}$ or $3 + (-2) = 1$: $\Delta_{13} = 0$)

B. For nonbasic variables or empty cells
1. $\Delta_{12} = C_{12} - (U_1 + P_2) = 5 - (3 + 1) = +1$
2. $\Delta_{14} = C_{14} - (U_1 + P_4) = 0 - [3 + (-2)] = -1$
3. $\Delta_{23} = C_{23} - (U_2 + P_3) = 4 - [1 + (-2)] = +5$
4. $\Delta_{24} = C_{24} - (U_2 + P_4) = 0 - [1 + (-2)] = +1$
5. $\Delta_{31} = C_{31} - (U_3 + P_1) = 7 - (2 + 3) = +2$
6. $\Delta_{33} = C_{33} - (U_3 + P_3) = 2 - [2 + (-2)] = +2$

If a different number had initially been picked[8] for variable U_1, a different system of row and column numbers would result, but the empty-cell evaluations would be unchanged. We can verify these evaluations by referring to Table 5.9, in which the steppingstone method yielded identical values.

At this point, just as before, iteration may be necessary. If so, we must revert to the basic steppingstone iteration technique. When all values in the empty-cell evaluations are nonnegative, optimality is reached. The modified distribution method is a computationally efficient method of evaluating ***empty*** cells without regard to the many closed loops that may exist. It is used in conjunction with the steppingstone method of shifting allocations to form a new solution basis. Especially for larger problems, the combination of these two techniques represents a complete iterative procedure that is more efficient than the steppingstone method alone.

The iterative procedure of the transportation algorithm is summarized diagrammatically in Figure 5.1.

5.3 The Assignment Problem

The Nature of the Problem

A variety of different problems, especially many network and scheduling problems, have the same basic structure as the transportation problem.

[8]For convenience of calculation, one can find the dual variable that appears most in these equations and set its value equal to zero. In this example, we could set U_1 equal to zero instead of 1.

Figure 5.1
Summary of the Transportation Algorithm

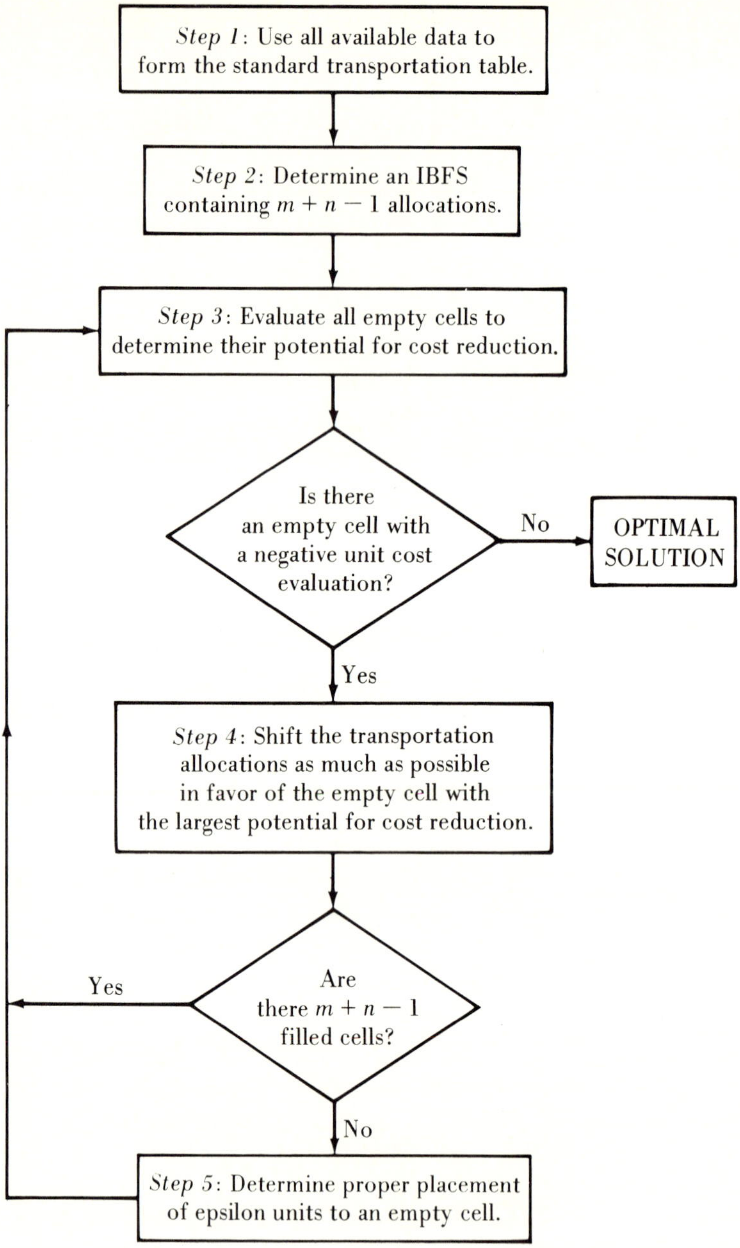

This section deals with the problem of assigning a range of jobs to machines or tasks to workers. The ***assignment problem*** is also a special case of the transportation problem. Minimization of total cost continues to be the objective. Faced with different costs of using machines or workers, the decision maker must optimally assign the jobs or tasks (which are analogous to shipping allocations in the transportation problem).

Several specific conditions characterize assignment problems. First, the number of tasks being assigned must ***equal*** the number of machines or workers available for accepting the assignments. Second, all assignments must be on a ***one-to-one-basis***; that is, each worker or machine must accept one and only one task. This one-to-one correspondence is inviolate; a one-to-many or many-to-one situation is not considered within the assignment classification. Third, the unit costs of completing tasks are on a total task basis, so the cost of completing each task by each productive resource is considered directly, not as the result of calculating an hourly or other periodic rate.

Assignment problems are essentially problems involving yes–no decisions. A task either is assigned or is not assigned to an available machine or worker. In a transportation type of table, an assignment is represented by a 1 (one task) and no assignment by a 0. Once an assignment is made, no other task can be assigned to the same resource. A table of tasks vs. productive resources must therefore be square, having the same number of rows as columns. The margin requirement of each row and column must be 1, because it is assumed that all tasks will be completed and all designated resources utilized. The total cost to complete all required tasks is simply the sum of all resource costs of the assigned tasks.

Suppose, for example, that the three tasks T_1, T_2, and T_3 must be assigned to three workers, W_1, W_2, and W_3, who vary in their productive efficiency and hence, ultimately, in the cost of performing the tasks. The individual cost differences may occur because of previous training, experience with different tasks, educational background, competitive pricing, or whatever. Suppose, then, that the worker–task costs for all combinations are as shown in Table 5.14.

We see that the first worker, W_1, can perform task 2 for \$23. The third worker would cost \$14 to complete the same task. Comparing worker 1's column of costs with that of worker 3, it is clear that the third worker can do all tasks less expensively than the first. Just the same, the third worker can be assigned only one task. The business manager's

Table 5.14
Cost Schedule for All Possible Task–Worker Combinations

Task \ Worker	W_1	W_2	W_3
T_1	\$18	\$12	\$15
T_2	23	20	14
T_3	32	15	10

problem is to determine the optimal utilization of ***all*** workers in the completion of ***all*** tasks.

Solution methods must already be springing to mind. Surely this is a linear programming problem that can be treated according to the techniques of Chapter 2. More appropriately, it fits the requirements of a transportation problem and can be organized within the format of a standard transportation table. Note, however, that the assignment problem is inherently degenerate with regard to either of these solution techniques. Assigning each worker ***one and only one*** task means that there will be n assignments in a problem of n workers and tasks. To avoid degeneracy, we would have to make $m + n - 1$ (or, since $m = n$, then $2n - 1$) assignments. Thus, in applying the simplex or transportation algorithms, we must use degeneracy-oriented techniques to find an optimal solution.

For smaller problems, a simple, brute-force solution procedure can be devised that involves the enumeration of all possible assignment alternatives, the calculation of total cost for each, and the selection of the least-cost assignment pattern. How many alternatives exist, in general? In a problem with n workers and tasks, each time a task is assigned, one less choice is available for the next assignment. Therefore, the number of possible alternatives must be $n \times (n - 1) \times (n - 2) \times \ldots \times 3 \times 2 \times 1$, or $n!$

Such calculations can be performed routinely by computer, but size limitations must exist. In the case of 3 workers and tasks, there are 3! or 6 alternatives to enumerate. As n grows to 5, we must examine $5! = 120$ alternatives. Examining all possible assignment patterns for a problem with 10 workers and tasks would require the enumeration and scanning of over 3.6 million alternatives—a healthy task even for an electronic computer. So the method of enumeration has very definite size restrictions depending on the calculating equipment available.

The Hungarian Method of Assignment

What seems to be a simple problem of making assignments should have a relatively simple procedure for finding optimal solutions, and this is indeed the case. The ***assignment method,*** also called the ***Hungarian method of assignment*** and ***Flood's technique***, is based on the determination of ***opportunity costs.*** Suppose, in Table 5.14, that a business manager arbitrarily decides to assign the first task to worker 1 at a task cost of \$18. Considering the alternative costs for this task, the arbitrary decision means that the \$12 task cost of worker 2 is forgone. The opportunity cost for this decision, \$6, might have been saved. Similarly, assigning task 1 to worker 3 involves an opportunity cost of \$3—the difference between task costs for worker 3 (\$15) and worker 2 (\$12).

Assigning this task to the least-cost worker results in zero opportunity cost. Similar calculations can be made for each task to determine row opportunity costs.

We can reverse the emphasis to consider the assignment of workers to tasks and then determine column opportunity costs. Since both types of opportunity costs are operating simultaneously, an optimal assignment pattern must have a total opportunity cost of zero.

The mechanical procedure for finding a zero-opportunity-cost solution is as follows. First, find all row opportunity costs by subtracting each row's least-cost value from all other cost values in the same row. For the preceding example, this is shown in Table 5.15. Second, find all column opportunity costs of the row-oriented table (Table 5.15) by subtracting each column's least-cost value from all other cost values in the same column. This represents a total opportunity cost table as shown in Table 5.16.

Having found total opportunity costs by combining both row and column opportunity costs, we can be sure that the zero positions now represent possible positions for the assignment of tasks. However, it is quite clear that the placement of zeros does not necessarily conform to the conditions of the problem—namely, assigning one and only one task to each worker. For example, if task 1 is assigned to worker 1, then the T_1–W_2 combination is no longer eligible for an assignment, even though a zero position is present. The two zeros located in the W_3 column present a similar situation. The problem has not yet been reduced to an equivalent representation containing enough zero positions for an optimal (zero-opportunity-cost) assignment pattern to be established.

Table 5.15
Row Opportunity Costs

Task \ Worker	W_1	W_2	W_3
T_1	\$ 6	\$0	\$3
T_2	9	6	0
T_3	22	5	0

Table 5.16
Column Opportunity Costs

Task \ Worker	W_1	W_2	W_3
T_1	\$ 0	\$0	\$3
T_2	3	6	0
T_3	16	5	0

To resolve the problem of finding at least one zero opportunity cost in each row and column of the total opportunity cost table, we determine the least possible number of lines—either vertical or horizontal—necessary to ***cover*** the existing zero cells. In this case, a horizontal line drawn through the T_1 row and a vertical line through the W_3 column will cover all existing zeros (see Table 5.16). If the number of lines were the same as the row-column size of the table, an optimal assignment would be available. But here there are only two lines needed to cover the zero cells in a 3-row-and-column table. Therefore optimal assignments cannot yet be identified.

A revised total opportunity cost table can be constructed that maintains the same relative cost characteristics of the original problem and allows the technique of using lines to cover zero cells to succeed in determining an optimal solution. To make this revision, we choose the lowest element of those that remain uncovered, and we ***subtract*** it from all uncovered elements and add it to any elements that are located at the intersection of the covering lines. Doing so contributes another zero to the table. In Table 5.16, the T_1 row and the W_3 column would be covered, and the least uncovered element, 3, should be both deducted from all other uncovered elements and added to the T_1–W_3 element. Table 5.17 results.

Again, as few lines as possible are applied to cover the zero cells of the table. In this case three are required, and, since three allocations must be made, enough zeros are present for us to find optimal assignment positions.

To find a cost-optimal assignment pattern for the completion of all tasks, make assignments to any zero position for which no other zero is found in either the same row or the same column. Then eliminate the row and column assigned and continue similarly with the next assignments. In Table 5.17 the T_3–W_3 zero position has only one zero in the third row, so make this the first assignment. Then, since we have eliminated the third row and the third column from consideration, the remaining two assignment alternatives fall out, each at locations where

Table 5.17
Revised Assignment Table Using the Hungarian Method

Task \ Worker	W_1	W_2	W_3
T_1	~~$ 0~~	~~$0~~	~~$6~~
T_2	0	3	0
T_3	13	2	0

the zero position is the only zero in either its row or its column—T_2–W_1 is one and T_1–W_2 the other. Thus the optimal assignment pattern for this problem is

T_1–W_2	@	\$12
T_2–W_1	@	\$23
T_3–W_3	@	\$10
Total (minimum) cost:		\$45

This procedure applies to assignment problems in general, regardless of their size.

A Flowchart Even though the assignment algorithm is not entirely numerical and relies partially on lines to cover zero elements, its logical flow is quite definite. Figure 5.2 will help us review the steps that we must follow to reach the optimal solution.

5.4 Summary

The transportation problem, a special case of the linear programming problem wherein the coefficients in the constraints are all either zero or 1, is concerned with the transfer of goods from factories (supply origins) to markets (demand destinations). The plan is to minimize total transportation costs subject to factory and market requirements.

The dual transportation problem not only provides an interesting economic interpretation, but it has also assumed central importance in the recent development of various transportation methods. The dual variable P_j represents the imputed price of the product corresponding to the jth market; the dual variable V_i measures the ith factory's comparative location advantage, known as ***location rent.*** Methods of solving the transportation problem compare the imputed market price with the sum of the factory location rent and the unit shipping cost along a given transportation route.

The special structure of the transportation problem has fostered the development of various transportation algorithms that are more efficient than the ordinary simplex method. Their variations can be classified as (1) alternative methods for determining an initial basic feasible solution and (2) alternative techniques for performing iteration.

Figure 5.2
Summary of the Assignment Algorithm

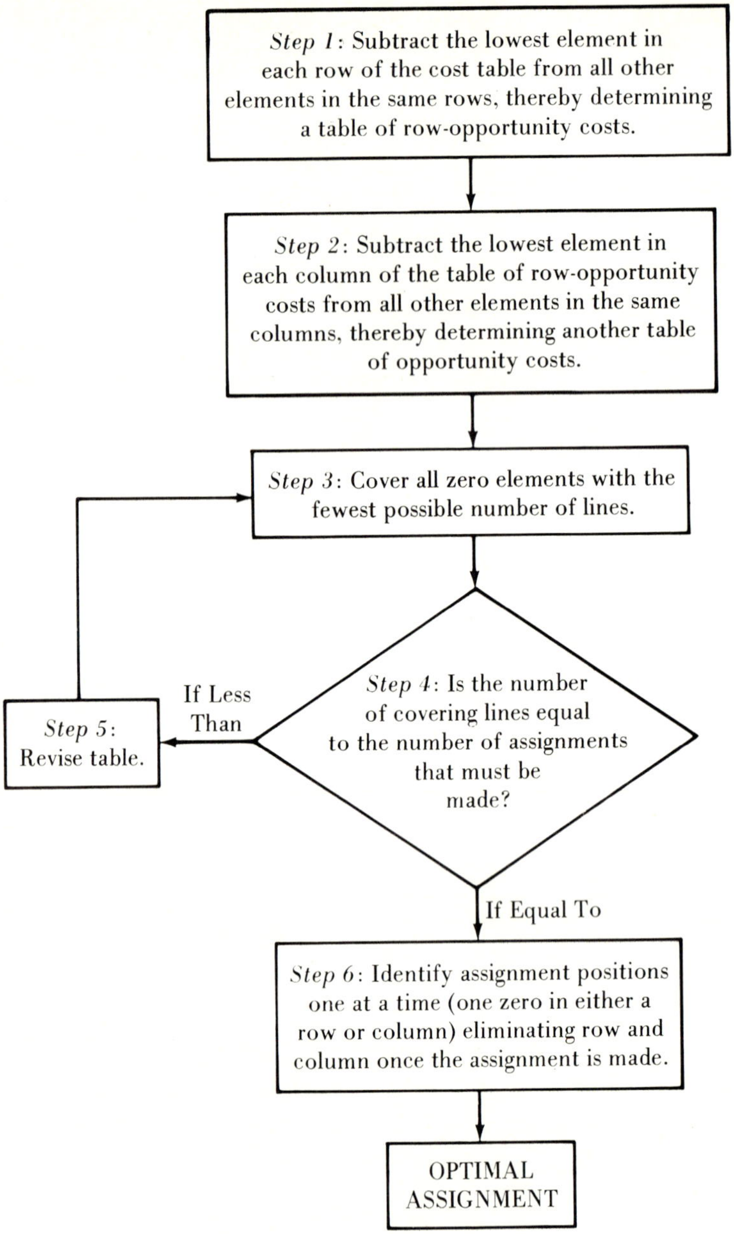

The assignment problem is a special case of the transportation problem. Because of the requirements of a one-for-one match of workers to tasks, it is characterized by inherent degeneracy. A specialized technique for finding optimal solutions to assignment problems is the Hungarian method, which, through its procedure of calculating relative opportunity costs, isolates the zero opportunity cost cells of an assignment table that are needed to determine an optimal solution.

Exercises

5.1 Define the following terms:
a. Transportation problem
b. Assignment problem
c. Opportunity cost

5.2 Refer to the following table to determine the initial basic feasible solution by using:
a. The northwest corner rule
b. The minimum cost search method

From \ To	Warehouse A	Warehouse B	Warehouse C	Supply
F_1	6	7	3	80
F_2	3	4	8	65
F_3	5	3	6	70
Demands	80	75	60	215

5.3 The Fly-By-Nite Transportation Company must ship its products from three plants to three markets. The weekly production of the plants is

Plant	Production
P_1	240
P_2	150
P_3	100
Total	490

Market	Requirement
M_1	200
M_2	180
M_3	110
Total	490

The shipping costs are

From \ To	M_1	M_2	M_3
P_1	$ 8	$11	$ 5
P_2	10	6	12
P_3	7	9	4

Formulate the minimum transportation cost schedule by using:

a. The mutually preferred method
b. The Vogel or penalty method
c. The modified distribution method

5.4 The Alpert Cement Company has three factories and four warehouses in different locations. Production data on factories and demand requirements for each warehouse are as follows:

Factories	Amount Available	Warehouse	Amount Needed
F_1	250	W_1	140
F_2	150	W_2	160
F_3	100	W_3	120
	500	W_4	80
			500

The costs of shipping are

Factory \ Warehouse	W_1	W_2	W_3	W_4
F_1	$ 5	$10	$15	$15
F_2	15	35	10	20
F_3	25	30	30	45

a. Formulate the transportation problem and write it out in mathematical form.

b. Write the dual problem corresponding to your answer to part (a).
c. Write the problems you formulated in parts (a) and (b) in sigma notation.
d. Give an economic interpretation of the dual problem.
e. Determine an optimal shipping schedule and the minimum total shipping cost.
f. Defend your opinion about whether multiple optimal solutions exist.

5.5 A manufacturer regularly consumes kerosene at four locations. She must now decide how much oil to purchase from three possible sellers. The kerosene companies have promised that they can supply the following amounts of oil during the next month:

400 gallons from company A
600 gallons from company B
750 gallons from company C

The demand at each location is

200 gallons at location 1
350 gallons at location 2
500 gallons at location 3
650 gallons at location 4

The transportation costs for each company furnishing each location are

Company \ Location	1	2	3	4
A	$18	$16	$14	$17
B	15	17	16	14
C	16	20	21	13

a. Formulate the decision problem as a linear programming model.
b. Is the model equivalent to a transportation problem? Explain.
c. Will a slack company or location be required? Why?

5.6 The cost table for a certain assignment problem is

Worker \ Task	A	B	C
W_1	\$7	\$3	\$9
W_2	4	2	5
W_3	6	1	4

a. Clearly, each worker is most efficient at doing task B. Why don't they let all do task B?
b. Using the northwest corner rule to set an IBFS, determine whether this is a degenerate problem. Isn't it true that all assignment problems are degenerate at every iteration? Why?

5.7 Refer to exercise 5.6.
a. Use the MODI method to solve this assignment problem.
b. Why can any assignment problem be solved by a transportation technique?

5.8 Using the Hungarian method of assignment, find the optimal solution for the assignment problem given in exercise 5.6.

5.9 The Oline Company has four jobs that can be completed by four machines. Each machine can handle only one job. Each job can be assigned to only one machine. The costs of performing each job on each machine are given in the following table:

Job \ Machine	M_1	M_2	M_3	M_4
J_1	\$21	\$11	\$16	\$ 8
J_2	15	9	7	12
J_3	17	13	12	15
J_4	26	21	28	18

a. Which job should be assigned to which machine?
b. How much will the Oline Company spend?
c. Why is it difficult to solve this problem by the transportation algorithm?

5.10 Review the iterative procedures of the transportation algorithms by drawing a flowchart.

5.11 Summarize the iterative procedures of the assignment problem diagrammatically.

5.12 Discuss the following statements. "The transportation problem is a special case of the linear programming problem." "The assignment problem is a special case of the transportation problem."

5.13 Evaluate this statement: "All transportation problems have the same structure in that the constraint coefficients are all either zero or 1."

5.14 The IBFS of a transportation problem must meet what criterion?

5.15 How do we know when we have reached an optimal solution in the transportation problem?

5.16 Use your knowledge of the simplex method to explain the logic of the following rules in the transportation algorithm.
   a. Use the steppingstone method to evaluate the incremental cost of empty cells.
   b. When one determines the number of units that can be shifted to an empty cell, the answer is no more than the least present value among the filled cells that must be decreased.

5.17 Using your knowledge of duality theory, give an economic interpretation of the MODI method.

5.18 Use your knowledge of the simplex method to evaluate the following statement. "If one or more cells turns out to be zero in the empty-cell evaluations in the optimal transportation table, then another solution exists that is no more or less costly."

5.19 Consider a transportation problem with two sources and three destinations, for which the problem statement is

$$\text{Min} \quad C_X = C_{11}X_{11} + C_{12}X_{12} + C_{13}X_{13} + C_{21}X_{21} + C_{22}X_{22} + C_{23}X_{23}$$

$$\begin{aligned}
\text{subject to} \quad & X_{11} + X_{12} + X_{13} \le S_1 \\
& X_{21} + X_{22} + X_{23} \le S_2 \\
& X_{11} + X_{21} \ge d_1 \\
& X_{12} + X_{22} \ge d_2 \\
& X_{13} + X_{23} \ge d_3 \\
\text{and} \quad & X_{ij} \ge 0 \quad \text{for all } i \text{ and } j
\end{aligned}$$

Using the notation shown in equation (5.2), write the corresponding dual problem and give an economic interpretation of:
a. The dual variables associated with the supply constraints
b. The dual variables associated with the demand constraints

c. The dual constraints
d. The dual objective function

5.20 A transportation company that owns five tractors has just signed a contract to pick up five trailers for a construction company. The five trailers are located at different construction sites. Assume that every tractor is capable of handling any of the trailers. The travel distances, in miles, from each tractor to each trailer are shown in the following table:

	From \ To (Trailer)	A	B	C	D	E
Tractor	T_1	20	40	18	50	30
	T_2	30	45	25	38	25
	T_3	40	48	35	27	19
	T_4	18	34	48	28	23
	T_5	43	20	33	18	47

What is the optimal assignment of tractors to trailers such that the total distance traveled is minimized?

Suggested Readings

Aarvik, Oddmund, and Paul Randolph. "The Application of Linear Programming to the Determination of Transmission Fees in an Electrical Power Network." *Interfaces*, 6, No. 1 (November 1975), 47–49.

Dantzig, George B. *Linear Programming and Extensions*. Princeton, N.J.: Princeton University Press, 1967, pp. 35–41, 299–313.

Dorfman, Robert, Paul A. Samuelson, and Robert M. Solow. *Linear Programming and Economic Analysis*. New York: McGraw-Hill, 1958. Chapter 5.

Hitchcock, F. L. "The Distribution of a Product from Several Sources to Numerous Localities." *The Journal of Mathematics and Physics*, August 1941, 224–230.

Hsiao, J. C. "An Economic Interpretation of the Transportation Problem." *American Journal of Agricultural Economics*, 53, No. 3 (August 1971).

Kantorovich, Leonid V. "On the Translocation of Masses." *Management Science*, 5, No. 1 (1958), 1–4.

Koopmans, Tjalling C. "Concepts of Optimality and Their Uses." *The American Economic Review*, June 1977 (copyright by the Nobel Foundation, 1976).

Koopmans, Tjalling C. "Optimum Utilization of the Transportation System." *Econometrica*, July 1949 (supplement).

Koopmans, Tjalling C., and Martin Beckmann. "Assignment Problems and the Location of Economic Activities." *Econometrica*, January 1957, 59–60.

Markland, Robert E. "Analyzing Multi-Commodity Distribution Networks Having Milling-in-Transit Features." *Management Science*, 21, No. 12 (August 1975), 1405–1416.

Summers, Edward L. "The Audit Staff Assignment Problem: A Linear Programming Analysis." *The Accounting Review*, July 1972, 443–453.

Wagner, Harvey M. *Principles of Operations Research*. Englewood Cliffs, N.J.: Prentice-Hall, 1969, pp. 50–58, 213–228.

6

Integer Programming

Linear programming is a powerful tool for solving many economic and business problems. It assumes that the decision variables are divisible—that is, that variables are permitted to take fractional values such as 1.5, $\frac{2}{3}$, and so on. Of course, there are cases in which this assumption is not realistic. Suppose, for example, that one wishes to decide whether to build a plant in a particular location. A linear programming solution of $X = 1$ means build the plant; $X = 0$ means don't build it. But if the solution were some noninteger value between zero and 1 (such as $X = 0.68$), the result would be meaningless. There are many problems for which a fractional solution does not provide a usable answer. Integer programming is designed to address problems such as these, wherein the answers must consist of some or all integer values.

6.1 Integer Programming

Let us again consider a standard, general linear programming problem:

$$\text{Max} \quad Z = \sum C_j X_j \tag{6.1}$$

$$\text{subject to} \quad \sum A_{ij} X_j \le b_i \quad \text{for } i = 1, 2, \ldots, m \tag{6.2}$$

$$\text{and} \quad X_j \ge 0 \quad \text{for } j = 1, 2, \ldots, n \tag{6.3}$$

In a linear programming problem, all decision variables X_j (for $j = 1, 2, \ldots, n$) can assume any nonnegative values. Such a problem with integer solution values is identified as ***pure integer programming.*** The integer programming problem is really a special case of ordinary linear programming where the constraint (6.3) can be restated as

$$X_j \text{ are nonnegative integers} \tag{6.3'}$$

If the problem requires some of the variables to assume integer values and the remaining variables to take on any other nonnegative values, the problem is referred to as ***mixed integer programming.*** A special case of integer programming is called ***zero–one programming.*** Here all decision variables are required to take on values of either zero or 1.

Round Off Solution One might wonder why it is not possible to obtain the integer solution simply by rounding off the noninteger solution values obtained from the ordinary linear programming solution. The trouble with such an approach is that there is no guarantee that it will yield an optimal integer solution. Very often the rounded integer value may be neither optimal nor feasible. The following simple example illustrates why.

$$\text{Max} \quad Z = 9X_1 + 27X_2 \tag{6.4}$$

subject to
$$3X_1 + 9X_2 \leq 16 \tag{6.5}$$

such that
$$X_1 \text{ and } X_2 \text{ are nonnegative integers} \tag{6.6}$$

In this simple problem, we can find the solution by inspection. The optimal integer solution is

$$X_1 = 2 \qquad X_2 = 1$$

or
$$X_1 = 5 \qquad X_2 = 0$$

so that
$$Z = 45$$

If we disregard the integer condition and solve (6.4) and (6.5) by ordinary linear programming techniques, the optimal noninteger solution is

$$X_1 = 0 \qquad X_2 = \tfrac{16}{9} \qquad Z = 48$$

Now, suppose the fractional value $X_2 = \frac{16}{9}$ (or $1\frac{7}{9}$) is rounded to an integer value, $X_2 = 2$ (and $X_1 = 0$). Obviously, this rounded solution is not feasible! Or consider a rounded-down solution, $X_2 = 1$ and $X_1 = 0$. This integer solution is feasible, but the optimal value for the objective function is Z = 27, which is significantly lower than the optimal integer solution, Z = 45.

As mentioned in Chapter 5, the special structure of the transportation problem makes the optimal solution of ordinary linear programming procedures satisfy the integer requirements as well. However, integer programming generally requires special algorithms. Before we learn the computation techniques, let's first investigate the integer programming formulation to gain insight into the structure, application, and importance of integer programming.

6.2 Formulations of Integer Programming

From (6.1), (6.2), and (6.3), we can see that the components of an integer programming problem are the same as those of an ordinary linear programming problem except that all decision variables are required to be integers. However, a myriad of business problems are concerned with ***whether-or-not*** and ***go–no-go*** decisions. To deal with these, we can often use the zero–one variables that are unique cases of integer programming models.

For example, we can let ($X = 1$) or ($X = 0$) correspond to the decision to either select an investment project or to reject it. Many managerial decisions that are seen as qualitative problems can be reformulated quantitatively through the zero–one variable device. We will explore several common situations that lend themselves to use of the zero–one integer programming formulation.

Capital Budgeting

Indivisibility and Interdependence Business firms and other enterprises are often confronted with a variety of potential investment projects, given a fixed capital fund. ***Capital budgeting*** refers to the decision-making procedures for the selection and financing of these projects. These decisions are probably some of the most crucial and difficult of managerial problems. The fundamental difficulty involves a common economic problem, scarcity—in this case the scarcity of capital funds. Because capital is limited, management should try to make maximum use of this scarce resource.

Suppose that a firm has n projects ($j = 1, 2, \ldots, n$), which are undertaken for T periods ($t = 0, 1, 2, \ldots, T$). Let

X_j = variable associated with project j

C_j = net present value of project j (the net present value is defined as the return of project j over the cost discounted in present dollar value)

K_t = amount of capital available for investment during each time period t

A_{jt} = amount of cash required during the period t to finance project j

The goal of the firm is to maximize the total yields of the present value of the expected future return for all projects. That is,

$$\text{Max} \quad Z = C_1X_1 + C_2X_2 + C_3X_3 + \ldots + C_nX_n$$

subject to

$$A_{01}X_1 + A_{02}X_2 + \ldots + A_{0n}X_n \leq K_0 \qquad (6.7)$$

$$\begin{aligned} A_{11}X_1 + A_{12}X_2 + \ldots + A_{1n}X_n &\leq K_1 \\ A_{21}X_1 + A_{22}X_2 + \ldots + A_{2n}X_n &\leq K_2 \\ &\ \ \vdots \\ A_{T1}X_1 + A_{T2}X_2 + \ldots + A_{Tn}X_n &\leq K_T \end{aligned} \qquad (6.8)$$

and

$$X_j = \begin{cases} 0 & \text{if project } j \text{ is rejected} \\ 1 & \text{if project } j \text{ is accepted} \end{cases} \quad \text{for all } j \qquad (6.9)$$

Note that the right-hand side of constraints (6.8) is interpreted as the capital available for each period, $t = 0, 1, 2, \ldots, T$. The left-hand side indicates the total capital required to finance all projects j ($j = 1, 2, \ldots, n$) in each of the time periods t ($t = 0, 1, 2, \ldots, T$). For example, the first constraint states that the sum of capital required in the initial period for all investment projects, $\Sigma A_{0j}X_j$, at most equals K_0, the total amount of capital available in this period. The remaining constraints are investments that can be interpreted similarly.

By the addition of constraint (6.9), we define a zero–one integer variable for each project. The model can now handle the indivisibility of projects by requiring all variables to be integers. This stipulation also forces a decision either to undertake or not to undertake a particular project. If $X_j = 1$, the jth project is undertaken; if $X_j = 0$, it is rejected.

Another special characteristic of the capital budgeting problem is that the alternative investment projects are interdependent. If two projects X_2 and X_3 are mutually exclusive, the zero–one integer programming model can handle this situation simply by our adding the constraint

$$X_2 + X_3 \leq 1 \qquad (6.10)$$

From the stipulations of (6.9) and (6.10), there can be no more than three possibilities:

$X_2 = 0, X_3 = 0$ (reject both projects)

$X_2 = 1, X_3 = 0$ (accept project 2, reject project 3)

$X_2 = 0, X_3 = 1$ (reject project 2, accept project 3)

Thus the integer programming solution permits either project 1 or project 2 to be undertaken, but not both. The possibility of rejecting ***both*** projects also exists.

If management wants at least one and possibly both projects to be included, we specify the constraint in the following form:

$$X_2 + X_3 \geq 1 \tag{6.11}$$

But if the decision requires that one of the two projects has to be included, then the constraint we impose must be an equality relationship:

$$X_2 + X_3 = 1 \tag{6.12}$$

We can further exploit the fact that X_j is a zero–one variable to deal with the problem of dependence among different investment projects. For example, when project 2 can be undertaken only if project 1 is accepted, the linear constraint becomes:

$$X_2 - X_1 \leq 0 \tag{6.13}$$

or

$$X_2 \leq X_1$$

We can easily verify that

If $X_1 = 0$, then X_2 must be 0.

If $X_1 = 1$, then X_2 may be either 0 or 1.

Note that project 2 cannot be undertaken unless project 1 is accepted.

Example ***Budgeting Capital Outlay*** The Board of Directors of Jay Davis Company is confronted with four 2-year investment projects. The net present value and capital requirement for each project during each year are shown in Table 6.1.

The company has \$15 million to invest for the initial year and \$11 million for the second year. For administrative reasons, project 3 cannot

Table 6.1
Capital Budgeting Information

Project	Net Present Value of the Project (millions)	Initial-Year Capital Requirement (millions)	Second-Year Capital Requirement (millions)
1	$4	$ 6	$ 1
2	3	7	4
3	2	4	3
4	1	2	5
Capital Available to Invest		$15 million	$11 million

be selected without project 4, but if project 4 is undertaken, project 3 can be either rejected or accepted. The integer programming formulations of the problem are

Let
$$X_j = \begin{cases} 0 & \text{if the } jth \text{ project is rejected} \\ 1 & \text{if the } jth \text{ project is accepted} \end{cases}$$

$$\text{Max } Z = 4X_1 + 3X_2 + 2X_3 + X_4$$

subject to
$$6X_1 + 7X_2 + 4X_3 + 2X_4 \leq 15$$
$$X_1 + 4X_2 + 3X_3 + 5X_4 \leq 11$$
$$X_3 - X_4 \leq 0$$

and
$$X_1, \ldots, X_4 \text{ may be either 0 or 1}$$

Transportation Problem with Fixed Charges

The transportation problems in Chapters 2 and 5 contained no fixed costs; the only costs were unit shipping costs from factory i to market j. Therefore, the total cost for ***a particular route*** is the product of the unit shipping cost and the number of units transported. That is,

$$TC_{ij} = C_{ij}X_{ij} \tag{6.14}$$

where TC_{ij} = total transportation cost from factory i ($i = 1, 2, \ldots, m$) to market j ($j = 1, 2, \ldots, n$)

C_{ij} = unit shipping cost from factory i to market j

X_{ij} = number of units transported from factory i to market j

The total transportation cost curve is shown in Figure 6.1. Clearly, C_{ij} is simply the slope of the total cost curve for the shipment from factory i to market j.

Figure 6.1
Total Transportation Cost

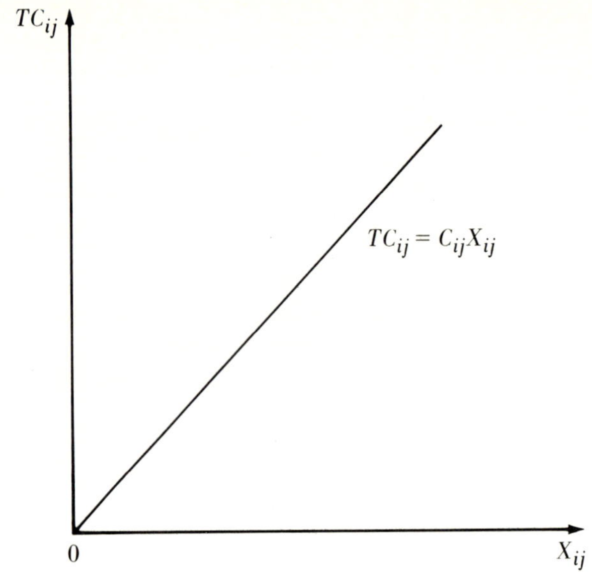

In this chapter, the transportation problem is revised to include a fixed cost charge for any shipment. The total cost for a particular route now becomes

$$TC_{ij} = F_{ij} + C_{ij}X_{ij} \tag{6.15}$$

The term F_{ij} represents the fixed cost charge for any shipment from factory i to market j. By definition, fixed cost is independent of the quantity shipped. Now the total cost, including this fixed charge, is shown in Figure 6.2. The fixed cost F_{ij} is defined as overhead costs that do not vary with the magnitude of X_{ij}. This means that, even if $X_{ij} = 0$, F_{ij} (a constant) is still positive.[1] We shall see in this section that the decision process involving the fixed charge problem requires integer programming.

Suppose that a firm has m ($i = 1, 2, \ldots, m$) factories and n ($j = 1, 2, \ldots, n$) markets, the capacity for each factory is S_i, and the minimum demand requirement for each market is d_j. In addition, define a new decision variable, Y_{ij}, which is associated with the fixed cost charge F_{ij} from factory i to market j. Then let

$$Y_{ij} = \begin{cases} 1 & \text{if } X_{ij} > 0 \quad \text{for all } i \text{ and } j \\ 0 & \text{if } X_{ij} = 0 \quad \text{for all } i \text{ and } j \end{cases} \tag{6.16}$$

[1]Economists call this the ***short-run phenomenon.*** In the short run a firm must honor commitments such as contractual wages and rentals, incurring costs even when it produces zero output. In the long-run, of course, all costs are variable and there is no fixed cost.

Figure 6.2
Total Transportation Cost with Fixed Charges

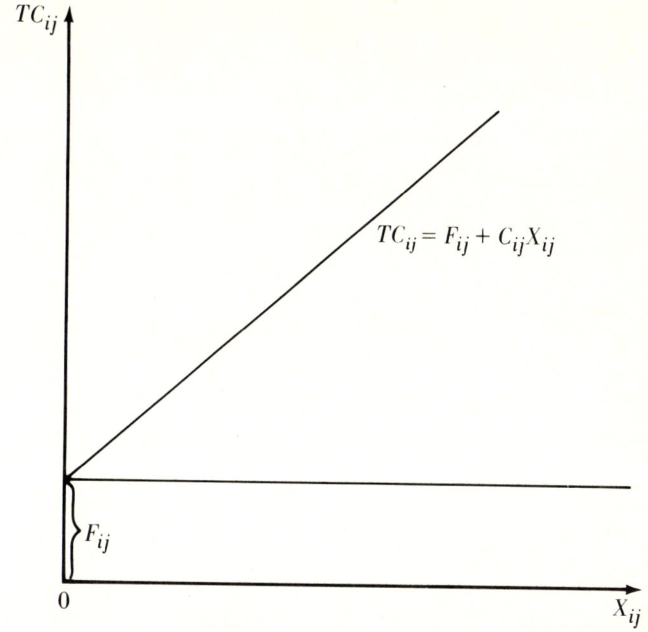

The firm seeks to minimize the sum of unit shipping costs and fixed cost charges. Consequently, the objective function becomes

$$\begin{aligned}\text{Min} \quad C = &(F_{11}Y_{11} + C_{11}X_{11}) + (F_{12}Y_{12} + C_{12}X_{12}) + \ldots + (F_{1n}Y_{1n} + C_{1n}X_{1n}) \\ &+ (F_{21}Y_{21} + C_{21}X_{21}) + (F_{22}Y_{22} + C_{22}X_{22}) + \ldots + (F_{2n}Y_{2n} + C_{2n}X_{2n}) \\ &+ (F_{m1}Y_{m1} + C_{m1}X_{m1}) + (F_{m2}Y_{m2} + C_{m2}X_{m2}) + \ldots + (F_{mn}Y_{mn} + C_{mn}X_{mn})\end{aligned} \tag{6.17}$$

which can be written as

$$\begin{aligned}\text{Min} \quad C = &(F_{11}Y_{11} + F_{12}Y_{12} + \ldots + F_{1n}Y_{1n} + F_{21}Y_{21} + F_{22}Y_{22} + \ldots + \\ &F_{2n}Y_{2n} + \ldots + F_{m1}Y_{m1} + F_{m2}Y_{m2} + \ldots + F_{mn}Y_{mn}) \\ &+ (C_{11}X_{11} + C_{12}X_{12} + \ldots + C_{1n}X_{1n} + C_{21}X_{21} + C_{22}X_{22} + \ldots + \\ &C_{2n}X_{2n} + \ldots + C_{m1}X_{m1} + C_{m2}X_{m2} + \ldots + C_{mn}X_{mn})\end{aligned}$$

The figures in the first set of parentheses represent the overall total fixed charges. The figures in the second set of parentheses represent the total shipping costs, similar to those discussed in Chapters 2 and 5.

The capacity limitations in the factories and the demand requirements in the markets are similar to those we encountered in the classic transportation problem discussed in Section 2.3:

$$\left.\begin{aligned} X_{11} + X_{12} + \ldots + X_{1n} &\le S_1 \\ X_{21} + X_{22} + \ldots + X_{2n} &\le S_2 \\ &\cdot \\ &\cdot \\ &\cdot \\ X_{m1} + X_{m2} + \ldots + X_{mn} &\le S_m \end{aligned}\right\} \text{capacity constraints} \qquad (6.18)$$

$$\left.\begin{aligned} X_{11} + X_{21} + \ldots + X_{m1} &\ge d_1 \\ X_{12} + X_{22} + \ldots + X_{m2} &\ge d_2 \\ &\cdot \\ &\cdot \\ &\cdot \\ X_{1n} + X_{2n} + \ldots + X_{mn} &\ge d_n \end{aligned}\right\} \text{demand constraints} \qquad (6.19)$$

and $$X_{ij} \ge 0 \quad \text{for all } i \text{ and } j \qquad (6.20)$$

By using sigma notation, we can rewrite the initial integer programming formulation of the problem (6.15) through (6.19) as follows:

$$\text{Min} \quad C = \sum_{i=1}^{m} \sum_{j=1}^{n} F_{ij} Y_{ij} + \sum_{i=1}^{m} \sum_{j=1}^{n} C_{ij} X_{ij} \qquad (6.21)$$

subject to $$\sum_{j=1}^{n} X_{ij} \le S_i \quad \text{for } i = 1, 2, \ldots, m \qquad (6.22)$$

$$\sum_{i=1}^{m} X_{ij} \ge d_j \quad \text{for } j = 1, 2, \ldots, n \qquad (6.23)$$

$$Y_{ij} = \begin{cases} 0 & \text{if } X_{ij} = 0 \quad \text{for all } i \text{ and } j \\ 1 & \text{if } X_{ij} > 0 \quad \text{for all } i \text{ and } j \end{cases} \qquad (6.24)$$

and $$X_{ij} \ge 0 \quad \text{for all } i \text{ and } j \qquad (6.25)$$

The model formulation is not completed yet. We want to ensure that, when $Y_{ij} = 0$, X_{ij} will not be positive. This can be achieved by substituting for (6.24) the following:

$$\begin{aligned} 0 \le Y_{ij} &\le 1 \\ X_{ij} &\le U_{ij} Y_{ij} \end{aligned} \qquad Y_{ij} \text{ an integer} \qquad (6.24')$$

where U_{ij} is a sufficiently large number so that $X_{ij} \leq U_{ij}$. We can now easily verify that, if $U_{ij} = 0$, X_{ij} must be zero. If $Y_{ij} = 1$, then X_{ij} ought to be positive. (Can you explain why?)

Note that the decision variable Y_{ij} is associated with the fixed charge F_{ij}. The economic interpretation is that the fixed charges $F_{ij}Y_{ij}$ are incurred only if the shipment takes place ($X_{ij} > 0$). On the other hand, the firm cannot impose the fixed charges (that is, $F_{ij}Y_{ij} = 0$) on the route from factory i to market j if no shipment takes place.

In short, we have examined the general formulation of a transportation problem with a fixed charge. The model involves both zero–one integer variables and a constraint ($X_{ij} - U_{ij}Y_{ij} \leq 0$) for each variable incurring a fixed charge.

Example ***A Transportation Problem with a Fixed Charge*** Given the transportation problem discussed in Section 2.3, the factory supply and market demand conditions along with unit transportation cost data are summarized in Table 6.2. On the basis of a new cost analysis, the company has decided to impose the new fixed charges shown in Table 6.3 for any shipment incurred.

Let X_{ij} be the quantity of shipment from factory i (for $i = 1, 2$) to market j (for $j = 1, 2, 3$), $U = 100$. Thus the transportation problem corresponding to (6.21) through (6.24) is formulated as follows:

$$\begin{aligned} \text{Min} \quad C - {} & (2.0Y_{11} + 6X_{11}) + (0.8Y_{12} + 5X_{12}) + (1.5Y_{13} + X_{13}) \\ & + (1.0Y_{21} + 4X_{21}) + (1.5Y_{22} + 2X_{22}) + (1.2Y_{23} + 4X_{23}) \end{aligned}$$

subject to

$$\begin{array}{llllllllllll}
X_{11} & + X_{12} & + X_{13} & & & & & & & & & \leq 18 \\
 & & & X_{21} & + X_{22} & + X_{23} & & & & & & \leq 15 \\
X_{11} & & & + X_{21} & & & & & & & & \geq 16 \\
 & X_{12} & & & + X_{22} & & & & & & & \geq 10 \\
 & & X_{13} & & & + X_{23} & & & & & & \geq 7 \\
X_{11} & & & & & & -100Y_{11} & & & & & \leq 0 \\
 & X_{12} & & & & & & -100Y_{12} & & & & \leq 0 \\
 & & X_{13} & & & & & & -100Y_{13} & & & \leq 0 \\
 & & & X_{21} & & & & & & -100Y_{21} & & \leq 0 \\
 & & & & X_{22} & & & & & & -100Y_{22} & \leq 0 \\
 & & & & & X_{23} & & & & & -100Y_{23} & \leq 0
\end{array}$$

Table 6.2
Transportation Data

From \ To	Market 1	Market 2	Market 3	Supply
Factory 1	\$ 6.0	\$ 5.0	\$1.0	18
Factory 2	4.0	2.0	4.0	15
Demand	16	10	7	

Table 6.3
Fixed Charges

Factory	Fixed Charge to Market 1	Fixed Charge to Market 2	Fixed Charge to Market 3
Factory 1	\$2.0	\$0.8	\$1.5
Factory 2	1.0	1.5	1.2

and

$$X_{ij} \geq 0 \quad \text{for all } i \text{ and } j$$

$$Y_{ij} = \begin{cases} 0 & \text{if } X_{ij} = 0 \quad \text{for all } i \text{ and } j \\ 1 & \text{if } X_{ij} > 0 \quad \text{for all } i \text{ and } j \end{cases}$$

Plant Location with Set-up Costs

The problem of plant location with set-up costs is similar in structure to the transportation problem with fixed charges. ***Set-up costs*** are expenses associated with constructing and operating a plant. The more plants built, the greater the fixed overhead costs incurred.

Suppose there are m possible sites at which plants could be located. The fixed set-up cost for a plant in the ith location is F_i (for $i = 1, 2, \ldots, m$). The production capacity for each plant is limited to K_i. The company has n markets, and the volume of minimum demand required for each market is d_j (for $j = 1, 2, \ldots, n$). The unit transportation cost from plant i to market j is C_{ij}. Let X_{ij} be the amount of shipment from the ith plant to the jth market.

The problem is to select the optimal number and location of plants so that the sum of the fixed set-up costs and the shipping costs is minimized. Note that the set-up cost F_i is assumed to be fixed and independent of the magnitude of X_{ij}, when $X_{ij} > 0$. And $F_i = 0$, when $X_{ij} = 0$. Accordingly, to formulate this problem as an integer programming problem, we have to introduce zero–one integer variables Y_i. Letting the new variable Y_i be associated with each of the possible plant locations, we have

$$Y_i = \begin{cases} 0 & \text{if the plant in the } i\text{th location is rejected} \\ 1 & \text{if the plant in the } i\text{th location is accepted} \end{cases}$$

Now we can formulate the problem as follows:

$$\begin{aligned}
\text{Min} \quad C = {} & (F_1Y_1 + F_2Y_2 + \ldots + F_mY_m) \\
& + (C_{11}X_{11} + C_{12}X_{12} + \ldots + C_{1n}X_{1n} \\
& \quad C_{21}X_{21} + C_{22}X_{22} + \ldots + C_{2n}X_{2n} \\
& \quad \vdots \\
& \quad C_{m1}X_{m1} + C_{m2}X_{m2} + \ldots + C_{mn}X_{mn})
\end{aligned}$$

subject to

$$\left.\begin{aligned}
X_{11} + X_{21} + \ldots + X_{m1} &\geq d_1 \\
X_{12} + X_{22} + \ldots + X_{m2} &\geq d_2 \\
&\vdots \\
X_{1n} + X_{2n} + \ldots + X_{mn} &\geq d_n
\end{aligned}\right\} \text{demand constraints} \qquad (6.25)$$

$$\left.\begin{aligned}
X_{11} + X_{12} + \ldots + X_{1n} &\leq S_1Y_1 \\
X_{21} + X_{22} + \ldots + X_{2n} &\leq S_2Y_2 \\
&\vdots \\
X_{m1} + X_{m2} + \ldots + X_{mn} &\leq S_mY_m
\end{aligned}\right\} \text{capacity constraints} \qquad (6.26)$$

and $\quad X_{ij} \geq 0 \quad$ for all i and j

$$Y_i = \begin{cases} 0 & \text{if the plant in the } i\text{th location is rejected} \\ 1 & \text{if the plant in the } i\text{th location is accepted} \end{cases} \qquad (6.27)$$

Note that (6.26) and (6.27) together ensure that

1. If $Y_i = 0$, then no plant is selected in the ith location, and $X_{i1} + X_{i2} + \ldots + X_{in} = 0$.
2. If $Y_i = 1$, then there is a plant selected in the ith location, and $X_{i1} + X_{i2} + \ldots + X_{in} > 0$.

By using sigma notation, we can rewrite this formulation as

$$\text{Min} \quad C = \sum_{i=1}^{m} F_i Y_i + \sum_{i=1}^{m} \sum_{j=1}^{n} C_{ij} X_{ij}$$

subject to

$$\sum_{i=1}^{m} X_{ij} \geq d_j \quad \text{for all } j$$

$$\sum_{j=1}^{n} X_{ij} \leq S_i Y_i \quad \text{for all } i$$

and

$$X_{ij} \geq 0 \quad \text{for all } i \text{ and } j$$

$$Y_i = \begin{cases} 0 & \text{if a plant is not selected in the } i\text{th site} \\ 1 & \text{if a plant is selected in the } i\text{th site} \end{cases}$$

Example ***Selecting Plant Location for Mini Computer, Inc.*** Mini Computer, Inc., is considering expanding its business by building three plants in three possible locations: Boston, Los Angeles, and New Orleans. The set-up cost and plant capacity for each location are shown in Table 6.4. The company has two distribution centers, New York and Chicago. A recent marketing survey indicates that the demand for minicomputers in each center for the next 5 years is as shown in Table 6.5. The unit shipping cost from each plant location to each distribution center is shown in Table 6.6.

The company's goal is to select the optimal number of plants and locations so as to minimize the sum of total transportation and set-up costs. Let X_{ij} be the volume of the shipments from location i (for i = 1, 2, 3) to distribution center j (for j = 1, 2). The integer programming model for the problem is

$$\text{Min} \quad C = (50{,}000Y_1 + 60{,}000Y_2 + 55{,}000Y_3) + (5X_{11} + 12X_{12} + 20X_{21} + 15X_{22} + 18X_{31} + 17X_{32})$$

subject to

$$X_{11} + X_{21} + X_{31} \geq 200{,}000$$

$$X_{12} + X_{22} + X_{32} \geq 300{,}000$$

$$X_{11} + X_{12} + X_{13} \leq 160{,}000Y_1$$

$$X_{21} + X_{22} + X_{23} \leq 250{,}000Y_2$$

$$X_{31} + X_{32} + X_{33} \leq 140{,}000Y_3$$

and

$$X_{ij} \geq 0 \quad \text{for } i = 1, 2, 3 \quad \text{and} \quad j = 1, 2$$

$$Y_i = \begin{cases} 0 & \text{if the plant is not selected in the } i\text{th location} \\ 1 & \text{if the plant is selected in the } i\text{th location} \end{cases}$$

Table 6.4
Set-up Cost and Capacity

Location	Set-up Cost, F_i (millions)	Production Capacity, S_i (units)
Boston	$0.50	160,000
Los Angeles	0.60	250,000
New Orleans	0.55	140,000

Table 6.5
Demand Projection

Distribution Center	Projected Demand (units)
New York	200,000
New Orleans	300,000

Table 6.6
Unit Shipping Cost

From \ To	New York	Chicago
Boston	$ 5	$12
Los Angeles	20	15
New Orleans	18	17

The solution to this model determines the optimal number of plants and locations. For example, if the computer program assigns a value of 1 to Y_2, the plant will be built in Los Angeles. As in the classic transportation problem, the solution also determines the optimal shipping schedule.

Other Formulation Devices

Batch Size Management may often require certain items X_j to be manufactured in at least the amount of L_j. In other words,

$$X_j \geq L_j$$

With a zero–one integer variable Y_j, we can handle this situation by using the following two constraints:

$$X_j - L_jY_j \geq 0$$

$$X_j - U_jY_j \leq 0$$

where U_j is a very large number such that the constraint $(X_j - U_j)$ is certainly satisfied. If $Y_j = 0$, both constraints inform us that there should be no production; $X_j = 0$. If $Y_j = 1$, the second constraint becomes ineffective, but the first constraint imposes the required condition,

$$X_j \geq L_j$$

Either–Or Relations Here is a situation that requires one constraint to hold, but not both. Suppose that there are two constraints specified as follows:

$$-A_{11}X_1 + A_{12}X_2 \leq b_1$$
$$A_{21}X_1 + A_{22}X_2 \leq b_2$$

The decision requires that either the first or the second constraint holds (is binding), but not both. By using the zero–one integer variable Y, we can express the two constraints in the following terms:

$$-A_{11}X_1 + A_{12}X_2 \leq b_1 + UY$$
$$A_{21}X_1 + A_{22}X_2 \leq b_2 + U(1 - Y)$$

where U is an arbitrarily large number. If $Y = 0$, the first constraint is binding and the second constraint becomes large and is ruled out. If $Y = 1$, the second constraint is binding and the first one is not.

6.3 Methods of Integer Programming Computation

There are basically two major algorithms that are designed to compute optimal solutions for an integer programming problem: the cutting-plane method and the branch-and-bound algorithm.

Cutting-Plane Method The ***cutting-plane method*** begins with an ordinary linear programming problem without regard to the integer requirement. Then an appropriate new constraint is added. This new constraint, called a ***cut,*** normally reduces the feasible region, but the shrunken feasible region includes every integer solution found in the feasible region of the original problem. If the solution to the restated problem has integer values, the optimal integer solution is found for the original problem. If not, we continue to add new cutting constraints.

Consider the following integer programming problem:

$$\text{Max} \quad Z = 6X_1 + 2X_2$$

subject to

$$4X_1 + 4X_2 \leq 9$$
$$X_1 + 3X_2 \leq 5$$

and

$$X_1 \text{ and } X_2 \text{ are integers}$$

The graphical solution in Figure 6.3 shows that the feasible region for the ordinary linear programming problem is 0*ABC*. The optimal non-integer solution is at point *C*: $X_1 = 2\frac{1}{4}$, $X_2 = 0$, $Z = 13\frac{1}{2}$. The dots within the feasible region represent all possible integer solutions (including the origin point). Note that the solutions to the ordinary problem occur on the boundary of the feasible region. But in Figure 6.3, none

Figure 6.3 Graphical Representation of the Example Problem

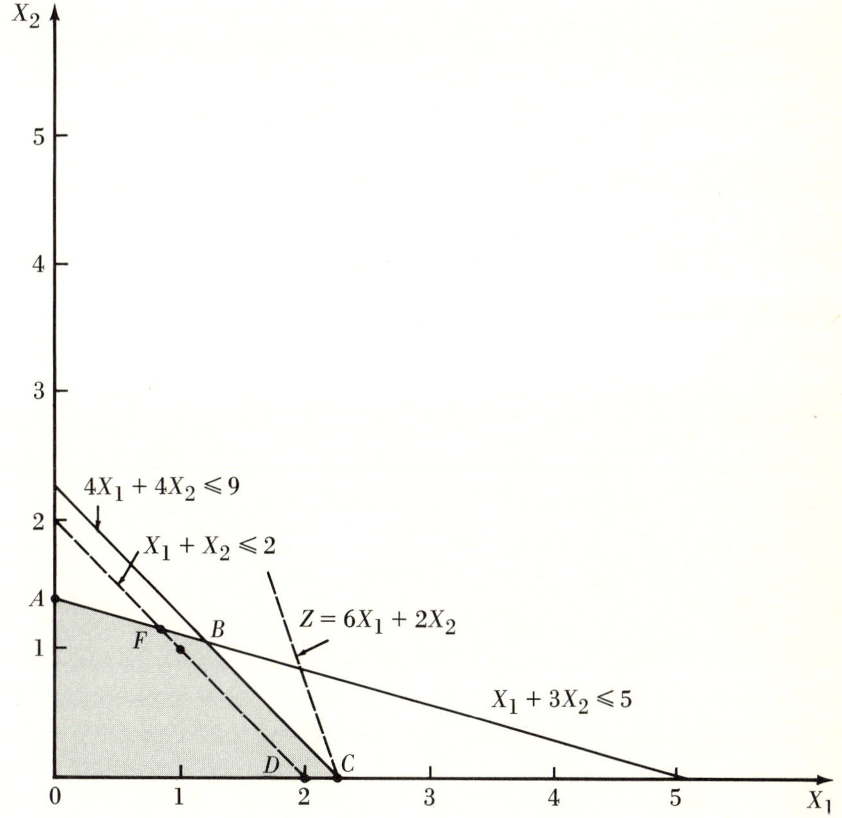

of the dots that represent possible integer solutions (except the origin) are on the boundary.

Suppose, then, that a new constraint is added—$X_1 + X_2 \leq 2$—which passes through two of the integer dots. This new constraint reduces the feasible region of the original problem from $0ABC$ to $0AFD$. The new constraint is called ***Gomory's fractional cut,*** or simply a cut, and it accomplishes two important things. (1) It reduces the feasible region of the original problem. (2) It forces the optimal solution to the new, modified problem to be an optimal integer solution to the original problem.

The central idea of the Gomory cutting algorithm is that, once the new constraint has been added, the augmented linear programming problem is solved. If the optimal solution is given in integer values, we are finished. If not, another constraint must be added and the new augmented linear programming problem solved. Note that, every time we add a new constraint (make a cut), we never eliminate any feasible integer solution contained in the original linear programming problem. After a finite number of cuts, it must be possible to find an optimal integer solution to the original problem, if such a solution exists.

Construction of the Cut The task to be considered now is how, procedurally, to make the cut or construct a constraint such as $X_1 + X_2 \leq 2$, as shown in Figure 6.3. Before describing how to construct the cut, however, we must review the simple technique of expressing a noninteger value as the sum of an integer and a nonnegative fraction. For example,

$$\begin{aligned} \tfrac{5}{4} &= 1 + \tfrac{1}{4} & 2.5 &= 2 + \tfrac{1}{2} \\ \tfrac{4}{5} &= 0 + \tfrac{4}{5} & -3.1 &= -4 + \tfrac{9}{10} \\ -\tfrac{4}{5} &= -1 + \tfrac{1}{5} & 3\tfrac{3}{4} &= 3 + \tfrac{3}{4} \end{aligned}$$

In the general case,

$$F \equiv F^* + f$$

where F represents a fractional value in the right-hand side (RHS) of the constraint. Thus $F \equiv F^* + f$ simply states that every noninteger value F is broken down into two parts—an integer part (F^*) and a nonnegative fractional part (f) less than 1. Similarly,

$$A_j \equiv A_j^* + f_j$$

where A_j is some noninteger coefficient associated with the jth variable, which can be broken down into two parts: an integer part (A_j) and a nonnegative fractional part (f_j). Using these definitions, we can now proceed to derive Gomory's fractional cut. Suppose that, by applying the simplex method, we have obtained the optimal solution for an ordinary linear programming problem. Let X_k be the basic variable in the ith row of the final simplex tableau. Then we can write the ith row in equation form as follows:

$$\underbrace{X_k}_{\text{basic variable}} + \underbrace{A_{i1}X_1 + A_{i2}X_2 + \ldots + A_{in}X_n}_{\text{nonbasic variables}} = \underbrace{F}_{\text{RHS}} \quad \text{(fractional value)} \tag{6.28}$$

In sigma notation,

$$X_k + \underbrace{\sum A_{ij}X_j}_{j \text{ nonbasic}} = F \tag{6.28$'$}$$

Note that F is a nonnegative fractional value in the RHS. Hence $X_k = F$ does not satisfy the integer requirement.

By the definitions of $F \equiv F^* + f$ and $A_j \equiv A_j^* + f_j$, we can write (6.28′) as

$$X_k + \sum (A_{ij}^* + f_{ij}) X_j = F^* + f \tag{6.29}$$

Now we move all the integer terms to the RHS:

$$\underbrace{\sum f_{ij}X_j}_{j \text{ nonbasic}} = f + \underbrace{(F^* - \sum A_{ij}^* X_j - X_k)}_{\text{some nonnegative integer}^2} \tag{6.29$'$}$$

If the left-hand side (LHS) is equal to f plus some nonnegative integer, the LHS must be greater than or equal to the value f alone, or

$$\underbrace{\sum f_{ij}X_j}_{j \text{ nonbasic}} \geq f \tag{6.30}$$

[2]Why nonnegative? Because $X_j \geq 0$, $F_{ij} \geq 0$, so LHS ≥ 0. This implies that RHS ≥ 0, because $1 < f \geq 0$, and therefore $(F^* - \sum A_{ij}^* X_j - X_k) \geq 0$.

To convert this inequality to equality, we subtract a slack variable S_i^g from the LHS:

$$-S_i^g + \underbrace{\sum f_{ij} X_j}_{j \text{ nonbasic}} = f$$

When we multiply both sides by -1, we have

$$S_i^g + \underbrace{\sum -f_{ij} X_j}_{j \text{ nonbasic}} = -f \qquad \text{(Gomory's fractional cut)} \qquad (6.31)$$

This procedure has accomplished a giant step—the construction of the cut. However, we must exercise caution. Note that S_i^g is a slack variable[3] and is required to be a nonnegative integer. When this constraint is added to the simplex tableau, a slight computational modification needs to be made before the ordinary simplex algorithm is applied to the augmented problem. We will illustrate this modification in a numerical example.

The initial simplex tableau for the numerical example is shown in tableau I of Table 6.7. The ordinary optimal noninteger solutions are shown in tableau II. They are

Basic Variables: $X_1 = 2\frac{1}{4}$, $S_2 = 2\frac{3}{4}$, $Z = 13\frac{1}{2}$

Nonbasic Variables: $X_2 = S_1 = 0$

Table 6.7 Linear Programming Solution of the Example Problem

	Row	Z	X_1	X_2	S_1	S_2	RHS
I	1	0	4	4	1	0	9
	2	0	1	3	0	1	5
	0	1	−6	−2	0	0	0
II	1	0	1	1	$\frac{1}{4}$	0	$2\frac{1}{4}$
	2	0	0	2	$-\frac{1}{4}$	1	$2\frac{3}{4}$
	0	1	0	4	$\frac{3}{2}$	0	$13\frac{1}{2}$

[3]Note that the superscript g indicates that the slack variable is associated with Gomory's fractional constraint. The subscript i reflects the order of the row, as usual.

To construct the cut, select the basic variable with the largest fractional part, S in row 2 of tableau II. Corresponding to equation (6.28), row 2 of tableau II can be written in the form

$$\underbrace{2X_2 - \tfrac{1}{4}S_1}_{\text{nonbasic}} + \underbrace{S_2}_{\text{basic}} = \underbrace{2\tfrac{3}{4}}_{\text{RHS}} \quad \text{(fractional value)}$$

By applying our definitions of F and A_j, we can break all coefficients and the RHS into two parts: an integer and a nonnegative fraction less than 1:

$$2 = 2 + 0 \qquad -\tfrac{1}{4} = -1 + \tfrac{3}{4} \qquad 1 = 1 + 0 \qquad 2\tfrac{3}{4} = 2 + \tfrac{3}{4}$$

Thus the equation corresponding to (6.29) becomes

$$(2 + 0)\,X_2 + (-1 + \tfrac{3}{4})\,S_1 + (1 + 0)\,S_2 = 2 + \tfrac{3}{4}$$

By moving all integer terms to the RHS, we get

$$\underbrace{0X_2 + \tfrac{3}{4}S_1 + 0S_2}_{\text{nonbasic variable}} = \tfrac{3}{4} + \underbrace{(2 - 2X_2 + S_1 - S_2)}_{\text{some nonnegative integer}}$$

We now have the following inequality corresponding to (6.30):

$$0X_2 + \tfrac{3}{4}\,S_1 + 0S_2 \geq \tfrac{3}{4}$$

By subtracting a slack variable S_3^g from the LHS, we get

$$-S_3^g + 0X_2 + \tfrac{3}{4}S_1 + 0S_2 = \tfrac{3}{4}$$

Multiplying both sides by -1, we have constructed Gomory's fractional cut corresponding to (6.31) as

$$S_3^g - 0X_2 - \tfrac{3}{4}S_1 - 0S_2 = -\tfrac{3}{4}$$

Once Gomory's constraint is established, we can add the coefficients of this cut to the bottom row of tableau II to form tableau III (see Table 6.8).

Table 6.8
Simplex Tableau with Gomory Constraint

	Row	Z	X_1	X_2	S_1	S_2	S_3^g	RHS	
	1	0	1	1	$\frac{1}{4}$	0	0	$2\frac{1}{4}$	
III	2	0	0	2	$-\frac{1}{4}$	1	0	$2\frac{3}{4}$	
	3	0	0	0	($-\frac{3}{4}$)	0	1	$-\frac{3}{4}$	(Gomory's cut)
	0	1	0	4	$\frac{3}{2}$	0	0	$13\frac{1}{2}$	
	1	0	1	1	0	0	1	2	
IV	2	0	0	2	0	1	$-\frac{1}{3}$	3	
	3	0	0	0	1	0	$-\frac{4}{3}$	1	
	0	1	0	4	0	0	2	12	

The augmented simplex tableau is ready for the next computation and search for an optimal solution. However, because of the negative element $-\frac{3}{4}$ in the RHS, the following solution set is ***not*** feasible:

$$X_1 = 2\tfrac{1}{4} \qquad S_2 = 2\tfrac{3}{4} \qquad S_3^g = -\tfrac{3}{4}$$
$$S_2 = S_1 = 0$$

To deal with such a situation, we have to perform the optimization by applying the so-called ***dual simplex method.*** This method differs from the ordinary simplex algorithm only in the way in which it selects the pivot element.

Dual Simplex Method

1. Select the negative element in the RHS as the pivot row, that is, the S_i^gth row.
2. Divide the coefficient of the nonbasic variables in the S_i^gth row into coefficients in row 0.
3. Select the maximum ratio (the minimum ratio for a minimization problem) that occurs in the *j*th column, ignoring ratios with zero or positive numbers in the denominator. The *j*th column is then chosen as the pivot column.

The computation for the example problem is illustrated in Table 6.9. Note that the ratio with zero in the denominator is ignored. The maximum ratio then is -2 (the only ratio in this problem) in the S_1 column. Given the pivot row 3 and the pivot column S_1, the entry where the pivot row and pivot column intersect, $(-\frac{3}{4})$, is circled as the pivot element (see Table 6.8).

Table 6.9
Dual Simplex Rule

Nonbasic Variables	X_2	S_1	
Coefficient in Row 0	4	$\frac{3}{2}$	
Coefficient in Row 3	0	$-\frac{3}{4}$	← (row 3 is pivot row)
Ratios	—	−2	
Maximum	ignore	−2	
		Pivot ↑ Column	

From here on, we carry out the same pivot operation as in the ordinary simplex method. The optimal simplex tableau, after completion of the pivot operation, is presented in tableau IV of Table 6.8. The associated basic solution is

$$X_1 = 2 \qquad S_1 = 3 \qquad S_2 = 1 \qquad Z = 12$$
$$X_2 = S_3^g = 0$$

The solutions for all basic variables are now optimal integers.

An Economic Interpretation Comparing this solution with the previous noninteger solution, we see that the value of X_1 drops from $2\frac{1}{4}$ to 2 and that the value of the objective function drops from $13\frac{1}{2}$ to 12. Economically, the reduction in the value of the objective function may be interpreted as the opportunity cost of the indivisibility requirement—that is, the loss incurred by the firm as a consequence of its inability to produce a fractional unit. In the example problem, the production of X_1 is reduced by a fraction, $\frac{1}{4}$. Given the profit per unit of X_1 as \$6, we can measure the opportunity cost as $\$6 \times \frac{1}{4} = \$1.5$.

Alternatively, one can view implementing Gomory's cut as equivalent to imposing an additional constraint on the company, a constraint that implies a reduction in the production options available to the management of the firm. Consequently, each additional Gomory's cut normally reduces the profit of the firm. The economic reasoning behind the cutting-plane method is that, as profit is reduced at each cut, the company will sooner or later be forced down to the profit level of the optimal integer solution.

To gain further understanding of the cutting-plane method, let's express the Gomory's fractional constraint in the example problem

$$S_3^g - \frac{3}{4}S_1 = -\frac{3}{4}$$

as an inequality in terms of the original variables X_1 and X_2. The first constraint of the original problem is

$$4X_1 + 4X_2 + S_1 = 9$$

or

$$S_1 = 9 - 4X_1 - 4X_2$$

Substituting S_1 into the Gomory constraint, we have

$$S_3^g - \tfrac{3}{4}(9 - 4X_1 - 4X_2) = -\tfrac{3}{4}$$

Rearranging the terms, we have

$$S_3^g + 3X_1 + 3X_2 = 6$$

Further, when we remove the slack variable S_3^g, the equation becomes an inequality:

$$3X_1 + 3X_2 \leq 6$$

or

$$\mathbf{X_1 + X_2 \leq 2}$$

It is interesting to note that this constraint, which is also known as a cutting-plane, is precisely the artificial constraint we graphed in Figure 6.3! From this derivation, the reader should be familiar with how Gomory's fractional cut is associated with the noninteger-valued original linear programming.

Recapitulation In this small problem, we obtain the optimal integer solution by the construction of only one Gomory's constraint and one iteration. Larger problems require more cuts and more iterations before an optimal solution is reached. The general procedure for Gomory's cutting method is as follows:

Step 1 Find the original linear programming solution with the simplex method.

Step 2 If the linear programming solution is an integer, terminate. Otherwise, add a cut derived from the row that has a noninteger variable with the largest fractional value.

***Step 3*.** Solve the argumented linear programming problem, and return to Step 2.

Figure 6.4
Flow Chart of the Cutting-Plane Algorithm

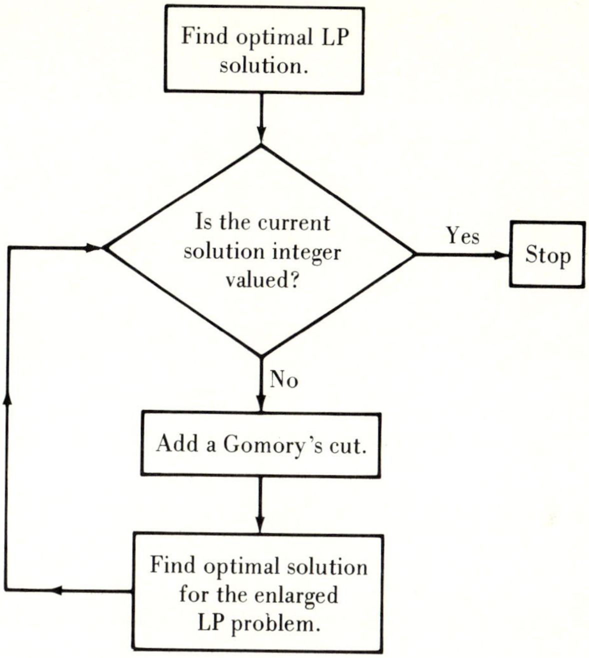

The foregoing discussion and steps of Gomory's cutting-plane algorithm for solving integer programming problems may be described in a flow chart, as shown in Figure 6.4.

Branch-and-Bound Method

The second method of solving integer programming problems is the ***branch-and-bound method.*** Let's restate our original example problem (now designated problem Z_0):

$$\text{Max } Z_0 = 6X_1 + 2X_2$$

subject to

$$4X_1 + 4X_2 \leq 9$$
$$X_1 + 3X_2 \leq 5$$

and

$$X_1 \text{ and } X_2 \text{ are integers}$$

As shown in Figure 6.3, there are only a few integer solutions (dots) to this problem. Suppose that X_1 and X_2 can take on three values (0, 1, and 2). There are nine ($3 \times 3 = 9$) integer solutions for this problem. All of them can be enumerated, and the solutions can be shown in a tree diagram (see Figure 6.5). Each branch of the tree represents a solution. Note that some of the solutions may not satisfy all constraints and hence are not feasible. For a small problem like this, we can evaluate

Figure 6.5
Tree Diagram Showing All Possible Solutions When X_1 and X_2 Take on the Values 0, 1, and 2

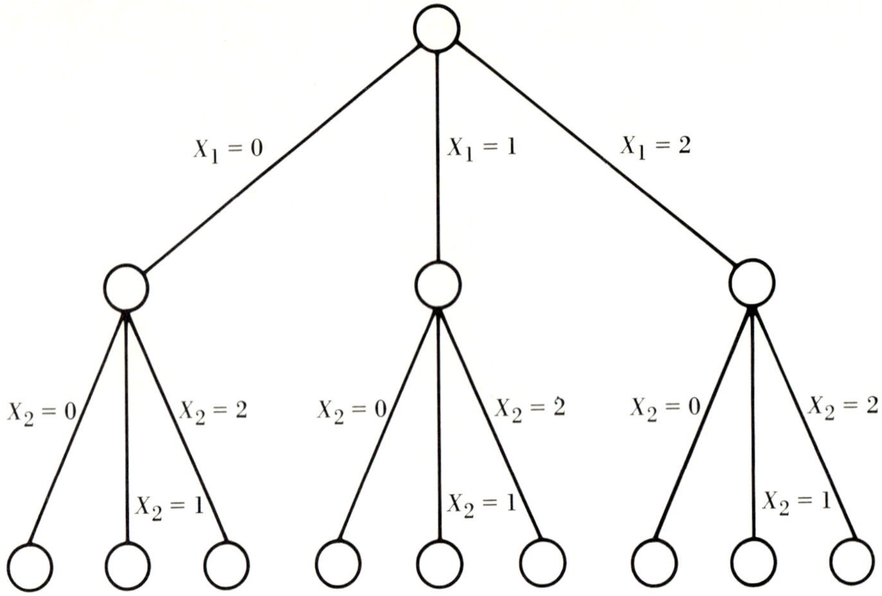

each branch and thereby find the one that optimizes the value of the objective function.

As a problem grows in size, however, complete enumeration becomes impractical. For example, consider a problem with only four variables, each of which can take on six integer values (0, 1, 2, 3, 4, and 5). There are 4^6, or 16,424, solutions or branches! And in practice this is still considered a relatively small problem. The complete enumeration and evaluation of all possible solutions would be a long and tedious process. Even if a computer were used to enumerate all the solutions, it would still be very time-consuming and economically impractical. The branch-and-bound technique is designed to enumerate only a small part of the total number of possible solutions by eliminating many of the branches or solutions from consideration.

The Concept of the Branch-and-Bound Method Suppose that we disregard the integer requirement in problem Z_0 and treat it as an ordinary linear programming problem. Let's call it problem Z_1.

$$\text{Max} \quad Z_1 = 6X_1 + 2X_2$$

subject to

$$4X_1 + 4X_2 \leq 9$$

$$X_1 + 3X_2 \leq 5$$

and

$$X_1 \geq 0, X_2 \geq 0$$

In the preceding discussion, we have seen that the optimal value of the objective function for the linear programming problem is greater than or at least equal to that of the integer programming problem. Let

Z_0^* = the optimal value of the objective function for the integer programming problem

Z_1^* = the optimal value of the objective function for the linear programming problem

This relationship between the two problems, known as the bounding relationship, may be formally stated as

$$Z_0^* \leq Z_1^*$$

The optimal solution value of the objective function for the integer programming problem (Z_0^*) is, at most, equal to that of the linear programming problem (Z_1^*). Hence Z_1^* is an upper bound for Z_0^*. If the optimal solution for the ordinary linear programming is found, we have an upper bound Z_1^* for problem Z_0. Thus no integer solution can have a value greater than Z_1^*, whether Z_1^* is an integer or not.

This binding relationship also reveals certain other properties. If an optimal solution to Z_1 is also feasible to Z_0, then it is also an optimal solution to Z_0. This is true because the objective function value Z_0 cannot exceed that of Z_1 as the maximum value of the objective function for problem Z_0. In this case, if the optimal solution to Z_1 is also feasible to Z_0, we have solved problem Z_0 and $Z_0^* = Z_1^*$.

On the other hand, if an optimal solution to problem Z_1 is infeasible to problem Z_0, we must proceed further by reformulating the problem. The process of formulating a new problem is called branching and bounding.

Branching and Bounding To construct branches, we can arbitrarily select a variable X_j that has the noninteger value b obtained from the optimal solution. Let k be the largest integer less than b. Thus a pair of branches are formulated:

X_j is upper-bounded by k; that is, $X_j \leq k$.

X_j is lower-bounded by $k + 1$; that is, $X_j \geq k + 1$.

Using these two branches, we can formulate two new linear programming problems. These two problems are identical to the previous linear programming problem, except that one is combined with the upper-bound branch and the other is combined with the lower-bound branch.

To illustrate this branching-and-bounding process, we turn to the linear programming problem Z_1, which has the optimal solution

$$X_1 = 2\tfrac{1}{4} \qquad X_2 = 0 \qquad Z_1^* = 13\tfrac{1}{2}$$

This solution is ***not feasible*** to the original integer programming problem Z_0. Choosing the noninteger variable $X_1 = 2\frac{1}{4}$, we have

$$b = 2\tfrac{1}{4} \quad \text{and} \quad k = 2$$

Hence the two new linear programming problems (Z_2 and Z_3) are

$$\text{Max} \quad Z_2 = 6X_1 + 2X_1$$

subject to

$$\begin{aligned} 4X_1 + 4X_2 &\leq 9 \\ X_1 + 3X_2 &\leq 5 \\ \mathbf{X_1} \qquad &\geq \mathbf{3} \qquad (X_j \geq k + 1) \\ X_1 \geq 0,\ X_2 &\geq 0 \end{aligned}$$

and

$$\text{Max} \quad Z_3 = 6X_1 + 2X_1$$

subject to

$$\begin{aligned} 4X_1 + 4X_2 &\leq 9 \\ X_1 + 3X_2 &\leq 5 \\ \mathbf{X_1} \qquad &\leq \mathbf{2} \qquad (X_j \leq k) \\ X_1 \geq 0,\ X_2 &\geq 0 \end{aligned}$$

We note that problem Z_2 is really problem Z_1 plus the upper-bounded constraint $X_1 \geq 3$ and that problem Z_3 is really problem Z_1 plus the lower-bounded constraint $X_1 \leq 2$.

Figure 6.6 presents a geometric picture of the two problems. The shaded area stands for the feasible region for problem Z_1. The dots within the shaded region signify the integer solutions for the original problem Z_1. The branch-and-bound process divides the feasible region of problem Z_1 into three parts: regions for problems Z_2 and Z_3 and that region in between which contains the optimal solution for problem Z_1.

Since our purpose is to find an integer solution, it is not possible for X_1 to have a value between 2 and 3 in Figure 6.6. Consequently, no feasible integer solution is eliminated when we chop this region off.

Figure 6.6
Problem Z_1 Branches into Two Problems, Z_2 and Z_3

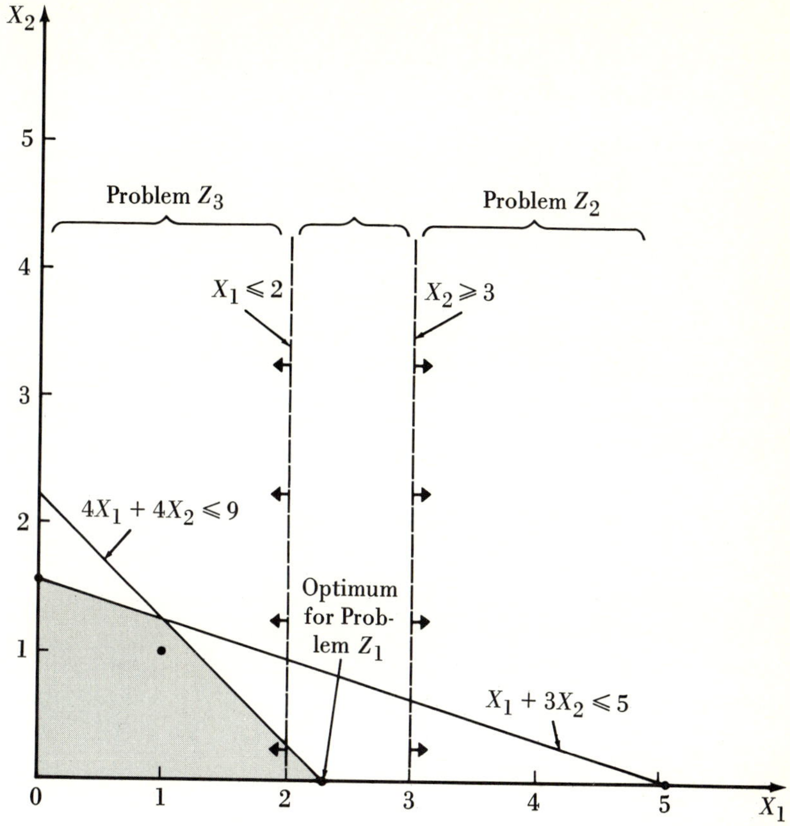

Let's investigate problem Z_2. By inspection, we discover that problem Z_2 itself is ***infeasible.*** (Why?) Accordingly, we eliminate this branch from further consideration and focus our attention on problem Z_3. The initial simplex tableau for problem Z_3 is shown as tableau I of Table 6.10. After only one iteration, we obtain the final simplex tableau (tableau III) with the optimal noninteger solution

$$X_1 = 2 \qquad X_2 = \tfrac{1}{4} \qquad Z_3^* = 12\tfrac{1}{2}$$

which is not feasible for problem Z_0. Therefore, we cannot yet cut off this branch. Further investigation is needed.

Select a noninteger variable X_2 from the optimal solution. The largest integer less than $\frac{1}{4}$ is zero, so two branches are formulated:

$$X_2 \leq 0 \qquad (X_j \leq k)$$

$$X_2 \geq 0 + 1 \qquad (X_j \geq k + 1)$$

Table 6.10
Simplex Solution to
Problem Z_3

	Row	Z_3	X_1	X_2	S_1	S_2	S_3	RHS
	1	0	4	4	1	0	0	9
	2	0	1	3	0	1	0	5
I	3	0	(1)	0	0	0	1	2
	0	1	−6	−2	0	0	0	0
	1	0	0	(4)	1	0	−4	1
	2	0	0	3	0	1	−1	3
II	3	0	1	0	0	0	1	2
	0	1	0	−2	0	0	6	12
	1	0	0	1	$\frac{1}{4}$	0	−1	$\frac{1}{4}$
	2	0	0	0	$-\frac{3}{4}$	1	2	$2\frac{1}{4}$
III	3	0	1	0	0	0	1	2
	0	1	0	0	$\frac{1}{2}$	0	4	$12\frac{1}{2}$

Problem Z_3 is now replaced by problem Z_4 and problem Z_5.

$$\text{Max} \quad Z_4 = 6X_1 + 2X_2$$

subject to

$$4X_1 + 4X_2 \leq 9$$
$$X_1 + 3X_2 \leq 5$$
$$X_1 \qquad \leq 2$$
$$\mathbf{X_2 = 0}$$
$$X_1 \geq 0, X_2 \geq 0$$

$$\text{Max} \quad Z_5 = 6X_1 + 2X_2$$

subject to

$$4X_1 + 4X_2 \leq 9$$
$$X_1 + 3X_2 \leq 5$$
$$X_1 \qquad \leq 2$$
$$\mathbf{X_2 \leq 1}$$
$$X_1 \geq 0, X_2 \geq 0$$

Observe that problems Z_4 and Z_5 differ from problem Z_3 only in the bounds on X_2. Since they have one more constraint than Z_3, the values of their objective functions cannot exceed that of Z_3. Therefore, the optimal value for $Z_3^* = 12\frac{1}{2}$ must be the upper bound for both Z_4 and Z_5. That is,

$$Z_4 \leq Z_3^* = 12\tfrac{1}{2}$$
$$Z_5 \leq Z_3^* = 12\tfrac{1}{2}$$

By simple inspection, we find that the optimal linear programming solution for problem Z_4 is

$$X_1 = 2 \qquad X_2 = 0 \qquad Z_4^* = 12$$

We observe that the linear programming solution for Z_4 is an integer. Therefore, it is feasible to the original integer programming problem Z_0.

Because the optimal solution for problem Z_4 is feasible to problem Z_0, we will not accept any integer-valued solution that is less than 12. $Z_4^* = 12$ is a lower bound for any possible integer solution that can subsequently be obtained.

Returning to problem Z_5, note that the fourth constraint ($X_2 \geq 1$) has the greater-than-or-equal-to sign. To formulate the IBFS (initial basic feasible solution), we add an artificial variable T in this constraint and assign 100 (a big number) as the coefficient of T in the objective function of Z_5. Through the algebraic manipulation discussed in Section 3.4, the IBFS is formulated and transformed in the regular simplex tableau (see tableau I in Table 6.11). After two iterations, the optimal solution is shown in the final tableau. It is

$$X_1 = \tfrac{5}{4} \qquad X_2 = 1 \qquad Z_5^* = 9\tfrac{1}{2}$$

This is a noninteger solution with the value of the objective function

$$Z_5^* = 9\tfrac{1}{2}$$

Do we need to select a noninteger value and branch into two other new problems? The answer is no. Since $Z_5^* = 9\frac{1}{2}$ is even less than the lower bound of $Z_4^* = 12$, we do not need to investigate further down this branch.

Now we have investigated all the branches for our example problem. The best integer solution obtained is $Z_4^* = 12$, which is feasible to problem Z_0. From the bounding relation

$$Z_0^* \leq Z_4^*$$

Table 6.11
Simplex Solution for Problem Z_5

	Row	Z	X_1	X_2	S_1	S_2	S_3	S_4	T	RHS
	1	0	4	4	1	0	0	0	0	9
	2	0	1	3	0	1	0	0	0	5
I	3	0	1	0	0	0	1	0	0	2
	4	0	0	1	0	0	0	−1	1	1
	0	1	−6	−102	0	0	0	100	0	−1000
	1	0	4	0	1	0	0	4	−4	5
	2	0	1	0	0	1	0	3	−3	2
II	3	0	1	0	0	0	1	0	0	2
	4	0	0	1	0	0	0	−1	1	1
	0	1	−6	0	0	0	0	−2	102	2
	1	0	1	0	$\frac{1}{4}$	0	0	1	−1	$\frac{5}{4}$
	2	0	0	0	$-\frac{1}{4}$	1	0	2	−2	$\frac{3}{4}$
III	3	0	0	0	$-\frac{1}{4}$	0	1	−1	1	$\frac{3}{4}$
	4	0	0	1	0	0	0	−1	1	1
	0	1	0	0	$\frac{6}{4}$	0	0	4	96	$9\frac{1}{2}$

we know that the optimal solution of the objective function for the integer programming problem Z_0 is at most equal to $Z_4^* = 12$. Therefore, the optimal solution for the original ***integer*** programming problem Z_0 is

$$X_1 = 2 \qquad X_2 = 0 \qquad Z_0^* = Z_4^* = 12$$

Recapitulation The general procedure of the branch-and-bound method is illustrated in Figure 6.7. The branch-and-bound algorithm can be summarized as follows:

Step 1 Select a linear programming problem. If all have been solved, terminate.

Step 2 Solve the chosen problem. If it has an infeasible solution, or if the value of the objective function is less than or equal to the value obtained in a previous solution, go to Step 1. Otherwise, go to Step 3.

Step 3 If the optimal problem solution is an integer, then record the solution if it is the best solution so far. Otherwise, proceed to Step 4.

Figure 6.7
Branch-and-Bound
Example Problem

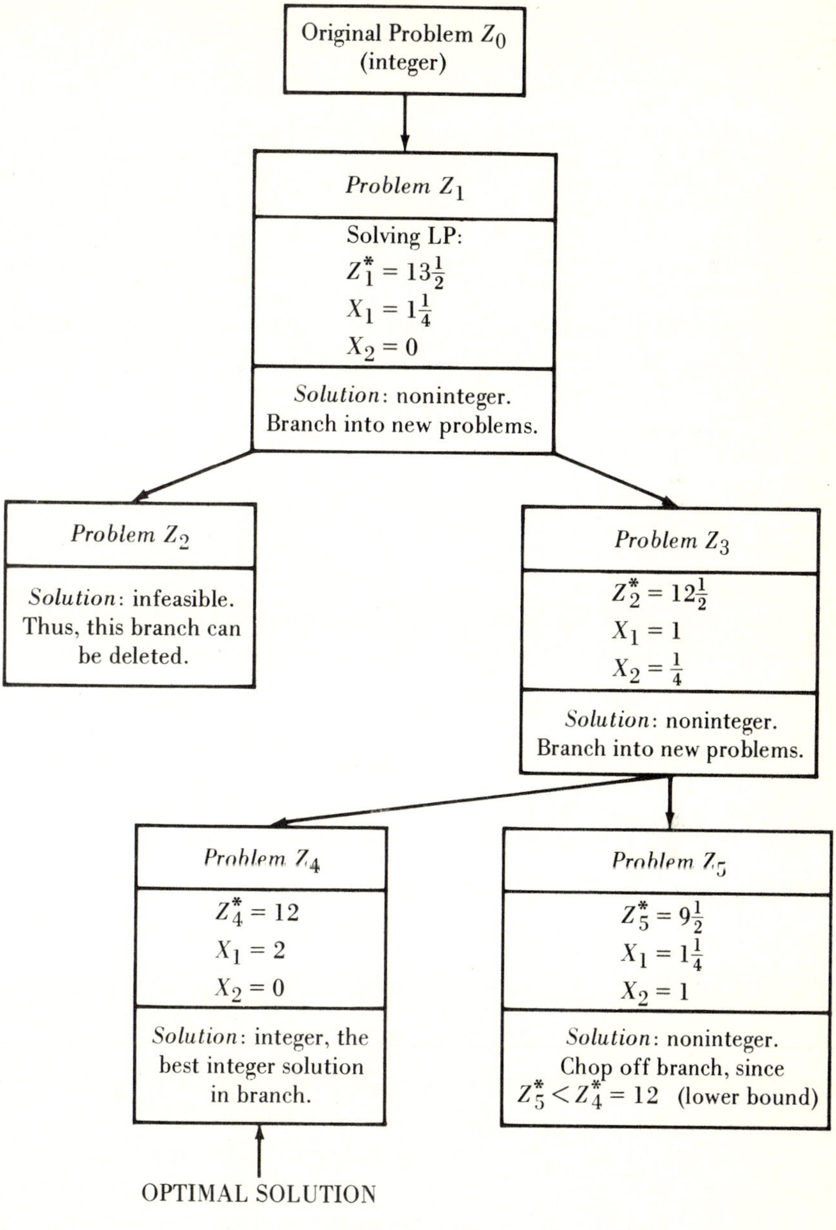

Step 4 Select a variable X_j with a noninteger value b. Let k be the largest integer less than b, then branch into two new problems. One problem is bounded by $X_j \leq k$, the other by $X_j \geq k + 1$. Return to Step 1.

As an aid to conceptual programming, we may also summarize the general procedure and steps of the branch-and-bound algorithm as a flow chart, shown in Figure 6.8.

Figure 6.8
Flow Chart of the Branch-and-Bound Algorithm

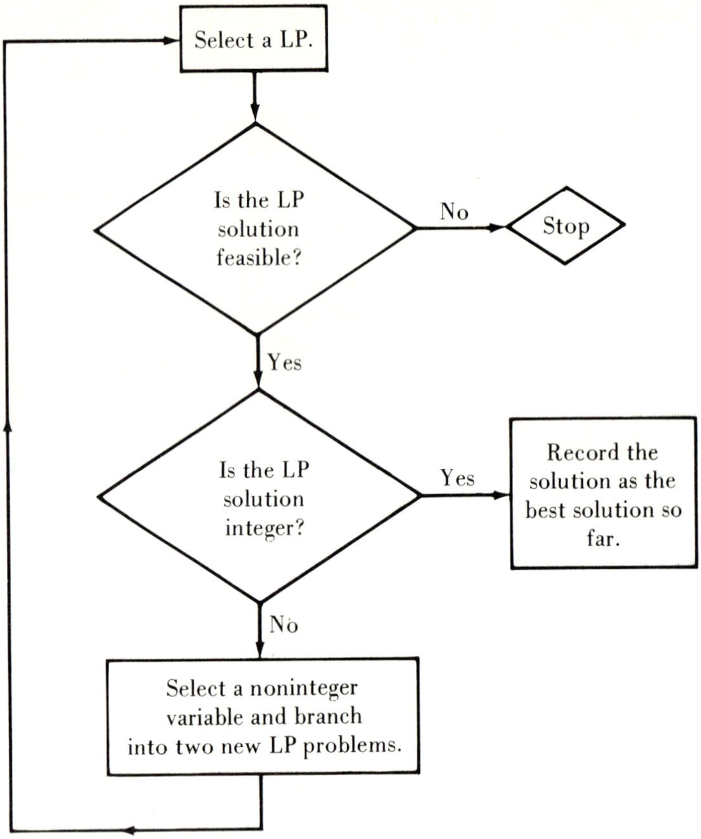

6.4 Summary

Integer programming is a special case of linear programming in which optimal solutions are required to be integers. If all decision variables are required to be integer values, the problem is referred to as pure integer programming. If only some of the variables must take on integer values, the problem is called mixed integer programming. Some problems that require the variables to be either zero or unity are called zero–one programming.

Many planning problems in business can be formulated into integer programming models. We have discussed several common models in this chapter. The essence of capital budgeting is the selection of investment projects and their financing. By stipulating zero–one variables, we can formulate the capital budgeting problem into integer programming form. The problem of indivisibility and interdependence among different projects can be directly incorporated into the integer programming formulation. Other problems, such as transportation with fixed charges, plant location with set-up costs, batch sizes, and go–no-go decisions, are examples of the integer programming formulations discussed in this chapter.

The many techniques for solving integer programming problems fall into two categories: the cutting-plane method and the branch-and-bound method. The cutting-plane method involves adding a new constraint known as Gomory's fractional cut, or simply a cut, to a linear programming problem to force the noninteger solution toward the optimal integer solution. The branch-and-bound method is an efficient enumeration technique for finding optimal integer programming solutions.

Are you comparing noninteger programming with integer programming here? The computations involved in integer programming are much more extensive than those for noninteger programming, because both cutting-plane and branch-and-bound methods require us to solve several linear programming problems. Fortunately, both algorithms can be efficiently coded into computer routines. Almost all real integer programming problems, particularly the zero–one problems, are sold in program format by computer companies.

There are no simple ways to solve zero–one problems by hand calculation. Many complex real problems require a computer. For this reason, our discussion has focused on problem formulation and the basic concept of the computation methods rather than on the mathematical and technical details of the algorithms.

Within the next few years, more progress will be made in the formulation of large-size problems. This will be reinforced by advances in computer technology. With more good computer programs available, integer programming may become a widely used technique in the business world.

Exercises

6.1 How does the integer programming model differ conceptually from the general linear programming model we have studied in previous chapters?

6.2 Define the following terms:
- a. Pure integer programming
- b. Mixed integer programming
- c. Zero–one programming
- d. Capital budgeting

6.3 Explain the following terms:
- a. Gomory's fractional cut
- b. Branch-and-bound method

6.4 When overhead costs are involved in a typical transportation problem, what are the trade-offs to be considered in management decision making?

6.5 Are the assignment problems discussed in Chapter 5 also integer programming problems? If yes, why?

6.6 The following is the final simplex tableau for a product-mix problem.

Row	Z	X_1	X_2	X_3	X_4	X_5	RHS
1	0	0	$\frac{5}{3}$	1	$-\frac{1}{3}$	$\frac{2}{3}$	$5\frac{2}{3}$
2	0	1	$\frac{4}{3}$	0	$\frac{1}{3}$	$\frac{1}{3}$	$7\frac{1}{3}$
0	1	0	$\frac{7}{3}$	0	$\frac{1}{3}$	$\frac{7}{3}$	$\frac{100}{3}$

- a. Construct the Gomory cut.
- b. Write down the enlarged simplex tableau.
- c. Using the dual simplex method, determine the pivot element.
- d. Find the optimal integer solution.

6.7 The following is the final simplex tableau for a production problem.

Row	Z	X_1	X_2	X_3	X_4	X_5	X_6	X_7	X_8	X_9	RHS
1	0	0	1	$\frac{15}{10}$	5	4	3	$\frac{1}{10}$	$-\frac{1}{2}$	0	$39\frac{1}{2}$
2	0	1	0	1	0	0	0	0	1	0	1
3	0	0	0	0	1	-1	0	0	0	1	0
0	1	0	0	95	470	180	110	5	55	0	2055

- a. Construct the Gomory cut.
- b. Write down the enlarged simplex tableau.
- c. Using the dual simplex method, determine the pivot element.
- d. Find the optimal integer solution.

6.8 Consider the following integer programming problem.

$$\text{Max} \quad Z = 8X_1 + 10X_2$$

subject to

$$2X_1 + X_2 \le 16$$
$$X_1 + 2X_2 \le 12$$

and

$$X_1 \text{ and } X_2 \text{ are integers}$$

a. Solve for the ordinary linear programming solution.
b. Give Gomory's fractional cut.
c. Using the dual simplex rule, determine the pivot element.
d. Find the optimal integer solution.
e. Derive the cutting plane. (***Hint***: Express Gomory's fractional cut in terms of the original variables X_1 and X_2 as an inequality.)
f. Graph the cutting plane you obtained in part (e) and the original constraints. Indicate the optimal solution you obtained in part (a) and the optimal solution in part (d) on the graph.

6.9 Refer to exercise 6.8.

a. Find the optimal integer solution by the branch-and-bound method.
b. Show the branch-and-bound procedure in a tree diagram (see Figure 6.7).
c. Graph the pair of branches (problems Z_2 and Z_3) on a diagram of problem Z_1 (see Figure 6.6).

6.10 Briefly discuss the rationale of the branch-and-bound method.

6.11 Given the product-mix problem

$$\text{Max} \quad Z = 8X_1 + 3X_2$$

subject to

$$6X_1 + 2X_2 \le 9$$
$$X_2 \le 1$$

and

$$X_1 \ge 0, X_2 \ge 0$$

The optimal simplex tableau is as follows:

Row	Z	X_1	X_2	X_3	X_4	RHS
1	0	1	0	$\frac{1}{6}$	$-\frac{1}{3}$	$1\frac{1}{6}$
2	0	0	1	0	1	1
0	1	0	0	$\frac{8}{6}$	$\frac{1}{3}$	$12\frac{1}{3}$

Using the cutting-plane method, find the integer programming solution to this problem. (***Hint:*** To reach the integer optimal solution, you may need three Gomory's fractional cuts.)

6.12 a. Use the branch-and-bound procedure to solve the following problem.

$$\text{Max} \quad Z = 8X_1 + 3X_2$$

subject to

$$6X_1 + 2X_2 \leq 9$$
$$X_2 \leq 1$$

and

$$X_1 \text{ and } X_2 \text{ are integers}$$

b. Graph your solutions in a tree diagram.

6.13 Consider the following problem.

$$\text{Max} \quad Z_0 = 8X_1 + 2X_2$$

subject to

$$6X_1 + 2X_2 \leq 3$$
$$X_1 \leq 1$$
$$X_2 \leq 1$$

and

$$X_1 \text{ and } X_2 \text{ are either 0 or 1}$$

a. Using the branch-and-bound method, solve this integer programming problem.
b. Graph your solution in a tree diagram.

6.14 A salesman is planning a trip to several department stores in his territory to display various vacuum cleaner models. The company has designed a special display table that has space for no more than 15 models. The salesman is limited to \$2,800 worth of vacuum cleaners, weighing no more than 70 pounds. The company also provides the sales forecast for the coming year for each model, the cost of each model, and the weight of each model. The problem the salesman faces is to select those models for his display table that will maximize the total expected sales for the models selected. Formulate a zero–one integer programming problem for the salesman. Do not solve it.

6.15 Refer to exercise 6.14. Suppose that the salesman is also confronted with the following additional constraints:

1. The company lists five models with special suction in its catalog, but he is allowed to display only three of them. These five models are numbered $j = 9$ through $j = 13$.
2. Three models (X_3, X_4, and X_5) are mutually exclusive alternatives. The company permits him to exhibit ***at most*** only one of these three models in the display.

3. Models X_2 and X_3 are not to be exhibited unless model X_1 is also included in the display.

Rewrite the salesman's optimization problem by incorporating these three constraints.

6.16 Eddie Murphy is a senior partner for a financial consulting firm in Dallas. He is in the process of reviewing four investment projects for one of his clients, Garbo and Company. The net present values for the four projects are estimated at $75 million, $15 million, $10 million, and $50 million, respectively. The company is committed to $18 million of capital funds for the first year and $14 million for the second year. The cash requirements for each project (in millions) in the two-year period are as follows:

Period \ Project	1	2	3	4
First Year	$ 5	$ 2	$ 1	$ 3
Second Year	3	4	2	4
Net Present Value	75 million	15 million	10 million	50 million

Projects 1 and 4 are mutually exclusive alternatives. Formulate a zero–one programming problem for Eddie Murphy. Do not solve this problem by hand calculation.

6.17 Raymond Johnson, Inc., is a subcontractor manufacturing batteries for National Aut Company. He makes two kinds of batteries, KS (X_1) and KW (X_2). Each unit of KS requires 1 hour of labor and 1 hour of machine time; each unit of KW uses up 7 hours of machine time and 1 hour of labor. Total hours of labor and machine time available for the given production period are 8 and 3, respectively. Profit per unit of KS is $2; profit per unit of KW is $24.

a. Given the goal of profit maximization, find the linear programming solution for Raymond Johnson, Inc. Is the solution realistic? If not, why not?
b. Write down Gomory's fractional cut and express it as inequalities in terms of the original variables X_1 and X_2.
c. If Raymond Johnson must produce integer quantities of batteries, what is the optimum integer mix?
d. Graph the inequalities in part (c) to see how Gomory's fractional cut is related to the noninteger linear programming problem you formulated in part (a).
e. What is the opportunity cost of indivisibility?

6.18 Jean Horwitz Associates is considering four investment projects. The net present value and resource requirement for capital and labor for each project are as follows:

Project	Capital (thousands)	Labor Power (thousands)	Net Present Value (thousands)
1	$15	$ 5	$50
2	3	4	5
3	10	15	15
4	4	2	8

The resources available for capital and labor power are $20 million and $15 million, respectively. For administrative reasons, projects 1 and 4 are mutually exclusive. The Associates want to find a mix of projects having the greatest total value. Formulate this problem as a zero–one integer programming problem. Do not solve it.

6.19 Refer to exercise 6.18. For technical reasons, project 3 cannnot be undertaken unless project 2 is also adopted, but project 2 can be adopted without project 3. Incorporate this condition into exercise 6.18.

6.20 The Fly-By-Nite Transportation Company must deliver its merchandise from two factories, A and B, to warehouses located in Los Angeles and New York City, respectively. The quantities available at the factories are

Factory	Quantity Available (boxes)
A	1500
B	2500

The demand requirements in the two warehouses are

Warehouse Location	Demand Requirement
Los Angeles	$1800
New York City	2200

There is a fixed charge for any shipment from a factory to a warehouse location. This fixed charge is independent of the quantity shipped. For example, the fixed charge from factory A to Los Angeles is $50 regardless of the amount of the shipment. Fixed charges for other routes are

From \ To	Los Angeles	New York City
A	$50	$35
B	30	40

The unit transportation costs for the shipments are

From \ To	Los Angeles	New York City
A	$10	$15
B	12	8

Find the shipment schedule for the company that will minimize the sum of fixed and transportation costs. Do not solve it by hand calculation.

6.21 Oil Land, Inc., is expected to increase its crude oil production from its newly discovered oil fields, Rich Oil Field and Victory Oil Field. The annual production of the former is 200 million barrels and that of the latter is 120 million barrels for each of the next ten years. The company wishes to build one or more refineries and has tentatively selected three locations, with initial set-up costs and annual refinery capacities as follows:

Location	Set-up Cost (millions)	Annual Capacity (million barrels)
East Harbor	$200	150
West Harbor	120	80
South Bay	300	200

The shipping costs per barrel of crude oil are

From \ To	East Harbor	West Harbor	South Bay
Rich Oil Field	$40	$20	$30
Victory Oil Field	50	35	20

Oil Land wishes to determine the best location and the best allocation of crude oil to the various refinery locations so that the sum of the total set-up costs for the refinery and the total shipping costs are minimal. Formulate the integer programming model for Oil Land. Do not solve it.

6.22 The Kahn Delivery Company has four crates to be carried by a truck with a capacity of 15,000 pounds. The weight and profit of each crate are

Crate	Weight (pounds)	Profit per Crate
A	4200	$500
B	3500	400
C	2500	300
D	1800	250

Note that each crate is indivisible but that the company can choose either to carry any particular crate or not to carry it. The company wishes to maximize profit. Formulate the truck-loading problem as a zero-one integer programming problem. Do not solve it.

6.23 The Atlantic Ship Line has a cargo ship with a weight capacity of 50,000 tons. The cargo ship has scheduled a route to carry chemical materials from New York to Tokyo. All materials are divided into different lots with the following characteristics:

Lot	Weight (tons)	Revenue per Ton
1	500	$50
2	700	30
3	800	20
4	1200	60
5	1800	20

The company wishes to maximize total revenue from the scheduled shipment. By contract specification, however, the ship must carry the entire given lot or none at all. Furthermore, certain lots are related. Lot 3 should not be carried unless lot 4 is also carried, but lot 4 can be shipped without lot 3. Formulate this problem as a linear integer programming problem. Do not solve it by hand calculation.

6.24 Margaret Doll, Inc., makes three models of dolls in a small shop. The name of the dolls are Alice, Bobby, and Jimmy. (Margaret Doll's production for a given day is constrained by two resources, labor and specially made metal.) These dolls require 5, 2, and 1 hours of labor for making Alice, Bobby, and Jimmy, respectively. In addition, every doll needs 1 pound of specially made metal. A total of 18 hours of labor and 14 pounds of metal are available for a given day. Formulate an optimization model for Margaret Doll, and suggest an optimal product mix.

6.25 A state government has asked for bids on various state construction projects for the coming year. Ten proposals have been submitted by different firms. After careful review and benefit–cost analysis for each proposal, the state came up with the following cost–benefit data:

Proposal	Cost (thousands)	Expected Social Benefit (thousands)
A	\$120	\$130
B	50	50
C	30	80
D	300	320
E	40	45
F	500	400
G	60	70
H	150	100
I	800	850
J	5	40

Three of the ten proposals (A, B, and C) come from firms out of state. Two of them (E and G) are submitted by one company within the state. For political reasons, the state cannot award more than one contract to an out-of-state company, and no company can be awarded more than one contract. For economic and technical reasons, project E should not be awarded unless project I is also awarded, but project I can be funded without project E. The total state budget for funding is \$2,000,000. The objective of the state is to select the contract mix offering the maximal total social benefit. Formulate this optimal organization problem for the state. Do not solve it by hand calculation.

6.26 Urban University is currently reviewing its security department to determine how to allocate security forces most efficiently. At different periods during the day, the university's security requirements are different. On the basis of a recent study of crime prevention, the director of the security department suggested the following minimal daily requirements for security guards:

Hours of 24-hour Day	Period of Day	Minimum Number of Security Guards Required for Each Period
8:00 A.M. – 12:00 noon	1	5
12:00 noon – 4:00 P.M.	2	6
4:00 P.M. – 10:00 P.M.	3	4
10:00 P.M. – 2:00 A.M.	4	2
2:00 A.M. – 6:00 A.M.	5	2
6:00 A.M. – 8:00 A.M.	6	3

By contract, each security guard works 8 hours per shift. Any overtime assignment results in double pay. The goal of the director is to construct a daily work schedule that minimizes the total number of security guards while meeting the minimal personnel requirement during each period. Formulate this situation as an integer programming problem. Do not solve it by hand calculation. Be sure to label all variables and to explain the relationships between variables. (***Hint:*** Consider that period 6 immediately precedes period 1.)

Suggested Readings

Garfinkel, R. S., and G. L. Nemhauser. "A Survey of Integer Programming Emphasizing Computation and Relations Among Models." In *Mathematical Programming.* Eds. T. C. Hu and Stephen M. Robinson. New York: Academic Press, 1973.

———. *Integer Programming.* New York: Wiley, 1972.

Geoffrion, A. M., and R. E. Marsten. "Integer Programming Algorithms: A Framework and State-of-the-Art Survey." *Management Science,* 18, No. 7 (March 1972).

Gomory, Ralph E. "Outline of an Algorithm for Integer Solutions to Linear Programs." *Bulletin of the American Mathematical Society*, 64 (September 1958).

Gomory, Ralph E., and William J. Baumol. "Integer Programming and Pricing." *Econometrica*, 28 (July 1960).

McMillan, Claude, Jr. *Mathematical Programming*. New York: Wiley, 1970. Chapters 11–12, Appendices C and H.

Wagner, Harvey M. *Principles of Operations Research*. Englewood Cliffs, N.J.: Prentice-Hall, 1969.

Weingartner, H. Martin. *Mathematical Programming and the Analysis of Capital Budgeting Problems*. Englewood Cliffs, N.J.: Prentice-Hall, 1963.

7

Goal Programming

In the preceding discussions, both transportation and integer programming problems have been presented as extensions or special cases of linear programming problems. In all of the linear programming models considered, the objective function has been unidimensional. That is, it is assumed that the decision maker strives for a single objective, such as profit maximization or cost minimization. In many real cases, however, multiple goals and subgoals must be considered. Various goals may be expressed in different units of measurement. Some may be complementary, and some may conflict with each other.

A second limitation of the standard linear programming model is that the decision maker must assign exact numbers as coefficients of the decision variables in the objective function. Numbers that express exact amounts, such as 1, 2, 7.5, 3.4, and the like, are known as ***cardinal values.*** The assignment of a cardinal value to each goal in linear programming forces management not only to rank the objectives in importance but also to assign weights indicating ***how much*** one goal is valued over the other. When these goals are not commensurable (for instance, one may be measured in dollars and another in physical units or in the satisfaction of desires), there is no valid ground on which to base cardinal ranking.

These two shortcomings—unidimensionality and commensurability—can be overcome by using a specific type of linear programming known as goal programming. This chapter presents the basic concepts of goal programming. To show the formulation of a goal programming model, we will use our familiar potato–tomato example. Finally, we will discuss the solution of a goal programming problem by using both the graphical approach and the simplex method.

7.1 The Concepts of a Goal Programming Problem

Goal programming is a modification and extension of linear programming that can be applied to a situation with multiple goals. In goal programming, all of the decision maker's objectives or goals are incorporated in one model that can be solved simultaneously. Furthermore, each goal may be expressed in different units of measurement in the objective function.

When using the goal programming technique, management must determine which goals are most important, but weighting the goals with cardinal numbers is not necessary. Instead, the decision maker assigns a goal an ***ordinal value,*** which is defined as its position in order of importance: first, second, third, and so on. Since different, and possibly incompatible, goals correspond to successive ranks in the model, solving the goal programming problem involves achieving some higher-order goals first, before the lower-order goals are considered. Once a higher-order goal is attained to the fullest extent possible, the goal programming model proceeds to find a satisfactory level for the lower-order goals.

The essence of business management is the allocation of scarce resources. When a firm or organization specifies multiple goals, it is not always possible to achieve every goal to the extent desired by the decision maker. The distinguishing feature of goal programming is that (instead of maximizing or minimizing certain goals directly as linear programming does) it seeks, within the given set of constraints, to ***minimize the deviations from established targets*** that were established.

Professor Herbert A. Simon, winner of the Nobel Prize in economics in 1977, has argued that management has largely given up the attempt to maximize or minimize anything, such as profit or sales. Instead, managers set some minimal standard of achievement. The real value of goal programming for decision analysis is that this technique reflects how a firm or organization really acts, not just how it ought to act if its decisions were all optimal.

The Single-Goal Model

Goal programming is a special type of linear programming. With only one goal, we could just as easily solve the problem by the standard linear programming technique. But starting our discussion with a single goal will help us understand multiple-goal programming. With linear programming, we attempt to optimize an objective function and make it as large or as small as possible. With the goal approach, we attempt to find values that, as closely as possible, exactly achieve the desired result.

To facilitate the comparison between the two, let's return to the potato–tomato example. As developed in Chapters 2 and 3, the linear programming format for the potato–tomato problem is

$$\text{Max} \quad Z = 40X_1 + 50X_2$$

subject to

$$X_1 + 2X_2 \leq 30 \qquad \text{(land)}$$

$$3X_1 + 2X_2 \leq 60 \qquad \text{(labor)}$$

$$2X_2 \leq 24 \qquad \text{(storage space)}$$

and

$$X_j \geq 0 \quad \text{for } j = 1, 2$$

Thus the linear programming problem is to maximize profit subject to the set of resource constraints. The optimal solution to this problem is to produce 15 units of potatoes (X_1) and 7.5 units of tomatoes (X_2) for a maximum profit of \$975. All land and labor resources are fully utilized, and the storage space is underutilized by 9 square feet.

Now let us examine the same problem from the point of view of goal programming, in which we move toward a specific goal. Suppose, for example, that the farmer wishes to attain a profit target of \$1000. The farmer realizes that he may not be able to reach the goal, but he would like to come as close to it as possible. This means that he wishes to minimize the deviations (both positive and negative) from his profit target. Mathematically, we can formulate this goal as follows:

$$40X_1 + 50X_2 + d_1^- - d_1^+ = 1000$$

where d_1^- and d_1^+ are ***deviational variables.***

d_1^- = amount of underachievement of the desired goal (the negative deviational variable)

d_1^+ = amount of overachievement or excess of the desired goal (the positive deviational variable)

This equation says that the profit obtained, $40X_1 + 50X_2$, plus any underachievement minus any overachievement must equal the profit target. Common sense tells us that, if a profit of more than \$1000 could be obtained, the farmer would be quite well off from a business standpoint. But should his profit turn out to be less than the desired figure, the result would be economically undesirable. Therefore, his objective is to minimize underachievement of the goal, or the value of d_1^-. The farmer is not concerned with overachievement of the profit goal, so the variable d_1^+ does not appear in the objective function. Presumably, one could assign d_1^+ a zero coefficient. The mathematical expression of the objective function is

$$\text{Min} \quad Z = d_1^-$$

subject to

$$\begin{aligned} X_1 + 2X_2 &\le 30 \\ 3X_1 + 2X_2 &\le 60 \\ 2X_2 &\le 24 \\ 40X_1 + 50X_2 + d_1^- - d_1^+ &= 1000 \end{aligned}$$

and

$$X_1 \ge 0,\ X_2 \ge 0,\ d_1^- \ge 0,\ d_1^+ \ge 0$$

The Simplex Method of Solution

After adding slack variables S_1, S_2, and S_3, we construct the initial simplex tableau shown as tableau I in Table 7.1. Note that no artificial variable is needed in the target profit constraint, because the deviational variable d_1^- can be used as a slack variable. However, the d_1^- column is not yet in the form of unit coefficients. To establish the IBFS, we must add the target profit constraint to the objective function ($Z - d_1^- = 0$). The resulting new objective function is

$$Z + 40X_1 + 50X_2 - d_1^+ = 1000$$

which is shown in row 0 of tableau I. The IBFS can now be read off as

$$\begin{aligned} S_1 &= 30 \quad \text{(land)} & X_1 = X_2 = d_1^+ = 0 \\ S_2 &= 60 \quad \text{(labor)} \\ S_3 &= 24 \quad \text{(storage space)} \\ d_1^- &= 1000 \end{aligned}$$

Since no production takes place, all resources must be idle. As expected, the amount of underachievement of the stated profit goal must be \$1000!

Now, by straightforward application of the simplex method, we reach the optimal tableau shown as tableau IV. The result is

$$\begin{aligned} X_1 &= 15 \quad \text{(potato)} & S_3 &= 9 \quad \text{(storage space)} \\ X_2 &= 7.5 \quad \text{(tomato)} & d_1^- &= 25 \quad \text{(underachievement)} \end{aligned}$$

Interestingly, the underachievement value indicates that total profit falls short of the desired goal of \$1000 by \$25. The actual profit is still

Table 7.1 Simplex Solution for the Potato–Tomato Problem with a Single Goal

	Row	Z	X_1	X_2	S_1	S_2	S_3	d_1^-	d_1^+	RHS
	1	0	1	2	1	0	0	0	0	30
I	2	0	3	2	0	1	0	0	0	60
	3	0	0	2	0	0	1	0	0	24
	4	0	40	50	0	0	0	1	−1	1000
	0	1	40	50	0	0	0	0	−1	1000
	1	0	1	0	1	0	−1	0	0	6
II	2	0	3	0	0	1	−1	0	0	36
	3	0	0	1	0	0	$\frac{1}{2}$	0	0	12
	4	0	40	0	0	0	−25	1	−1	400
	0	1	40	0	0	0	−25	0	−1	400
	1	0	1	0	1	0	−1	0	0	6
III	2	0	0	0	−3	1	2	0	0	18
	3	0	0	1	0	0	$\frac{1}{2}$	0	0	12
	4	0	0	0	−40	0	15	1	−1	160
	0	1	0	0	−40	0	15	0	−1	160
	1	0	1	0	$-\frac{1}{2}$	$\frac{1}{2}$	0	0	0	15
IV	2	0	0	0	$-\frac{3}{2}$	$\frac{1}{2}$	1	0	0	9
	3	0	0	1	$\frac{3}{4}$	$-\frac{1}{4}$	0	0	0	7.5
	4	0	0	0	$-\frac{35}{2}$	$-\frac{15}{2}$	0	1	−1	25
	0	1	0	0	$-\frac{35}{2}$	$-\frac{15}{2}$	0	0	−1	25

\$975. Thus we attain the same solution with single-goal programming as with linear programming.

It is also interesting to note that we cannot have both underachievement and overachievement simultaneously. If d_1^- is positive, d_1^+ must be zero, and vice versa. They cannot both be zero unless the goal is exactly achieved.

Equally Ranked Goals

Suppose that the potato–tomato farmer has another goal. In addition to the desired profit goal of \$1000, he also wants to produce 5 units of tomatoes. If these two goals are of ***equal importance*** to management, a \$1 deviation from the profit-target goal is just as important as a deviation of 1 unit of tomatoes. Let

d_1^- = amount of underachievement of the desired profit goal

d_1^+ = amount of overachievement or excess of the desired profit goal

d_2^- = amount of underachievement of the tomato goal

d_2^+ = amount of overachievement of the tomato goal

The objective function and constraints of this goal programming problem can be expressed as follows:

$$\text{Min} \quad Z = d_1^- + d_2^-$$

subject to

$$X_1 + 2X_2 \leq 30 \qquad \text{(land)}$$

$$3X_1 + 2X_2 \leq 60 \qquad \text{(labor)}$$

$$2X_2 \leq 24 \qquad \text{(storage space)}$$

$$40X_1 + 50X_2 + d_1^- - d_1^+ = 1000 \qquad \text{(profit goal)}$$

$$X_2 + d_2^- - d_2^+ = 5 \qquad \text{(tomato goal)}$$

and

$$X_1 \geq 0, X_2 \geq 0, d_1^- \geq 0, d_1^+ \geq 0, d_2^- \geq 0, d_2^+ \geq 0$$

Table 7.2 Simplex Solution for the Potato–Tomato Problem with Two Equally Ranked Goals

	Row	Z	X_1	X_2	S_1	S_2	S_3	d_1^-	d_2^-	d_1^+	d_2^+	RHS
	1	0	1	2	1							30
	2	0	3	2		1						60
I	3	0	0	2			1					24
	4	0	40	50				1		−1		1000
	5	0	0	1					1		−1	5
	0	1	40	51						−1	−1	1005
		⋮										
	1	0	1	0	$-\frac{1}{2}$	$\frac{1}{2}$	0	0	0	0	0	15
	2	0	0	0	$-\frac{3}{2}$	$\frac{1}{2}$	1	0	0	0	0	9
V	3	0	0	0	$\frac{3}{4}$	$-\frac{1}{4}$	0	0	−1	0	1	2.5
	4	0	0	0	−17.5	7.5	0	1	0	−1	0	25
	5	0	0	1	$\frac{3}{4}$	$-\frac{1}{4}$	0	0	0	0	0	7.5
	0	1	0	0	−17.5	−7.5	0	0	−1	−1	0	25

Table 7.2 is constructed from this system, after the addition of three slack variables, S_1, S_2, and S_3. We obtain the objective function, row 0, by substituting, in the objective function, the following algebraic expressions of the deviations:

$$d_1^- = 1000 - 40X_1 - 50X_2 + d_1^+ \qquad \text{(from profit goal constraint)}$$

$$d_2^- = 5 - X_2 + d_2^+ \qquad \text{(from tomato goal constraint)}$$

Thus the objective function can be rewritten as

$$Z = d_1^- + d_2^- = 1005 - 40X_1 - 51X_2 + d_1^+ + d_2^+$$

or

$$Z + 40X_1 + 51X_2 - d_1^+ - d_2^+ = 1005$$

which appears in row 0 in tableau I.

Once the IBFS is established as shown in tableau I, we can apply the simplex routine directly to this problem. The final optimal solution, after four more iterations, is presented in tableau V as

$$X_1 = 15 \qquad S_1 = S_3 = d_2^- = d_1^+ = 0$$
$$X_2 = 7.5$$
$$S_3 = 9$$
$$d_1^- = 25$$
$$d_2^+ = 2.5$$

The result, of course, confirms the solution we obtained previously. The amount of underachievement, $d_1^- = 25$, indicates that we have fallen short of our desired profit goal of \$1000 and have attained only a \$975 profit. The firm's second goal of 5 tomatoes, however, is fulfilled and even surpassed by 2.5 units ($d_2^+ = 2.5$).

It should be emphasized that only one deviational variable (either underachievement or overachievement) assigned to each goal is included in the solution at a positive level. Here we have $d_1^- = 25$, $d_1^+ = 0$; and $d_2^+ = 2.5$, $d_2^- = 0$.

As we have seen, in either the case of a single goal or the case of equally ranked multiple goals, ***the objective function is contained in only one row.*** The goal programming solutions in this case differed only slightly from those obtained through linear programming. The real value of goal programming emerges when we encounter complex decision problems that involve multiple, incompatible, and incommensurable goals.

7.2 Examples of Multiple-Goal Programming Formulation

The decision maker is always confronted with the problem of allocating scarce resources, whether time, money, or physical inputs. To solve this problem the manager must set goals. Because the resources are scarce, however, attaining all or even some of the goals could prove impossible within the given decision environment. Perhaps the most efficient way to approach this situation is for management to assign priorities to different goals and rank them in order of importance.

Priority-Ranked Goals

In goal programming, whether there are two or more goals competing for scarce resources, the decision maker must be able to determine which goal should be met first, which second, and so on.

Suppose that management has established a set of goals and has assigned them priorities symbolized by P's (P_1, P_2, P_3, and so on). The P's used here are ***preemptive priority factors***, which indicates that they represent different levels of priority. The P's are not given actual values. They are simply a convenient way of indicating that the P_1 goal is more important than the P_2 goal, that the P_2 goal is more important than the P_3 goal, and so on. Furthermore, the P_2 goal will never be achieved until the P_1 is fulfilled. The P_2 goal, in turn, will be satisfied to the fullest extent possible before the P_3 goal is considered.

Back to the Potato–Tomato Problem

Let's return to the potato–tomato problem illustrated in Chapter 2. The maximum quantities of land and storage space available are 30 acres and 24 square feet, respectively. Standard or regular labor hours available for the production period are still 60 hours, but the farmer's sister in the city has decided to send her college-age son to the farm so that he will learn the true meaning of social value through manual labor. She has stipulated that the boy will work unpaid, provided that his total labor does not exceed 10 hours.

Suppose that the farmer has established the following goals for the production period and has assigned them the priorities:

First, fully utilize the regular labor hours available.
Second, limit the overtime allowed for farm work to 10 hours.
Third, fully utilize available land.
Finally, reach a profit target of $1200.

We now formulate the following constraints:

Land Constraint Each unit of potatoes and tomatoes requires 1 and 2 acres of land, respectively. Thus we have

$$X_1 + 2X_2 + d_1^- = 30$$

where X_1 = amount of potato production

X_2 = amount of tomato production

d_1^- = amount of underutilization of land resources

Since no overuse is possible, the positive deviation variable (overutilization of land) can be omitted.

Regular Labor Hours Regular labor hours available to the farmer are limited to 60 hours. The farmer himself may, under some circumstances, provide some extra hours of work if necessary. Thus the regular labor constraint could be set up as follows:

$$3X_1 + 2X_2 + d_2^- - d_2^+ = 60$$

where d_2^- = amount of underutilization of available regular working hours

d_2^+ = amount of extra available hours provided by the hardworking farmer himself

Overtime The farmer would like to limit the college student's work on the farm to 10 hours. Now a new constraint should be introduced:

$$d_2 + d_{21}^- - d_{21}^+ = 10$$

where d_2 = actual work time of the college student

d_{21}^- = difference as a shortfall between the actual work time of student and the desired 10 hours

d_{21}^+ = student work time in excess of the desired 10 hours

Both negative and positive deviations from the allowed 10 hours are included, because the actual time can be less than, equal to, or even more than 10 hours. To achieve the second goal, the farmer can minimize the deviational variable d_{21}^+.

Alternatively, the student's time could have been incorporated directly into the regular labor hours. That is, we could simply add the desired 10 hours to the right-hand side of the regular labor constraint, which would yield

$$3X_1 + 2X_2 + d_2^- - d_2^+ = 70$$

We can choose either of the two constraints to solve the problem.

Profit Goals The achievement of a $1200 profit is the last-priority goal. It is susceptible to either over- or underachievement, depending on the conditions necessary to fulfill the higher-order goals. Given the profit per unit of potato as $40 and that of tomato as $50, the final profit constraint is

$$40X_1 + 50X_2 + d_4^- - d_4^+ = 1200$$

where d_4^- = amount of underachievement of the desired profit goal

d_4^+ = amount of overachievement of the desired profit goal

Multiple Objective Functions With priority-ranked goals, we have to formulate one objective function for ***each goal*** in the programming model. In this example, the highest-ranked goal is to maximize utilization of the regular labor hours. This is equivalent to minimizing the deviation variable d_2^- (the amount of underachievement of the regular labor hours). Thus the objective function corresponding to the first-priority goal is

$$\text{Min} \quad Z_1 = P_1 d_2^-$$

The second-ranked goal is to limit labor overtime to 10 hours. In other words, the farmer wants to minimize the deviational variable d_{21}^+, the boy's overtime in excess of the desired 10 hours. Mathematically, the objective function for the second-priority goal is:

$$\text{Min} \quad Z_2 = P_2 d_{21}^+$$

The third-ranked goal is to utilize available land as fully as possible. This means minimizing d_1^-, the amount of underutilization of land resources:

$$\text{Min} \quad Z_3 = P_3 d_1^-$$

The last-ranked goal in this problem is to make a profit of \$1200, or to minimize the deviational variable d_4^-, the amount of underachievement of the desired profit:

$$\text{Min} \quad Z_4 = P_4 d_4^-$$

At this point we have formulated one objective function for each goal. The farmer's overall objective is to minimize the total of deviations from all these goals. Letting Z stand for the total of the unattained portions of the farmer's goals expressed in terms of priority factors, we can write the overall objective function as follows:

$$\text{Min} \quad Z = P_1 d_2^- + P_2 d_{21}^+ + P_3 d_1^- + P_4 d_4^-$$

Combining the constraints and the objective function, we can now formulate the complete goal programming model for this problem:

$$\begin{aligned}
&\text{Min} \quad Z = P_1 d_2^- + P_2 d_{21}^+ + P_3 d_1^- + P_4 d_4^- \\
&\text{subject to} \quad X_1 + 2X_2 + d_1^- = 30 \\
&\qquad 3X_1 + 2X_2 + d_2^- - d_2^+ = 60 \\
&\qquad 2X_2 + d_3^- = 24 \\
&\qquad d_2^- + d_{21}^- - d_{21}^+ = 10 \\
&\qquad 40X_1 + 50X_2 + d_4^- - d_4^+ = 1200 \\
&\text{and} \quad X_1, X_2, d_1^-, d_2^-, d_2^+, d_{21}^-, d_{21}^+, d_3^-, d_4^-, d_4^+ \geq 0
\end{aligned}$$

The General Format Having presented the formulation of multiple-goal programming through a specific example, we can now express the model in its general form:

$$\text{Min} \quad Z = \sum_{i=1}^{m} d_i^- + \sum_{i=1}^{m} d_i^+$$

$$\text{subject to} \quad \sum_{j=1}^{n} A_{ij} X_j + d_i^- - d_i^+ = b_i \qquad i = 1, 2, \ldots, m$$

$$\text{and} \quad X_j \geq 0,\ d_i^- \geq 0,\ d_i^+ \geq 0 \quad \text{for all } i, j$$

where X_j stands for the choice variables for $j = 1, 2, \ldots, n$. Assuming that there are m goals, let $i = 1, 2, \ldots, m$. Since each goal is incorporated in a constraint, we must have m constant terms b_i on the right-hand side of the system. A_{ij} represent the coefficients for the jth choice variable in the ith constraint. Both d_i^- and d_i^+ are deviational variables representing the amount of under- and overachievement of the ith goal.

The deviational variables must be ranked by preemptive priority factors according to their order of importance. Failure to assign weights other than unity indicates that the two deviations are of equal importance to the decision maker. This priority ranking is assumed to be absolute in the sense that one goal is more important than another. Assuming that there are goals in m ranks, the relationship among these preemptive factors can be expressed in the following notation:

$$P_i > kP_{i+1} \quad \text{for } k \text{ arbitrarily large}$$
$$\text{for } i = 1, 2, \ldots, m$$

This relation means that there is no k large enough to make the product kP_{i+1} greater than P_i. Consequently, a lower-priority goal will never be achieved at the expense of a higher-priority goal.

The objective, then, is to minimize the value of the sum of d_i^- and d_i^+. Exact achievement of this goal results in a zero value for the sum of d_i^- are d_i^+. If both d_i^- and d_i^+ are zero, goal b_i is exactly achieved. Otherwise, the ith goal is underachieved (d_i^- is positive) or overachieved (d_i^+ is positive) for a specific value of the choice variable X_j. One can see that d_i^- and d_i^+ are complementary by nature. Their relationship can be expressed as $d_i^- \times d_i^+ = 0$. If either assumes a positive value, the other must be zero, and vice versa.

7.3 Solving a Goal Programming Model

The graphical method of solving goal programming models is quite similar to the method we used in Chapter 2 with linear programming. In linear programming, the method is implemented to maximize or minimize an objective function with one goal, whereas in goal programming, one always strives to ***minimize the total deviation from a set of multiple goals.*** As we have demonstrated, the decision maker strives to fulfill a set of goals according to a priority-ranked sequence. The deviation from the goal with the highest priority is minimized to the fullest extent possible before deviation from the next goal is minimized.

In this section, we will examine the two-variable graphical method of goal programming, using the familiar potato–tomato problem.

Graphical Analysis of Solution

To facilitate the discussion, the goal programming model for the potato–tomato problem is rewritten as follows:[1]

$$\text{Min} \quad Z = P_1 d_2^- + P_2 d_5^+ + P_3 d_1^- + P_4 d_4^-$$

subject to

$X_1 + 2X_2 + d_1^-$	$= 30$	(land)
$3X_1 + 2X_2 + d_2^- - d_2^+$	$= 60$	(regular labor)
$2X_2 + d_3^-$	$= 24$	(storage space)
$40X_1 + 50X_2 + d_4^- - d_4^+$	$= 1200$	(profit goal)
$3X_1 + 2X_2 + d_5^- - d_5^+$	$= 70$	(regular plus overtime labor)

and $\quad X_1, X_2, d_1^-, d_2^-, d_3^-, d_4^-, d_5^-, d_2^+, d_4^+, d_5^+ \geq 0$

The first step in solving the problem by the graphical method is to plot all the constraints on a graph, as shown in Figure 7.1. Because the overutilization of land is impossible but its underutilization is permissible, the deviational variable d_1^- must be on or below the land constraint, as indicated by the arrow at d_1^- in Figure 7.1. Turning to the regular labor constraint, we find that the amount of labor hours employed may be less than, equal to, or even greater than 60 hours. Thus the feasible region can be on either side of the line, as indicated by the arrows pointing toward both sides of the constraint at d_2^- and d_2^+.

Similarly, we can plot the constraints for storage space, profit goal, and sum of regular time plus overtime. Once all the constraints have been plotted on the graph, the feasible region of the goal programming model for the potato–tomato problem is confined to the shaded area $0ABC$.

The next step is to analyze each goal in the objective function in search of the optimal solution within the feasible region. In this example,

[1]For convenience of graphical presentation, the separate overtime constraint, $d_2^+ + d_{12}^- - d_{12}^+ = 10$, is replaced by the alternative constraint with the sum of regular and overtime labor on the right-hand side and the choice variable on the left-hand side—that is, $3X_1 + 2X_2 + d_5^- - d_5^+ = 70$.

Figure 7.1 Graphical Representation of the Potato-Tomato Problem

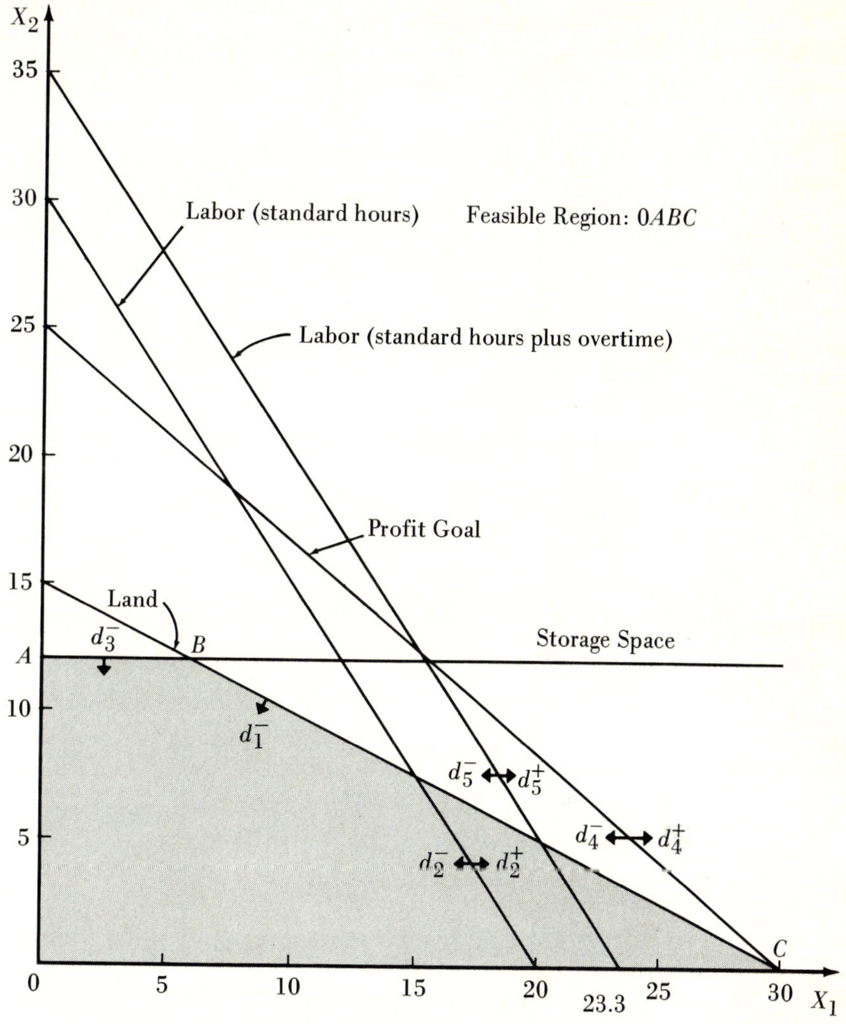

the first goal is to utilize all available regular working hours. In other words, management wants to minimize the value of the deviational variable d_2^-, the underutilization of working hours, to zero. As d_2^- approaches zero, the area of feasible solutions shrinks to the area *EDC* shown in Figure 7.2.

The second goal, which is to limit the farmer's nephew's work time to 10 hours, can be achieved by driving the deviational variable d_5^+ to zero. When we do so, the area of feasible solutions shrinks to the shaded area *EDGM* shown in Figure 7.3. Management's first two most important goals are attained as long as the production of potatoes and tomatoes takes place within the shaded area *EDGM*.

Figure 7.2 Feasible Region: *EDC*

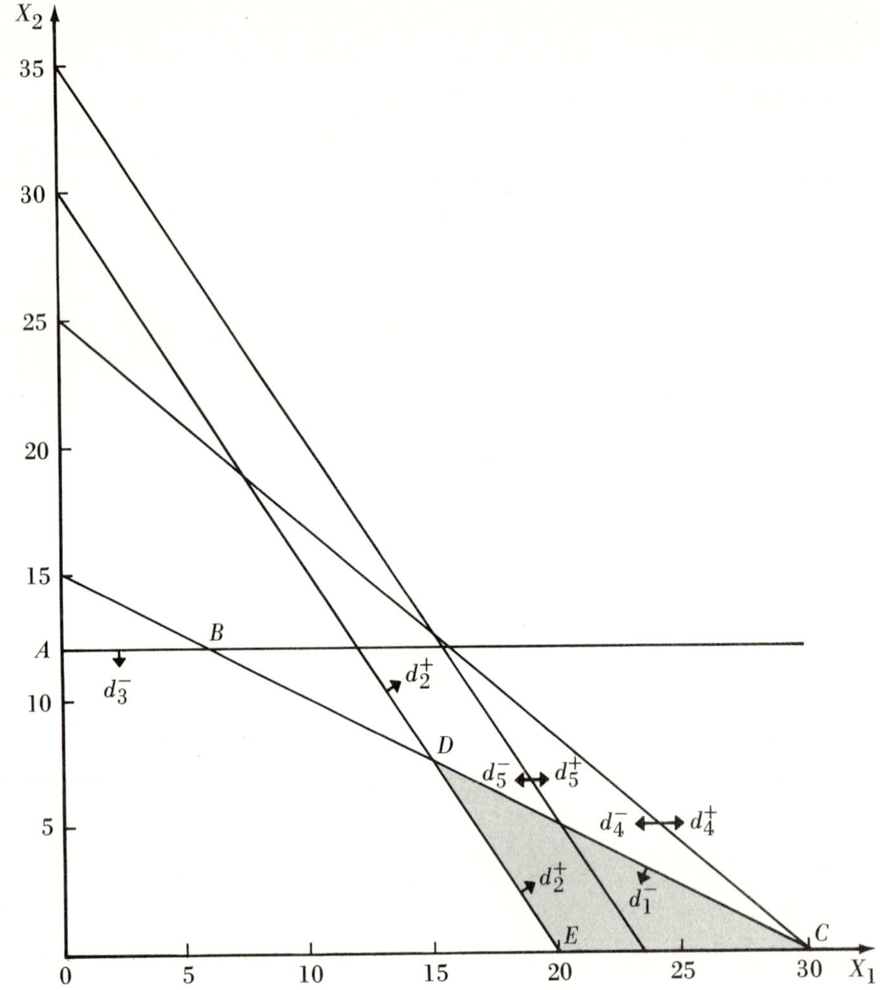

Management's third goal is to utilize all available land resources—that is, to minimize d_1^-, the amount of underutilization of land, to zero. This goal will be achieved on the heavy line segment *DG* shown in Figure 7.3. Any point on this line indicates full utilization of all available land.

Finally, the farmer's lowest-priority goal is to come as close as possible to the profit target of \$1200. Maximization of the profit goal is unattainable, because the profit constraint lies outside *DG*. Our first three goals could not be achieved on any point of the profit line. Since the decision maker does not want to achieve the last goal at the expense of the three higher-priority goals, the desired profit level of \$1200 cannot be achieved within the given decision environment. The farmer must

Figure 7.3
Optimal Solution:
$X_1 = 20$, $X_2 = 5$,
$d_4^- = 150$

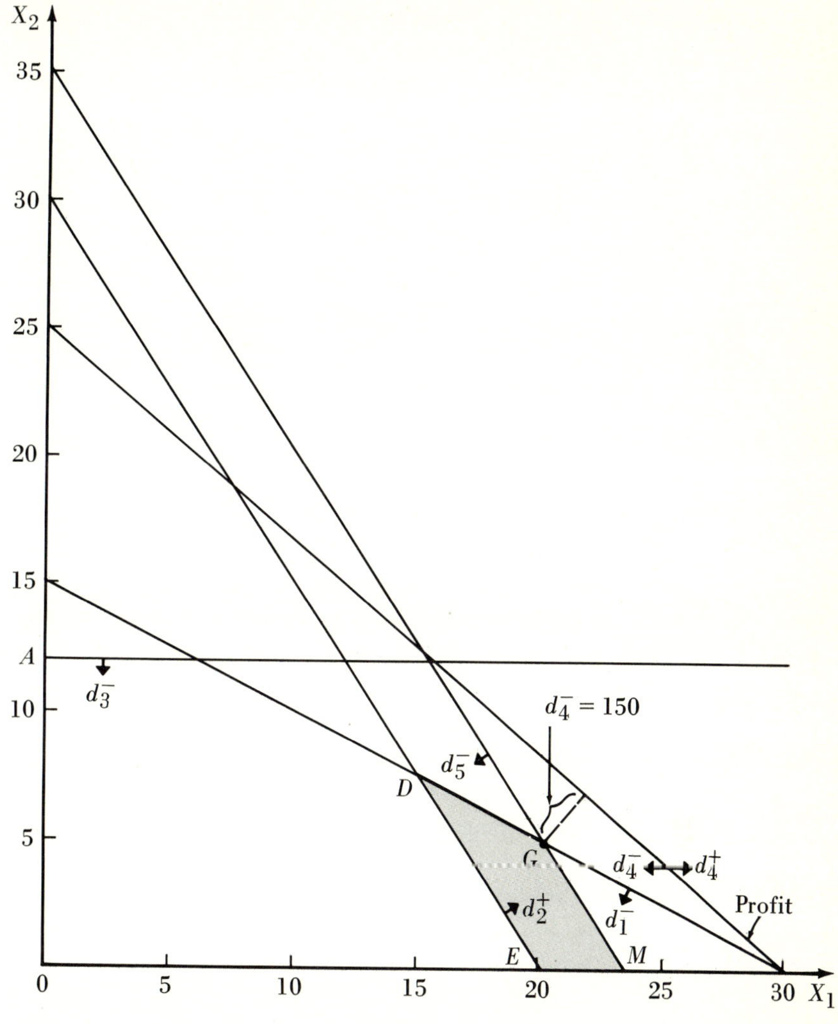

be willing to settle for the largest possible profit below the desired level. Given the feasible solution on line DG, which satisfies our first three goals, the decision maker looks for the point on this line that is closest to the \$1200 profit constraint. By inspection,[2] we see that the minimum distance between the line DG and the profit constraint is the point G in Figure 7.3. The solution at point G is

$$X_1 = 20 \qquad X_2 = 5$$

[2]We find this point by moving the isoprofit line, $X_2 = \frac{Z}{50} - \frac{40}{50} X_1$, toward the origin until the line touches the highest-profit point in the feasible region (line DG). This unique point is point G.

Table 7.3 Goal Attainment for the Potato–Tomato Problem

Priority	Goal	Attainment
P_1	Use all regular working hours.	Achieved
P_2	Limit overtime.	Achieved
P_3	Use all land resources.	Achieved
P_4	Reach target profit.	Not achieved

Thus total profit is (\$40 × 20) + (\$50 × 5) = \$1050.

Note that the total profit falls \$150 short of our desired goal of \$1200. That is, the value of the deviational variable d_4^- is 150, which is measured by a dotted line in Figure 7.3.

Having established these graphs and completed our analysis of each goal of the problem, we conclude that the optimal solution is at point G. The optimal production is 20 units of potatoes and 5 units of tomatoes, yielding a profit of \$1050. Table 7.3 summarizes the results in terms of goal attainment.

We have presented this graphical analysis mainly to illustrate the underlying concept of goal programming. The major drawback of the graphical method is that it is limited to only two structural variables. To solve general problems of goal programming with more than two dimensions, we must use a modified simplex method.

The Modified Simplex Method of Solution

With slight modifications introduced by Lee,[3] the standard simplex method can be used to solve goal programming problems. Consider again the farmer's goal programming model for the potato–tomato problem:

$$\text{Min} \quad Z = P_1d_2^- + P_2d_{21}^+ + P_3d_1^- + P_4d_4^-$$

$$\begin{aligned}
\text{subject to} \quad X_1 + 2X_2 + d_1^- &= 30 \\
3X_1 + 2X_2 + d_2^- - d_2^+ &= 60 \\
2X_2 + d_3^- &= 24 \\
40X_1 + 50X_2 + d_4^- - d_4^+ &= 1200 \\
d_2^+ + d_{21}^- - d_{21}^+ &= 10
\end{aligned}$$

$$\text{and} \quad X_1, X_2, d_1^-, d_2^-, d_3^-, d_4^-, d_{21}^-, d_2^+, d_{21}^+, d_4^+ \geq 0$$

The initial simplex tableau for this problem is presented in Table 7.4. The first five rows of the initial tableau are set up in the same way as

[3] Sang M. Lee, *Goal Programming for Decision Analysis* (Philadelphia: Auerbach Publishers, 1972), Chapters 5–6.

Table 7.4 Initial Simplex Tableau

Row	Z_1	Z_2	Z_3	Z_4	X_1	X_2	d_1^-	d_2^-	d_3^-	d_4^-	d_{21}^-	d_2^+	d_4^+	d_{21}^+	RHS
1					1	2	1								30
2					(3)	2		1				−1			60
3					0	2			1						24
4					0	0					1			−1	10
5					40	50				1			−1		1200
P_4				1	40	50							−1		1200
P_3			1		1	2									30
P_2		1			0	0								−1	0
P_1	1				3	2						−1			60

for a linear programming problem, with the coefficients of the associated variables placed in the appropriate entries. Beneath the dotted line that separates the constraints from the objective function, however, there is no longer just a single row 0 representing the objective function. Instead there are four rows. ***Each row stands for a priority goal level.*** For reasons that will be explained shortly, the highest preemptive priority goal (P_1) is listed on the bottom. Above this we place the lower-ranked goals (P_2, P_3, and so on) in ascending order.

To formulate the IBFS, we need to perform some algebraic operations on each goal so that every basic variable is associated with a unit-coefficient column in the tableau. For example, the first preemptive priority goal of the potato–tomato problem is to minimize the value of d_2^-:

$$\text{Min} \quad Z_1 = d_2^-$$

Since $d_2^- = 60 - 3X_1 - 2X_2 + d_2^+$, this first goal can be rewritten as

$$\text{Min} \quad Z_1 + 3X_1 + 2X_2 - d_2^+ = 60$$

which is presented in the P_1 row of Table 7.4. Similarly, we can enter the other rows corresponding to the other priority goal levels of the problem, shown in Table 7.5 in the order P_2, P_3 and P_4.

Having constructed the initial simplex tableau, we are able to read off the IBFS as follows:

$$d_1^- = 30 \qquad d_4^- = 1200$$
$$d_2^- = 60 \qquad d_{21}^- = 10$$
$$d_3^- = 24$$

The nonbasic solutions are

$$X_1 = X_2 = d_2^+ = d_4^+ = d_{21}^+ = 0$$

The values of the goal attainments are

$$Z_1 = 60 \qquad Z_3 = 30$$
$$Z_2 = 0 \qquad Z_4 = 1200$$

The economic interpretation of the IBFS is interesting. Since the solution is at the point of origin with no production, all resources are idle. Thus all deviation variables that represent the amount of underachievement (d_1^-, d_2^-, d_3^-, d_4^-, and d_{21}^-) are in the solution.

How should we interpret the value of the objective function at IBFS? Remember that in goal programming we are minimizing deviations from the goals. The first goal is to minimize the value of d_2^-, the amount of underutilization of labor. Since no production has taken place, all labor must be idle and the first goal is completely unattained. Thus we have $Z_1\ (= d_2^-) = 60$ in the solution.

With no production no overtime is needed, so d_{21}^+ must be zero. Thus the second goal of minimizing overtime in excess of the desired 10 hours is achieved. This is why $Z_2\ (= d_{21}^+) = 0$ is in the IBFS!

Turning to the third goal, utilization of all land resources, we have $Z_3\ (= d_1^-) = 30$, which is obviously unattained.

Management's last goal is to minimize d_4^- from the desired profit target of \$1200. With no production, the profit goal is bound to be unachieved. No wonder that $Z_4\ (= d_4^-) = \$1200$ is in the solution of the initial tableau!

Once the IBFS is established in the initial tableau, we can apply the standard simplex method for minimization in a linear programming problem, with a few modifications. First, in choosing the pivot column, we must select the largest positive coefficient in the highest-priority level—that is, in the P_1 row. The idea is to satisfy the highest-ranked goal to the fullest extent possible, then move to the second priority, and so forth. In this case, the largest positive element in the P_1 row is 3. Thus we choose the variable X_1 as our pivot column. The economic reasoning behind choosing the column with the largest positive coefficient as the pivot column can be demonstrated by rewriting the P_1 row as an equation:

$$Z_1 = 60 - 3X_1 - 2X_2 - d_2^+$$

If one of the variables on the right-hand side of the equation is chosen as the incoming variable to replace one of the IBFS, X_1 can obviously contribute most to the minimization of the first goal, because it has the negative coefficient with the greatest absolute value.

By following exactly the same standard simplex procedures, we divide the constants on the RHS by the corresponding coefficients in the pivot column (ignoring zero and negative coefficients) and select the row with the smallest ratio as the pivot row. The smallest ratio in this example, 20, occurs in the second row. Accordingly, we select row 2 as the pivot row. The intersection between the pivot row and the pivot column is the pivot element. This element, 3, is circled in Table 7.4.

From this point on, we can follow the standard simplex pivoting procedure discussed in Chapter 3. The pivot column is transformed into a unit coefficient, and we wind up with Table 7.5, which gives the following solution:

$$X_1 = 20 \qquad d_4^- = 400$$
$$d_1^- = 10 \qquad d_{21}^- = 10$$
$$d_3^- = 24$$

and

$$Z_1 = 0 \qquad Z_3 = 10$$
$$Z_2 = 0 \qquad Z_4 = 400$$

Now d_2^- has been replaced by X_1. Interestingly, by producing 20 units of potatoes, the farmer has utilized all regular hours of labor, because it takes 3 hours to produce 1 unit of potatoes ($3 \times 20 = 60$). Hence his

Table 7.5 Second Simplex Tableau

Row	Z_1	Z_2	Z_3	Z_4	X_1	X_2	d_1^-	d_2^-	d_3^-	d_4^-	d_{21}^-	d_2^+	d_4^+	d_{21}^+	RHS
1						($\frac{4}{3}$)	1	$-\frac{1}{3}$				$\frac{1}{3}$			10
2					1	$\frac{2}{3}$		$\frac{1}{3}$				$-\frac{1}{3}$			20
3						2			1						24
4						0					1	1		-1	10
5						$\frac{70}{3}$		$-\frac{40}{3}$		1		$\frac{40}{3}$	-1		400
P_4				1		$\frac{70}{3}$		$-\frac{40}{3}$				$\frac{40}{3}$	-1		400
P_3			1			$\frac{4}{3}$		$-\frac{1}{3}$				$\frac{1}{3}$			10
P_2		1				0		0				0		-1	0
P_1	1					0		-1				0			0

first goal of driving d_2^- to zero is completely fulfilled. Looking at the P_1 row, we see that all elements are nonpositive (except the unit coefficient of Z). This means that the value of the objective function (the first goal in this case) has been optimized.

We move to the next most important goal, P_2. But all the values in the P_2 row are ***nonpositive,*** which means that its objective function in terms of the second goal is fulfilled. Remember that Z_2 ($= d_{21}^+$) $= 0$ and thus is still satisfied.

Moving up directly to the third-priority level, P_3, we select the largest positive coefficient in the P_3 row to determine the pivot column. The second modification of the standard simplex method must be introduced at this point: ***No pivot column can be chosen unless it has zero value(s) on rows for the higher-priority goals.*** In other words, when there is a positive coefficient corresponding to a higher-priority goal, we cannot bring that variable into the solution, because such a positive value might reduce the degree of satisfaction we already attained by satisfying a higher-priority goal. Following this rule, we select the variable X_2 as the pivot column in this problem. It has the most positive coefficient ($\frac{4}{3}$) in the P_3 row, and there are two zero coefficients for the higher-priority goals beneath it.

The pivot row is row 1 in Table 7.5. Accordingly, the intersection of the pivot column and the pivot row determines the pivot element as $\frac{4}{3}$, which is circled in Table 7.5. By converting the pivot column into a unit column, through pivoting we arrive at Table 7.6. Because all coefficients in the P_3 row are nonpositive (ignore the unit value in the Z_3 column), the farmer's third goal is optimized. Also there are three zeros in the RHS of Table 7.6, which indicates that the first three goals are satisfied.

Table 7.6 Third Simplex Tableau

Row	Z_1	Z_2	Z_3	Z_4	X_1	X_2	d_1^-	d_2^-	d_3^-	d_4^-	d_{21}^-	d_2^+	d_4^+	d_{21}^+	RHS
1						1	$\frac{3}{4}$	$-\frac{1}{4}$				$\frac{1}{4}$			$\frac{30}{4}$
2					1		$-\frac{1}{2}$	$\frac{1}{2}$				$-\frac{1}{2}$			15
3							$-\frac{3}{2}$	$\frac{1}{2}$	1			$-\frac{1}{2}$			9
4							0	0			1	(1)		-1	10
5							$-\frac{35}{2}$	$-\frac{15}{2}$		1		$\frac{15}{2}$	-1		225
P_4				1			$-\frac{35}{2}$	$-\frac{15}{2}$				$\frac{15}{2}$	-1		225
P_3			1				-1	0				0			0
P_2		1					0	0				0		-1	0
P_1	1						0	-1				0			0

In attempting to satisfy the fourth goal, we choose the variable d_2^+ as the pivot column. This decision is justified because (1) its associated coefficient, $\frac{15}{2}$, is the largest positive value in the P_4 row, and (2) there are three zeros in the same column on rows corresponding to the three higher-priority goals.

Row 4 is the pivot row, and the circled coefficient, 1, is the pivot element. The next iteration leaves us with Table 7.7. In the P_4 row, there is still a positive value of $\frac{15}{2}$ in the d_{21}^+ column. However, we ***cannot*** use this column as an incoming variable. Why not? Although there is a positive value in the fourth-priority goal under the d_{21}^+ column, there is also a negative value -1 in the same column for the second-priority goal. This means that bringing the variable d_{21}^+ into the solution would improve the value of the fourth goal, but only at the expense of the second. According to the farmer's ranked preferences, his second goal is more important than his fourth goal. Since no trade-off is possible within the given management priority structure, there is no need for further iteration. Table 7.7 represents the optimal solution to the problem. The optimal results are

$$X_1 = 20 \qquad d_3^- = 14$$

$$X_2 = 5 \qquad d_2^+ = 10$$

$$d_4^- = 150$$

which are identical to the results we obtained for the potato–tomato problem by the graphical method.

Table 7.7 Optimal Simplex Tableau

Row	Z_1	Z_2	Z_3	Z_4	X_1	X_2	d_1^-	d_2^-	d_3^-	d_4^-	d_{21}^-	d_2^+	d_4^+	d_{21}^+	RHS
1						1	$\frac{3}{4}$	$-\frac{1}{4}$				$-\frac{1}{4}$		$-\frac{1}{4}$	5
2					1		$-\frac{1}{2}$	$\frac{1}{2}$				$\frac{1}{2}$		$-\frac{1}{2}$	20
3							$-\frac{3}{2}$	$\frac{1}{2}$	1			0		$\frac{1}{2}$	14
4							0	0			1	1		-1	10
5							$-\frac{35}{2}$	$-\frac{15}{2}$		1		$-\frac{15}{2}$		$\frac{15}{2}$	150
P_4				1			$-\frac{35}{2}$	$-\frac{15}{2}$				$-\frac{15}{2}$		$\frac{15}{2}$	150
P_3			1				-1	0						0	0
P_2		1					0	0						-1	0
P_1	1						0	-1						0	0

Goal programming is becoming increasingly important. It has been applied in solving a wide range of problems, including production planning, corporate planning, municipal economic planning, and budgeting and accounting control.[4] Most of the problems to which goal programming models are applied involved many variables. They are too complex to solve by hand, and computers must be used.

7.4 Summary

Goal programming is a special type of linear programming. One of the limitations of linear programming is that its objective function has to be unidimensional—either for maximizing or for minimizing a particular variable. The primary advantage of goal programming is its ability to handle decision problems involving multiple, incompatible goals according to the importance assigned to them. The decision maker strives to achieve some higher-priority goals to the fullest degree possible and accepts a satisfactory level of achievement for some lower-priority goals. In the goal programming procedure, the lower-ranked goals are examined only after the higher-ranked goals have been achieved to the fullest extent possible.

In formulating a goal programming model, we must state all goals in the form of constraints. New variables known as deviational variables are introduced to represent deviations, either underachievement or overachievement, from the desired goals. Whereas the objective criterion is to be maximized or minimized directly in linear programming, in goal programming we always strive indirectly to minimize deviations from the goals. Hence these deviational variables must appear, and they are the only ones in the objective function. All deviational variables must be ranked by preemptive priority factors to reflect their order of importance from most important to least important.

Once the goal programming problem is formulated, the problem can easily be solved by the graphical method if it has only two choice variables. In using graphical techniques to search for the optimal solution, one must analyze each of the goals according to its priority. To solve more complex goal programming problems, one must use the simplex

[4]For applied examples, see Lee, *Goal Programming*. See also the Suggested Readings at the end of this chapter.

algorithm. Two minor modifications are needed when we use the simplex technique to solve goal programming problems.

1. In the simplex tableau, instead of a single row 0 signifying the objective function, there are ***multiple rows***, each row representing one goal of the objective function.
2. In selecting the pivot column, we can introduce the variable with the most positive coefficient into the solution only if the values beneath it are all zero.

The iteration procedures of the simplex method of solving goal programming problems are basically the same as those of ordinary linear programming. The steps are summarized in Figure 7.4.

Exercises

7.1 Identify the major differences between linear programming and goal programming.

7.2 Explain the following terms:
   a. Deviational variable
   b. Priority-ranked goals
   c. Preemptive priority factors

7.3 Explain the difference between cardinal value and ordinal value.

7.4 Exotic Lighting, Inc., makes two kinds of products, desk lamps and floor lamps, for a furniture chain store. The net profit margin from the sale of a desk lamp is \$60; from the sale of a floor lamp it is \$120. The owner of the company has set a goal of achieving a net profit of \$1200 for the next month.
   a. Formulate a goal programming model for the owner of this company.
   b. Find the optimal solution by inspection. Is the solution unique?
   c. Has the firm's goal been achieved? What are the values of the deviational variables?

7.5 Refer to exercise 7.4. Suppose that the order from a chain store for next month is limited to 10 desk lamps and 9 floor lamps.
   a. Formulate a new goal programming model for the company.
   b. Solve it by inspection.
   c. Has the firm's goal been fulfilled? If not, what are the values of the deviational variables?

Figure 7.4
Flow Chart of the Simplex Method of Goal Programming

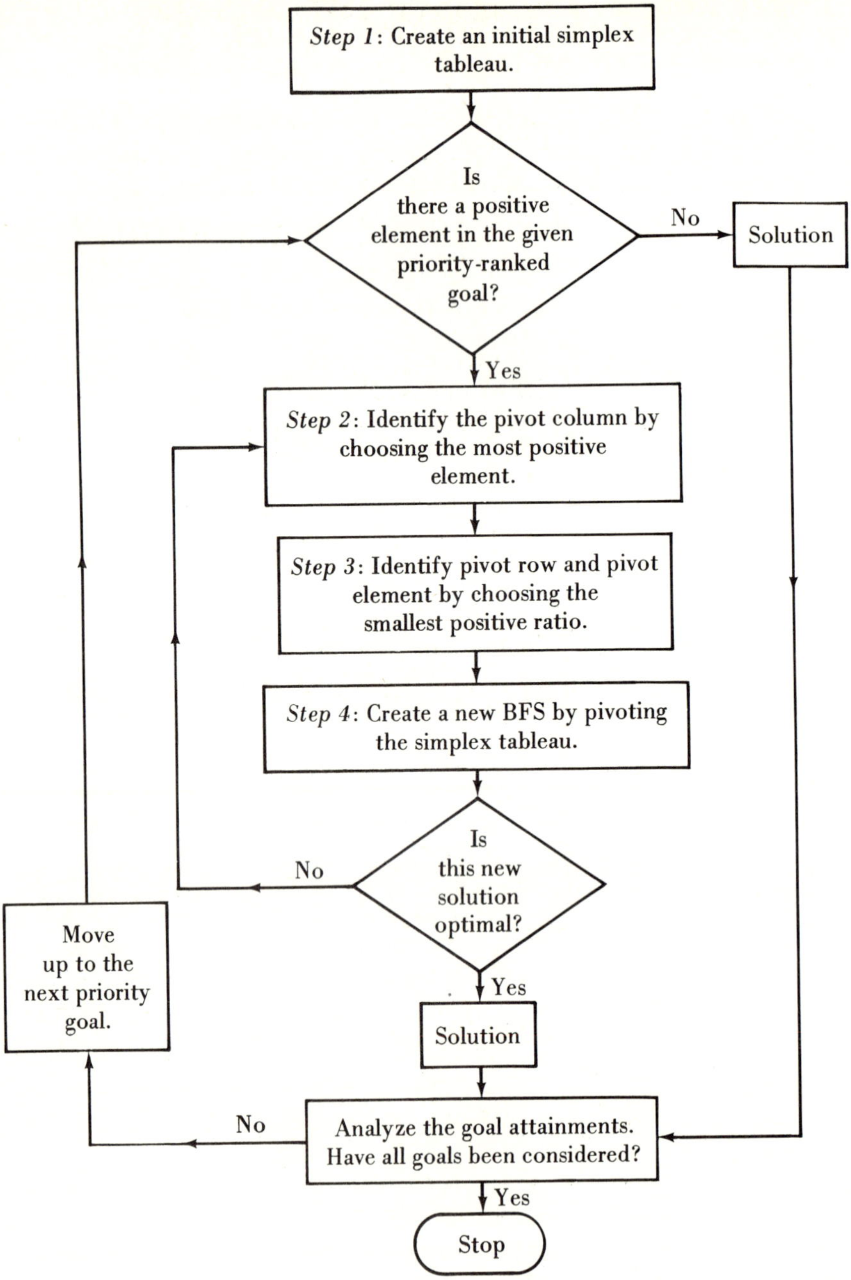

7.6 Refer to exercise 7.4. Suppose that, in addition to achieving his desired monthly profit goal of $1200, the owner also wants to meet a sales goal of 10 desk lamps and 5 floor lamps.

a. Formulate a goal programming model for the owner's decision problem.
b. Solve it by inspection.
c. Were all the goals attained?

7.7 Refer to exercise 7.4. Suppose that producing each unit of desk lamp or floor lamp requires 2 hours of machine time. The maximum production capacity is 40 hours per month. The sales limitation imposed by the furniture chain store is 10 units of desk lamps and 9 units of floor lamps. The owner of the company has listed the following goals in the order of their importance.

First, he wants to avoid underutilization of production capacity.

Second, he likes to maximize sales. And because the net profit margin for floor lamps is twice that for desk lamps, he feels that selling the floor lamp is twice as important as selling the desk lamp.

Third, he wants to minimize the overtime operation of the machine.

a. Formulate a goal programming model of the owner's problem and assign a preemptive priority factor to each of the goals.
b. Solve the model by either graphical analysis or the simplex method.

7.8 "The manufacturing plant of an electronics firm produces television sets, both color and black and white. Production of either a color or a black and white set requires 1 hour in the plant. The plant has a maximum production capacity of 10 hours a week. Because of the limited sales capacity, the maximum numbers of color and black and white sets that can be sold are 6 and 8 sets per week, respectively. The net profit margin from the sale of a color set is $80, whereas it is $40 from a black and white set."[5]

The president of the company wants to achieve the following goals, listed in ordinal rank of importance:

[P_1] Avoid any underutilization of production capacity.

[P_2] Sell as many television sets as possible. Because the net profit margin from the sale of a color set is twice that from a black and white set, she wants to achieve the sales goal for color television sets twice as much as she wants to meet the goal for black and white sets.

[5]This problem is adapted from Sang M. Lee, "Decision Analysis Through Goal Programming," *Decision Sciences*, 2, No. 2 (April 1971), 176. Used by permission.

$[P_3]$ Minimize overtime as much as possible.

a. Formulate a goal programming model.
b. Solve it by the graphical method.
c. Solve it by the simplex method.

7.9 Deborah Lehman is the manager and owner of a retail store that sells jeans and similar items in a suburban mall. Currently, the store employs 5 full-time and 4 part-time workers as sales personnel. The full-time salespeople regularly work 80 hours and the part-time sales people 40 hours per 2-week pay period. Performance records show that the average sales for the full-time salespeople are 5 pairs of jeans per hour, while the part-time personnel sell only 2 pairs per hour. The hourly wage for each full-time salesperson is \$3; it is \$2 for part-time workers. The average profit per item is \$2.50.

A special promotional strategy of the mall leads Lehman to estimate that the sales of her store should reach a target level of 2750 items every two weeks. To cope with the increased sales, clerks are expected to work overtime. For a full-time clerk, the wage rate for overtime is \$3.50 per hour, and for a part-time clerk it is still \$2. However, the owner feels that, to maintain "fresh working attitudes," her full-time employees should not work more than 50 hours of overtime during each pay period. Lehman has established a set of goals and has assigned them ordinal priorities as follows:

1. Reach a sales goal of 2750 items.
2. Limit the overtime of full-time salespeople to 50 hours.
3. Provide job security to sales personnel. Full-time employees, however, are twice as important as part-time employees.
4. Minimize the sum of overtime for both full-time and part-time workers.

a. Formulate and explain the economic meaning of each constraint of the goal programming model.
b. Summarize the complete goal programming model.

7.10 Refer to exercise 7.9. Using a graphical analysis, determine the optimal solution. Indicate which of the goals specified by management have been fully achieved and which have not been fully achieved.

7.11 Solve the goal programming model in exercise 7.9 by the simplex method. Check the results with the solution you obtained by the graphical method in exercise 7.10.

7.12 Table E7.1 shows a simplex tableau for the goal programming problem in exercise 7.9.

Table E7.1
A Simplex Tableau for Lehman's Sales Problem

Row	Z_1	Z_2	Z_3	Z_4	X_1	X_2	d_1^-	d_2^-	d_3^-	d_{21}^-	d_1^+	d_2^+	d_3^+	d_{21}^+	RHS
1							$\frac{1}{2}$	$-\frac{5}{2}$	-1	$-\frac{5}{2}$	$-\frac{1}{2}$		1	$\frac{5}{2}$	90
2					1			1		1				-1	450
3						1	$\frac{1}{2}$	$-\frac{5}{2}$		$-\frac{5}{2}$	$-\frac{1}{2}$			$-\frac{5}{2}$	250
4										1		1		-1	50
P_4				1		$\frac{3}{2}$	$-\frac{15}{2}$	-3		$-\frac{13}{2}$	$-\frac{3}{2}$			$\frac{13}{2}$	320
P_3			1				-2	-1							0
P_2		1												-1	0
P_1	1					-1									0

a. Is this the optimal solution? If so, write down the solution. If not, why not?
b. If this is an optimal solution, analyze the goal attainments.

7.13 How is the fact that a goal is to be achieved exactly incorporated in the objective function of a goal programming model?

7.14 How is the fact that overachievement of a goal should be avoided incorporated in the objective function of a goal programming model?

7.15 Formulate a general goal programming model, defining your terms.

7.16 Massrail is considering adding another train to help serve more people in the downtown area. Train A will run at off-peak hours and train B will run at peak hours. Massrail would like to receive $10,000 in additional revenue for adding either train. The cost to commuters will be $5 per ticket for train A and $10 per ticket for train B. However, there is a limit to the electricity available for the additional train. In particular, 700 units are allowed for train A and 600 units are allowed for train B. The goals of management, in order of priority, are as follows:

[P_1] Achieve the desired profit of $10,000.

[P_2] Avoid using any more electricity than necessary in the operation of the least profitable train, A.

[P_3] Avoid using any more than the permitted 600 units of electricity in the operation of the peak-hour train, B.

a. Formulate a goal programming model for Massrail.
b. Solve it by the simplex method.

7.17 Finest Candy, Inc., is preparing its Easter line of merchandise. The company has decided to produce two types of chocolate rabbits—white chocolate and dark chocolate. Each type of rabbit can be produced at the rate of a dozen per hour. Because the vats are used for other products besides rabbits, the time available for producing Easter inventory is limited to 160 hours per month. The demand for the products and the nature of competition are such that sales are expected to be high, but no greater than 140 units of dark chocolate rabbits and 90 units of white chocolate rabbits. (A unit consists of a dozen rabbits.) White chocolate sells for $50 per unit and dark chocolate sells for $30 per unit.

The president of the company has set the following goals, arranged in order of importance:

[P_1] Avoid underutilization of production capacity.

[P_2] Limit overtime operation to 20 hours per month.

[P_3] Achieve the sales goal of 140 units of dark rabbits and 90 units of white rabbits.

[P_4] Minimize the overtime operation of the plant as much as possible.

Formulate a goal programming model for Finest Candy.

7.18 Table E7.2 shows a simplex tableau for exercise 7.18.

a. Is this an optimal solution? If so, write down the solution. If not, why not?

b. If this is an optimal solution, analyze the goal attainments.

c. In the P_3 row, there is a positive element 3 under the column d_{11}^+. Could we pick column d_{11}^+ as the pivot column? If not, why not?

d. In the P_4 row, could we introduce d_{11}^- into the next solution? If not, why not?

7.19 Donald Guitars Company is a musical instrument store located in Oakland, California. Donald specializes in the sale of guitars and accessories, and he would like to optimize sales of his two main guitar lines, Gibson and Fender, for the coming month. The Gibson model sells for an average of $450 per unit, with a contribution to profit of $75. The Fender line sells for an average of $375 per unit, with a contribution to profit of $50. Donald has one full-time salesperson working for him, whose job consists of demonstrating guitars to the customers. Donald has calculated that the average time needed to sell the guitars is 30 minutes for the Gibson and 20 minutes for the Fender.

Before it can sell a certain kind of guitar, a music store must be awarded the dealership by the guitar manufacturer. The guitar companies that authorize these dealerships set minimum sales standards that the store must meet to earn the right to renew a dealership. Renewals are reviewed every 6 months. The minimum monthly sales level

Table E7.2
A Simplex Tableau for Finest Candy's Problem

Row	Z_1	Z_2	Z_3	Z_4	X_1	X_2	d_1^-	d_2^-	d_3^-	d_{11}^-	d_1^+	d_{11}^+	RHS
1						1	1	−1	0	1	0	−1	40
2					1		0	1	0	0	0	0	140
3							−1	1	1	−1	0	1	50
4							0	0	0	1	1	−1	20
P_4				1			0	0	0	11	0	−1	20
P_3			1				−3	−2	0	−3	0	3	150
P_2		1					0	0	0	0	0	−1	0
P_1	1						−1	0	0	0	0	0	0

for Gibson is 75 guitars, whereas the Fender standard is slightly lower at 50 guitars.

Donald has set the following goals, listed in order of their importance, in his quest to optimize sales of the two guitar lines:

[P_1] Meet the monthly minimums required to retain both dealerships.
[P_2] Maximize his salesperson's work.
[P_3] Meet a sales goal of 250 guitars.
[P_4] Maximize the store's profits.

Formulate a goal programming model for the store.

7.20 Consider your analysis of the goal attainments in exercise 7.19. If Donald feels that profit maximization is more important than achieving a certain sales level, what would he do?

7.21 St. Mary's Hospital is located in a suburb of a large city on the West Coast. Patient care in the hospital is divided into nursing units, each headed by a nursing supervisor and each having a 30-bed capacity. The nursing unit employs two types of registered nurses. The first are the full-time equivalent nurses (FTENs) who are employed by the hospital. The FTENs work a 40-hour week and are paid $5 per hour.

By regulation of the Public Health Service, the hospital is required to provide a minimum of 4 hours of nursing care per day to each patient. When the number of patients in the unit is too great for the FTENs to provide this service, the nursing supervisor must hire registry nurses from an independent agency. The cost to the hospital for this outside help is $7 per hour.

On the basis of time-series data, the nursing supervisor has forecast the expected number of patients for each of the next four weeks as follows:

Week	1	2	3	4
Expected number of patients	20	25	27	16

At the beginning of each four-week period, the nursing supervisor must determine the number of FTENs the unit needs. Once set, this number remains constant for the period.

The supervisor has set the following multiple goals, listed in ordinal importance, to guide her in determining the optimal number of FTENs:

[P_1] Provide at least the minimum Public Health Service standard of 4 hours of care per patient per day.

[P_2] Minimize the cost of nursing care.

[P_3] Maximize the time of the FTENs above 4 hours per patient per day.

a. Formulate and explain the economic meaning of each constraint of the goal programming model.
b. Write down the complete goal programming model.

Hint: (1) Define Y = 1 FTEN at 40 hours per week

X_i = number of registry nurse hours in the ith week for $i = 1, 2, 3, 4$

(2) The cost constraint is set equal to an arbitrary value of \$2000.

7.22 From your own observation or imagination, construct a problem wherein you think goal programming would be applicable. Formulate a goal programming model.

Suggested Readings

Auerbach, S., J. Ecker, and W. Wallace. "A Note: Hidden Nonlinearities in the Application of Goal Programming." *Management Science*, 22, No. 8 (April 1976).

Bailey, W. Boe, and T. Schnack. "The Audit Staff Assignment Problem: A Comment." *Accounting Review* (July 1974).

Balintfy, Joseph L. "A Mathematical Programming System for Food Management Applications." *Interfaces,* 6, No. 1 (November 1975).

Burton, Johnathan. *A Model Using Goal Programming in Elementary School Administration.* Philadelphia, Pa.: ORSA/TIMS, April 1976.

Charnes A., and W. W. Cooper. *Management Models and Industrial Applications of Linear Programming.* Vol. I. New York: Wiley, 1961.

———. "A Goal Programming Model for Media Planning." *Management Science,* 14, No. 8 (April 1968), 423–430.

———. "An Extended Goal Programming Model for Manpower Planning." Management Science Research Paper No. 188. Carnegie-Mellon University, June 1969.

Charnes, A., C. Colantoni, W. Cooper, and K. Kortanek. "Economic, Social, and Enterprise Accounting and Mathematical Models." *The Accounting Review* (January 1972).

Chesser, Dalton L., and James W. Rozendaal. "Increasing Effectiveness." *Federal Home Loan Bank Board Journal* (T-HLBB), August 1975.

Dyer, J. "Interactive Goal Programming." *Management Science,* 19, No. 1, (September 1972).

Goodman, D. "A Goal Programming Approach to Aggregate Planning of Production and Work Force." *Management Science,* 20, No. 12 (August 1974).

Ignizio, J. P. *Goal Programming and Extensions.* Lexington, Mass.: D.C. Heath, 1976.

Ijiri, Juji. *Management Goals and Accounting Control.* Amsterdam, Netherlands: North-Holland Publishing Company, 1965.

Kornbluth, J. S. "A Survey of Goal Programming." *Omega* (April 1973).

———. "Accounting in Multiple Objective Linear Programming." *The Accounting Review* (April 1974).

Lee, Sang M. *Goal Programming for Decision Analysis.* Philadelphia: Auerbach Publishers, 1972.

———. "Decision Analysis Through Goal Programming." *Decision Sciences,* 2, No. 2 (April 1971) and No. 3 (July 1971).

Lee, Sang M., and Laurence J. Moore. "Optimizing University Admissions Planning." *Decision Sciences,* 5, No. 3 (July 1974).

Lee, Sang M., and R. Nicely. "Goal Programming for Marketing Decisions: A Case Study." *Journal of Marketing,* 38 (January 1974).

Lee, Sang M., O. E. Park, and S. C. Economides. "Resource Planning for Multiple Projects." *Decision Sciences,* 9, No. 1 (January 1978).

Sartoris, William L., and M. L. Spruill. "Goal Programming and Working Capital Management." *Financial Management,* 3, No. 1 (Spring 1974).

Schroeder, R. "Resource Planning in University Management by Goal Programming." *Operations Research,* 22, No. 4 (July–August 1974).

Welam, U. "Comments on Goal Programming for Aggregate Planning." *Management Science,* 22, No. 6 (February 1976).

8

Quadratic Programming

The linear programming (LP) model is defined as the optimization of a ***linear*** objective function, subject to a set of linear constraints. This chapter presents a ***quadratic programming (QP) model***, which is defined as the optimization of a ***quadratic*** objective function (instead of being linear, the objective function is a second-degree polynomial function), subject to a set of linear constraints. This special case of nonlinear analysis is important for at least two reasons.

1. Since most industries operate in an imperfect market, the horizontal demand curve—constant value weights associated with the various decision variables of an LP objective function—is often not realistic. A downward-sloping linear demand curve may be more representative, so the quadratic objective function is preferable.[1]
2. With the contributions made by Wolfe,[2] Hutton,[3] and Takayama and Judge,[4] QP problems can be modeled into a primal–dual formulation that can be solved by standard linear programming routines.

[1]There have been wide applications of QP. For an earlier application of QP in an empirical study, see J. C. Hsiao and M. W. Kottke, *Spatial Equilibrium Analysis of the Dairy Industry in the Northeast Region—An Application of Quadratic Programming*, Agricultural Experiment Station, Bulletin 405 (Storrs, Conn.: The University of Connecticut, July 1968). For application to a multidivision firm problem, see J. C. Hsiao, "Equilibrium Analysis via Quadratic Programming and Decentralized Decision Making in a Multidivision Firm." In *Recent Developments in Decision Sciences*, ed. David Murphy. N.E. Conference of the American Institute of Decision Sciences (Boston, Mass.: Boston College, May 1972). See also Jerome E. Hass, "Transfer Pricing in a Centralized Firm," *Management Science*, 14, No. 6 (February 1968). For application to risk problems, see R. J. Freund, "The Introduction of Risk into a Programming Model," *Econometrica*, 24, July 1956.

[2]P. Wolfe, "The Simplex Method for Quadratic Programming," *Econometrica*, 27, 1959.

[3]Robert Hutton, *An Introduction to Quadratic Programming*, Agricultural Experi-

The purpose of this chapter is to illustrate the application of the QP primal–dual formulation and its extension to a more complicated QP problem without becoming engrossed in sophisticated mathematical detail. Our presentation of this technique should be understandable to anyone with a working knowledge of LP. Let's look at a simple numerical example to demonstrate the computations involved.

8.1 The LP Primal–Dual Model

First, we examine the logic of formulating the LP ***primal–dual*** model. The primal of an LP problem can be specified as

$$\text{Max} \quad Z_X = C_1X_1 + C_2X_2 \tag{8.1}$$

subject to
$$a_{11}X_1 + a_{12}X_2 \leq b_1$$
and
$$X_1 \geq 0, X_2 \geq 0 \tag{8.2}$$

The corresponding dual is

$$\text{Min} \quad Z_Y = b_1Y_1 \tag{8.3}$$

subject to
$$a_{11}Y_1 \geq C_1$$
$$a_{12}Y_1 \geq C_2 \tag{8.4}$$
and
$$Y_1 \geq 0$$

Now we define a new primal–dual objective function subject to the constraints in ***both*** the primal and the dual:

$$\text{Max} \quad Z_{X,Y} = C_1X_1 + C_2X_2 - b_1Y_1 \tag{8.5}$$

subject to
$$a_{11}X_1 + a_{12}X_2 + S_1 = b_1$$
$$a_{11}Y_1 - V_1 = C_1 \tag{8.6}$$
$$a_{12}Y_1 - V_2 = C_2$$
and
$$X_1, X_2, S_1, Y_1, V_1, V_2 \geq 0$$

---

ment Station, A. E. & R. S. No. 41 (University Park, Pa.: The Pennsylvania State University, June 1963).

[4]T. Takayama and G. G. Judge, "Equilibrium Among Spatially Separated Markets: A Reformulation," *Econometrica*, 32, No. 4 (October 1964).

Table 8.1 Primal–Dual Simplex Tableau in an LP Format

Row	Z	X_1	X_2	S_1	Y_1	V_1	V_2	T_1	T_2	RHS
1	0	a_{11}	a_{12}	1						b_1
2	0				a_{11}	-1		1		C_1
3	0				a_{12}		-1		1	C_2
0	1	0	0	0	0	0	0	M	M	0

where S_1 is a slack variable, and V_1 and V_2 are surplus (or disposal) activities corresponding to the primal and dual constraints, respectively. By the fundamental duality theorem discussed in Chapter 4, the primal–dual objective function in (8.5) is bounded from above by zero. The LP simplex tableau corresponding to the primal–dual formulation in (8.5) and (8.6) is shown in Table 8.1, where T_1 and T_2 are artificial variables and M ***(big M)*** is a large, arbitrary constant.

Clearly, the primal–dual simplex tableau consists simply of the chain of primal and dual constraints. Note that the column entries for Y_1 are the same as X_1 and X_2 in the first row of the primal. All value weights in ***both*** the primal and the dual objective functions are incorporated or ***internalized*** as elements in the right-hand side (RHS). Thus each coefficient corresponding to a variable in the objective function is zero, as shown in row 0 of Table 8.1. We deduced from (8.5) that the optimal value of the objective function in the primal–dual model is zero. As we know, the optimal solution of a given primal (or dual) program provides enough information for us to solve its counterpart dual (or primal) program. By solving the simple LP problem stated in (8.1) and (8.2), we simultaneously arrive at all dual information contained in (8.3) and (8.4). There is really no reason to discuss the LP primal–dual model, as we did in (8.5) and (8.6), and the presentation of the primal–dual simplex tableau is unnecessary. We offer the LP primal–dual format here mainly to introduce the following QP primal–dual formulation.

8.2 The QP Primal–Dual Model

Very often the value weights assigned to decision variables in the objective function are not predetermined constants. For example, suppose the C_1 in (8.1) is a linear, demand function of X_1. That is,

$$C_1 = e_1 - d_1X_1 \qquad e_1, d_1 \geq 0 \tag{8.7}$$

Then e_1 and d_1 are the C_1 intercept and the slope, respectively, for a linear demand relation between C_1 and X_1. As a result, the objective function in (8.1) assumes the following quadratic form:

$$\text{Max} \quad Z_X = e_1X_1 - d_1X_1^2 + C_2X_2 \tag{8.8}$$

subject to $\quad a_{11}X_1 + a_{12}X_2 \leq b_1$

and $\quad X_1 \geq 0, X_2 \geq 0 \quad$ (8.9)

Given the quadratic problem stated in (8.8) and (8.9), our task is to convert it into an LP problem. To do this, we apply the reducibility theorem without proof. Following the contribution made by Takayama and Judge, we know that, if the QP problem has an optimum solution at X_1, the following primal LP problem has a solution set at a point where $X_1 = X_1^*$:

$$\text{Max} \quad Z_X = (e_1 - 2d_1X_1^*)\,X_1 + C_2X_2 \tag{8.10}$$

subject to $\quad a_{11}X_1 + a_{12}X_2 \leq b_1$

and $\quad X_1 \geq 0, X_2 \geq 0 \quad$ (8.11)

The dual problem corresponding to (8.10) and (8.11) is specified as follows:

$$\text{Min} \quad Z_Y = b_1Y_1 \tag{8.12}$$

subject to $\quad a_{11}Y_1 \geq e_1 - 2d_1X_1^*$

$\quad a_{12}Y_1 \geq C_2 \quad$ (8.13)

and $\quad Y_1 \geq 0$

Thus it is evident that the linear primal–dual problem corresponding to (8.10) through (8.13) must be stated as follows:

$$\text{Max} \quad Z_{XY} = (e_1 - 2d_1X_1^*)\,X_1 + C_2X_2 - b_1Y_1 \tag{8.14}$$

subject to

$$a_{11}X_1 + a_{12}X_2 + S_1 = b_1 \tag{8.15}$$

$$a_{11}Y_1 - V_1 = e_1 - 2d_1X_1^* \tag{8.16}$$

$$a_{12}Y_1 - V_2 = C_2 \tag{8.17}$$

and

$$X_1, X_2, Y_1, S_1, V_1, V_2 \geq 0 \tag{8.18}$$

where S_1 and V_1, V_2 are disposal variables for the primal and the dual, respectively. By the duality theorem, the objective function (8.14) is bounded from above by zero. This means that the value of the primal must equal the value of the dual ***at the optimum point.*** Therefore, ***the optimal value of the objective function in the LP primal–dual formulation of the problem is zero*** when X_1 equals X_1^*, when X_2 equals X_2^*, and when Y_1 equals Y_1^*.

If we replace X_1^* with X_1 in (8.10), however, the objective function (8.14) is again bounded from above by zero. By replacing X^* with X in (8.14) and (8.16), we cause the corresponding QP model, (8.14) through (8.18), to become (8.14′) through (8.18′):

$$\text{Max} \quad Z_{X,Y} = (e_1 - 2d_1X_1)\,X_1 + C_2X_2 - b_1Y_1 \tag{8.14′}$$

subject to

$$a_{11}X_1 + a_{12}X_2 + S_1 = b_1 \tag{8.15′}$$

$$a_{11}Y_1 - V_1 = e_1 - 2d_1X_1$$

or

$$2d_1X_1 + a_{11}Y_1 - V_1 = e_1 \tag{8.16′}$$

$$a_{12}Y_1 - V_2 = C_2 \tag{8.17′}$$

and

$$X_1, X_2, Y_1, V_1, V_2 \geq 0 \tag{8.18′}$$

Consequently, the QP problem of (8.8) and (8.9) becomes the primal–dual model specified in (8.14′) through (8.18′). The corresponding QP simplex tableau is presented in Table 8.2.

In this simplex tableau, the variables V_1 and V_2 that serve as surplus or disposal activities in the dual are said to be the ***counterparts*** (that is, the complements) of X_1 and X_2 in the primal. These counterpart relationships between primal variables X_1 and X_2 and their corresponding dual disposal variables V_1 and V_2 are linked by solid arrows in Table 8.2. The variable S_1, which served as a slack or disposal variable in the primal, is the counterpart of Y_1 in the dual. This counterpart relationship is indicated by a broken-line arrow in Table 8.2.

Table 8.2 Primal–Dual Simplex Tableau in a QP Format (One Quadratic Term)

Row	Z	X_1	X_2	S_1	Y_1	V_1	V_2	T_1	T_2	RHS
		Counterpart Relationships								
1	0	a_{11}	a_{12}	1						b_1
2	0	$2d_1$			a_{11}	-1		1		e_1
3	0				a_{12}		-1		1	C_2
0	1	0	0	0	0	0	0	M	M	0

By virtue of the equilibrium theorem (Chapter 4), which states the so-called ***complementary slackness*** relationship between the decision variables X_1 and X_2 in the primal and the surplus or disposal variables V_1 and V_2 in the dual, the following conditions exist:

(i) $X_jV_j = 0 \quad \text{for } j = 1, 2$

(ii) $S_1Y_1 = 0$

This complementary slackness relationship between the primal and the dual suggests Wolfe's algorithm[5] of the simplex method for QP. Wolfe's basic criterion, as it applies to this problem, may be stated as follows:

(i′) If X_j is in the basis, do not admit V_j, and vice versa.

(ii′) If S_1 is in the basis, do not admit Y_1, and vice versa.

That is, in obtaining solutions for the QP primal–dual model, we cannot put both a decision variable and its counterpart in the basic solution at nonzero levels at the same time. A simple numerical example that shows the modified simplex calculation will be presented later in this chapter.

8.3 Comparisons Between the LP and QP Simplex Tableaux and an Economic Interpretation

Comparisons Between the LP and QP Simplex Tableaux

As indicated earlier, we include LP primal–dual simplex tableaux in our discussion because they can enhance our understanding of the QP primal–dual model. But now we must consider the similarities and differences between Tables 8.1 and 8.2. Both tables contain programs of the primal and the dual. The simplex tableaux are arranged exactly the same. Each program appropriately combines the primal ***and*** the dual. Since the value weights associated with all variables in the primal–dual formulation have been internalized in the RHS, the values of the coefficients in the objective function (row 0) are all zero. To formulate the initial basis, we include artificial variables in both tableaux. Consequently, the ***big M*** coefficients are assigned to the artificial variable column of row 0.

[5]See P. Wolfe, "The Simplex Method."

In this problem, the only difference between the LP and the QP simplex tableaux lies in the second row. Note that the element $2d_1$ appears in the row 2, X_1 column of Table 8.2, whereas this position was empty in Table 8.1. Also, the element in the RHS of row 2 in Table 8.2 is e_1 instead of the C_1 that we find in Table 8.1. Given that X_1 has a value-weight expression of $(e_1 - d_1X_1)$ in the QP model, instead of C_1 as in the LP model, a new term is to be added in the X_1 column in the dual constraint corresponding to X_1. The new term is the coefficient of X_1 (d_1 in the value-weight expression) multiplied by 2 (see equation 8.16′). Thus the term $2d_1$ is added in the X_1 column and the corresponding dual equation (row). The sign of $2d_1$ is determined by mathematical logic as well as the economic reasoning discussed in the next section.

Economic Interpretation of the QP Tableau

Let us turn our attention to the first column, X_1, of the two tableaux. What is the economic implication of the ***extra*** element $2d_1$ in the QP simplex tableau? In the QP model the value weight for X_1 is no longer a predetermined constant C_1, as in the LP model, but rather a linear function of X_1—namely, $C_1 = e_1 - d_1X_1$. Thus the value weight C_1 is inversely related to the decision variable X_1 in the QP model. The value-weight expression C_1 itself is linear, but its contribution to the objective function for each unit of X_1 produced is $(e_1 - d_1X_1)X_1$ or $e_1X_1 - d_1X_1^2$. Therefore, the original quadratic objective function in (8.8) shows clearly that the contribution in terms of ***marginal value*** for each additional unit of X_1 to the value of the objective function is $e_1 - 2d_1X_1$.[6]

Economically, the change in sign of $2d_1$ from minus to plus under the primal activity X_1 means that, as the X_1 activity increases, additional resources are required from the dual activity Y_1. The unit contribution of the X_1 activity to the objective function increases, but at a ***decreasing rate.*** This rate, of course, is $2d_1$, and it is measured in this case by the dual counterpart Y_1.

Conversely, should C_1 be in a direct relationship with X_1 (for example, $C_1 = e_1 + d_1X_1$), then the coefficient $2d_1$ would have entered. The negative element $2d_1$ under the primal activity X_1 would mean that, as the X_1 activity increases, resources are ***produced*** that correspond to the dual activity Y_1. The unit contribution of the X_1 activity to the objective function (for example, $Z = eX_1 + d_1X_1^2 + C_2X_2$) would increase, but at an ***increasing rate.*** This rate would be $2d_1$, and it would be measured by the dual counterpart Y_1.

[6]Given the quadratic objective function $Z = e_1X_1 - d_1X_1^2 + C_2X_2$, the derivative of the expression with respect to X_1 is $(e_1 - 2d_1X_1)$.

8.4 Extension to More Complex Quadratic Problems

More Than One Quadratic Decision Variable

The model we have discussed so far involves only one decision variable that has a quadratic term. Suppose now that the value weight of X_2 were also a linear function of X_2:

$$C_2 = e_2 - d_2X_2$$

Then the corresponding objective function would be

$$\text{Max} \quad Z_X = e_1X_1 - d_1X_1^2 + e_2X_2 - d_2X_2^2$$

Consequently, the term $2d_2$ would appear in the X_2 column in the third row of Table 8.3. Likewise, the element C_2 in the RHS of Table 8.2 would be replaced by e_2, as shown in Table 8.3.

General Case

We are ready to proceed to a more complex QP problem. The addition of more decision variables and constraints can be handled by the same rules we have already outlined in this chapter. Table 8.4 presents a general case of n decision variables with quadratic terms and m constraints in the primal. The general pattern of Table 8.4 is that the ***column*** entries for Y_1, for instance, are the same as the X_{1j} (for $j = 1, 2, \ldots, n$) entries in the ***first row of the primal.*** The same relationship holds for coefficients of the Y_2 column and for X_{2j} in row 2 of the primal.

Note that there are n decision variables with quadratic terms, m constraints, and m slack variables in the primal. Therefore, there are n rows and $(m + n)$ columns (m dual variables plus n dual surplus variables) in the dual (see Table 8.4). Thus the dimensions for the primal–dual QP model (primal–dual combined) is as follows:

$$\left.\underbrace{m}_{\substack{\text{number of rows}\\ \text{from primal}}} + \underbrace{n}_{\substack{\text{number of rows}\\ \text{from dual}}}\right\} \text{rows, or } (m + n) \text{ rows}$$

$$\left.\underbrace{(n + m)}_{\substack{\text{number of}\\ \text{columns}\\ \text{from primal}}} \quad \underbrace{(m + n)}_{\substack{\text{number of}\\ \text{columns}\\ \text{from dual}}}\right\} \text{columns, or } 2(m + n) \text{ columns}$$

Table 8.3
Primal–Dual Simplex Tableau in a QP Format (Two Quadratic Terms)

Row	Z	X_1	X_2	S_1	Y_1	V_1	V_2	T_1	T_2	RHS
1	0	a_{11}	a_{12}	1						b_1
2	0	$2d_1$			a_{11}	-1		1		e_1
3	0		$2d_2$		a_{12}		-1		1	e_2
0	1	0	0	0	0	0	0	M	M	0

For clarity, the artificial variables are excluded from Table 8.4. If artificial variables were included, then ***big M*** coefficients would have been assigned in the objective function (row 0) of Table 8.4. The sign of the entry $2d_j$ (for $j = 1, 2, \ldots, n$), whether positive or negative, is determined by the sign of the coefficients of the associated quadratic term. If the quadratic term has a negative coefficient, the entry $2d_j$ is positive; otherwise, it is negative. The elements e_j in the RHS of Table 8.4 would also be zero if the constant term e associated with the value weight (for example, $C = e - dX$) if X were zero.

8.5 A Numerical Example

A Quadratic Problem in the Primal–Dual Model

Consider the following decision problem faced by Sparta Company. The company produces two types of clothing, X_1 and X_2. The profit (value weight) per unit of X_2 is \$15, but the value weight for the product X_1 is inversely related to the amount of X_1 produced. This relationship is estimated as $(4 - 2X_1)$. The only constraint for the company is capital, which is limited to 80 units. The goal of Sparta Company is to maximize profits. This problem translates into the following quadratic programming model:

$$\text{Max } Z_X = (4 - 2X_1)X_1 + 15X_2 \quad \text{or} \quad \text{Max } Z_X = 4X_1 - 2X_1^2 + 15X_2$$

$$\text{subject to} \qquad X_1 + 2X_2 \geq 80$$

$$X_1 \geq 0,\ X_2 \geq 0$$

This quadratic problem can now directly apply to the primal–dual formulation presented in Table 8.2, and tableau I in Table 8.5 is the simplex tableau of this quadratic problem. The large ***big M*** number is chosen to be 100, as shown in row 0 under the artificial variables of T_1 and T_2.

Table 8.4 Primal–Dual Simplex Tableau in a QP Format: General Case with n Decision Variables and m Constraints

Row	Z	X_1	X_2	$\cdots$	X_n	S_1	S_2	$\cdots$	S_m	Y_1	Y_2	$\cdots$	Y_m	V_1	V_2	$\cdots$	V_n	RHS
1	0	a_{11}	a_{12}	$\cdots$	a_{1n}	1												b_1
2	0	a_{21}	a_{22}	$\cdots$	a_{2n}		1											b_2
·		·	·		·			·										·
·		·	·		·			·										·
·		·	·		·			·										·
m	0	a_{m1}	a_{m2}	$\cdots$	a_{mn}				1									b_m
$m + 1$	0	$\pm 2d_1$								a_{11}	a_{21}	$\cdots$	a_{m1}	-1				e_1
$m -+ 2$			$\pm 2d_2$							a_{12}	a_{22}	$\cdots$	a_{m2}		-1			e_2
·				·						·	·		·			·		·
·				·						·	·		·			·		·
·				·						·	·		·			·		·
$m + n$	0				$\pm 2d_n$					a_{1n}	a_{2n}	$\cdots$	a_{mn}				-1	e_n
0	1	0	0	$\cdots$	0	0	0	$\cdots$	0	0	0	$\cdots$	0	0	0	$\cdots$	0	0

Table 8.5
Simplex Tableaux of the Sparta Company Problem

	Row	Z	X_1	X_2	S_1	Y_1	V_1	V_2	T_1	T_2	RHS
I	1	0	1	2	1						80
	2	0	4			1	−1		1		4
	3	0				2		−1		1	15
	0	1	0	0	0	0	0	0	100	100	0
II	1	0	1	2	1				0	0	80
	2	0	(4)		0	1	−1		1	0	4
	3	0			0	2		−1	0	1	15
	0	1	−400	0	0	−300	100	100	0	0	−1900
III	1	0	0	(2)	1	$-\frac{1}{4}$	$\frac{1}{4}$	0	$-\frac{1}{4}$	0	79
	2	0	1		0	($\frac{1}{4}$)	$-\frac{1}{4}$		$\frac{1}{4}$	0	1
	3	0	0		0	2		−1		1	15
	0	1	0	0	0	−200	0	100	100	0	−1500
IV	1	0	0	1	$\frac{1}{2}$	$\frac{1}{8}$	$\frac{1}{8}$	0	$-\frac{1}{8}$	0	$\frac{79}{2}$
	2	0	1	0	0	($\frac{1}{4}$)	$-\frac{1}{4}$	0	$\frac{1}{4}$	0	1
	3	0		0	0	2	0	−1	0	1	15
	0	1	0	0	0	−200	0	100	100	0	−1500
V	1	0	$\frac{1}{2}$	1	$\frac{1}{2}$	0	0	0	0	0	40
	2	0	4	0	0	1	−1	0	1	0	4
	3	0	−8	0	0	0	(2)	−1	2	1	7
	0	1	800	0	0	0	−200	100	300	0	−700
VI	1	0	$\frac{1}{2}$	1	$\frac{1}{2}$	0	0	0	0	0	40
	2	0	0	0	0	1	0	$-\frac{1}{2}$	1	1	7.5
	3	0	−4	0	0	0	1	$-\frac{1}{2}$	1	1	3.5
	0	1	0	0	0	0	0	0	500	200	0

Note that an IBFS (initial basic feasible solution) is not yet available in tableau I, because the T_1 and T_2 columns have not been converted into unit columns. By adding $-100X$ (row 2 plus row 3) to row 0 in tableau I, we convert the T_1 and T_2 columns into unit columns, as shown in tableau II. We are now able to read off the IBFS from tableau II. It is $S_1 = 80$, $T_1 = 4$, $T_2 = 15$. Nonbasic variables are $X_1 = X_2 = Y_1 = V_1 = V_2 = 0$, and $Z = -1900$.

The Simplex Solution The simplex method can now be applied in substantially the same way, except for two modifications suggested by Wolfe (see Section 8.3). Since this is a maximization problem, the X_1 column that has the most negative coefficient in row 0 of tableau II is chosen as the pivot column. A straight application of the simplex method leads to simplex tableau III of Table 8.5.

A problem arises with the next iteration. According to the simplex method, we could select Y_1 as the incoming variable (pivot column) in the next basis, because the most negative element, -200, occurs in row 0 of the Y_1 column of tableau III. Furthermore, the entry $\frac{1}{4}$ (dashed circle) could be circled as the pivot element. Y_1 is the counterpart of S_1, however, and S_1 is currently in the basis, so Wolfe's criterion does not allow us to admit its counterpart Y_1.

Instead, we select X_2 by inspection (its counterpart, V_2, is not currently in the basis) as the incoming variable. The entry 2, circled in tableau III, is selected as the pivot element. Repeating the pivoting procedures, we obtain the results shown in tableau IV. But note that, due to the fact that the profit contribution coefficient in row 0 of the X_2 column is zero (see tableau III), this iteration achieves no improvement in the value of the objective function.

Examining tableau VI, we find that S_1 is *not* in the basis, so we may admit its counterpart Y_1 (with the most negative coefficient, -200, in row 0) to the next basis. The subsequent steps are nothing but the simplex algorithm repeated. Because all coefficients in row 0 of the simplex tableau are nonnegative, no further iteration is needed. The final optimal solution is shown in tableau VI. It is

$$X_2 = 40,\ Y_1 = 7.5,\ V_1 = 3.5 \qquad (X_1 = S_1 = V_2 = T_1 = T_2 = 0)$$

It is interesting to note that, after tableau II, each successive tableau (except tableau IV for the reason we mentioned before) improved the value of the objective function. As the final optimal is reached in tableau VI, the value of the quadratic objective function in the primal–dual simplex tableau, as we expected, is zero. It should be clear that, in the QP primal–dual formulation, all the information on ***value weights*** in both the primal and the dual has been ***internalized*** into the QP objective function (see equation 8.5). Thus, by the duality theory introduced in Chapter 4, the value of the primal objective function must, at the optimal point, equal the value of the dual. Consequently, the value of the quadratic objective function, which ***monitors*** the difference between the primal and the dual programs, is bounded by zero at the optimal point.

Once the decision variables contained in the primal and the dual are obtained from the optimal simplex tableau, the value of the original quadratic objective function can be calculated indirectly:

$$
\begin{aligned}
Z_X &= (4 - 2X_1)X_1 + 15X_2 \\
&= [4 - 2(0)]X_1 + 15(40) \\
&= \$600
\end{aligned}
$$

(From primal information, $X_1 = 0$ and $X_2 = 40$.)

or

$$
\begin{aligned}
Z_Y &= 80(Y) \\
&= 80(7.5) \\
&= \$600
\end{aligned}
$$

(From dual information, $Y = 7.5$.)

8.6 Summary

Quadratic programming problems are important for at least two reasons. (1) The predetermined value weights associated with decision variables in the classic linear programming objective function form may not be realistic. In many applications, a quadratic form of objective function is preferable. (2) Quadratic programming problems can be modeled in a primal–dual formulation that can be solved by standard linear programming routines.

The purpose of this chapter has been to demonstrate the quadratic programming primal–dual formulation. For purposes of explicating QP primal–dual formulation, we presented an LP primal–dual format, which incorporates primal and dual into a single tableau. The economic interpretation was used to illustrate the reasoning underlying the QP problem. A simple numerical example illustrated the compilation of QP by the modified simplex method. The rules outlined here can be applied to more complex quadratic programming problems.

Exercises

Note: The purpose of this chapter is to show the quadratic programming primal–dual formulation. As the size of the problem increases, we must obviously rely on computer assistance. Anyone who encounters a QP in business management or academic research should consult the QP routines that are normally available in most of the research-oriented computer centers.[7] Because of the computational effort required for even a very simple problem, this chapter provides fewer exercises than the other chapters in the book.

8.1 Cite the differences and similarities between the essential components of QP and LP.

8.2 What specific assumption is made when a constant value weight is asociated with a decision variable in an LP model? Explain why a decision variable is inversely (or directly) related to the amount of value that the decision variable has taken.

8.3 What is Wolfe's basic criterion?

8.4 Consider the following problem:

$$\text{Max} \quad Z_X = C_1X_1 + C_2X_2$$

subject to $$X_1 + 2X_2 \leq 60$$

and $$X_1 \geq 0, X_2 \geq 0$$

where $$C_1 = 80 - 2X_1, C_2 = 120$$

a. Is this a QP problem? If so, formulate a primal–dual model.
b. Solve it by the simplex method.
c. Does this problem encounter Wolfe's basic criterion? If so, indicate it in the calculation.

8.5 The only effective resource constraint for a manufacturing firm is 50 units. This resource is the basis of two outputs. Output A uses 1 unit of the resource per unit level and output B uses 2 units. The value of output A is 100 per unit and that of B is 160.[8]

a. Formulate this problem in a linear programming model. Solve it by the simplex method.
b. Reformulate the problem in a primal–dual model and solve it. Are you supposed to get the same solution you got in part (a)? If yes, why?

8.6 Referring to exercise 8.5, assume that X_1 has a value weight of $(100 - 2.5X_1)$ instead of 100. The value weight of X_2 and other information remain the same.

[7]A QP computer routine called ZORILLA, developed at Iowa State University, has incorporated the simplex method with a procedure for choosing incoming and outgoing variables, and it seems to be computationally efficient for large problems.

[8]Exercises 8.5 and 8.6 are adapted from the work of Hutton, *An Introduction to Quadratic Programming*, pp. 2, 10. Used with permission.

a. Formulate the problem in a QP problem.
b. Formulate the QP primal–dual model and solve it.
c. Compare your QP solution with the LP solution you obtained in part (a) of exercise 8.5, and give an economic explanation of the difference, if there is any, between the QP and LP solutions.

8.7 Kesslo Company manufactures two products, for which the only constraint resource for a given period is 800 units of capital. Each unit of product I uses two units of capital; each unit of product II uses 3 units of capital. The net profits from products I and II are $120 and $60 per unit, respectively.
a. Formulate the problem in a linear programming problem.
b. Solve it by inspection.
c. Solve it by the simplex method.
d. Formulate the problem in an LP primal–dual model. Do not solve it.

8.8 Refer to exercise 8.7. The marketing department of Kesslo Company estimates that the profit (value weight) for product I is no longer a constant at $120 but that it is inversely related to the quantity of product I produced. The relationship is estimated as $(120 - 2X_1)$.
a. Formulate the problem in a QP model.
b. Formulate the QP primal–dual model and solve it.
c. Compare your QP solution with the LP solution you obtained in exercise 8.7. Is there any difference between the final solutions? If not, why not?

8.9 Formulate a QP primal–dual simplex tableau for the following problem.

$$\text{Max } Z_X = (e_1 - d_1X_1)X_1 + (e_2 - d_2X_2)X_2 + (e_3 + d_3X_3)X_3$$

subject to

$$a_{11}X_1 + a_{12}X_2 + a_{13}X_3 \leq b_1$$
$$a_{21}X_1 + a_{22}X_2 + a_{23}X_3 \leq b_2$$
$$a_{31}X_1 + a_{32}X_2 + a_{33}X_3 \leq b_3$$

and

$$X_j \geq 0 \quad \text{for } j = 1, 2, 3$$

Suggested Readings

Boot, J. C. G. *Quadratic Programming*. Amsterdam, Netherlands: North-Holland Publishing Company, 1964.
Freund, R. J. "The Introduction of Risk into a Programming Model." *Econometrica*, 24 (July 1956).

Hass, Jerome E. "Transfer Pricing in a Centralized Firm." *Management Science*, 14, No. 6 (February 1968).

Hsiao, J. C., and M. W. Kottke. *Spatial Equilibrium Analysis of the Dairy Industry in the Northeast Region—An Application of Quadratic Programming.* Agricultural Experiment Station, Bulletin 405. Storrs, Conn.: The University of Connecticut, July 1968.

Hsiao, J. C. "Equilibrium Analysis via Quadratic Programming and Decentralized Decision Making in a Multidivision Firm." In *Recent Developments in Decision Sciences,* ed. David Murphy. N.E. Conference of the American Institute of Decision Sciences. Boston, Mass.: Boston College, May 1977.

Hutton, Robert. *An Introduction to Quadratic Programming.* Agricultural Experiment Station, A. E. & R. S. No. 41, The Pennsylvania State University, University Park, Pennsylvania, June 1963.

Taha, Hamdy A. *Operations Research: An Introduction.* New York: Macmillan, 1971. Chapter 17.

Takayama, T., and G. G. Judge. "Equilibrium Among Spatially Separated Markets: A Reformulation." *Econometrica,* 32, No. 4 (October 1964).

Van de Panne, C., and A. Whinston. "The Simplex and the Dual Method for Quadratic Programming." *Operations Research Quarterly,* 15, 1964, pp. 355–388.

Wolfe, P. "The Simplex Method for Quadratic Programming." *Econometrica,* 27, 1959.

9

Dynamic Programming

Dynamic programming is a quantitative technique that we use to solve certain types of problems that involve optimizing in a series of interrelated decisions. There are many problems wherein decisions must be made, not just at one time, but sequentially over many periods of time. The decision made at one period influences the next period and all future periods. Under these circumstances, we apply dynamic programming techniques to obtain an overall solution. For example, a firm may wish to make a series of production decisions over different time intervals in order to minimize the total production cost for all periods. The overall solution may not be the same as the minimum-cost solutions of the individual periods taken collectively. A dynamic approach provides solutions that assure overall effectiveness.

Dynamic implies a time-related or multistage interpretation of a problem. It contrasts with ***static***, which implies a single time or stage of development. Linear programming is normally a static approach to optimization, and dynamic programming is not a variation of linear programming techniques. Nor does it fall out in such a well-defined manner with standard solution techniques (such as the simplex method). Since dynamic solutions vary greatly with the situation, many different types of dynamic models can be developed. In this chapter, we present several different dynamic models to demonstrate the variety of approaches that fall into the more general category of dynamic programming.

9.1 A Multistage, Shortest-Route Problem

Arthur Kerr, a 58-year-old native of Salt Lake City, Utah, vows to make a year-long journey from Los Angeles to Boston in a covered two-horse wagon to advocate a new tax system in America. At each of a number of cities along the way he wants to collect tea bags, which he plans to dump into Boston Harbor to recall the Boston Tea Party.

Through a travel agency, Kerr learned the distances of alternative routes from Los Angeles to Boston. He then drew the highway network map shown in Figure 9.1. The city of origin, Los Angeles, is city 1. The destination city, Boston, is city 10. Other cities where Kerr will stop are given the numbers 2–9. The arrows represent routes between cities, and the mileage is indicated for each route. Arthur Kerr's problem is to find the shortest route that covers all of the selected cities from Los Angeles to Boston.

Solving the Problem by the Backwards Process

To solve this problem, Kerr divides it into a series of ***stages***. Each stage consists of a set of cities. For reasons that will become clear later, he solves the problem backwards, working stage by stage from the destination to the origin.

Stage 1 There are two cities, city 8 and city 9, at stage 1. As indicated in Figure 9.1, each city has only one direct route to Boston. Obviously, the ***direct*** routes from cities 8 and 9 to Boston, with immediate distances of 500 and 900 miles, respectively, are optimal in both cases. Table 9.1 shows the solutions for the stage 1 problem. The lengths of the shortest distances are stored in boxes above cities 8 and 9, as shown in Figure 9.2.

Figure 9.1
Highway Network Map

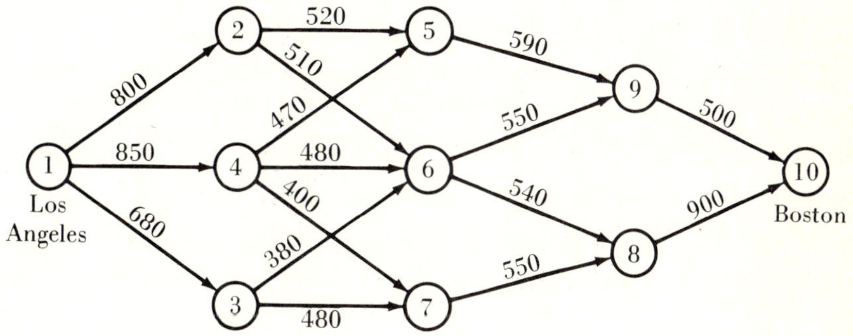

Table 9.1
Stage 1: Cities 8 and 9

City	Immediate Distance to Boston	Optimal Route to Boston
8	500 miles	8 → Boston
9	900 miles	9 → Boston

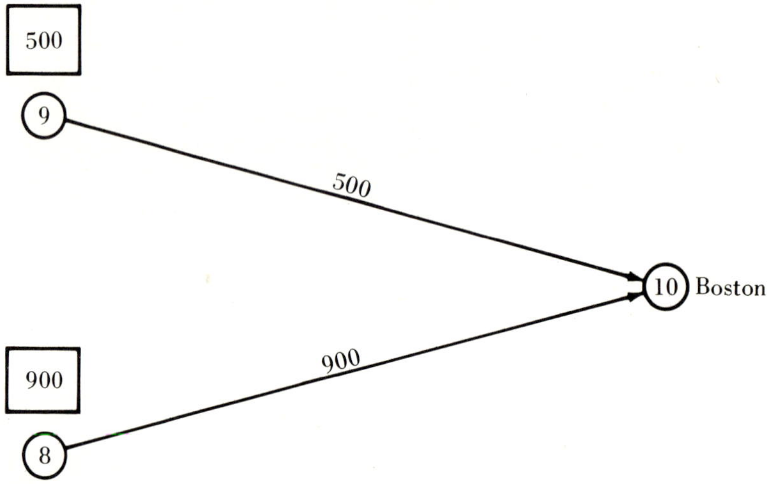

Figure 9.2
Solution to Stage 1 Problem

Stage 2 Stage 2 consists of cities 5, 6, and 7. Figure 9.1 shows that there is only one route from city 5 to a stage 1 city, and that is from city 5 to city 9, with a shortest distance (only distance) of 590 miles. From stage 1, Kerr already knows that the optimal additional distance from city 9 to Boston is 500 miles. So the total distance from city 5 to the destination city, Boston, is 1090 miles (590 + 500). Similarly, the total distance from city 7 to the destination city is 1,450 miles (550 + 900).

Turning to city 6, we note that there are two routes to Boston. One route is city 6 → city 9 → Boston, with a distance of 1050 miles (500 + 550). The other is city 6 → city 8 → Boston, with a distance of 1440 miles (540 + 900). Clearly, city 6 → city 9 → Boston is the optimal route. The results of stage 2 are given in Table 9.2, and the solution based on this information is represented in Figure 9.3. We use the optimal distance enclosed in the boxes above cities 5, 6, and 7 to find the shortest route in the next stage.

Stage 3 Cities 2, 4, and 3 make up stage 3. Arbitrarily, Kerr chooses city 2 as the beginning point. Starting here, he has cities 5 and 6 to choose between, with distances of 520 and 510 miles, respectively. From the stage 2 results, he knows that the optimal remaining distances from

Table 9.2 Stage 2: Cities 5, 6, and 7

Entering City	To City	(Immediate Distance	+	Optimal Additional Distance to Boston)	=	Total Distance	Optimal Route
5	→ 9	(590	+	**500**)	=	1090	5 → 9 → Boston
6	→ 9	(550	+	**500**)	=	1050	6 → 9 → Boston
	→ 8	(540	+	**900**)	=	1440	
7	→ 8	(550	+	**900**)	=	1450	7 → 9 → Boston

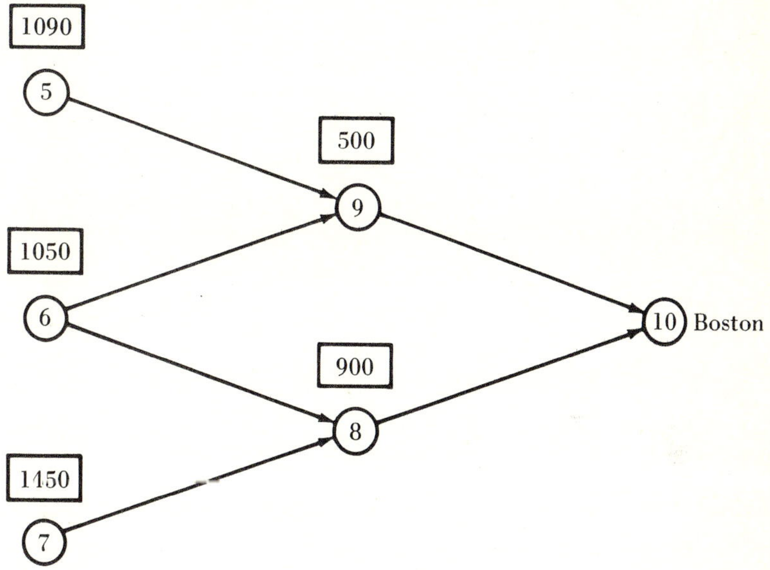

Figure 9.3
Solution to Stage 2 Problem

cities 5 and 6 to Boston are 1090 and 1050 miles, respectively. He compares the distance 1610 (520 + **1090**) for the route from city 2 to city 5 with the distance 1560 (510 + **1050**) for the route from city 2 to city 6. The route from city 2 to city 6 is preferred.

Turning to city 4, Kerr can go to any one of three cities, cities 5, 6, and 7, with immediate distances of 470, 480, and 400 miles, respectively. Again, by using the optimal route information already available from stage 2, he can evaluate routes city 4 → city 5, city 4 → city 6, and city 4 → city 7, with the respective distances of 1560 (470 + **1090**), 1530 (480 + **1050**) and 1850 (400 + **1450**). Thus, route 4 → 6 is preferred. If he leaves from city 4, the optimal route for Mr. Kerr is city 4 → city 6 → city 9 → Boston—a total of 1530 miles.

Table 9.3 Stage 3: Cities 2, 3, and 4

Entering City	To City	(Immediate Distance	+	Optimal Additional Distance to Boston)	=	Total Distance	Optimal Route
2	5	(520	+	**1090**)	=	1610	
	6	(510	+	**1050**)	=	1560	2 → 6 → 9 → Boston
4	5	(470	+	**1090**)	=	1560	
	6	(480	+	**1050**)	=	1530	4 → 6 → 9 → Boston
	7	(400	+	**1450**)	=	1850	
3	6	(380	+	**1050**)	=	1430	3 → 6 → 9 → Boston
	7	(480	+	**1450**)	=	1930	

Figure 9.4
Solution to Stage 3 Problem

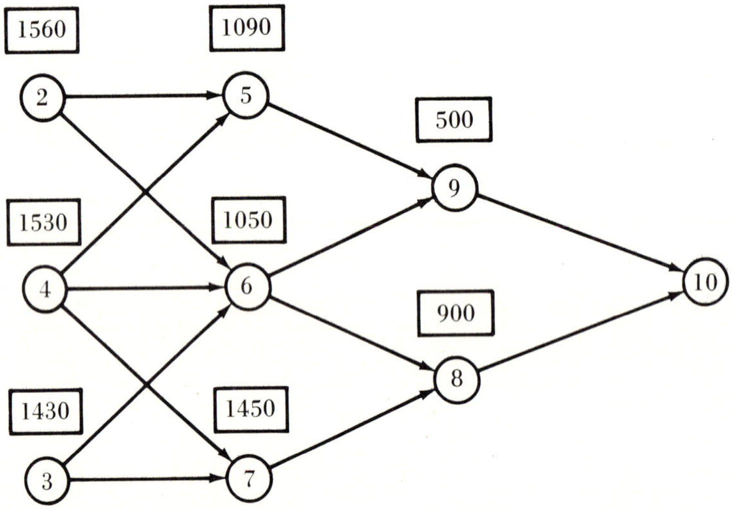

In a similar fashion, he can evaluate routes city 3 → city 6 and city 3 → city 7 when city 3 is the starting point. The travel distance from city 3 to city 6 is 1430 (380 + **1050**). The travel distance from city 3 to city 7 is 1930 (480 + **1450**). Consequently, the route from city 3 to city 6 is chosen. If Kerr leaves from city 4, the optimal route is city 3 → city 6 → city 9 → Boston, with a total distance of 1430 miles. The results of stage 3 are shown in Table 9.3, and the solution of the stage 3 problem appears in Figure 9.4.

Table 9.4 Stage 4: City 1 (Los Angeles)

Entering City	To City	(Immediate Distance	+	Optimal Additional Distance to Boston)	=	Total Distance	Optimal Route
1 (Los Angeles)	2	(800	+	**1560**)	=	2360	
	4	(850	+	**1530**)	=	2480	
	3	(680	+	**1430**)	=	2110	1 → 3 → 6 → 9 → Boston

Figure 9.5
Solution to Stage 4 Problem

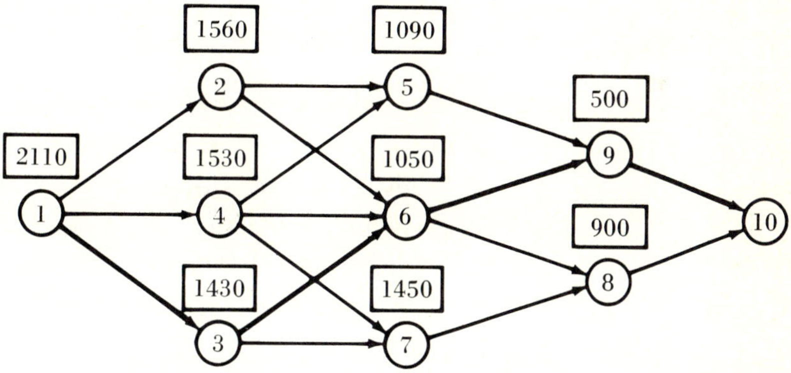

Stage 4 There is only one city in stage 4. Looking at Figure 9.1, Kerr sees that the immediate distances from the city of origin, Los Angeles, to cities 2, 4, and 3 are 800, 850, and 680 miles, respectively. By adding each of the immediate distances to the corresponding optimal route obtained in stage 3, Kerr finds that he should go from city 1 to city 3 (see Table 9.4). This means that, if Mr. Kerr starts from Los Angeles, the optimal route is Los Angeles → city 3 → city 6 → city 9 → Boston, with a total distance of 2110 miles. Figure 9.5 shows the solution to stage 4.

Mr. Kerr solved his shortest-route problem by first breaking down the problem into different stages or subproblems and then solving the overall problem backwards. That is, he worked stage by stage from the destination city (Boston) to the original city (Los Angeles). As each stage (subproblem) was solved, he recorded the optimal answer in an enclosed box, right above the city in question. This information was then used to find the shortest route in the next stage. Finally, the length of the shortest route from the city of origin to the destination city emerged—

in this case, 2110 miles. The optimal route is traced by a heavy line in Figure 9.5.

The key idea is that all Mr. Kerr had to consider at each stage was the immediate distance from the entering city to the exit city plus its optimal distance from the previous stage. This notion is fundamental to our subsequent discussion of dynamic programming in this chapter.

The Dynamic Recursive Relationship

Now we will use the multistage, shortest-route problem to demonstrate the formulation of the dynamic programming problem. For a more systematic approach to dynamic programming models, we will adopt the following terminology and notations:

n = number of stages (a stage consists of a group of cities)

s = state variable that describes a specific city at any stage

$d_{s,t}$ = immediate distance (return) from entering state s to exit state t

$f_n(s)$ = optimal return function (minimum distance) when the decision maker is in state s with n more stages to go to the final destination

$t_n(s)$ = a policy decision of selecting the exit route that yields the return function $f_n(s)$

The beginner in dynamic programming should not be frightened by these definitions. In plain English, the letter f in the term $f_n(s)$ stands for the objective ***f***unction. The letter s signifies that the value of the objective function depends on the **s**tate (in this case, the ***state*** is the specific city) of the problem. The subscript n indicates the ***n***umber of stages (groups of cities) remaining to go to the final destination when Mr. Kerr is entering state s. For the last term, $t_n(s)$, the letter t designates the policy decision of selecting the exit route to ***t***ravel at state s and stage n. The optimal policy is a policy that optimizes the value of the objective or return function $f_n(s)$.

We know from the preceding discussion that, in making a decision, the key idea is to consider the sum of the immediate distances, going from state s (a specific entering city) to state t (exit city), and its optimal distance from the previous stage. Now, let $f_{n-1}(t)$ be the known distance from the previous stage. In a general case for any state s at any stage n, then, the optimal return function for the shortest-route problem can be expressed as follows:

$$f_n(s) = \text{Min} \; [\underbrace{d_{s,t}}_{\substack{\text{immediate}\\\text{return}\\\text{(distance}\\\text{from state}\\s\text{ to state }t)}} + \underbrace{f_{n-1}(t)}_{\substack{\text{known}\\\text{optimal}\\\text{distance out}\\\text{of state }t\text{ from}\\\text{previous stage}}}] \qquad \text{for } n = 1, 2, 3, 4 \tag{9.1}$$

This formula says that the optimal policy decision at any state and any stage is to choose the minimum of each possible sum of immediate distances from entering state s to exit state t and the optimal distance out of state t in the previous stage. The right-hand side of this formula indicates that, once the term $f_{n-1}(t)$ is determined, there is no problem in finding the return function $f_n(s)$.

In the shortest-route problem, we work backwards by starting with the destination city, Boston. That is, let $n = 1$ (the first stage). When Mr. Kerr reaches state 10, or Boston, he stops because there are no more stages left. Thus the optimal value from the ***previous stage*** is

$$f_0(10) = 0 \qquad \text{for} \quad t_0(10) = \text{stop}$$

If we treat this as the known distance in the previous stage, the immediate distances for entering state 8 or state 9 in stage $n = 1$ are $d_{8,10} = 900$ or $d_{9,10} = 500$, respectively (see Figure 9.1). By equation (9.1), we can calculate all values of the return function $f_1(s)$, namely $f_1(8)$ and $f_1(9)$. They are

For entering state $s = 8$	$f_1(8) = d_{8,10} + f_0(10) = 900 + \mathbf{0} = 900$
For entering state $s = 9$	$f_1(9) = d_{9,10} + f_0(10) = 500 + \mathbf{0} = 500$

Zero is printed in heavy type to indicate that this value is already known from the previous stage. Once $f_1(s)$ is known, we can calculate the values of the return function $f_2(s)$ for the stage $n = 2$, namely $f_2(5)$, $f_2(6)$, and $f_2(7)$. That is,

For entering state 5	$f_2(5) = d_{5,9} + f_1(9) = 590 + \mathbf{500} = 1090$
For entering state 6	$f_2(6) = d_{6,9} + f_1(9) = 550 + \mathbf{500} = 1050$
	$f_2(6) = d_{6,8} + f_1(8) = 540 + \mathbf{900} = 1440$
For entering state 7	$f_2(7) = d_{7,8} + f_1(8) = 550 + \mathbf{900} = 1450$

Similarly, having already determined $f_2(s)$, we can calculate the values of $f_3(s)$ (these are $f_3(2)$, $f_3(3)$, and $f_3(4)$ at stage 3). The entire problem is solved once we know the value of $f_4(1)$—the optimal value of the return function when the decision maker is at the city of origin (Los Angeles) with 4 more stages to go to the final destination city, Boston.

In essence, (9.1) simply states that, once we know the values of $f_0(s)$, we can calculate the value of $f_1(s)$, which allows us to find the value of $f_2(s)$, and so on until the entire problem is solved. For this very reason, equation (9.1) is known as the ***dynamic recursive relation.*** This computational procedure is often referred to as a ***recursive algorithm.***

Computational Procedures

The shortest-route problem was solved by a backwards process. To show the dynamic recursive relation, however, it is often better to present the computational data for each stage in tabular form. There are four stages; they are shown in Tables 9.5 through 9.8.

In each table, there is a row for each possible entering state and a column for each possible travel decision. Thus there is one column for each possible exit from the stage in question.

Table 9.5 represents the solution for the stage 1 problem. Note that there are two rows for entering states 8 and 9, but there is only one column for exit state 10, because state 10 (Boston) is the only designated city for both entering states 8 and 9. As we have just said, once $f_0(10) = 0$ is known, we obtain the entries such as $900 + \mathbf{0} = 900$ and $500 + \mathbf{0} = 500$ by simply adding the value of $f_0(10)$ to the values of $d_{8,10}$ and $d_{9,10}$, respectively. These numbers are shown in the body of the table.

Consider next the stage 2 problem. The entering state is either state 5, state 6, or state 7, so there are three rows in Table 9.6. There are two exit states, either state 8 or state 9, so two columns are needed. The letters **n.f.** indicate that it is not feasible to travel from the row

Table 9.5
Stage 1 Problem ($n = 1$)

Formula:
$f_1(s) = d_{s,t} + f_0(s)$

Entering State	**Travel Decision: Exit State t**	**Optimal Policy Decision**	**Min of Each Sum (in a given row)**
s	**10**	$t_1(s)$	$f_1(s)$
8	$900 + \mathbf{0} = 900$	$t_1(8) = 10$	$f_1(8) = 900$
9	$500 + \mathbf{0} = 500$	$t_1(9) = 10$	$f_1(9) = 500$

state to the column state. The numbers shown in the body of the table, again, represent the sum of the immediate distances, going from the entering state to the exit state, and the shortest distance out of the exit state in the previous stage. For example, the value of $f_1(8) = \mathbf{900}$ is added to each $d_{s,8}$ in the $t = 8$ column, and the value of $f_1(9) = \mathbf{500}$ is added to each $d_{s,9}$ in the $t = 9$ column. The last two columns represent the optimal policy decision, $t_2(s)$, for the exit state and the optimal distance associated with this decision. For example, given entering state 6, the optimal policy decision is $t_2(6) = 9$. This decision yields an optimal distance $f_2(6) = 1050$ miles, which is the minimum of the corresponding row of the table.

The computations for $n = 3$ are presented in Table 9.7. In this stage, the entering states are states 2, 3, and 4, and the exit state can be state 5, state 6, or state 7.

When $n = 4$, there is only one state (and thus only one row) required in Table 9.8. The optimal travel decision is to go from state 1 to state

Table 9.6 Stage 2 Problem ($n = 2$)

Formula: $f_2(s) = d_{s,t} + f_1(s)$

Entering State s	Travel Decision: Exit State t		Optimal Policy Decision $t_2(s)$	Min of Each Sum (in a given row) $f_2(s)$
	8	9		
5	n.f.	590 + **500** = 1090	$t_2(5) = 9$	$f_2(5) = 1090$
6	540 + **900** = 1440	550 + **500** = 1050	$t_2(6) = 9$	$f_2(6) = 1050$
7	550 + **900** = 1450	n.f.	$t_2(7) = 8$	$f_2(7) = 1450$

Table 9.7 Stage 3 Problem ($n = 3$)

Formula: $f_3(s) = d_{s,t} + f_2(s)$

Entering State s	Travel Decision: Exit State t			Optimal Policy Decision $t_2(s)$	Min of Each Sum (in a given row) $f_3(s)$
	5	6	7		
2	520 + **1090** = 1610	510 + **1050** = 1560	n.f.	$t_2(2) = 6$	$f_3(2) = 1560$
3	n.f.	380 + **1050** = 1430	480 + **1450** = 1930	$t_2(3) = 6$	$f_3(3) = 1430$
4	470 + **1090** = 1560	480 + **1050** = 1530	400 + **1450** = 1850	$t_2(4) = 6$	$f_3(4) = 1530$

Table 9.8 Stage 4 Problem ($n = 4$) — **Formula:** $f_4(s) = d_{s,t} + f_3(s)$

Entering State s	Travel Decision: Exit State t			Optimal Policy Decision	Min of Each Sum (in a given row)
	2	3	4	$t_3(s)$	$f_4(1) = 2110$
1	800 + **1560** = 2360	680 + **1430** = 2110	850 + **1530** = 2380	$t_3(1) = 3$	$f_4(1) = 2110$

Table 9.9
Optimal Decision At Each Stage

Stage	Entering State (city)	Exit State (City)	Route	Distance (miles)
4	1	3	$1 \to 3$	680
3	3	6	$3 \to 6$	380
2	6	9	$6 \to 9$	550
1	9	10	$9 \to 10$	500
			Total =	2110

3, with a minimum distance of 2110 miles. As we expected, this is exactly the distance we calculated earlier.

To see the complete routing, we must work forward by going through the tables from stage 4 to stage 1. At stage 4 (Table 9.8), the optimal route is to go to state 3. From Table 9.7 ($n = 3$), we see that, from the entering state 3, the optimal travel decision is to go to state 6. Progressing to Table 9.6 for $n = 2$, we see that the optimal travel decision is to go from state 6 to state 9. Finally, having entered state 9, we see that the optimal travel decision (as shown in Table 9.5 for $n = 1$) is to move directly to state 10. Table 9.9 illustrates the process. Note that the exit state (city) in stage 4 is the stage 3 entering state (city) and that the exit state in stage 3 is the stage 2 entering state, and so on. In summary, the shortest route is state 1 $\to$ state 3 $\to$ state 6 $\to$ state 9 $\to$ state 10. The total distance from Los Angeles to Boston is 2110 miles (check: 680 + 380 + 550 + 500 = 2110). This is exactly the same distance that we obtained in our previous dynamic programming calculations.

Principle of Optimality

It is important to note that calculation of the dynamic recursive relation is based on Bellman's ***principle of optimality***, which states that "an optimal policy has the property that, wherever the initial state and the initial decision are, the remaining decisions must constitute an optimal policy with regard to the state resulting from the first decision."[1] In accordance with the principle of optimality, the optimal policy decision at any given state of any stage depends only on that state and not on the history of how that state was reached. For example, an optimal policy to leave state 6 does not depend on which route we took to enter state 6.

In theory, it is the principle of optimality that allows us to break the total problem into a sequence of stages, the last one of which can be solved independently of the rest. Then we can solve the total problem by working backwards to the original entering state. All multistage problems are linked by the recursive objective function (9.1). We have observed that the decisions at one stage influence other stages through the state variable. Since the linkage relationship may vary from problem to problem, there is no general algorithm for the computation of dynamic programming. The only way to appreciate the appropriate formulation and the wide-ranging applicability of the dynamic programming process is through practice. For this very reason, we will discuss several economic and business problems to illustrate the formulation and unique characteristics of dynamic programming.

9.2 A Dynamic Programming Approach to an Inventory–Production Problem

Sheridan Manufacturing Company produces large industrial equipment. The company has received orders for its products in the period from September to December, as shown in Table 9.10.

The cost of production for the firm involves a set-up cost of $50,000 and an average variable cost of $30,000 per unit. In addition, there is an inventory holding cost of $5000 per unit per month. Because of

Table 9.10 Sales Orders for Sheridan Manufacturing Company

Month	Units Ordered
September	2
October	3
November	4
December	3

[1]R. E. Bellman, *Dynamic Programming* (Princeton, N.J.. Princeton University Press, 1957), p. 83.

limited production capacity and storage space, the firm cannot produce more than 5 units in any month. Assume that the firm has zero inventory on hand at the beginning of September. The problem is to find a production schedule that will minimize the total cost (production cost plus inventory cost), subject to the restrictions on production capacity and to the demand requirements on time.

Dynamic Characterization Before we examine the dynamic phenomena of inventory processes, let's define the following notations:

n = stages, each month (period) being viewed as a stage, for $n = 1$ (December), $n = 2$ (November), $n = 3$ (October), and $n = 4$ (September)

i = state variable representing the level of beginning inventory in any stage

X_n = decision variable representing the level of production at the nth stage

d_n = quantity demanded at the nth stage

In terms of these definitions, the firm's cost function, which includes both production cost and inventory holding cost for each period, is

$$\text{Cost function} = 5 + \underbrace{3X_n}_{\text{production cost}} + \underbrace{0.5i}_{\text{inventory holding cost}} \qquad \text{for } X_n > 0 \tag{9.2}$$

Note that the cost of production is $30,000 per unit plus a set-up cost of $50,000. In any period, we assume that there is no set-up cost if no production takes place. The only cost, in this case, would be for inventory holding.

We should also note that the beginning inventory is presented as the state variable. It links different periods together through the so-called ***material balance equation***:

$$i_{n+1} = i_n + X_n - d_n \qquad \text{for } n = 1, 2, 3, 4 \tag{9.3}$$

which means that

$$\begin{bmatrix} \text{Inventory} \\ \text{level at} \\ \text{the end of} \\ \text{period } n \end{bmatrix} = \begin{bmatrix} \text{Inventory at} \\ \text{the beginning} \\ \text{of period } n \end{bmatrix} + \begin{bmatrix} \text{Production} \\ \text{in period} \\ n \end{bmatrix} - \begin{bmatrix} \text{Demand} \\ \text{in period} \\ n \end{bmatrix}$$

Clearly, it is the level of inventory that links consecutive time periods. These time-staged linkages relating inventory in one period to inventory in the next period are the basic characteristics of multiperiod dynamic production models.

To simplify the notation, we have designated i as the level of beginning inventory. The firm's cost function corresponding to (9.2) in a general case can be written as follows:

$$\text{Cost function} = C_n(X_n, i + X_n - d_n) \qquad \text{for } n = 1, 2, \ldots, N \quad (9.4)$$

where the quantity $(i + X_n - d_n)$ is simply inventory at the ***end*** of the stage (period) n. Let us now define two more terms.

$f_n(i)$ = minimum cost when the beginning inventory is at level i with n more stages to go (this function is called the ***return function***)

$X_n(i)$ = a level of production decision yielding $f_n(i)$

When $n = 1$, given the beginning inventory level i and the demand requirement d_1, the level of production must be the exact difference between these two specific amounts so that the ending inventory in December is zero:

$$i + X_1 - d_1 = 0$$

Thus the return function in the period $n = 1$ becomes

$$\begin{aligned} f_1(i) &= \min C_1(X_1, i + X_1 - d_1) \\ &= \min C_1(X_1, 0) \end{aligned} \qquad (9.5)$$

For $n = 2$, we compute the associated cost by minimizing the sum of production cost and inventory holding cost plus the cost in the previous period (stage). That is,

$$f_2(i) = \min C_2(X_2, i + X_2 - d_2) + f_1(i + X_2 - d_2) \qquad (9.6)$$

As in the shortest-route problem, once we know the values for $f_2(i)$, we can find the values for $f_3(i)$, and so on. When $n = 3$, we have

$$f_3(i) = \min C_3(X_3, i + X_3 - d_3) + f_2(i + X_3 - d_3) \qquad (9.7)$$

In the general case, then, the dynamic recursion for the nth period is

$$f_n(i) = \min \underbrace{C_n(X_n, i + X_n - d_n)}_{\substack{\text{costs in the}\\ \text{immediate}\\ \text{period } n}} + \underbrace{f_{n-1}(i + X_n - d_n)}_{\substack{\text{known minimum}\\ \text{cost from}\\ \text{previous}\\ \text{period } n-1}} \tag{9.8}$$

for $n = 1, 2, \ldots, N$.

As in the shortest-route problem, the formula says that, given the entering inventory level i, the optimal policy decision at any stage (period) is to choose the minimum of each possible sum of cost for that stage (period) plus the known optimal costs from the previous stage (period). In the case of the Sheridan Manufacturing Company problem, the policy decision in each period involves selection of the level of production X_n for each i. However, the value of X_n is constrained by the production capacity, $X_n \leq 5$. On the other hand, the firm's production and inventory must be sufficient to meet the demand requirement at each period, namely $i + X_n \geq d_n$.

The Computational Process

There are four stages (periods) in this example. Calculations for each stage can be presented in a table. The format of the computational table is quite similar to that used in the shortest-route problem. Working backwards, we have $n = 1$ (December) as the starting period. Given the beginning inventory i, we must determine the level of production such that in this period demand is met exactly and the ending inventory is zero. Therefore, the specific return function corresponding to (9.5) can be expressed as

$$f_1(i) = [(5 + 3X_1) + 0.5(0)]$$

which is presented in Table 9.11. In order for us to meet the zero ending inventory requirement, the first column for beginning inventory i cannot go beyond 3 units. Accordingly, the column for production decision X_1, shown in Table 9.11, is also restricted to no more than 3 units.

For $n = 2$, the formula for the return function in this period is

$$f_2(i) = \min [(5 + 3X_2) + 0.5(i + X_2 - d_2)] + f_1(i + X_2 - d_2)$$

which consists of three parts: the production cost at period two, the inventory holding cost at period two, and the optimal known cost cal-

Table 9.11
Stage 1 Problem
(December), $d_1 = 3$

Formula:
$f_1(i) = [(5 + 3X_1) + 0.5(0)]$

Beginning Inventory i	**Production Decision:** X_1	$f_1(i)$
0	3	$f_1(0) = 14$
1	2	$f_1(1) = 11$
2	1	$f_1(2) = 8$
3	0	$f_1(3) = 0$

culated from period one. The numerical computation is presented in Table 9.12. There are five rows, one for each feasible value of i.

In each cell of Table 9.12 (except the n.f. cells), the first two values in each column are the production cost and the inventory cost, respectively, in period two. The third entry is the value of the optimal known cost from Table 9.11 for period one. For example, in the cell corresponding to $i = 4$, $X_2 = 1$ in Table 9.12, the numerical calculation of the value of $f_2(i)$ can be explained schematically as follows:

$$\underbrace{8}_{\substack{\text{production cost:}\\ (5 + 3X_2)\\ = 5 + 3(1)\\ = 8}} + \underbrace{0.5}_{\substack{\text{ending inventory cost:}\\ 0.5\,(i + X_2 - d_2)\\ = 0.5\,(4 + 1 - 4)\\ = 0.5}} + \underbrace{11}_{\substack{\text{optimal cost in}\\ \text{period one:}\\ f_1\,(i + X_2 - d_2)\\ = f_1\,(4 + 1 - 4)\\ = f_1\,(1)\\ = 11}} = 19.5$$

We can compute the values of other entries in the body of Table 9.12 similarly.

Given a level of i, we find the value of $f_2(i)$ by selecting the minimum sum for ***that*** row. For example, given $i = 2$, there are 4 sums in this row—25, 25.5, 26, and 29. Clearly, the minimum sum is 25. An asterisk is used to mark the optimal value of $f_2(i)$ for the given level of beginning inventory $i = 3$. For each row, the minimum sum is placed under the $f_2(i)$ column. The optimal policy decision for the level of production that yields $f_2(i)$ is designated in the $X_n(i)$ column. For example, the optimal production decision that yields $f_2(i) = 18.5$ is $X_2(i) = 4$ (see Table 9.12).

Because of the demand requirement in this period ($d_2 = 4$), any combination of inventory and production that is less than 4 units is not feasible. Thus n.f. is entered in the table. Also, all the combinations of production level (with $i = 0$) is 4. With $d_2 = 4$, there is no ending

Table 9.12 Stage 2 Problem (November), $d_2 = 4$

Beginning Inventory i	Production Decision: X_2		
	0	1	2
0	n.f.	n.f.	n.f.
1	n.f.	n.f.	n.f.
2	n.f.	n.f.	11 + 0 + 14 = 25*
3	n.f.	8 + 0 + 14 = 22	11 + 0.5 + 11 = 22.5
4	0 + 0 + 14 = 14*	8 + 0.5 + 11 = 19.5	11 + 1 + 8 = 20
5	0 + 0.5 + 11 = 11.5*	8 + 1 + 8 = 17	11 + 1.5 + 0 = 12.5

Table 9.13 Stage 3 Problem (October), $d_3 = 3$

Beginning Inventory i	Production Decision: X_3		
	0	1	2
0	n.f.	n.f.	n.f.
1	n.f.	n.f.	11 + 0 + 31 = 42
2	n.f.	8+ 0 + 31 = 39	11 + 0.5 + 28 = 39.5
3	0 + 0 + 31 = 31*	8 + 0.5 + 28 = 36.5	11 + 1 + 25 = 37
4	0 + 0.5 + 28 = 28.5*	8 + 1 + 25 = 34	11 + 1.5 + 18.5 = 31
5	0 + 1 + 25 = 26*	8 + 1.5 + 18.5 = 28	11 + 2 + 14 = 27

inventory and production that are greater than the sum of the two periods' demand requirements ($d_1 + d_2 = 7$) are not feasible, because the ending inventory must be zero. For example, the combination of $i = 5$ and $X_2 = 3$ is greater than the two periods' demand requirement of 7, so the nonfeasible alternative is labeled as such in the corresponding entry of the table.

In a similar fashion, when $n = 3$ (October), we can calculate the values for $f_3(i)$ that are shown in Table 9.13. The first two terms of the formula are $(5 + 3X_3)$ and $0.5\,(i + X_3 - d_3)$. We obtain the values for the third term, $f_2(i + X_3 - d_3)$, from Table 9.12.

Proceeding to $n = 4$, using the recursive formula shown at the top of Table 9.14 yields the calculations for $f_4(i)$ that are presented in this table. Since the beginning inventory in this period (September) is given as zero units, we have only one row in Table 9.14. Thus, given $i = 0$,

Formula: $f_2(i) = \min [(5 + 3X_2) + 0.5(i + X_2 - d_2)] + f_1(i + X_2 - d_2)$

Production Decision: X_2			Optimal Policy Decision	
3	4	5	$X_2(i)$	$f_2(i)$
n.f.	17 + 0 + 14 = 31*	20 + 0 + 14 = 34	4	$f_2(0) = 31$
14 + 0 + 14 = 28*	17 + 0.5 + 11 = 28.5	20 + 0.5 + 11 = 31.5	3	$f_2(1) = 28$
14 + 0.5 + 11 = 25.5	17 + 1 + 8 = 26	20 + 1 + 8 = 29	2	$f_2(2) = 25$
14 + 1 + 8 = 23	17 + 1.5 + 0 = 18.5*	n.f.	4	$f_2(3) = 18.5$
14 + 1.5 + 0 = 15.5	n.f.	n.f.	0	$f_2(4) = 14$
n.f.	n.f.	n.f.	0	$f_2(5) = 11.5$

Formula: $f_3(i) = \min [(5 + 3X_3) + 0.5(i + X_3 - d_3)] + f_2(i + X_3 - d_3)$

Production Decision: X_3			Optimal Policy Decision	
3	4	5	$X_3(i)$	$f_3(i)$
14 + 0 + 31 = 45*	17 + 0.5 + 28 = 45.5	20 + 1 + 25 = 46	3	$f_3(0) = 45$
14 + 0.5 + 28 = 42.5	17 + 1 + 25 = 43	20 + 1.5 + 18.5 = 40*	5	$f_3(1) = 40$
14 + 1 + 25 = 40	17 + 1.5 + 18.5 = 37	20 + 2 + 14 = 36*	5	$f_3(2) = 36$
14 + 1.5 + 18.5 = 34	17 + 2 + 14 = 33	20 + 2.5 + 11.5 = 34	0	$f_3(3) = 31$
14 + 2 + 14 = 30	17 + 2.5 + 11.5 = 31	n.f.	0	$f_3(4) = 28.5$
14 + 2.5 + 11.5 = 28	n.f.	n.f.	0	$f_3(5) = 26$

the optimal production level is 5, and the minimum cost with 4 more periods to go is 52.5, or $525,000.

To determine the overall optimal production decision at each stage, we start at stage 4 (Table 9.5) and work ***forward***, using the tables that have already been computed. Given the beginning inventory of zero units in September, the optimal production level is 5 units. With the demand requirement at 2 units, the ending inventory in September must be 3. The total cost, which is the sum of production and inventory holding costs for this period, is 21.5. This information is given in the first row of Table 9.15.

From Table 9.13 ($n = 3$), we see that, given the entering inventory of 3 and the demand requirement of $d_3 = 3$, the best production level is zero, which results in a zero level of ending inventory in October. Going on to Table 9.12 for $n = 2$ in November, we see that the optimal

Table 9.14 Stage 4 Problem (September), $d_4 = 2$

Formula:

$$f_4(i) = \min [(5 + 3X_4) + 0.5\,(i + X_4 - d_4)] + f_3\,(i + X_4 - d_4)$$

Beginning Inventory i	Production Decision: X_4						Optimal Policy Decision	
	0	1	2	3	4	5	$X_4(i)$	$f_4(i)$
0	n.f.	n.f.	11 + 0 + 45 = 56	14 + 0.5 + 40 = 54.5	17 + 1 + 36 = 54	20 + 1.5 + 31 = 52.5*	5	$f_4(0) = 52.5$

Table 9.15 Optimal Production Decision at Each Stage

Stage n	Period	Demand	Beginning Inventory	Optimal Production	Ending Inventory	Cost
4	September	2	0	5	3	21.5
3	October	3	3	0	0	0
2	November	4	0	4	0	17
1	December	3	0	3	0	14
					Total	52.5

inventory in November. Finally, we move to Table 9.11 for $n = 1$, and find that the best production decision must be exactly 3 units so that there is no ending inventory in December, as required by the management of the firm.

Table 9.15 summarizes the optimal production decision at each stage. Interestingly, just like the multistage shortest-route problem, the ending inventory in September (exit) is the beginning inventory (entry) in October. The table illustrates the time-staged linkages relating inventory in one period to inventory in subsequent periods. This particular problem happens to have no ending inventory in the optimal solution from October through December. The total cost, shown in Table 9.15, is 52.5, or $525,000.

Once the optimal production plan and the optimal value of the return function are obtained, management can evaluate the sensitivity of the optimal solution to any changes in the parameters of the model. For example, the following questions could be examined. (1) What effect will a change in the cost of inventory have? (2) What effect will a change in the amount of starting inventory have? (3) What effect will a change in the restriction on production have? (4) How would the optimal solution be different if the change is an increase in production cost and a decrease in inventory cost, or vice versa? In addition to revealing the sensitivity of the solution to changes in parameters, the analysis provides additional valuable information. For example, as we shall see in the next section, it provides insight into the problem of resource allocation.

9.3 The Dynamic Programming Approach to Other Resource Allocation Problems

In this section, we will use the dynamic programming approach to solve a set of hypothetical but suggestive resource allocation problems that occur in economics and business.

Allocation of Auditors

(Example 1) Consider a problem faced by a financial consulting firm. The firm has five auditors to cover five territories. Estimated cost-revenue data suggest that the profit generated from each territory is a function of the number of auditors assigned. The profit function for each territory is shown in Table 9.16.

We can think of each territory as a different stage, and the unassigned auditors are functionally similar to inventory. Thus, as in the multiperiod inventory production problem, the subproblems of the multiterritory problem can be linked together by the unassigned auditors. Let's define the following variables and notations:

X_n = number of auditors to be assigned to stage (territory) n

A = total number of auditors available for assignment

A_n = state variable representing the number of unassigned auditors at stage n

$f_n(A_n)$ = optimal return function when A_n auditors are allocated in a stage with n more stages to go

$R_n(X_n)$ = level of assignment decision that yields $f_n(A_n)$

To be consistent with the process of calculating backwards, we designate $n = 1$ for territory 3, $n = 2$ for territory 2, and $n = 3$ for territory 1. But this designation is arbitrary; we could have designated territory 1 or 2 as the starting point.

Now we can write a series of equations that define the return function for each stage. At stage $n = 1$ (territory 3), the return function is

$$f_1(A_1) = \max R_1(X_1) \tag{9.9}$$

Table 9.16 Estimated Monthly Return (unit = $10,000)

Number of Auditors Assigned	Expected Return from Territory 1	Expected Return from Territory 2	Expected Return from Territory 3
0	$ 0	$ 0	$ 0
1	7	5	2
2	13	10	6
3	16	10	10
4	17	17	14
5	23	18	17

Entering stage $n = 2$, we can write the return function as

$$f_2(A_2) = \max R_2(X_2) + f_1(A_2 - X_2) \qquad (9.10)$$

which is the maximum sum of the immediate return resulting from the allocation of X_2 auditors to stage 2 plus the optimal known return from the allocation of the remaining $(A_2 - X_2)$ auditors to stage 1.

In the general case, the dynamic programming recursion at any stage n can be written as follows:

$$f_n(A_n) = \max [\underbrace{R_n(X_n)}_{\substack{\text{immediate}\\ \text{return}\\ \text{from}\\ \text{stage } n}} + \underbrace{f_{n-1}(A_n - X_n)}_{\substack{\text{optimal known}\\ \text{returns from}\\ \text{subsequent}\\ \text{stage}}}] \qquad \text{for } n = 1, 2, 3 \ldots, N \qquad (9.11)$$

In other words, at each stage we find the optimal return by maximizing the immediate return from territory n plus the known optimal returns from the previous stage (territory).

To find the numerical solution, we start with stage 1 (territory 3). At this stage, we could allocate from 0 to 5 unassigned auditors. The return function is simply the estimated monthly return, as shown in Table 9.17.

Turning to stage 2, we see that the number of unassigned auditors in territory 2 can range from 0 to 5. Thus there are 6 rows, as shown in Table 9.18. Note that the format of this table is similar to that of

Table 9.17
Allocation Problem in Stage 1 (Territory 3)

Formula:
$f_1(A_1) = \max R_1(X_1)$

Number of Unassigned Auditors A_1	Number of Auditors Assigned X_1	Immediate Return from Territory 3 $R_1(X_1)$	Optimal Return Function $f_1(A_1)$
0	0	0	$f_1(0) = 0$
1	1	2	$f_1(1) = 2$
2	2	6	$f_1(2) = 6$
3	3	10	$f_1(3) = 10$
4	4	14	$f_1(4) = 14$
5	5	17	$f_1(5) = 17$

Table 9.18 Allocation Problem in Stage 2 (Territory 2) **Formula:** $f_2(A_2) = \max R_2(X_2) + f_1(A_2 - X_2)$

Number of Unassigned Auditors A_2	Assignment Decision: X_2						Optimal Policy Decision $R_2(X_2)$	Max Sum $f_2(A_2)$
	0	1	2	3	4	5		
0	0 + 0 = 0	n.f.	n.f.	n.f.	n.f.	n.f.	0	$f_2(0) = 0$
1	0 + 2 = 2	5 + 0 = 5*	n.f.	n.f.	n.f.	n.f.	1	$f_2(1) = 5$
2	0 + 6 = 6	5 + 2 = 7	10 + 0 = 10*	n.f.	n.f.	n.f.	2	$f_2(2) = 10$
3	0 + 10 = 10	5 + 6 = 11	10 + 2 = 12*	10 + 0 = 10	n.f.	n.f.	2	$f_2(3) = 12$
4	0 + 14 = 14	5 + 10 = 15	10 + 6 = 16	10 + 2 = 12	17 + 0 = 17*	n.f.	4	$f_2(4) = 17$
5	0 + 17 = 17	5 + 14 = 19	10 + 10 = 20*	10 + 6 = 16	17 + 2 = 19	18 + 0 = 18	2	$f_2(5) = 20$

Table 9.19 Allocation Problem in Stage 3 (Territory 1) **Formula:** $f_3(A_3) = \max R_3(X_3) + f_2(A_3 - X_3)$

Number of Unassigned Auditors A_3	Assignment Decision: X_3						Optimal Policy Decision $R_3(X_3)$	Max Sum $f_3(A_3)$
	0	1	2	3	4	5		
5	0 + 20 = 20	7 + 17 = 24	13 + 12 = 25	16 + 10 = 26*	17 + 5 = 22	19 + 0 = 19	3	$f_3(5) = 26$

many of the tables developed earlier in this chapter. On the basis of the formula $f_2(A_2) = R_2(X_2) + f_1(A_2 - X_2)$, the computation consists largely of two parts: the immediate return at stage 2 and the optimal known return in stage 1. For example, given the number of unassigned auditors $A_2 = 3$ (row), we could assign $X_2 = 2$ (column) in territory 2, with the immediate return of 10, and the remaining auditor ($A_2 - X_2 = 1$) to territory 3, with a known return $f_1(1) = 2$. Thus the total return at the entry of row $A_2 = 3$ and column $X_2 = 2$ is 12 (see Table 9.18).

Given the number of unassigned auditors A_2, the desired result is to determine the assignment in this row yielding the maximum value of $f_2(A_2)$. For the row $A_2 = 3$, we see that the optimal policy assignment is at $X_2 = 2$, or $R_2(X_2) = 2$, yielding a maximum value of $f_2(3) = 12$. Again, an asterisk indicates the maximum sum for ***that*** row. The resulting values of other $f_2(A_2)$ are computed in the last column of Table 9.18. Note that any assignment for $X_2 > A_2$ is impossible. The resulting n.f. alternatives are labeled as such in Table 9.18.

The analysis for the final stage $n = 3$ (territory 1) is shown in Table 9.19. Since we work backwards in dynamic programming, this stage is the beginning point in our actual allocation process. Therefore, all auditors are available for assignment ($A_3 = A = 5$), and we have only one row in this table. The maximum value for $f_3(A_3)$ is $260,000, which corresponds to an optimal assignment of 3 auditors ($X_3 = 3$) in territory 1.

To get the optimal allocation of auditors in each territory, as shown in Table 9.20, we start at stage 3 (territory 1) and work forward. We determine the optimal assignments for territories 2 and 3 by working through Table 9.18 and Table 9.17. Table 9.20 indicates that the optimal allocation is to assign 3 and 2 auditors to territories 1 and 2, respectively;

Table 9.20
Optimal Assignment at Each Territory

Stages	Number of Unassigned Auditors A_n	Territory	Optimal Number of Auditors Assigned X_n	Remaining Auditors $A_n - X_n$	Return
3	5	1	3	2	16
2	2	2	2	0	10
1	0	3	0	0	0
				Total =	26

no auditor is assigned to territory 3. The total monthly return is verified again as \$260,000.

It is interesting to note that, at the optimal solution in this problem, none of the auditors is assigned to territory 3. This is not surprising, because Table 9.16 reveals that the expected return from the third territory is less than that from the others. For marketing reasons, the management of the firm might consider providing additional auditors to cover the third territory. Sensitivity analysis can help answer the important question of how much each additional unit would be worth in terms of increasing expected return.

A Cargo-Loading Problem

(Example 2) The manager of a transportation company faces a cargo-loading problem. On a particular flight, he has three items (A, B, and C) to be carried. These items have the characteristics shown in Table 9.21. His decision problem is to find the number of units of each item to be carried such that the total profit is maximized. The maximum allowable weight capacity for the cargo plane is 10 tons.

If fractional amounts were allowed, one should obviously load the item with the greatest profit-weight ratio first. However, since only integer quantities of each item can be carried, the problem does not lend itself to an easy linear programming solution. On the other hand, one could formulate an integer programming problem like those we discussed in Chapter 6. To do so, let

X_n = number of units of item n taken
W = total available weight
W_n = state variable representing the remaining (unassigned) weight at stage n
a_n = unit weight of item n
P_n = profit per unit of item n

The integer programming model is then

$$\text{Max} \quad Z = P_1X_1 + P_2X_2 + P_3X_3$$

subject to $$a_1X_1 + a_2X_2 + a_3X_3 \leq W$$

and X_1, X_2, and X_3 are all integers

At this point we are interested in transforming this integer programming problem into a dynamic programming model. Consider each item

Table 9.21 Cargo-Loading Problem

Item	Unit Weight (tons)	Profit Per Unit
A	3	20
B	1	5
C	2	15

as a stage, and the remaining weight to be distributed, denoted by W_n, as the state variable. The remaining variables are defined as follows:

$f_n(W_n)$ = optimal return function when available weight is W_n with n more stages (items) to be distributed

$R_n(X_n)$ = quantity of each item yielding $f_n(W_n)$

The dynamic recursion relationship can be expressed as

$$f_n(W_n) = \max [\underbrace{R_n(X_n)}_{\substack{\text{immediate}\\ \text{return}\\ \text{from}\\ \text{stage } n}} + \underbrace{f_{n-1}(W_n - a_nX_n)}_{\substack{\text{optimal}\\ \text{known return}\\ \text{from previous}\\ \text{stage}}}] \quad \text{for } n = 1, 2, 3, \ldots, N \tag{9.12}$$

Table 9.22 Immediate Profit Function for Each Item

Weight Available W_n	**Optimal Unit X_1**	**Return from Item C $R_1(X_1) = P_1X_1$**	**Optimal Unit X_2**	**Return from Item B $R_2(X_2) = P_2X_2$**	**Optimal Unit X_3**	**Return from Item A $R_3(X_3) = P_3X_3$**
0	0	0	0	\$5 × 0 = \$ 5	0	0
1	0	0	1	5 × 1 = 5	0	0
2	1	\$15 × 1 = \$15	2	5 × 2 = 10	0	0
3	1	15 × 1 = 15	3	5 × 3 = 15	1	\$20 × 1 = \$20
4	2	15 × 2 = 30	4	5 × 4 = 20	1	20 × 1 = 20
5	2	15 × 2 = 30	5	5 × 5 = 25	1	20 × 1 = 20
6	3	15 × 3 = 45	6	5 × 6 = 30	2	20 × 2 = 40
7	3	15 × 3 = 45	7	5 × 7 = 35	2	20 × 2 = 40
8	4	15 × 4 = 60	8	5 × 8 = 40	2	20 × 2 = 40
9	4	15 × 4 = 60	9	5 × 9 = 45	3	20 × 3 = 60
10	5	15 × 5 = 75	10	5 × 10 = 50	3	20 × 3 = 60

Table 9.23 Stage 1 (Item C) Problem ($A_1 = 2$ tons, $P_1 = \$5$)

Formula: $f_1(W_1) = \max R_1(X_1)$

Available Weight W_1	Unit of X_1	Immediate Return $R_1(X_1)$	$f_1(W_1)$
0	0	0	$f_1(0) = 0$
1	0	0	$f_1(1) = 0$
2	1	15	$f_1(2) = 15$
3	1	15	$f_1(3) = 15$
4	2	30	$f_1(4) = 30$
5	2	30	$f_1(5) = 30$
6	3	45	$f_1(6) = 45$
7	3	45	$f_1(7) = 45$
8	4	60	$f_1(8) = 60$
9	4	60	$f_1(9) = 60$
10	5	75	$f_1(10) = 75$

Note that the term $(W_n - a_nX_n)$, which is the difference between weight W_n available at state n less the total weight a_nX_n allocated at state n, represents the weight remaining at stage $n - 1$. Again the recursive dynamic programming relationship (9.12) conforms to the principle of optimality. At each stage, we find the optimal decision, maximizing the profit for that stage n plus the profits from previous stages.

Table 9.24 Stage 2 (Item B) Problem ($A_2 = 1$, $P_2 = \$5$)

Available Weight W_2	Allocation Decision: X_2				
	0	1	2	3	4
0	0 + 0 = 0	n.f.	n.f.	n.f.	n.f.
1	0 + 0 = 0	5 + 0 = 5*	n.f.	n.f.	n.f.
2	0 + 15 = 15*	5 + 0 = 5	10 + 0 = 10	n.f.	n.f.
3	0 + 15 = 15	5 + 15 = 20*	10 + 0 = 10	15 + 0 = 15	n.f.
4	0 + 30 = 30*	5 + 15 = 20	10 + 15 = 25	15 + 0 = 15	20 + 0 = 20
5	0 + 30 = 30	5 + 30 = 35*	10 + 15 = 25	15 + 15 = 30	20 + 0 = 20
6	0 + 45 = 45*	5 + 30 = 35	10 + 30 = 40	15 + 15 = 30	20 + 15 = 35
7	0 + 45 = 45	5 + 45 = 50*	10 + 30 = 40	15 + 30 = 45	20 + 15 = 35
8	0 + 60 = 60*	5 + 45 = 50	10 + 45 = 55	15 + 30 = 45	20 + 30 = 50
9	0 + 60 = 60	5 + 60 = 65*	10 + 45 = 55	15 + 45 = 60	20 + 30 = 50
10	0 + 75 = 75*	5 + 60 = 65	10 + 60 = 70	15 + 45 = 60	20 + 45 = 65

We obtain the value of the immediate profit by multiplying profit per unit by the number of units; that is,

$$R_n(X_n) = P_n \times X_n$$

Given available weights ranging from 0 to 10 tons, the resulting profit function is as shown in Table 9.22.

Since the unit weight for item C is 2 tons, the X_1 column shows that we cannot allocate 1 unit of item C unless the available weight capacity to be loaded is at least 2 tons. We cannot load 2 units of item C unless the available weight is 4 or 5 tons. Once we know the allocation of the optimal unit of X_1, the immediate profit function $R_1(X_1)$ is easily calculated as P_1X_1, shown in the third column of Table 9.22. Then we calculate the $R_2(X_2)$ and $R_3(X_3)$ columns in a similar way, as shown in Table 9.22.

Proceeding with our recursive dynamic calculations, we again work backwards. At stage 1 ($n = 1$), all the remaining available weights W_1, viewed as state variables, ranging from 0 to 10 tons could be allocated to the last item C. Given the formula $f_1(W_1) = \max R_1(X_1)$, we obtain the stage 1 results (Table 9.23) directly from Table 9.22.

Moving to stage 2, we note that the available weight W_2 could also be any amount between 0 and 10 tons. The optimal profit function is calculated by

$$f_2(W_2) = \max [R_2(X_2) + f_1(W_2 - a_2X_2)]$$

Formula: $f_2 (W_2) = \max [R_2 (X)_2 + f_1 (W_2 - A_2X_2)]$

Allocation Decision: X_2							
5	6	7	8	9	10	$R_2(X_2)$	$f_2(W_2)$
n.f.	n.f.	n.f.	n.f.	n.f.	n.f.	0	$f_2(0) = 0$
n.f.	n.f.	n.f.	n.f.	n.f.	n.f.	1	$f_2(1) = 5$
n.f.	n.f.	n.f.	n.f.	n.f.	n.f.	0	$f_2(2) = 15$
n.f.	n.f.	n.f.	n.f.	n.f.	n.f.	1	$f_2(3) = 20$
n.f.	n.f.	n.f.	n.f.	n.f.	n.f.	0	$f_2(4) = 30$
25 + 0 = 25	n.f.	n.f.	n.f.	n.f.	n.f.	1	$f_2(5) = 35$
25 + 0 = 25	30 + 0 = 30	n.f.	n.f.	n.f.	n.f.	0	$f_2(6) = 45$
25 + 15 = 40	30 + 0 = 30	35 + 0 = 35	n.f.	n.f.	n.f.	1	$f_2(7) = 50$
25 + 15 = 40	30 + 15 = 45	35 + 0 = 35	40 + 0 = 40	n.f.	n.f.	0	$f_2(8) = 60$
25 + 30 = 55	30 + 15 = 45	35 + 15 = 50	40 + 0 = 40	45 + 0 = 45	n.f.	1	$f_2(9) = 65$
25 + 30 = 55	30 + 30 = 60	35 + 15 = 50	40 + 15 = 55	45 + 0 = 45	50 + 0 = 50	0	$f_2(10) = 75$

Formula:

$$f_3(W_3) = \max\,[R_3(X_3) + f_2(W_3 - a_3X_3)]$$

Table 9.25 Stage 3 (Item A) Problem ($A_3 = 3$, $P_3 = \$20$)

Available Weight W_3	Allocation Decision: X_3				
	1	2	3	$R_3(X_3)$	$f_3(W_3)$
10	20 + 50 = 70	40 + 30 = 70	60 + 5 = 65	1, 2	$f_3(10) = 70$

Table 9.26 Optimal Allocation for Each Item (Stage)

Stage n (Item)	Weight Available W_n	Optimal Unit of Allocation X_n	Total Weight Allocated to an Item A_nX_n	Total Weight Remaining $W_n - A_nX_n$	Total Profit
3 (item A)	10	1	1 × 3 tons = 3 tons	7 tons	\$20
2 (item B)	7	1	1 × 1 ton = 1 ton	6 tons	5
1 (item C)	6	5	3 × 2 tons = 6 tons	0 tons	45
				Total =	\$70
Alternative Solution:					
3 (item A)	10	2	2 × 3 tons = 6 tons	4 tons	\$40
2 (item B)	4	0	0	4 tons	0
1 (item C)	4	2	2 × 2 tons = 4 tons	0 tons	30
				Total =	\$70

which says that, given each available weight W_2, total profit is the sum of the immediate returns from the allocation of units of item B (stage 2) plus the optimal allocation of the remaining weight in the previous item C (stage 1). The computation process is shown in Table 9.24. Note that, once we know the optimal unit of X_2, we can obtain the value of $R_2(X_2)$ directly from the corresponding column in Table 9.22. And we can obtain the value of the second term, $f_1(W_2 - a_2X_2)$, from the last column of Table 9.23. The nonfeasible allocations are again labeled n.f. in the table.

At stage 3 there is only one row in the table, because the available weight is 10 tons. Table 9.25 indicates that the optimal allocation is either $X_3 = 1$ or $X_3 = 2$; they both yield a maximum profit of \$70.

The optimal allocations at each stage (item) are summarized in Table 9.26, which indicates that 1 unit is assigned for both items A and B and 3 units for item C. Alternatively, we could allocate 2 units for both items A and C and no units for item B. Either pattern of allocation yields a total profit of $70 and is optimal.

Product-Mix Problem

(Example 3) Judy Ball Manufacturing makes three models of porcelain (1, 2, and 3), designated by X_1, X_2, and X_3, respectively. The raw materials required and the cash return for each product are shown in Table 9.27. The total number of boxes of raw materials available for the given period is 10. Judy Ball wants to select a product mix that maximizes the total cash return. Since a fractional unit of porcelain is meaningless, the product must be measured in integer values. Thus, we have the following integer programming problem:

$$\text{Max} \quad Z = 4X_1 + 7X_2 + 10X_3$$

subject to $\quad 2X_1 + 3X_2 + 4X_3 \leq 10$

and $\quad X_1, X_2,$ and X_3 are all integers

As in the cargo-loading problem, we can solve the integer programming problem by using dynamic programming techniques. To do so, we consider each product as a stage and the unallocated raw material as a state variable. Let

B = total number of boxes of raw materials for allocation

B_n = state variable representing the total number of boxes of unallocated raw materials at stage n

X_n = number of units of product n

b_n = number of boxes of raw materials required to produce 1 unit of product n

Table 9.27
Product-Mix Problem

Model	Number of Boxes of Raw Material Required for Each Unit of Product	Profit Per Unit
1	4	$10
2	3	7
3	2	4

$f_n(B_n)$ = return function when B_n boxes of raw materials are optimally allocated at stage n (item n) with n more stages (items) to be allocated

$R_n(X_n)$ = level of product n yielding $f_n(B_n)$

Table 9.28 Immediate Return Function for Each Product

Available Boxes of Raw Materials B_n	Unit of Product 3 X_1	Return from Product 3 $R_1(X_1) = P_1X_1$	Unit of Product 2 X_2	Return from Product 2 $R_2(X_2) = P_2X_2$	Unit of Product 1 X_3	Return from Product 1 $R_3(X_3) = P_3X_3$
0	0	0	0	0	0	0
1	0	0	0	0	0	0
2	1	4	0	0	0	0
3	1	4	1	7	0	0
4	2	8	1	7	1	10
5	2	8	1	7	1	10
6	3	12	2	14	2	20
7	3	12	2	14	2	20
8	4	16	2	14	2	20
9	4	16	3	21	3	60
10	5	20	3	21	3	60

Formula:
$f_1(B_1) = \max R_1(X_1)$

Table 9.29 Stage 1 (Product 3) Problem ($n = 1, A_1 = 2$)

Available Boxes of Raw Materials B_1	Unit of Product C X_1	Return from Product C $R_1(X_1)$	$f_1(B_1)$
0	0	0	$f_1(0) = 0$
1	0	0	$f_1(1) = 0$
2	1	4	$f_1(2) = 4$
3	1	4	$f_1(3) = 4$
4	2	8	$f_1(4) = 8$
5	2	8	$f_1(5) = 8$
6	3	12	$f_1(6) = 12$
7	3	12	$f_1(7) = 12$
8	4	16	$f_1(8) = 16$
9	4	16	$f_1(9) = 16$
10	5	20	$f_1(10) = 20$

Table 9.30 Stage 2 (Product 2) Problem ($n = 1, A_2 = 3$)

Formula: $f_2(B_2) = \max [R_2(X_2) + f_1(B_2 - A_2X_2)]$

Available Boxes of Raw Materials B_2	Allocation Decision: X_2 0	1	2	3	$R_2(X_2)$	$f_2(B_2)$
0						
1	0 + 0 = 0				0	$f_2(1) = 0$
2	0 + 4 = 4*				0	$f_2(2) = 4$
3	0 + 4 = 4*	4 + 0 = 4*			0, 1	$f_2(3) = 4$
4	0 + 8 = 8*	4 + 0 = 4			0	$f_2(4) = 8$
5	0 + 8 = 8*	4 + 4 = 8*			0, 1	$f_2(5) = 8$
6	0 + 12 = 12	4 + 4 = 8	14 + 0 = 14*		2	$f_2(6) = 14$
7	0 + 12 = 12	4 + 8 = 12	14 + 0 = 14*		2	$f_2(7) = 14$
8	0 + 16 = 16	4 + 8 = 12	14 + 4 = 18*		2	$f_2(8) = 18$
9	0 + 16 = 16	4 + 12 = 16	14 + 4 = 18	21 + 0 = 21*	3	$f_2(9) = 21$
10	0 + 20 = 20	4 + 12 = 16	14 + 8 = 22*	21 + 0 = 21	2	$f_2(10) = 22$

Table 9.31 Stage 3 (Product 1) Problem ($n = 3, A_3 = 4$)

Formula: $f_3(B_3) = \max [R_3(X_3) + f_2(B_3 - A_3X_3)]$

Available Boxes of Raw Materials B_3	Allocation Decision: X_3 1	2	$R_3(X_3)$	$f_2(B_3)$
10	10 + 14 = 24	20 + 0 = 20	1	$f_3(10) = 24$

Table 9.32 Optimal Allocation of Raw Materials for Each Product

Stage n (Product)	Available Boxes of Raw Materials B_n	Optimal Unit of X_n	Total Boxes of Raw Materials Allocated B_nX_n	Total Boxes of Raw Materials Remaining	Total Profit
3 (product 1)	10	1	1 × 4 = 4	6	10
2 (product 2)	6	2	2 × 3 = 6	0	14
1 (product 3)	0	0	0	0	0
					Total 24

The recursive dynamic programming relationship is then

$$f_n(B_n) = \max \underbrace{[R_n(X_n)}_{\substack{\text{immediate}\\ \text{return}\\ \text{from}\\ \text{stage } n}} + \underbrace{f_{n-1}(B_n - b_nX_n)]}_{\substack{\text{optimal known}\\ \text{return from}\\ \text{previous}\\ \text{stage } n-1}} \quad \text{for } n = 1, 2, 3, \ldots, N \tag{9.13}$$

The term $(B_n - b_nX_n)$, which is the difference between the total available raw material and the amount used up in producing product n, represents the remaining raw materials at stage $n - 1$. Equation (9.13) states that, at each stage, we find the optimal return by maximizing the immediate return from product n (stage n) plus the returns from preceding products (stage $n - 1$).

The immediate return function for each product is shown in Table 9.28. If we allocate between 2 and 3 boxes of raw materials to product 3, only 1 unit of this product can be produced. If we allocate less than 4 boxes of raw materials to product 1, we cannot produce this product at all.

The stage 1 results of our dynamic programming calculation, obtained directly from Table 9.28, are reproduced in Table 9.29. Going on to stage 2 (product 2) and stage 3 (product 1), we ask the reader to verify the results shown in Table 9.30 and Table 9.31. Furthermore, the reader should derive the summary of the optimal allocation of raw material for each product, as shown in Table 9.32.

9.4 A Dynamic Programming Model with Two State Variables

Each example we have discussed has had a one-dimensional (one-constraint) state variable. In the following example, we show how the dynamic programming model can be extended to two state variables.

In the preceding product-mix problem, suppose that we have a machine time constraint in addition to the raw material limitation. Let

P_n = profit per unit of product n for $n = 1, 2, \ldots, N$

B = total number of boxes of raw materials for allocation

X_n = number of the unit of product n

b_n = number of boxes of raw material required to produce 1 unit of product n

T = total amount of machine time available

t_n = amount of machine time needed to produce 1 unit of product n

With $n = 1, 2, \ldots, N$, the integer programming model for that product-mix problem is

$$\text{Max} \quad Z = \sum_{n=1}^{N} P_n(X_n)$$

subject to

$$\sum_{n=1}^{N} b_n X_n \le B$$

$$\sum_{n=1}^{N} t_n X_n \le T$$

and

$$X_n \text{ are integers for all } n$$

To formulate this as a dynamic programming problem, we can generalize from the one-constraint-for-one-state-variable situation. Since a one-dimensional state variable was needed in the one-constraint case, it is reasonable to expect that a two-dimensional state variable will be required with two constraints. Let

B_n = stage variable associated with the first constraint, representing, as before, the total number of boxes of raw material unallocated at stage n (product n)

T_n = state variable associated with the second constraint, representing the total amount of unused machine time to be allocated to stage n

$f_n(B_n, T_n)$ = return function when available boxes of raw material B_n and available amount of machine time T_n are optimally allocated over stage n for $n = 1, 2, \ldots, N$

The appropriate dynamic recursive relation is then

$$f_n(B_n T_n) = \max \left[P_n(X_n) + f_{n-1}(B_n - b_n X_n, T_n - t_n X_n)\right] \quad \text{for all } n \tag{9.14}$$

Conceptually, formulating a dynamic recursion problem with two state variables is really no different from the case that we have just studied with one state variable. Computationally, however, in searching for an optimal return we must calculate all possible combinations of the two state variables at each stage. This obviously multiplies the number of computations at each stage, but the addition of a new constraint in a linear programming problem causes only a slight increase in computation time. Furthermore, in a well-defined linear programming model, the optimization problem can be solved simultaneously by using the standard algorithm—the simplex method.

By contrast, the dynamic programming approach attacks the optimization problem by splitting it into different stages in which optimization takes place. There is no general efficient computer program to handle all dynamic programming problems. But the recursion models with only one state variable that we discussed earlier in this chapter are simple enough for the calculation normally to be performed by a specially written computer programming routine. In a dynamic programming problem with two state variables, however, the calculation process is not easily handled by computer programming routines.

9.5 Summary

The critical aspect of formulating a dynamic programming model is the ability to distinguish among the following concepts and terms:

Stage A point in the problem situation where a decision is made. Stages frequently represent time periods, but they can also represent places (a group of cities), people, or other entities.

State Information that describes various conditions at a stage. A specific city is referred to as a state variable in any stage of the shortest-route problem. Variables such as beginning inventory, number of unassigned auditors, weight of an item, and quantity of raw material for allocation are all state variables that link together the various stages in a multistage decision problem.

Decision or Policy Variable The decision made at each stage. The policy variable transforms the state variable from any given stage into a state associated with the next stage.

Return or Objective Function One per stage, it indicates the amount of return, cost, distance, or whatever determined by the decision variable and state at each stage. We measure the overall value of the return function by incorporating the returns from each stage.

Principle of Optimality Guideline for optimizing the overall return function which states that, regardless of how a particular state and stage were entered, all remaining decisions should be made in an optimal manner.

Recursive Return Function In accordance with the principle of optimality, the optimal return function is found by maximizing (minimizing) the immediate return (cost) from stage n plus the known optimal return (cost) from the previous stage $n - 1$.

Dynamic Recursive Relation On the basis of the principle of optimality, the multistage problem is solved by first attacking the problem in the last stage, then working backwards and solving the problem in the next-to-last stage, and so on until the first-stage problem is solved. This computational procedure is also referred to as a recursive algorithm.

With these concepts and terms in mind, we can summarize the general procedure for formulating and solving a dynamic program as follows:

1. Define the decision or policy variables and stages. Determine the state variables, and characterize the dynamic relation by which the state in one stage is linked with the state in the next stage.
2. Formulate the recursive function, either maximum or minimum. Specify the return function at stage 1 and work backwards.
3. Construct the appropriate tables to show the computational analysis for values of the return function at each stage.
4. Determine the overall optimal decision at each stage by working forward, using tables that have already been computed.

Constructing dynamic programming models is something like an art, and the most effective way to develop this ability is by practice. In this chapter, we have chosen some representative problems to illustrate the essential concepts and elements common to most dynamic programming models. Throughout the discussion, we have tried to demonstrate the general approach to model formulation, which is quite similar in most dynamic programming problems. After studying this chapter, the reader should have a good idea of how to handle dynamic programming problems with a one-dimensional state variable.

Exercises

9.1 Be sure that you understand the following terms:
a. Stage
b. State
c. Dynamic programming
d. Recursive algorithm

9.2 State the principle of optimality.

9.3 Consider the route map shown in Figure E9.1.
a. Formulate a dynamic programming model to minimize the length from O (origin) to D (destination).
b. Solve the model and find the length of the shortest path from O to D.
c. Trace the shortest path.

9.4 Refer to the route map given in exercise 9.3.
a. Formulate a dynamic programming model to maximize the length from O to D.
b. Solve the model and find the longest path.
c. Trace the longest path.

9.5 What is the dynamic recursive relation?

9.6 Debbie Rausch, executive vice-president of Round Corporation in Denver, has to attend a meeting in New York. Before she goes to the meeting, she wants to visit one of the regional sales offices located in the midwest (Detroit, Chicago, or Cleveland) and one located in the south (Miami, New Orleans, or Richmond). Since she wishes to make this trip a surprise inspection, she does not want to reveal her itinerary. Her administrative assistant has prepared the road map shown in Figure E9.2 with the airline ticket price between cities indicated. Rausch wants to minimize the total travel cost of her trip.

Figure E9.1

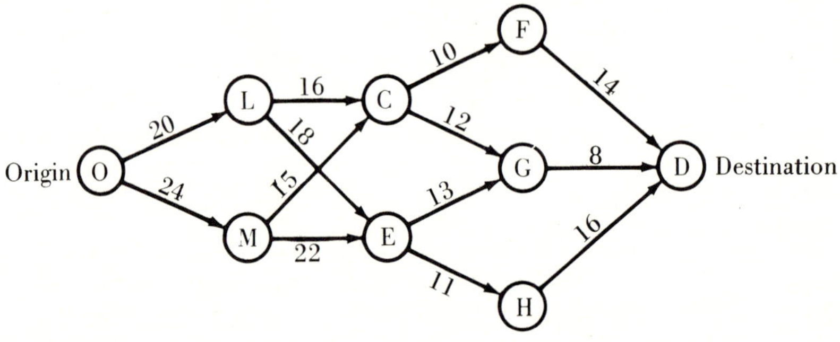

Figure E9.2

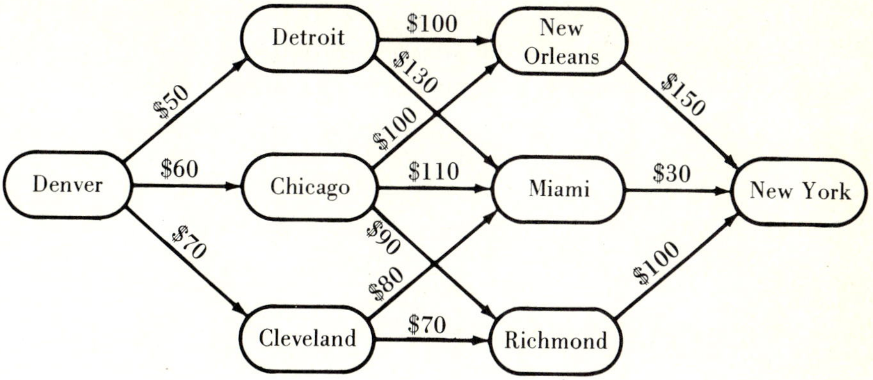

a. Using the "backwards" process, find an optimal route that Debbie could take to New York.
b. Formulate a recursive dynamic programming model for Debbie.
c. Solve the model and find the minimum cost and its associated optimal route.

9.7 Refer to exercise 9.6. If airline services from Richmond to New York are not available, what is the cheapest route from Denver to New York?

9.8 Refer to exercise 9.6.
a. Rausch's son lives in Detroit. Find an optimal route from Denver to New York that goes through Detroit.
b. Rausch may want to return to Denver after her meeting in New York. What is the cheapest route?

9.9 a. What is the material balance equation?
b. Let

i_0 = specific level of initial inventory
X_n = production quantity at period n
D_n = quantity demanded at period n

With n = 1, 2, 3, and 4, write the coefficients of different period equations in matrix form, and move all constants to the right-hand side.
c. Show that

$$X_1 + X_2 + X_3 + X_4 = \sum_{n=1}^{4} D_n - i_0$$

9.10 Refer to the Sheridan Manufacturing Company problem discussed in Section 9.2. If the inventory holding cost increased from $0.50 to $2.00 per unit, how would this change affect the optimal solution? Formulate a recursive dynamic program and solve it. Show the changes in terms of production and inventory.

9.11 Meck Manufacturing Company wants to establish a production schedule by which to manufacture an item during the next spring from January through April. The company has projected a stationary demand of 3 units for each month. Production cost depends on the number of units produced, as shown in the following table:

Production (Units per Month)	0	1	2	3	4	5
Cost ($000)	0	40	70	90	100	110

In addition, there is an inventory cost of $20,000 per unit for any units holding at the end of the month. The company has 1 unit of inventory at the beginning of January and wants 2 units of inventory at the end of April. Production capacity in any month is restricted to no more than 5 units. The level of ending inventory in any month is limited to 5 units. Find the optimal production decision for the company.

9.12 "Mini Ha-Ha" is a 10-ton barge owned by Atlantic Ship, Inc. For one particular trip from Atlantic City to New York, there are 4 types of commodities to be carried. They have the characteristics shown in the following table:

Commodity	**Unit Weight (tons)**	**Profit per Ton**
A	4	$100
B	2	50
C	3	80
D	1	20

Given the total allowable weight of 10 tons, management's problem is to determine the number of units of ***each*** of the 4 commodities to carry to maximize the total profit.

a. Why would a linear programming model be inappropriate in this problem?
b. Formulate an integer programming model.
c. Convert the integer programming model into a recursive programming model.
d. Solve the model and give the optimal solution.

9.13 Phyllis Noble wishes to invest $50,000 among three possible investment projects suggested by her bank's investment analyst. She could invest

Table E9.1

Amount of Investment ($000)	Expected Return from Project ($000)		
	A	B	C
0	0	0	0
10	8	9	12
20	15	14	16
30	21	25	24
40	26	30	28
50	30	34	32

all, part, or none of her $50,000 in any one of the projects, but she has to invest in units of $10,000. The expected return, which depends on the amount of money invested, is shown in Table E9.1.

a. What is the policy or decision variable?
b. How can the problem be expressed in term of stages?
c. What characterizes the state of the problem at each stage?
d. Formulate a recursive dynamic programming model for any stage.
e. Find the optimal pattern of allocation of funds—the pattern that yields the maximum return.

9.14 Jack Moss, a junior majoring in business administration at Western Texas University, has to take a final examination for three courses—mathematics, management science, and statistics. He has only 8 more hours to review all material. Jack has a habit of taking a coffee break after each 2 hours of study, so he divides his total available time into 4 periods. In each period he will continuously devote 2 hours of study to a particular subject. The university has a 4-point grade system. That is, A = 4, B = 3, C = 2, and D = 1. According to Jack's estimate, the relationships between his grade-point in any subject and the hours of time he spends studying that subject are as shown in Table E9.2.

a. What is the policy or decision variable?
b. How can the problem be analyzed in term of stages?
c. What characterizes the state of the problem at each stage?
d. Formulate a recursive dynamic programming model at any stage.
e. Find the optimal pattern of allocating time—the pattern that yields the maximum grade-point total for Jack Moss.

9.15 Jean Adams, a graduate student in accounting at Chicago Western College, is preparing for her CPA examination. Her review efforts are focused on three areas of concentration: (1) accounting theory, (2) audit and taxation, and (3) business law and quantitative methods. She has only 5 days left. Table E9.3 indicates the relationships between the

Table E9.2

Block of Time Available	Course		
	Mathematics	Management Science	Statistics
0	0	1	0
2	1	1	1
4	3	2	2
6	4	3	3
8	4	4	3

Table E9.3

Block of Hours	Accounting Theory	Audit and Taxation	Business Law and Quantitative Methods
0	0	0	0
1	40	30	20
2	65	50	40
3	75	60	50
4	90	70	70
5	100	80	90

expected grade in a particular subject and the block of time spent studying it.

a. Identify the stage, decision variable, and state variable.
b. Formulate a dynamic programming model for Jean Adams to maximize the numerical total of her grades.
c. Solve the allocation problem for Jean Adams so that her total score is maximized.

9.16 Senator Como is running for re-election to the United States Senate on an independent ticket. His district is divided into 3 precincts, precincts 1, 2, and 3. He plans to allocate 5 campaign workers among these precincts. Table E9.4 shows that the increase in his plurality in each precinct depends on the number of campaign workers assigned.

a. Formulate a dynamic programming model for Senator Como.
b. Solve this model and indicate how many campaign workers are assigned to each precinct.
c. Are the decision variables in your model integer-valued?
d. Are the decision variables in your model proportional to the expected increase in plurality?

9.17 The D. R. G. Publishing Company has hired 5 new sales representatives to cover 3 territories in which they will sell college textbooks. Market

Table E9.4

Number of Campaign Workers	Precinct 1	Precinct 2	Precinct 3
0	0	0	0
1	10	30	20
2	30	50	30
3	45	80	45
4	60	90	65
5	70	98	76

Table E9.5

	Expected Net Return		
Number of Sales Representatives	Territory 1	Territory 2	Territory 3
0	0	0	0
1	$150	$110	$100
2	260	200	200
3	350	280	280
4	400	340	350
5	420	380	410

studies reveal that the net return (sales less cost) is a function of the number of sales representatives assigned to each territory, as shown in Table E9.5. The company wants to determine the number of representatives to assign in each territory so that the total net return is maximized.

a. Formulate a recursive dynamic programming model for this problem.
b. Solve the model and provide an optimal assignment for the company.

9.18 Refer to exercise 9.17. The D. R. G. Publishing Company is considering hiring an additional sales representative. How much expected net return would the new person contribute to the company?

9.19 Refer to exercises 9.17 and 9.18. Why would a linear programming model be inappropriate?

9.20 The First National Auto Dealer is considering running a number of advertisements on local radio stations A, B, and C. The spot commercials will be aired for the next 6 months. Management has estimated the following sales-response relationship between the expected net return (expected revenue less advertising cost) and the amount of money allocated to spot commercials on each station. These estimates are shown in Table E9.6. The total budget is limited to $50,000, and each spot

Table E9.6

Amount of Money Allocated ($000)	Expected Net Return for Radio Stations ($000)		
	A	B	C
0	0	0	0
10	30	50	60
20	50	80	80
30	65	100	90
40	70	110	95
50	80	120	110

commercial costs a unit price of $10,000. Formulate a dynamic programming model for the firm and find an optimal purchasing plan.

9.21 Consider the following decision problem.

$$\text{Min} \quad \sum_{j=1}^{3} C_j X_j$$

subject to

$$\sum_{j=1}^{3} X_j = N$$

and $\qquad X_j$ are all nonnegative integers

where X_j = jth product

C_j = cost per unit of jth product

N = available quantity of raw materials to be allocated

Transform this model into a dynamic programming model. Identify the stages and state variables, and write down the dynamic recursion formula.

9.22 Describe the similarities and differences between linear programming and dynamic programming.

9.23 Suppose that, in the product-mix problem, we had not only the material limitation but also a budget constraint. With k products, the problem becomes

$$\text{Max} \quad \sum_{n=1}^{k} P_n X_n$$

subject to

$$\sum_{n=1}^{k} A_n X_n \le A$$

$$\sum_{n=1}^{k} b_n X_n \le B$$

and X_n are all noninteger values

where X_n = jth product

P_n = profit per unit of product j

A = total quantity of raw materials

A_n = number of units of raw materials required to produce 1 unit of product j

B = total allocational budget

b_n = cost of producing 1 unit of X_j

a. Identify the stages and state variables.
b. Convert this problem into a recursive dynamic programming model.

9.24 Computationally, why is a dynamic programming model with two-dimensional variables more complicated than the one-dimensional case?

Suggested Readings

Bellman, R. E. *Dynamic Programming.* Princeton, N.J.: Princeton University Press, 1957.

Debanne, J. G. "Management Science in Energy Policy—A Case History and Success Story." *Interfaces,* 5, No. 2, Pt. 2 (February 1975), pp. 1–21.

Hadley, G. *Nonlinear and Dynamic Programming.* Reading, Mass.: Addison-Wesley, 1964.

Howard, R. A. *Dynamic Programming and Markov Processes.* Cambridge, Mass.: M.I.T. Press, 1960.

Nemhauser, George L. *Introduction to Dynamic Programming.* New York: Wiley, 1966.

Peterson, E. R. "A Dynamic Programming Model for the Expansion of Electric Power Systems." *Management Science,* 20, No. 4, Pt. II (December 1973), pp. 656–664.

Rothstein, Marvin. "A Dynamic Programming Model for Periodical Selection." *Decision Sciences,* 4, No. 2 (April 1973), pp. 237–246.

Taylor, P. T. "A Dynamic Programming Approach to the Design of Natural Gas Pipelines." Paper presented at the Fourteenth Annual TIMS Conference, August 1967, Mexico City.

Wagner, Harvey M. *Principles of Operations Research.* 2nd ed. Englewood Cliffs, N.J.: Prentice-Hall, 1975.

10

Project Planning and Control Using PERT/CPM

In the preceding chapters, linear programming and its extensions have been presented to demonstrate modern analytical methods of determining the efficient allocation of resources. We have seen that, in a production process, the optimal allocation of machine centers to production needs results in maximum profits. In a transportation problem, the optimal routing of goods between various supply points and demand centers results in minimal transportation costs. In this chapter the emphasis shifts to efficient project management, wherein the organization of time becomes the crucial factor.

Projects with many activities require careful coordination. Some functions must precede others, whereas other functions can occur simultaneously. All parts of a project must lead to its timely and successful completion. ***Overlapping, dove-tailing, scheduling,*** and ***coordinating*** are some of the practices familiar to a successful project manager. The techniques of PERT and CPM provide an analytical framework for the efficient organization and supervision of complex projects.

10.1 PERT/CPM: Basic Concepts

PERT, the ***program evaluation and review technique,*** is a relatively recent arrival in the field of applied quantitative methods for business. Developed jointly in 1958 by the United States Navy and the management consulting firm of Booz, Allen, and Hamilton, its original purpose was to expedite the Polaris ballistic missile project. Since then, the usefulness of PERT has led to its widespread application in government and industry, including construction projects, industrial development, product planning, contract completion, systems design, space exploration, complex maintenance and repair situations, and development of new weapons systems.

CPM, or ***critical path method,*** is a similar project management technique that was developed independently by the DuPont Company at about the same time as PERT. The development of CPM for industrial purposes, as contrasted with PERT's original military purposes, is a distinction that lacks real importance, since both are concerned with effective project control. However, on a conceptual basis, the two techniques may be differentiated according to their individual treatment of activity times and time-cost relationships. With regard to the former, PERT allows for the completion time of activities to be uncertain or probabilistic, whereas CPM treats them as fixed, or deterministic. Regarding the latter, CPM incorporates specific treatment of time reduction through the application of greater resources at increased cost, whereas PERT does not. These are largely historical distinctions that have been dropped as the best of both techniques have been melded into a common approach to project management that bears the combined name, ***PERT/CPM.***

A few basic concepts are fundamental to nearly all project-planning situations. First, a project generally consists of numerous activities that must be coordinated, each of which contributes to the overall completion of the project. Second, a project usually progresses through stages of completion that are marked by events or milestones. Project initiation and project completion are events of great significance, and many other intermediate events occur as individual activities are begun or completed. ***Events,*** then, represent points of recognizable achievement. Third, there is generally a definite interdependency among all project activities such that relationships of precedence are clearly established. Specifying the interdependencies of a project is fundamental both to understanding the order of precedence of all project activities and to good project planning. PERT/CPM analysis relies heavily on the accurate specification or portrayal of all project activities in the form of a ***network,*** the lines of which trace through the project in an appropriate and organized fashion.

A sample of a complex PERT network—one that was developed by the Connecticut State Department of Education—appears in Figure 10.1 (which, incidentally, shows only about half of the entire project).

Figure 10.1 Part of an Extensive PERT Diagram Taken from a Practical Project-Planning Application

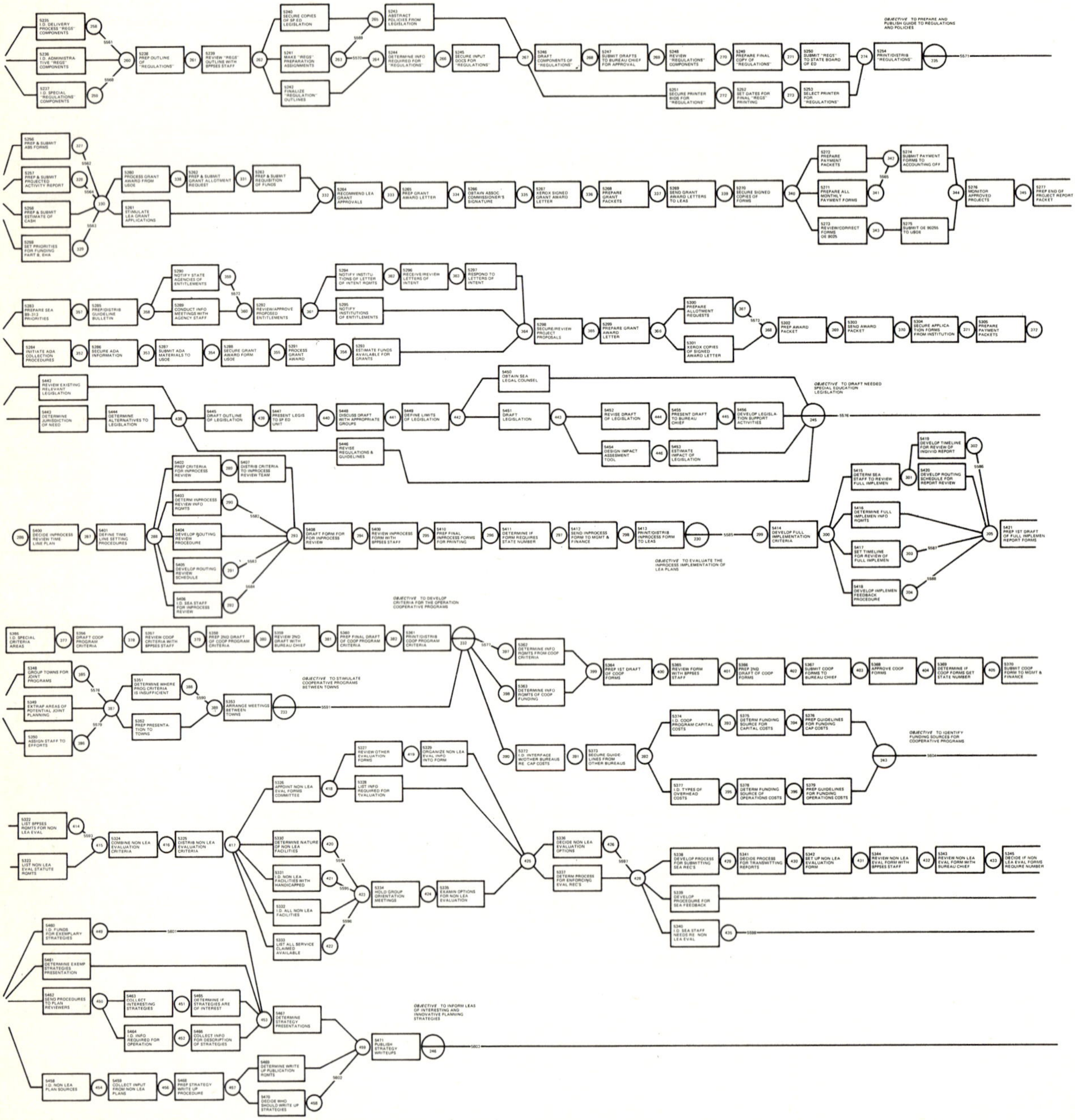

Numerous activities are identified by lines and rectangles, and the order of precedence of activities throughout the network is clearly indicated. Whereas such a network is too complex to illustrate in this introductory chapter, some of the most effective applications of PERT/CPM occur in very complex situations. The concepts and techniques developed in this chapter extend to applications of all sizes and complexity. With the aid of PERT/CPM computer routines, efficient project planning and control are possible in situations that defy proper coordination by ordinary intuitive approaches.

10.2 Project Portrayal—The Gantt Chart

The first step in planning a project for PERT analysis is to list all relevant activities. Project activities must be distinctly separable so that each is well defined unto itself. Furthermore, each activity must be completely predictable in the sense that it represents an integral part of the whole project. All activities must be completed before the final project objective can be reached.

Suppose, for example, that you must organize the logistics of a space shuttle launch—that is, the loading of people and materials in a timely and efficient way so that "lift-off" can proceed according to a given schedule. Assume that 9 basic activities have been identified. These activities and the time required to complete each are listed in Table 10.1.

Table 10.1
Logistics for a Space Shuttle Launch

Activity	**Time Required (minutes)**
1. Uncovering the Launch Pad	40
2. Check-in of Scientists	110
3. Assembling of Astronauts	55
4. Boarding of Astronauts	50
5. Security Clearance of Scientists	55
6. Baggage, Food, and Freight Loading	90
7. Boarding of Scientists	75
8. Radio Communications and Systems Checks	115
9. Final Countdown	60

Two characteristics of the listed activities must be noted. First, although the listing leads generally from the beginning to the end of this project, a specific designation of the order of precedence for the activities is lacking. This must be supplied as a next step. It must be clear, for example, that the assembling of astronauts precedes their boarding of the shuttle. Likewise, the possibility that some activities will proceed simultaneously should be evident. For example, baggage, food, and freight loading can reasonably occur at the same time that scientists are receiving their security clearances. A second fundamental characteristic of this particular listing of activities is that the times allotted to every activity are single, fixed values, which is a typical CPM presentation of fixed, or determined, activity times. These two very basic characteristics are extended with the techniques that follow.

One of the primary planning devices that was used before PERT/CPM (and that continues to be used even now, in conjunction with PERT/CPM) is the ***Gantt chart***—a graph or chart that plots against a time scale the duration of activities as they are planned or expected to occur. Figure 10.2 shows a Gantt chart that has been developed for the space shuttle logistics project. This chart, which can be used for planning and control, presents a complete picture of the timing of activities—all in terms of a common time line. Overall, the logistics project will require 300 minutes to move from beginning to end, with some activities succeeding others and some occurring simultaneously. The usefulness of a Gantt chart can be summarized as follows:

1. It shows clearly the timing of each activity in relation to all others.
2. It shows which activities have been planned to follow others and which are overlapping.
3. It allows for project planning by manipulation. Project planners can intuitively arrange activities in the Gantt chart on the basis of their experience with similar projects and their knowledge of scheduling and available resources.
4. It marks milestones in project completion—in particular, the beginning and end points of activities.
5. It reflects implicit precedence relationships among project activities.

10.3 The PERT Network

Although a Gantt chart portrays all project activities in relation to a common time frame, it fails to provide the explicit interconnections

Figure 10.2
A Gantt Chart

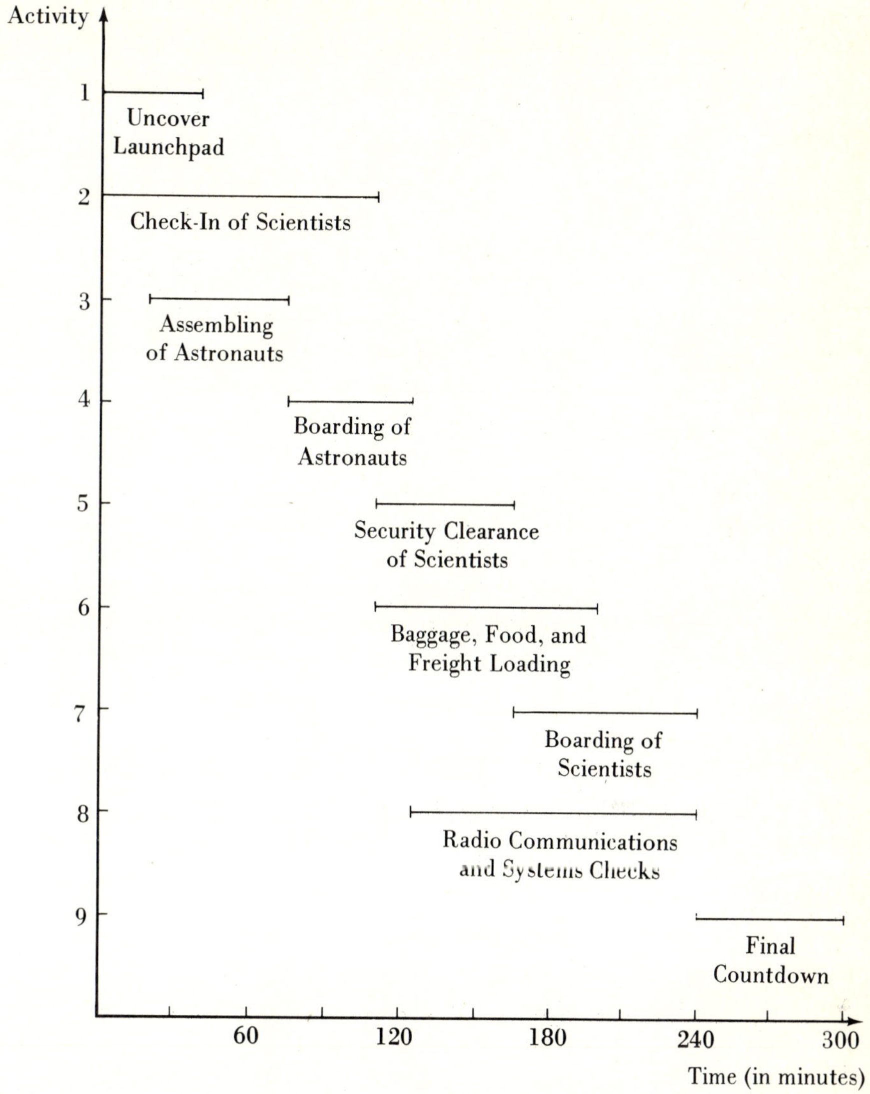

between activities that make possible precise analysis of complex projects. A PERT network does this. It portrays the same project activities in a network diagram such that all interrelationships are shown among activities. The correspondence of each activity to a common time scale is lost when we specify a network rather than a Gantt chart, but the detailed analysis offered by a PERT network provides even more accurate and more useful time-related information.

Before addressing time calculations made using PERT/CPM, let's look at a few of the fundamentals of network presentation. The basic unit of a PERT network is the individual activity. Various visual presentations of activities are used. Generally, however, we use either an arrow or a straight line—representing activity progress—to connect circles or ***nodes***—representing events. For example, activity 9, "Final Countdown," might be represented much as it is shown in the Gantt chart simply by adding beginning and ending event designations (see Figure 10.3a). The length of the line connecting the two events is chosen for convenience of diagramming, not so that it will be proportional to elapsed time.

As we connect a network of activities, one activity's beginning event becomes another activity's ending event. For example, the beginning event for "Final Countdown" coincides with the ending event for "Radio Communications and Systems Checks." (This approach is used in Figure 10.1.) Each event is numbered. Events that have major significance for project completion are called ***milestones*** and are represented by a larger circle with a line extending through it. Ordinary lines are used instead of arrows, and descriptions are given in the rectangles drawn along activity lines.

In Figure 10.3b, the representation of an activity reflects standard flow chart techniques. Although this approach might be entirely appropriate for a particular project, flow chart presentations of PERT

Figure 10.3
Alternative Methods of Representing Activities in a PERT Network

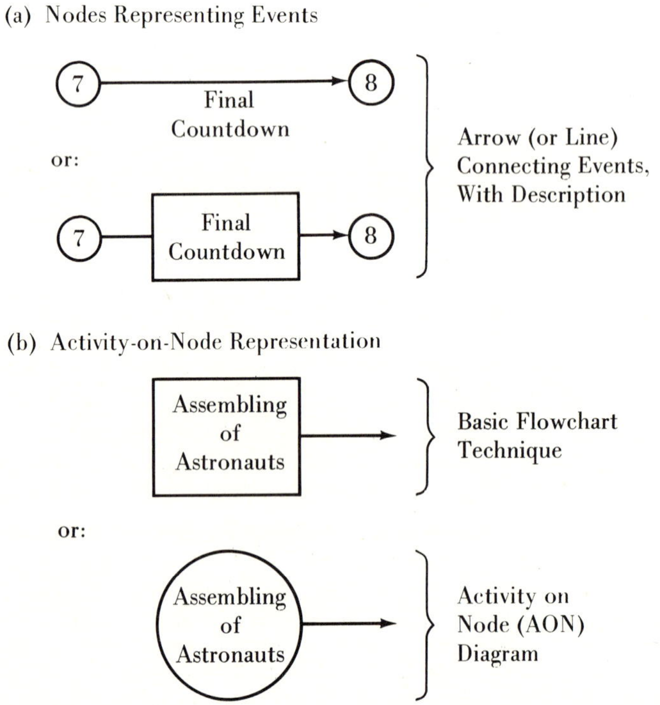

networks are uncommon. This is because flow charting tends to emphasize the boxes as activities more than their interconnections. The activity-on-node, or AON, diagram (Figure 10.3b) is another activity-oriented method of presentation. In this case, the circles or nodes of a network represent the activities themselves. This contrasts with Figure 10.3a, wherein the nodes of a network are the events marking the end of one activity and the beginning of another. Event-oriented activity representations have the distinct advantage for PERT/CPM analysis of identifying and labeling all events in a network of activities. As a result, they provide a convenient bookkeeping method for the interconnections of activities in a network. This will become evident in the analysis of PERT networks that follows.

Now let us consider the development of a complete PERT network for the space shuttle logistics report. All order-of-precedence relationships must be reasoned out before a proper network can be drawn. Beginning with the final project objective—which is a timely lift-off of the shuttle with all of its passengers and equipment aboard—and then working backwards to the beginning of the project, we must itemize all necessary or desirable precedence relationships. For example:

1. Lift-off must be preceded by "Final Countdown.
2. Three activities—"Radio Communications and Systems Checks," "Baggage, Food, and Freight Loading," and "Boarding of Scientists"—must precede "Final Countdown."
3. "Boarding of Astronauts" and "Security Clearance of Scientists" must precede "Boarding of Scientists."
4. "Assembling of Astronauts" precedes "Boarding of Astronauts," but "Uncovering the Launch Pad" must also precede "Boarding of Astronauts."
5. "Uncovering the Launch Pad" must precede "Baggage, Food, and Freight Loading."
6. Finally, "Check-in of Scientists" must precede "Security Clearance of Scientists."

Granted, this is a backwards way of looking at the project, but there is good reason for proceeding in this manner. The logic of organizing a project is often based on answering the question, "What activity or activities must have been completed before a given activity can be initiated?" This follows the logic of finding the ***immediate predecessor(s)*** of a given activity. The emphasis is on establishing order of precedence.

In practice, sketching a PERT network may help us conceptualize the order-of-precedence relationships that must be maintained. Construct-

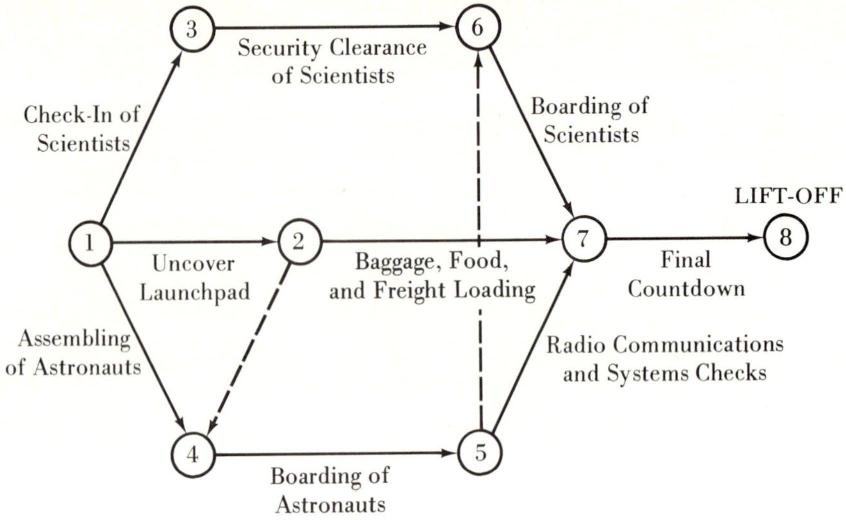

Figure 10.4
A PERT Network for the Space Shuttle Logistics Project

ing the network requires drafting and redrafting until all appropriate interconnections between activities have been specified. A PERT network for the space shuttle logistics project was prepared in this way and is presented in Figure 10.4.

In this network, there are three ways to start at the beginning (node 1) and reach the end of the project (node 8). These are called ***paths*** through the network. They are identified by the string or succession of project nodes covered—for example, path 1-3-6-7-8, path 1-2-7-8, and path 1-4-5-7-8, in this particular case. A path through the network is measured by the time required to complete all activities along that path. Referring to Table 10.1, which shows the time required for all activities, the reader can quickly compute the time required to complete each of the paths. These calculations are given in Table 10.2.

Clearly, the longest path (path 1, requiring 300 minutes), has a controlling effect on the overall completion time for the entire network. If an activity on this path were to increase by 5 minutes, completion time for the project would increase by 5 minutes. If an activity on this path required 15 fewer minutes to complete, total project completion time also would decrease by 15 minutes. This time-controlling effect of the longest path has obvious implications for project management. All activities along the longest path must proceed on schedule if overall project completion is to occur on time. Because of its critical importance to project completion schedules, the longest network path is called the ***critical path.***

Project paths other than the critical path do not have the same time-controlling effect as the critical path. Consider, for example, a 10-minute

Table 10.2 Time Required Along Each Path in the Space Shuttle Network

Path 1		Path 2		Path 3	
Activity	Time (minutes)	Activity	Time (minutes)	Activity	Time (minutes)
1 – 3	110	1 – 2	40	1 – 4	55
3 – 6	55	2 – 7	90	4 – 5	50
6 – 7	75	7 – 8	60	5 – 7	115
7 – 8	60		190	7 – 8	60
	300				280

delay in uncovering the launch pad. As a consequence of this delay, the launch pad is not clear until 50 minutes after the beginning of the project, rather than the originally scheduled 40 minutes. How does this delay affect total project completion? Not at all. It does not delay the final countdown, because path 1 is longer than path 2 by 110 minutes. Neither does it affect the boarding of astronauts, because the assembling of astronauts, another prior step, requires 55 minutes. Time flexibility of this sort in a noncritical path is called ***slack***. For this example, there are 15 minutes of slack time associated with uncovering the launch pad; that is, 15 minutes can be added to activity 1 – 2 without causing a delay in the start of the next immediate successor (boarding of astronauts, which starts 55 minutes after project initiation). Flexibility due to slack sometimes allows the project manager an option in the allocation of resources to a project. A worker who is idle because of temporary slack along one particular path of activities might be assigned to activities that lie on the critical path—at least until the slack time has expired. The shifting of available resources between critical and noncritical activities can be an effective project-management tool for expediting overall completion.

Two activities illustrated in Figure 10.4 have not been included in any network path. These are activity 2 – 4 and activity 5 – 6, which are drawn with a broken line or arrow, and which are regarded as ***dummy activities***. There is no ***real*** activity at all in either of these cases; their inclusion in the network indicates order of precedence only. Thus, although there is no actual activity between the uncovering of the launch pad and the boarding of astronauts, the former must be completed before the latter can begin. And although there is no actual activity between the boarding of astronauts and the boarding of scientists, these activities must follow in order of precedence. Each of these activities merely adds a constraint to the interdependence relationships of the network. Dummy activities require no time; they illustrate precedence relationships only.

10.4 PERT-Time Analysis

The PERT network has already added more to our understanding of project requirements and relationships than the Gantt chart. The concept of a critical path, the concept of slack on noncritical paths, and a specific treatment of order of precedence relationships have emerged from our development of network portrayal methods.

Elementary network analysis of the sort presented in the previous section might be sufficient for project-management purposes if all projects were as straightforward as the space shuttle project. However, complicated PERT networks may have more paths than we would care to enumerate, and complex network relationships require more efficient methods of network analysis. Together with other enhancements that serve to more realistically simulate actual project conditions, PERT represents a collection of analytical techniques that extend significantly beyond the building and inspection of a network. We will examine these techniques of analysis in this section. The use of time as the only project-planning consideration is the reason for classifying the following methods as ***PERT-time.***

One fundamental enhancement of the elementary PERT concepts we have discussed involves the treatment of time estimates for activities. Estimates such as those given in Table 10.1 are called single-point time estimates; a single time requirement is given for each activity, and there is no consideration of variability in these time requirements. This is the CPM deterministic time approach, according to which any deviation from the single-point time estimate is considered abnormal. Realistically, however, the time required to complete an activity is often variable. Moreover, variability in activity times may occur simply because of inaccuracy in estimating the times, as when no past experience is available. The PERT technique for dealing with variability in time estimates calls for the formulation of ***three-point time estimates.*** The following three estimates are made for each activity:

1. ***The most optimistic estimate***: the shortest time that might be required for completion of the activity
2. ***The most likely estimate***: the amount of time that would most often be required for completion of the activity
3. ***The most pessimistic estimate***: the longest time that might be required for completion of the activity

For each activity, the three estimates are combined algebraically in a weighted average that yields an ***expected time requirement.*** The generally accepted formula[1] for this average, in which the most likely estimate receives a weight four times as great as the other two estimates, is

$$t_e = \frac{a + 4m + b}{6}$$

where t_e = expected time requirement
a = most optimistic estimate
m = most likely estimate
b = most pessimistic estimate

Let us now extend the space shuttle example using three-point time estimates. Suppose that, in addition to the most likely time estimates presented in Table 10.1, the most optimistic and the most pessimistic estimates are collected. Hypothetical values prepared for the purpose of illustration are given in Table 10.3.

Return to the Gantt chart (based on single-point time estimates) shown in Figure 10.2, and consider the path followed by the astronauts. It includes assembling, boarding, radio checks, and countdown. In the Gantt chart, astronauts begin to assemble 20 minutes after initiation of the project, and each subsequent step in this path follows through, with

Table 10.3 Hypothetical Three-Point Estimates for the Space Shuttle Project

Activity/ Events	**Description**	**Time Estimates (minutes)**			
		a	m	b	t_e
1 – 2	Uncovering the Launch Pad	30	40	50	40
1 – 3	Check-in of Scientists	90	110	112	107
1 – 4	Assembling of Astronauts	54	55	56	55
2 – 4	(Dummy Activity)	0	0	0	0
4 – 5	Boarding of Astronauts	45	50	55	50
3 – 6	Security Clearance of Scientists	20	55	60	50
5 – 6	(Dummy Activity)	0	0	0	0
2 – 7	Baggage, Food, and Freight Loading	55	90	95	85
6 – 7	Boarding of Scientists	63	75	81	74
5 – 7	Radio and Systems Checks	110	115	150	120
7 – 8	Final Countdown	60	60	60	60

[1]Statistical justification for the expected time formula will not be developed in this text.

no slack, to the final countdown. If the 20 minutes at the beginning were eliminated, earliest completion of the assembling activity would be only 55 minutes after project initiation. The latest allowable completion for this same activity is 75 minutes after project initiation, as shown in the Gantt chart. Any later completion would result in a delay in the final countdown. This difference between earliest possible completion and latest allowable completion represents slack in the system along this particular path.

By calculating the earliest possible completion time and the latest allowable completion time for all events in the network, PERT algorithms identify the critical path and provide measures of slack. The earliest possible completion of an event is the earliest time that this event can be expected to occur, on the basis of expected times of all activities that ***precede*** it. Conversely, the latest allowable completion of an event is the latest time that an event can occur without causing delay in overall project completion. The latest allowable time depends on the expected times of all activities that ***follow*** the given event in the network. Differences between latest allowable and earliest completion times represent slack. Along the critical path there is no slack—at least not if scheduled completion is not allowed to extend beyond the project's earliest possible completion. The earliest possible completion time is identical to the latest allowable completion time. These concepts are further developed in the example that follows.

First, consider the earliest possible completion of the events in the space shuttle network. In general, an activity can begin no earlier than its immediate predecessor ends. If more than one predecessor exists, completion time of the last predecessor governs the earliest start of the given activity. Add to that the expected time of the activity itself, and you have identified the time of the event marking the activity's earliest possible completion. Performing these simple additions through an entire network determines the earliest possible completion for all events. Table 10.4 illustrates this process for the space shuttle example. (The results are transferred to Table 10.6 in the column labeled T_E, the symbol used to represent earliest possible completion.)

Next, consider the calculation of latest allowable completion times for all events in a network. In general, the event marking completion of an activity can occur no later than the latest allowable beginning of the activity that follows it. Latest allowable completion, then, must be the latest completion time of the successor event minus the expected time of the following activity. When more than one activity follows the given event, this calculation must be made for each of the succeeding activities, and the lowest result should be applied. This assures that a

Table 10.4
Calculation of Earliest Possible Completion Times

Earliest Completion of Event Number		plus	Estimated Time for Activity		equals	Earliest Completion of Event Number	
1	0 min		1 – 2	40 min		2	40 min
1	0 min		1 – 3	107 min		3	107 min
1	0 min		1 – 4	55 min		4	55 min
2	40 min		2 – 4	0 min		4	40 min
4	55 min*		4 – 5	50 min		5	105 min
3	107 min		3 – 6	50 min		6	157 min
5	105 min		5 – 6	0 min		6	105 min
2	40 min		2 – 7	85 min		7	125 min
6	157 min*		6 – 7	74 min		7	231 min
5	105 min		5 – 7	120 min		7	225 min
7	231 min*		7 – 8	60 min		8	291 min

*Faced with more than one alternative, we choose the largest value.

Table 10.5
Calculation of Latest Allowable Completion Times

Latest Completion of Event Number		minus	Estimated Time for Activity		equals	Latest Completion of Event Number	
—			—			8	291 min
8	291 min		7 – 8	60 min		7	231 min
7	231 min		6 – 7	74 min		6	157 min
7	231 min		5 – 7	120 min		5	111 min*
6	158 min		5 – 6	0 min		5	157 min
5	111 min		4 – 5	50 min		4	61 min
6	158 min		3 – 6	50 min		3	107 min
7	231 min		2 – 7	85 min		2	146 min
4	61 min		2 – 4	0 min		2	61 min*

*We choose the lowest value in a situation that presents alternatives.

time allowance is made for the longest of the succeeding activities. These calculations are presented in detail in Table 10.5. They also appear in Table 10.6 under the column marked T_L, the symbol for latest allowable completion.

Finally, we determine slack as the difference between the latest allowable and the earliest possible completion times (see Table 10.6). Since total estimated project completion time is 291 minutes—both T_E and T_L—a critical path is readily identifiable as the string of events for which there is no identifiable slack. This, again, is the path 1-3-6-7-8. Path 1-4-5-7-8 has 6 minutes of slack along its entire length, except where it coincides with the critical path. The greatest amount of slack

Table 10.6
Calculation of Earliest Possible and Latest Allowable Times

Activity/ Events	t_e	T_E	T_L	Slack
1 – 2	40	40	61	21
1 – 3	107	107	107	0
1 – 4	55	55	61	6
2 – 4	0	40	61	21
4 – 5	50	105	111	6
3 – 6	50	157	157	0
5 – 6	0	105	157	52
2 – 7	85	125	231	106
6 – 7	74	231	231	0
5 – 7	120	225	231	6
7 – 8	60	291	291	0

is found along the third path, path 1-2-7-8. Activity 1 – 2 can vary as much as 21 minutes before the boarding of astronauts can take place. Activity 2 – 7 has 106 minutes of slack between uncovering the launch pad and final countdown.

10.5 PERT-Cost Extensions

Careful planning and scheduling for the efficient completion of a project is sufficient for most project management purposes, and PERT-time is very helpful in this regard, especially with large and complex projects. PERT can effect time savings that translate directly into cost savings. The old adage, "Time is money," underscores this.

Various conditions, however, may require that we consider both time and cost simultaneously. For example, consider the case of a business that performs projects on a contractual basis and competes with other contractors by bidding to obtain contract awards. The due date for completion of a contract may well affect the costs incurred, because more resources are generally needed to perform tasks in a shorter period of time. Thus the bid submitted should reflect any special costs that result from a need to hasten final completion. A similar situation would arise within an organization if a manager wanted to know how much it would cost to reduce project time to less than the time that is usually required. ***PERT-cost*** is an extension of the methods already developed. It is an outgrowth of the original CPM techniques dealing with time-cost relationships and makes possible the explicit treatment of costs in situations where additional resources can be used to reduce activity times.

Planning for the efficient completion of a project using PERT-time techniques is based primarily on averaged time estimates, or expected times, for each activity. The normal time needed to complete a given activity is its expected time. In the case of single-point time estimates, the normal time of an activity is the estimate itself for that activity. PERT-cost analysis uses the term ***normal time*** to mean the time ordinarily required to complete an activity, as opposed to an activity time that has been diminished by applying more resources. Theoretically, there must be some lower limit to the time required to perform an activity, no matter how many additional resources are brought to bear. This lower limit is called the ***crash time*** for an activity. Hence, depending on the resources applied, an activity can be completed along a time scale ranging from the crash time to the normal time for that activity.

The relationship between time and cost for individual activities is strictly a matter of the way in which resources must be applied in order to reduce activity time. At the very least, one can assume an inverse relationship between these two variables: it costs money to complete an activity in less than normal time. Beyond that, depending on the circumstances, the relationship might be stepwise or discrete; it might be linear or curved. The generally accepted approach of PERT-cost is first to estimate total direct costs for completing an activity on a normal basis and then to establish total direct costs for completing this activity on a crash basis. This provides two points along the time-cost relationship. Indeed, they lie at the extremes of the relationship, because completion times greater than normal or less than crash are not relevant to the practical situation. PERT-cost assumes simply that the straight line connecting these two points is an adequate representation of the time–cost relationship. For any given activity, this relationship may be graphed as shown in Figure 10.5.

The straight-line, downward-sloping cost relationship gives us a good idea of the direct cost required to perform an activity over any time from normal to crash completion. The steeper the slope of the line, the more expensive it is to reduce the completion time. Of course, the slope of the line is a measure of cost-per-time-unit reduction, and it provides a convenient measure for comparing activities in time-reduction anal-

Figure 10.5 The PERT-Cost Assumed Relationship Between Time and Cost for a Single Activity

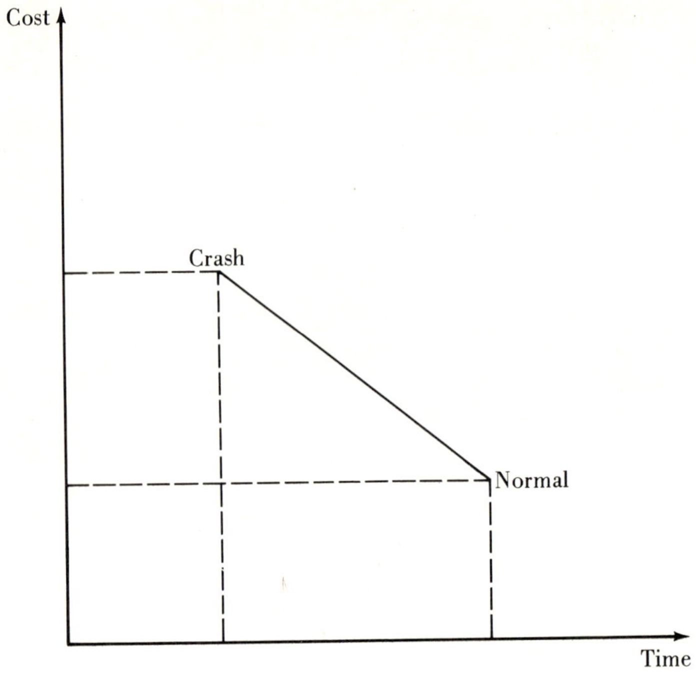

ysis. This measure is referred to as ***incremental cost***, or the cost of reducing activity time by one increment. It is calculated as follows:

$$\text{Incremental cost} = \frac{\text{crash cost} - \text{normal cost}}{\text{normal time} - \text{crash time}}$$

Let's apply these concepts to the space shuttle example. Suppose that normal activity time and expected time (t_e) are equated. Suppose also that, for each activity, estimates for crash completion time and the corresponding costs for normal and crash times are obtained. Hypothetical values for this example are given in Table 10.7. The last column of this table shows the incremental costs, which were obtained by using the formula just cited.

For purposes of illustration only, the time–cost relationships for each activity can be drawn together on a single graph, as shown in Figure 10.6. For time-saving purposes, it is more important to consider the slope of these relationships than the absolute cost level or location on the graph. An activity with a steep slope (such as activity 1 – 2) is more expensive to crash than one with a shallow slope (such as activity 1 – 4).

Table 10.7
Estimates of Time and Cost for the Space Shuttle Project

Activity	Time		Cost		Incremental Cost
	Normal	Crash	Normal	Crash	
1 – 2	40	30	$ 1,400	$ 2,700	$130.00
1 – 3	107	57	1,800	3,000	24.00
1 – 4	55	15	200	200	0
2 – 4	0	0	0	0	(not applicable)
4 – 5	50	10	500	1,000	12.50
3 – 6	50	25	2,700	3,600	36.00
5 – 6	0	0	0	0	(not applicable)
2 – 7	90	75	400	1,900	100.00
6 – 7	74	24	800	1,400	12.00
5 – 7	120	100	3,100	3,200	5.00
7 – 8	60	60	5,200	5,200	(not applicable)
			$16,100		

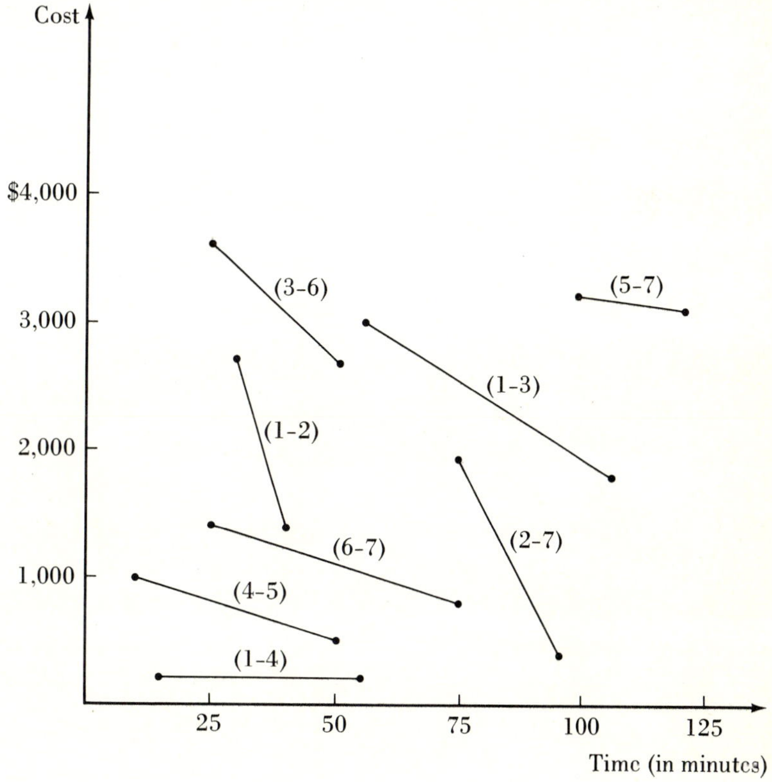

Figure 10.6
Time-Cost Relationships for Each Activity in the Space Shuttle Project

An attempt to reduce the time required to prepare the space shuttle for lift-off (which might be due to other requirements, such as subsequent link-up schedules) must be worked out stepwise, by applying resources to activities that have the lowest incremental costs and that lie on the critical path. Consider once again the results of our PERT-time analysis.

Path 1 (critical): 1-3-6-7-8
Time required: 107 + 50 + 74 + 60 = 291 minutes

Path 2: 1-2-7-8
Time required: 40 + 85 + 60 = 185 minutes

Path 3: 1-4-5-7-8
Time required: 55 + 50 + 120 + 60 = 285 minutes

Table 10.7 reveals that completing the project using normal activity times would cost a total of $16,100.

To compress the project time schedule, it is necessary to reduce the critical path. The lowest incremental cost incurred for any activity along the critical path is that of activity 6 – 7. Reducing the time of this activity by 6 minutes causes path 1 to be of the same length as path 3; that is, both become critical simultaneously. Thus the network is reduced as follows:

Path 1 (critical): 1-3-6-7-8
Time required: 107 + 50 + 68 + 60 = 285 minutes

Path 2: 1-2-7-8
Time required: 40 + 85 + 60 = 185 minutes

Path 3 (critical): 1-4-5-7-8
Time required: 55 + 50 + 120 + 60 = 285 minutes

Increased costs of $72 (6 minutes times $12 per minute) cause the total project cost to increase under this level of activity to $16,172.

With two critical paths now in effect, activity in both paths must be reduced to further reduce total project time. For activity 6 – 7, 44 minutes of further reduction can be made before reaching crash time (76 minutes of normal time minus 6 minutes prior reduction minus 24 minutes of crash time). Along the path 1-4-5-7-8, activity 1 – 4 has the lowest incremental cost and can be reduced by 40 minutes. Thus the network now can be reduced by 40 minutes as follows:

Path 1 (critical): 1-3-6-7-8
Time required: 107 + 50 + 28 + 60 = 245 minutes

Path 2:	1-2-7-8
Time required:	40 + 85 + 60 = 185 minutes
Path 3 (critical):	1-4-5-7-8
Time required:	15 + 50 + 120 + 60 = 245 minutes

Now costs have increased another $480 (40 minutes times $12 per minute plus 40 minutes times $0 per minute). Total project cost is now $16,652, and activity 1 – 4 (assembling of astronauts) has been reduced to a minimum—that is, to crash time.

Activity 6 – 7 can still be reduced by 2 minutes, after which activity 1 – 3 will be least expensive along path 1. Activity 5 – 7 is the next-least-expensive activity along path 3. Reducing these paths simultaneously by 20 minutes further reduces total project time:

Path 1 (critical):	1-3-6-7-8
Time required:	91 + 50 + 24 + 60 = 225 minutes
Path 2:	1-2-7-8
Time required:	40 + 85 + 60 = 185 minutes
Path 3:	1-4-5-7-8
Time required:	15 + 50 + 100 + 60 = 225 minutes

With these changes, total cost increases $348 (4 minutes times $12 for activity 6 – 7; 16 minutes times $12.50 for activity 1 – 3; and 20 minutes times $5 for activity 5 – 7) to a new level of $17,000.

Still more time reductions can be made. Picking the next-least-expensive activities, reduce activities 1 – 3 and 4 – 5 simultaneously by 34 minutes (all that remains to be reduced for activity 1 – 3) for the following result:

Path 1 (critical):	1-3-6-7-8
Time required:	57 + 50 + 24 + 60 = 191 minutes
Path 2:	1-2-7-8
Time required:	40 + 85 + 60 = 185 minutes
Path 3 (critical):	1-4-5-7-8
Time required:	15 + 16 + 100 + 60 = 191 minutes

Accordingly, total cost increases $1241 (34 minutes times $24 for activity 1 – 3 and 34 times $12.50 for activity 4 – 5) to $18,241. Activities 6 – 7, 1 – 4, 1 – 3, and 5 – 7 have been reduced to their crash times.

Together with activity 3 – 6, activity 4 – 5 can be reduced another 6 minutes, but this makes path 2 become critical:

Path 1 (critical): 1-3-6-7-8
Time required: 57 + 44 + 24 + 60 = 185 minutes
Path 2 (critical): 1-2-7-8
Time required: 40 + 85 + 60 = 185 minutes
Path 3 (critical): 1-4-5-7-8
Time required: 15 + 10 + 100 + 60 = 185 minutes

At this point, all slack disappears from the network. All paths are critical paths. The last 6-minute reductions have added $291 (6 times $36 for activity 3 – 6 and 6 times $12.50 for activity 4 – 5) to total cost, raising it to $18,532. All activities along path 3 are now at their crash times, so no further reductions in project time can be accomplished.

A summary of these steps provides insight into the project as a whole. Table 10.8 lists the total project times as they were successively reduced by crashing appropriate activities in the network. Corresponding costs are included. The table makes the overall time–cost trade-off clear. Normal project completion would result in $16,100 of direct costs and would require 291 minutes. By applying more resources to various activities, total project time can be reduced to a minimum of 185 minutes, at which level total project cost rises to $18,532. Decision makers have all the time and cost figures they need to choose an appropriate and informed course of action.

This example has demonstrated the general procedure for determining the relationship between time and cost for an entire project on the basis of time–cost estimates for individual project activities. First, identify the critical path and other alternative paths through the network.

Table 10.8
Time Versus Cost for the Space Shuttle Project

Total Project Time (minutes)		Total Project Cost
291	(normal)	$16,100
285		16,172
245		16,652
225		17,000
191		18,241
185	(minimum)	18,532

Second, obtain time and cost estimates for each activity for normal and crash processing, and calculate the resultant incremental costs. Third, based always on the principle of reducing time in activities that have the lowest incremental cost, shorten the critical path until an alternative path also becomes critical. Then reduce time in both critical paths simultaneously until yet another path becomes critical, and so on. We continue shortening critical paths simultaneously until all activities along one or more of the paths have been reduced to their crash times. At the end of each time-reducing step we calculate and record time and cost changes and prepare a listing of these time-cost alternatives as the end result of PERT-cost analysis.

Although linear programming techniques can be applied to network problems, PERT models are usually much more efficiently analyzed by using PERT techniques directly. Especially where PERT-cost analysis is concerned, linear programming solutions may require many variables and constraints. For example, using linear programming to minimize cost for a given total project time would require as many variables in the linear programming model as there are activities and events combined—and many more constraints. Large PERT networks are best analyzed by using specialized computational routines that have been programmed for computer processing.

10.6 Summary

PERT/CPM is a project-oriented analytical technique that provides a systematic framework for the complete planning and efficient achievement of project objectives. To this end, it provides estimates of completion time both for the project as a whole and for all individual activities. It identifies the ***critical path*** through a network of project activities, and it points out all slack between activities.

To apply PERT/CPM to practical situations, it is necessary first to carefully define all components of the project and to arrange them in the form of a PERT network that reflects all precedence relationships. Then, time estimates for each activity must be collected and expected times computed. Finally, computation of earliest possible and latest allowable completion times identifies the critical path and slack times for events throughout the network. Through PERT analysis, the project manager can closely follow the actual progress of a project and can evaluate, report, direct, and (if necessary) reallocate resources.

Based on the original CPM analysis, PERT-cost is an extension of the standard PERT concepts. It allows for reducing the time necessary to complete an activity by allocating additional resources to it (and consequently incurring increased costs). On the basis of a linear cost relationship between the normal time and the crash time for completion of an activity, the costs of reducing total project time can be calculated, and a time–cost relationship for the entire project can be derived. Reducing total project time can be accomplished only by shortening the critical path, so PERT-cost is largely concerned with finding the least-cost time-saving alternatives along a critical path (or paths) through the network.

PERT/CPM supplies basic information about all parts of a project—especially those parts that must be watched most carefully and those that may leave resources idle. It is a proven and effective tool for project planning and management. Proper use of PERT/CPM analysis leads to increased efficiency in the scheduling of project activities and better utilization of available resources.

Exercises

10.1 Explain each of the following terms:

a. PERT/CPM
b. Activity
c. Event
d. Network
e. Gantt chart

10.2 What are the three-point time estimates for each activity in PERT analysis? Show how one uses these estimates to compute the average or expected time requirement.

10.3 For each of the following three-point estimates (in minutes) of activity duration, calculate the expected activity time.

a. 23, 34, 39
b. 51, 54, 59
c. 2, 9, 15
d. 82, 98, 106
e. 65, 68, 128
f. 132, 182, 195
g. 458, 492, 532
h. 207, 223, 239

10.4 A manufacturer of minicomputers must supervise a network of activities on every computer installation. Table E10.1 lists these activities and their time estimates.

Table E10.1

Activity	Description	Time Estimates *a*	*m*	*b*
1 – 2	Organize Staff	60	66	67
1 – 3	Electrical Wiring	7	7	12
2 – 4	Specify Software	34	45	52
3 – 4	Install Computer	51	58	69
2 – 5	Train Staff	31	34	46
3 – 6	Finish Physical Facilities	80	83	93
4 – 7	Engineering Checks	24	26	31
5 – 7	Final Staff Checks	82	93	99
6 – 7	Add Manuals and Supplies	16	23	31

a. Draw the appropriate PERT network for this installation project.
b. Perform all PERT-time calculations to determine the earliest possible and latest allowable completion times, the critical path, and slack times.

10.5 Draw a Gantt chart for the project presented in exercise 10.4.

10.6 A chemical research laboratory discovers a new compound that should have widespread consumer use, and a plan for bringing the product to the consumer marketplace is developed. This plan consists of the activities and time estimates shown in Table E10.2. Perform a complete PERT/time analysis for this project.

Table E10.2

Activity/ Event	Description	Time Estimates *a*	*m*	*b*
1 – 2	Hire Production Manager	35	36	38
1 – 3	Product Design	4	4	13
1 – 4	Hire Marketing Director	60	75	91
2 – 3	—	0	0	0
2 – 5	First Production Run	64	71	84
2 – 6	Make Pricing Decisions	48	50	61
3 – 7	Product Testing	92	96	119
4 – 7	Plan Advertising Strategy	60	81	81
5 – 8	Ship to Warehouses	14	26	35
6 – 8	Organize Sales Force	8	11	17
7 – 8	Conduct Advertising Campaign	4	12	20
7 – 9	Review Advertising Effectiveness	94	107	111
8 – 10	Take Orders	37	47	60
9 – 10	Consumer Satisfaction Poll	69	71	78

Table E10.3

Activity/ Event	Description	Time Estimates		
		a	*m*	*b*
1 – 2	Lay Foundation	262	265	290
2 – 3	Framework	333	353	383
2 – 4	—	0	0	0
3 – 5	Roof	60	75	96
4 – 5	Chimney	85	90	98
5 – 6	Plumbing and Electricity	525	547	566
5 – 7	Finishing of Interior and Exterior	231	282	289
6 – 8	Painting	100	114	119
7 – 8	—	0	0	0
8 – 9	Landscaping	96	124	128

Table E10.4

Activity/ Event	Description	Time Estimates		
		a	*m*	*b*
1 – 2	Assemble Wings	29	35	39
1 – 3	Assemble Framework	15	15	25
2 – 3	Attach Wings	13	17	22
3 – 4	Finish Fuselage	46	47	49
2 – 5	Add Landing Gear	11	15	28
4 – 5	Install Engine	37	40	50
4 – 7	Connect Pilot Flight Controls	8	16	17
5 – 6	Connect Radios, Avionics	13	19	28
6 – 7	Install Seats, Interior	5	5	5
6 – 8	Add Propeller	7	13	14
7 – 8	Paint Exterior	12	17	17

10.7 One of the major selling points used by a supplier of prefabricated houses is the outstanding efficiency of the prefab building project. This efficiency is based on the results of a PERT project analysis, the details of which are given in Table E10.3. Time values represent hours of labor required.

a. Draw the PERT network for the entire project.
b. Calculate the estimated time for all activities.
c. Compute the earliest possible and latest allowable completion times for all network events.
d. Determine the critical path and all slack points.

Table E10.5

Activity	Time		Cost	
	Normal	Crash	Normal	Crash
(a)	67	33	$4300	$5200
(b)	72	70	5000	9800
(c)	38	15	4700	8000
(d)	50	25	6400	9400
(e)	66	29	7600	9200
(f)	81	76	8300	8600
(g)	55	1	6200	7700
(h)	42	14	2400	6600

Table E10.6

Activity/ Event	Production Process Designation	Time Estimates		
		a	*m*	*b*
1 – 2	P.D. 413	7	10	11
1 – 3	P.D. 320	6	8	10
1 – 4	P.D. 425	19	20	25
2 – 5	P.D. 316	4	7	8
3 – 5	P.D. 303	1	3	5
4 – 6	P.D. 415	17	18	20
4 – 7	P.D. 305	3	6	7
5 – 6	P.D. 422	3	5	9
6 – 8	P.D. 428	11	12	14
6 – 9	P.D. 431	6	9	9
6 – 10	P.D. 308	20	22	30
7 – 9	P.D. 437	14	15	18
8 – 10	P.D. 312	13	16	21
9 – 10	P.D. 318	12	14	15

10.8 On the basis of the PERT analysis of the project in exercise 10.7 draw a Gantt chart of the activity flow.

10.9 Perform a complete PERT-time analysis for the activities and time estimates shown in Table E10.4, which describe the assembly line production of airplanes. Include a drawing of the PERT network, all earliest possible and latest allowable completion times, the critical path, and slack.

10.10 Calculate the incremental cost for crashing the activities shown in Table E10.5.

Table E10.7

Activity	Normal Time	Normal Cost	Crash Time	Crash Cost
1 – 2	1	\$5	1	\$5
1 – 3	2	3	1	5
2 – 4	2	4	1	7
3 – 4	3	1	1	3
4 – 5	1	1	1	1

10.11 The network shown in Table E10.6 represents a complex flow of activities that are necessary for the production of a scientific instrument.

a. Sketch the network, and determine the earliest possible and latest allowable completion times, the amount of slack for each activity, and the critical path.

b. Give an interpretive analysis of the use of time in the flow of activities relating to this network. Where are the bottlenecks? What production activities are kept waiting for significant periods of time before they can start? Assuming their transferability and compatibility, how might resources be shifted in order to smooth out the time flows and create a more even movement of the production process?

10.12 What is the meaning of and the reasoning behind a crash effort in an activity? When would such an effort be used?

10.13 Outline some project management problems wherein you think PERT techniques might be applicable. Be as specific as possible.

10.14 Table E10.7 represents a system of activities in a project that must be completed.

a. Draw and label the PERT network.

b. On the basis of normal work rates, calculate the earliest possible and latest allowable completion times for all events.

c. Determine the critical path, total project time, and total project cost.

d. Reduce the network to crash time. Determine the critical paths, total time, and total cost.

Suggested Readings

Department of the Navy. *PERT, Program Evaluation Research Task, Summary Report Phase I*. Washington, D.C.: Government Printing Office, July 1958.

Evarts, H. F. *Introduction to PERT*. Boston, Mass.: Allyn and Bacon, 1964.

Green, Thad B. "A Statistical Analysis of the Utilization Effectiveness of a PERT Program." *Decision Sciences,* 4, No. 3 (July 1973).

Hu, T. C. "Revised Matrix Algorithms for Shortest Paths." *SIAM Journal on Applied Mathematics,* 15, 1967, 207–218.

I.B.M. *General Information Manual PERT.* International Business Machines Corporation, White Plains, New York (No. E20-8067-01).

Moder, J., and C. R. Phillips. *Project Management with CPM and PERT.* New York: Reinhold Publishing Company, 1970.

National Aeronautics and Space Administration. *NASA PERT Handbook.* Washington, D.C.: Government Printing Office, September 1961.

Van Slyke, R.M. "Monte Carlo Methods and the PERT Problem." *Operations Research,* 11, No. 5 (1963), 839–860.

Wiest, J. D., and F. K. Levy. *A Management Guide to PERT/CPM.* Englewood Cliffs, N.J.: Prentice-Hall, 1969.

11

Bayesian Decision Theory and Its Applications

Certain areas of decision theory—which is derived from the broader field of statistical analysis—have been adopted and further developed within operations research for the specific purposes of effective business decision making. Just as the models of queuing typically are based on the theories and techniques of statistics but extend beyond pure statistical analysis, similarly decision theory as it relates to operations research is based on a foundation of statistical concepts and branches out to suit the special requirements of operations research. In this chapter the basics of probability and statistics will be used to develop efficient methods of business decision making under conditions of uncertainty. Readers who are not familiar with basic probability concepts are referred first to this chapter's appendix, which gives a condensed review of basic fundamentals.

11.1 Bayesian Versus Classical Decision Theory

Bayesian decision theory is based largely on calculations of conditional probability and on the formulation of strategies involving expected outcomes or expected payoffs. ***Classical decision theory,*** by contrast, deals fundamentally with assessing the probability of making a wrong decision in either accepting or rejecting a hypothesis about an event or a state of nature on the basis of a predetermined, maximum acceptable level of risk. This chapter is an introduction to Bayesian decision analysis. The concepts of classical decision theory are not treated here; they can be found in any comprehensive textbook dealing with traditional statistical methods.

Conscious or subconscious use of probability in making business decisions is very widespread. Consider, for example, the automobile dealer who judges how likely customers are to select certain options in order to anticipate the colors, styles, and equipment that will sell best. Too, some airlines squeeze greater revenue out of booked-up flights by anticipating the probability that a few passengers will not arrive at the airport in time for departure and then selling some of these potentially unoccupied seats to other passengers. Virtually every business operation faces unknown variables that probability assessment, formal or informal, can clarify. Probability assessments are typically oriented toward an objective such as expected profits, expected utility, or an expected payoff. ***Bayesian decision theory*** aids in the assessment of subjective probabilities through conditional probability calculations. It allows us to derive decision criteria through the systematic determination of expected payoffs.

The man whose name is synonymous with this aspect of decision theory was the Reverend Thomas Bayes, who lived during the eighteenth century and was a member of the English clergy. His scholarly interest in probability led to the development and publication of the fundamentals on which our modern concepts are based.[1] Although some discussion of the Bayesian concepts was recorded during the nineteenth century, it was largely during the past several decades that his fundamental ideas have been extended, adding significantly both to theoretical statistics and to the applied areas of decision making and operations research. This chapter demonstrates some Bayesian techniques that contribute to more effective decision making for business purposes.

11.2 Decision Criteria and the States of Nature

Variations in the operating environment of any functioning system cause uncertainty about its operation. Once the system has completed its function or functions, however, the unknown characteristics are known

[1]Thomas Bayes, "An Essay Toward Solving a Problem in the Doctrine of Chance," originally published in 1763 in *Philosophical Transactions of the Royal Society* and reprinted more recently in *Biometrica*, 45, 1958, 293–315.

and we say that the ***state of nature*** has been revealed. The ability to predict outcomes aids in the reduction of uncertainty—but usually only at a distinct cost and with varying degrees of reliability. The problem is having to act, or make decisions, prior to the time that the state of nature is revealed, either fully or in part. Thus the Bayesian decision-making process deals with alternative events or states of nature in situations wherein alternative courses of action are available. The object of analysis is to formulate a decision strategy, or decision rule, that will yield the best expected results under the given circumstances.

With regard to the states of nature, two types of situations can be specified. The first is a situation for which a prior probability distribution is available for the relevant outcomes, or states of nature. This prior probability distribution may have been scientifically determined through experimentation or examination of past records, or it may reflect the decision maker's subjective perception of the situation. The subjective assignment of probabilities is common in business decision problems. Even when past records are available, the derived probabilities may still be subjective in the sense that there is nothing to guarantee that things will be the same in the future as they were in the past or, indeed, that the underlying probabilities were constant in the past. In the world of business and economics, things are constantly changing.

The second type of situation is one for which it is possible both to specify a prior probability distribution governing the states of nature and to determine a posterior probability distribution. As in the first case, the prior probabilities may be subjective probabilities, but here additional information may be available that will help in determining probabilities for the various possible states of nature. This additional information is generally an observation of an event or events that are known to relate to the ultimate outcome and that consequently allow one better to assess or revise the prior probabilities. We can obtain additional information by running a preliminary experiment or conducting a survey. The effect of cost is important in this regard. It would be unwise to spend more money obtaining additional information about the states of nature than that information is worth in terms of the likely gain attributable to the prediction activity.

Conditional probability analysis is fundamental to the second of these two types of analysis. For example, one must determine the probabilities of the states of nature given that a particular event, which represents additional information, has occurred. Bayes derived the way to calculate these conditional probabilities (as will be shown in Section 11.4 of this chapter). Consequently Bayesian decision theory is often considered synonymous, in a simplified way, with the calculation of conditional probabilities. In fact, Bayesian decision theory is better characterized by the type of decision criterion that is employed—maximizing the expected payoff that results from the decision process. This applies whether or not conditional probabilities enter into the analysis.

A third, non-Bayesian, situation occurs when no prior probability distribution can be given for the possible states of nature. Without such a distribution of probabilities, it would not be possible to employ an expected-payoff decision criterion. ***Expected payoff*** means literally a payoff that is based on the assigned probabilities. Other, non-Bayesian, decision criteria (such as ***maximin*** and ***minimax***) have been developed for this type of situation, and these are presented later in this text in the chapter on game theory.

11.3 A Zero Back-Order, Zero Salvage Value Problem

Ordering or stocking products for resale is the way in which most wholesale and retail businesses operate, and wisely choosing the amount of goods to stock can significantly enhance profits. The business firm is always affected by having money tied up in an inventory of goods. This section deals with the peculiarities of selling a perishable product—such as food or newspapers—while operating in a market that requires having fresh stock on hand for customers to purchase when they arrive. On the one hand, unsold units will perish and will not be sold at all if too much is stocked. On the other hand, if too little is stocked to meet the market demand of a given period, customers who do not find what they want will go to a competitor rather than wait for a back-order to arrive. How does the manager most advantageously stock such products?

As an example of this type of situation, let us consider the Nashville–New Orleans Express, a nonstop train running daily between the capitals of country music and Dixieland jazz. Fixed menu dinner service is available, offering first class meals in a special dining car. The problem is to determine how many meals should be prepared and how to efficiently draw the greatest profit from the meal service operation. Only some of the passengers eat dinner on the train, and the number varies from trip to trip. Estimating the total number of passengers and the number of meals that will be needed is complicated by many unknown factors. Assume also that food purchased for meal service cannot effectively be saved for the next day; fresh food is required at the beginning of each run.

Suppose that food costs are approximately \$3.25 per meal when all of the items of a given menu are added together. Suppose also that the customer is charged \$9.25 per meal. Other costs, such as the wages of waiters and kitchen personnel and the maintenance and transportation of the dining car—reduce this margin of operation. These costs, however, are considered fixed if the service is to be provided. For this analysis it is the stocking of meals versus the selling of them that is important.

If the number of meals served varies from 10 to 30, past experience suggests that the prior probability distribution of meals served per run is as shown in Table 11.1. Given this information, consider the various possibilities for planning the train run.

What happens when the equivalent of 10 meals is taken on board? All 10 meals will be sold and no food will be wasted, but an actual demand of greater than 10 meals occurs 90% of the time. What happens when the equivalent of 15 meals is taken on board? Since exactly 10 meals will be demanded 10% of the time and exactly 15 meals will be demanded 10% of the time, more than 15 meals will be demanded 80% of the time, causing potential customers to be turned away. What happens when the equivalent of 20 meals is provided? As before, exactly 10 meals will be demanded 10% of the time, exactly 15 meals will be demanded 10% of the time, and exactly 20 meals will be demanded 40% of the time. A demand of greater than 20 meals will occur the remaining 40% of the time, and a demand of fewer than 20 meals will occur 20% of the time. What happens when food for 25 meals is stocked? Since exactly 25 meals will be demanded 30% of the time, less than 25 meals

Table 11.1 Prior and Cumulative Probabilities for the Random Variable, Demand

Random Variable	Prior Probabilities	Probability of Turning Customers Away	Probability of Wasting Food
Meals Demanded per Run X	The Probability of Demand Being Exactly x_i Meals per Run, $P(X = x_i)$	The Probability of Demand Being Greater than x_i per Run $P(X > x_i)$	The Probability of Demand Being Less than x_i per Run $P(X < x_i)$
$x_1 = 10$	.10	.90	0.00
$x_2 = 15$	.10	.80	.10
$x_3 = 20$	.40	.40	.20
$x_4 = 25$	.30	.10	.60
$x_5 = 30$	.10	0.00	.90
	1.00		

will be demanded 60% of the time, causing food to be wasted. And since more than 25 meals will be demanded 10% of the time, potential customers will be turned away. Finally, when provision for 30 meals is made, there will be food left over in varying amounts 90% of the time, but no potential customers will be turned away.

Conditional Profits

Resolving all the possibilities of Table 11.1 into an optimal stocking decision requires specification of profits for all combinations of actual demand and meals available for purchase. Using the figures for food cost ($3.25 per meal) and revenue ($9.25 per meal), we can prepare a table of ***conditional profits,*** payoffs that depend on the actual level of

Table 11.2 Procedure for Calculating Conditional Profit Values

Meals Demanded	Meals Stocked	Status	Payoff
10	10	Match	$9.25 × 10 sold −$3.25 × 10 available = $60.00
15, 20, 25, 30	10	Shortage	$60.00, as above
10	15	5 Surplus	$9.25 × 10 sold − $3.25 × 15 available = $43.75
15	15	Match	$9.25 × 15 sold − $3.25 × 15 available = $90.00
20, 25, 30	15	Shortage	$90.00, as above
10	20	10 Surplus	$9.25 × 10 sold − $3.25 × 20 available = $27.50
15	20	5 Surplus	$9.25 × 15 sold − $3.25 × 20 available = $73.75
20	20	Match	$9.25 × 20 sold − $3.25 × 20 available = $120.00
25, 30	20	Shortage	$120.00, as above
10	25	15 Surplus	$9.25 × 10 sold − $3.25 × 25 available = $11.25

Table 11.2 (continued)

Meals Demanded	Meals Stocked	Status	Payoff
15	25	10 Surplus	\$9.25 × 15 sold − \$3.25 × 25 available = \$57.50
20	25	5 Surplus	\$9.25 × 20 sold − \$3.25 × 25 available = \$103.75
25	25	Match	\$9.25 × 25 sold − \$3.25 × 25 available = \$150.00
30	25	Shortage	\$150.00, as above
10	30	20 Surplus	\$9.25 × 10 sold − \$3.25 × 30 available = −\$5.00
15	30	15 Surplus	\$9.25 × 15 sold − \$3.25 × 30 available = \$41.25
20	30	10 Surplus	\$9.25 × 20 sold − \$3.25 × 30 available = \$87.50
25	30	5 Surplus	\$9.25 × 25 sold − \$3.25 × 30 available = \$133.75
30	30	Match	\$9.25 × 30 sold − \$3.25 × 30 available = \$180.00

demand. (Table 11.3 is such a table.) Calculation of each of the table's conditional profit values is summarized in Table 11.2.

The results of these calculations are more conveniently placed in a table of payoffs or conditional profits, such as Table 11.3. It is important to notice that no more meals can be served than were stocked.

In general, calculating conditional profits is a matter of determining differences between sales revenue and preparation cost, where the number of units actually sold need not necessarily equal the number of units prepared for sale. Thus if π_{ij} is conditional profit based on a combination of the jth action and the ith state of nature, then

$$\pi_{ij} = (p \times x_i') - (v \times a_j) \qquad \text{for all } i, j \tag{11.1}$$

Table 11.3 Payoffs for All Possible Combinations of Actions and States of Nature

Meals Demanded X	Conditional Profits Meals Stocked A				
	$a_1 = 10$	$a_2 = 15$	$a_3 = 20$	$a_4 = 25$	$a_5 = 30$
$x_1 = 10$	\$60.00	\$43.75	\$ 27.50	\$ 11.25	\$ −5.00
$x_2 = 15$	60.00	90.00	73.75	57.50	41.25
$x_3 = 20$	60.00	90.00	120.00	103.75	87.50
$x_4 = 25$	60.00	90.00	120.00	150.00	133.75
$x_5 = 30$	60.00	90.00	120.00	150.00	180.00

where x_i' represents actual units sold, a_j represents the units supplied for sale (or the action taken), and p and v are per-unit price and variable cost, respectively. The actual units sold, x_i', must always equal the lesser of x_i (the value of the random variable X) and a_j (the units supplied for sale).

Expected Profits The prior probability distribution for meals demanded (recall Table 11.1 and the reasoning relating to it) reveals that 10 out of 100 train runs will find only 10 people wanting meal service, 10 out of 100 train runs will find exactly 15 people wanting meal service, in 40 out of 100 runs there will be exactly 20 people desiring meal service, and so on. Considering the entire distribution of relative frequencies, what is the average profit per train run to be derived for a given action repeated over many train runs? This ***average,*** in fact, must be a weighted average, or expected value, such that the weights reflect the probability distribution of demand for meal service. Thus the average or expected profit is the expected value of conditional profits per run for each possible stocking action. Given a table of conditional profits π_{ij} and a prior probability distribution $P(X)$ for n possible states of nature, we calculate expected profits, $E\pi_j$, as follows:

$$E(\pi)_j = P(X = x_1)\pi_{1j} + P(X = x_2)\pi_{2j} + \cdots + P(X = x_n)\pi_{nj} \quad (11.2)$$

$$= \sum_{i=1}^{n} P(X = x_i)\pi_{ij} \quad \text{for all } j$$

Returning to our example, expected profits for each stock action are presented in Table 11.3. These calculations in greater detail are as follows:

1. Action a_1, 10 meals stocked
   Expected profit = $.1 \times \$60 + .1 \times \$60 + .4 \times \$60 + .3 \times \$60 + .1 \times \$60 = \$60$

2. Action a_2, 15 meals stocked
   Expected profit = $.1 \times \$43.75 + .1 \times \$90 + .4 \times \$90 + .3 \times \$90 + .1 \times \$90 = \$85.38$

3. Action a_3, 20 meals stocked
   Expected profit = $.1 \times \$27.50 + .1 \times \$73.75 + .4 \times \$120 + .3 \times \$120 + .1 \times \$120 = \$106.13$

4. Action a_4, 25 meals stocked
   Expected profit = $.1 \times \$11.25 + .1 \times \$57.50 + .4 \times \$103.75 + .3 \times \$150 + .1 \times \$150 = \$108.38$

5. Action a_5, 30 meals stocked
   Expected profit = $.1 \times -\$5 + .1 \times \$41.25 + .4 \times \$87.50 + .3 \times \$133.75 + .1 \times \$180 = \$96.76$

In this step, the prior probabilities are applied to the table of conditional profits. Although the calculations using these probabilities are simple, the individual probabilities in the prior probability distribution are critically important. The final results depend completely on the accuracy of these prior probabilities, and the overall reliability of the analysis hinges on good prior probabilities to start with.

The results of these calculations, which show an optimum strategy of 25 meals stocked, can now be interpreted. The expected value of providing 10 meals is \$60. In this case all food will always be sold, so the expected profit of \$60 is simply the difference between the price of \$9.25 per meal and the cost of \$3.25 per meal (\$6) multiplied by the 10 meals sold. However, 90% of the time customers will have to be turned away because of a lack of food. Providing 15 meals increases expected profit to \$85.38. In this case customers will be turned away 80% of the time; the remaining 20% of the time there will be either enough meals (15 meals demanded) or more than enough (10 meals demanded). Similarly, the expected profits of the 20-meal and 25-meal stocking actions are larger than the preceding values. In the case of the 30-meal stocking action, no one will ever be refused a meal, but 90% of the time food will be left over and will not be sold, so the 30-meal strategy yields a smaller expected profit.

Table 11.4 Calculation of Expected Payoffs

Meals Demanded X	$P(X = x_i)$	Conditional Profits Meals Stocked A					Expected Profits Meals Stocked A				
		$a_1 =$ 10	$a_2 =$ 15	$a_3 =$ 20	$a_4 =$ 25	$a_5 =$ 30	$a_1 =$ 10	$a_2 =$ 15	$a_3 =$ 20	$a_4 =$ 25	$a_5 =$ 30
$x_1 = 10$	.10	$60.00	$43.75	$ 27.50	$ 11.25	$−5.00	$ 6.00	$ 4.38	$ 2.75	$ 1.13	$−0.50
$x_2 = 15$	.10	60.00	90.00	73.75	57.50	41.25	6.00	9.00	7.38	5.75	4.13
$x_3 = 20$	.40	60.00	90.00	120.00	103.75	87.50	24.00	36.00	48.00	41.50	35.00
$x_4 = 25$	.30	60.00	90.00	120.00	150.00	133.75	18.00	27.00	36.00	45.00	40.13
$x_5 = 30$	.10	60.00	90.00	120.00	150.00	180.00	6.00	9.00	12.00	15.00	18.00
	1.00						$60.00	$85.38	$106.13	$108.38	$ 96.76

Given the circumstances of this problem, the best decision strategy is to prepare 25 meals and thereby maximize expected profits at a level of $108.38. Such a strategy will result in the turning away of no more than 5 customers per train run, and this will occur with only 10% probability. This strategy carries a 60% chance that food will be left over. However, because the cost of food is low relative to its sales value, it is not surprising that the results favor serving customers at the expense of having some unsold (and hence wasted) food.

11.4 Expected Opportunity Loss

An equivalent way to analyze the decision-making situation faced by the Nashville–New Orleans Express is to shift the emphasis from maximizing profits to minimizing losses. ***Loss*** is to be interpreted here in the economic sense—that is, an ***opportunity loss,*** the opportunity forgone by not having made the best possible decision for any given state of nature.

It is convenient, though not absolutely necessary, to find conditional opportunity losses by examining the conditional profits table. In Table 11.2, the best possibilities for making profits occur where the number of meals provided in advance exactly matches the subsequently determined demand by customers for meal service. This means simply that the largest conditional profit figures for the given states of nature are the elements of the table that lie on the diagonal running from the upper left to the lower right. Comparing all the elements of any row with the diagonal element that lies in that row gives the economic opportunity loss. For example, preparing for 25 meals results in an opportunity loss of $30 if 30 people come for meal service: the difference between actual profits realized—$150.00—and the conceivable profits—$180.00—of taking the best possible action for the given level of demand.

We calculate conditional losses for all combinations of actions and states of nature as follows:

Row 1: x_1 = 10 and diagonal element (Table 11.2) = $60

$60 − 60	$60 − 43.75	$60 − 27.50	$60 − 11.25	$60 − (−5)
= 0.0	= 16.25	= 32.50	= 48.70	= 65.00

Row 2: x_2 = 15 and diagonal element (Table 11.2) = $90

$90 − 60	$90 − 90	$90 − 73.75	$90 − 57.50	$90 − 41.25
= 30.00	= 0.0	= 16.25	= 32.50	= 48.75

Row 3: x_3 = 20 and diagonal element (Table 11.2) = \$120

\$120 − 60	\$120 − 90	\$120 − 120	\$120 − 103.75	\$120 − 87.50
= 60.00	= 30.00	= 0.0	= 16.25	= 32.50

Row 4: x_4 = 25 and diagonal element (Table 11.2) = 150

\$150 − 60	\$150 − 90	\$150 − 120	\$150 − 150	\$150 − 133.75
= 90.00	= 60.00	= 30.00	= 0.0	= 16.25

Row 5: x_5 = 30 and diagonal element (Table 11.2) = 180

\$180 − 60	\$180 − 90	\$180 − 120	\$180 − 150	\$180 − 180
= 120.00	= 90.00	= 60.00	= 30.00	= 0.0

Comparing each element of the conditional profits table with the diagonal element in the same row enables us to derive a conditional opportunity loss table. Then, using the prior probability distribution for the states of nature, we can calculate expected opportunity losses for each possible action. We perform these expected-value calculations in the same way that we calculated expected profits previously, on the basis of the given prior probability distribution and the table of conditional payoffs. The results of this set of calculations are presented in Table 11.5.

In general, if the best possible conditional profit for any row (the main diagonal element that falls in the given row) is represented as π_i^*, then by definition,

$$\pi_i^* = \pi_{ij} \quad \text{where } i = j \tag{11.3}$$

We calculate conditional losses as ***the difference between the conditional profits of the best possible action for a given state of nature and the conditional profits actually realized.*** That is,

$$L_{ij} = \pi_i^* - \pi_{ij} \quad \text{over all } j\text{, for each } i \tag{11.4}$$

where L_{ij} is the conditional opportunity loss for the combination of any action a_j and event x_i. Clearly, (11.4) is an economic opportunity loss formula indicating the difference between potential and realized profits, not a formula for ordinary loss (total cost exceeding total revenue).

What is the decision strategy indicated by the opportunity loss analysis? Minimizing expected opportunity losses will always lead to the same optimal action as maximizing expected profits; the two methods are equivalent. In the train example, expected opportunity losses are least (\$17.62) when 25 meals are prepared. Uncertainty makes it

Table 11.5 Calculation of Conditional and Expected Opportunity Losses

Meals Demanded X	$P(X = x_i)$	Conditional Losses Meals Stocked A					Expected Losses Meals Stocked A				
		$a_1 =$ 10	$a_2 =$ 15	$a_3 =$ 20	$a_4 =$ 25	$a_5 =$ 30	$a_1 =$ 10	$a_2 =$ 15	$a_3 =$ 20	$a_4 =$ 25	$a_5 =$ 30
$x_1 = 10$	.10	$ 0	$16.25	$32.50	$48.75	$65.00	$ 0	$ 1.62	$ 3.25	$ 4.87	$ 6.50
$x_2 = 15$	.10	30.00	0	16.25	32.50	48.75	3.00	0	1.62	3.25	4.87
$x_3 = 20$	.40	60.00	30.00	0	16.25	32.50	24.00	12.00	0	6.50	13.00
$x_4 = 25$	.30	90.00	60.00	30.00	0	16.25	27.00	18.00	9.00	0	4.87
$x_5 = 30$	.10	120.00	90.00	60.00	30.00	0	12.00	9.00	6.00	3.00	0
	1.00						$66.00	$40.62	$19.87	$17.62	$29.24

impossible always to make the best possible decision, but providing for 25 meals minimizes opportunity losses due to uncertainty.

11.5 Expected Profit Under Certainty and EVPI

Any clever manager will by now have asked the question, "What must I do in order always to match the units prepared for sale with the units demanded?" Or, put another way, how can the state of nature be predicted, and what level of expected profit results when an absolutely reliable prediction process is adopted? If it were possible to predict the states of nature in advance, the best possible action could always be made, and opportunity losses would always be zero. Conditional profits for each state of nature, when correctly predicted, would simply be the diagonal elements π_i^* of the conditional profits table. Furthermore, being able to predict the states of nature in advance means that expected profits, then, must be the sum of products of the appropriate probabilities times these diagonal elements. This result, which assumes elimination of uncertainty, is called the ***expected profit under certainty.***

One should note carefully that elimination of uncertainty through a reliable prediction process does not imply elimination of the random variable. The states of nature will still occur in a random fashion governed, presumably, by the underlying prior probability distribution. Uncertainty is eliminated in the sense that, whatever state of nature may occur, some prediction process will enable the decision maker to know in advance which it is and will allow enough time for this person to act accordingly.

In our train example, the expected profit under certainty is calculated as follows:

$$\begin{aligned}\text{Expected profit under certainty} &= .1 \times \$60 + .1 \times \$90 \\ &\quad + .4 \times \$120 + .3 \times \$150 \\ &\quad + .1 \times \$180 = \$126\end{aligned}$$

Naturally, this value is larger than the greatest possible expected profit with uncertainty, which was \$108.38. It is no coincidence that the difference between these values equals the minimum expected opportunity loss, or \$17.62, which is the cost of uncertainty. To remove uncertainty is to improve expected profits by the value of the expected opportunity

Table 11.6 Summary of Expected Profits and Expected Opportunity Losses

Action A	Expected Profit	Expected Opportunity Loss	Expected Profit under Certainty
a_1 = 10	$60.00	$66.00	$126.00
a_2 = 15	85.38	40.62	126.00
a_3 = 20	106.13	19.87	126.00
a_4 = 25*	108.38	17.62	126.00
a_5 = 30	96.76	29.24	126.00

*Optimal decision strategy under uncertainty.

loss, and this is true regardless of the action (optimal or otherwise) that is considered (see Table 11.6).

If perfect information about the states of nature can be obtained in advance, what additional cost is it worth to the decision maker? In the case of an optimal decision strategy under uncertainty, the ***expected value of perfect information,*** or EVPI, is the amount of money that it is worth for a decision maker to obtain a perfect prediction. We have shown in our train example that, when perfect information is supplied, expected profits improve $17.62 over the maximum expected profit obtainable under uncertainty. Hence, it would be unprofitable to pay ***more than*** this amount for perfect information. However, any cost less than $17.62 would improve the decision maker's expected profits, and it would then be worth the expense to reliably predict the state of nature.

11.6 Revising Estimates of Prior Probabilities

A further extension of the problem the Nashville–New Orleans Express faces can be used to demonstrate Bayesian methods that, via sampling, provide additional information to the decision maker without necessarily removing uncertainty. The additional information can then be used to derive revised estimates of the prior probabilities or to derive a distribution of posterior probabilities (probabilities based on experimentation) for the states of nature. Whatever additional information can be obtained serves to revise the decision maker's outlook on the operating environment. This section will demonstrate how to properly assess the implications of such additional information.

Bayes' Theorem Suppose that ordering food for the meals served on the dining car entails the purchase of wine to be served with the meals. Whereas the wine offered is always listed as "superior," the actual wine received from the supplier is sometimes superior and sometimes mediocre, depending on the batch from which it is bottled. Past experience indicates that three-quarters of the wine supplied is from a superior batch and that one-quarter is from a mediocre batch. The managers of meal service on the train are concerned about the rate of rejection of wine by customers on the grounds that it is mediocre. Of course, rejection of a mediocre wine is significantly more probable than rejection of a superior one.

A classical probability analysis of this problem would stress the probabilities of acceptance or rejection given the superior or mediocre quality of the wine. Suppose that, of the past 100 cases of wine served, 75 were superior in quality and that only 5 of these were rejected by finicky customers. Suppose that a larger proportion, 5 cases out of 25, involved the rejection of mediocre wine. We can then specify the two-way probability table shown in Table 11.7.

Classical probability analysis reasons from the state of nature to the reaction taken. That is, given a particular wine quality, it determines the probability of a customer accepting or rejecting the product. For this example, let A mean "Accept," R mean "Reject," S mean "Superior," and M mean "Mediocre." We have the following conditional probabilities:

$$\left.\begin{aligned} P(\mathrm{A}|\mathrm{S}) &= \frac{P(\mathrm{A,S})}{P(\mathrm{S})} = \frac{.7}{.75} = .93 \\ P(\mathrm{R}|\mathrm{S}) &= \frac{P(\mathrm{R,S})}{P(\mathrm{S})} = \frac{.05}{.75} = .07 \end{aligned}\right\} 1.00$$

$$\left.\begin{aligned} P(\mathrm{A}|\mathrm{M}) &= \frac{P(\mathrm{A,M})}{P(\mathrm{M})} = \frac{.20}{.25} = .80 \\ P(\mathrm{R}|\mathrm{M}) &= \frac{P(\mathrm{R,M})}{P(\mathrm{M})} = \frac{.05}{.25} = .20 \end{aligned}\right\} 1.00$$

Table 11.7
A Two-Way Probability Table for the Wine Example

Wine Quality	**Customer Reaction** Accept (A)	Reject (R)	
Superior (S)	.70	.05	.75
Mediocre (M)	.20	.05	25
	.90	.10	1.00

Whether or not the wine is superior, each customer is asked to either accept or reject.

Bayesian probability analysis reverses the reasoning of the classical approach. A typical Bayesian analysis attempts to determine the probabilities of the states of nature, given the reaction taken. Thus, for example, a Bayesian approach might be to revise the prior probability of a superior wine having been served, given that the customer rejected it. Or it might be to revise the prior probability of a mediocre wine having been served, given that the customer accepted it. Put more simply, classical probability analysis reasons from cause (the state of nature) to effect (the reaction or outcome), whereas Bayesian probability analysis reasons from effect to cause. The crucial distinction here is that it may not be possible to discern the state of nature without observing outcomes that have been caused by that unknown state. In such cases a prior probability distribution for the states of nature must be considered judgmental, rather than absolute, and subject to revision on the basis of related experimental outcomes.

As a practical matter, the Bayesian approach necessitates a modification in our calculation of the conditional, ***revised*** probabilities. For example, without knowing whether a particular wine is superior or mediocre, suppose we find that an attempt to serve it results in a rejection. If the prior distribution of probabilities was originally .75 for superior and .25 for mediocre, how does this additional information change our estimates of the prior probabilities? We start with the classical formula for conditional probability:

$$P(\text{Superior}|\text{Reject}) = \frac{P(\text{S,R})}{P(\text{R})} \qquad (11.5)$$

A rejection might occur with either a superior or a mediocre wine. Hence,

$$P(\text{R,S}) = P(\text{S})\,P(\text{R}|\text{S})$$

and

$$P(\text{R,M}) = P(\text{M})\,P(\text{R}|\text{M}) \qquad (11.6)$$

Although we do not know whether or not a superior wine has been served, we can calculate the joint probabilities under dependence (equations 11.6) for each possibility. Also, because these are the only two types of wine under consideration, their sum must equal the unconditional probability of a rejection. That is,

$$P(\text{S})\,P(\text{R}|\text{S}) + P(\text{M})\,P(\text{R}|\text{M}) = P(\text{R,S}) + P(\text{R,M}) = P(\text{R}) \qquad (11.7)$$

Combining (11.5), (11.6), and (11.7) yields the following formula, which in the general case is ***Bayes' theorem:***

$$P(\mathrm{S}|\mathrm{R}) = \frac{P(\mathrm{S})\,P(\mathrm{R}|\mathrm{S})}{P(\mathrm{S})\,P(\mathrm{R}|\mathrm{S}) + P(\mathrm{M})\,P(\mathrm{R}|\mathrm{M})} \tag{11.8}$$

Note that Bayes' theorem for conditional probability is the ratio of a joint probability to an unconditional probability, just as in the classical conditional probability formula. Remember that Bayes' theorem is an extension of the classical treatment of conditional probability, not something completely new and unique unto itself.

Applying Bayes' Theorem

We can revise our estimates of prior probabilities conveniently in tabular form, which facilitates doing all calculations systematically. Returning to the question of using a rejection as the first bit of additional information about a batch of wine, Table 11.8 demonstrates the steps required for this application. First, a column is prepared containing the only possible states of nature, superior and mediocre, and next to it a second column specifies the prior probabilities of the states of nature. In the third column, the conditional probabilities of a rejection (the experimental result) are presented for each possible state of nature. These are calculated as follows (see equations 11.6 and Table 11.7):

$$P(\text{Reject}|\text{Superior}) = \frac{P(\mathrm{R,S})}{P(\mathrm{S})} = \frac{.05}{.75} = 0.07$$

$$P(\text{Reject}|\text{Mediocre}) = \frac{P(\mathrm{R,M})}{P(\mathrm{M})} = \frac{.05}{.25} = 0.20$$

In the fourth column, the joint probabilities required by Bayes' theorem are calculated and totaled. The sum of the joint probabilities is the

Table 11.8
Revising Estimates of Prior Probabilities on the Basis of Sample Information

State of Nature E	Prior Probabilities $P(E)$	Conditional Probability of Experimental Result $P(\text{Reject}|E)$	Joint Probability $P(E) \times P(\mathrm{R}|E)$	Posterior, Revised Probability $P(E|\mathrm{R})$
Superior	.75	.07	.0525	.5122
Mediocre	.25	.20	.0500	.4878
	1.00		.1025	1.0000

unconditional probability of the experimental result, or the denominator of (11.8). These calculations are performed as follows:

$$P(\text{S}) \times P(\text{R}|\text{S}) = .75 \times .07 = .0525$$
$$P(\text{M}) \times P(\text{R}|\text{M}) = .25 \times .20 = \underline{.0500}$$
$$P(\text{R}) = .1025$$

Finally, and again following Bayes' theorem as given in equation (11.8), the fifth column of Table 11.8 presents the ratio of each joint probability to the unconditional probability of the experimental result. That is,

$$P(\text{S}|\text{R}) = \frac{.0525}{.1025} = .5122$$

and

$$P(\text{M}|\text{R}) = \frac{.0500}{.1025} = .4878$$

On the basis of one observed rejection, the prior probability distribution, which is 3 to 1 in favor of a superior quality of wine, must be revised to approximately even odds, or 51.2% for superior and 48.8% for mediocre.

Bayes' theorem does not apply only to samples of size 1. Any experiment that offers additional information can serve as a basis for revising prior probability estimates. Indeed, successive experiments can be performed such that a single unit at a time is observed and the probabilities revised in a stepwise fashion. Such a procedure often entails graphing the revised probability as a function of each additional experimental unit that is observed. This technique is well suited to quality control situations wherein a batch of items must be checked one at a time until a conclusion can be drawn about the entire lot.

11.7 Bayesian Decision Theory and Revised Probabilities

The revision of prior probabilities can be combined with Bayesian decision theory to modify the calculation of expected payoffs. Suppose that the wine merchant who acts as supplier to the Nashville–New Orleans Express guarantees the wine by offering complete replacement of any shipment judged mediocre. However, returning a shipment for replace-

Table 11.9
The Conditional and Expected Costs Without Sampling

State of Nature *E*	Prior Probability *P*(*E*)	Conditional Costs		Expected Costs	
		Keep	Return	Keep	Return
Superior (7% rejection rate)	.75	$6.00	$10.00	$4.50	$7.50
Mediocre (20% rejection rate)	.25	$18.00	$10.00	$4.50	$2.50
	1.00			$9.00	$10.00

ment carries a $10 handling charge. For $1, a sample of the wine being supplied is included for taste-testing before the train's departure time.

Thirty bottles of wine are ordered at $3 each for the meals of each trip. As previously calculated, a superior wine has a 7% rejection rate, or 2 bottles per trip, and a mediocre wine has a 20% rejection rate, or 6 bottles per trip. Thus the costs of keeping the wine shipment and having some bottles rejected can be weighed against the $10 cost of returning a shipment. At $3 per bottle, $6 will be lost through rejections with a superior wine and $18 will be lost with a mediocre wine.

Consider first the expected costs without sampling. Conditional and expected payoffs are given in Table 11.9. Based solely on the 3:1 odds in favor of superior wine from this supplier, the expected cost of keeping the wine is less than that of returning it.

Next, suppose that the $1 sample for taste-testing is acquired and offered to an impartial taste-tester (perhaps an early passenger). If the passenger accepts the proposition that the wine truly is superior, then it should be kept. But what if the passenger rejects the wine as mediocre? Revising the distribution of probability estimates results in a posterior probability distribution of a 51.2% probability that the batch is superior and a 48.8% probability that the batch is mediocre. Assuming that the rejection rate is constant, expected costs can be recalculated on the basis of the posterior probability distribution. This is shown in Table 11.10.

Given a negative result in the taste-testing experiment, the revised probabilities move the expected cost of keeping the wine shipment above the expected cost of returning it. In this case, it would be wise from the standpoint of expected costs to return the shipment for replacement with a new batch before the train's departure.

Table 11.10
The Conditional and Expected Costs on the Basis of Preliminary Rejection

State of Nature E	Posterior Probability $P(E\|R)$	Conditional Costs		Expected Costs	
		Keep	Return	Keep	Return
Superior (7% rejection rate)	.5122	\$6 + \$1	\$10 + \$1	\$3.59	\$5.63
Mediocre (20% rejection rate)	.4878	\$18 + \$1	\$10 + \$1	\$9.27	\$5.37
	1.0000			\$12.86	\$11.00

11.8 Summary

A common thread can be found in the examples of Bayesian analysis presented in this chapter. First, the Bayesian approach is oriented toward formulating optimal decision strategies that are based on expected payoffs. Second, Bayesian analysis offers methods of dealing with judgmental prior probability distributions and, in particular, methods of revising these distributions when additional information is available. Third, the idea of incorporating additional information is typically Bayesian. This applies as much to hypothetical consideration of the effect of perfect information as to revising estimates of prior probabilities on the basis of the results of an actual probabilistic experiment. Finally, the cost of obtaining additional information is realistically incorporated in Bayesian analysis so that the decision maker can adequately assess overall payoffs. Decision models based on Bayesian techniques have broad applicability and have proved themselves useful in a wide variety of circumstances.

Exercises

11.1 Explain the following terms:
a. Bayes' theorem
b. Conditional profits
c. Expected profits

d. Expected opportunity losses
e. EVPI

11.2 Briefly explain the major conceptual differences between Bayesian decision theory and classical, statistical decision theory.

11.3 Give examples of types of business situations that can be specified as "states of nature."

11.4 Ms. Rogers is mailing a package to her relatives abroad. "Would you like to buy insurance coverage for your package?" the postmaster inquires. "How much?" "Well, it depends on the value of your package." Suppose that the market value of Ms. Rogers' package is \$500, the insurance fee is \$5, and the probability of the package being lost is .001.
a. What is the probability distribution function?
b. What criterion should Ms. Rogers use in deciding whether to buy the insurance coverage?

11.5 Distinguish between objective probability and subjective probability.

11.6 Consider the following payoff matrix:

	Action				
Events	a_1	a_2	a_3	a_4	**Probabilities**
E_1	\$90	\$100	\$200	\$40	0.5
E_2	70	150	60	20	0.3
E_3	50	50	10	90	0.2

a. Calculate the expected payoff for each course of action.
b. Indicate the expected payoff for the optimal course of action under uncertainty.
c. Calculate the expected payoff under certainty.
d. How much would it be worth to be able to make this decision under certainty?

11.7 Consider the payoff table given in exercise 11.6.
a. Develop the opportunity loss table.
b. Calculate the expected opportunity loss for each course of action.
c. Select the optimal course of action with the lowest expected loss.

11.8 a. Refer to exercises 11.6 and 11.7, and show that the action with the highest payoff also has the lowest expected opportunity loss. Why is this so?
b. Show also that the expected opportunity loss of the optimal action is the same as the expected value of perfect information (EVPI).

11.9 A company's past sales data show that, for a given product,

10 cases were sold on 9 business days
11 cases were sold on 18 business days
12 cases were sold on 36 business days
13 cases were sold on 27 business days

Profits from the sale of this item depend on the number of cases in stock and the number demanded, according to the following table:

Cases Demanded	Cases Stocked 10	11	12	13
10	30	28	26	24
11	30	33	31	29
12	30	33	36	34
13	30	33	36	39

a. Which number of cases stocked each day will maximize long-run or expected profits? Perform all calculations.
b. What profits can be expected when the company has access to perfect information about demand?
c. How much is this perfect information worth, on the average, to this company?
d. What is the expected loss of each stock action? What is the minimal expected loss of any possible action?
e. Describe fully the relationship between the minimal expected loss you found in part (d) and the expected value of perfect information.
f. What is an expected value? How are expected values calculated?

11.10 Businessman Jones receives shipments of ice cubes each day in 2-pound bags, which he stocks to sell to his customers under conditions of uncertainty. His refrigerator space limits the number of bags of ice that he can carry to 3, and any bags left unsold at the end of the day are unfit for sale by the next day. Last month, Jones' records show that, on 4 of the 20 business days, no ice was sold; on 8 business days, 2 pounds were sold; on 6 business days, 4 pounds were sold; and on 2 business days, 6 pounds were sold. Ice costs Jones \$.25 a pound and he sells it for \$.40 a pound.

a. On the basis of last month's figures, what quantity of ice should Jones have available to sell each day to maximize his long-run daily profits in this product?

b. Compared with his best action under uncertainty, how much larger would one expect Jones' profits to be if he could always stock exactly the same number of bags of ice as he can sell?

11.11 A businesswoman estimates that she has a 50% chance of selling exactly 20 units on any given day of an item that is perishable and that is supplied no more than once a day. Likewise, she estimates that there is a 30% chance of her selling 15 units and a 20% chance of her selling 25 units on any given day. If the retail price is $80 (after having been marked up 60% of the wholesale price), how many of these items should she stock daily in order to maximize her long-run expected profits? What would her expected profits be if she had certain information about any day's demand level? Should she be willing to pay $80 for certain information? Why? $100? Why? $150? Why?

11.12 Consider a firm that makes a product that sells for $1.50 and has a variable cost per unit of $1.30. Assume that this is a perishable product and that it is not possible to back-order when supply runs out. Given the following probability distribution for demand, what level of product should be made available for sale in any given period, and what will expected profits be at this level? Also, what are the expected opportunity losses for stock actions that match the various demand levels? What is the EVPI?

Demand Levels	Probability
100	.3
200	.4
300	.2
400	.1

11.13 a. Show in tabular form the methods of revising estimates of prior probabilities. Be careful to specify each type of probability that must be calculated.

b. What is Bayes' theorem? Show how the table you drew up in part (a) facilitates the use of Bayes' theorem.

c. Explain the significance of prior versus posterior probability distributions in Bayesian analysis. In particular, what justification is there for revising a prior probability distribution?

11.14 Two types of weighted or biased dice are placed in an urn and thoroughly mixed together. Both types of dice are identical in outward appearance, but three-quarters of them (type 1) produce an ace 30% of the time and the rest (type 2) come up ace 60% of the time.

a. One die is drawn at random and rolled. It produces an ace. What is the prior probability that the die that has been drawn is a type 1 die? What is the posterior probability that this die is a type 1 die?
b. All dice are mixed again and, as before, one is drawn at random. This time the selected die is rolled twice and yields two aces. What is the revised probability that this die is a type 1 die?
c. Starting once again with all dice mixed together in the urn, what is the probability of a randomly selected die being a type 1 die if it is rolled and produces no aces in three rolls?

11.15 A barrel of bolts, it is realized, could have come from either of 2 different batches of machine output. Out of every 4 batches, 1 batch is thought to have come from machine operator A, whose inexperience has been found to cause faulty bolts about 20% of the time. The rest should have been made by machine operator B, whose production of faulty bolts averages only 1%. The barrel is tested by randomly drawing, measuring, and replacing 4 bolts, 1 at a time. Suppose that no faulty bolts were detected in the test procedure, and revise the prior probability estimate of the batch origin of the bolts in order to take this observed outcome into account. What would be the revised probability distribution if 1 faulty bolt were discovered? 2 faulty bolts? 3 faulty bolts? 4 faulty bolts?

11.16 The barrel of bolts you considered in exercise 11.15 is used in a manufacturing process. Bad bolts require assembly workers to spend time sorting out the good from the bad. This sorting can be performed more efficiently by a person who is set to the task, which is called ***preprocessing.*** Depending on the batch from which the bolts come, the daily wage costs of preprocessing and of not preprocessing are as follows:

	Preprocess	**Do Not Preprocess**
Batch A	\$10	0
Batch B	\$15	\$20

Use the posterior probability distributions found in exercise 11.15 (for 0, 1, 2, 3, and 4 faulty test bolts) to show which situations should be preprocessed to minimize costs.

11.17 What are the basic assumptions and what are the limitations of Bayesian analysis?

Suggested Readings

Chernoff, Herman, and Lincoln Moses. *Elementary Decision Theory.* New York: Wiley, 1959. Chapter 5.

Feller, William. *An Introduction to Probability Theory and Its Applications,* Vol. 1. 3rd ed. New York: Wiley, 1968.

———. *An Introduction to Probability Theory and Its Applications,* Vol. 2. New York: Wiley, 1966.

Halter, Albert N., and Gerald W. Dean. *Decisions Under Uncertainty.* Cincinnati, Ohio: South-Western Publishing Co., 1971. Chapters 5 and 12.

Morgan, Bruce W. *An Introduction to Bayesian Statistical Decision Processes.* Englewood Cliffs, N.J.: Prentice-Hall, 1968.

Schleifer, Robert. *Probability and Statistics for Business Decisions.* New York: McGraw-Hill, 1959.

Appendix to
Chapter 11

Basic Probability Concepts and Distribution

11A.1 Measuring Probability

The specification of a probability is simply a measurement. Just as one measures temperature on a Fahrenheit or Celsius scale and distance on a scale of miles or kilometers, one measures the likelihood of the occurrence (or nonoccurrence) of events on a probability scale. The most common scale used for measuring probability ranges from 0 to 1 (see Figure 11A.1). The value 0 represents absolute certainty that an event ***will not*** occur, and the value 1 represents absolute certainty that the event ***will*** occur. Between these extremes is the entire range of values that represent varying degrees of risk.

It is also common to express a probability value as a percentage rather than a proportion. A probability value of .64 represents sixty-four one-hundredths, or 64%. The two measures are equivalent.

11A.2 Basic Concepts

***A Posteriori* Probabilities** Sometimes probabilities can be derived from experimentation. For example, one can derive the probability of obtaining heads on the flip of

Figure 11A.1 The Scale of Probability

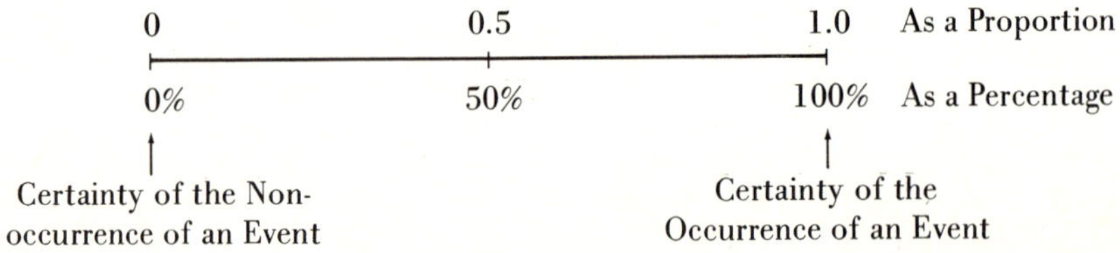

a coin by recording the results of many tosses and making a ratio of the number of heads to the total number of tosses. These probabilities are derived ***after the fact*** (based on experimentation) and hence are called ***a posteriori probabilities.*** They are also called ***posterior probabilities.*** We calculate them by forming the ratio of observed outcomes to the total number of trials:

$$P(\mathrm{A}) = \frac{f_\mathrm{A}}{N}$$

where $P(\mathrm{A})$ = probability of event A occurring
f_A = frequency of observed occurrence of event A
N = total number of trials under observation

Thus the ***a posteriori*** definition of probability (also called the ***relative frequency*** definition of probability) estimates the probabilities of events on the basis of their observed relative frequency of occurrence. This definition is also sometimes referred to as ***statistical probability.***

A Priori Probabilities By contrast, one can often reason the probability of occurrence of an event without experimentation. For example, the toss of a coin has only two possible outcomes, each of which should be equally likely. Therefore, the probability of getting heads should equal the probability of getting tails, or

$$P(\mathrm{H}) = P(\mathrm{T}) = .5$$

Determining probabilities in this way is reasoning ***before the fact*** (before experimentation), and such probabilities are called ***a priori probabilities,*** or simply ***prior probabilities.*** This is the ***classical*** approach to probability. If an event can occur in N mutually exclusive ways that are equally likely and collectively exhaustive, and if N_A of the outcomes have a given attribute A, the probability of A occurring is N_A/N. Thus the probability of obtaining two on the roll of a die is 1/6; the probability of drawing a heart from a deck is 13/52, or 1/4; the probability of obtaining two heads in the flip of two coins is 1/4; and so on.

Mutually exclusive means that two outcomes cannot happen simultaneously. ***Equally likely*** means that with a given number N of possible outcomes, each has the same probability as all others, $1/N$. ***Collectively exhaustive*** means that every possible outcome has been listed or accounted for.

Objective Versus Subjective Probabilities

These ***a priori*** and ***a posteriori*** definitions of probability relate only to the assessment of ***objective probabilities***—probabilities for which historical evidence can be supplied for substantiation. Duplication of the environment and the actions that result in events must be possible. When substantiation is not possible, a subjective approach must be applied. For example, the probability of a particular horse winning the Kentucky Derby must be a ***subjective probability.*** The running of the Derby with a given group of horses takes place only once. Historical evidence is neither available nor can it be established. Moreover, even though the list of horses is collectively exhaustive, winning the race is not equally likely for every horse, considering the different breeding, training, and past performance of the individual horses and their riders. Horse races, political elections, weather forecasts, and all other such situations are subjective probabilities.

Basic Axioms

I. The probability of any event must be greater than or equal to 0.

II. The probability of all of the possible outcomes of an experiment must equal 1; that is, some one of the outcomes must occur in the performance of an experiment.

III. Given a set of mutually exclusive agents $A_1, A_2, \ldots, A_n$, the probability of A_1 occurring, or A_2, or . . ., or A_n is the sum of the probabilities of the individual events. In other words, the probability of mutually exclusive events is additive (Figure 11A.2).

The probability of a single event, $P(A)$, is sometimes called an ***unconditional*** or ***marginal probability.*** In Figure 11A.3, the two events are not mutually exclusive. Hence mutually exclusive means that

$$P(\text{A and B}) = 0$$

The intersection of sets A and B is the null set.

The probability of two events occurring simultaneously is called a ***joint probability.*** Where two events are independent, their joint probability is the product of the individual probabilities:

$$P(\text{A and B}) = P(\text{A}) \times P(\text{B}) \qquad \text{(independence)}$$

Figure 11A.2
Additivity Based on Mutually Exclusive Events

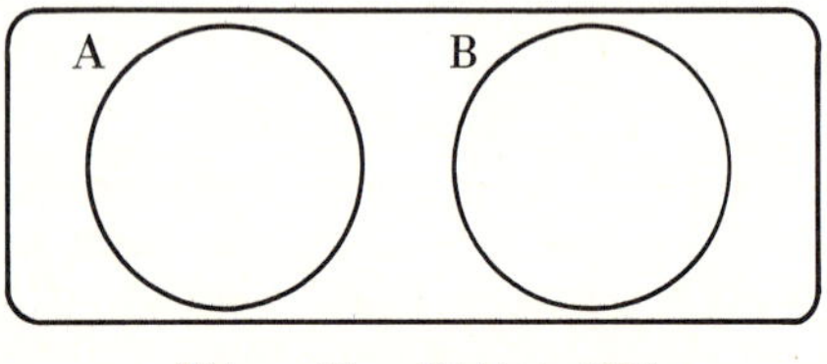

$P(\text{A or B}) = P(\text{A}) + P(\text{B})$

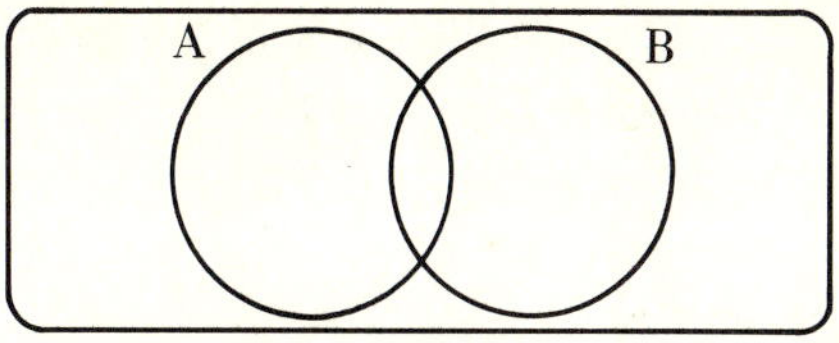

Figure 11A.3 General Additivity Based on Events That Are Not Mutually Exclusive

$P(\text{A or B}) = P(\text{A}) + P(\text{B}) - P(\text{A and B})$

Joint probabilities are written not only as $P(\text{A and B})$.

If the probability of one event is affected by the occurrence of another event, the probability of the first event is called a ***conditional probability***: the probability of event A given that event B has occurred. The conditional probability $P(\text{A given B})$ is generally written as $P(\text{A}|\text{B})$. We can calculate conditional probabilities by using the following formula:

$$P(\text{A}|\text{B}) = \frac{P(\text{A and B})}{P(\text{B})} \qquad \text{(dependence)}$$

Here the joint probability $P(\text{A and B})$ cannot be calculated as the product of the individual probabilities, because event A depends on event B. When this is not the case,

$$P(\text{A}|\text{B}) \times P(\text{B}) = P(\text{A and B}) = P(\text{A}) \times P(\text{B}) \qquad \text{(independence)}$$

Consequently, if $P(\text{A}|\text{B}) = P(\text{A})$ then the probability of occurrence of event A does not depend on the occurrence or nonoccurrence of event B. Event A is independent of event B.

11A.3 Probability Distributions

Random Variable A ***random variable*** is a variable the value of which is determined by random experiment. Practical application of probability and statistical concepts requires an understanding of some basic probability distributions. ***Probability functions*** describe the relationship between a random variable and the probability of occurrence of any value of the random variable. A random variable is random only in the sense that the values of the variable occur unpredictably. Nevertheless, the probability of occurrence of particular values of the random variable is considered definite. The specification of all possible probabilities for a random variable represents a ***probability distribution.***

Capital letters are generally used to denote random variables, and in cases where symbols are required, small letters denote given values of the random variable. Hence the notation

$$P(X = x) \quad \text{for } x = 0, 1, 2$$

represents the probabilities of occurrence of all values x of a random variable X.

According to the range of possible values of a given random variable, its probability distribution may be either ***discrete*** or ***continuous.***

The ***expected value*** of a random variable is a measure of the mean or average value of the probability distribution. It is a weighted average and is represented as

$$E(X) = \sum_i x_i f(x_i) \quad \text{for all outcomes, } x_i, \text{ of variable } X$$

where $E(X)$ = expected value of the random variable X

$f(x_i)$ = value of the probability function at the point $x = x_i$

This method of calculating expected values applies to all cases of discrete random variables. Determining the expected value of a continuous random variable requires the summation of weighted values via calculus.

Uniform Distribution

With the ***uniform distribution***, all possible values of the random variable are equally likely and none is more likely to occur than any other. The observance of heads on the flip of one coin is a simple example. Heads is as likely to occur as tails, and each has a probability of .5. The observance of the face value of a fair die is another example of a uniform distribution. Each of the possible faces is as likely to occur as any other. Each of the possibilities from 1 to 6 carries a 1/6 probability.

In the general case of a uniform distribution, the expected value is

$$E(X) = \sum_i x_i f(x_i) = \frac{1}{n}x_0 + \frac{1}{n}x_1 + \ldots + \frac{1}{n}x_n$$

$$= \frac{1}{n}(x_0 + x_1 + \ldots + x_n)$$

which is simply the unweighted arithmetic average of all possible values of the random variable.

The Bernoulli Process

One of the most fundamental of probability experiments was investigated in the seventeenth century by the Swiss mathematician Jacob Bernoulli, and a basic probability distribution is named after him. A

Figure 11A.4 Probabilities for Heads with Two Coins

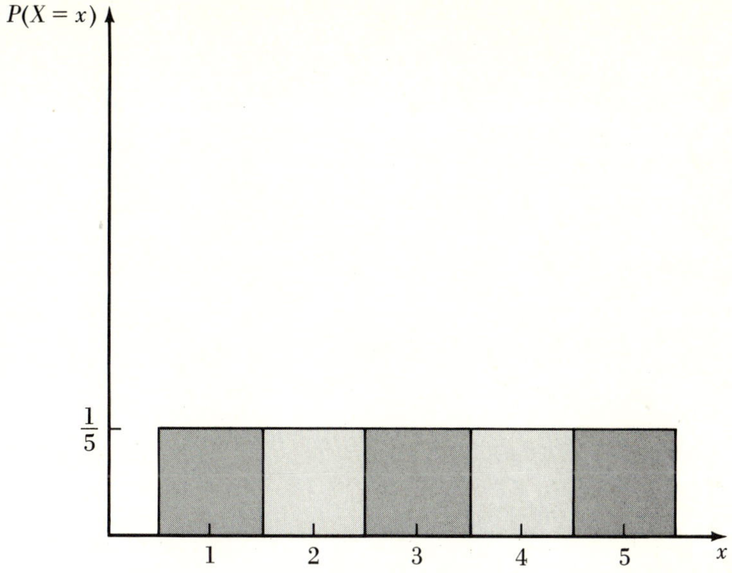

Bernoulli process is a single experiment for which either success or failure is observed. If the probability of success is given as p, the probability of a failure must be $(1 - p)$. A success can be defined to have a value of 1 and a failure to have a value of 0, in which case the Bernoulli distribution is as follows:

Random Variable X	***P(X = x)***
Success: $x_1 = 0$	$1 - p$
Failure: $x_2 = 1$	p

The expected value of the Bernoulli distribution is

$$E(X) = \sum_i x_i f(x_i) = 0(1 - p) + (1 \times p) = p$$

The probability of successes in more than one Bernoulli process is merely an extension, albeit an important one, of the Bernoulli distribution. An example of this is the number of heads (successes) in the flip of two coins:

0 Heads	**1 Heads**	**2 Heads**
T T	H T	H H
	T H	

The probability of 0 heads is 1/4, of 1 head is 1/2, and of 2 heads is 1/4.

The random variable that represents the number of observed heads

Table 11A.1
The Probabilities of Successes in a Given Number of Trials

Trials (Number of fair coins)	Number of Successes						
	0	1	2	3	4	5	6
0	1						
1	$\frac{1}{2}$	$\frac{1}{2}$					
2	$\frac{1}{4}$	$\frac{2}{4}$	$\frac{1}{4}$				
3	$\frac{1}{8}$	$\frac{3}{8}$	$\frac{3}{8}$	$\frac{1}{8}$			
4	$\frac{1}{16}$	$\frac{4}{16}$	$\frac{6}{16}$	$\frac{4}{16}$	$\frac{1}{16}$		
5	$\frac{1}{32}$	$\frac{5}{32}$	$\frac{10}{32}$	$\frac{10}{32}$	$\frac{5}{32}$	$\frac{1}{32}$	
			etc.				

based on three fair coins flipped simultaneously varies from 0 to 3, and the ways of obtaining the possible outcomes are

0 Heads	1 Heads	2 Heads	3 Heads
T T T	H T T	H H T	H H H
	T H T	H T H	
	T T H	T H H	

The probabilities are thus 1/8, 3/8, 3/8, and 1/8, for X equal to 0, 1, 2, and 3, respectively. Similarly, if four coins are under consideration, enumeration of all possible outcomes indicates the probabilities 1/16, 1/4, 3/8, 1/4, and 1/16 for X equal to 0, 1, 2, 3, and 4, respectively.

From this process of enumeration, a pattern emerges (Table 11A.1).

Pascal's Triangle

Pascal's Triangle, it will be recalled, is a concept of basic algebra that provides coefficients in the expansion of binomial equations (Table 11A.2). The same pattern occurs in the numerator of the fractional probability values presented in Table 11A.1.

As a result, Pascal's triangle gives the number of ways of combining a given number of successes when the number of trials has been determined. For example, flipping three coins there is one way to get no heads, three ways to get 1 head, three ways to get 2 heads, and one way to get 3 heads. These are the row 3 coefficients of Pascal's triangle. The triangle itself works according to a system of adding any two elements across a row to obtain the coefficient in the next row located directly below the right-hand element used to create the sum. Zeros are assumed where no elements exist.

A more efficient way to find the coefficients of Pascal's triangle requires us only to recognize that the number of successes r in n trials is the same as the number of combinations that can be formed of r successes and $(n - r)$ failures. Thus any coefficient found in Pascal's

Table 11A.2
Pascal's Triangle

Trials	Number of Successes 0	1	2	3	4	5	6
0	1						
1	1	1					
2	1	2	1				
3	1	3	3	1			
4	1	4	6	4	1		
5	1	5	10	10	5	1	

triangle can be calculated directly as the number of ways of combining n objects taken r at a time, or $C_{n,r}$, defined as follows:

$$C_{n,r} = \frac{n!}{r!(n-r)!}$$

where $n!$ (read "n factorial") is $n(n-1)(n-2)\cdots(2)(1)$. Also, by definition, $0!$ equals 1.

As an example, consider the number of ways of obtaining 3 successes in 5 trials of an experiment:

$$C_{5,3} = \frac{5!}{3!2!} = \frac{5 \times 4 \times 3 \times 2 \times 1}{(3 \times 2 \times 1)(2 \times 1)} = 10$$

Similarly, the number of ways of obtaining 3 successes in 6 trials of an experiment is 20. These are direct calculations of the coefficients given in Pascal's triangle.

The Binomial Distribution When we generalize the pattern that arises when we calculate binomial probabilities by enumerating all possible outcomes, we obtain a valid computational formula. Once the number of ways of obtaining a given number of successes has been determined—or $C_{n,r}$—the desired probability is $C_{n,r}$ times the probability of any one of the combinations of a given number of successes and failures. The most convenient of these combinations to work with is the combination with all successes grouped first and all failures last. Thus the general formula for this probability distribution, called the ***binomial*** probability distribution, is as follows:

$$P(r \text{ successes in } n \text{ trials} | p = \text{the probability of a success})$$

$$= C_{n,r} \times \underbrace{[p \times p \times \cdots \times p]}_{\left[\begin{array}{c} r \text{ independent} \\ \text{successes} \end{array}\right]} \times \underbrace{[(1-p) \times (1-p) \times \cdots \times (1-p)]}_{\left[\begin{array}{c} (n-r) \text{ independent} \\ \text{failures} \end{array}\right]}$$

$$= C_{n,r}\,[p^r(1-p)^{n-r}]$$

We can verify the calculations of Table 11A.2 with a simple example. What is the probability of obtaining 4 heads in 5 independent flips of a fair coin?

$$P(n,r|p) = P\left(5,4|p = \frac{1}{2}\right) = \frac{5!}{4!1!}\left(\frac{1}{2}\right)^4\left(\frac{1}{2}\right)^1 = \frac{5}{32}$$

For another example, what is the probability of obtaining either 4 or 5 or 6 six's when rolling 8 dice?

$$P\left(4 \text{ or } 5 \text{ or } 6 \text{ six's in } 8 \text{ trials}|p = \frac{1}{6}\right)$$

$$= P\left(8,4|p = \frac{1}{6}\right) + P\left(8,5|p = \frac{1}{6}\right) + P\left(8,6|p = \frac{1}{6}\right)$$

$$= \frac{8!}{4!4!}\left(\frac{1}{6}\right)^4\left(\frac{5}{6}\right)^4 + \frac{8!}{5!3!}\left(\frac{1}{6}\right)^5\left(\frac{5}{6}\right)^3 + \frac{8!}{6!2!}\left(\frac{1}{6}\right)^6\left(\frac{5}{6}\right)^2$$

$$= .0260 + .0042 + .0004$$

$$= .0306$$

In a quality control examination process, what is the probability of getting at least 19 good parts in a random sample of 20 when the production of these parts is known to be 99% reliable? In this case, we would use the binomial distribution formula as follows:

$$P(19 \text{ successes or } 20 \text{ successes in } 20 \text{ trials}|p = .99)$$

$$= P(19 \text{ successes in } 20 \text{ trials}|p = .99)$$

$$+ P(20 \text{ successes in } 20 \text{ trials}|p = .99)$$

$$= \frac{20!}{19!1!}(.99)^{19}(.01)^1 + \frac{20!}{20!0!}(.99)^{20}(.01)^0$$

In cases such as this wherein calculations are somewhat complex, one can either use a good electronic calculator or look up the answers in tables of the binomial distribution. Tables are especially easy to use. Refer to Appendix A.2, "Table of Values of the Binomial Distribution," and find the desired probabilities under $n = 20$, $r = 19$ (and 20), and $p = .99$.

$$P(20,19|.99) + P(20,20|.99) = .165 + .818 = .983$$

The Poisson Distribution

In cases where the probability of success is small and the number of trials is large, we can use the ***Poisson*** probability distribution to determine very good approximations of binomial probabilities without encountering these difficulties of calculation.

We find Poisson probabilities by using the following formula:

$$P(x \text{ successes}|\lambda = np) = \frac{e^{-\lambda}\lambda^x}{x!}$$

where e = 2.71828 (the base of the Naperian system of logarithms)
x = number of successes being considered
λ = average success rate for a given number of trials, or np

How large should the number of trials be, and how small should the probability of success be, for us to get good approximations of binomial probabilities using the Poisson distribution? As a rule of thumb, if n is larger than 20 and the average success rate np is less than 5, the Poisson distribution can be used.

Typical business applications of the Poisson distribution are found in the study of waiting lines, or queuing problems, where the probability of an "arrival" is small and the number of trials—or time intervals—is large. Problems of this sort will be considered in detail in Chapter 13. To ease the burden of calculation, a table of values of the Poisson distribution can be used (see Appendix A.3).

The Normal Distribution

Whereas the foregoing distributions are all based on discrete random variables, the ***normal*** distribution is continuous. It is the familiar, bell-shaped distribution that is perhaps the most important of all probability distributions (Figure 11A.5).

Figure 11A.5 The Normal Distribution: Device for Randomly Generating Numbers from One to Five with Equal Probability

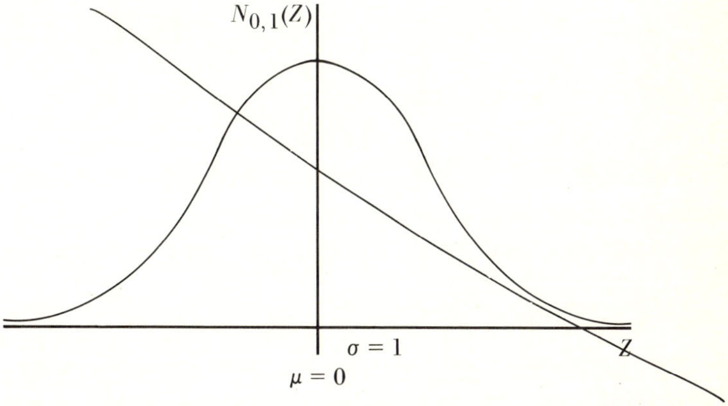

The ***standard normal*** distribution, shown in Figure 11A.5, is a normal probability distribution that has a mean, μ, of 0 and a standard deviation, σ, equal to 1. Its formula is

$$N_{0,1}(Z) = \frac{1}{\sqrt{2\pi}} = e^{-1/2(Z^2)}$$

where π is constant (about 3.142) and e is also constant (about 2.718).

We usually find values of the normal probability distribution by using tables of ordinates or tables of areas under the curve (see Appendix A.4).

Normal distributions may have any conceivable mean μ and standard distribution σ. A simple conversion allows us to use probabilities of the standard normal distribution in relation to any other normal distribution. This calculation

$$Z = \frac{x - \mu}{\sigma}$$

simply converts the given normal distribution to a standard normal distribution. Then we can obtain probabilities from tables of the standard normal distribution (see Appendix A.4).

For instance, if the average life of standard 40-watt light bulbs is 1500 hours and the standard deviation of this distribution is measured to be 425 hours, what, assuming a normal distribution of light bulb life, is the probability that a given bulb will last no more than 900 hours before burning out? First, convert to a Z value for reference to the standard normal distribution. That is,

$$Z = \frac{x - \mu}{\sigma} = \frac{900 - 1500}{425} = -1.41$$

Then refer to the table of areas to the left of Z under the standard normal distribution. Finding the value of $Z = -1.41$ yields

$$\begin{aligned} &P(\text{900-hour life or less, given } \mu = 1500 \text{ and } \sigma = 425) \\ &= P(Z \leq -1.41) \\ &= .0793 \\ &\cong 8\% \end{aligned}$$

Probability Density Function versus Cumulative Distribution Function

A ***density function*** (see Figure 11A.6) gives probabilities for all possible values of the random variable. The total area under a density function is 1.

A second and equally useful method of representing a probability distribution is by its ***cumulative distribution function.*** The cumulative distributive function gives the probability that a value of the random variable will be less than or equal to a given value. Any individual

Figure 11A.6
A Uniform Distribution of Probabilities

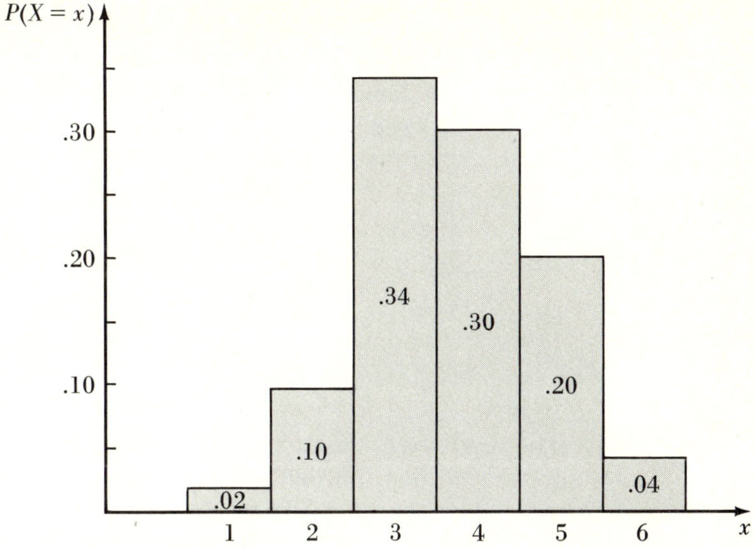

cumulative probability is found by summing all probabilities less than or equal to the given value. Thus, for the foregoing probability density function, the equivalent cumulative distribution function is as shown in Table 11A.3 and as illustrated in Figure 11A.7.

Figure 11A.7
The Cumulative Distribution Function

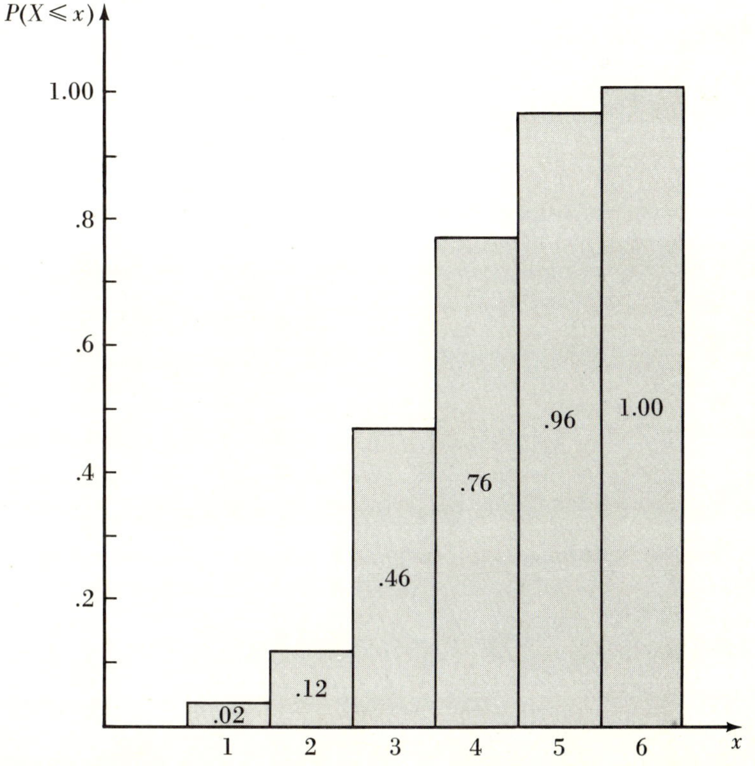

Table 11A.3
Probability Density Function Versus Cumulative Distribution Function

Random Variable X	Probability Density Function $P(X = x)$	Cumulative Distribution Function $P(X \leq x)$
1	.02	.02
2	.10	.12
3	.34	.46
4	.30	.76
5	.20	.96
6	.04	1.00

The reader will quickly recognize that the representation of the standard normal distribution given in Appendix A.4 is a cumulative distribution function. It gives areas under the distribution to the left of a given value. That is, it indicates the probability of a variable Z being less than or equal to the listed value.

Suggested Readings

Bierman, Harold, Jr., Charles P. Bonini, and Warren H. Hausman. *Quantitative Analysis for Business Decisions.* 5th ed. Homewood, Ill.: Irwin, 1977.

Drake, Alvin W. *Fundamentals of Applied Probability Theory.* New York: McGraw-Hill, 1967.

Feller, W. *An Introduction to Probability Theory and Its Applications,* Vol. 1. 3rd ed. New York: Wiley, 1968.

Ewart, P. J., J. S. Ford, and C. Y. Lin. *Probability for Statistical Decision Making.* Englewood Cliffs, N.J.: Prentice-Hall, 1974.

Goldberg, Samuel. *Probability: An Introduction.* Englewood Cliffs, N.J.: Prentice-Hall, 1960.

Hays, W. L., and R. L. Winkler. *Statistics.* New York: Holt, 1970.

Hodges, L. J., Jr., and E. L. Lehmann. *Elements of Finite Probability.* 2nd ed. San Francisco, Calif.: Holden-Day, 1970.

Kemeny, J. G., A. Schleifer, Jr., J. L. Snell, and G. L. Thompson. *Finite Mathematics with Business Applications.* 2nd ed. Englewood Cliffs, N.J.: Prentice-Hall, 1972.

Mosteller, F., R. E. Rourke, and G. B. Thomas, Jr. *Probability with Statistical Applications.* 2nd ed. Reading, Mass.; Addison-Wesley, 1970.

Neter, John, William Wasserman, and G. A. Whitmore. *Fundamental Statistics for Business and Economics.* 4th ed. Boston, Mass.: Allyn and Bacon, 1975, pp. 93–138.

Parzen, E. *Modern Probability Theory and Its Applications.* New York: Wiley, 1960.

Yamane, Taro. *Statistics: An Introductory Analysis.* 3rd ed. New York: Harper and Row, 1973, pp. 81–127, 735–745.

12

Inventory Control Models

Storing things is not so glamorous as producing and selling them, but the efficient control of inventories is an important business activity and ranks high on any list of sound business management practices. Attesting to this, the president of Satellite Business Systems—a leader in modern communications technology—recently stated in a published interview that, for his organization, even small percentage reductions in inventory levels could translate into sizable savings in the costs of operation. Similar situations exist in many business operations, and potential savings can be important on a relative basis whether a firm is large or small. Managing inventory efficiently means knowing one's costs and how they respond to varying inventory levels. It means determining an optimal level of average inventory for each stock item. Most of all, it means knowing when to reorder inventory items routinely and how much to reorder. These are the objectives of inventory analysis, and we strive to achieve them in practice by using carefully designed ***inventory control models.*** The primary goal of ***inventory analysis*** is to minimize inventory-related costs.

12.1 Economics of Inventory

Functionally, holding inventories results in decoupling the production processes from the consumption or utilization of goods. Some businesses operate solely from inventories; they include the independent gasoline station, the business supplies distributor, and most supermarkets. Manufacturing enterprises generally work from inventories of raw materials or intermediate goods in order to create inventories of processed goods with added value. In either case, the formation of inventories allows production and distribution to proceed smoothly, rather than in spurts, as they would if each order were filled from a production batch or if production runs had to await the arrival of raw materials. Thus an inventory of goods acts as a buffer to absorb intermittent arrivals of shipments and sales to customers—also known as supply and demand.

For the individual firm, as for the economy as a whole, the status of inventories reflects the balance or imbalance of supply and demand. If inventories accumulate or dwindle beyond expectation, the production or ordering of goods must be adjusted accordingly. Consequently, the inventory buffer, or decoupling process, does not make the production and distribution of goods completely independent. Indeed, the difference between expected (or ***ex ante***) and actual (or ***ex post***) demand for inventories ultimately governs increases or decreases in production.

The operation of inventories requires careful record keeping. The stock room generally records all transactions for each inventory item, including dates, amounts received or issued, the parties to each transaction ("issued by . . ." and "received by . . ."), and running totals. Reorder points should be readily available for comparison with the running totals, and the initiation of purchase orders (or job runs) should occur routinely. Records may be kept in a variety of forms from card files to computer systems.

The periodic valuation of business inventories is an essential accounting function that includes both the verification of records by thorough inspection of all amounts and the "costing" of each item. For various practical or financial reasons, methods such as FIFO ("first in, first out") or LIFO ("last in, first out") may be employed. In the former system, those units that arrive first in inventory are the first to be issued (examples include the storage of food or other perishable items and any bin or pipeline arrangement where units are filled in at the top and taken out at the bottom). In the latter system, the last unit received is the first unit issued (as in any stacking arrangement that both receives and draws from the top of the stack—store shelves, for example).

Economic Motivations Relating to Inventory

The motivations for holding an item of inventory may extend beyond providing a buffer for production. Although money itself is not usually regarded as an inventory item, the motivations for holding ordinary inventories are analogous to those for holding money. The prevailing economic theories about the demand for a stock of money offer three primary motivations:

1. A transactionary demand
2. A precautionary demand
3. A speculative demand

A regular inventory item may be needed to cover the transactions—input and output—of ordinary production operations. Holding an inventory item may be motivated by the desire to take precautions against unexpected shortages or "stockouts." And inventories may be maintained in order to take advantage of expected price changes—in other words, for speculative purposes. Let us now consider the application of inventory control models in specific business situations.

Basic Characteristics of Inventory Situations and Models

The ways in which inventory accumulation and depletion occur are numerous, and they vary significantly with the particular business situation, the practices of suppliers, and demand requirements. In order to be fully applicable, an inventory model should be suited to the particular situation a given business faces. If it is not specifically related to the conditions that exist, using it may lead to inaccurate conclusions. For this reason, a large assortment of inventory models has been developed.

This chapter presents a sampling of fundamental inventory models, each of which is based on different assumptions about the operating environment for a hypothetical inventory situation. It is instructive to learn how to use these models in situations that match the given assumptions, but one should also try to understand how models are developed. The possibilities for different types of models are virtually endless, so developing the skills required to build new models is as desirable as mastering the use of standard ones.

Inventory models can be classified largely according to the assumptions on which they rest. Three considerations are of primary importance in characterizing any inventory system. They are

1. Characterization of the supply of an item to inventory
2. Characterization of demand for an item of inventory
3. Characterization of inventory-related costs

Table 12.1 presents the details of these three considerations in outline form.

Table 12.1
Basic Characteristics of Inventory Systems

I. *The Supply of an Item to Inventory by Reorder (or Manufacture)*
   A. Instantaneous Reorder (or Set-Up)
      1. Entire order will arrive in one batch
      2. Order flows into inventory
         a. In discrete quantities
         b. Continuously
   B. Positive and Constant Lead Time
      1. Entire order will arrive in one batch
      2. Order flows into inventory
         a. In discrete quantities
         b. Continuously
   C. Positive and Random (Probabilistic) Lead Time

II. *The Demand for an Item of Inventory*
   A. Constant Demand Rate per Time Period (Deterministic)
      1. Uniform constant demand rates in all time intervals
         a. Occurring in discrete quantities
         b. Occurring continuously
      2. Different constant demand rates in different time intervals
         a. Occurring in discrete quantities
         b. Occurring continuously
   B. Variable Rate of Demand per Time Period (Deterministic)
      1. Uniform and determined in each time interval
         a. Occurring in discrete quantities
         b. Occurring continuously
   C. Intermittent Demand (Deterministic)
      1. Constant rate when functioning
      2. Variable rate when functioning
   D. Random Demand (Probabilistic)

III. *Costs*
   A. Cost per unit of an Inventory Item (Purchased or Manufactured)
      1. Constant
      2. Subject to "quantity discounts" or "price breaks"
   B. Inventory Carrying Cost per Unit of Time
      1. Determined as a dollar amount per unit of average inventory
      2. Determined as a percentage of average inventory value
      3. Determined continuously
   C. Stockout (Shortage) Cost per Unit of Time
      1. Constant
         a. Infinite (precluding stockouts)
         b. Finite
      2. Variable over time
   D. Ordering Cost (to Purchase) or Set-Up Cost (to Manufacture)
   E. Depreciation of Inventory Over Time

Inventory models run the gamut of modeling techniques. They may be "relatively" deterministic in situations where uncertainty is small and flows are fairly constant, or they may be probabilistic. As the complexity of assumptions in deterministic situations increases, the mathematical manipulations may become quite intricate, extending well beyond the scope of this text. In probabilistic models, if two or more variables act randomly, simulation models such as those described in Chapter 13 on queuing may be the most efficient means of analysis. Where a single variable is probabilistic, Bayesian analysis may apply. Indeed, the examples used in Chapter 11 on Bayesian decision theory was essentially an inventory model—a model that determined what quantity to stock at fixed time intervals. Under different circumstances, linear programming, quadratic programming, and dynamic programming techniques may apply. The most complete models may even tie together the determination of optimal production processes with inventory control analysis, rather than treat each independently.

In the following sections, four inventory control models are presented. The first three of these models deal with deterministic cases for which the rate of demand is considered constant and known. Two of the three deterministic models involve ordering; the third applies to a production-to-inventory situation. The last model is a probabilistic model that addresses random demand fluctuations occurring during the reorder period.

Notation The algebraic notation used in this chapter's inventory models is as follows:

Supply and Demand

X_o = number of units ordered (supplied) per shipment

D = demand in units (usage) of inventory per standard time period

N = number of orders placed per standard time period

Costs

C_T = total inventory-related costs per standard time period

C_o = total ordering costs per standard time period

γ_o = ordering cost per order placed

C_c = total carrying cost per standard time period

γ_c = cost per unit of average inventory

Time

t_o = time interval between orders measured as a fractional part of the standard time period

12.2 The Basic Deterministic Model

Let's use a typical inventory situation in its simplest form to illustrate inventory conditions and analysis. Consider the common problem of a manufacturer who requires parts for a production process. An inventory of parts is maintained to be drawn from according to the requirements of production, and production rates establish a relatively constant demand pattern. Inventory is supplied by batch from a distributor. Thus inventory for a given item (or part) is depleted at a steady rate over time but is replenished all at once, or instantaneously.

The least complicated supply condition is one for which units ordered are delivered and made available for production immediately upon placement of an order. This would occur, for example, in the case of a supplier whose warehouse is next door or at least close enough to deliver the ordered goods with a negligible waiting period. Thus the ***lead time***, or the time lapse between placing an order and receiving it, is cut, in this simplest of cases, to zero. In this situation, the manufacturer can wait to reorder an inventory item until the stock level reaches zero. Ordering earlier would only increase ***carrying costs***, or the costs that result from investment in inventory and storage requirements. (Indeed, in such an ideal situation the manufacturer would be well advised to avoid holding inventory altogether and to obtain units directly from the supplier as they are needed for production.) Of course, the ***ordering costs*** (the costs of preparing and handling paperwork for requisitions, purchase orders, and other accounting requirements, as well as the usual process of inspecting received goods) must also be reckoned. Quite clearly, if the quantity ordered decreases, the average level of inventory kept on hand also decreases and carrying costs are reduced. But counteracting this reduction in carrying costs, ordering costs increase. This sort of trade-off must be resolved in any basic inventory situation. What quantity ordered is optimal in reducing total inventory costs (carrying and ordering costs) to a minimum?

To be more specific, the assumptions of this basic deterministic model are as follows:

1. Supply instantaneous on reorder
2. Demand constant and uniform (assumed continuous)
3. Inventory carrying cost determined as a dollar amount per unit of average inventory
4. No stockouts (therefore an infinite stockout cost)
5. Positive ordering costs
6. Negligible depreciation of inventory over time

Figure 12.1
Average Inventory and the Basic Deterministic Model

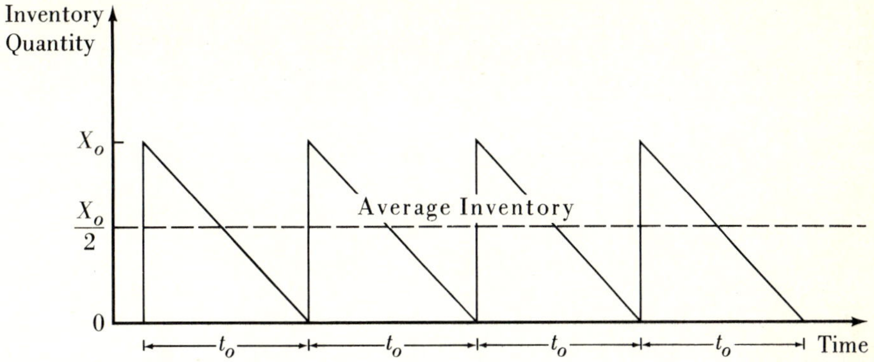

Fluctuation in inventory levels for a given item over time reflects the repetitive cycles of depletion and replenishment. Shown on a graph, the relationship between quantity in inventory and time describes a "saw-tooth" pattern (see Figure 12.1). Since actual amounts in inventory fluctuate constantly, we simplify computations related to inventory level by using average inventory. For any number of complete depletion–replenishment cycles, computation of average inventory is equivalent to the detailed accumulation of actual amounts over many very short time periods. With a constant rate of demand, average inventory is simply the arithmetic average of maximum and minimum levels. That is,

$$\text{Average inventory} = \frac{\text{maximum level} + \text{minimum level}}{2}$$

In this model, where the minimum level is zero and the maximum level equals the amount ordered X_o,

$$\text{Average inventory} = \frac{X_o}{2}$$

Determining the Economic Order Quantity

What cost relationships apply to the basic model? We have seen that, when a given level of demand must be satisfied, ordering costs vary inversely with the size of the order placed. For example, if the yearly requirement is 1000 units and orders of 10 are placed, the ordering cost is greater than if orders of 100 are placed (the number of orders is greater for smaller order sizes). Overall, the yearly ordering cost is simply the number of orders placed (total yearly requirement divided by the order size) times the cost per order. When we use the notation specified earlier, this relationship is expressed as

$$C_o = \gamma_o \times \frac{D}{X}$$

The other cost relationship that must be specified is total yearly carrying cost. This cost depends on the amount of inventory held. It is found as the product of carrying cost per unit times average inventory:

$$C_c = \gamma_c \times \frac{X_o}{2}$$

Total yearly inventory cost is the sum of yearly ordering costs and yearly carrying costs:

$$C_T = C_o + C_c$$

or

$$C_T = \gamma_o \frac{D}{X_o} + \gamma_c \frac{X_o}{2} \tag{12.1}$$

As an example, suppose that ordering cost per order is \$2.25, that carrying cost per unit is \$.06, and that annual demand for the inventory item is 1200 units. These numbers have been used to calculate yearly ordering cost, yearly carrying cost, and total yearly inventory cost for various possible order sizes ranging from 50 to 500, and the results appear in Table 12.2. Clearly, yearly ordering costs are decreasing and yearly carrying costs are increasing as the order quantity increases. Total costs reach a minimum (\$18) at an order quantity of 300. This minimum

Table 12.2 Calculation of EOQ in Tabular Form for the Basic Deterministic Model

Order Quantity X_o	Number of Orders per Year N	Yearly Ordering Cost C_o	Average Inventory $X_o/2$	Yearly Carrying Cost C_c	Total Yearly Inventory Cost $C_o + C_c$
50	24	\$54.00	25	\$ 1.50	\$55.50
100	12	27.00	50	3.00	30.00
150	8	18.00	75	4.50	22.50
200	6	13.50	100	6.00	19.50
250	4.80	10.80	125	7.50	18.30
300	4	9.00	150	9.00	18.00
350	3.43	7.71	175	10.50	18.21
400	3	6.75	200	12.00	18.75
450	2.67	6.00	225	13.50	19.50
500	2.40	5.40	250	15.00	20.40

Figure 12.2 Cost Functions for the Basic Deterministic Model

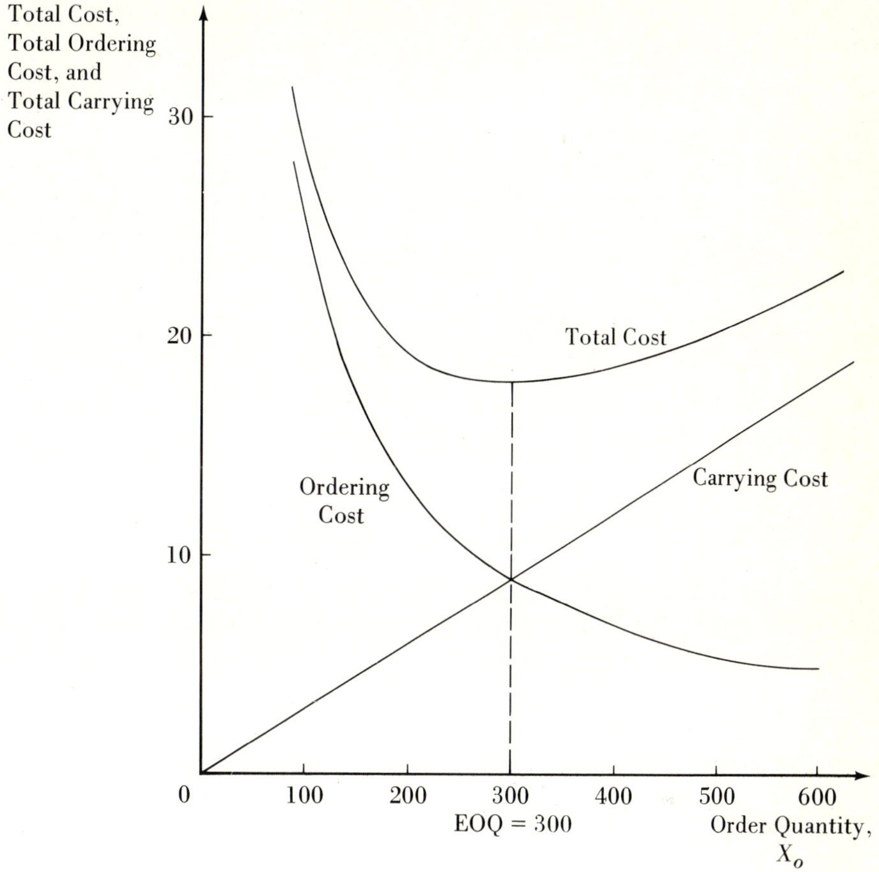

is called the ***economic order quantity*** or EOQ; it is the order quantity that minimizes total yearly inventory costs.

Figure 12.2, a graph of the cost functions shown in Table 12.2, demonstrates several important characteristics of the basic deterministic model. First, ordering cost, which varies with the inverse of the order quantity, generates a downward-sloping hyperbola, and carrying cost an upward-sloping line. The trade-off is quite clear: one cost function increases as the other decreases. Second, the total cost function has a minimum that identifies the economic order quantity of 300. Third, EOQ occurs exactly where ordering cost equals carrying cost. This last characteristic is a necessary and sufficient condition for EOQ in the basic model. EOQ occurs if and only if

$$\text{Ordering cost} = \text{carrying cost}$$

Applied algebraically, the EOQ condition is

$$C_o = C_c \quad \text{for EOQ}$$

Therefore,

$$\gamma_o \frac{D}{X_o} = \gamma_c \frac{X_o}{2}$$

Isolating X_o, we find that

$$\frac{2\gamma_o D}{\gamma_c} = X_o^2$$

Thus optimal X_o (EOQ) is derived to be

$$X_o(\text{EOQ}) = \sqrt{\frac{2\gamma_o D}{\gamma_c}}$$

With this formula, we can calculate EOQ directly. Applying it to the example for which a tabular solution has already been found yields

$$X_o(\text{EOQ}) = \sqrt{\frac{2\gamma_o D}{\gamma_c}} = \sqrt{\frac{2 \times 2.25 \times 1200}{.06}} = \sqrt{90{,}000}$$
$$= 300 \text{ units per order}$$

The Marginal Principle

An alternative method of determining EOQ is based on the principles of marginal analysis, which are employed widely in economic reasoning. Briefly, ***marginal analysis*** is concerned with incremental change, or the change in one variable that is induced by a unit change in another variable. Although these concepts provide possibilities for the direct application of differential calculus, the student whose background does not include calculus can follow the same reasoning by repeating some very elementary calculations. The marginal principle that applies here applies to trade-off situations of this sort generally. If the marginal ***increase*** in one variable (carrying cost) equals the marginal ***decrease*** in an opposing variable (ordering cost), the total of the two variables (total inventory cost) is at a minimum.

Marginal costs are calculated as a ratio of the change in one variable to the corresponding change in a related variable. The resulting quotient represents incremental or per-unit change in a dependent variable.

Here ordering cost, carrying cost, and total cost all depend on, or are functions of, order quantity. For example, Table 12.2 reveals that, for each increase of 50 in order quantity, yearly carrying cost increases by \$1.50; therefore, marginal carrying cost is \$1.50/50 = \$.03.

In general, if a variable y depends on the value of another variable x, then y is a function of x, or $y = f(x)$. The marginal value of y is its change due to a unit change in x. That is,

$$\text{Marginal value of } y = \frac{\text{change in } y}{\text{change in } x}$$

Often the expression "change in" is symbolized by a capital Greek delta, so that

$$\text{Marginal } y = \frac{\Delta y}{\Delta x} = \frac{y_1 - y_0}{x_1 - x_0}$$

where (x_0,y_0) and (x_1,y_1) are points in some interval on $f(x)$.[1]

Whereas marginal carrying cost is constant for all intervals of Table 12.1, marginal ordering cost varies according to the interval chosen. This difference occurs because the carrying cost relationship is linear whereas the ordering cost relationship is hyperbolic, or curved. Since the marginal cost calculation loses accuracy over large intervals on curves, a table should be prepared that has relatively small intervals to maintain the necessary degree of accuracy. Table 12.3 does this for order quantities in the vicinity of EOQ, which is already known to be 300 units. The calculations for orders per year, total ordering cost, average inventory, yearly carrying cost, and total yearly inventory cost are the same as those that were performed for Table 12.2. Marginal ordering cost is calculated as follows:

$$\frac{9.247 - 9.310}{272 - 290} = -.032$$

$$\frac{9.184 - 9.247}{294 - 292} = -.032$$

$$\frac{9.122 - 9.184}{296 - 294} = -.031$$

and so on

[1]In terms of trigonometric relationships, this calculation is the same as dividing "side opposite" by "side adjacent" to determine the tangent of an angle in a right triangle. Hence, the marginal relationship is a tangential relationship expressing the slope of a function over the given interval.

Table 12.3 Marginal Ordering and Carrying Costs in the Vicinity of Minimum Cost, EOQ

Order Quantity X_o	Number of Orders per Year N	Yearly Ordering Cost C_o	Marginal Ordering Cost $\Delta C_o/\Delta X_o$	Average Inventory $X_o/2$	Yearly Carrying Cost C_c	Marginal Carrying Cost $\Delta C_c/\Delta X_o$	Total Yearly Inventory Cost $C_o + C_c$
290	4.138	\$9.310		145.00	\$8.70		\$18.01
292	4.110	9.247	−.032	146.00	8.76	+.030	18.006
294	4.082	8.184	−.032	147.00	8.82	+.030	18.004
296	4.054	9.122	−.031	148.00	8.88	+.030	18.002
298	4.027	9.060	−.031	149.00	8.94	+.030	18.0004
300	4.000	8.000	−.030	150.00	9.00	+.030	18.0000
302	3.974	8.940	−.030	151.00	9.06	+.030	18.0004
304	3.947	8.882	−.029	152.00	9.12	+.030	18.002
306	3.922	8.824	−.029	153.00	9.18	+.030	18.004
308	3.896	8.766	−.029	154.00	9.24	+.030	18.006
310	3.871	8.710	−.028	155.00	9.30	+.030	18.01

Marginal carrying cost is calculated in the same way. Each increment of 2 units in order quantity increases carrying cost \$.06, so marginal carrying cost is \$.03 for each interval.

Table 12.3 demonstrates that marginal ordering cost equals marginal carrying cost (in absolute values) at the economic order quantity of 300. At this level, total yearly inventory cost is at a minimum, \$18. Parenthetically, the coincidence of marginal costs in Table 12.3 for order quantities of 300 and 302 is due to rounding in the calculations. If, while maintaining small intervals, we kept enough places in all calculations, the marginal principle would apply ***uniquely*** to EOQ = 300.

Other Characteristics Although it is sufficient to express EOQ as an order quantity, other characteristics of the inventory situation should often be specified as well. Once we have determined the optimal level of X_o, these other characteristics generally follow directly. For example, we find minimum total inventory cost by using equation (12.1) with the optimal value of X_o:

$$C_T = \gamma_o \frac{D}{X_o} + \gamma_c \frac{X_o}{2}$$

The optimal number of orders placed per year, N, is the ratio of yearly demand to the optimal order quantity, or

$$N = \frac{D}{X_o} \tag{12.2}$$

In terms of EOQ, this becomes

$$N = \frac{D}{\sqrt{\dfrac{2\gamma_o D}{\gamma_c}}}$$

which simplifies to

$$N = \sqrt{\frac{\gamma_c D}{2\gamma_o}} \tag{12.3}$$

The optimal length of time between orders (duration of supply) is simply 1 year divided by the optimal number of orders per year. Let this value be T. Expressed as a fraction of a year, it is simply $1/N$. Expressed as the number of months' supply per order, it is $12/N$. The optimal number of weeks' supply per order is $52/N$; an optimal days' supply is $365/N$. These constants may be revised to properly fit the business situation. For example, if only 250 days of the year are production days, the optimal production days' supply is $250/N$. Let the constant (1, 12, 52, or 365) that expresses the number of intermediate periods per year be K. Then, since the optimal number of orders per year, N, has itself been presented as an algebraic relationship (see 12.3), the optimal duration of supply is

$$T = \frac{K}{\sqrt{\dfrac{\gamma_c D}{2\gamma_o}}}$$

which simplifies to

$$T = \sqrt{\frac{2\gamma_o K^2}{\gamma_c D}} \tag{12.4}$$

These relationships provide a fairly complete picture of the optimal inventory situation. For the preceding example, the equations can be applied to determine the following:

Economic order quantity:
X_o (EOQ) = 300 units per order
Minimum total yearly inventory cost:
C_T = \$18 per year
Optimum number of orders placed per year:
N = 4 per year
Optimum number of days supply per order:
T = 91.25 days (based on 365 days per year)

12.3 A Deterministic Model with Periodic Stockouts

The basic deterministic model can be extended to include periodic stockouts. Being out of stock at a time when stock is needed usually results in additional cost. Production time may be lost; sales may be forgone. In the previous section, stockout costs were assumed to be so great as to preclude ever having a stockout. Such a condition may be actual (for example, any case where a substantial penalty results from being out of stock) or it may be imposed as a matter of preference (for example, when management decides always to have stock available even if it costs more to do so).

The assumptions of this model are the same as those of the basic deterministic model, with the following stockout modification:

1. Regular stockouts may occur.
2. A finite stockout cost exists.

A graph of the deterministic model with periodic stockouts is shown in Figure 12.3. As before, the saw-tooth pattern is described, but the minimal stock level is allowed to fall below zero. This means that demand for inventory continues whether or not it is available. Unsatisfied demand builds up during the period of stockout in the form of ***back-orders.*** When back-orders accumulate to a predetermined maximum, an order for more inventory is placed and immediately received. All back-orders are filled first, on receipt of units ordered.

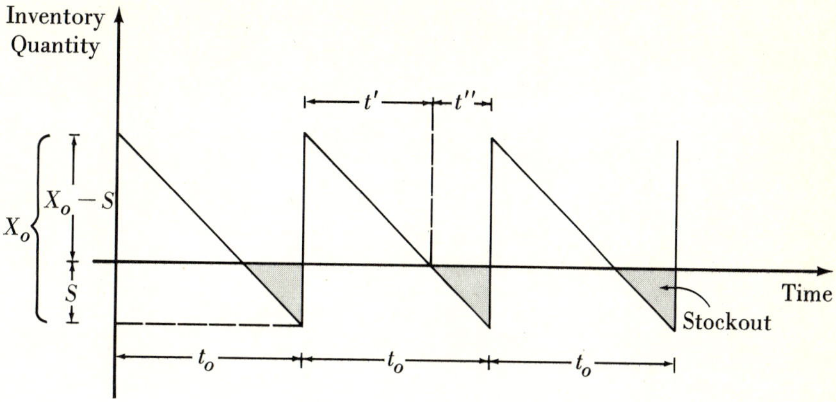

Figure 12.3 A Deterministic Model with Periodic Stockouts

Some additional algebraic notation is required to handle this case:

S = units on back-order during the stockout period which, when reached, initiate a reorder of inventory (maximum allowable back-order quantity)

C_s = total yearly stockout cost

γ_s = stockout cost per unit of average back-ordered inventory

t' = portion of time period t_o during which stock is available

t'' = portion of time period t_o during which there is a stockout and back-ordering occurs

Total yearly inventory cost in this model has three individual cost components: (1) ordering cost, (2) carrying cost, and (3) stockout cost. Expressed algebraically,

$$C_T = C_o + C_c + C_s \tag{12.5}$$

Ordering cost C_o is no different from ordering cost in the previous model:

$$C_o = \gamma_o \frac{D}{X_o} \tag{12.6}$$

Carrying cost depends, as before, on average inventory. Given a maximum level of $(X_o - S)$ and a minimum number of units in inventory of zero (see Figure 12.3),

$$\text{Average inventory} = \frac{X_o - S}{2}$$

Because of the periodic stockouts, the time during which inventory is carried is t', which is only part of the total cycle time t_o. Therefore, carrying cost per cycle is

$$\gamma_c \left[\frac{X_o - S}{2} \right] t'$$

and the yearly carrying cost over N cycles is

$$C_c = \gamma_c \left[\frac{X_o - S}{2} \right] Nt' \tag{12.7}$$

This relationship between t' and t_o is one of proportion. The triangles embedded in Figure 12.3 reveal that the ratio of t' to t_o must equal the ratio of $(X_o - S)$ to X_o (corresponding sides of similar triangles). Hence,

$$\frac{t'}{t_o} = \frac{X_o - S}{X_o}$$

As a result,

$$t' = \frac{X_o - S}{X_o} t_o \tag{12.8}$$

Then, combining equations (12.7) and (12.8) yields the following equation for carrying cost:

$$C_c = \gamma_c \left[\frac{(X_o - S)^2}{2X_o} \right] Nt_o$$

But, because t_o is the fraction of a year that elapses between successive orders and N is the number of orders placed per year, Nt_o equals 1 and

$$C_c = \gamma_c \left[\frac{(X_o - S)^2}{2X_o} \right] \tag{12.9}$$

Finally, stockout cost is represented in terms of average stockout (back-order) size, or S/2. Yearly stockout cost is therefore

$$C_s = \gamma_s \frac{S}{2} Nt''$$

Once again, the proportionality of corresponding sides of similar triangles in Figure 12.3 reveals that

$$\frac{t''}{t_o} = \frac{S}{X_o}$$

so

$$C_s = \gamma_s \frac{S^2}{2X_o} N t_o$$

As before, $Nt_o = 1$ and

$$C_s = \gamma_s \frac{S^2}{2X} \tag{12.10}$$

The three components of total yearly inventory costs have now been derived. Total cost is the sum of the three individual cost components. Combining (12.5), (12.6), (12.9), and (12.10), we get

$$C_T = \gamma_o \frac{D}{X_o} + \gamma_c \frac{(X_o - S)^2}{2X_o} + \gamma_s \frac{S^2}{2X_o} \tag{12.11}$$

Suppose that the manufacturer we considered in the previous section is curious about the cost consequences of incurring stockouts. As before, the ordering cost per order is \$2.25, carrying cost per unit of average inventory is \$.06, and total yearly demand is 1200 units. Estimated stockout cost is \$.25 per unit of average back-ordered inventory. On the basis of the previous EOQ of 300 units, (12.11) is applied for stockout levels varying from 0 to 150 units, and total inventory costs are recorded. The results are shown in Table 12.4.

We are not surprised that the first row of Table 12.4 indicates \$18 as the total yearly inventory cost for a stockout size of 0, because this is the same total yearly cost that we obtained in the model without stockouts. Indeed if we simplify (12.11) by using $s = 0$, then

$$\begin{aligned} C_T &= \gamma_o \frac{D}{X_o} + \gamma_c \frac{(X_o - 0)^2}{2X_o} + \gamma_s \frac{0^2}{2X_o} \\ &= \gamma_o \frac{D}{X_o} + \gamma_c \frac{X_o}{2} \end{aligned}$$

Table 12.4
Total Inventory Costs for Various Stockout Amounts (based on EOQ of 300)

Stockout Size (units)	Total Inventory Costs $C_o + C_s + C_c$
0	$18.00
10	17.45
20	17.01
30	16.67
40	16.43
50	16.29
60	16.26
70	16.33
80	16.51
90	16.79
100	17.17
110	17.65
120	18.24
130	18.93
140	19.73
150	20.63

This result is the same as (12.1). Consequently, the basic deterministic model is a special case of this section's deterministic model with periodic stockouts.

The remainder of Table 12.4 shows inventory costs decreasing until a back-order value of about 60 units is reached. At the lowest cost value in the table, $16.26, inventory costs with periodic stockouts are almost 10% less than costs without stockouts. The decreasing costs between 0 and 60 units reflect a more rapid rate of decrease in carrying cost than the corresponding rate of increase in stockout costs. Thereafter, the accumulated stockout costs rise to a point where total costs begin to increase with further increases in the stockout size.

What is EOQ for this model? First, it is apparent that the carrying-cost-equals-ordering-cost condition for EOQ does not apply in this situation, because there are three types of costs altogether. Second, in cases where the per-unit stockout cost is of approximately the same magnitude as the per-unit carrying cost, an in-depth analysis of the total cost function shows that the absolute minimum for total yearly inventory costs occurs at a relatively large stockout size compared with the size of order quantities. If the per-unit stockout cost does not include an ***inconvenience factor*** (a measure of actual inconvenience resulting from not having inventory when it is needed), which usually is substantial, the absolutely optimal solution may well be more inconvenient than would normally be desired.

Because periodic stockouts of a relatively small size may decrease total inventory cost, it is convenient to determine independently a maximal level of stockout size that is tolerable under the given operating conditions. For example, suppose that the manufacturer referred to in this chapter decides that, in order to reduce inventory costs, a recurring stockout situation of no more than 30 units is acceptable. Given this value, one first should verify that inventory costs are indeed falling (as was done in Table 12.4) with the original EOQ of 300 units. Having verified that this is so, one should calculate a revised EOQ that reflects the periodic stockout situation.

In general, optimization techniques rely heavily on calculus, but we can avoid calculus in this situation by applying the marginal principle for a trade-off situation. In this model, as (12.11) shows, carrying cost is increasing as order quantity increases, and ordering and stockout costs are decreasing. For this trade-off, then, when the marginal value of the combined decreasing costs equals the marginal value of the increasing cost (in absolute values) a minimal total cost has been reached. Using (12.11) and the marginal cost calculation presented earlier, Table 12.5 reveals EOQ for a periodic stockout policy of 30 units.[2]

12.4 A Production-to-Inventory Model

Suppose that, rather than purchasing an item for inventory, a manufacturing firm produces the item itself by scheduling a production run. For example, it is common for manufacturing companies to have a machine shop with tools that can be set up to make special parts not easily acquired elsewhere, and that may also allow for the production of one or more inventory items. Another case of this type occurs when the output of a firm varies in styling, thickness, color, or some other

[2]If we were to use calculus, we would obtain the equation

$$X_o(\text{EOQ}) = \sqrt{\frac{2\gamma_o D + (\gamma_c + \gamma_s)S^2}{\gamma_c}}$$

by partial differentiation. For a stockout size of 30 units, X_o(EOQ) is calculated to be 307.65 units, compared with the 308 units we obtained using marginal analysis.

Table 12.5 EOQ with Built-In Stockout (30 units)

		Decreasing Costs with Increasing X_o				Increasing Costs with Increasing X_o		
Order Quantity X_o	Number of Orders per Year N	Total Ordering Cost C_o	Total Stockout Cost C_s	Ordering Plus Stockout Cost $C_o + C_s$	Marginal Ordering, Stockout Costs $\Delta(C_o + C_s)/\Delta X_o$	Total Carrying Cost C_c	Marginal Carrying Cost $\Delta C_c/\Delta X_o$	Total Yearly Inventory Cost $C_o + C_s + C_c$
296	4.054	$9.12	$.38	$9.50		$7.17		$16.67
300	4.000	9.00	.38	9.38	−.032	7.29	.030	16.67
304	3.947	8.88	.37	9.25	−.031	7.41	.030	16.66
308	3.896	8.77	.36	9.13	−.030	7.53	.030	16.66
312	3.846	8.65	.36	9.01	−.029	7.65	.030	16.66
316	3.797	8.54	.36	8.90	−.029	7.77	.030	16.67
320	3.750	8.44	.35	8.79	−.028	7.88	.030	16.67

attribute, and various production runs occur throughout the year to be placed in inventory for later sales. In either case, inventory items are not ordered; they are produced.

The ***production-to-inventory model*** assumes that the production process provides a steady flow of items into inventory and that this influx lasts for the duration of each production run. By the end of the production run, inventory will have built up to a predetermined maximum. Whereas the supply of inventory takes place intermittently according to the scheduling of production runs, it is assumed that the demand for inventory remains constant and uniform over time. Note that this is not a batch-supply situation, as was assumed in the other models we have discussed in this chapter. Certainly, a production run ***might*** result in a batch of output that would be added to inventory all at once. If this were the case, the model would resemble the basic deterministic model, but there would be two differences. (1) Order costs in the basic model would be represented as set-up costs in the production model. (2) The order quantity of the basic model would be a production lot size in the production model. A simple redefinition of terms is enough to account for these exceptions, and the solution for EOQ corresponds exactly to the solution for an optimal lot size. By replacing the batch-supply assumption with a steady-flow-of-supply assumption, we generate a new model, which is shown in Figure 12.4.

The assumptions of this model (which can be discerned in part from the diagram) are as follows:

1. Supply begins immediately following production set-up.
2. Supply ends when lot size of production run is reached.

Figure 12.4
A Production-to-Inventory Model

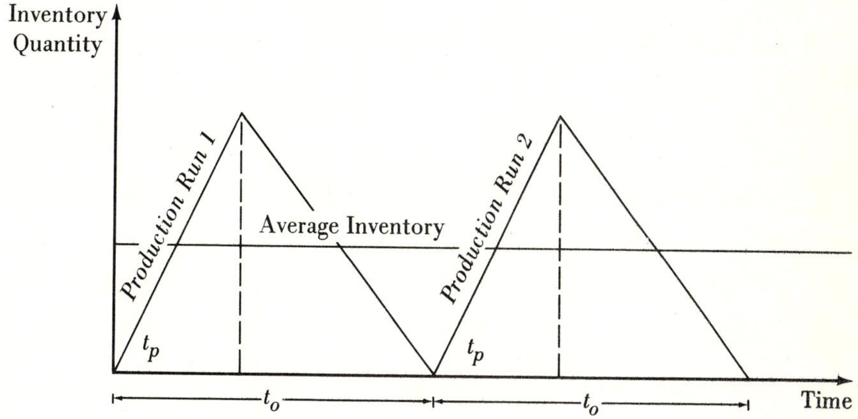

3. There is a constant and uniform (continuous) rate of supply during the production run.
4. Demand is constant and uniform (continuous).
5. Inventory carrying cost is determined as a dollar amount per unit of average inventory.
6. There are no stockouts (an infinite stockout cost).
7. There is a positive set-up cost.
8. There is negligible depreciation of inventory over time.

New notation for this model is as follows:

X_p = production run lot size

N = number of production runs per year

C_p = total set-up costs per year

γ_p = set-up cost for each production run

r_p = production rate in units per time period

r_d = demand rate in units per time period

t_p = length of production run in days

Now, the total cost function is the sum of set-up costs and carrying costs, or

$$C_T = C_p + C_c \tag{12.12}$$

Set-up costs are analogous to ordering costs in the basic model—that is, the number of set-ups times the set-up cost per production run:

$$C_p = \gamma_p \frac{D}{X_p} \tag{12.13}$$

Carrying costs are derived, as before, on the basis of average inventory. It is important to recognize that, due to simultaneous demand for and supply of the inventory item during the time of a production run, the maximum inventory level will never be as large as the production lot size when the time of the production run, t_p, is finite. In fact, the rate of increase of inventory during a production run is the difference between the production (or supply) rate and the demand rate. Therefore, at the end of the run, the quantity in inventory—which is a maximum inventory level—is the time of the run times the net rate of increase:

$$\text{Maximum inventory quantity} = t_p\,(r_p - r_d)$$

The minimum inventory level is zero, so

$$\text{Average inventory} = \frac{t_p(r_p - r_d)}{2}$$

Of course, the time of a production run is simply the number of units, or lot size, divided by the rate of production ($t_p = X_p/r_p$), so that

$$\text{Average inventory} = \frac{X_p(r_p - r_d)}{2r_p}$$

Finally, carrying cost is the cost per unit of average inventory times the average inventory level:

$$C_c = \gamma_c \frac{X_p(r_p - r_d)}{2r_p} \tag{12.14}$$

Combining (12.12), (12.13), and (12.14), we get a total yearly inventory cost of

$$C_T = \gamma_p \frac{D}{X_p} + \gamma_c \frac{X_p(r_p - r_d)}{2r_p} \tag{12.15}$$

We can apply this equation in a tabular way to find the minimum-cost production lot size, or we can derive an algebraic solution for optimal lot size. First, consider the manufacturer, once again, for whom carrying cost remains \$.06 per unit of average inventory and yearly demand is 1200 units. If the relevant number of days per year is 240, the daily demand rate is 5 units per day. Suppose that the production rate is twice the rate of demand, or 10 units per day, and that the set-up cost is \$2 per production run. The tabular solution has been calculated using equation (12.15) and is presented in Table 12.6. The optimal lot size is found to be 400 units, which would mean 3 production runs per year to satisfy the 1200-unit yearly demand.

Here again, the marginal approach can be used. Because set-up costs are decreasing and carrying costs are increasing as production quantity

Table 12.6 Lot Size Calculation in Tabular Form for a Production-to-Inventory Model

Production Quantity X_p	Number of Runs per Year N	Total Set-Up Cost C_p	Average Inventory $\frac{r_p - r_d}{r_p} \times \frac{X_p}{2}$	Total Carrying Cost C_c	Total Yearly Inventory Cost $C_p + C_c$
50	24.000	$48.00	12.5	$ .75	$48.75
100	12.000	24.00	25	1.50	25.50
150	8.000	16.00	37.5	2.25	18.25
200	6.000	12.00	50	3.00	15.00
250	4.800	9.60	62.5	3.75	13.35
300	4.000	8.00	75	4.50	12.50
350	3.429	6.86	87.5	5.25	12.11
400	3.000	6.00	100	6.00	12.00
450	2.667	5.33	112.5	6.75	12.08
500	2.400	4.80	125	7.50	12.30
550	2.182	4.36	137.5	8.25	12.61
600	2.000	4.00	150	9.00	13.00

Table 12.7 Marginal Set-Up and Carrying Costs in the Vicinity of Optimal Lot Size

Production Quantity X_p	Number of Runs per Year N	Total Set-Up Cost C_p	Marginal Set-Up Cost $\Delta C_p/\Delta X_p$	Average Inventory $\frac{r_p - r_d}{r_p} \times \frac{X_p}{2}$	Total Carrying Cost C_c	Marginal Carrying Cost $\Delta C_c/\Delta X_p$	Total Yearly Inventory Cost $C_p + C_c$
380	3.158	$6.316		95	$5.700		$12.02
385	3.117	6.234	−.016	96.25	5.775	.015	12.01
390	3.077	6.154	−.016	97.5	5.850	.015	12.004
395	3.038	6.076	−.016	98.75	5.925	.015	12.001
400	3.000	6.000	−.015	100	6.000	.015	12.000
405	2.963	5.926	−.015	101.25	6.075	.015	12.001
410	2.927	5.854	−.014	102.5	6.150	.015	12.004
415	2.892	5.783	−.014	103.75	6.225	.015	12.01
420	2.857	5.714	−.014	105	6.300	.015	12.01

increases, the fact that the marginal set-up cost equals the marginal carrying cost (in absolute values) can be used to verify lot size for minimum total cost. Calculations in the vicinity of the optimal lot size, 400 units (which was found in Table 12.6), are presented in Table 12.7. These calculations demonstrate again the marginal principle and confirm that 400 units are the optimal lot size.

The algebraic approach is more direct. As in the basic deterministic model, the total cost function given by (12.12) and (12.15) has two opposing components, set-up costs and carrying costs, and a minimal total cost occurs when these two costs are equal. Therefore, referring again to (12.12), (12.13), (12.14), and (12.15), we find that the optimal-lot-size condition is

$$\text{Set-up cost} = \text{carrying cost}$$

which means that

$$C_p = C_c$$

or

$$\gamma_p \frac{D}{X_p} = \gamma_c \frac{X_p(r_p - r_d)}{2r_p}$$

Solving for the optimal lot size, we get

$$\frac{\gamma_p}{\gamma_c} \times \frac{2r_p}{r_p - r_d} \times D = X_p^2$$

or

$$X_p = \sqrt{\frac{\gamma_p}{\gamma_c} \frac{2r_p}{(r_p - r_d)} D} \tag{12.16}$$

Applying this equation to our example, we find that

$$X_p = \sqrt{\frac{2.00}{.06} \frac{2 \times 10}{(10 - 5)} \times 1200}$$
$$= 400 \text{ units} \qquad \text{optimal lot size}$$

The solution of a production-to-inventory model can be described more completely by converting the result for optimal lot size into other related characteristics. In particular, we can specify total yearly inventory costs by using (12.15). The number of production runs per year is a ratio of total demand to optimal lot size:

$$\text{Production runs per year} = \frac{D}{\text{optimal } X_p}$$

or

$$N = \frac{D}{\sqrt{\dfrac{\gamma_p}{\gamma_c}\dfrac{2r_p}{(r_p - r_d)}D}}$$

which simplifies algebraically to

$$N = \sqrt{\frac{\gamma_c(r_p - r_d)D}{2\gamma_p r_p}} \qquad (12.17)$$

The length of each lot-size production run is the ratio of units produced per run to the production rate:

$$t_p = \frac{\text{optimal } X_p}{r_p}$$

or

$$t_p = \frac{\sqrt{\dfrac{\gamma_p}{\gamma_c}\dfrac{2r_d}{(r_p - r_d)}D}}{r_p}$$

which simplifies to

$$t_p = \sqrt{\frac{\gamma_p}{\gamma_c}\frac{2D}{r_p(r_p - r_d)}} \qquad (12.18)$$

When the rate at which production takes place becomes very large compared with the demand rate, the time needed to build inventory to its maximum level shortens. Carried to extremes, such a model would resemble the basic deterministic model. Algebraically, the ratio $r_p/(r_p - r_d)$ approaches a value of unity as r_p grows to infinity. In this case, (12.16) becomes

$$X_p = \sqrt{\frac{\gamma_p}{\gamma_c} \times 2 \times 1 \times D}$$

or

$$X_p = \sqrt{\frac{2\gamma_p D}{\gamma_c}} \qquad (12.19)$$

Clearly, (12.19) is of the same form as the equation for EOQ, the only difference being that set-up costs per run in the production-to-inventory model are interpreted as ordering costs per order in the basic model. Thus, for a very rapid rate of supply of inventory, the basic deterministic model is identical to the model that allows for varying rates of supply.

Once again, the basic model is found to be a special case of a more complex model.

12.5 A Model for Probabilistic Demand and Stockouts

Each of the three models that we have discussed in this chapter has assumed a lead time (the time lapse between placing an order, or scheduling a production run, and receiving new inventory) equal to zero. In other words, there is no waiting. Although situations such as this do exist, it is more common to wait to receive an order that has been placed. This section treats specifically the precautionary strategies that one can implement to guard against unexpected stockouts due to uncertainty during the reorder period.

It is easy to alter a completely deterministic model to make it accommodate a positive and fixed lead time. On the basis of a known rate of demand and a determined lead time, inventory should be reordered as soon as the inventory quantity equals the amount that will be used during the reorder period. This ***reorder level*** is calculated as follows:

$$\begin{aligned}\text{Reorder level} &= \text{amount of inventory used during lead time}\\ &= \text{rate of demand for inventory} \times \text{lead time}\end{aligned}$$

The reorder of inventory, then, is timed so that its arrival coincides exactly with zero inventory. A completely deterministic model with positive lead times is shown graphically in Figure 12.5. Should there be a need for a minimum inventory level other than zero, the reorder-level equation would be adjusted accordingly:

$$\text{Reorder level} = (\text{rate of demand})\,(\text{lead time}) + (\text{minimum level})$$

The reorder-level concept can be applied to our familiar manufacturer whose EOQ has been found to be 300 units. The total yearly demand of 1200 units is equivalent to a daily rate of demand for inventory of 3.288 units per day (based on a year of 365 days). If the lead time for reorder is 7 days, the reorder level would be

$$\begin{aligned}\text{Reorder level} &= 3.288 \text{ units per day} \times 7 \text{ days' lead time}\\ &= 23 \text{ units}\end{aligned}$$

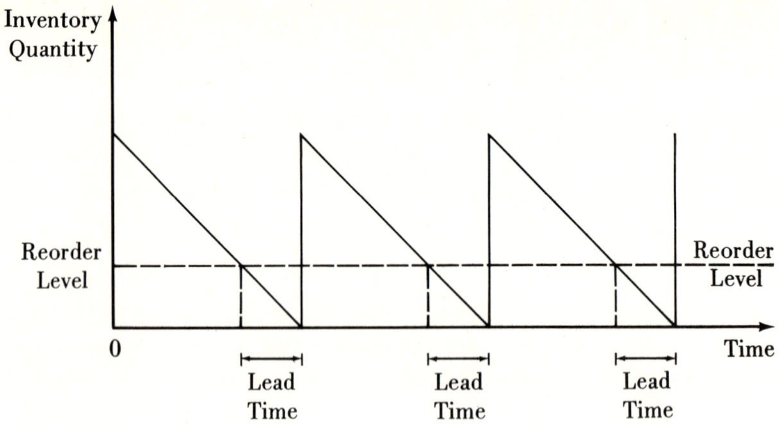

Figure 12.5
Reorder Level and Lead Time in a Deterministic Model

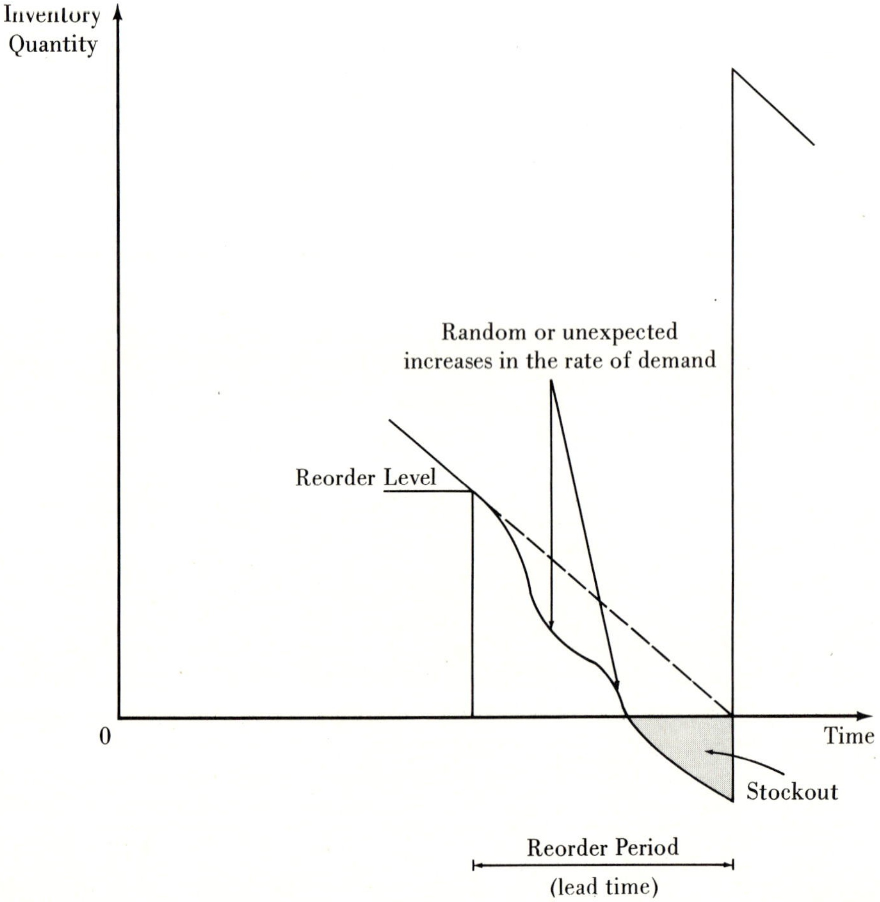

Figure 12.6
Stockout Arising from Random Increase in the Rate of Demand During Reorder Period (No Safety Stock)

Reality, in the form of uncertainty, dictates a somewhat more sophisticated approach to lead time and reorder level. The arrival of shipments can be a notoriously uncertain affair; likewise, the rate of demand for inventory may be uncertain during the reorder period. In either case, having already placed an order for more inventory, one is left utterly dependent on the accuracy of the reorder-level calculation. If either the rate of demand or the lead time should change unexpectedly, stock levels may be depleted either more rapidly or less rapidly than expected. Since the ordinary reorder-level calculation anticipates inventory falling to a minimum of zero, depletion of inventory more rapidly than expected means the occurrence of a stockout (see Figure 12.6). Conversely, depletion slower than anticipated during the reorder period leaves one with more inventory on hand (see Figure 12.7).

Clearly, the only way to avoid stockouts is to raise the reorder level, which is equivalent to establishing a positive minimum-inventory level, or ***safety stock.*** Random changes in demand or lead time during the reorder period that would otherwise cause stockouts are absorbed instead by the safety stock (see Figures 12.7 and 12.8). Obviously, carrying

Figure 12.7
Drawing from Safety Stock to Avoid Stockouts Arising from Random Demand Increases

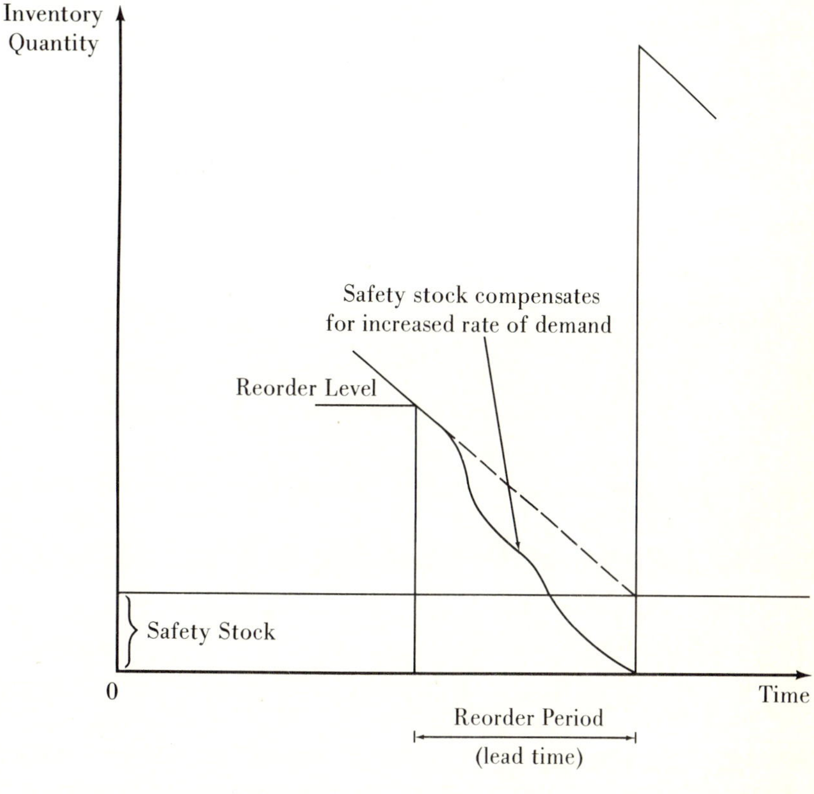

Figure 12.8
Idle Safety Stock with a Random Decrease in the Rate of Demand for Inventory

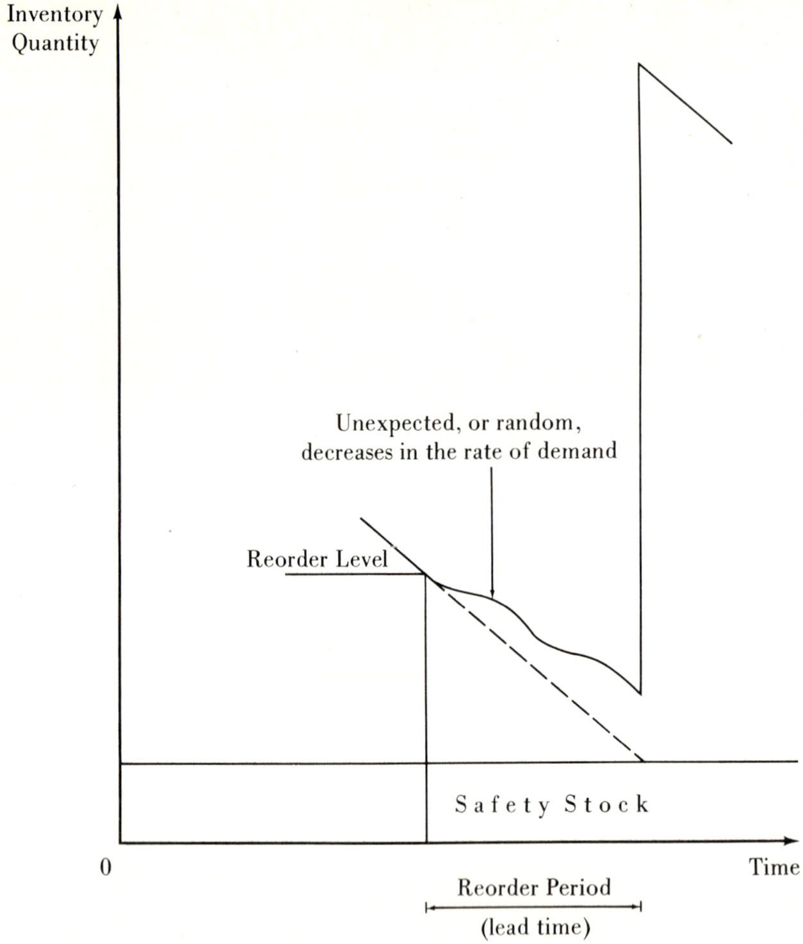

more stock prevents stockouts, so we reduce or eliminate stockout costs by incurring increased carrying costs. Again, there is a trade-off between two types of costs—a trade-off that the analyst must resolve by determining an optimal level of safety stock.

The probabilistic model we will examine in this section focuses particularly on the reorder period, or lead time, and it assumes that the rate of demand during lead time is a random variable. In fact, demand may be probabilistic at all times, but, because of potential stockouts, fluctuations become critical only during the reorder period. At other times during the inventory cycle, a linear approximation of the inventory depletion process may be quite sufficient. Indeed, this model follows the deterministic approach to establishing EOQ. Demand uncertainty relates only to the reorder period and affects only the safety stock decision. Lead time is assumed to be constant, so only one factor in the determination of reorder level—the rate of demand—is considered probabilistic. Should lead time, in fact, be probabilistic, a somewhat different model would be appropriate.

Let us again consider the same manufacturer who holds inventory. Calculations presented in this and earlier sections have established the following characteristics of this inventory situation:

EOQ: 300 units per order

Demand: 1200 units per year (3.288 units per day)

Orders: 4 per year

Days' supply per order: 91.25

Lead time: 7 days

Reorder level: 23 units

Carrying cost: $.06 per unit

Ordering cost: $2.25 per order

Stockout cost: $.25 per unit

Suppose that the rate of demand varies randomly during the reorder period so that actual usage of lead time may vary anywhere from 19 to 27 units. Stockroom records reveal the following probability distribution of usage:

Demand during Lead Time	**Probability**
19	.02
20	.09
21	.12
22	.15
23	.27
24	.12
25	.11
26	.08
27	.04
	1.00

Coinciding with the reorder level of 23 units, the expected value of demand during the reorder period is

$$(19 \times .02) + (20 \times .09) + (21 \times .12) + (22 \times .15) + (23 \times .27)$$
$$+ (24 \times .12) + (25 \times .11) + (26 \times .08) + (27 \times .04)$$
$$= 23 \text{ units}$$

If no safety stock is provided, stockouts will occur whenever demand during the reorder period exceeds 23. Working backwards through the probability distribution, we find that, if a safety stock of 4 units is added to the reorder level of 23 units (that is, if enough safety stock is provided to handle even the largest lead-time demand possible), then the probability of a stockout is zero. If a safety stock of 3 units is provided, the probability of a stockout is 0.04—the probability that lead-time demand is 27 units. If a safety stock of 2 units is provided, the probability of a stockout is 0.12 (0.04 + 0.08)—or the probability of either 26 or 27 units being required during the lead time. If 1 unit of safety stock is provided, the probability of a stockout is 0.23 (0.04 + 0.08 + 0.11); and so on. The following table gives stockout probabilities for all safety stock values of zero and above.

Reorder at	Implied Safety Stock	Probability of Stockout
23 units	0 units	0.35
24	1	0.23
25	2	0.12
26	3	0.04
27	4	0.00

These figures alone may be sufficient to allow a business manager to decide on the desired safety stock. The manager may know that, for reasons other than cost, stockouts should never be tolerated (4 units of safety stock) or that a probability of stockout no larger than 4% is acceptable (3 units of safety stock). Nevertheless, let us continue to find the minimum-cost basis for a managerial decision on safety stock.

The following is a simple application of Bayesian decision theory. First, a table of conditional costs for shortages is prepared and used to derive expected stockout costs for varying levels of safety stock. Total yearly expected costs must be calculated and combined with the additional carrying cost due to safety stock to determine the minimal-cost safety stock policy.

First, what is the cost of a shortage for any combination of usage during lead time and safety stock level? The unit cost of stockout is \$.25. Any lead-time demand of 23 units or less will not cause stockouts regardless of the size of safety stock. A lead-time demand of 24 units will occur 12% of the time and will cause 1 unit of stockout if the safety stock is zero, for a \$.25 stockout cost. A lead-time demand of 25 units will occur 11% of the time and will cause 2 units of stockout for zero safety stock (a \$.50 stockout cost) or 1 unit of stockout if safety stock is 1 unit (a \$.25 stockout cost). Table 12.8 presents conditional stockout costs for this situation.

We find expected stockout costs per lead time by multiplying the probability of demand by the corresponding conditional stockout costs. These calculations are given in Table 12.9.

Expected stockout costs per lead time have now been determined. Naturally, they decrease as the size of safety stock increases. The expected stockout cost for zero safety stock is \$.1850; for 1 unit of safety stock, \$.0775; for 2 units of safety stock, \$.04; for 3 units of safety stock, \$.01; and for 4 units of safety stock, no cost.

The next step is elementary. Yearly carrying costs due to safety stocks are \$.06 per unit—or 0, 6, 12, 18, and 24 cents for safety stocks in the range of from 0 to 4 units. These costs and the yearly expected stockout costs are combined in Table 12.10. Table 12.10 shows clearly the inventory trade-off between expected stockout cost and the carrying cost of safety stock. The total cost reaches a minimum at the safety stock

Table 12.8 Conditional Stockout Costs

Lead-Time Demand	Probability of Demand	Safety Stock 0	1	2	3	4
Less Than or Equal to 23 units	.65	\$ 0	\$ 0	\$ 0	\$ 0	\$ 0
24	.12	.25	0	0	0	0
25	.11	.50	.25	0	0	0
26	.08	.75	.50	.25	0	0
27	.04	1.00	.75	.50	.25	0
	1.00					

Table 12.9 Expected Stockout Costs

Lead-Time Demand	Safety Stock 0	1	2	3	4
Less Than or Equal to 23 units	\$ 0	\$ 0	\$ 0	\$ 0	0
24	.0300	0	0	0	0
25	.0550	.0275	0	0	0
26	.0600	.0400	.0200	0	0
27	.0400	.0300	.0200	.0100	0
	\$.1850	\$.0775	\$.0400	\$.0100	0

Table 12.10 Costs of Safety Stock Policies

A Size of Safety Stock	B Expected Stock-out Cost per Lead Time	C Expected Yearly Stockout Cost $C = B \times 4$	D Yearly Carrying Cost $D = \$.06 \times A$	E Total Yearly Cost
0	$.1850	$.74	$ 0	$.74
1	.0775	.31	.06	.37
2	.0400	.16	.12	.28
3	.0100	.04	.18	.22
4	0	0	.24	.24

size of 3 units. This means that an order for more inventory should be placed whenever the inventory quantity falls to 26 units (reorder level of 23 units plus safety stock of 3 units). Accordingly, stockouts will occur 4% of the time. It would be somewhat more costly to avoid stockouts completely by carrying more safety stock.

12.6 Summary

Whatever their very specific characteristics, inventory control models are usually cost-minimization models, and they typically exhibit different types of costs that counteract each other. Resolving the trade-off between relevant costs in a given situation means finding a minimum-total-cost solution. The business analyst's job is to determine how to quantitatively represent an actual inventory situation to identify total costs and obtain cost-saving results. The results are a prescription for the business enterprise. They are the basis for policies, practices, systems, and procedures that will efficiently control inventory activities and bring meaningful benefits to the firm.

In practice, some items of inventory move at fairly predictable rates, and the corresponding inventory control models show good reliability. However, the difficulty of predicting demand for inventories is a crucial aspect of this type of model building. Fluctuations in firm competitiveness, industry growth, and overall economic conditions are some of the independent factors that affect inventories generally and can directly influence the demand for specific items of inventory as well. The relative success of all business functions—inventory control and others—is governed by the decision maker's ability to recognize and adapt to these less predictable demand conditions.

Exercises

12.1 Explain each of the following terms:
a. EOQ
b. Safety stock
c. Reorder point
d. Lead time

12.2 What are the basic types of inventory costs? What do these inventory costs include?

12.3 What are the assumptions of the EOQ model? Give some situations in which the EOQ model may apply.

12.4 A wholesale distributor of finished goods estimates essentially constant demand for one of its items at the rate of 640 units per year. If carrying costs are estimated at $1 per unit per year and ordering costs add up to $5 per order, what is the most economical quantity to order? How many orders should be placed per year? At EOQ, how much is total annual ordering cost, and how much is total annual carrying cost?

12.5 a. Determine a formula for EOQ in a situation where yearly carrying costs are expressed as a percentage of the value of average inventory. Start by specifying algebraic expressions for yearly ordering cost and yearly carrying cost; then solve for minimum-cost order quantity. Let the per-unit cost of inventory be v and the carrying cost measured as a percentage of average inventory be $\gamma\%$.
b. Using the equation you found for EOQ, determine the minimum-cost order quantity for an inventory item for which 600 units are required per year, ordering costs are $3 per order, cost per unit of inventory is $2, and carrying costs are 2% of average inventory. How many times per year must orders be placed? How much are total inventory costs for this EOQ?

12.6 Find the economic order quantity, number of orders per year, ordering cost per year, and total yearly ordering cost for a company that uses 750,000 units of a production part yearly, where the ordering cost is $125 per order and carrying cost is $30 per unit.

12.7 A manufacturer maintains inventory for an item that yearly costs 17 cents per unit of average inventory to carry and is used at the rate of 35,280 units per year. Ordering cost per order is estimated to be $1.70. Find EOQ, total yearly inventory cost, optimal number of orders to be placed per year, and optimal number of days' supply per order (assume 252 business days per year).

12.8 How are the motivations for holding money analogous to those for holding ordinary inventories?

12.9 What are the assumptions for a basic deterministic inventory model?

12.10 What are the assumptions for a production-to-inventory model?

12.11 Show how the fundamental economic concepts involved in inventory control are similar to the environmental issues discussed in Section 1.5. Make your comparison in diagrams.

12.12 Timly Watch Company is producing Electro brand watches. According to production plans, the company will need 40,000 pounds of platinum metal. A contract has been signed to assure delivery of platinum during the next year. By contract, the company can choose the order size, but the supplier charges $1600 handling cost for the processing of each order, which includes the costs of packaging and mailing and miscellaneous fees. In addition, there is a holding cost of $800 per pound held in inventory per year. Calculate the economic order quantity for this contract.

12.13 Refer to exercise 12.13. Suppose that the unit order cost is increased by 50%. How would this change in cost affect EOQ? Is this EOQ model sensitive to small variations or errors in estimating unit order cost?

12.14 Explain the relationship between a reorder point and EOQ.

12.15 You are given the following information:

Annual demand = 100 units
Ordering cost per order = $5
Inventory carrying cost = $1 per unit per year

a. What is the economic order quantity?
b. What is the carrying cost of this quantity?
c. What is the cost of ordering this quantity?
d. What is the total inventory cost of this quantity?
e. What is the optimal number of orders per year?
f. What is the optimal number of days' supply per order?

12.16 The Bike Manufacturing Company makes 60,000 three-speed bicycles per year. Tires are ordered from another company at a cost of $2 per pair. The ordering cost is estimated as $30 per order, and the inventory carrying costs are 20% per pair per year. Determine the minimum-cost order quantity (EOQ), the annual ordering costs and carrying costs at EOQ, and the optimal number of orders per year.

12.17 A mail-order retailer reduces annual inventory costs on a particular item of inventory by purposely allowing stockouts as large as 15% of the no-stockout EOQ.

a. Find the no-stockout EOQ when demand is at an annual rate of 51,200 units, carrying cost is $.07 per unit of average inventory, and ordering cost is $.28 per order. What is the total yearly cost of inventory in this situation?

b. Assuming that stockout cost is \$.40 per unit of average stockout size, prepare a table of total inventory cost on the basis of the no-stockout EOQ for stockouts varying in size up to 15% of the no-stockout EOQ level. Are these costs decreasing? Finally, on the basis of the 15% stockout level, find EOQ with stockout and determine the percentage reduction in total yearly inventory cost compared with the cost of no-stockout EOQ.

12.18 Determine an optimal stockout policy when the cost per unit of stockout in exercise 12.17 is \$10.

12.19 Determine the optimal lot size and the optimal number of production runs per year for a firm that produces an inventory item and places it into inventory, by batches, at the end of each production run. Perform calculations on the basis of a set-up cost of \$6.52 per production run, an annual demand of 288 units, and a carrying cost per unit of average inventory of \$1.63. How many production runs must be scheduled during the course of a year?

12.20 Ronald Ink, the manager of a tool-manufacturing company, is using an EOQ formula in the planning and management of inventories. One of the problems he faces is double-digit inflation. There is no sign that the inflation rate will decline in the future. How does high inflation affect Mr. Ink's inventory policy?

12.21 Items for inventory are being produced by a manufacturing company at the rate of 40 units per week. Demand is constant and uniform at half this rate and, for a 48-week year, total yearly demand is 961 units. Set-up costs are \$.84 per production run and per-unit carrying cost is \$.21. Find the optimal lot size for production runs, the optimal length of production run for the determined lot size, and the optimal number of production runs to schedule per year.

12.22 A tire producer makes 1200 tires per day and sells them at approximately half that rate. Accounting figures show that the production set-up cost is \$1109.76 and that carrying cost per unit is \$.50. If annual demand is 120,000 tires, what is the optimal lot size and how many production runs should be scheduled per year?

12.23 E. W. Gift Store predicts the demand for an imported gift to be 500 units per year. If carrying costs per unit are approximately \$1 and if ordering costs are \$40 per order, what is the minimum-cost order quantity? Also find the total inventory costs of stocking this item. If demand were 320 units per year, how would the inventory costs change?

12.24 Refer to exercise 12.5. What is the reorder point when, in a 300-day year, the lead time for ordering is 5 working days, given a stockout cost of \$20 per unit and the following probability distribution for demand during lead time:

Demand	Probability
0	.10
1	.25
2	.30
3	.25
4	.10

a. Find the expected value of the demand distribution.
b. On the basis of cost alone, find the optimal level of safety stock.

12.25 You have the following information about a manufacturing enterprise:

Demand: 5800 units per year
Work weeks per year: 50
Lead time: 3 weeks (batch supply)
Ordering cost: $42.05
Carrying cost: $1.45 per unit
Stockout cost: $2.50 per unit

The probability of usage during the reorder period is as follows:

Units	Probability
33	.15
34	.20
35	.30
36	.20
37	.10
38	.05
	1.00

Determine EOQ, the reorder point, the optimal number of orders per year, and the optimal safety stock.

Suggested Readings

Buffa, Frank P. "A Model for Allocating Limited Resources When Making Safety-Stock Decisions." *Decision Sciences*, 8, No. 2 (April 1977), pp. 415–426.

Buffa, E. S., and W. H. Taubert. *Production-Inventory Systems: Planning and Control.* Homewood, Ill.: Irwin, 1972.
Churchman, C. W., R. L. Ackoff, and E. L. Arnoff. *Introduction to Operations Research.* New York: Wiley, 1958.
Hanssmann, Fred. *Operations Research in Production and Inventory Control.* New York: Wiley, 1962.
Hebbar, B. A., and A. R. Brani. "Inventory Control System." *Journal of Industrial Engineering* (February 1976), pp. 41–45.
Kapner, Sylvan L. "How to Control Elusive In-Process Inventory Costs." *Modern Materials Handling* (December 1962).
Lucas, John D. "Material Control—The Key to Manufacturing." *Material Handling Engineering* (May 1961).
Magee, J. F., and D. M. Magee. *Production Planning and Inventory Control,* 2nd ed. New York: McGraw-Hill, 1967.
Reed, R., Jr., and W. E. Stanley. "Optimizing Control of Hospital Inventories." *Journal of Industrial Engineering* (Jan./Feb. 1965), pp. 48–51.
Smith, S. B. "An Input-Output Model for Production and Inventory Planning." *The Journal of Industrial Engineering* (Jan./Feb. 1965), pp. 64–69.
Starr, M. K., and D. W. Miller. *Inventory Control: Theory and Practice.* Englewood Cliffs, N.J.: Prentice-Hall, 1962.
Stockton, R. *Basic Inventory Systems: Concepts and Analysis.* Boston: Allyn and Bacon, 1965.
Trueman, Richard E. "Incremental (Marginal) Analysis of Basic Inventory Models." *Decision Sciences,* 2 (July 1971), pp. 341–355.
Wagner, Harvey M. *Principles of Operations Research,* 2nd ed. Englewood Cliffs, N.J.: Prentice-Hall, 1975.
———. "The Design of Production and Inventory Systems for Multi-facility and Multi-warehouse Companies." *Operations Research,* 22, No. 2 (March-April, 1974), pp. 278–291.

13

Queuing Models

Queuing, or waiting in line, is a common problem in business, particularly when efficient and cost-effective systems are desired. The transportation industry provides numerous examples of queuing situations. Whether an airplane, ship, truck, train, or automobile is involved, waiting one's turn to use transportation facilities is a familiar experience. Likewise, the passenger on public transportation is confronted with waiting lines in both purchasing tickets and boarding the vehicle. Even manufacturing processes are complicated by the need to wait for one stage of production to end before another can begin. In general, applications of queuing analysis can be found in almost any situation where customers are to be served by one or more attendants and where excessive waiting times are to be avoided. Ticket counters at airports, toll booths on parkways, tellers' windows at banks, and order stations at hamburger stands are but a few of the queuing situations that confront the average person almost daily.

Among the first serious analyses of queuing problems are those done early in the twentieth century by A. K. Erlang, a Danish telephone analyst, for problems of telephone switching. His publications, "Solution of Some Problems in the Theory of Probabilities of Significance in Automatic Telephone Exchanges" (1917) and "The Theory of Probabilities and Telephone Conversations" (1909) are credited with being the first important contributions to the study of queuing problems.[1]

In this chapter, we will consider two broad areas of analysis. The first is a ***theoretical–statistical approach*** that uses specific probability dis-

[1]For translated articles and further information, see E. Brockmeyer, H. L. Halstrom, and A. Jensen, "The Life and Works of A. K. Erlang," Copenhagen Telephone Company, Copenhagen, 1948.

tributions to derive mathematical solutions. The second is a ***simulation approach*** wherein complex models can be created in abstraction and studied by manipulating important parameters of the models. Specialized computer languages for constructing simulation models make possible the analysis of very large and involved queuing situations. Likewise, the computer can be used to test queuing models with many repetitions and under complex combinations of conditions. Both theoretical and simulated analyses help the decision maker understand the characteristics of queuing situations and the decision options available under the prevailing circumstances.

13.1 Basic Queuing Models and Their Classification

In a basic ***queuing model*** there are elements of a system, such as customers; there is provision for a waiting line, if necessary; there is a service facility to which the system elements are directed; and there is a time-related service procedure from which the serviced elements leave the system. Diagrammatically, everything takes place along a real time line, as shown in Figure 13.1.

There is usually expense in both the servicing and the waiting aspects of a queuing system, and, in both cases, the premium is generally related to time. Labor hours of service attendants' time translate into a dollar expenditure. Similarly, waiting expenses can be a real consideration. Take for example the fuel consumed by a large airplane circling overhead, or the business lost when customers become intolerant of long lines. Because there is usually a trade-off between service costs and waiting costs, in most cases the objective is to minimize the total expenditure associated with a system. However, objectives may vary from one type of situation to another. One might wish, for example, only to maintain the average length of a waiting line, or the average time spent waiting, at a desired minimum.

Figure 13.1
The Basic Queuing Model

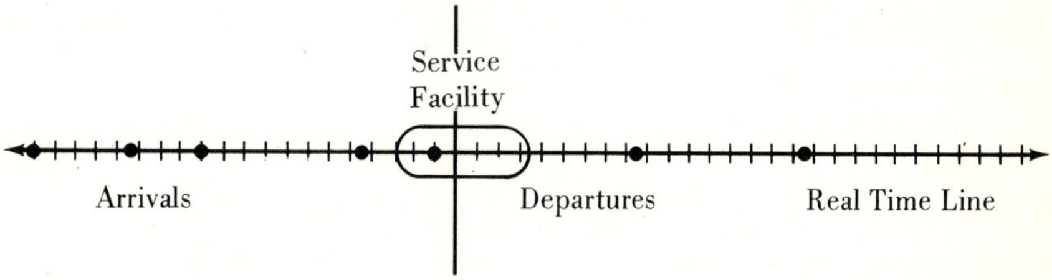

Many queuing problems are worked out on a daily basis without rigorous analysis, and some business managers would be quick to point out that nonanalytical solutions to queuing problems can be applied with substantial success. The customer flow through a service facility might reliably be judged on the basis of past experience combined with intuition. Especially in cases where there is flexibility in the assignment of employees, managers can adapt to the situation at hand simply by observing the prevailing conditions and directing the work force accordingly. However, the analysis of a queuing model often can help us construct facilities that later can be managed without further analysis.

Furthermore, special problems that arise from a changing environment are best analyzed abstractly so that the effects of decision options are understood before modifications are made. It is usually easier and less expensive to find efficient ways to proceed by experimenting with a good model rather than manipulating the actual conditions. Especially in situations where trial and error are the only other alternatives, an abstract, analytical approach has definite advantages.

The various queuing situations give rise to different types of models. Queuing models are usually classified in terms of the number of serving lines, the number of servers, the serving process, and the way in which arrivals and servicing occur over time. The simplest of models is the one-line, one-server situation that is typical of a car wash. Local barber shops that employ several barbers operate on a one-line, multiple-server basis. Multiple lines and multiple servers may occur either with or without line switching, according to the queuing discipline that prevails. Voting procedures often require that one not switch lines, because one must stand in the line in which one's name appears on the alphabetically or geographically organized voting lists. Situations that do not allow line switching can often be divided up and treated as several problems of the one-line, one-server type. A standard supermarket check-out area is a good example of queuing with line switching. Queuing models may also follow a ***station-to-station*** scheme, wherein sequential processing occurs. Complex situations of this type require processing by different stations depending on the characteristics or desires of the individual served. Such a system is typical of student registration procedures at many large universities.

Although one generally assumes a standard ***first come, first served*** discipline in waiting lines, other queuing disciplines do occur. For example, there may be a system of customer preference or priority rating that allows high-priority customers to move in ahead of low-priority customers. ***Line balking,*** or refusing altogether to wait in line, is another queuing phenomenon that sometimes needs to be built into models.

The further classification of queues identifies the timing of arrivals for service and their processing. These characteristics may occur in any combination with others of the foregoing characteristics. The simplest model assumes uniform time intervals between arrivals and constant service time. However, one or the other of these two factors is usually variable, so one may design models with random arrivals and constant service time, with uniform arrivals and random service time, or with random arrivals and random service time

These last characteristics of queuing problems—the average rate of arrivals and the average rate of servicing—are absolutely fundamental to queuing models, and a common notation is used for their specification. Let

λ = average arrival rate (number of units arriving for service per unit of time)

μ = average service rate (number of units being serviced per unit of time)

For example, the arrival rate may be 6 units, or customers, per hour ($\lambda = 6$), and the service rate may be 10 units per hour ($\mu = 10$). Note that the inverses of these values also have significant meaning:

$\frac{1}{\lambda}$ = interarrival time

$\frac{1}{\mu}$ = service time

Thus if $\lambda = 6$, the average interarrival time is $\frac{1}{6}$ hour per customer, or 10 minutes. Given $\mu = 10$, the average time required to service a customer is $\frac{1}{10}$ hour, or 6 minutes.

Generally we are interested in the analysis of situations for which the average rate of arrival is less than the average rate of servicing. The ratio of these values, the ratio of λ to μ, is called the ***clearing ratio*** of the system. It is expressed as ρ and defined as follows:

$$\rho = \frac{\lambda}{\mu}$$

If λ is less than μ, the clearing ratio is less than 1, and the arrival rate is less than the servicing rate. Of course, even with a clearing ratio less than 1, if arrivals and servicing are not equally spaced, the variability of the system will sometimes cause waiting lines and sometimes not.

Nevertheless, on average the rate of arrivals is less than the rate of servicing. The long-run average characteristics of such a system, if they exist, are called the ***steady state*** or ***stable*** conditions of the system. A system that is moving toward its steady state is in a ***transient*** condition.

A queuing situation for which the clearing ratio is greater than 1 involves a waiting line that grows without bound. This is called an ***explosive*** condition, and the business manager would probably want to alter it by introducing measures that would reduce the clearing ratio. Other systems may display oscillating characteristics wherein the swing, or amplitude, of the oscillations may be exploding, steady or dampened over time.

13.2 The Theoretical–Statistical Approach

The basic queuing model can be manipulated mathematically to obtain solutions for the average system characteristics. The most common case assumes random arrivals and random servicing. If the real time line is divided into many small intervals (seconds or minutes), most commercial applications show service facility arrivals or departures having a very small probability of occurrence. Indeed, many time intervals are empty, exhibiting neither an arrival nor a departure. If an arrival does occur in a given time interval, only one will be considered, because the probability of more than one arrival in the same time interval is negligible. Furthermore, each arrival is independent of all others. As a result, the assumptions of randomness and small time intervals mean that n, the number of observed time intervals, is large and that np is small, where p is the probability of an arrival. Both the arrival/no-arrival and the departure/no-departure phenomena are analogous to success/failure experiments, and the Poisson distribution (which assumes a low success rate) can be adopted for model-building purposes.

With regard to the rate of servicing, we are typically concerned with the time required for servicing more than a given number of units per hour. If the service rate is distributed according to the Poisson distribution, it can be shown that the service time varies according to the negative exponential distribution. This relationship is derived as follows. Consider a given time interval in which 1 element is serviced. Such an interval T represents the service time measured from beginning to end. The probability that the random variable T exceeds any given value, $P(T > t)$, is simply the probability that servicing continues for the given element. The fundamental probability equation

$$P(T > t) = 1 - P(T \leq t) \tag{13.1}$$

shows that the probability of a given service time is 1 minus the cumulative distribution function for T. During servicing, no departures from the service facility occur, and the departure rate, being random, is distributed according to the Poisson distribution. Hence, the probability of a given service time is the same as the probability of no departures during this time:

$$P(T > t) = P(t,0) = \frac{e^{-\mu t}(\mu t)^0}{0!} = e^{-\mu t} \tag{13.2}$$

Equations (13.1) and (13.2) combined yield the cumulative distribution function for service time:

$$P(T \leq t) = 1 - e^{-\mu t} \tag{13.3}$$

This is a representation of the negative exponential distribution, for which the probability density function is

$$P(T = t) = e^{-\mu t} \tag{13.4}$$

and which is illustrated in Figure 13.2.

On the basis of this derivation, we can describe the elementary queuing model with random arrivals and random service time as one for which arrivals are distributed according to the Poisson distribution and service times according to the negative exponential distribution. Moreover, as a result of these basic assumptions, the two distributions

Figure 13.2
The Negative Exponential Distribution

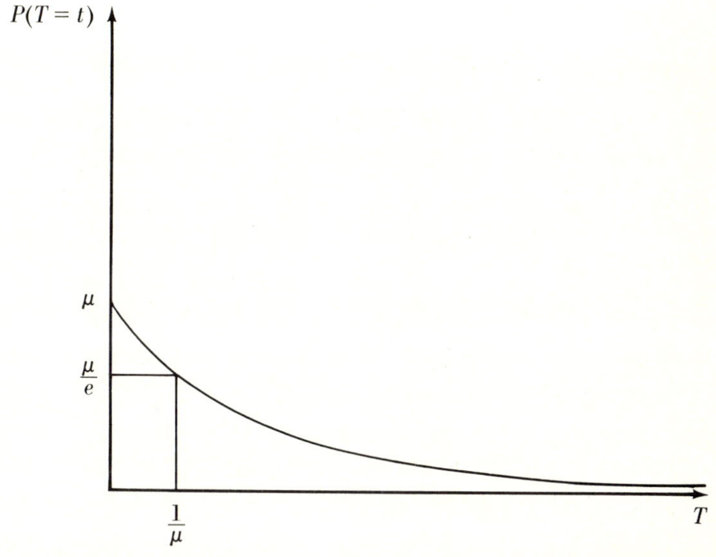

can be combined mathematically (refer to in-depth presentations of queuing theory) to derive the following system characteristics:

1. The average number of elements waiting and being served is

$$E(N_{ws}) = \frac{\lambda}{\mu - \lambda}$$

2. The average number of elements waiting in line for service is

$$E(N_{w}) = \frac{\lambda^2}{\mu(\mu - \lambda)}$$

3. The average time spent both waiting in line and being served is

$$E(T_{ws}) = \frac{1}{\mu - \lambda}$$

4. The average time spent waiting before being served is

$$E(T_{w}) = \frac{\lambda}{\mu(\mu - \lambda)}$$

In these equations,

E = expected value of the indicated random variable
N_{ws} = number of elements waiting and being served
N_{w} = number of elements waiting for service
T_{ws} = time spent waiting and being served
T_{w} = time spent waiting before being served
λ = average arrival rate
μ = average service rate

Considering the algebraic complexity of the underlying probability distributions, these are simple ratios to calculate.

13.3 Application of the Theoretical–Statistical Model to a Typical Queuing Example

Now consider the following example. Deciding whether to acquire a duplicating machine, the manager of an organization must formulate procedures for efficient duplication of materials. In doing so, the manager wishes to minimize the combined cost of operating the machine and waiting in line to use it. Two alternatives exist. According to the first, all employees would be allowed to duplicate freely on a first come, first served basis. Waiting to use the machine would occur if others who came earlier had not yet completed their copying. The second alternative would be to hire a full-time machine operator who would accept the materials to be duplicated, process them, and return them to the proper person when completed. In this case, the only time regular employees would spend would be a fixed number of minutes filling out a slip indicating the number of copies needed, any special requests, and where to return the completed job.

Suppose that, for the first alternative, the average arrival rate is observed to be 8 employees per hour and that the average service time spent using the machine on an individual basis (first alternative) is 4.8 minutes. The service rate is therefore $(1/4.8) \times 60$, or 12.5 per hour. Secretaries earning \$3.50 per hour are the prime users of the duplication facilities. Under the second alternative, an attendant's wage would be \$3 per hour, and filling out slips would take 2.4 minutes each. Which of the two alternatives would be least costly?

In each case, we must arrive at some measures of the time expended during each phase. Multiplied by their appropriate wage rates and accumulated, these measures yield the overall cost of operating the system. Random arrivals and servicing lead, respectively, to the assumptions of the Poisson and the negative exponential distributions. In fact, these might not apply; but suppose that a statistical validation procedure is successfully applied to the observed data to support this assumption.

The total costs for each alternative during a 60-minute period are calculated as follows:

Alternative 1:

$$\begin{aligned}
\text{Total cost} &= (\text{average time in hours spent by each secretary both waiting in line and using the machine}) \\
&\quad \times (\text{average number of secretaries per hour}) \\
&\quad \times (\text{secretarial wage rate}) \\
&= \left(\frac{1}{\mu - \lambda}\text{ hours per secretary}\right) \times (\lambda \text{ secretaries per hour}) \\
&\quad \times (\$3.50 \text{ per hour}) \\
&= \frac{1}{12.5 \quad 8} \times 8 \times \$3.50 \\
&= \$6.22
\end{aligned}$$

Alternative 2: Total cost = (time in hours required for each secretary to fill out a processing slip)

× (average number of secretaries each hour)

× (secretarial wage rate)

+ (attendant's hourly wage rate)

$$= \frac{2.4 \text{ minutes}}{60 \text{ minutes per hour}} \times 8 \text{ secretaries per hour}$$

$$\times \$3.50 \text{ per hour} + \$3 \text{ per hour}$$

$$= \$4.12$$

The calculations for this example show that reducing the time spent waiting and operating the duplicating machine under alternative 1 more than compensates for the cost of the attendant in alternative 2. Therefore, the second alternative is less expensive than the first.

13.4 The Simulation Approach

It is not unusual to encounter a queuing situation that either does not fit the assumptions for using the theoretical–statistical approach or is too complex mathematically for us to find solutions equivalent to those in the type of model with basic random arrivals and random servicing. In such cases, simulation techniques are often used.

Underlying probability distributions must be determined for arrivals and servicing just as before, but in the simulation approach, one records information about the actual situation so that observed probability distributions can be used. Thus the only assumption is that the observed probabilities will persist in the future and that no changes in the underlying probability functions will occur.

The simulation approach relies on random numbers to generate arrivals and servicing. Doing this in a way that simulates the observed probability distributions is called the ***Monte Carlo method.*** Simply stated, this technique assigns probabilities to values of a random variable (such as the number of arrivals or the time for servicing) according to the selection of random numbers and according to a preassigned correspondence designed to duplicate the observed probabilities.

For example, suppose that observation of a service facility yields the probability distribution for arrivals shown in Table 13.1.

Table 13.1
Observed Probability Distribution for Arrivals

Random Variable X	Probability $P(X = x)$
$x_1 = 0$	$P_1 = .50$
$x_2 = 1$	$P_2 = .35$
$x_3 = 2$	$P_3 = .10$
$x_4 = 3$	$P_4 = .05$

Table 13.2
The Cumulative Probability Distribution and Monte Carlo Assignment

Random Variable X	Probability $P(X \leq x)$	Monte Carlo Random Number Assignment	Probability of Random Number
$x_1 = 0$	$P_1 = .50$	01–50	.50
$x_2 = 1$	$P_1 + P_2 = .85$	51–85	.35
$x_3 = 2$	$P_1 + P_2 + P_3 = .95$	86–95	.10
$x_4 = 3$	$P_1 + P_2 + P_3 + P_4 = 1.00$	96–99 and 00	.05
			1.00

Since a cumulative distribution function ranges from 0 to 1 (or 0% to 100%), we can set up an equivalence with all 2-digit random numbers ranging from 00 to 99 such that the probabilities of the random numbers coincide with the observed probability distribution. Using the probability distribution in Table 13.1, Table 13.2 creates the corresponding cumulative probability distribution and illustrates the assignment of random numbers for simulation.

We get random numbers we need to use the Monte Carlo method either from tables of random numbers or from a random number generator. Random numbers are generated on the basis of the uniform distribution; for instance, any 2-digit number appears with a probability of .01. Such a table of random numbers is given in Appendix A.1. The user should randomly enter the table at different points each time the table is used, thereby avoiding repetitive lists of numbers. One can further randomize the process by altering the method of drawing numbers—either across rows or down columns. If a random number generator is used, choosing a different seed value to start each use of the generator will also ensure nonrepetitive results.

The Monte Carlo method governs the occurrence of events according to the draw of random numbers. For example, if the process of arrivals described in Table 13.2 is to be simulated, random numbers are selected from the random-number table, and, with each selection, the corresponding number of simulated arrivals is recorded. Suppose that we enter the random number table in Appendix A.1 at the beginning of the block of numbers that is over 8 and down 4 from the upper-left-hand corner (beginning with the digits 8434). Selecting 2-digit numbers in a vertical column from this starting point, the Monte Carlo method generates arrivals as follows (see also Table 13.2):

Random number 84 corresponds to 1 arrival
Random number 12 corresponds to 0 arrivals
Random number 08 corresponds to 0 arrivals
Random number 93 corresponds to 2 arrivals
Random number 88 corresponds to 2 arrivals
Random number 99 corresponds to 3 arrivals
Random number 59 corresponds to 1 arrival
Random number 17 corresponds to 0 arrivals
Random number 26 corresponds to 0 arrivals
Random number 48 corresponds to 0 arrivals
and so on

Each number selected indicates the number of arrivals in a given time interval, and many short intervals of this type are generally constructed to cover a longer time period. Because of the correspondence established between the random numbers and the assigned number of arrivals, this process simulates the underlying probability distribution.

Suppose, for example, that this simulation approach is applied to alternative 1 in the duplicating machine example and that the observed distribution of arrivals given in Table 13.1 is the distribution of secretary arrivals that is to be simulated. Building a simulation model requires that observations be taken on service times so that a probability distribution for service times can be derived and simulated. Such a distribution and the random number assignments for the Monte Carlo method are given in Table 13.3.

The last component of this simulated model is to establish rules for the queuing discipline. In this case, a straightforward system of first come, first served is assumed. There is no line balking.

Conceptually, the simulation model is now complete, and a flow chart of the model (see Figure 13.3) contains all of the basic components—simulated arrivals (generated with random numbers), simulated queuing, simulated servicing (generated with another set of random numbers), and system departures.

Table 13.3 Probability Distribution for Service Times and Monte Carlo Assignment

Service Time (minutes)	Observed Probability	Cumulative Probability	Monte Carlo Random Number Assignment
3	.05	.05	01–05
4	.40	.45	06–45
5	.30	.75	46–75
6	.25	1.00	76–99 and 00
	1.00		

The actual working of the model is represented in the form of a table that shows the status of the system for successive time periods in terms of the number of arrivals, the queuing, the time needed for servicing, and the overall time spent by each element in the system. Table 13.4 presents these basic data for 5-minute time intervals over a period of 2 hours. In each time interval, a 2-digit random number is selected and the number of arrivals is recorded according to Table 13.2. If more than 1 arrival occurs in a single time period, the arrivals are spread evenly throughout the 5-minute interval (for example, 2 arrivals in the time interval beginning at 1:10 are assumed to appear at 1:10 and 1:12.5, respectively). Service times for each element are determined using another 2-digit random number and the assignment rule developed in Table 13.3. No secretary can begin to use the duplicating machine until secretaries who arrived earlier have finished their work. Thus the second of the two arrivals in the 1:10 interval must wait $2\frac{1}{2}$ minutes until the first finishes 5 minutes of copying. These basic characteristics are preserved throughout the simulation of 2 hours of activity.

Finally, at the end of the simulation, we calculate totals in order to derive the average characteristics of the system. With 19 arrivals simulated during the 2-hour period, the average arrival rate is 9.5 per hour. Likewise, total service time divided by the number of secretaries serviced yields an average service time per secretary of 4.6 minutes. The average time spent both in waiting and in copying is the total time spent by all secretaries divided by the number of secretaries, or 8.92 minutes. Secretaries spend an average of 8.92 minutes waiting and copying, and there are 9.5 secretaries per hour, each of whom earns $3.50 per hour. Therefore, the average cost in time for waiting and servicing is $4.94 per hour. The average value of secretarial time used in copying is an important decision criterion. It can be compared with other service alternatives to determine the least-cost method of running the facility.

Of course, only 2 hours of activity have been simulated. In practice, we might wish to repeat the simulation many times on the basis of either

Table 13.4 Simulation of a Self-Service Duplicating Machine Facility (2 Hours)

Time Period (5 minutes beginning)	Random Number Arrivals	Arrivals	Time Servicing Begins	Random Number Servicing	Minutes Servicing	Time Servicing Ends	Minutes Spent in System
1:00	64	1	1:00	13	4	1:04	4
1:05	04	0					
1:10	94	2	1:10	71	5	1:15	5
			1:15	88	6	1:21	8.5
1:15	62	1	1:21	74	5	1:26	11
1:20	90	2	1:26	10	4	1:30	10
			1:30	46	5	1:35	12.5
1:25	00	3	1:35	23	4	1:39	14
			1:39	15	4	1:43	16
			1:43	11	4	1:47	18
1:30	13	0					
1:35	40	0					
1:40	51	1	1:47	78	6	1:51	11
1:45	50	0					
1:50	12	0					
1:55	68	1	1:55	31	4	1:59	4
2:00	55	1	2:00	11	4	2:04	4
2:05	05	0					
2:10	94	2	2:10	91	6	2:16	6
			2:16	99	6	2:22	9.5
2:15	69	1	2:22	57	5	2:27	12
2:20	51	1	2:27	28	4	2:31	11
2:25	28	0					
2:30	73	1	2:31	18	4	2:35	5
2:35	10	0					
2:40	34	0					
2:45	71	1	2:45	32	4	2:49	4
2:50	56	1	2:50	21	4	2:54	4
2:55	21	0					
		19			88		169.5

Simulation Results

Average arrival rate: 9.5/hour (19 arrivals/2 hours)
Average service time: 4.6 minutes/secretary (88 minutes/19 secretaries serviced)
Average time in system: 8.92 minutes (169.5 minutes/19 secretaries serviced)
Average cost of waiting and servicing: \$4.94/hour [8.92 minutes/hour (60 minutes)
× 9.5 secretaries/hour
× \$3.50/hour]

Figure 13.3
A Simulation Flow Chart of the Duplicating Machine Facility

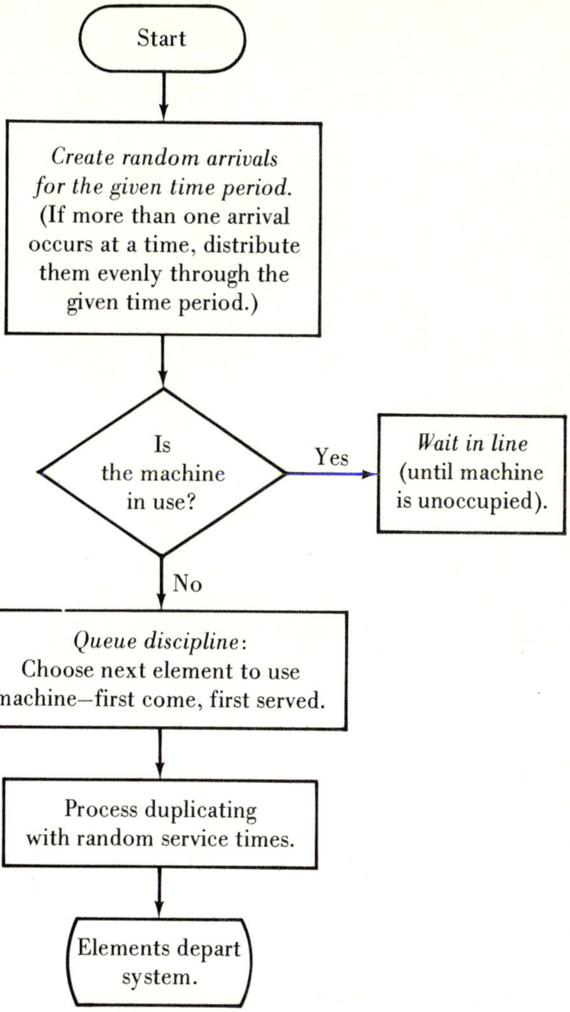

2 hours or longer periods of time. Averaging the results (which themselves are averages) would then paint a reliable picture of the system characteristics.

The tediousness of repetitive calculations for simulation models can be removed by computerization of the model. Computer routines are commonly available for generating random numbers. Beyond that, virtually any computer programming language can be used to specify the conditions of the model and to perform the same types of calculations, listings, and summary results presented in our example.

A standard requirement for computer simulation is to set up a flow chart of the system under consideration. These flow charts may be complex, involving many branches and stages, according to the systems being simulated. Although the FORTRAN language can be used advantageously for simulation purposes, just as it is used in many other scientific or quantitative computer applications, the types of tasks needed for simulation purposes are fairly standard and lend themselves to generalization. As a result, a number of programming languages have been designed specifically for use in building computerized simulation models. One such simulation language, which is based on FORTRAN and uses FORTRAN simulation subroutines, is called GASP II. This language allows standardized specification of system attributes, generation of random events, and preparation of statistical reports, all of which would require more programming effort if FORTRAN alone were used.

Of the numerous other simulation languages that have been developed and are available for use at computer centers, one called the General Purpose Simulation System, or GPSS, is especially convenient to use. GPSS relies heavily on standardized flow-charting of the systems to be simulated. Once a complete flow chart has been prepared and put in the form of a GPSS block diagram, the GPSS listing can be derived, for the most part, by a one-for-one specification of the blocks in the flow chart. It is a very convenient and time-saving tool for building simulation models by computer.

13.5 Summary

Queuing, or waiting line analysis, can be performed by using either a theoretical–statistical approach or the techniques of simulation. Both methods rely fundamentally on the specification of probability distributions for arrivals and servicing. In the former case, these distributions are judged by the researcher to be essentially the same as theoretical or statistical distributions. For example, queuing situations with random arrivals and service times are often described effectively by the Poisson and negative exponential distributions. In the latter case, distributions for arrivals and servicing are simulated on the basis of extensive observation of the system in operation and through use of the Monte Carlo technique. In actual applications, the choice between these methods depends largely on the complexity of the system to be analyzed and on the degree of justification for selecting theoretical distributions rather than distributions based on actual observations. Both types of analysis can be applied effectively to a wide variety of actual problems.

Exercises

13.1 What is a queuing problem? What are some of the basic characteristics of a queuing system?

13.2 Explain the essential economic similarity between queuing problems and inventory problems.

13.3 How can a queuing model be used to improve service in:
a. The duplicating room (Xerox machines) at city hall
b. The take-out counter in a downtown restaurant
c. A bank branch in a shopping mall
d. A radio repair shop

13.4 a. Give one or two examples of queuing situations that confront you in your everyday life.
b. Give some examples of business problems that demonstrate queuing situations.

13.5 As mentioned in the text, there is generally a trade-off between service costs and waiting costs, and in most cases the objective is to minimize the total expenditure associated with both costs in the queuing system. Let

C_s = service costs per unit of time

C_w = waiting costs of an arrival per unit of time

C_t = total cost (the sum of service costs and waiting costs)

Show these cost relationships in a diagram. What is the goal of the decision maker? Indicate the optimal decision point on your diagram. How is this model conceptually similar to the treatment of environmental issues mentioned in Chapter 1?

13.6 Explain the following concepts:
a. Average length of a waiting line
b. Average arrival rate
c. Average service rate
d. Interarrival time
e. Service time

13.7 What is the clearing ratio? Discuss the meaning of each of the following:
a. Stable condition
b. Transient condition
c. Explosive condition

13.8 Requests for landing by airliners at a metropolitan airport are known to occur randomly according to a Poisson distribution at an average rate of 3.1 requests per 5-minute period. The guiding of aircraft to a safe landing once clearance has been given is exponentially distributed and takes an average of $1\frac{1}{4}$ minutes each. The cost of waiting (in fuel expended) is approximately \$4.60 per minute.

a. Determine the average number of airliners waiting to land.
b. What is the average time that airliners spend waiting to land?
c. What is the average time spent by airliners both in waiting and in landing?
d. Determine the average waiting costs of airliners at this airport.
e. A group of airlines is considering the shared expense of constructing an additional runway that would cut in half the average time required to guide aircraft to a safe landing. If 115 airliners per day land at the airport under these conditions and if construction costs of the additional runway are \$300,000, how long will it take before the shared runway costs are earned back in reduced costs due to shorter waiting time?

13.9 Delta Computer Systems, Inc., employs a mechanic to repair electronic meters for its customers at a service center on its premises. For the most part, the mechanic can fix the meters at once. Customer arrivals are Poisson distributed at the rate of 6 per hour. For meters that can be fixed at once, the repair service rate is 10 units per hour and is exponentially distributed.

a. Determine the clearing ratio of the system.
b. Find the proportion of time that the service center is empty. (***Hint:*** Determine P_0, the probability of no one being in the system.)
c. Find the probability of having 2 customers in the service center.

13.10 Refer to exercise 13.9. Calculate:

a. The average number of customers waiting to be served
b. The average time spent waiting to be served
c. The average number of customers waiting to be served and being served
d. The average time spent waiting to be served and being served

13.11 A typical truck driver of the Fly-By-Night Transportation Company earns \$18 profit per hour. The company has 100 trucks in operation. Truck drivers arrive in a Poisson fashion at the rate of 50 per hour, whereas the service rate, which is exponentially distributed, is 70 per hour. Furthermore, a truck driver eats breakfast in 10 minutes at a company diner.

a. What is the profit lost for the truck drivers waiting in the queue?
b. What is the profit lost while truck drivers are being served?
c. Calculate the profit lost while truck drivers are actually eating breakfast.

d. Determine the total profits lost for all three of these service functions.

13.12 The Registration Office of a city college is faced with the problem of determining the number of staff to use during the rush hours of the college's registration day. The Registration Office has observed that students arrive on the average of every 2 minutes and that the average time required to complete 1 student's registration is 3 minutes. A study by the college's Institution Research Office indicates that the pattern of student arrivals follows the Poisson distribution and that the service rate, which is exponentially distributed, is 1.5 per minute.

a. What is the rate of utilization for the existing registration system?
b. What is the expected number of students waiting and being served in the system?
c. What is the expected number of students waiting in line for service?
d. What is the average time spent waiting before being served?

13.13 The manager of the Dellato Machine Shop needs to hire a mechanic to repair a certain type of machine. The frequency of machine breakdown is Poisson distributed and occurs at a rate of 1.5 machines per hour. Any machine out of service loses $50 per hour. Two applicants have already been interviewed by the manager of the company. The first applicant asks for $15 per hour and is able to repair machines at a rate of 2 machines per hour. The second applicant, who is less experienced, asks for $10 per hour and repairs an average of 1.5 machines per hour. Which of the two applicants should be hired to minimize total cost?

13.14 The oil company that owns his station gives a gas station operator the option of converting entirely to self-service pumps and completely eliminating automobile repair functions. Doing so would cause the price charged to drop $.05 per gallon, customer demand would increase, and the job of a hired auto mechanic would be eliminated. On the basis of the Poisson and negative exponential distributions, weigh the alternatives to determine which option is financially most attractive to the station operator. What are the expected waiting line characteristics of the current facility? What are the expected waiting line characteristics of the self-service facility?

	Remain As Is	**Self-Service**
Price Charged	$.65/gallon	$.60/gallon
Average Arrival Rate	10/hour	22/hour
Average Service Time	2.5 minutes	2.5 minutes
Average Purchase	7 gallons	11 gallons
Earnings on Repairs	$4/hour	none

13.15 A waiting line system is known to average 4.3 minutes between arrivals, and 3.65 minutes is the average time required for servicing. Answer the following questions on the basis of the Poisson and negative exponential distributions.

a. What is the average number waiting in line?
b. What is the average length of time spent waiting?
c. What is the average time spent in the system?

13.16 A parking garage finds that, during certain peak periods, the average rate at which automobiles exit is 112 per hour. Service times are found to vary randomly, largely due to the time it takes drivers to find their money and attendants to make change. The average service time for an attendant is 30 seconds. Three booths are available for collecting fees from drivers as they leave. The number of cars that can safely be allowed to stack up waiting for departure from the garage is limited by management to an average of 4. How many attendants need to be on duty during peak periods? What are the basic waiting line characteristics of the system using 1 attendant? 2 attendants? 3 attendants?

13.17 Use the Monte Carlo technique to simulate arrivals in a system with the following observed distribution of arrivals during 5-minute intervals:

Number of Arrivals	Number of Observations
0	8
1	15
2	38
3	82
4	67
5	14
6	2

Do the simulation for a 2-hour period.

13.18 Perform a 2-hour simulation of arrivals in a system with the following observed characteristics:

Minutes Between Arrivals	Number of Observations
Fewer than 1	14
1 up to 2	27
2 up to 3	39
3 up to 4	30
4 up to 5	6

13.19 An airline offers telephone reservation services with two reservation clerks. A growing business has led the airline management to install a recorded message that asks callers to wait when both clerks are busy. Monitoring this device makes it apparent that some customers choose to hang up (presumably to call a competing airline) rather than to wait at the request of a recorded message. Thus the airline decides to have enough clerks available so that it will not be necessary for any more than 1 customer in 10 to wait at the request of the answering device. Simulate this system for 2 hours, using 2 or more clerks, to determine the number of clerks necessary to meet the requirements that management has specified. Past records reveal that telephone calls come in as follows:

Number of Calls per 5-Minute Period	Frequency of Occurrence
3	5
4	20
5	35
6	20
7	15
8	5

The performance of each clerk in handling calls has the following observed distribution:

Minutes per Call	Frequency of Occurrence
1	82
2	80
3	26
4	10
5	2

If each reservation has an average value to the airline of $138 in revenue and each clerk earns $4.50 per hour, what is the net amount saved per hour if every caller who is asked to wait calls another airline instead? What is this amount if only one-fourth of all such callers switch to another airline?

13.20 Visit a supermarket, a fast-food restaurant, a bank, a laundromat, a toll station, or some other such business in your vicinity. Observe the overall system. What are the stages of activity in the system? Provide a detailed flow chart of all aspects of the system. Over a period of time, record the times or rates of arrivals and servicing. Develop a simulation model of the system. Using the Monte Carlo technique to do simulations, manipulate the characteristics of servicing or arrivals to see how the model reacts. After manipulating the model, draw conclusions about the best way to manage the system in terms of costs, the length of waiting lines, the time spent waiting, or other relevant factors.

Suggested Readings

Budnick, F. S., R. Mojena, and T. E. Vollman. *Principles of Operations Research for Management.* Homewood, Ill.: Irwin, 1977.

Feller, William. *An Introduction to Probability Theory and Its Applications,* Vol. 1. 3rd ed. New York: Wiley, 1968.

———. *An Introduction to Probability Theory and Its Applications,* Vol. 2. New York: Wiley, 1966.

Grass, D., and C. M. Harris. *Fundamentals of Queuing Theory.* New York: Wiley, 1974.

Kaufmann, Arnold. *Methods and Models of Operations Research.* Englewood Cliffs, N.J.: Prentice-Hall, 1963.

Morse, P. M. *Queues, Inventories, and Maintenance.* New York: Wiley, 1958.

Newell, G. F. *Applications of Queuing Theory.* London: Chapman S. Hall, 1971.

Panico, Joseph A. *Queuing Theory.* Englewood Cliffs, N.J.: Prentice-Hall, 1969.

Saaty, T. L. *Elements of Queuing Theory.* New York: McGraw-Hill, 1961.

Wagner, Harvey M. *Principles of Management Science.* Englewood Cliffs, N.J.: Prentice-Hall, 1975.

White, J. A., J. W. Schmidt, and G. K. Bennett. *Analysis of Queuing Systems.* New York: Academic Press, 1975.

14

Simulation

In Chapter 13, queuing problems were analyzed and solved according to either the theoretical–statistical approach or simulation methods. Since simulation methods are widely used in many areas of analysis, this chapter devotes special attention to them and shows how simulation techniques are useful in business management and research. By using simulation techniques, we can gain insight into real working systems without experimenting with the real systems themselves. Thus we can examine relationships and interactions in systems that may be too complex to judge directly and too costly to tamper with in practice.

14.1 The Applicability of Simulation Techniques

Advantages and Disadvantages

The primary advantage of using simulation to model a real system is that this approach allows us to study the system without actually manipulating the system itself. The effects of various factors can be determined systematically, either one at a time or in combination. Design considerations can be handled under controlled, experimental conditions. Alternatives can be assessed. For systems that are very costly to change, it is wise to be certain of the basic operating characteristics before set-up or revision takes place, and thereby to avoid undue modification expenses that arise from afterthoughts.

Simulation methods also can be a highly effective training device for the inexperienced operator of a complex system. The details of various control situations can be presented to the trainee in a way that teaches appropriate responses so that the risks of training under real circumstances are avoided. Sufficient training on a simulator can lead to operation of the real system—first under the supervision of an experienced operator and later with full responsibility.

Simulation techniques are appropriate when the use of resources for a simulation is both practicable and cost-effective. In other words, simulation techniques are advantageous when the system under consideration is capable of being simulated and when studying it by simulation consumes less resources than actually manipulating it. If either of these conditions is not met, simulation may prove disadvantageous. For example, attempting to develop a simulation model of the stock market would be futile. The complexity of relevant factors (including world events, psychological attitudes of investors, political interactions, and so on) is just too great for any simulation model to duplicate reliably. Under these conditions there is no substitute for informed judgment and practical experience. Cost-effectiveness should also be considered before a working system is simulated. If it is relatively inexpensive to experiment with the real system, and if the associated risks are small or acceptable, the relatively more expensive simulation approach should be avoided.

Other factors can contribute to the possible disadvantages of simulation. If the time available for making changes is short, it may be impractical to simulate the operation of the system before taking real action. Or, if one can reliably predict outcomes on the basis of experience or other knowledge of systems interactions, the results of simulation are redundant. In such cases, it is better to move ahead and get the job done. Finally, we must remember that a simulation model is not real and that critical assumptions must be evaluated in the light of reality. That is, field tests of simulation results versus real results may be required. Hidden assumptions must be rooted out to determine their impact on simulation results. Ultimately, advantages and disadvantages have to be considered in terms of the ability of a simulation model to reflect real conditions and the degree to which valuable resources are saved.

Computer Simulation

Electronic computers make possible the development of highly sophisticated simulation models for specialized applications. Complex analysis of many interrelated factors can be handled by computer. The computational power of a computer and its ability to handle involved logic operations and to manage volumes of data make it the ideal simulation tool. Some of the computer-related aspects of simulation were discussed in Chapter 13, and an example of computer simulation is given in Chapter 18. This chapter demonstrates the process of setting up and using a simulation model. It does not cover computer processing but proceeds in a way that exposes all the details and steps required to create and use a simulation model.

Basic System Characteristics

What are the characteristics of systems that an analyst may seek to simulate in the business environment? Simulation models are typically applied to ***stochastic*** systems, systems wherein randomness or probabilistic outcomes are found. By contrast, a ***deterministic*** system may be analyzed without simulation—for example, the transportation problem, assignment problem, or other situations in which computational techniques yield solutions directly.

Generally, business-oriented simulation is applied to stochastic systems that are ***discrete*** systems—that is, systems in which the stochastic variables take on a finite number of values. This type of probabilistic process can be described appropriately in terms of particular discrete values or discrete intervals of values. By contrast, a ***continuous*** system varies over an infinite number of values in a continuum. Discrete systems move from one state to another in steps. Continuous systems move smoothly or continuously. Whereas discrete stochastic systems lend themselves to analysis by simulation, continuous systems are often analyzed via the calculus of differential equations, a topic that is beyond the scope of this book.

There are two basic types of computers, digital and analog computers. A ***digital computer***, by virtue of its computation with digits, is ideally suited for use with discrete systems. Its computational power allows highly complex and repetitious analysis to be performed with speed and accuracy. Because they can be programmed for specific purposes, digital computers are widely applicable. By contrast, ***analog computers*** are generally applied to continuous systems. They work on the basis of some physical analogy and are usually specified for use in the analysis of particular continuous systems. Thus they lack the general applicability of digital computers. Digital computers can also be used to simulate continuous systems. Calculations relating to continuous variables can be performed either directly on the basis of known mathematical equations, or by precise approximation methods. Representing systems through a physical analogy, the analog computer seldom offers the degree of precision that one can obtain with digital computers. However, for specialized continuous systems it can be easier to use. Examples of such analog computers are driver-training and flight-training simulators. Due to their computational power, versatility, and widespread availability, digital computers provide the fundamental capabilities necessary for meaningful simulation of discrete stochastic systems.

Finally, simulation models can be either ***static*** or ***dynamic*** in nature.

Static models provide "snapshot" system descriptions that are unrelated to time. The preceding and succeeding system characteristics are not considered. For example, the stochastic systems that we analyzed in Chapter 11 using Bayesian decision theory were static decision models. Each period is treated independently of other periods. Dynamic models are time-related models, such as those we discussed in Chapter 9. The outcomes of one time period affect the decisions of the next, and the next, and so on ad infinitum. Business-oriented simulation often seeks solutions to time-related, dynamic problems. For example, the queuing simulation we performed in Chapter 13 provided a detailed account of waiting-line characteristics over many time periods. In a similar fashion, this chapter demonstrates the dynamic simulation of a discrete, stochastic decision-making process.

14.2 Simulation—The Process

Model Building In order to build a useful simulation model, we must study all aspects of an actual situation in order to properly identify the fundamental characteristics and translate them into a working model. A number of basic steps must be performed. First, for an existing system, it is important to observe its operation in all relevant details. If the simulation approach is intended to anticipate the requirements of a new system, a thorough conceptualization of the system under consideration is necessary. Lessons learned from the operation of similar systems elsewhere should be incorporated in the conceptualization. This process of observation and conceptualization should identify key system variables that will later become part of the simulation model. Wherever possible, keep records on the movement of probabilistic variables to derive probability distributions. As an example, see Table 14.1.

Second, itemize all basic assumptions about the workings of the system. Operating conditions must be stated and interrelationships between variables specified. These specifications need to be thorough, complete, and exact. If possible, system functions should be expressed as mathematical equations. The basic pieces of the model will emerge, and the fundamental parameters will be identified.

Third, combine the pieces of the model to see that the specifications are complete. A working model should accept identifiable inputs, including the decisions of managers, and derive outputs that simulate the working of an actual system. Variables determined outside the working of the model (such as decision variables) are called ***exogenous variables.***

Table 14.1 Derivation by Observation of Probabilities in a Stochastic Process: The Flow of Cars Through a Traffic Light While It Is Green, During Rush Hour

Number of Cars	Number of Observations: Tally	Number of Observations: Total	Derived Probabilities	Monte Carlo: Cumulative Probabilities	Monte Carlo: Two-Digit Random Numbers
5 or fewer	𝍷	1	.01	.01	01
6	𝍸 𝍷𝍷𝍷	8	.06	.07	02–07
7	𝍸 𝍸	10	.08	.15	08–15
8	𝍸 𝍸 𝍸 𝍸 𝍷𝍷𝍷𝍷	24	.18	.33	16–33
9	𝍸 𝍸 𝍸 𝍸 𝍸 𝍸 𝍸 𝍷𝍷	37	.28	.61	34–61
10	𝍸 𝍸 𝍸 𝍸 𝍸 𝍷𝍷𝍷	28	.22	.83	62–83
11	𝍸 𝍸 𝍸 𝍷	16	.12	.95	84–95
12	𝍷𝍷𝍷𝍷	4	.03	.98	96–98
13 or more	𝍷𝍷	2	.02	1.00	99 & 00
			1.00		

Variables determined within, or as a result of, the working of the model (such as variables that represent outcomes) are called ***endogenous variables.*** In a complete model, specification of all inputs should be sufficient to derive the resulting output values. Such a model is called ***determined,*** because it is sufficient to determine the results. However, if one segment is missing such that no results can be derived, the model is ***underdetermined,*** or in need of further definition. Occasionally, we may find that the pieces of a model are more than necessary to obtain values for output variables, in which case the model is said to be ***overdetermined.***

Finally, we record and evaluate simulation results over many repetitions of model use. If simulation results are judged realistic, the model has succeeded. If not, the problem(s) should be identified, and the parameters of the model should be modified for improved results. This fine tuning of the simulation model is an important step.

14.3 Demonstration of Techniques—Two Competing Firms

Conceptualization Let's develop a simulation model for a hypothetical business decision-making situation. Consider the situation faced by two business firms competing against one another only (this is called a ***duopoly*** market environment), and assume that the purpose of the simulation is to offer instruction in decision making for future business managers who may be faced with the same duopoly market characteristics. Suppose that both firms are essentially equal in size and have similar production costs. Suppose also that their products are perceived by consumers to be undifferentiated; in other words, people see no substantial differences between the product of one firm and that of the other. Consumer demand is a function of price, availability, and response to advertising promotions. Market share is a probabilistic or stochastic variable that depends on random consumer reactions. Key variables for the simulation model must include the assets of each firm, production amounts, costs, price, sales, market share, advertising, and quantity demanded by consumers.

In order to identify the two firms, let the first be called Allied and the second Norton. A complete list of the variables and their definitions, follows.

Q = total market demands, for a given period
P = sales price in the market place
X_A = production of Allied during a given period
X_N = production of Norton during a given period
S = total market supply, for a given period
TC_A = total cost of Allied, for a given period
TC_N = total cost of Norton, for a given period
A_A = advertising expenditures by Allied, for a given period
A_N = advertising expenditures by Norton, for a given period
m = Allied's markup over average cost, for a given period
Y_A = quantity sold by Allied during a given period
Y_N = quantity sold by Norton during a given period
R_A = Allied's competitiveness ratio, expressed as a percent, for a given period
MS_A = market share of Allied, for a given period
MS_N = market share of Norton, for a given period
TR_A = total revenue of Allied, for a given period
TR_N = total revenue of Norton, for a given period

$Prof_A$ = profit earned by Allied, for a given period

$Prof_N$ = profit earned by Norton, for a given period

CP_A = cash position of Allied

CP_N = cash position of Norton

I_A = inventory level of Allied

I_N = inventory level of Norton

Assumptions, Conditions, and Interrelationships

Assume that Allied is a price leader and Norton a price follower; that is, Norton will follow with whatever price is set by Allied. The higher the price, the lower the quantity demanded by consumers. Let this demand function be a straight-line relationship specified as follows (see also Figure 14.1):

$$Q = 10{,}000 - 50P \tag{14.1}$$

Quantity supplied in the market place is the sum of the amounts Allied and Norton produce for the given period:

$$S = X_A + X_N \tag{14.2}$$

Figure 14.1
Simulation Model Demand Function

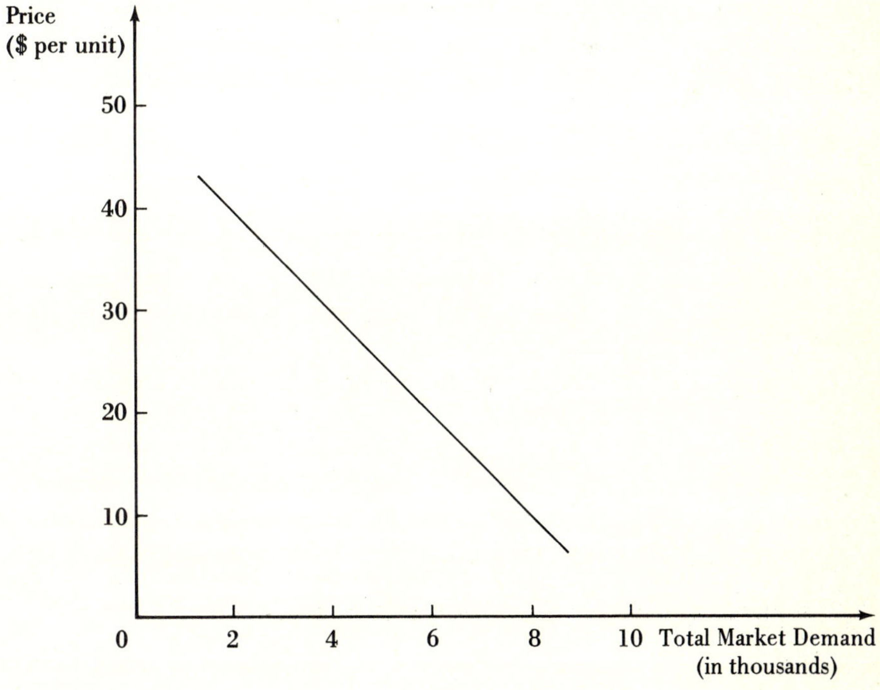

Any product not sold during the period is returned to inventory. If more of either firm's product is demanded than is produced in a given period, sales are made out of inventory.

Inputs, Decisions, and Outcomes

Fixed costs of production are \$1000 per period for each firm. These are standard overhead costs, but advertising expenditures—a decision variable—are itemized as a separate fixed cost. Variable cost per unit for each firm is \$50. Thus

$$TC_A = \$1000 + A_A + 50X_A \tag{14.3}$$

$$TC_N = \$1000 + A_N + 50X_N \tag{14.4}$$

Total costs divided by the production quantity yield an average cost per unit. Assume that Allied makes its pricing decision on the basis of a markup ratio m. This decision is made at the beginning of each period. Hence the price charged by Allied (and adopted by Norton) is

$$P = \frac{TC_A}{X_A}(1 + m) \tag{14.5}$$

Price determines quantity demanded, Q, in the market place according to the demand function. But quantity sold by either firm is determined by the market share that it wins, or

$$Y_A = MS_AQ \tag{14.6}$$

$$Y_N = MS_NQ \tag{14.7}$$

The market share of either firm is a function of both product attractiveness—as perceived by consumers on the basis of advertising effort—and product availability—the quantity of product manufactured and distributed for sale in the market place. Assume that the determination of market share is a stochastic process. First, a competitiveness ratio is derived on the basis of either firm's proportions of total advertising and distribution of new product. For the purposes of calculating this ratio, take Allied as a frame of reference. The ratio itself is the average of advertising and distribution proportions, converted to a percentage, as follows:

$$R_A = \frac{1}{2}\left[\frac{A_A}{A_A + A_N} + \frac{X_A}{X_A + X_N}\right] \times 100\% \tag{14.8}$$

Then, depending on the competitiveness ratio that is derived, market shares are determined according to a probability distribution, as shown in Table 14.2. For example, if Allied is highly competitive (with, say, a 78% competitiveness ratio), its market share is determined by the random action of consumers such that a market share for Allied of 60% has a probability of .20, a market share of 70% has a probability of .30, and so on. If Allied's competitiveness rates only 43%, however, market shares of 20%, 30%, 40%, and 50% have probabilities of .2, .3, .35, and .15, respectively. This stochastic process has been designed to have comparable probability distributions for any competitiveness ratio R_A.

We simulate action in the market place by using the Monte Carlo technique (see Chapter 13). That is, we select random numbers such that, for a large number of selections, the underlying, hypothetical distribution is preserved. In this case, Monte Carlo simulation assigns market shares using uniformly distributed random numbers, as follows:

Hypothetical probabilities:	.20	.30	.35	.15
Cumulative probabilities:	.20	.50	.85	1.00
Corresponding two-digit random numbers:	01–20	21–50	51–85	86–99 & 00
Resulting Market Shares—Allied, Norton:	(Read from the scale in Table 14.3 according to the derived competitiveness ratio.)			

Table 14.2 Probabilities of Given Market Shares for Various Possible Competitiveness Ratios

Competitiveness Ratio R_A	**Market Share, Firm A**										
	0%	**10%**	**20%**	**30%**	**40%**	**50%**	**60%**	**70%**	**80%**	**90%**	**100%**
0–35%	.20	.30	.35	.15							
35–40%		.20	.30	.35	.15						
40–45%			.20	.30	.35	.15					
45–50%				.20	.30	.35	.15				
50–55%					.20	.30	.35	.15			
55–60%						.20	.30	.35	.15		
60–65%							.20	.30	.35	.15	
65% & over								.20	.30	.35	.15
	100%	**90%**	**80%**	**70%**	**60%**	**50%**	**40%**	**30%**	**20%**	**10%**	**0%**
	Market Share, Firm N										

Table 14.3 Random-Number Assignments to Determine Market Shares for Varying Competitiveness Ratios, According to the Monte Carlo Technique

Competitiveness Ratio R_A	Market Share, Firm A										
	0%	10%	20%	30%	40%	50%	60%	70%	80%	90%	100%
0–35%	01–20	21–50	51–85	86–99 & 00							
35–40%		01–20	21–50	51–85	86–99 & 00						
40–45%			01–20	21–50	51–85	86–99 & 00					
45–50%				01–20	21–50	51–85	86–99 & 00				
50–55%					01–20	21–50	51–85	86–99 & 00			
55–60%						01–20	21–50	51–85	86–99 & 00		
60–65%							01–20	21–50	51–85	86–99 & 00	
65% & over								01–20	21–50	51–85	86–99 & 00
	100%	90%	80%	70%	60%	50%	40%	30%	20%	10%	0%
	Market Share, Firm N										

The sum of the market shares for Allied and for Norton, of course, totals 100%, so

$$MS_N = 100\% - MS_A \tag{14.9}$$

Revenue received is price times quantity sold; that is,

$$TR_A = PY_A \tag{14.10}$$

$$TR_N = PY_N \tag{14.11}$$

Profits are the difference between total revenue and total cost:

$$\text{Prof}_A = TR_A - TC_A \tag{14.12}$$

$$\text{Prof}_N = TR_N - TC_N \tag{14.13}$$

Finally, the new positions of Allied and Norton, in terms of cash balances and inventory amounts, are determined according to the changes that transpired during the period. Thus

$$CP_A\,(\text{new}) = CP_A\,(\text{initial}) + \text{Prof}_A \tag{14.14}$$

$$CP_N\,(\text{new}) = CP_N\,(\text{initial}) + \text{Prof}_N \tag{14.15}$$

$$I_A\,(\text{new}) = I_A\,(\text{initial}) + X_A - Y_A \tag{14.16}$$

$$I_N\,(\text{new}) = I_N\,(\text{initial}) + X_N - Y_N \tag{14.17}$$

Implementation Having specified all assumptions, conditions, interrelationships and decision variables, we are ready to try this model out. Let the period of time under consideration be 1 month, and let's set as our initial objective the simulation of 4 months. We need to devise a worksheet to record all positions, decisions, and outcomes. And we need a table of random numbers for reference. In this demonstration, random numbers have been selected from the table of random numbers given in Appendix A.1, starting with the top row of the table and reading across, left to right.

Let both of the firms start on an equal footing, with cash reserves of $250,000 and inventories of 500. Allied picks a markup ratio of 25%, decides to produce 3000 units, and plans advertising expenditures of $15,000. For its part, Norton wants to make a strong initial showing by producing a lot—5000 units—and advertising a lot—$25,000, or 10%

of its total cash reserves. As a result (see Table 14.4), the market price is \$69.17 [equation (14.5)], total supply is 8000 units [equation (14.2)], and total demand at this price is 6542 units [equation (14.1)]. Equation (14.8) determines Allied's relative competitiveness at 38%, and the random number 85 (the first two digits in the upper-left-hand corner of Appendix A.1) simulates a consumer reaction favoring Norton with 70% of the market (see Table 14.3). Consequently, Norton sells approximately 4600 units for a profit of \$40,726, while Allied loses \$30,260 on sales of 1963. The results given in Table 14.4 and in all subsequent tables are calculated without rounding but are shown rounded to the nearest dollar or unit, except for the market price, which is rounded to the nearest cent.

The strategies of Allied and Norton now unfold. Allied has a large, unintended buildup in its inventory of over 1000 units and received only 30% of market sales. Due to losses during the first period, Allied's cash position is down to approximately \$220,000 from the original \$250,000. Allied needs to increase its market attractiveness and restore profitable operations.

Table 14.4 Simulation—First Month

	Allied		Norton
Initial Positions			
Cash	\$250,000		\$250,000
Inventory	500		500
Decisions (beginning of each period)			
Markup ratio	0.25		
Production quantity	3,000		3,000
Advertising	\$15,000		\$25,000
Outcomes			
Price on market		\$69.17	
Total market supply		8,000	
Total market demand		6,542	
Relative competitiveness	38%		
Random number		85	
Market share	30%		70%
Quantity sold	1,963		4,579
Revenue	\$135,740		\$316,726
Total cost	\$166,000		\$276,000
Profit	\$(30,260)		\$40,726
New Positions			
Cash	\$219,740		\$290,726
Inventory	1,538		921

By contrast, Norton has benefited from favorable market action during the first period and has sold nearly all it produced. The outlook here is good, and management should be inclined to continue this initial strong showing. Selecting a production level to meet market demand will be the primary decision-making consideration.

Allied's need to improve its situation prompts a decision to embark on an extensive advertising campaign. Expenditures of $45,000 are approved for this purpose. Considering the buildup in inventory, production is cut in half to 1500 units, and finally, to keep price as low as possible, the markup ratio is cut from 0.25 to 0.20. Norton chooses simply to continue with the same level of advertising and to produce 4000 units, expecting to sell from inventory if demand should exceed this amount.

To be sure, Allied's attractiveness (or relative competitiveness) improves, as can be seen in Table 14.5. But the Monte Carlo simulation of random market action continues to award only 30% of total market sales to Allied. As a result, Allied makes almost enough profit to restore

Table 14.5 Simulation—Second Month

	Allied		Norton
Initial Positions			
Cash	$219,740		$290,726
Inventory	1,538		921
Decisions (beginning at each period)			
Markup ratio	0.20		
Production quantity	1,500		4,000
Advertising	$45,000		$25,000
Outcomes			
Price on market		$96.80	
Total market supply		5,500	
Total market demand		5,160	
Relative competitiveness	46%		
Random number		18	
Market share	30%		70%
Quantity sold	1,548		3,612
Revenue	$149,846		$349,642
Total cost	$121,000		$226,000
Profit	$28,846		$123,642
New Positions			
Cash	$248,586		$414,367
Inventory	1,490		1,309

its initial cash balance of about $250,000. Slightly more than the quantity produced by Allied is sold, resulting in a minimal reduction of total inventory.

In the second period (Table 14.5), Norton continues to thrive. With 70% of market sales, Norton is the volume leader, and, due largely to increased market price, profits are three times those of the prior period. Norton's cash position increases to $414,367 and its inventory rises by approximately 400 units.

During the third and fourth periods (Tables 14.6 and 14.7), Allied persists with low production quantities and progressively larger advertising expenditures. The markup ratio continues to be reduced. But since production is low, unit costs increase and the market price continues to rise. Under these conditions, there are fewer production units contributing to covering fixed and advertising costs. Of course, total market demand drops off as price increases. This leads Norton to cut back on production, and, seeing how much more advertising there is

Table 14.6
Simulation—
Third Month

	Allied		Norton
Initial Positions			
Cash	$248,586		$414,367
Inventory	1,490		1,309
Decisions (beginning of each period)			
Markup ratio	0.18		
Production quantity	1,000		3,500
Advertising	$55,000		$35,000
Outcomes			
Price on market		$125.08	
Total market supply		4,500	
Total market demand		3,746	
Relative competitiveness	42%		
Random number		44	
Market share	30%		70%
Quantity sold	1,123		2,622
Revenue	$140,565		$327,985
Total cost	$106,000		$211,000
Profit	$34,565		$116,985
New Positions			
Cash	$283,151		$531,352
Inventory	1,366		2,187

Table 14.7
Simulation—
Fourth Month

	Allied		Norton
Initial Positions			
Cash	$283,151		$531,352
Inventory	1,366		2,187
Decisions (beginning of each period)			
Markup ratio	0.15		
Production quantity	1,000		1,500
Advertising	$60,000		$25,000
Outcomes			
Price on market		$127.65	
Total market supply		2,500	
Total market demand		3,618	
Relative competitiveness	55%		
Random number		22	
Market share	60%		40%
Quantity sold	2,171		1,447
Revenue	$277,064		$184,710
Total cost	$111,000		$101,000
Profit	$166,064		$83,710
New Positions			
Cash	$449,215		$615,062
Inventory	195		2,240

for Allied products, Norton increases its advertising in the third period.

Market outcomes continue to favor Norton until the fourth period, when Allied's increased competitiveness combines with the favorable market action to sell all of what Allied produced, together with most of its inventory. This fourth-period action yields a sizable profit for Allied ($166,064), and business suddenly looks very much better. Norton continues its profitable operations through these two periods but experiences a buildup of its inventory.

In practice, one would continue this simulation over many periods. Indeed, you should continue with this sequence of business operations, doing your own decision making and calculating the results. However, a number of basic decision-making concepts are demonstrated in only four periods. First, there is the inverse relationship between price and quantity demanded, which is fundamental to the decision-making process. Second, scheduling of production must combine the effects of a number of important factors, some of which are unpredictable—namely total market demand, market attractiveness through advertising and availability, market share, and inventory management. Third, one must be aware of the relationship between average per-unit costs (including fixed costs) and the quantity of production: large quantities greatly reduce per-unit costs. And finally, the decision maker must contend with random market actions that reflect hidden probability distributions and require judgmental formulation of strategies under conditions of uncertainty.

14.4 Summary

Simulation is an analytical approach that can reveal expected outcomes on the basis of complex system interrelationships. When we use simulation, we experiment with a reliable working model of the system under consideration and observe the reactions of the model to controlled conditions. Insofar as the model is a precise simulation of the real system, the results provide basic information that can be used in the efficient design or control of system elements. Thus simulation methods can be used as an aid in effective decision making.

The typical business use of simulation techniques is related to discrete, stochastics systems that are dynamic, or progress through time. Digital computers provide the necessary tool to operate simulation models and to repeat system operations over many hypothetical time periods. The usual ingredients of simulation models are mathematical equations to represent the way variables interact, a random-number generator, Monte Carlo simulation of discrete stochastic processes, and statistical specifications that may govern system action or summarize and evaluate results. Once system functions have been defined, inputs (including decisions) determine how the system acts. Fitting the pieces of a simulation model together requires intimate knowledge of system interrelationships and an ability to make all the specifications and select all the parameters that are necessary. Ultimately, the usefulness of these techniques lies in the analysis of records of system results, as shown in period-by-period listings and computed averages of important system characteristics.

This chapter has demonstrated the process of developing and implementing a simulation model. Simulation techniques have widespread applicability in a world where stochastic processes abound, and business analysts should be alert to spot and capitalize on situations where these techniques can be beneficially applied.

Exercises

14.1 Define or explain the following terms:
a. Simulation
b. Static versus dynamic models
c. Digital versus analog computers
d. Continuous versus discrete systems
e. Endogenous versus exogenous variables
f. Underdetermined versus overdetermined models

14.2 Explain how simulation techniques may be more appropriately applied to stochastic than to deterministic systems. Why do simulation models not necessarily seek optimal solutions to decision-making problems?

14.3 Give several examples of systems that could benefit from management's use of simulation models. In each case, explain how the simulation approach would be useful, and give your interpretation of the key variables, the inputs required, and the type of results expected.

14.4 Refer to the Allied–Norton duopoly model demonstrated in this chapter. Develop a detailed flow chart that diagrams the interconnection of system elements and shows the progression of inputs, decisions, and results from period to period.

14.5 On the basis of the flow chart you developed in exercise 14.4, develop a computer program or a set of instructions for a programmable desk calculator. Using your programmed model, simulate at least five more periods of competition between Allied and Norton, starting where the fourth period given in this chapter left off. Organize small groups of decision makers and use the model as the basis of decision-making competitions (in this case, start from scratch).

14.6 Having performed numerous periods of simulation with the Allied–Norton duopoly model, review your results to determine, if possible, any steady-state characteristics of the model. For example, do price, production, advertising, and profits tend to "home in" on any particular values?

14.7 P. J. Sutton, the famed stockbroker, feels that, in order to get better order execution for his customers, he needs a simulation of the way market prices move during the course of a day. He hypothesizes that prices randomly step to one side or the other from a prior trade. This suits the "random walk" theory postulated by leading economists who have analyzed price behavior in the stock market. Therefore, Sutton asks analysts to develop a simulation model that, on a day of increasing prices, starts with a stepping function biased to the down side of the opening price until the daily minimum is reached. Then the process reverses its bias to the up side until the maximum is reached. Finally, a reversal of probabilities takes place again, and the process finally ends at the closing price of the day. First, develop this stepping model for generally increasing prices. Then modify the model to allow the reverse process to occur on a day of decreasing prices. Set up the model on worksheets or a computer, and, using the following daily stock market price listings, simulate the action of prices for each open-high-low-close combination. List the stepping process and tally the number of steps required to complete a given day's price activity.

Day	Open	High	Low	Close
1	20	$22\frac{1}{8}$	$19\frac{5}{8}$	$21\frac{1}{2}$
2	$21\frac{1}{2}$	22	20	$20\frac{1}{2}$
3	$20\frac{1}{2}$	$21\frac{7}{8}$	$19\frac{7}{8}$	$21\frac{5}{8}$
4	$21\frac{5}{8}$	$22\frac{3}{4}$	$20\frac{1}{2}$	$22\frac{1}{4}$
5	$22\frac{1}{4}$	$22\frac{1}{2}$	20	$20\frac{7}{8}$
6	$20\frac{7}{8}$	$23\frac{5}{8}$	$20\frac{7}{8}$	23
7	23	$24\frac{3}{8}$	$22\frac{3}{4}$	$24\frac{3}{8}$
8	$24\frac{3}{8}$	$24\frac{5}{8}$	$23\frac{1}{8}$	$23\frac{7}{8}$
9	$23\frac{7}{8}$	25	$22\frac{3}{4}$	$23\frac{1}{8}$
10	$23\frac{1}{8}$	$25\frac{1}{2}$	23	25

The stepping function should move in increments of one-eighth of a point at a time. Use probabilities of 60% and 40% to create upward or downward bias, as required. Does this simulation reveal common characteristics that could be useful for trading purposes? On the basis of this analysis, what results, evaluations, or recommendations should be forwarded to Sutton?

14.8 A campus dormitory provides cafeteria service during normal meal hours. Students arrive randomly and are served food in either one or two lines, according to the conditions. Students routinely enter the first cafeteria line and then are allowed to move to a second, parallel service line if it is open. The second line is set to open when waiting builds up to 10 or more students. The second line is allowed to close again only when the first line is moving with no waiting for service, and it does not then reopen during this meal time. Simulate cafeteria operations hours on the basis of the following distribution of arrivals:

Number of Arrivals in One Minute	Probability
0	.10
1	.25
2	.30
3	.25
4 or more	.10

The time required co serve at the key station—hot foods—determines the amount of waiting (there is no cash checkout; students pay in advance for a semester's meal service), and this distribution is as follows:

Time Spent Being Served	Probability
$\frac{1}{4}$ minute or less	.15
$\frac{1}{4}$ to $\frac{1}{2}$ minute	.45
$\frac{1}{2}$ to $\frac{3}{4}$ minute	.25
$\frac{3}{4}$ to 1 minute	.10
1 minute or more	.05

Simulate this queuing system over a period of 2 hours and determine its average characteristics. Does the rule of thumb, 10 or more students waiting before opening the second line, seem realistic? Is there a better alternative? If so, what does the simulation analysis indicate?

14.9 Develop a simulation model for the operation of any multielevator facility of your choice. Determine adequacies or inadequacies of operation. Make your model as realistic as possible. What recommendations would you make about the operation of this facility? What average characteristics does it have that involve the elevator rider?

14.10 Use the data given in Table 14.1 as your basis for a simulation of traffic flow in the one direction indicated through a traffic light. Set up a process of arrivals that varies randomly according to each of the following assumptions and, on the basis of simulation results, describe how the traffic pattern works for each assumption.

Number of Cars Arriving During Each Traffic Light Cycle	Probabilities Based on Assumption I	II	III
5 or fewer	.10	0	0
6	.25	.10	0
7	.30	.25	.10
8	.25	.30	.25
9	.10	.25	.30
10	0	.10	.25
11 or more	0	0	.10

Suggested Readings

Brenner, M. E. "Selective Sampling—A Technique for Reducing Sample Size in Simulation for Decision-Making Problems." *Journal of Industrial Engineering*, 14, No. 6 (1963), 291–296.

Clark, Robert M., and James I. Gillean. "Analysis of Solid Waste Management Operations in Cleveland, Ohio: A Case Study." *Interfaces*, 6, No. 1, Pt. 2 (November 1975), 32–42.

Emshoff, J. R., and R. L. Sisson. *Design and Use of Computer Simulation Models*. New York: Macmillan, 1970.

Evans, G. W., G. F. Wallace, and G. L. Sutherland. *Simulation Using Digital Computers*. Englewood Cliffs, N.J.: Prentice-Hall, 1967.

Gitlow, H. S. "A Methodology for Determining the Optimal Design of a Free Standing Abortion Clinic." *Management Science*, 22, No. 12 (August 1976), pp. 1289–1298.

Godin, V. B. "The Dollars and Sense of Simulation." *Decision Sciences*, 7, No. 2 (April 1976), pp. 331–342.

Hertz, D. B. "Risk Analysis in Capital Investment." *Harvard Business Review* (January–February 1964).

Hess, Sidney W. "Design and Implementation of a New Check-Clearing System for the Philadelphia Federal District." *Interfaces*, 5, No. 2, Pt. 2 (February 1975), 22–36.

Holgman, A. G., and D. B. Johnson. "A Simulation Model of the College Admission Process." *Interfaces*, 5, No. 3 (May 1975), pp. 55–64.

Hsiao, J. C. "The Learning Effectiveness of Micoeconomics Simulation." *Education*, 95 (Spring 1975), pp. 270–275.

IBM Corporation. *Bibliography on Simulation*. White Plains, N.Y.: IBM Corporation, 1966.

King, W. R. "Methodological Simulation in Marketing." *Journal of Marketing*, 34 (April 1970), pp. 8–13.

Maisel, H., and G. Gnugnoli. *Simulation of Discrete Stochastic Systems*. Chicago, Ill.: Science Research Associates, 1972.

Meier, R. C., W. T. Newell, and H. L. Pazer. *Simulation in Business and Economics*. Englewood Cliffs, N.J.: Prentice-Hall, 1969.
Naylor, T. H. *Computer Simulation Experiments with Models of Economic Systems*. New York: Wiley, 1971.
———, J. L. Balintfy, D. S. Burdick, and K. Chu. *Computer Simulation Techniques*. New York: Wiley, 1966.
Philippakis, A. S. "A Simulation Study of Decentralized Decision Making." *Decision Sciences*, 3, No. 1 (January 1972), pp. 59–72.
Schmidt, J. W., and R. E. Taylor. *Simulation Analysis of Industrial Systems*. Homewood, Ill.: Irwin, 1970.
Schriber, Thomas J. *Simulation Using GPSS*. New York: Wiley, 1974.
Shannon, Robert E. *Systems Simulation: The Art and Science*. Englewood Cliffs, N.J.: Prentice-Hall, 1975.
Wagner, Harvey M. *Principles of Operations Research*, 2nd ed. Englewood Cliffs, N.J.: Prentice-Hall, 1975.
Wiest, J. D. "A Heuristic Model for Scheduling Large Projects With Limited Resources." *Management Science*, 13, No. 6 (February 1967), pp. 359–377.

15

Game Theory: Decision Making Under Conflict

Game theory is concerned with a type of decision problem characterized by conflict or competition among different decision makers. The linear optimization models that we studied in Chapters 2 through 8 involve a decision maker or an organization with a well-defined goal of maximizing profit or minimizing cost. In such models, it is assumed that the decision maker is in complete control of all relevant factors pertaining to the problem. However, if the decision problem is one in which there are individuals or groups with diverging interests, an optimal solution for one may be far from optimal for another. The outcome resulting from a decision made by one individual depends not only on that individual's choice, but also on the course of action taken by other interested parties. In a decision problem under conflict, a decision maker is not interested only in what she or he is doing as an individual, but also in what her or his opponent is doing, and vice versa.

Game theory clarifies the basic characteristics of competitive situations. Using it, one can analyze and develop rules and procedures for decision makers who must face other decision makers with conflicting goals. The basic concepts of game theory were originally presented in von Neumann and Morgenstern's monumental work, *The Theory of Games and Economic Behavior.*[1]

[1]J. von Neumann and O. Morgenstern, *The Theory of Games and Economic Behavior*, 3rd ed. (Princeton, N.J.: Princeton University Press, 1953).

15.1 Two-Person, Zero-Sum Games

This chapter is primarily concerned with ***two-person, zero-sum games.*** As the name implies, this simplest of cases involves two competitors who are vying for a common, fixed source of reward. Depending on the situation, the reward might be market share, prize money, or some other winnings. The implementation of decision strategies governs the gains or losses incurred. Considering the conflicting situation and the fixed source of reward, one competitor's gain must be another's loss, and vice versa.

Union–Management Bargaining

Consider a management–union conflict in which a new contract is being drafted because the active one expires next month. The actions taken by representatives from either side will ultimately dictate the outcome of the negotiations. Consequently, the selection of representatives for both sides is of paramount importance. After years of bargaining, the management group has arrived at a predetermined set of alternative courses of action, or ***strategies,*** based on the types of negotiations to be used. These strategies can be specified as M_1, M_2 M_3, and M_4, where

M_1 = an innovative company man

M_2 = a conservative and hard-line company man

M_3 = a company woman who uses a restrained and analytical approach

M_4 = a conciliatory company man who tries to bring all parties together

Because management does not know the thrust of the union team of negotiators, its strategy is not easy to determine. The union, like management, has a set of selected representatives or strategies to employ in the negotiation process. They can be specified as U_1, U_2, U_3, and U_4, where

U_1 = an innovative union man

U_2 = a conservative and hard-line union man

U_3 = a union woman who uses a restrained and analytical approach

U_4 = a conciliatory union man who tries to bring all parties together

What wage-rate increment (in cents per hour) can the union achieve? The answer depends not only on which individual or strategy the union chooses to emphasize but also on management's chosen strategy. Essential to this type of situation is the fact that neither the company nor the union knows in advance what type of individual (strategy) the opposition will choose. Furthermore, once the representatives of both sides are selected and appear at the bargaining table, neither side can alter its original choice.

Payoff Matrix In such a management–union conflict, each side has four strategies or courses of action at its disposal. The total number of possible outcomes is therefore 16 (4 × 4). These outcomes are illustrated in Table 15.1. This rectangular table, which shows the outcomes of a game as the players implement their particular strategies, is known as the ***payoff matrix.***

To read the payoff matrix, let us consider one pair of strategies. If the union selects strategy U_1 (an innovative union man) and management chooses strategy M_2 (a conservative and hard-line company man), the contract will include a 5¢-per-hour increase in wages. This amount is the labor union's payoff. If management chooses strategy M_1 in response to U_1, the union's payoff is even better—a 10¢ increase in hourly wages. However, if management adopts strategy M_3 (a woman who uses a restrained and analytical approach) against U_1, the union's payoff is nothing!

Since, in a zero-sum game, gain for one player (union) spells loss for the other (management), it is customary to record the payoff matrix for only one player (union). There is no need to record the opposition's payoff.

In the general case for games with two players, we assume that the number of strategies for each player is infinite. The payoff may be described in a matrix with m rows and n columns, where m and n

Table 15.1
Payoff Matrix

		Management Strategies				
		M_1	M_2	M_3	M_4	**Row Minima**
	U_1	10¢	5¢	0¢	1¢	0
Union	U_2	11	4	2	3	2
Strategies	U_3	9	(6)	7	8	6 ← maximin
	U_4	4	5	5	7	4
Column Maxima:		11	6 ↑ minimax	7	8	

Table 15.2
Payoff Matrix in the General Case

		B's Strategies			
		B_1	B_2	$\cdots$	B_n
A's Strategies	A_1	a_{11}	a_{12}	$\cdots$	a_{1n}
	A_2	a_{21}	a_{22}	$\cdots$	a_{2n}
	$\cdot$	$\cdot$	$\cdot$		$\cdot$
	$\cdot$	$\cdot$	$\cdot$		$\cdot$
	$\cdot$	$\cdot$	$\cdot$		$\cdot$
	A_m	a_{m1}	a_{m2}		a_{mn}

represent the finite number of strategies available to the two players. (See Table 15.2.)

By convention, the rows denote player A's strategies and the columns denote player B's strategies. Then the elements a_{ij} (for $i = 1, 2, \ldots, m$; $j = 1, 2, \ldots, n$) represent the payments to player A by player B for any combination of strategies. Thus the entries a_{ij} show that, if A chooses strategy A_i, and B chooses strategy B_j, then A's payoff made by B is the amount a_{ij}. Each round of the game consists of a simultaneous choice of strategy A_i by player A and strategy B_j by player B. The payoff is then equal to a_{ij} for player A. Of course, the payment made to B must be $-a_{ij}$.

15.2 Pure Strategies: Games with Saddle Points

Even given the information of the payoff matrix, the final solution of the game is still unknown to both players. How to select the best strategy for each player without knowledge of the opponent's strategy is the basic problem of game theory. In the established theory, both players are assumed to be cautious, or risk averters. Given this premise, player A will naturally act in such a way that his or her possible gain is ***at least*** equal to the highest payoff among all the ***least gains*** possible. For this reason, player A is called the ***maximizer***. Player B, in turn, will act so as to make his or her loss (that is, the gain to player A) equal to the lowest among all the ***highest losses*** possible. For this reason, player B is called the ***minimizer***.

Maximin and Minimax Strategies

To further analyze the solution of two-person, zero-sum games, we should examine the reasoning behind the play of the game in the management–labor problem. The first row in Table 15.1 shows that, if the union chooses strategy U_1, management should select strategy M_3. Management reasons that this choice would reduce the union's payoff to its minimal wage increment, 0¢. In Table 15.1 this minimum payoff (or least value) of the first row is written on the extreme right-hand side of the matrix, beneath the heading Row Minima. Similarly, if the union selects U_2, management should adopt M_3 to minimize the union's payoff (2¢). Again, this figure is entered in Table 15.1 as the Row Minima value (or lower value) corresponding to row U_2. When we repeat this reasoning for U_3 and U_4, we find that the corresponding minimal payoff levels are 6¢ and 4¢, respectively, which are recorded in the Row Minima column.

Thus the minimal value in each row represents the least payoff guaranteed to the union if a particular strategy is chosen. All of these values are represented in Table 15.1 under Row Minima. Referring to Table 15.1, one can see that the union will maximize its minimal payoff by choosing strategy U_3. The union's decision rule—seeking the maximum among these minimal gains (or lower values)—is therefore called the ***maximin strategy.*** Management, on the other hand, likes to minimize its losses. If it chooses its first strategy, M_1, the maximal loss to the company is 11¢ (in the first column) if the union selects strategy U_2. Similarly, the maximal losses corresponding to strategies M_2, M_3, and M_4 (the highest figure in each column) are indicated in Table 15.1 as Column Maxima (or upper values). Clearly, the company is trying to minimize its maximal losses. This value is 6¢, corresponding to company strategy M_2 in the Column Maxima row of Table 15.1. The management decision rule—seeking the minimum among these maximal losses (or upper values)—is therefore called the ***minimax strategy.***

Saddle-Point Solution

In the management–union example, the solution occurs when each party chooses its own optimal strategy: the union selects strategy U_3 and management selects strategy M_2. Consequently, the solution or ***value of the game*** is 6¢. It is important to note that the union's guaranteed payoff from its maximin strategy, U_3, is exactly the same as the value that management expects the union to receive when management plays its minimax strategy M_2. The circled entry in Table 15.1, which indicates both the maximum of the row minima and the minimum of the column maxima, is referred to as a ***saddle point.*** This is because it is a maximum from one player's point of view (union), and a minimum from the other player's point of view (management). The saddle point represents the equilibrium solution of the game in the sense that, once this point is reached, neither player is tempted to change strategies. Clearly, playing the game repeatedly would result in each player always choosing the same strategy. In such a situation, with optimal strategy choices and a saddle point, the strategies are known as ***pure strategies.***

Let's summarize. In a general two-person (A and B), zero-sum game, the procedures for finding a saddle-point solution, if it exists, are as follows:

1. For each row, list the minimal entry[2] under the Row Minima column and mark the maximum among the minimal values with an arrow. This establishes the maximin strategy for player A.
2. For each column, list the maximal entry[2] under the Column Maxima row and mark the minimum among the maximal values with an arrow. This establishes the minimax strategy for player B.
3. If the circled element derived from step (1) is equal to that of step (2)—more specifically, if the maximin (lower) value equals the minimax (upper) value—the value of the game (where the corresponding row and column intersect) defines the saddle point. This solution is referred to as a minimax or maximin solution. It yields the optimal strategy for the game.
4. If the first two steps result in different entries (unequal elements), the payoff matrix contains no saddle point. The value of the game falls in the range of the upper value (minimax) and the lower value (maximin). That is,

$$\text{Maximin (lower) value} \leq \text{value of the game} \leq \text{minimax (upper) value}$$

This game contains no saddle point, because the minimax value is greater than the value of the maximin. It follows that neither player can use a pure strategy as his or her optimal choice. The value of the game may be improved by selecting a combination of strategies. We will discuss this procedure in Section 15.3.

Dominance The concept of dominance allows us to reduce the dimension of a larger game by carefully eliminating certain rows and/or columns. Consider, for example, a 2 × 3 game characterized by the payoff matrix given in Table 15.3.

Note that every element of row A_1 (strategy 1 for player A) is greater than every element of row A_2 (strategy 2 for player A). It would be

[2]If the smallest entry is not unique, write all equal values.

Table 15.3
Payoff Matrix

		Player B		
		B_1	B_2	B_3
Player A	A_1	8	3	4
	A_2	−7	−2	2

unwise for player A to adopt strategy A_2 if strategy A_1 is available. Thus, A_1 is a ***preferred*** strategy and is said to ***dominate*** A_2, which is an ***inferior*** strategy. A_2 will not be played and is therefore discarded from further consideration with no effect on the optimal strategies of the players or the solution value of the game.

After the elimination of row A_2, the reduced matrix is

$$\begin{bmatrix} 8 & 3 & 4 \end{bmatrix}$$

which indicates that there is only one strategy for player A. The optimal strategy for player B is to select column B_2 (strategy 2), which minimizes player B's losses. Thus the solution value of the game is 3.

Consider next the payoff matrix shown in Table 15.4, which represents a two-person, zero-sum game. Using the maximin and minimax principle already developed, the reader can verify the saddle-point solution, which is illustrated by the arrows. The optimal strategy for player A is to select strategy A_2, whereas the optimal strategy for player B is to adopt strategy B_2. Thus the value of the game is 6.

A search for dominance shows that A_2 dominates A_3, so A_3 can be discarded. Domination can also occur among columns. Note that every entry in the B_1 column is higher than the corresponding entry in column B_2. Strategy B_1 is dominated by strategy B_2 (from player B's viewpoint).

Table 15.4
Payoff Matrix with the Saddle-Point Solution

		Player B			
		B_1	B_2	B_3	**Row Minima**
	A_1	10	5	4	4
Player A	A_2	9	(6)	7	6 ←
	A_3	8	4	1	1
Column Maxima:		10	6	7	
			↑		

Table 15.5
Reduced Payoff Matrix

	Player B		Row Minima
Player A	5	4	4
	(6)	7	6 ←
Column Maxima:	6	7	
	↑		

Clearly, then, player B should never choose strategy B_1, and this strategy should be removed from further consideration.

After the elimination of row A_3 and column B_1, the original payoff matrix is reduced as shown in Table 15.5. Note that the saddle-point solution indicated by the circled value 6 and the optimal strategies for both players remain unaffected.

15.3 Mixed Strategies: Games without Saddle Points

Mixed Strategies Consider the union–management problem again. Suppose that in the contract negotiations the leadership of the union has only two strategies—an innovative approach U_1 and a conservative, hard-line approach U_2. Company management is considering the same two alternative strategies, M_1 and M_2. Let the simple 2 × 2 payoff matrix for the union be as shown in Table 15.6.

By the criterion of maximin (pure) strategy, the union should stick with strategy U_2, for which a payoff of 3¢ is guaranteed. Management, on the other hand, will adopt the minimax strategy M_1. This pure strategy guarantees that the union will have a payoff no larger than 5¢. However, the maximin and minimax payoffs do not coincide in the same payoff entry. Hence, the game does not have a saddle point and union

Table 15.6
Payoff Matrix without Saddle Point

		Management M_1	Management M_2	Row Minima
Union	U_1	(5)	2	2
	U_2	(3)	9	3 ← maximin
Column Maxima:		5	9	
		↑ minimax		

and management cannot use maximin–minimax strategies as their best strategies. Why? When one player persists with the same pure strategy, this persistence is equivalent to revealing that player's chosen strategy to the opponent. For example, if the union knows that management is *certain* to stay with M_1 (according to management's minimax principle), the union should adopt U_1 (not U_2) as a counterstrategy to improve the union's payoff from 3¢ to 5¢. On the other hand, if management is convinced that the union will employ U_1 (nonmaximin criterion), management will choose strategy M_2 as its counterstrategy, thereby cutting the union's payoff from 5¢ to 2¢! In the absence of a saddle point, the game clearly lacks an equilibrium pair of strategies. Both players face a situation wherein "He knows that I know that he knows." The kind of strategy (maximin or nonmaximin) that the union will use depends on what kind of strategy management will employ, and vice versa.

Facing the problem of uncertainty, a player should keep the opponent in doubt. Even though the union would like to select a particular, pure strategy that would maximize its wage gains for the coming contract period, it appears to be of greater importance for the union to select a set of strategies that will allow it to maximize its wage gain in the long run. In other words, where there is no saddle point, the optimal strategy for the union is to keep the opposition guessing. Thus the union would not use a pure maximin strategy but would implement a set of strategies chosen randomly according to some probability distribution imposed on each particular pure strategy (U_1 and U_2). This process is referred to as a ***mixed strategy.***

With a policy of mixed strategies, the union will choose either one of the two strategies *randomly*. One way is to toss a balanced coin, adopting U_1 if it lands heads and U_2 if tails. The expected value of a mixed strategy is a probabilistic combination of the two strategies. For example, suppose that there are more conservative and hard-line union members U_2, who usually get their way 30 times out of 40 ($\frac{3}{4}$ of the time) and that the innovative members U_1, who can speak well, are real firebrands and get their way 10 times out of 40 ($\frac{1}{4}$ of the time). Consequently, in a particular mixture of this problem, the relative frequency of having U_1 and that of having U_2 for the union in the long run are $\frac{1}{4}$ and $\frac{3}{4}$, respectively. If management adopts M_1, the expected payoff E in a probability sense for the union is the weighted average

$$\tfrac{1}{4}\,(5¢) + \tfrac{3}{4}\,(3¢) = 3.5¢$$

If management is assumed to use M_2, the union's expected payoff is

$$\tfrac{1}{4}\,(2¢) + \tfrac{3}{4}\,(9¢) = 7.25¢$$

Note that either one of these two outcomes is greater than 3¢, which is guaranteed by the pure and predeterministic maximin strategy. By using the mixed strategy and keeping the opponent guessing, the union has been able to improve its payoff from 3¢ to 3.5¢, regardless of which strategy management uses.

Graphical Solution Note that the specific pair of probability values $(\frac{1}{4}, \frac{3}{4})$ in the foregoing example are ***arbitrarily*** chosen. Because there are an infinite number of probability values (from 0 to 1) available to a player, the real issue becomes selecting probabilities to go with the strategies. In our 2 × 2 union–management example, let X_1 and X_2 be the probabilities that the union assigns to each of the randomly chosen strategies. Needless to say, the sum of these probabilities must be 1 (that is, $X_1 + X_2 = 1$). The goal is to determine the optimal values of X_1 and X_2—union's best randomly mixed strategies. Thus, if management selects M_1, the union's expected payoff E_1 is

$$E_1 = 5X_1 + 3X_2$$

And, if management selects M_2, the union's expected payoff E_2 is

$$E_2 = 2X_1 + 9X_2$$

Since $X_1 + X_2 = 1$, substituting $(1 - X_1)$ for X_2 yields

$$\begin{aligned} E_1 &= 5X_1 + 3(1 - X_1) \quad \text{or} \quad E_1 = 2X_1 + 3 \\ E_2 &= 2X_1 + 9(1 - X_1) \quad \text{or} \quad E_2 = -7X_1 + 9 \end{aligned} \tag{15.1}$$

Both E_1 and E_2 are linear functions of X_1, and we can easily plot these two equations (Figure 15.1). Figure 15.1 clearly indicates that the union's expected payoff depends on which strategy management selects. At the point where the two lines intersect, the payoff is the same for the union no matter which counterstrategy management uses. We find this unique payoff by setting E_1 equal to E_2 and solving for X_1.

$$2X_1 + 3 = -7X_1 + 9$$

$$\therefore \overline{X}_1 = \tfrac{2}{3}$$

and

$$\overline{X}_2 = 1 - \tfrac{2}{3} = \tfrac{1}{3}$$

Figure 15.1
Plotting the Two Payoff Equations

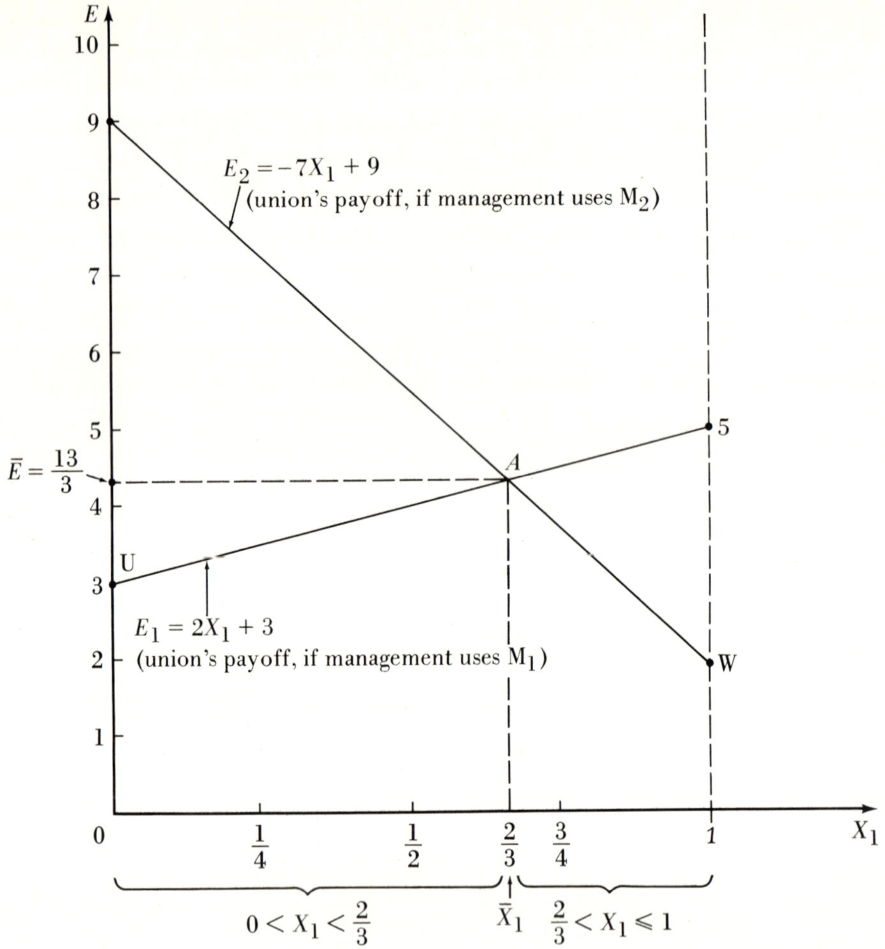

Then, using the solution $\overline{X}_1$ in the equation for E_1 (or E_2) in (15.1), we have

$$\overline{E} = 2(\tfrac{2}{3}) + 3 = \tfrac{13}{3}¢$$

The solutions for $\overline{X}_1$ and $\overline{E}$ are both shown in Figure 15.1. A perceptive reader may ask, "Is the solution $\overline{E}$ the optimal payoff for the union?" The following analysis focuses on this question.

For $0 < X_1 < \frac{2}{3}$ in Figure 15.1, the union's expected payoff E_1 is lower than E_2, and management reasons that it should select strategy M_1. For $\frac{2}{3} < X_1 \leq 1$, the union's expected payoff E_2 is lower than E_1, so management should adopt strategy M_2. The kinked curve *UAW* delineates all the possible lower (secured) expected payoffs for the union. Using the principle of maximin, the union should choose the maximum among all the minimal expected payoffs. This optimal value, the solution of the game, occurs at $\overline{E} = \frac{13}{3}$ when $\overline{X}_1 = \frac{2}{3}$.

Given the simple union–management problem, what is the best mixed strategy for management? Guided by the minimax principle, management should also select a pair of probabilities, Y_1 and Y_2, for its strategies such that it will minimize the maximum expected payoffs to the union (expected losses to management). Thus, if the union picks strategy U_1, management's expected loss (L_1) is

$$L_1 = 5Y_1 + 2Y_2$$

Similarly, if the union picks strategy U_2, management's expected loss (L_2) is

$$L_2 = 3(Y_1) + 9(Y_2)$$

Since $$Y_1 + Y_2 = 1 \quad \text{or} \quad Y_2 = 1 - Y_1$$

then $$\begin{aligned} L_1 &= 3Y_1 + 2 \\ L_2 &= -6Y_1 + 9 \end{aligned} \qquad (15.2)$$

Next the two equations can be graphed as linear functions of Y_1, as shown in Figure 15.2. To solve for Y_1, equate the two equations:

$$3Y_1 + 2 = -6Y_1 + 9$$

$$\therefore \overline{Y}_1 = \frac{7}{9}$$

It follows that

$$\overline{Y}_2 = 1 - \frac{7}{9} = \frac{2}{9}$$

Substituting $\overline{Y}_1$ into L_1 (or L_2) of equation (15.2), we find that management's expected loss is

$$\overline{L} = 3(\tfrac{7}{9}) + 2 = \tfrac{13}{3}¢$$

One should note that the kinked curve *SFK* in Figure 15.2 delineates the set of all possible expected losses for management (or all maximum expected payoffs to the union). For $0 < Y_1 < \frac{7}{9}$, the maximum expected loss to management is *SF*, when the union adopts U_2. For $\frac{7}{9} < Y_1 \leq 1$, management's maximum loss is *FK*, when the union picks U_1. Guided by the principle of minimax, management must pick the set of mixed strategies that will result in the minimum loss among all the maximums. This unique solution occurs at point *F*, where management adopts the

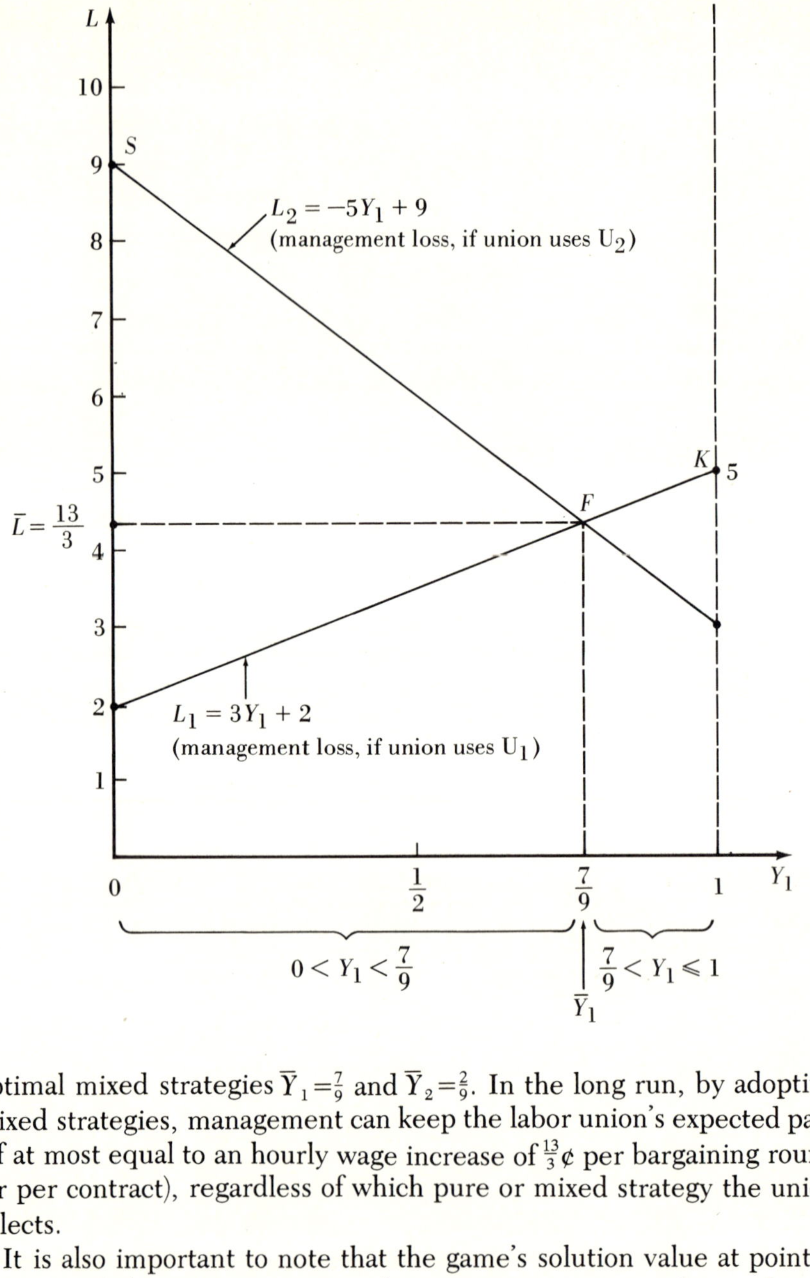

Figure 15.2 Plotting the Two Loss Equations

optimal mixed strategies $\bar{Y}_1 = \frac{7}{9}$ and $\bar{Y}_2 = \frac{2}{9}$. In the long run, by adopting mixed strategies, management can keep the labor union's expected payoff at most equal to an hourly wage increase of $\frac{13}{3}$¢ per bargaining round (or per contract), regardless of which pure or mixed strategy the union selects.

It is also important to note that the game's solution value at point *F* (Figure 15.2) using management's minimax criterion and its solution value at point A (Figure 15.1) using the union's maximin criterion are exactly the same: $\frac{13}{3}$¢! This is true even when there is no saddle point. This observation reveals the fundamental theorem of modern game theory. ***For any zero-sum, two-person game, there exists an equilibrium solution at which the values of the maximin expected payoff and the***

minimax expected payoff are equal to each other. This fundamental theorem was originally proved by J. von Neumann, the founder of modern game theory.

15.4 Optimal Mixed Strategies Using Linear Programming

Transforming the Game into a Linear Programming Problem

So far, the graphical solution we have examined is confined to only two strategies or two courses of action. For a game with strategies of more than two dimensions, we must free ourselves from the graphical method. Fortunately, linear programming and the basic theory of games are intimately related. Solving a game with $m \times n$ dimensions is mathematically equivalent to solving a linear programming problem. We will first show how the 2×2 game is transformed into a linear programming problem. Then the conversion of a game with $m \times n$ dimensions will be demonstrated in a straightforward manner.

Returning to the payoff matrix given in Table 15.6, let X_1 and X_2 be the probabilities assigned to union strategies U_1 and U_2, respectively. Since both union and management are cautious, they assume the worst and act accordingly. The union's payoff is secured at a minimum level E when management uses its various strategies. In light of Table 15.6, the expected payoff (E) to the union is at least E when management uses strategy M_1. That is,

$$5X_1 + 3X_2 \geq E$$

Similarly, when management adopts M_2, the union's minimum payoff is at least E; that is,

$$2X_1 + 9X_2 \geq E$$

By the maximin criterion, the union's goal is to find the maximum among these minimum expected payoffs. Therefore, the union's linear programming model is formulated as follows:

$$\text{Max } E$$

subject to

$$\begin{aligned} &\text{(a)} \quad 5X_1 + 3X_2 \geq E \\ &\text{(b)} \quad 2X_1 + 9X_2 \geq E \qquad (15.3) \\ &\text{(c)} \quad X_1 + X_2 = 1 \end{aligned}$$

and

$$\text{(d)} \quad X_1 \geq 0,\ X_2 \geq 0,\ E \geq 0$$

Constraints (a) and (b) in system (15.3) state that, regardless of what strategy management uses, the union's payoff must be at least E. Since X_1 and X_2 are probabilities, their sum must equal 1 and neither can be negative, as required by constraints (c) and (d), respectively.

What is the sign of the variable E? The standard simplex method of linear programming requires all variables to be nonnegative. In this union–management example, all of the payoff values are positive, so the expected payoff E must be nonnegative.

If the payoff matrix contains one or more negative elements, we have to add a suitable constant k to all entries a_{ij} in the payoff table such that the resulting table contains all nonnegative entries. It is convenient to let the value of k be determined by the absolute value of the smallest entry. Then, in interpreting the solution, we subtract the constant k from the final value of the game to recover the true value of E.

Consider, for example, the payoff matrix

$$\begin{bmatrix} -8 & -5 \\ -4 & -3 \end{bmatrix}$$

By adding a constant 8 (the smallest entry), we transform this matrix into

$$\begin{bmatrix} 0 & 3 \\ 4 & 5 \end{bmatrix}$$

which contains all nonnegative entries. Note that this transformation has no effect on the optimal strategies. The only adjustment necessary is that the constant 8 be subtracted from the final solution of the game.

Finally, the objective function in system (15.3) states that the union's program objective is to determine the values of the variables X_1 and X_2 such that the minimum expected payoff E is a maximum, subject to constraints (a)–(d). By defining $Z \equiv E$, we can rewrite the objective function in system (15.3) in the customary form:

$$\text{Max} \quad Z = 0X_1 + 0X_2 + E$$

To apply the simplex method, we must make a minor modification. The problem specified in system (15.3) is rewritten as

$$\text{Max} \quad Z = 0X_1 + 0X_2 + E$$

subject to

$$\begin{aligned}
&(a') \quad -5X_1 - 3X_2 + E \leq 0 \\
&(b') \quad -2X_1 - 9X_2 + E \leq 0 \\
&(c') \quad X_1 + X_2 \leq 1
\end{aligned} \qquad (15.3')$$

and

$$(d) \quad X_1 \geq 0, X_2 \geq 0, E \geq 0$$

Note that, by multiplying by -1 in constraints (a) and (b) of system (15.3), we have reversed the direction of inequality. Also, constraint (c) in system (15.3) has been changed from an equal-to to a less-than-or-equal-to relationship. This conversion is justified so long as the expected value E is positive. We lose no generality by assuming that all payoff elements are positive. If one or more of these entries is negative, we can use the transformation introduced earlier by adding an appropriate constant to all of the entries to make all the payoff elements nonnegative. This does not affect the optimal strategies. Granting the expected payoff to be positive, whether or not this arises from the addition of some constant k to the original payoff matrix, the labor union would certainly not forfeit any opportunity to play the game. That is, it would play each time that the opportunity is granted. If so, the ***effective*** constraint is $X_1 + X_2 = 1$. On the other hand, the constraint may be $X_1 + X_2 < 1$ instead if one player chooses not to use up all the available opportunities in the game. If $E = 0$, neither case $X_1 + X_2 = 1$ nor case $X_1 + X_2 < 1$ makes any difference.

The union's problem can now be seen as a standard linear programming maximization problem that can be solved by the simplex method we discussed in Chapter 3!

The Simplex Solution

Slack variables—S_1, S_2, and S_3—are added to the foregoing system to convert the inequalities in system (15.3′) into equalities. The simplex method is now fully applicable with the ready-made IBFS shown in tableau I of Table 15.7. Proceeding with the simplex calculation, we select column E, with the most negative value (indeed the only one), as the pivot column. Degeneracy now arises, because in attempting to identify the pivot row, we found two equal and minimum ratios, each zero, in rows 1 and 2. To break the tie, we arbitrarily displace the basic variable with the leftmost entry in the simplex tableau (S_1 in this case). Consequently, the entry at the intersection of row 1 and column E is circled as the pivot element, and the current basic variable S_1 is converted into a nonbasic variable in the next simplex tableau (tableau II). Through pivoting procedures, column E is converted into a unit column in the next tableau (tableau II), with a unit coefficient in row 1 and zeros

Table 15.7

Tableau	Row	Z	X_1	X_2	E	S_1	S_2	S_3	RHS
	1	0	−5	−3	(1)	1	0	0	0
I	2	0	−2	−9	1	0	1	0	0
	3	0	1	1	0	0	0	1	1
	0	1	0	0	−1	0	0	0	[0]
	1	0	−5	−3	1	1	0	0	0
II	2	0	(3)	−6	0	−1	1	0	0
	3	0	1	1	0	0	0	1	1
		1	−5	−3	0	1	0	0	[0]
	1	0	0	−13	1	$-\frac{2}{3}$	$\frac{5}{3}$	0	0
III	2	0	1	−2	0	$-\frac{1}{3}$	$\frac{1}{3}$	0	0
	3	0	0	(3)	0	$\frac{1}{3}$	$-\frac{1}{3}$	1	1
	0	1	0	−13	0	$-\frac{2}{3}$	$\frac{5}{3}$	0	[0]
	1	0	0	0	1	$\frac{7}{9}$	$\frac{2}{9}$	$\frac{13}{3}$	$\frac{13}{3}$
IV	2	0	1	0	0	$-\frac{1}{9}$	$\frac{1}{9}$	$\frac{2}{3}$	$\frac{2}{3}$
	3	0	0	1	0	$\frac{1}{9}$	$\frac{1}{9}$	$\frac{1}{3}$	$\frac{1}{3}$
	0	1	0	0	0	$\frac{7}{9}$	$\frac{2}{9}$	$\frac{13}{3}$	[$\frac{13}{3}$]

elsewhere. Through two more straightforward applications of the simplex algorithm, we reach an optimal solution in tableau IV. Due to degeneracy, the tableaux resulting from pivoting in tableaux II and III both fail to make any improvement in the value of the objective function until the final tableau (tableau IV).

The optimal solution for the union's problem, yielded by the simplex method as shown in tableau IV, is

$$\overline{X}_1 = \tfrac{2}{3}$$

$$\overline{X}_2 = \tfrac{1}{3}$$

$$\overline{E} \equiv \overline{Z} = \tfrac{13}{3} \qquad \text{(by the definition of the objective function)}$$

This means that the union's optimal strategy is $(\frac{2}{3}, \frac{1}{3})$ and that the associated expected payoff to the union is $\frac{13}{3}$. Clearly, the linear programming solution is exactly the same as the graphical solution. These results verify the maximin principle that the union pursues in this problem.

The Dual Linear Program of a Game and Its Economic Interpretation

Chapter 4 pointed out that every linear programming problem has two representations—a primal and a dual. If the union's problem is a primal, it is interesting to ask whether the dual program can be interpreted in terms of management's real situation. The answer is yes. In fact, the associated dual program yields management's minimax loss principle (the least among all possible maximal payoffs to management).

Let Y_1 and Y_2 be the probabilities of the mixed strategies for management, and let L be the expected loss. Given the union's primal problem specified by system (15.3′), we can write the corresponding dual problem for management directly as follows:

$$\text{Min} \quad Z_Y = 0Y_1 + 0Y_2 + L$$

$$\begin{array}{lll} \text{subject to} & \text{(a)} & -5Y_1 - 2Y_2 + L \geq 0 \quad \text{or} \quad 5Y_1 + 2Y_2 \leq L \\ & \text{(b)} & -3Y_1 - 9Y_2 + L \geq 0 \quad \text{or} \quad 3Y_1 + 9Y_2 \leq L \\ & \text{(c)} & Y_1 + Y_2 \geq 1 \\ \text{and} & \text{(d)} & Y_1 \geq 0,\ Y_2 \geq 0,\ L \geq 0 \end{array} \tag{15.4}$$

Constraint (a) of (15.4) states that, if the union chooses strategy U_1, the expected loss to management is at most L. Similarly, constraint (b) of (15.4) represents management's highest expected loss if union chooses strategy U_2. The interpretation of constraint (c) of (15.4) sounds somewhat artificial, but it is interesting. It is known that union's payoff is positive. Again, we lose no generality by assuming that all payoff elements are positive. If one or more of these entries are negative, we can use the transformation introduced earlier by adding an appropriate constant to all the entries to make payoff elements nonnegative. This does not affect the optimal strategies. Given the union's positive payoff, the expected value E to management is actually negative whenever the game is played: management would probably prefer not to negotiate at all and thereby have a loss of zero. Of course, not playing the game (not negotiating) will bring a different kind of loss—in this case, lost production and selling capacity through prolongation of the strike. Therefore, the sign of constraint (c) in (15.4) is imposed in the greater-than-or-equal-to form ("at least") instead of the less-than-or-equal-to form ("at most"). Finally, management's goal is to minimize L, its expected loss, as shown in the objective function system of (15.4).

What, then, is the solution of the dual problem? According to the duality theory demonstrated in Chapter 4, solving one of these linear programming problems automatically gives the solution to the other problem. Thus the optimal simplex tableau of the union's problem must contain the optimal solution for management's problem. Turning to the last tableau in Table 15.7, we can read the solution immediately from the coefficients of row 0:

$$\bar{Y}_1 = \tfrac{7}{9}$$
$$\bar{Y}_2 = \tfrac{2}{9}$$
$$\bar{L} = (\bar{Z}_Y) = \tfrac{13}{3} \qquad (\bar{L} = \bar{Z}_Y, \text{ by definition})$$

This means that the optimal mixed strategy for management is $(\frac{7}{9}, \frac{2}{9})$ and the associated expected loss is $\frac{13}{3}$. Note that this solution is identical to the one obtained by the graphical method in Figure 15.2. These results verify the minimax principle that management pursues in this problem.

Conversion of Games into Linear Programming Problems

The 2 × 2 Payoff Matrix To facilitate our discussion, the conversion of a 2 × 2 payoff matrix into a linear programming problem is presented in the following general form:

$$\text{Player A} \overset{\text{Player B}}{\begin{bmatrix} a_{11} & a_{12} \\ a_{21} & a_{22} \end{bmatrix}}$$

The corresponding linear programming problem for player A is

$$\text{Max } Z_X = 0X_1 + 0X_2 + E$$

subject to

$$\begin{aligned} -a_{11}X_1 - a_{21}X_2 + E &\le 0 \\ -a_{12}X_1 - a_{22}X_2 + E &\le 0 \\ X_1 + X_2 &\le 1 \end{aligned} \qquad (15.5)$$

and

$$X_1 \ge 0,\ X_2 \ge 0,\ E \ge 0$$

The dual of the linear programming model that will yield the optimal solution for player B is

$$\text{Min } Z_Y = 0Y_1 + 0Y_2 + L$$

subject to

$$\begin{aligned} -a_{11}Y_1 - a_{12}Y_2 + L &\ge 0 \\ -a_{21}Y_1 - a_{22}Y_2 + L &\ge 0 \\ Y_1 + Y_2 &\ge 1 \end{aligned} \qquad (15.6)$$

and

$$Y_1 \ge 0,\ Y_2 \ge 0,\ L \ge 0$$

The General Case The rules for transforming a game problem into a standard (primal) linear programming format are:

1. Assign zero coefficients to the probability variables X_1 and X_2 and a unit coefficient to the expected payoff variable E in the objective function that is to be maximized from player A's viewpoint. (If any entry in the payoff matrix is negative, add a constant k to make all entries nonnegative.)
2. A ***column*** of the payoff matrix will become the negative coefficient in the corresponding ***row*** constraint of the linear programming problem. A variable E with a positive algebraic sign is added to each constraint (not including the probability constraint). The inequality sign is in the less-than-or-equal-to form, with a zero on the right-hand side of the inequality.
3. Add the probability constraint—that is, $X_1 + X_2 \leq 1$.
4. All variables X_1 and X_2 and E are nonnegative.

These conversion procedures can be readily applied to a general game with an $m \times n$ payoff matrix.

$$\text{Player A} \quad \overset{\text{Player B}}{\begin{bmatrix} a_{11} & a_{12} & \cdots & a_{1n} \\ a_{21} & a_{22} & \cdots & a_{2n} \\ \cdot & \cdot & & \cdot \\ \cdot & \cdot & & \cdot \\ \cdot & \cdot & & \cdot \\ a_{m1} & a_{m2} & \cdots & a_{mn} \end{bmatrix}}$$

Following the conversion rules just outlined, we can now formulate the corresponding linear programming problem for player A in a straightforward manner:

$$\text{Max} \quad Z_X = 0X_1 + 0X_2 + \cdots + 0X_m + E$$

subject to

$$\begin{aligned} -a_{11}X_1 - a_{21}X_2 - \cdots - a_{m1}X_m + E &\leq 0 \\ -a_{12}X_1 - a_{22}X_2 - \cdots - a_{m2}X_m + E &\leq 0 \\ &\cdot \\ &\cdot \\ &\cdot \\ -a_{1n}X_1 - a_{2n}X_2 - \cdots - a_{mn}X_m + E &\leq 0 \\ X_1 + X_2 + \cdots + X_m &\leq 1 \end{aligned} \tag{15.7}$$

and

$$X_i \geq 0 \, (i = 1, 2, \ldots, m) \, E \geq 0$$

Accordingly, player B would conclude that his or her optimal mixed strategy is given by the optimal solution of the corresponding dual linear programming problem:

$$\text{Max} \quad Z_Y = 0Y_1 + 0Y_2 + \cdots + 0Y_n + L$$

subject to

$$\begin{aligned}
-a_{11}Y_1 - a_{12}Y_2 - \cdots - a_{1n}Y_n + L &\geq 0 \\
-a_{21}Y_1 - a_{22}Y_2 - \cdots - a_{2n}Y_n + L &\geq 0 \\
&\vdots \\
-a_{m1}Y_1 - a_{m2}Y_2 - \cdots - a_{mn}Y_n + L &\geq 0 \\
Y_1 + \quad Y_2 + \cdots + \quad Y_n \quad &\geq 1
\end{aligned} \tag{15.8}$$

and

$$Y_j \geq 0 \; (j = 1, 2, \ldots, n) \; L \geq 0$$

15.5 Limitations and Extensions

Our discussion has disclosed some of the limitations we encounter when we apply game theory to real-life situations. The simple case of two-person, zero-sum games does provide a unique optimal solution—a situation in which both players gain their minimax (expected payoff) or maximin (expected loss). Even in such a simple case, however, the solution is based on several implicit and explicit restrictions.

One assumption we made is that both players have complete knowledge of the payoff table before the game is played. In a real-life situation (like the union–management example used in this chapter), the opposing players may not always have all the information for each payoff associated with every possible combination of strategies contained in this table. Furthermore, will the payoff matrix next year be the same as the payoff matrix this year, and likewise for successive years after that? Probably not. Negotiation will center on different issues and demands and have different payoffs every year.

With a zero-sum game, it must also be assumed that the behavior of the players has no effect on their combined payoff. In practice, this may not be the case. Two players could often affect the total size of the game through collusion or cooperation. For example, cooperation between labor and management may increase the total payoff for both. This may result from other factors that enter into the discussion; for instance, the union may offer a shorter strike as compensation for a larger wage boost. We no longer have a zero-sum situation.

Recently, a great deal of research has been directed toward solving non-zero-sum games, such as the collusion situation exemplifies. Non-zero-sum games are much more complicated to solve, and we leave their treatment to books dealing with advanced concepts in game theory.

Another obvious extension in real-life situations requires analysis of games having more than two players. When this is the case, the existing theory is less satisfactory than it is for two-person games. The major difficulty in *n*-person games arises from the possibility of coalitions and side payments among the participants. Imagine a case where three players, A, B, and C, just learned that they won \$3000 with a jointly owned lottery ticket. A ***fair*** solution would be for each to receive \$1000. But things may not be that simple. If player A, who is in possession of the winning ticket, threatens (for whatever reason) to burn the ticket unless his or her winning share equals \$2000, only \$1000 would remain to be divided between B and C. Player B might be willing to form a coalition with player C against player A in an effort to secure, between them, \$2500, leaving the remaining \$500 to A. Now player A faces the same situation (share of winnings equaling \$500) that the other two players would have faced. Player A could also offer either member of the coalition, say B, a side payment of \$1300 so that player B is better off by breaking away from C to join A against C. This process can go on indefinitely, and it negates the possibility of a unique equilibrium solution. It becomes even more complex with more than three players, as the number of possible coalitions and side payments multiplies.

15.6 Summary

Game theory deals with a type of decision problem characterized by conflict or competitive situations among different decision makers. The consequences of an action taken by one person depend not only upon that person's choice but also on the courses of action chosen by other interested parties. In a two-person, zero-sum game, two competitors are opposed in such a way that the sum of their gains is zero for every play of the game.

The rectangular table that shows the outcomes of a game as the players execute their particular strategies is known as the payoff matrix. A strategy is a predetermined set of alternative courses of action. A player who seeks the maximum among these minimal gains is said to use a maximin strategy. A player who seeks the minimum among these maximal losses is said to use a minimax strategy. The point indicating both the maximum of the row minima and the minimum of the column maxima is referred to as a saddle point. A player who chooses only one strategy is said to use a pure strategy. A player who uses some combination of strategies chosen randomly, according to some probability distribution imposed on each particular pure strategy, is said to use mixed strategies. For any zero-sum, two-person game, there exists an equilibrium solution at which the values of the maximin expected payoff and the minimax expected payoff are equal.

For a two-person game with two strategies, one can find the optimal mixed strategies by using a two-dimensional graph. Solving a game with $m \times n$ dimensions is mathematically equivalent to solving a linear programming problem. Interestingly, if player A's optimal mixed strategies are given by the primal linear programming problem, player B's optimal mixed strategies are given by the corresponding dual linear programming problem.

Like other quantitative methods, game theory has both strengths and weaknesses. It cannot provide a categorical solution to many competitive problems in complex real-life situations. But the theory of the zero-sum game has strength as well. A businessperson or policy maker, facing the vexing and competitive world of business and politics, can use game theory to assist in formulating the most appropriate defensive measures against a rival's most profitable or advantageous counterstrategy.

Exercises

15.1 Define the following terms:
a. Maximin principle
b. Minimax principle
c. Two-person, zero-sum game

15.2 Two companies, A and B, dominate an entire industry. The total market share for these companies in a zero-sum game is 100%. Compose a matrix for company B, given each of the following payoff matrices for player A:

a. $\begin{bmatrix} 65 & 35 \\ 75 & 50 \end{bmatrix}$ b. $\begin{bmatrix} 40 & 60 \\ 85 & 20 \end{bmatrix}$

15.3 Two players, Mary and Ted, agree to play matching pennies. If the two tossed coins turn out to be a combination of two heads or two tails, Ted pays Mary 10¢. Write a payoff matrix for matching pennies.

15.4 Anderson and Brown agree to draw balls, red or yellow, from two urns. Anderson draws one ball, red or yellow, from one urn. Simultaneously, Brown draws one ball, red or yellow, from the other urn. The colors are then compared and the payoff is determined on the basis of the matching colors. Interpret the following payoff matrix:

		Brown	
		Red	Yellow
Anderson	Red	25¢	−15¢
	Yellow	−10¢	15¢

15.5 The following payoff matrix represents a game to be played between players A and B. Each entry in the matrix stands for the payoff to player A (and the loss to player B).

	Player B	
Player A	8	10
	4	7

a. What is player A's optimal strategy?
b. What is player B's optimal strategy?
c. Does the game have a saddle-point solution? If so, what is it?

15.6 The following payoff matrix represents a game to be played between players A and B. Each entry in the matrix stands for the payoff to player A (and the loss to player B).

	Player B	
Player A	−3	−5
	8	−2

a. What strategy should player A pursue?
b. What strategy should player B pursue?

c. Does the game have a saddle-point solution? If so, what is it?
d. What is the payoff to player A?

15.7 Consider the following payoff matrix:

$$\begin{bmatrix} 18 & 12 & 8 \\ 16 & 13 & 14 \\ 6 & 11 & 15 \end{bmatrix}$$

a. Write out the row minima, and identify the maximin.
b. Write out the column maxima, and identify the minimax.
c. Does the game have a saddle-point solution? If so, what is it?
d. Does the saddle-point solution satisfy the condition specified in step (3) on page 461? Explain.

15.8 The payoff matrix in exercise 15.7 is changed to

$$\begin{bmatrix} 18 & 12 & 8 \\ 16 & 20 & 14 \\ 6 & 11 & 15 \end{bmatrix}$$

Answer the same four questions asked in exercise 15.7.

15.9 For each of the following games, find the saddle point and the optimal strategies by making use of the relations of dominance.

a. $\begin{bmatrix} 10 & 5 & 7 \\ 12 & 7 & 8 \\ 7 & -1 & 11 \end{bmatrix}$ b. $\begin{bmatrix} -3 & -2 & -1 & -4 & 1 \\ -1 & 0 & 1 & -1 & 2 \\ 1 & -3 & 2 & -5 & 3 \end{bmatrix}$

15.10 Consider the following payoff matrix:

		Player B	
		B_1	B_2
Player A	A_1	4	8
	A_2	10	6

a. List the row minima, and find the maximin payoff that selecting a pure strategy assures player A.
b. List the column maxima, and find the minimax payoff that selecting a pure strategy assures player B.

c. Is there a saddle point? If not, which conditions (3) or (4), specified on page 461, does this matrix satisfy?
d. What is the optimal mixed strategy for player A?
e. Find a graphical solution for player A.
f. What is the optimal mixed strategy for player B?
g. Find a graphical solution for player B.
h. What is the expected payoff of the game when both A and B follow the mixed strategies?

15.11 The payoff matrix given in exercise 15.10 is changed to

$$\begin{array}{cc} & \text{Player B} \\ & \begin{array}{cc} B_1 & B_2 \end{array} \\ \text{Player A} \begin{array}{c} A_1 \\ A_2 \end{array} & \begin{bmatrix} 7 & 9 \\ 11 & -4 \end{bmatrix} \end{array}$$

Answer the same eight questions asked in exercise 15.10.

15.12 Refer to the payoff matrix specified in exercise 15.10.
a. Convert the game into a corresponding linear programming problem.
b. Write out the corresponding dual linear program.
c. Using the simplex method, solve the linear programming problem you found in part (a), determine the optimal strategies for both players, and give the expected payoff of the game.
d. Check your answer to part (c) against the results you obtained in exercise 15.10.

15.13 Two rival duopolists, Douglas, Inc. and McLine Company, are both battling for a share of the market. To improve its market share, Douglas decides to launch the following strategies:

D_1 = Home delivery services

D_2 = Mail order services

D_3 = Free gift for customer

As a countermove, the McLine Company decides to use media advertising to promote its product:

M_1 = Radio

M_2 = Magazine

M_3 = Newspaper

Past experience and recent studies reveal that the payoff matrix to Douglas for any combination of strategies is

		McLine		
		M_1	M_2	M_3
	D_1	55	45	70
Douglas	D_2	40	35	20
	D_3	60	40	45

What is the ***best*** strategy for Douglas to employ without knowing what counterstrategy its opponent will choose? What is the ***best*** strategy for McLine Company to select without knowing Douglas's countermove?

15.14 In a state–employee collective bargaining situation, the bargaining unit for the state employee is the labor union, and management represents the state. The union's bargaining position is summarized as follows:

U_1 = 18% wage increase
U_2 = Improvement in fringe benefits, including an extra 10 days of sick leave with pay and a dental insurance program

The position adopted by management is as follows:

M_1 = 7% wage increase
M_2 = 5 days of sick leave with pay

The payoff matrix from union's point of view is

		Management	
		M_1	M_2
Union	U_1	35	5
	U_2	10	20

a. Is this bargaining a two-person, zero-sum game? If so, why?
b. Is there any dominant strategy for either side? If not, why not?
c. Is there a saddle-point solution? If not, why not? If so, what is it?
d. Are mixed strategies needed for either party? If so, what are the optimal mixed strategies for the union?

15.15 Transform the following game matrices into their corresponding primal and dual linear programming problems:

a. $\begin{bmatrix} a_{11} & a_{12} & a_{13} \\ a_{21} & a_{22} & a_{23} \\ a_{31} & a_{32} & a_{33} \end{bmatrix}$ b. $\begin{bmatrix} 5 & 2 \\ 1 & 3 \\ 3 & 0 \end{bmatrix}$ c. $\begin{bmatrix} 2 & 3 & 0 \\ 1 & -1 & 1 \\ -1 & 2 & 4 \end{bmatrix}$

15.16 Write out the corresponding game matrix for the following linear programming problem:

$$\text{Max} \quad Z = X_3$$

subject to

$$-6X_1 - 4X_2 + X_3 \le 0$$
$$-3X_1 - 5X_2 + X_3 \le 0$$
$$X_1 + X_2 \le 1$$

and

$$X_1 \ge 0, X_2 \ge 0, X_3 \ge 0$$

Suggested Readings

Baumol, William J. *Economic Theory and Operations Analysis.* 3rd ed. Englewood Cliffs, N.J.: Prentice-Hall, 1972.

Chiang, Alpha C. *Fundamental Methods of Mathematical Economics.* 2nd ed. New York: McGraw-Hill, 1974.

Dorfman, Robert, P. A. Samuelson, and R. M. Solow. *Linear Programming and Economic Analysis.* New York: McGraw-Hill, 1958.

Johnson, Ross H., and P. R. Winn. *Quantitative Methods for Management.* Boston: Houghton-Mifflin, 1976.

Kemeny, John G., A. Schleifer, J. L. Snell, and G. L. Thompson. *Finite Mathematics with Business Applications.* Englewood Cliffs, N.J.: Prentice-Hall, 1962.

Luce, R. D., and H. Raiffa. *Games and Decisions.* New York: Wiley, 1957.

Richmond, S. B. *Operations Research for Management Decisions.* New York: Ronald Press, 1968.

Shubik, M., ed. *Game Theory and Related Applications to Social Behavior.* New York: Wiley, 1964.

Thompson, G. E. *Management Science: An Introduction to Modern Quantitative Analysis and Decision Making.* New York: McGraw-Hill, 1976.

Vajda, S. *An Introduction to Linear Programming and the Theory of Games.* New York: Wiley, 1960.

von Neumann, J., and O. Morgenstern. *Theory of Games and Economic Behavior*. 3rd ed. Princeton, N.J.: Princeton University Press, 1953.
Williams, J. D. *The Compleat Strategyst*. Rev. ed. New York: McGraw-Hill, 1966.

16

Markov Processes

In Chapter 15, it became clear that game theory solutions are limited in the number of rivals or competitors that they can handle effectively. Furthermore, we can deal with many real situations more effectively by using known or derivable probability distributions. This chapter introduces the techniques of ***Markov analysis***, for which two-person, zero-sum situations can be analyzed in a dynamic as opposed to static way—moving from one time period to another ad infinitum—and for which probability distributions that govern the dynamic process can be applied. Although it is possible to analyze situations with large numbers of competitors using matrix algebra, this chapter presents situations involving no more than three competitors.

16.1 The Use of Markov Processes in Market Share Analysis

One important type of multiperiod two-person, zero-sum situation for which Markov processes are well suited is the analysis of market shares. Over a number of periods, customers are able to shift their purchases from one producer to another. On a percentage basis, the market share is distributed among all producers in the given market, so one producer's gain in market share is achieved at the expense of another producer or producers. Let's analyze this shifting situation using Markov processes.

Markov Processes Applied to a Hypothetical Airline Situation

Suppose that airline service for a certain region of the United States is limited to two major airlines, Air Hopeful (airline A) and Big Air (airline B). The current market share of Air Hopeful is 25% and that of Big Air is 75%. According to an independent market survey conducted by an airline regulatory authority, the likelihood of an Air Hopeful passenger traveling the next time with Big Air is .30. Conversely, the likelihood of a Big Air passenger traveling the next time with Air Hopeful is .20. Algebraically, these conditions can be stated as follows:

(a) $P(A_t|A_{t-1}) = .70$

(b) $P(B_t|A_{t-1}) = .30$

(c) $P(B_t|B_{t-1}) = .80$

(d) $P(A_t|B_{t-1}) = .20$

Specifically, the notation in (a) states: Given that the passenger was traveling with Air Hopeful at period $t - 1$, the probability that this passenger will travel the same airline the next period, t, is equal to .70. The notation in (b) states: Given that the passenger was traveling Air Hopeful at period $t - 1$, the probability that this passenger will travel Big Air the next period, t, is equal to .30. Similar interpretations apply to notations (c) and (d). Of course, these are conditional probabilities related to shifts in the patronizing of one airline versus the other in different time periods.

The probabilities may also be arranged in tabular form, as shown in Table 16.1. Clearly, the probability of a passenger's choice of an airline in period t depends on the airline that passenger flew in period $t - 1$. Each probability in Table 16.1 must therefore be a conditional probability, as indicated earlier. The table shows all possible conditional probabilities for transitions from the initial states of nature to subsequent ones.

Transition Diagrams and Probability Trees

Although the table of transition probabilities serves as the primary tool of analysis for applying Markov processes, the underlying transition from one period to another can be demonstrated more fully with two types

Table 16.1
Table of Transition Probabilities for Passenger Shifts Between Airlines

		Period $t - 1$	
	To \ From	A (Air Hopeful)	B (Big Air)
Period t	A (Air Hopeful)	.70	.20
	B (Big Air)	.30	.80

of diagrams. The first of these, called simply a ***transition diagram,*** shows fully the transition possibilities, or shifts, that can occur in any particular situation between succeeding time periods. Here the emphasis is on the flow of the shifting process. The second type of diagram that is often used to demonstrate a Markov process is the traditional ***probability tree diagram,*** which, as the name indicates, emphasizes the probabilities and their connection through periods of time. Let's look at each of these diagrams for our example of the two airlines.

The transition diagram illustrates the underlying process, which in this case is straightforward: either continue to use the airline patronized previously, or shift to the competitor airline. Thus, between any two time periods $t - 1$ and t, a transition diagram for the given process might look like Figure 16.1.

Variations of this transition diagram exist, but the necessary ingredients remain the same. First, all possible states of nature must be displayed. In a transition diagram, it usually is assumed that the possible states of nature do not change from one period to the next. In this case, the two states of nature are the passenger choices of either airline A or airline B. Second, the patterns of all possible actions between periods for any element in the system are displayed. Figure 16.1 shows that a passenger of airline A during one time period may remain with that airline or shift to the other during the succeeding time period. Likewise, a first-stage passenger of airline B may shift to airline A or continue to use airline B in the next stage. Note that this process considers only passengers who use either airline A or airline B in both time periods. There is no provision for these passengers traveling irregularly from time period to time period. Thus this particular pattern of possible

Figure 16.1
Transition Diagram

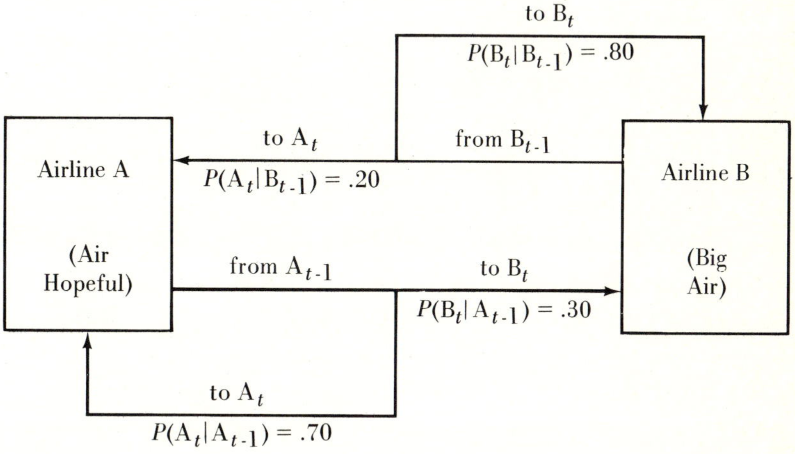

actions illustrates the occurrence of either a different state or the same state in the chain of events. The third ingredient of a transition diagram is the indication of appropriate probabilities for the various possible interperiod actions of elements of the system. These, of course, are the same conditional probabilities that were described before.

Probability tree diagrams show movement from one period to another along all possible branches or paths that may connect events over time. Also shown in such diagrams are the outcomes that might occur in a succession of events and the appropriate probabilities at each stage of the process. Such a probability tree diagram for our airline example is given in Figure 16.2. The probabilities between time periods are con-

Figure 16.2 A Probability Tree for the Airline Example

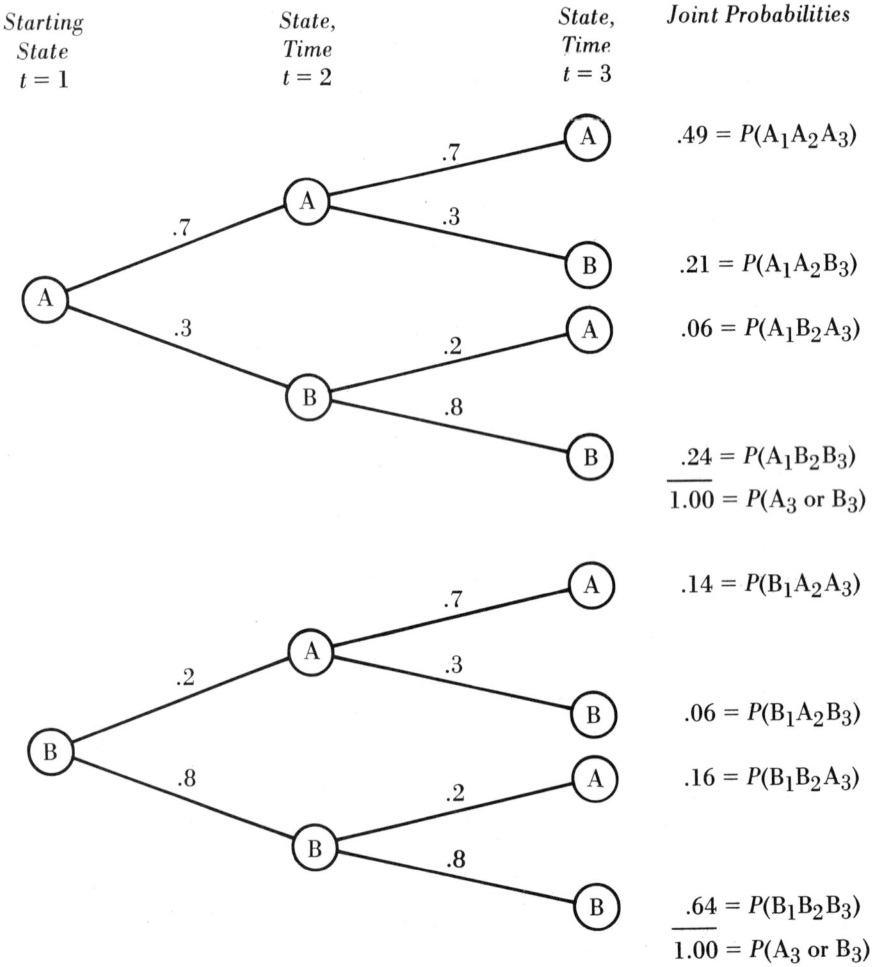

ditional probabilities (for example, $P(A_2|B_1) = .2$), because each depends on the state of nature in the preceding time period. The probabilities of the joint occurrence of any two successive outcomes are joint probabilities under dependence and are calculated as the product of the probabilities found along any given path of the diagrams. Since probability trees involve progressive time periods, the branching process could be extended for as many periods as desired. The number of possible branches increases exponentially—in this case, according to 2^t.

Probability Calculations

Suppose that the decision maker in the airline example wants to know the probability of a passenger flying Air Hopeful at the end of the third period. One must first know the initial state of the process. Suppose that the passenger starts out flying Air Hopeful (state A). Then the probability of that passenger patronizing Air Hopeful in the third period is the probability of AAA or ABA, which is .49 (.7 × .7) plus .06 (.2 × .3) or .55. That is,

$$P\begin{pmatrix}\text{state A} & \text{state A} \\ \text{at third period} & \text{at first period}\end{pmatrix}$$
$$= P\begin{pmatrix}\text{state A} & \text{state A} \\ \text{at third period} & \text{at second period}\end{pmatrix} P\begin{pmatrix}\text{state A} & \text{state A} \\ \text{at second period} & \text{at first period}\end{pmatrix}$$
$$+ P\begin{pmatrix}\text{state A} & \text{state B} \\ \text{at third period} & \text{at second period}\end{pmatrix} P\begin{pmatrix}\text{state B} & \text{state A} \\ \text{at second period} & \text{at first period}\end{pmatrix}$$

When we use standard probability notation, this becomes

$$\begin{aligned} P(A_3|A_1) &= P(A_3|A_2)\,P(A_2|A_1) + P(A_3|B_2)P(B_2|A_1) \\ &= (.7)(.7) + (.2)(.3) \\ &= .49 + .06 \\ &= .55 \end{aligned}$$

Note that the probability tree shown in Figure 16.2 facilitates this and other calculations. One can simply multiply the probabilities taken from the appropriate branches of the tree—in this case, (.7)(.7) and (.2)(.3). Since the joint occurrence of these two branches is mutually exclusive, the probabilities .49 and .06 are added together.

What is the probability that a given passenger is in state B (Big Air) at the end of the third period, given that this passenger started out in state A (Air Hopeful) in the first period? By the same reasoning, one obtains the following probability (see Figure 16.2):

$$\begin{aligned} P(B_3|A_1) &= P(B_3|A_2)P(A_2|A_1) + P(B_3|B_2)P(B_2|A_1) \\ &= (.3)(.7) + (.8)(.3) \\ &= .21 + .24 \\ &= .45 \end{aligned}$$

Alternatively, because a given passenger must use one of the two airlines in the third period, we recognize that

$$P(A_3|A_1) + P(B_3|A_1) = 1.00$$

Consequently, we can calculate the same result for $P(B_3|A_1)$, as follows:

$$\begin{aligned} P(B_3|A_1) &= 1 - P(A_3|A_1) \\ &= 1 - .55 \\ &= .45 \end{aligned}$$

Now consider the probability that a passenger is in state A at the end of the third period, given that this passenger started out in state B in the first period. From Figure 16.2, this probability is .30:

$$\begin{aligned} P(A_3|B_1) &= P(A_3|A_2)P(A_2|B_1) + P(A_3|B_2)P(B_2|B_1) \\ &= (.7)(.2) + (.2)(.8) \\ &= .14 + .16 \\ &= .30 \end{aligned}$$

Finally, the probability that a passenger will be in state B at the end of the third period, given that this passenger started off in state B in the first period, is .70:

$$\begin{aligned} P(B_3|B_1) &= P(B_3|A_2)P(A_2|B_1) + P(B_3|B_2)P(B_2|B_1) \\ &= (.3)(.2) + (.8)(.8) \\ &= .06 + .64 \\ &= .70 \end{aligned}$$

Alternatively, we can calculate this probability as follows:

$$P(A_3|B_1) + P(B_3|B_1) = 1$$

Then,

$$P(B_3|A_1) = 1 - P(A_3|B_1)$$
$$= 1 - .30$$
$$= .70$$

Note that the probabilities we have discussed so far consider no more than three periods. More computation is involved when there are more periods, but the procedure remains the same. As the number of periods increases, the probability computations become more tedious. Fortunately, as the number of periods increases, the probability of reaching any particular state often approaches some limiting value, which (as we shall see) represents an equilibrium or steady-state condition.

Equilibrium or Steady State

It is important to repeat that the transition probabilities are assumed to be constant, regardless of which successive time periods are considered. That is, the probability of a passenger traveling with a particular airline does not change over time:

$$P(A_t|A_{t-1}) = .7 \quad \text{and} \quad P(A_t|B_{t-1}) = .2 \quad \text{for all } t \tag{16.1}$$

Given this assumption, then

$$P(A_t) = .7P(A_{t-1}) + .2P(B_{t-1}) \tag{16.2}$$

Equation (16.2) states that the probability of state A at ***any period t*** is equal to .7 times the probability that the passenger was in state A in the preceding period, plus .2 times the probability that the passenger was in state B in the preceding period. When we use (16.2), calculating $P(A_t)$, the probability of a passenger being in state A in any future periods, becomes ***recursive***; that is, each period depends on the preceding one. (See Table 16.2.)

Table 16.2 shows that the probability of the passenger being in state A in any future period, given that the passenger originated in state A, approaches the limiting value of .40 as the number of periods becomes larger. Once again, since

$$P(A_t) + P(B_t) = 1 \tag{16.3}$$

then

$$P(B_t) = 1 - P(A_t) \tag{16.4}$$

Table 16.2 Recursive Calculation of the Probabilities of Starting and Ending in State A

Period t	$P(A_t)$	$P(B_t) = 1 - P(A_t)$	$P(A_{t-1}) - P(A_t)$
1	$P(A_1) = 1.00$	0	
2	$P(A_2) = .70$	.3	.3
3	$P(A_3) = .7P(A_2) + .2P(B_2) = (.7)(.7) + (.2)(.3) = .55$	.45	.15
4	$P(A_4) = .7P(A_3) + .2P(B_3) = (.7)(.55) + (.2)(.45) = .475$	.525	.075
5	$P(A_5) = .7P(A_4) + .2P(B_4) = (.7)(.475) + (.2)(.525) = .4375$	.5625	.0375
6	$P(A_6) = .7P(A_5) + .2P(B_5) = (.7)(.4375) + (.2)(.5625) = .41875$	.58125	.01875
7	$P(A_7) = .7P(A_6) + .2P(B_6) = (.7)(.41875) + (.2)(.58125) = .409375$	.590625	.009375
8	$P(A_8) = .7P(A_7) + .2P(B_7) = (.7)(.40375) + (.2)(.590625) = .4046875$	.5953215	.0046875

(These calculations are also presented in Table 16.2.) In other words, the probability of the passenger being in state B in any particular period, given that the passenger originated in state A, approaches the value of .6 as the number of periods becomes large.

The last column of Table 16.2 contains the changes in probabilities between any two successive periods; namely, the difference between $P(A_{t-1})$ and $P(A_t)$. As shown in Figure 16.3, the changes from one period to the next start at a fairly high magnitude and gradually decrease. The changes get smaller and smaller and will become infinitesimally small, as the number of periods increases. Theoretically, as the number of periods approaches infinity, the changes in probabilities between period t and period $t - 1$ are so small that they may be treated as zero. Therefore, the limiting or extreme case becomes

$$\begin{aligned} P(A_t) &= P(A_{t-1}) \\ P(B_t) &= P(B_{t-1}) \end{aligned} \tag{16.5}$$

These equations formally define the equilibrium or steady-state condition of the problem. We calculate the probability values at equilibrium or ***steady state*** by combining (16.5) and (16.2) to get

$$P(A_t) = .7P(A_t) + .2P(B_t) \tag{16.6}$$

Figure 16.3 Change in Probabilities through Successive Periods

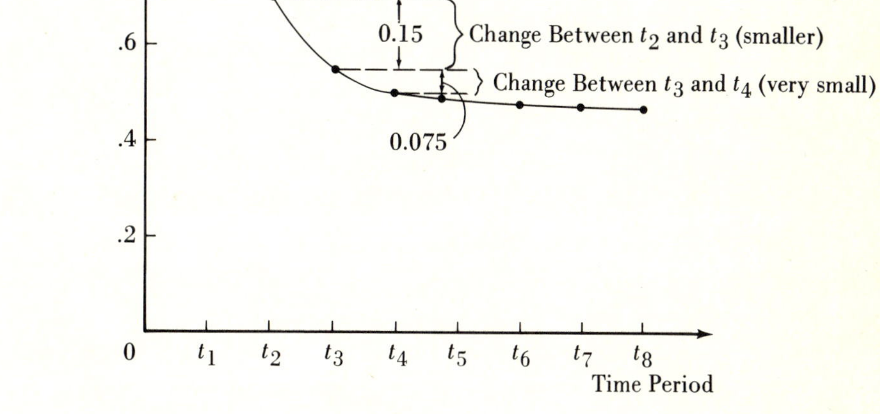

Rearranging terms yields

$$.3P(A_t) = .2P(B_t) \qquad (16.7)$$

or

$$P(A_t) = \tfrac{2}{3}P(B_t)$$

$$= \tfrac{2}{3}[1 - P(A_t)] \qquad \text{[from (16.4)]}$$

$$\therefore P(A_t) = \tfrac{2}{5} = .40$$

and

$$P(B_t) = 1 - P(A_t)$$

$$= 1 - .40 = .60$$

This means that, in the long run, if the assumption of constant probabilities specified in (16.1) persists, the final market share for Air Hopeful is 40% and for Big Air is 60%.

Note that we derived the equilibrium value using only transition probabilities and with no reference to the starting state. In other words, the probability of the passenger reaching state A will eventually approach .40, regardless of the initial state. The reader may verify this by constructing a table similar to Table 16.2 showing the successive probabilities of the passenger being in state A in a future period, given that this passenger originated in state B. (See exercise 16.3.)

16.2 Extending the Example to Three Airlines

Transition Matrix and Its Interpretation

Suppose that a third airline, Catch-up Airways, enters into the market and that this results in a loss of market share for each of the two established airlines. Assume also that the data shown in Table 16.3 were collected by independent analysis. Finally, assume that no new passengers enter the market and no old passengers leave it.

Table 16.3 Numbers and Movement of Passengers over an Observation Period

Airline	Number of Passengers in Period 1	Gain from			Loss to			Number of Passengers in Period 2
		A	B	C	A	B	C	
A	100	0	9	18	0	20	10	97
B	180	20	0	24	9	0	9	206
C	60	10	9	0	18	24	0	37

On the basis of the data given in Table 16.3, we can compute all three airlines' transition probabilities. You will recall that transition probabilities are simply the probabilities that each airline will retain its own passengers—or lose them to its competitors. The following matrix, derived from these transition probabilities, is known as the ***transition matrix.***

From: Passengers in Period 1

To: Passengers in Period 2	A	B	C
A	$\frac{70}{100} = .70$	$\frac{9}{180} = .05$	$\frac{18}{60} = .30$
B	$\frac{20}{100} = .20$	$\frac{162}{180} = .90$	$\frac{24}{60} = .40$
C	$\frac{10}{100} = .10$	$\frac{9}{180} = .05$	$\frac{18}{60} = .30$

This is nothing more than a table of transition probabilities like Table 16.1.

From: Passengers in Period 1

To: Passengers in Period 2	A	B	C
A	.70	.05	.30
B	.20	.90	.40
C	.10	.05	.30

How do we interpret the terms in the matrix? First, reading the rows of the matrix yields certain information. These transition probabilities for shifts between periods may be interpreted as follows:

1. The first row shows that airline A retains 70% of its own passengers, gains 5% of airline B's passengers, and gains 30% of airline C's passengers.
2. The second row shows that B gains 20% of A's passengers, retains 90% of its own passengers, and gains 40% of C's passengers.
3. The third row shows that C gains 10% of A's passengers, gains 5% of B's passengers, and retains 30% of its own passengers.

Likewise, the columns of the matrix are interpreted as follows:

1. The first column shows that A retains 70% of its own passengers, loses 20% of its passengers to B, and loses 10% of its passengers to C.
2. The second column shows that B loses 5% of its passengers to A, retains 90% of its own passengers, and loses 5% of its passengers to C.
3. The third column shows that C loses 30% of its passengers to A, loses 40% of its passengers to B, and retains 30% of its own passengers.

In widely applied market research models, the probabilities in the major diagonal are often referred to as ***brand loyalty probabilities*** and the probabilities off the major diagonal are often referred to as ***brand switching probabilities.*** Note that calculating transition probabilities is based on the fact that "From" states are located at the top of the matrix and "To" states are presented vertically on the left-hand side. In some other textbooks and articles, the arrangement of rows and columns is reversed. In this case, the interpretation of off-diagonal probabilities in terms of gains and losses is reversed as well. One interpretation of the transition matrix is summarized in the schematic diagram shown in Figure 16.4.

Calculation of the Equilibrium or Steady-State Probabilities

The Markov process is now applied to a case with three firms for the purpose of predicting whether or not an equilibrium or steady-state market share will be established and, if so, what the percentage market share for each airline will be at equilibrium. Assume again that the matrix of transition probabilities remains unchanged over time.

Before determining the equilibrium market share, we can intuitively see that airline B will ultimately dominate the market while airline C's market share will dwindle to a small amount. Why? Because the probability of passengers remaining loyal to airline B is .9, which is relatively higher than the chances of loyalty to either A (.7) or C (.3). Also, airline B gains passengers from C at a rate of 40%, whereas C captures only 5% of B's passengers. Mathematical calculation of the equilibrium or steady-state probabilities should confirm this intuitive prediction.

The probability of passengers traveling with Air Hopeful at any future period t is equal to .7 times the passengers it retained in the preceding period $(t-1)$, plus .05 times the market share gained from B in the preceding period, plus .3 times the market share gained from C in the preceding period. Thus, A's market share in any future period may be expressed as follows:

Figure 16.4
Interpretation of the Transition Matrix through a Schematic Diagram

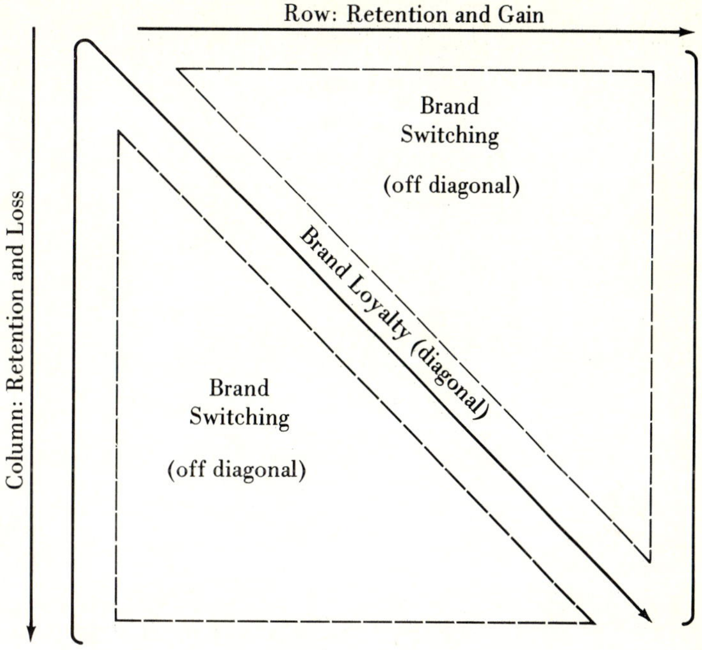

$$\underbrace{A_t}_{\text{A's market share in } t} = \underbrace{.7A_{t-1}}_{\text{number of passengers A retained from period } t-1} + \underbrace{.05B_{t-1} + .3C_{t-1}}_{\text{number of passengers A gained from B and C from period } t-1}$$

Similarly, B's and C's market shares are calculated as follows:

$$B_t = .2A_{t-1} + .9B_{t-1} + .4C_{t-1}$$
$$C_t = .1A_{t-1} + .05B_{t-1} + .3C_{t-1}$$

At equilibrium, the probability values in periods t and $t - 1$ are only infinitesimally different, so

$$P(A_t) = P(A_{t-1})$$
$$P(B_t) = P(B_{t-1})$$

and

$$P(C_t) = P(C_{t-1})$$

Combining all equations yields

$$A = .7A + .05B + .3C \qquad (16.8a)$$

$$B = .2A + .90B + .4C \qquad (16.8b)$$

$$C = .1A + .05B + .3C \qquad (16.8c)$$

We next rearrange terms so that each equation is set equal to zero:

$$-.3A + .05B + .3C = 0 \qquad (16.9a)$$

$$.2A - .10B + .4C = 0 \qquad (16.9b)$$

$$.1A + .05B - .7C = 0 \qquad (16.9c)$$

With three equations and three unknowns, it should be possible to solve simultaneously for the unknowns, but only if the equations are independent. Unfortunately, they are ***not.*** By the very nature of the transition matrix, one of the equations is actually redundant. For example, if we add (16.9a) and (16.9b):

$$\begin{array}{rr} & -.3A + .05B + .3C = 0 \\ + & 0.2A - .10B + .4C = 0 \\ \hline & -.1A - .05B + .7C = 0 \end{array}$$

The result is

$$.1A + .05B - .7C = 0$$

which is equation (16.9c). In other words, (16.9c) is merely the sum of the first two equations. Consequently, we can drop (16.9c) without fear of losing any information that is not contained in the other two equations.[1]

There is another condition. The sum of the three market shares must be 1:

$$A + B + C = 1.00 \qquad (16.9d)$$

[1] In general, the number of simultaneous equations to be solved will always be one fewer than the number of rows. Since the transition matrix is always square (the number of rows equals the number of columns), there is a set of $n - 1$ simultaneous equations with n unknowns. However, because the sum of the steady-state probabilities is required to be 1, adding this required equation will give us n equations and n unknowns.

Given the three simultaneous equations (16.9a), (16.9b), and (16.9d), we find the equilibrium or steady-state market share as follows:

Step One Multiply (16.9b) by .5 and add it to (16.9a).

$$
\begin{array}{rrl}
 & -.3A + .0\cancel{5}B + .3C = 0 & (16.9a) \\
+ & .1A - .0\cancel{5}B + .2C = 0 & (16.9b) \times .5 \\
\hline
 & -.2A \qquad + .5C = 0 & \\
 & \therefore A = 2.5C & (16.10a)
\end{array}
$$

Step Two Multiply (16.9a) by 2 and add it to (16.9b) multiplied by 3.

$$
\begin{array}{rrl}
 & -.\cancel{6}A + .1B + \ \ .6C = 0 & (16.9a) \times 2 \\
+ & .\cancel{6}A - .3B + 1.2C = 0 & (16.9b) \times 3 \\
\hline
 & -.2B + 1.8C = 0 & \\
 & \therefore B = 9C & (16.10b)
\end{array}
$$

Step Three Substitute (16.10a) and (16.10b) into (16.9d). This yields

$$C = .08$$

Next, from (16.10a) and (16.10b) we know that

$$A = .20$$

$$B = .72$$

Hence, the solutions for equilibrium or steady-state market share are

Air Hopeful:	20% of the total market	
Big Air:	72% of the total market	(16.11)
Catch-up Airways:	8% of the total market	

As expected, the switching pattern of passengers among the three airlines causes Big Air to remain the dominant firm in the market.

Alternative Formulation of the Equilibrium or Steady-State Model Our previous discussion showed that, as the equilibrium period is approached, the gains and losses accruing to each airline become infinitesimally small. For each airline, the number of passengers lost must, at the equilibrium state, equal the number of passengers the other airlines gain. Accordingly, the condition for equilibrium or steady-state may be stated as follows:

$$\text{Switching out (loss)} = \text{switching in (gain)} \tag{16.12}$$

From the first row of the transition matrix, we see that 70% of A's passengers were loyal to A, which means that 30% were lost. Specifically, 20% went to B and 10% went to C. On the other hand, 5% of B's passengers and 30% of C's passengers switched to A. Then, according to equation (16.12),

$$\begin{aligned} .30A &= .05B + .30C \\ .10B &= .20A + .40C \\ .70C &= .10A + .05B \end{aligned} \tag{16.13}$$

Rearranging terms, we can rewrite these equations as follows:

$$\begin{aligned} -.30A + .05B + .30C &= 0 \\ .20A - .10B + .40C &= 0 \\ .10A + .05B - .70C &= 0 \end{aligned} \tag{16.13$'$}$$

Interestingly, but not surprisingly, equations (16.13′) are the same as equations (16.9).

16.3 Altering Transition Probabilities through Advertising

A Cash Rebate Program

In our airline example, airline C can expect only 8% of the market share in the long run. Suppose that the management of airline C decides to launch an advertising campaign designed to retain more passengers. To discourage customers from switching to competing airlines, Catch-up Airways advertises a cash rebate program for passengers who purchase tickets in two succeeding time periods. For purposes of comparison, two transition matrices are presented. The first is the original matrix of transition probabilities, and the second represents the transition matrix after the cash rebate program is implemented.

Original Matrix of Transition Probabilities

		Period $t-1$ A	B	C
Period t	A	.70	.05	.30
	B	.20	.90	.40
	C	.10	.05	.30

After Cash Rebate Program

		Period $t-1$ A	B	C
Period t	A	.70	.05	.25
	B	.20	.90	.35
	C	.10	.05	.40

The retention probabilities for both A and B in the new matrix remain the same, but, due to the cash rebate program, the passenger's retention probability for C increases by 10% (from 30% to 40%). Consequently, the probabilities of A and B gaining passengers from C drop from 30% to 25% and from 40% to 35%, respectively.

By using the alternative formulation for equilibrium described in (16.12) and (16.13), we find the following set of simultaneous equations corresponding to the transition matrix after the cash rebate program begins:

$$\begin{aligned}
&\text{(a)}\ .30A = .05B + .25C \\
&\text{(b)}\ .10B = .20A + .35C \\
&\text{(c)}\ .60C = .10A + .05B \\
&\text{(d)}\ A + B + C = 1
\end{aligned} \tag{16.14}$$

This system of equations can be rearranged as follows:

$$\begin{aligned}
&\text{(a)}\ -.3A + .05B + .25C = 0 \\
&\text{(b)}\ \quad .2A - .10B + .35C = 0 \\
&\text{(c)}\ \quad .1A + .05B - .60C = 0 \\
&\text{(d)}\ A + B + C = 1
\end{aligned} \tag{16.14$'$}$$

Once again, since (16.14′c) is the sum of (16.14′a) and (16.14′b), we can drop one equation as redundant without losing any information. We solve (16.14′a), (16.14′b), and (16.14′d) simultaneously to yield the following approximate market shares at equilibrium:

$$\begin{aligned} &\text{A: } 20.2\% \text{ of the total market} \\ &\text{B: } 70.5\% \text{ of the total market} \\ &\text{C: } \ \ 9.1\% \text{ of the total market} \end{aligned} \tag{16.15}$$

Under the circumstances, should airline C proceed with the rebate campaign? Suppose that the total market consists of 20 million passengers, that the per-unit contribution of booking a passenger is \$5, and that the total advertising cost is \$1.5 million. With the advertising, C's market share would increase from 8% to 9.1%. In other words, 0.22 million additional passengers (20 million passengers × the 1.1% increase) would be served. This means an increased contribution to profits of \$1.1 million (\$5 × 0.22 million) but only after a total advertising expenditure of \$1.5 million. Since the return is less than the cost, the management of Catch-up Airways should ***not*** implement the cash rebate program.

An Alternative Advertising Strategy

Under an alternative advertising strategy, airline C focuses on ***gaining*** passengers from airlines A and B, rather than increasing the retention rate of its own passengers. The transition matrix for this alternative is

$$\begin{array}{c} \text{From:} \\ \begin{array}{cc} & \begin{array}{ccc} \text{A} & \text{B} & \text{C} \end{array} \\ \begin{array}{r} \text{A} \\ \text{To: B} \\ \text{C} \end{array} & \begin{bmatrix} .60 & .05 & .30 \\ .20 & .85 & .40 \\ .20 & .10 & .30 \end{bmatrix} \end{array} \end{array}$$

Now airline C's probability of retaining its own customers remains the same (30%), but the probability of passengers switching from A and B to C increases from 10% to 20% and from 5% to 10%, respectively. Because of C's gain in customers from A and B, both A's and B's probability of retaining their own customers has dropped.

To evaluate this alternative advertising campaign, we formulate the following set of simultaneous equations associated with the transition matrix:

$$\begin{aligned} .4A &= .05B + .30C \\ .15B &= .20A + .40C \\ .70C &= .20A + .10B \\ A + B + C &= 1 \end{aligned} \tag{16.16}$$

Solving these simultaneous equations reveals that the equilibrium market shares after the alternative advertising campaign is implemented are as follows:

A: 19% of the total market

B: 66% of the total market (16.17)

C: 15% of the total market

The proposed alternative advertising strategy would increase airline C's market share from 8% to 15%, thereby bringing an additional 1.4 million passengers (7% times 20 million) and would increase the contribution to profits by $7 million ($5 times 1.4 million). If this second advertising strategy also costs $1.5 million, the net benefit would be $5.5 million and the campaign would make good business sense.

First-Order and Higher-Order Markov Processes

The basic assumption in Markov analysis is that the passenger decisions shift from one airline to another in accordance with the decisions made in the past. A first-order Markov process assumes that the probability of the next event depends only on the outcome of the prior event. A second-order process assumes that the probability of the next event may depend on the two previous outcomes. Likewise, a third-order process assumes that the probability of the next event can be calculated best by observing and taking account of the outcomes of the past three periods.

We have limited our analysis only to the first-order Markov process for two reasons. First, empirical study indicates that using first-order assumptions proves to be a reliable forecasting tool for the prediction proposed. This is particularly valid if the transition probabilities remain stable over time. Secondly, the mathematics involved in the computation of higher-order Markov processes is burdensome and beyond the scope of this book.

16.4 Summary

The basic concepts of Markov processes have been discussed in this chapter through the use of simple examples. The underlying Markov process of transition from one period to another was demonstrated fully by two types of diagrams. The transition diagram shows all transition probabilities that can occur in any particular situation between succeeding periods. The probability tree diagram emphasizes the probabilities and their connection through periods of time along all possible branches or paths. The probability of moving from one period to another is referred to as the transition probability. Because the probability of moving to one period depends on what happened in the preceding period, the transition probability is a conditional probability.

As the number of periods becomes larger and larger, the changes in probabilities between any two successive periods approach infinitesimally small limiting values. These limiting values are called the steady-state or equilibrium probabilities.

Markov analysis has been widely applied in managerial decision making to predict market share and brand switching. To apply Markov models successfully in market share or other analysis, one must bear in mind the underlying assumptions:

1. The transition probabilities remain constant over time.
2. The transition probabilities depend only on the outcome of the immediately preceding period.
3. When the problem concerns market share, the total market size, the counterstrategies of the rival or rivals and other market conditions remain unchanged over time.

Exercises

16.1 Define or explain the following concepts:
   a. Markov process
   b. Transition probabilities
   c. Matrix of transition probabilities
   d. Equilibrium or steady state

16.2 Given the table of transition probabilities (Table 16.1), calculate the probability that a passenger will be in state A (Air Hopeful) at the end of the fourth period, assuming that she or he started in state B (Big Air) during the first period.

16.3 On the basis of the transition probabilities shown in Table 16.1, construct a corresponding table (similar to Table 16.2) showing the probabilities that a passenger will be in state A in any future period, given that she or he started in state B in the first period. Then answer the following questions:

a. Does the probability value approach the limiting value of .40 . . .?
b. What is the probability of the passenger being in state B (Big Air) in any future period, given that she or he started off in state B in the first period?
c. Does the probability value you obtained in part (b) approach the limiting value of .60 . . .?
d. Compute the exact probability value of the equilibrium or steady-state condition.
e. Does the probability value of the equilibrium condition or steady state that you obtained in part (d) differ from the one obtained in equation (16.7)? Explain.

16.4 Refer to exercise 16.3. Draw a corresponding diagram (similar to Figure 16.3), and show the changes in probabilities between any two successive periods.

16.5 a. Solve the set of simultaneous equations (16.14′) step by step, and check the solution with (16.15).
b. Solve the set of simultaneous equations (16.16) step by step, and check the solution with (16.17).

16.6 According to the data collected by the Agricultural Experiment Station in Lexington County, the number of dairy farms retained and the number of farms changed in herd size during the two survey periods are as follows:

Representative Type	Range in Herd Size	Number of Farms in Period t Survey Sample	Number of Farms Exit and Change in Size	Number of Farms Retained	Probability of Retain
A	11–30	80	75	5	$\frac{5}{80} = .063$
B	31–50	200	50	150	$\frac{150}{250} = .750$
C	51–70	150	5	145	$\frac{145}{150} = .970$

The pattern of dairy farm growth and decline during the survey period is as follows:

Repesenta-tive Type	Range in Herd Size	Number of Farms in Period t	Gain from			Loss to			Survey Samples in Period $t+1$
			A	B	C	A	B	C	
A	11–30	80	0	2	0	0	50	25	7
B	31–50	200	50	0	5	2	0	48	205
C	51–70	150	25	48	0	0	5	0	218

a. Calculate the transition probabilities.
b. Predict the equilibrium or steady-state condition for each representative type of dairy farm in Lexington County.
c. What are the assumptions that you include in your prediction in part (b)?

16.7 Find the steady-state probabilities for the Markov processes given by the following transition probability matrices:

a. From: States at t; To: States at $t+1$

$$\begin{bmatrix} 0.2 & 0.6 \\ 0.8 & 0.4 \end{bmatrix}$$

b. From: States at t; To: States at $t+1$

$$\begin{bmatrix} 0 & 0.4 & 0.3 \\ 0.2 & 0 & 0.7 \\ 0.8 & 0.6 & 0 \end{bmatrix}$$

16.8 A market survey conducted by Kleenex Company shows that 70% of the consumers who bought Kleenex this time will buy it again next time but that the remaining 30% will buy some other brand next time. The analysis also indicates that 15% of the consumers who bought other brands this time will shift to Kleenex next time, but that 85% will continue to buy other brands. Write down the transition probability matrix and interpret each row and column.

16.9 Three rival companies, A, B, and C, simultaneously introduce products that are very similar. By the end of the given period, an independent market-research organization conducts a survey and provides the following matrix of transition probabilities:

From: A B C

$$\text{To: } \begin{matrix} A \\ B \\ C \end{matrix} \begin{bmatrix} .50 & .05 & .50 \\ 0 & .90 & 0 \\ .50 & .05 & .50 \end{bmatrix}$$

a. Interpret the data presented in the matrix.
b. Form a transition diagram of the problem, and insert the corresponding transition probabilities on its arrows.
c. By inspection of the data presented in the matrix (without any calculation), can you predict the eventual market share for company A? (Assume, of course, that consumer buying patterns remain constant.)
d. What will be the equilibrium market condition?

16.10 Given the following transition matrix, determine and analyze the equilibrium market share for each company. Which firm will eventually gain all the customers? Why?

$$\begin{array}{c} \\ \text{Co. A} \\ \text{Co. B} \\ \text{Co. C} \end{array} \begin{array}{c} \begin{array}{ccc} \text{Co. A} & \text{Co. B} & \text{Co. C} \end{array} \\ \begin{bmatrix} .2 & .1 & 0 \\ .3 & .6 & 0 \\ .5 & .3 & 1.0 \end{bmatrix} \end{array}$$

16.11 a. Given the following transition matrix, determine the equilibrium market share for each company.

$$\begin{array}{c} \\ \text{Co. X} \\ \text{Co. Y} \\ \text{Co. Z} \end{array} \begin{array}{c} \begin{array}{ccc} \text{Co. X} & \text{Co. Y} & \text{Co. Z} \end{array} \\ \begin{bmatrix} .25 & .05 & .10 \\ .25 & .85 & .20 \\ .50 & .10 & .70 \end{bmatrix} \end{array}$$

b. In an effort to improve its market share, company X considers two marketing strategies. The first is to provide a coupon with its product that the customer can apply to his or her next purchase. Data indicate that this strategy affects the loyalty of company A's own customers as reflected in the following transition matrix:

$$\begin{array}{c} \\ \text{Co. X} \\ \text{Co. Y} \\ \text{Co. Z} \end{array} \begin{array}{c} \begin{array}{ccc} \text{Co. X} & \text{Co. Y} & \text{Co. Z} \end{array} \\ \begin{bmatrix} .50 & .05 & .10 \\ .10 & .85 & .20 \\ .40 & .10 & .70 \end{bmatrix} \end{array}$$

Instead of improving retention probabilities, the second marketing strategy is designed to gain customers from company Y and company Z. The transition matrix resulting from the second market strategy is as follows:

	Co. X	Co. Y	Co. Z
Co. X	.25	.10	.20
Co. Y	.25	.85	.10
Co. Z	.50	.05	.70

Suppose that the costs for both market strategies are the same. If you were the market analyst for company X, which market strategy would you recommend? Why?

16.12 The accounting department of a large department store provides the following matrix that represents all transition probabilities for accounts receivable in three categories: pay on time, delinquent, and unpredictable. These breakdown data are based on the past behavior of the store's customers in paying their monthly bills.

		From:	
	Pay on Time	Delinquent	Unpredictable
To: Pay on Time	.95	.30	.40
To: Delinquent	.05	.60	.40
To: Unpredictable	0	.10	.20

What percentage of credit customers fall into each category, according to the Markovan model of prediction?

16.13 Throughout many older American cities, residential abandonment is spreading like wildfire. The Urban Planning Department of Johnson City has conducted an intensive survey of the city's housing abandonment. The department has classified the city's existing housing according to the quality of housing services, as (1) high-quality, (2) moderate-quality, or (3) low-quality. Statistics indicate that, during the last 10 years, the following changes for each category of housing took place:

1. High-quality housing retained 90% of its families and lost 10% to moderate-quality housing. Nobody moved from high- to low-quality housing.
2. Moderate-quality housing retained 50% of its families and lost 47% to high-quality housing and 3% to low-quality housing.
3. Low-quality housing retained 30% of its families, and lost 60% to moderate-quality housing and 10% to high-quality housing.

By using these data, construct a transition probability matrix. Assume that the total housing market in terms of number of families does not change. What percentage of the total number of families is each form of housing likely to have in the equilibrium or steady-state condition? What are the implications of this equilibrium solution in terms of housing abandonment?

Suggested Readings

Chung, Kai Lai. *Markov Chains with Stationary Transition Probabilities.* Berlin, Germany: Springer-Verlag, 1960.

Derman, C. *Finite State Markov Decision Processes.* New York: Academic Press, 1970.

Hillier, Frederick S., and Gerald J. Lieberman. *Introduction to Operations Research.* San Francisco, Calif.: Holden-Day, 1967. Chapter 13.

Kenney, John G., and J. Laurie Snell. *Finite Markov Chains.* Englewood Cliffs, N.J.: Prentice-Hall, 1960.

Levin, Richard I., and Charles A. Kirkpatrick. *Quantitative Approaches to Management.* 3rd ed. New York: McGraw-Hill, 1976.

Martin, J. J. *Bayesian Decision Problems and Markov Chains.* New York: Wiley, 1967.

Sands, Gary, and Lewis L. Bower. *Vacancy Chains in the Local Housing Market.* Ithaca, N.Y.: Center for Urban Development Research, Cornell University, 1974. Pages 215–28, 257–65.

Thompson, Gerald E. *Management Science: An Introduction to Modern Quantitative Analysis and Decision Making.* New York: McGraw-Hill, 1976. Chapter 17.

17

Forecasting Techniques

Predicting the future when money is at stake is risky. Tangible gains or losses gage the accuracy of such predictions. Good results can contribute significantly to the success, or profits, of any business enterprise.

Future events that affect business operations can be complex. All types of situations arise. For example, the cost of fuel affects consumer driving habits, thereby influencing sales in shopping centers that are primarily accessible by car. Weather affects the size of crop harvests, be it rain in the midwest, freezing temperatures in Florida's citrus groves, or frost in the coffee-growing regions of Brazil. The concoctions of a Parisian dress designer may change the style of fashionable clothing overnight—or they may not. A competitor's advertising campaign can cause shifts in market proportions. Government subsidies may greatly affect an industry's efforts in research and development; space technology and exploration for crude oil are good recent examples. Unemployment affects auto sales. And so on. Future events play an important part in the operation of business enterprises. Shrewd managers forecast regularly, either intuitively or scientifically, in an attempt to improve their performances. This chapter presents various basic forecasting techniques that have proved useful in practice.

17.1 Types of Forecasting

Classical versus Econometric Approaches

Two broad categories of forecasting models exist. The first is the traditional, or classical, approach. ***Classical forecasting*** is based on an analysis of time-series data over regular intervals of time. Specific components of the movement in a series of data are determined and then used for predictive purposes. Assuming that an underlying process will repeat itself, one attempts to decipher the patterns that have arisen in the past and use them to predict the future. To the extent that such patterns are regular and discernible, forecasting based on classical techniques can be productive.

A second class of forecasting techniques is found in econometric analysis. ***Econometric forecasting*** relies heavily on the interplay of cause and effect in a structured, probability-based model of the system or process under consideration. Econometric models often contain simultaneous equations that, in combination, satisfactorily explain much of the observed variability in a series of data. Once constructed, tested, and fine-tuned, such models can be highly effective as forecasting tools in situations where complex, interactive, causal relationships exist. Due to the complexity of even a fairly elementary econometric model, econometric analysis will not be presented in this book.

Basically, classical forecasting techniques look only at ***patterns which a variable itself portrays*** that can be used for predictive purposes. By contrast, econometric analysis is concerned with explaining fluctuations in a variable in terms of ***the causal movement of other variables.*** The classical approach is largely descriptive with little or no explicit specification of causes and effects. Econometric techniques are probability-oriented and founded primarily on causal relationships.

The Usefulness and Accuracy of Forecasting

Good business management requires forecasting to support administrative and planning activities. Inventory purchases, production levels, hiring and firing, budgeting, expenditures for plant and equipment, and outlays for research and development are all standard procedures that require decisions to be made on the basis of future expectations. And above all others, sales is the business variable that one is most likely to forecast.

No technique or combination of techniques guarantees that the forecasted results will occur. However, one can generalize to some extent about the relative accuracy of forecasts under different conditions. Quite clearly, a process that yields erratic and highly fluctuating values over time is less likely to be accurately predicted than a smooth series. Thus a disaggregated series of data (such as individual sales reports) is generally more erratic and more difficult to predict than data that represent broad aggregates (such as sales reports for the total activity of divisions or companies). Similarly, short-term forecasts are usually subject to less error than forecasts made further into the future. Over a longer period of time, more extraneous and unforeseen factors can occur to change the expected results.

Forecasting techniques should suit the purpose for which the forecasting results will be used. Long-term forecasts are most useful for decisions that do not require a high degree of accuracy. For example, a forecasted 30–50% increase in sales over 5 years might call for increased investment in plant or production capacity; less than 30% growth would mean canceling plans for expansion. Likewise, short-term forecasts should be more accurate or highly specific. For example, short-term forecasts might govern the number of sales personnel needed to handle expected business activity or the number of attendants needed to manage an operating facility.

17.2 Simple Forecasting Techniques

A basic hypothesis of classical forecasting techniques is that the future will continue to yield results similar to the results observed in the past. The various forecasting approaches dealt with in this chapter are all based on this fundamental concept. We shall deal with ***time-series data,*** or periodic data measurable at specific time intervals. How to interpret the past in order to predict the future is the problem that confronts a forecaster.

Naive Models The simplest of the ***naive forecasting models*** takes the most recent observed value of a time series and predicts that the next value to occur in the future will be the same. Thus the most elementary of the naive models is

$$\hat{X}_{t+1} = X_t \tag{17.1}$$

where X_t is the observed value of a time-series variable at time period t. The "hat," or inverted v, over the value of X_{t+1} signifies that this is an ***estimated*** value for variable X at time $t + 1$, not necessarily the actual value. We will learn the error of this estimate when we observe the actual value of variable X. Thus

$$\text{Predictive error} = \hat{X}_{t+1} - X_{t+1} \tag{17.2a}$$

Predictive error can also be measured as a percentage:

$$\text{Percentage error} = \frac{\hat{X}_{t+1} - X_{t+1}}{X_{t+1}} \times 100\% \tag{17.2b}$$

Although this first attempt at interpreting the past is simplistic to say the least, it is often used in situations where there is, first, an underlying belief that things are staying fairly constant and, second, a desire to avoid calculations and complex analysis. For example, it is quite common for financial analysts, prior to the announcement of monthly Consumer Price Index figures, to indicate an "expected" rate of inflation that is the same as the last month's recorded rate of inflation. Without any reason to expect otherwise, and wanting to avoid costly sampling or other analysis to improve the accuracy of the estimate, forecasters will pick the last observed value in the series of values.

Certainly, where there is reason to expect change, one might forecast by adding to, or subtracting from, the last observed amount. Thus another naive model for forecasting, the ***additive forecasting model,*** is

$$\hat{X}_{t+1} = X_t + k \tag{17.3}$$

where k is an additive constant. What value should we pick for the constant? Intuitively, we add the amount of change most recently observed in the past:

$$k = X_t - X_{t-1}$$

so that (17.3) becomes

$$\hat{X}_{t+1} = X_t + (X_t - X_{t-1}) \tag{17.4}$$

Alternatively, if the change between time periods fluctuates so much that any one period's change might be unreliable as the additive constant, we might use an average of changes over two or more periods. The following model uses an averaged additive constant over n prior time periods:

$$\hat{X}_{t+1} = X_t + \frac{(X_t - X_{t-1}) + (X_{t-1} - X_{t-2}) + \cdots + (X_{t-n+1} - X_{t-n})}{n} \tag{17.5}$$

Let's consider an example of this approach. Solar Panels, Inc., a firm that produces and sells solar heating units for new homes, has been in business for four years and wishes, for routine planning purposes, to project next year's sales, in units, on the basis of past performance. First, the firm's planner and marketing analyst gather past sales data to see where the firm has been. These figures are given in Table 17.1.

The simplest of the naive approaches would project 1981 sales to be the same as 1980 sales, or 268 units (17.1). But these data can hardly

Table 17.1
Sales, in Units, of Solar Panels, Inc.

Year	Sales	Change over Prior Year
1977	87	
		} +51
1978	138	
		} +62
1979	200	
		} +68
1980	268	

be assumed to be constant. An additive constant equal to the change of 1980 over 1979 would yield a projection of 268 + 68 = 336 units (17.4). Finally, averaging the yearly changes to determine an average additive constant (17.5) yields

$$\hat{X}_{1980} = 268 + \frac{51 + 62 + 68}{3}$$
$$= 268 + 60$$
$$= 328 \text{ units}$$

Where alternative forecasting methods exist, the analyst must use his or her knowledge of the business climate, past and present, to select the forecasting model that most closely fits the conditions that exist. The assumptions that accompany a forecast can be as important as the forecast itself, and they should usually be stated. In this case, a projection of 328 units for 1980 sales assumes that future sales will increase in additive amounts roughly equal to the average yearly changes for the past three years. If agreement is reached on the assumptions, a forecast based on these assumptions must be accepted. If projections are consistently in error, one may wish to question the assumptions and apply techniques that more closely reflect the real situation.

Time-series data may also change according to a growth factor, or a multiplicative constant. Thus another variation of the naive approach projects future amounts on the basis of a constant times the last observed value. This ***multiplicative forecasting model*** is as follows:

$$\hat{X}_{t+1} = kX_t \tag{17.6}$$

where k represents a multiplicative constant. The constant itself may be chosen as the last proportionate change in the observed data; that is,

$$\hat{X}_{t+1} = \left(\frac{X_t}{X_{t-1}}\right) X_t \tag{17.7}$$

Table 17.2
Proportionate Growth in Sales of Solar Panels, Inc.

Year	Sales	Proportionate Change
1977	87	
		} 158.6%
1978	138	
		} 144.9%
1979	200	
		} 134.0%
1980	268	

Alternatively, one may wish to average the proportionate changes from a number of prior periods to determine an average constant of proportionate change:

$$\hat{X}_{t+1} = \frac{\left(\frac{X_t}{X_{t-1}} + \frac{X_{t-1}}{X_{t-2}} + \cdots + \frac{X_{t-n+1}}{X_{t-n}}\right)}{n} \times X_t \qquad (17.8)$$

In our Solar Panels example, suppose the forecasting analysts decide that the process that best describes sales changes is not additive but multiplicative—deriving from proportionate changes or factors of growth. Under these assumptions, the historical data are reanalyzed to determine yearly growth factors from the past. These are given in Table 17.2.

On the basis of these data, we may choose to project future sales using either the most recent proportionate change or the average of observed proportionate changes as the multiplicative constant. In the first case, 1981 sales are predicted to be 134% of actual 1980 sales, or 268 × 1.34 = 359 units. In the second case, the average of the last three years of proportionate changes is used as the multiplicative constant:

$$\hat{X}_{1981} = \frac{158.6\% + 144.9\% + 134.0\%}{3} \times 268$$
$$= 1.458 \times 268$$
$$= 391 \text{ units}$$

Again, results should be accompanied by a careful statement of our assumptions. In this case, we have assumed that sales increase annually by proportionate amounts—that is, by a ***growth factor.***

Moving Averages Often the time-series data are so variable that a forecast that smooths out the choppiness in the data is more useful than one that does not. This is especially true when erratic movements in forecasted amounts are to be avoided and when the underlying, significant movements in the data should be stressed. The process of smoothing relies on averages to reduce statistical variability.

A ***moving average*** is an average of a selected number of terms in a series of data which always represents the latest or most recent terms in the series. Thus, when a new observation is added to the series because of the passage of time, the average moves ahead to include the newest value. Maintaining a fixed number of terms in the average requires dropping the oldest term included in the average of the prior period. The mathematical equation for a four-term moving average is

$$\overline{X}_t = \frac{X_t + X_{t-1} + X_{t-2} + X_{t-3}}{4}$$

where $\overline{X}_t$ is the value of the moving average. In general, the equation for an n-term moving average is

$$\overline{X}_t = \frac{X_t + X_{t-1} + X_{t-2} + \cdots + X_{t-n+1}}{n} \tag{17.9}$$

For example, an organization maintains records that indicate the number of sick days its employees accrue each month. One year's data for a single unit of employees are presented in Table 17.3. Management wishes to produce three-term and seven-term moving averages as a means of smoothing the data and better assessing the underlying pattern of absence due to illness. Calculation of the moving averages is performed in the table. Note, in particular, the process of ***picking up a new term and dropping off an old term*** to maintain a fixed number of terms in the moving average over time.

Figure 17.1 demonstrates the effect of moving averages in reducing the variability of data ("smoothing"). It is a graph of the raw data and the two moving averages from Table 17.3. Note that the choppy aspect of the original data is greatly reduced by the three-term moving average—and even more so by the seven-term moving average. Generally, the greater the number of terms that are included in the moving average, the greater the amount of smoothing the average provides. It is also apparent from the graph that the moving averages lag behind changes in the original data. Here again we can generalize: The greater the number of terms in a moving average, the slower the moving average is to respond to changes in the original data. Consequently, ***choosing the number of terms for a moving average is a trade-off between the***

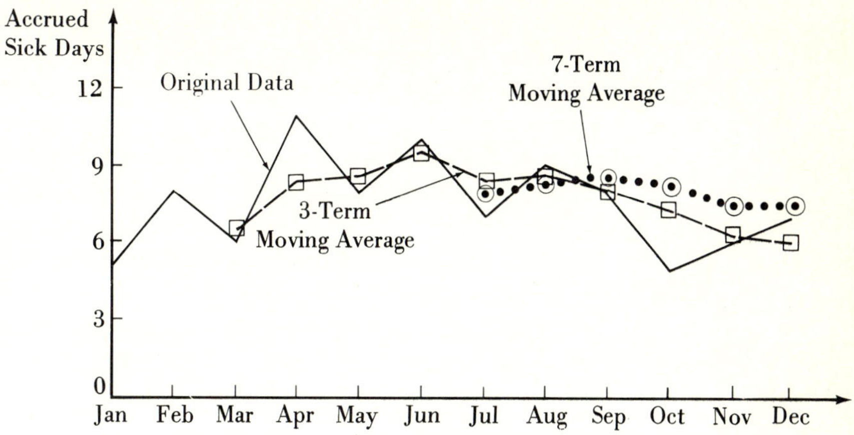

Figure 17.1 Graphical Presentation of Smoothing by Using Moving Averages

Table 17.3 Moving Averages Applied to Accrued Sick Days

Time Period	Days Accrued	Moving Averages: Three-Term	Moving Averages: Seven-Term
Jan.	5		
Feb.	8		
Mar.	6	(5 + 8 + 6)/3 = 6.3	
Apr.	11	(8 + 6 + 11)/3 = 8.3	
May	8	(6 + 11 + 8)/3 = 8.3	
Jun.	10	(11 + 8 + 10)/3 = 9.7	
Jul.	7	(8 + 10 + 7)/3 = 8.3	(5 + 8 + 6 + 11 + 8 + 10 + 7)/7 = 7.9
Aug.	9	(10 + 7 + 9)/3 = 8.7	(8 + 6 + 11 + 8 + 10 + 7 + 9)/7 = 8.4
Sep.	8	(7 + 9 + 8)/3 = 8.0	(6 + 11 + 8 + 10 + 7 + 9 + 8)/7 = 8.4
Oct.	5	(9 + 8 + 5)/3 = 7.3	(11 + 8 + 10 + 7 + 9 + 8 + 5)/7 = 8.3
Nov.	6	(8 + 5 + 6)/3 = 6.3	(8 + 10 + 7 + 9 + 8 + 5 + 6)/7 = 7.6
Dec.	7	(5 + 6 + 7)/3 = 6.0	(10 + 7 + 9 + 8 + 5 + 6 + 7)/7 = 7.4

degree of smoothing and the degree of responsiveness one seeks to obtain from the average.

In addition to their usefulness in smoothing erratic data and creating an improved picture of underlying trends in time-series data, moving averages can be used for prediction. The most common approach for this purpose is to use the basic naive model. In its simplest form, a naive model that employs a moving average predicts that the next value of a time series will equal the last value of the moving average, or

$$\hat{X}_{t+1} = \overline{X}_t \tag{17.10}$$

Thus the latest value of the moving average becomes the predicted next actual value of the time series. Under what conditions is this approach successful? The basic characteristics of moving averages provide an explanation. They are best suited to situations that are highly variable from period to period and wherein the purpose of making the prediction is to take actions on the basis of the underlying movement of the data. One should also remember that ***a moving average characteristically lags behind movements in the actual data,*** and the seriousness of this lag effect in a prediction procedure must be evaluated. Moreover, the degree to which the moving average should provide predictions that are responsive to changes in the actual data necessarily affects the choice of the number of terms to be included in the average. The greater the number of terms, the less responsive the moving average is.

Time-series data that are moving in a significant trend are not appropriately predicted via the ordinary moving-averages approach. Because moving averages are always "trying to catch up" to the trend in the actual data, predictions using this simple approach always provide underestimates with rising trends and overestimates with falling trends. To demonstrate this problem, let us further analyze the Solar Panels sales data and apply two alternative prediction methods.

To provide more detail, suppose that the Solar Panels data are broken down on a quarterly basis. Such data are provided in Table 17.4; note that they are moving steadily upward. A simple four-term moving average has been applied, quarter by quarter, always as a means of predicting the next term in the series. For example, the prediction of 19 units for the next quarter is an average of the prior four quarterly sales values. The next predicted value, 22 units, is also an average of its prior four sales values, and so on. It is clear that predicted values obtained with this approach lag consistently behind the upward-trending actual data, with percentage differences of from −15% to −24%.

For further illustration, consider using the forecasting approach presented in (17.5), and, to remain consistent, consider the particular case of averaging four prior changes in the data:

$$\hat{X}_{t+1} = X_t + \frac{(X_t - X_{t-1}) + (X_{t-1} - X_{t-2}) + (X_{t-2} - X_{t-3}) + (X_{t-3} - X_{t-4})}{4} \quad (17.$$

This average is, of course, a four-term moving average of differences in the data. It is a moving average because, as time progresses, the computation picks up the latest computed difference and drops the oldest difference to maintain a four-term average. Thus the forecasting approach represented in (17.5) and (17.11) adds to the most recently ob-

Table 17.4
Solar Panels Sales Data and Quarterly Forecasts, Using a Four-Term Moving Average

Yearly Sales	Year and Quarter	Quarterly Sales	Prediction $\hat{X}_{t+1} = \bar{X}_t$	Percentage Error
	1976 IV	15		
87	1977 I	17		
	II	21		
	III	24		
	IV	25	19	−24.0%
138	1978 I	28	22	−21.4%
	II	33	25	−24.2%
	III	37	28	−24.3%
	IV	40	31	−22.5%
200	1979 I	44	35	−20.5%
	II	49	39	−20.4%
	III	52	43	−17.3%
	IV	55	46	−16.4%
268	1980 I	59	50	−15.3%
	II	65	54	−16.9%
	III	70	58	−17.1%
	IV	74	62	−16.2%
			67	

served value of a time series the average differences over a given number of time periods. The moving average of differences is used as an estimate of the difference between the most current value of the time series and the next value to occur in the future.

Now let's apply this approach to the sales data of Solar Panels, Inc.—the data that were presented in Table 17.4. This analysis is given in Table 17.5, in which, first, the differences are computed; second, a four-term moving average of differences is calculated (and rounded to the nearest tenth of a unit); and finally, the calculated average difference is added to the most recently observed value to predict the next term in the series. The results are strikingly better than those that the ordinary moving-averages approach yielded (Table 17.4). They range from a +1.9% to a −6.7% error, and most of the predicted values are within 2% of the actual term in the series.

There are good reasons for the improved results shown in Table 17.5. Most important, the actual data in the time series are trending steadily upward, causing the ordinary moving-averages predictor to lag behind the actual data. The size of this lag, alone, is sufficient to cause a constant error of considerable proportions. By shifting to a moving average of

Table 17.5 Quarterly Forecasts Using a Four-Term Moving Average of Differences

Year and Quarter	Quarterly Sales	Differences $X_t - X_{t-1}$	Four-Term Moving Averages of Differences $\hat{X}_t$	Prediction $\hat{X}_{t+1} = X_t + \bar{X}_t$	Percentage Error
1976 IV	15				
1977 I	17	2			
II	21	4			
III	24	3			
IV	25	1	2.5		
1978 I	28	3	2.8	25 + 2.5 = 27.5	−1.8%
II	33	5	3.0	28 + 2.8 = 30.8	−6.7%
III	37	4	3.3	33 + 3.0 = 36.0	−2.7%
IV	40	3	3.5	37 + 3.3 = 40.3	0.8%
1979 I	44	4	4.0	40 + 3.5 = 43.5	−1.1%
II	49	5	4.0	44 + 4.0 = 48.0	−2.0%
III	52	3	3.8	49 + 4.0 = 53.0	1.9%
IV	55	3	3.8	52 + 3.8 = 55.8	1.5%
1980 I	59	4	3.8	55 + 3.8 = 58.8	−0.3%
II	65	6	4.0	59 + 3.8 = 62.8	−3.4%
III	70	5	4.5	65 + 4.0 = 69.0	−1.4%
IV	74	4	4.8	70 + 4.5 = 74.5	0.7%
				74 + 4.8 = 78.8	

differences, we eliminate this lag effect. The latter approach focuses instead on the average difference between consecutive values in the series. A moving average of differences becomes a predictor of the next difference that will occur. Adding the predicted difference to the last observed value then provides a more accurate forecast of the next value in the series. Since the differences are small relative to the actual quarterly sales, and since the trend effect among the differences themselves is small, predictive error is greatly reduced.

Another aspect of the particular data used in this example is worth noting. A graph of the quarterly differences (see Figure 17.2) reveals a ***seasonal movement.*** This means, simply, that the observed differences exhibit a pattern that is based on the time of year. In particular, the largest difference of each year is the difference between second- and first-quarter sales; the smallest is consistently the difference between

Figure 17.2
Four-Term Moving Average of Differences, Solar Panels Data

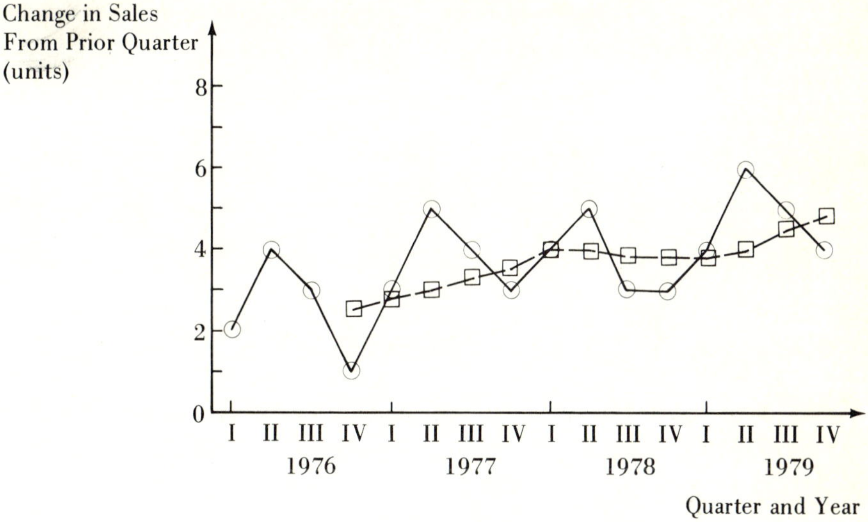

fourth- and third-quarter sales. This pattern repeats itself every four quarters.

Superimposed on the graph of differences is the smoothed series—that is, the four-term moving average of differences. In this case, since the seasonal pattern repeats itself every four quarters, the four-term average is especially well suited to smoothing the peaks and troughs in the data. This is so because the number of terms in the moving average just matches the number of observations necessary for one complete run through the seasons, or one cycle in the data. Therefore, the moving average never contains two peaks or two troughs simultaneously. Whatever the starting point, each four-term average encompasses exactly one full cycle of data. Consequently, the smoothing achieved with a four-term moving average should be better than that achieved with a moving average based on a larger or smaller number of terms. Generally, where data display a regular seasonal pattern, moving averages that are ***in phase*** with the seasonal cycle provide the best smoothing.

Ordinary Weighted Moving Averages

One often finds time-series data for which prediction is best accomplished by emphasizing knowledge of the most recently observed data. In the physical world, this characteristic is found in any tracking problem involving irregular movement. (The type of tracking that military personnel employ with unknown aircraft or submarines that might purposely not hold to a set course is a good example.) One might obtain data that are erratic, highly variable, and even "deceptive." Lacking an identifiable, predictive pattern or trend, such data might lend themselves to smoothing, just as other data to which we might apply moving averages. But we face a special problem when the predictive usefulness of the most recently observed values outweighs the usefulness of more distant values from the past. We must apply special adaptive procedures to such problems to reflect the increased predictive usefulness of the most recently observed data.

A ***weighted moving average*** is calculated as follows:

$$\overline{X}_t = \frac{w_1X_t + w_2X_{t-1} + \cdots + w_nX_{t-n+1}}{w_1 + w_2 + \cdots + w_n} \tag{17.12}$$

where w_i are weighting constants and X_i are observed data values. Of course, a trivial special case of a weighted moving average occurs when all weighting constants are set equal to 1. Then,

$$\overline{X}_t = \frac{X_t + X_{t-1} + \cdots + X_{t-n+1}}{n} \tag{17.13}$$

which is simply the formula for an ordinary moving average.

Various weighting schemes can be employed, but a weighted moving average usually applies progressively lower weights to older terms in the average. Thus we would typically specify weights such that

$$w_1 > w_2 > \cdots > w_n$$

Again, a differences approach is often most productive when we are applying weighted moving averages. Just as before, this is true whenever tracking and predicting the direction of movement are important. Combining the latest known position with the latest forecasted direction and amount of change affords a prediction of the next period's position or value. This is the approach used in (17.5) and (17.8) and in Table 17.5. However, when the latest observed direction is considered a better indicator of future movement than any other observed movement in the data, it is most appropriate to apply a weighted moving average to observed differences. This tracking and predicting process is analogous to the aircraft or submarine problem we mentioned. The direction of movement of physical objects is measured by the differences between coordinates of physical location. The direction in which economic or business variables are moving is measured by the differences between observed values of a time series.

Many economic and business variables are suitably forecast using direction, differences, and weighted moving averages. In particular, industry sales (automobiles, for example) are typically reported on the basis of change over the prior month. For the economy overall, industrial production is reported monthly in the same manner. More immediate to the needs of an individual firm, sales and inventory levels are both appropriately presented in terms of percentage change from the prior month.

Consider, for example, the hypothetical sales data given in Table 17.6 for an automobile manufacturing firm. These data have purposely been constructed to incorporate sudden, substantial changes that will affect production and other management decisions. The technique of analysis and prediction is to smooth the differences by using a weighted average but, moreover, to employ a weighted moving average that will respond to the rapid changes in direction occurring in the data.

Since the changes in the data are expressed in proportionate or percentage terms, a predictive model of the sort given in (17.8) would be appropriate, except that now we will use a weighted moving average of the proportionate changes. Suppose that a four-term moving average is chosen and suppose, furthermore, that the weights for each of the terms from most recent to most distant are 0.4, 0.3, 0.2, and 0.1. Then the weighted moving average is calculated as follows:

$$\overline{P}_t = \frac{0.4P_t + 0.3P_{t-1} + 0.2P_{t-2} + 0.1P_{t-3}}{(0.4 + 0.3 + 0.2 + 0.1) = 1} \tag{17.14}$$

where P_t is the proportionate rate of change observed at time period t and $\overline{P}_t$ is the four-term weighted moving average of proportionate changes. The denominator is equal to 1 only because the sum of the weights equals 1. If weights had been chosen otherwise, the denominator might not equal 1; ***it must always equal the sum of the weights.***

As before, when using moving averages for predictive purposes, we use the most recent value of the weighted average to predict the next future value of the weighted average. That is,

$$\hat{P}_{t+1} = \overline{P}_t \tag{17.15}$$

Consequently, on the basis of proportionate changes between observed values of the time-series data, we predict the next term in the series to be

$$\hat{X}_{t+1} = X_t \times \hat{P}_{t+1} \tag{17.16}$$

Table 17.6 Actual and Predicted Gross Sales, in Thousands of Units, for the American Automobile Manufacturing Company, Inc.

Year and Month	Units Sold (thousands)	Percentage Change over Prior Month	Weighted Moving Averages of Percentage Changes	Predicted Sales Next Month
1978				
J	23.5	+4.2%		
F	24.7	+4.9%		
M	25.6	+3.7%		
A	26.9	+5.1%	+4.55%	
M	27.2	+1.0%	+3.16%	28.1
J	26.6	−2.3%	+0.77%	28.1
J	26.7	+0.4%	+0.18%	26.8
A	25.4	−4.8%	−2.16%	26.7
S	24.1	−6.4%	−4.15%	24.9
O	23.9	−0.9%	−3.20%	23.1
N	23.2	−3.0%	−3.23%	23.1
D	23.6	+1.6%	−1.08%	22.5
1979				
J	24.9	+5.5%	+1.99%	23.3
F	25.8	+3.6%	+3.11%	25.4
M	26.2	+1.5%	+2.94%	26.6
A	26.9	+2.8%	+2.84%	27.0
M	27.2	+1.2%	+1.98%	27.7
J	27.5	+3.4%	+2.43%	27.7
J	26.6	−3.3%	+0.22%	28.2
A	26.9	+1.3%	+0.33%	26.7
S	28.2	+4.7%	+1.95%	27.0
O	29.1	+3.3%	+2.66%	28.7
N	28.2	−3.0%	+0.86%	29.9
D	26.6	−5.6%	−2.01%	28.4
1980				
J	25.3	−4.7%	−3.83%	26.1
F	23.3	−7.9%	−5.99%	24.3
M	22.2	−4.9%	−5.83%	21.9
A	21.6	−2.5%	−4.52%	20.9
				20.6

Figure 17.3
Proportionate Changes Smoothed with a Weighted Moving Average, American Automobile Manufacturing Data

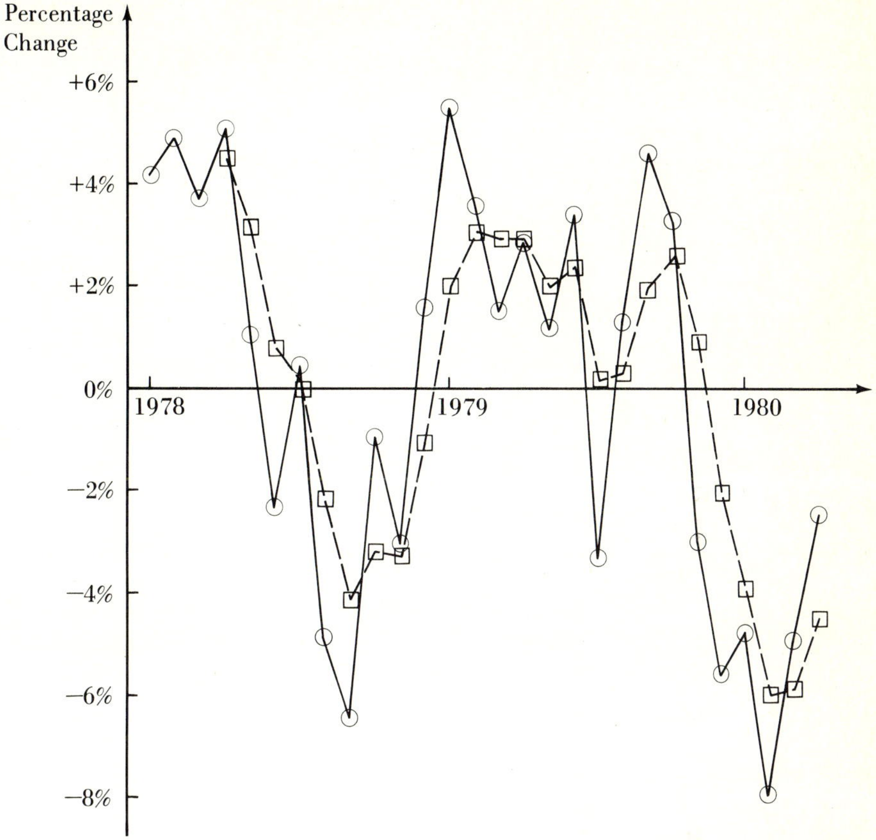

This sequence of calculations—first, determining the weighted moving averages of percentage changes; second, selecting the latest average proportionate change to use for prediction; third, estimating the next value in the series on the basis of the predicted proportionate change—is the same sequence of calculations used to complete Table 17.6. The actual proportionate changes are graphed in Figure 17.3, together with a superimposed drawing of the values of the weighted moving average. Both from the table of actual numbers and from the graph of proportionate values, it is clear that the weighted moving average reacts responsively to movements in the series of proportionate changes. Later in this chapter we will discuss responsiveness further and compare the different types of moving averages.

Exponentially Weighted Moving Averages

The weighting scheme we have just discussed is a convenient one based on a four-term moving average. Indeed, the possibilities for combining different weighting schemes with various numbers of terms to be included in the average are limitless. The choice of an appropriate combination of terms and weights usually depends on the data and the user's needs. Although quantitative measures can be found that are meant to optimize the predictive ability of moving averages, such choices are often made by analysts on the basis of general suitability and appropriateness.

A variation of the weighted-moving-averages approach uses weights drawn from a geometric, or exponential, series, and hence is called an ***exponentially weighted moving average.*** As before, we assign the greatest weight to the most recent value in the series and declining weights to progressively more distant values. Once again, this approach is intended to be more ***adaptive,*** or responsive to sudden changes in direction and amount in the time series.

For convenience, suppose that we start with a geometric series such as

$$1, \tfrac{1}{2}, \tfrac{1}{4}, \tfrac{1}{8}, \ldots, \left(\tfrac{1}{2}\right)^{n-1}$$

Each term in this geometric series is obtained by raising the fraction $\frac{1}{2}$ to an appropriate power, and each term in the series is smaller than the prior term by a factor of $\frac{1}{2}$.

In the general case, a geometric series of this type can be formed with any fraction or, in fact, any proportionate amount between 0 and 1. Consequently, the general case of this geometric series is

$$1, (1 - a), (1 - a)^2, (1 - a)^3, \ldots, (1 - a)^{n-1}$$

where $0 < a < 1$.

Such a series establishes a sequence of exponentially declining values that can be used appropriately as weights in a weighted moving average. The most recent value of the time series receives the greatest weight. Thus an exponentially weighted moving average is calculated as follows:

$$\overline{X}_t = \frac{1X_t + (1 - a)X_{t-1} + (1 - a)^2X_{t-2} + \cdots + (1 - a)^{n-1}X_{t-(n-1)}}{1 + (1 - a) + (1 - a)^2 + \cdots + (1 - a)^{n-1}} \quad (17.17)$$

Especially if the number of terms in this expression is large, the calculation required appears at first glance to be overly burdensome. But various simplifications greatly reduce the computational burden. To begin with, the denominator of (17.17) can be simplified because it is the sum of terms in a geometric series. In particular, where the number of terms in a geometric series is large and the ratio r between terms lies between 0 and 1, the sum s of the geometric series is

$$s = \frac{-1}{r - 1} \tag{17.18}$$

In this case, the ratio between terms of the geometric series is $(1 - a)$; therefore, the sum is simply

$$s = \frac{-1}{(1 - a) - 1} \quad \text{or} \quad \frac{1}{a} \tag{17.19}$$

Consequently, we can simplify (17.17) by combining it with the result of (17.19), which yields

$$\overline{X}_t = a[X_t + (1 - a)X_{t-1} + (1 - a)^2X_{t-2} + \cdots] \tag{17.20}$$

We can further simplify by analyzing the process of calculation between time periods. For example, the moving average for the prior time period is

$$\overline{X}_{t-1} = a[X_{t-1} + (1 - a)X_{t-2} + (1 - a)^2X_{t-3} + \cdots] \tag{17.21}$$

The difference between exponentially weighted moving averages from one time period, $t - 1$, to the next, t, is therefore

$$\overline{X}_t - \overline{X}_{t-1} = a[X_t - X_{t-1} - (1 - a)X_{t-2} - (1 - a)^2X_{t-3} - \cdots] \tag{17.22}$$

which is the same as

$$\overline{X}_t - \overline{X}_{t-1} = a[X_t - \overline{X}_{t-1}] \tag{17.23}$$

Consequently

$$\overline{X}_t = aX_t + \overline{X}_{t-1} - a\overline{X}_{t-1}$$

or

$$\overline{X}_t = aX_t + (1 - a)\overline{X}_{t-1} \tag{17.24}$$

This result greatly simplifies the process of calculating exponentially weighted moving averages. It shows that ***the current value of the exponentially weighted average is a constant times the most recently ob-***

served value of the time series plus the same constant subtracted from 1, times the last-computed moving average value. It is a very useful result in applications that require both responsiveness of weighted moving averages and ease of computation.

The constant a that enters into the calculation of exponentially weighted moving averages can be selected to be any value between 0 and 1. It is called the ***smoothing constant,*** and, as the name suggests, it affects the degree of smoothing obtained. A value of a close to 0 provides the most smoothing and the least responsiveness. In terms of the variability of the moving average itself, such a low smoothing constant provides a moving average equivalent to a regular moving average consisting of a large number of terms. Of course, the exponentially weighted moving average still responds more readily to the most recently observed values in the time series than an equivalent regular moving average does. Conversely, a value of a that is farther away from 0 gives more weight to current data and thus provides less smoothing and greater responsiveness. It causes the exponentially weighted moving average to act more like a regular moving average that has very few terms. In ordinary practice, the range of the smoothing constant used with exponentially weighted moving averages is from about 0.1 to 0.4, with greater smoothing provided by the lower values.

For an example of the use of exponentially weighted moving averages, let's return to the data for American Automobile Manufacturing. Table 17.7 gives an exponentially weighted moving average of percentage changes, using the same data as before for units sold. A smoothing constant of $a = 0.4$ has been chosen—a value that will provide responsiveness comparable to that of the four-term weighted moving average computed in Table 17.6.

Since an exponentially weighted moving average is computed using the most recent period's exponentially weighted average as part of the computation (a value not known initially), a brief discussion of how one gets started is in order. One must begin the computational process with some "guesstimate" about what the most recent period's moving average would be if it were known. Various techniques can be used for this. When dealing with moving averages of rates of change, one can simply assume zero to be the starting point. If this assumption is incorrect, one must recognize that the first calculations of the exponentially weighted average will be in error and should not be used. Over a few periods, the moving average will adjust itself and quickly eliminate any initial error.

Another "rule-of-thumb" method for getting an exponentially weighted moving average started is to assume that the most recent period's av-

Table 17.7
An Exponentially Weighted Moving Average Applied to Percentage Changes in Monthly Sales Data of the American Automobile Manufacturing Company

Year and Month	Percentage Change over Prior Month	Exponentially Weighted Moving Averages of Percentage Changes	
1978			
J	4.2%		
F	4.9%	Initial	
M	3.7%	Average: 4.475%	
A	5.1%		
M	1.0%	(.4 × 1.0) + (.6 × 4.475) =	3.085%
J	−2.3%	(.4 × −2.3) + (.6 × 3.085) =	0.931%
J	0.4%	etc.	0.72%
A	−4.8%		−1.49%
S	−6.4%		−3.45%
O	−0.9%		−2.43%
N	−3.0%		−2.66%
D	1.6%		−0.96%
1979			
J	5.5%		1.63%
F	3.6%		2.42%
M	1.5%		2.05%
A	2.8%		2.35%
M	1.2%		1.89%
J	3.4%		2.49%
J	−3.3%		0.18%
A	1.3%		0.63%
S	4.7%		2.26%
O	3.3%		2.67%
N	−3.0%		0.40%
D	−5.6%		−2.00%
1980			
J	−4.7%		−3.08%
F	−7.9%		−5.01%
M	−4.9%		−4.96%
A	−2.5%		−3.89%

erage is the same as the first value of the series to which the moving average will be applied. This also may or may not be a correct assumption, so the first few moving-average values computed should be discounted. Perhaps the most reliable method of getting started with an exponentially weighted average is to use an ordinary arithmetic average of several of the first terms in the series and then assume that this value will closely approximate the starting point of the exponentially weighted average.

In Table 17.7, the first four percentage changes were averaged to provide a starting value for the exponentially weighted moving average. Thenceforth, the computations proceed according to (17.24), where a is 0.4.

A comparison of the weighted moving averages in Tables 17.6 and 17.7 shows very similar results. One approach is not necessarily better than the other. The analyst must choose which system of moving averages operates most satisfactorily for the data being used and the purposes to which the moving average will be put. Note, however, that experimenting with different moving averages is easiest with exponentially weighted averages, because one needs to change only a single constant in order to obtain different averaging characteristics. In the end, the final choice of a moving average depends on both a proper balance of desired characteristics and an intuitive feeling that the selected average performs suitably under the given conditions.

Moving Averages Summarized A moving average that is relatively more responsive provides relatively less smoothing, and vice versa. Working with moving averages always involves a trade-off between smoothing and responsiveness. Weighted moving averages, whether weighted exponentially or otherwise, provide more rapid adaptation to sudden changes in the direction of time-series data. Finally, one should also consider whether to apply a selected moving average to the actual data one is working with or to changes in values of data in the series. Where the latter is the case, one should consider the appropriateness of working with actual or proportionate changes. The decision maker who gives proper attention to all of these factors can develop simple but effective predictive models that can help considerably in a variety of business forecasting situations.

17.3 Trend Analysis

In business and economics, one often encounters time-series data that portray a fairly consistent trend in their movement. Forecasting techniques can take advantage of this consistency of movement by assuming, quite simply, that the observed data will continue into the future largely along the same trend that they have shown in the past. These techniques are basically extrapolation procedures that project past data into the future.

Typical Characteristics of Trend Data

Although ***trend analysis*** is appropriate for many types of data, data that are broad-based aggregates and data viewed over a relatively long period of time often fall into this category. For example, most national economic time series show consistent trends through the postwar years.

For business decision-making purposes, analysis of trends in the national economy helps provide a proper perspective on the overall business climate. And businesses face many variables more immediately, such as energy costs, salary levels, regional population growth, market share, costs of raw materials, property values, and government defense contracts. Wherever a reliable trend exists, and in any case in which it is reasonable to assume a continuing trend in the future, projections based on the past trend can, and if necessary should, be made. Many such forecasts suit long-range planning needs. Whether short-term or long-term, whether for planning or other purposes, trend analysis can be a very useful predictive device.

Data that exhibit a trend over time often fluctuate according to recognizable patterns, and forecasters usually attempt to dissect this complex movement to determine its specific components. Depending on the given data, any or all of the following components may exist:

1. The underlying trend itself
2. A cyclical pattern
3. Seasonal fluctuations
4. Irregular or random movement

The ***trend*** is the basic, consistent directional movement of the data, which may appear straight or curved when graphed. There may be ***cyclical movement*** in the data, which can be recognized as a relatively smooth oscillation about the trend. For most business and economics applications, this oscillation will cycle over a period of years and therefore, like the trend component, represents long-term patterns of movement. Seasonal fluctuations occur generally within the duration of a single year of data. The last component, ***irregular movement***, is whatever is left over after other components have been identified. It is choppy, short-term movement that represents random variation in the variable being observed.

A good way to start factoring out components of a time series is to graph the data, thereby allowing for visual recognition of any patterns that exist. Various sophisticated computer techniques can be used to assist in the factoring process, but these are based on statistical procedures that extend beyond the scope of this book. In the sections that follow, techniques for determining trends are covered in detail, and all other variation is assumed to be irregular.

Trend Lines, Computation, and Projection

Aside from purely visual analysis, the basic problem of trend analysis is to identify the mathematical equation that best describes the underlying trend exhibited by a given set of data. The mathematical equation then becomes a representation of expected movement in the data. It can be used for projecting into the future and for analyzing past deviations from the expected.

The simplest mathematical form that can be applied to trend analysis is the ordinary straight line. For a given variable Y that moves with a dependence on time t, the linear trend relationship is

$$Y_t = a + bt \tag{17.25}$$

The specific line that best describes a given set of data is identified by a particular combination of parameters a and b in (17.25). To determine these parameters is to determine the trend line. The technique for doing so is called ***regression analysis.*** Whereas the topic of regression is treated at great length in the study of statistics and econometrics, its treatment here will be limited to trend lines of the sort described in (17.25). In a nutshell, using basic regression techniques allows us to determine a trend line that best fits a given set of data. Projecting the trend line into the future is then a useful forecasting technique.

Consider, for example, a major machine tool manufacturer that knows from experience that there is a strong relationship between its own production levels and the total domestic investment expenditures in the economy and therefore follows business investment statistics closely as a key indicator of its own situation. Past data have been collected on a yearly basis extending back to 1946. These are presented in Table 17.8. The problem now is to find the trend line that best fits these data and to forecast future business investment expenditures for the year 1985.

Although a complete mathematical derivation of the regression procedure will not be given here, the following discussion should explain the fundamentals and the computational process. The observed values in Table 17.8 represent a trend, but they do not all lie on a single line. These observations, then, are a scatter of points for which a trend line must be found. For any line that one might pick to represent the trend in these data, there will be numerous differences between what the trend would indicate as an expected value of expenditures and what the actual expenditures were observed to be. Conceptually, therefore, the trend line that fits best should be the one for which these differences are a minimum. Indeed, the statistical criterion for a ***best-fit regression line*** is that the sum of the squares of deviations between the regression

Table 17.8
Gross Private Domestic Investment Expenditures, 1946–1978

Year	Expenditures (billions of dollars)
1946	30.7
1947	34.0
1948	45.9
1949	35.3
1950	53.8
1951	59.2
1952	52.1
1953	53.3
1954	52.7
1955	68.4
1956	71.0
1957	69.2
1958	61.9
1959	77.6
1960	76.4
1961	74.3
1962	85.2
1963	90.2
1964	96.6
1965	112.0
1966	124.5
1967	120.8
1968	131.5
1969	146.2
1970	140.8
1971	160.0
1972	188.3
1973	220.0
1974	214.6
1975	190.9
1976	243.0
1977	297.8
1978	344.5

Source: *Economic Report of the President*, 1979, p. 199.

line and the observed values is a minimum. This is often called ***least-squares regression,*** or the least-squares fit.

As in any linear algebraic relationship, the parameters a and b of the regression trend line (see equation 17.25) represent the Y intercept and the slope of the line, respectively. Briefly reviewing these simple algebraic concepts, observe that, if the value of t is set equal to 0 in (17.25), then $Y_t = a$. In other words, the parameter a represents the value of Y_t when $t = 0$, which is the point where the line intercepts the Y axis, or the Y intercept. The parameter b determines the amount that Y_t changes for each incremental increase in the value of t; hence, it represents the slope of the line. A slope of 0 indicates a horizontal line. A slope of 1 indicates a line inclined at an angle of 45° from the horizontal; in this case, 1 unit of increase in t results in exactly 1 unit of increase in Y_t.

To calculate the values of a and b, one must use two equations, each containing various sums of the data, sums of squares, and sums of cross-products. These equations are

$$b = \frac{\Sigma tY - \dfrac{\Sigma t \Sigma Y}{n}}{\Sigma t^2 - \dfrac{(\Sigma t)^2}{n}} \tag{17.26}$$

and

$$a = \frac{1}{n}(\Sigma Y - b\Sigma t) \tag{17.27}$$

To interpret these two formulas, first review the various terms that indicate summation. Both the sum of values of t and the sum of the values of Y are required. Equation (17.26) also calls for a sum of cross-products (the products of corresponding pairs of t and Y), and there is a sum of the values of t squared. This requires some detailed computation, and suddenly these procedures appear very much more statistical than mathematical.

A worksheet has been prepared for all of the necessary calculations. It contains the paired values of t and Y, which represent observations on the investment-expenditures variable. It contains the columns of cross-products and t values squared. And, as a computational device, it contains a recoded list of the years under observation. This serves to simplify all of the computations involving values of t, because these values are now kept to small and manageable numbers. Review this worksheet, which is presented in Table 17.9, and verify all calculations.

Table 17.9 Worksheet for Computing the Trend Line

Year	Year Recoded t	Expenditures Y	$t \times Y$	t^2
1946	1	30.7	30.7	1
1947	2	34.0	68.0	4
1948	3	45.9	137.7	9
1949	4	35.3	141.2	16
1950	5	53.8	269.0	25
1951	6	59.2	355.2	36
1952	7	52.1	364.7	49
1953	8	53.3	426.4	64
1954	9	52.7	474.3	81
1955	10	68.4	684.0	100
1956	11	71.0	781.0	121
1957	12	69.2	830.4	144
1958	13	61.9	804.7	169
1959	14	77.6	1086.4	196
1960	15	76.4	1146.0	225
1961	16	74.3	1188.8	256
1962	17	85.2	1448.4	289
1963	18	90.2	1623.6	324
1964	19	96.6	1835.4	361
1965	20	112.0	2240.0	400
1966	21	124.5	2614.5	441
1967	22	120.8	2657.6	484
1968	23	131.5	3024.5	529
1969	24	146.2	3508.8	576
1970	25	140.8	3520.0	625
1971	26	160.0	4160.0	676
1972	27	188.3	5084.1	729
1973	28	220.0	6160.0	784
1974	29	214.6	6223.4	841
1975	30	190.9	5727.0	900
1976	31	243.0	7533.0	961
1977	32	297.8	9529.6	1024
1978	33	344.5	11368.5	1089
Totals:	561	3822.7	87046.9	12529

The focus of this worksheet eventually falls on the column totals, which we need in order to apply (17.26) and (17.27) to derive the parameters of the trend line.

Note that we must calculate the slope b first, because we must know the value of the slope to use the formula for a. Therefore, starting with (17.26), we calculate the first parameter:

$$b = \frac{\Sigma tY - \dfrac{\Sigma t \Sigma Y}{n}}{\Sigma t^2 - \dfrac{(\Sigma t)^2}{n}}$$

$$= \frac{87{,}046.9 - \dfrac{561 \times 3822.7}{33}}{12{,}529 - \dfrac{(561)^2}{33}}$$

$$= 7.37$$

Then we calculate the Y intercept:

$$a = \frac{1}{n}(\Sigma Y - b\Sigma t)$$

$$= \frac{1}{33}[3822.7 - (7.37 \times 561)]$$

$$= -9.51$$

Thus the best-fit trend line has been determined for these given data. It is

$$Y_t = -9.51 + 7.37t$$

where $t = 1$ represents 1946.

To predict a future value of this series of data via the trend line, one calculates the expected value of Y on the trend line for the given future value of t. Thus the prediction for 1985 (corresponding to $t = 40$) is

$$\dot{Y}_{1985} = -9.51 + 7.37(40)$$

$$= 285.3 \qquad \text{(billion dollars)}$$

A graph of the data and the trend line, which has been superimposed, is shown in Figure 17.4.

Figure 17.4
Gross Domestic Investment Expenditures, 1946–1978, with a Linear Trend

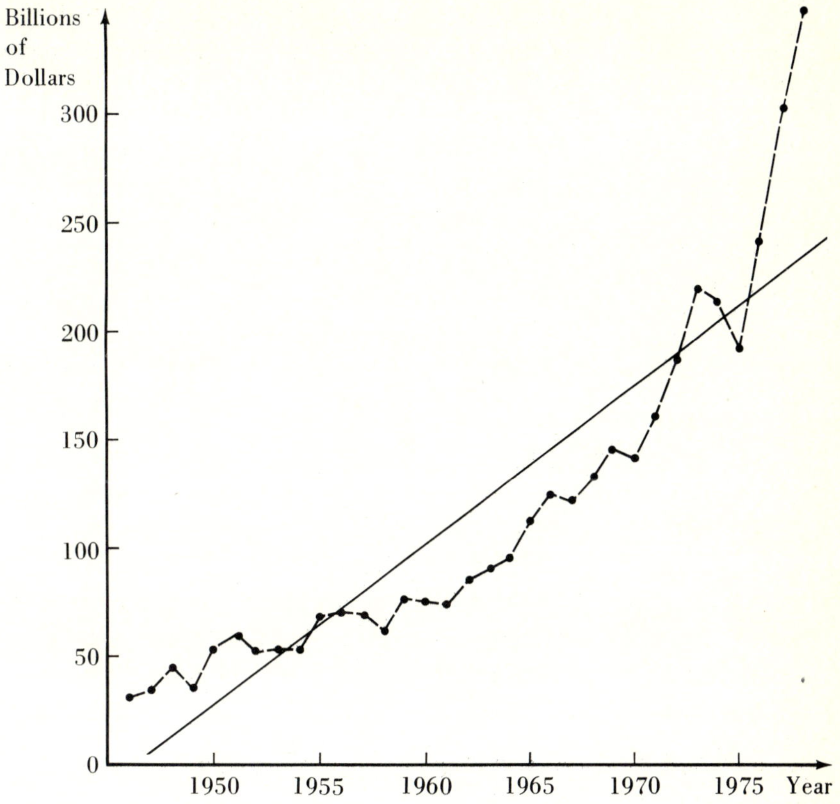

Semilogarithmic Trends

Calculating a trend line using regression techniques is only part of a good forecaster's background and training. Finding an appropriate forecasting model that provides reasonable accuracy can be at least as demanding as doing the calculations. In this section, various trend analysis models are explored that are not ordinary linear models. We seek to answer the question, "What type of trend model, or models, can be used for situations in which a variable describes a consistent trend, but one that is curved rather than linear?" The best approach is to continue with the linear regression techniques we have already developed, but to modify them in ways that yield curved, or ***curvilinear,*** results.

It has long been recognized in business, finance, economics, and statistics that growth variables, which increase generally in constant proportion over each time period, are nonlinear and constantly increasing in slope when plotted on ordinary graph paper. This is because the graph is constructed with arithmetic scales of measurement, whereas the growth phenomenon fosters increases that are compounding over time. Consequently, special graph paper has been constructed to show constant growth as an apparently linear relationship. This is the familiar semilogarithmic graph paper that is widely used with business and economics time-series data—that is, with growth variables. It is called ***semilogarithmic***, because only one of the two axes, the vertical axis, is measured on a logarithmic scale. The other, horizontal, axis which usually represents time, is measured on an ordinary arithmetic scale.

We will briefly review the use of semilogarithmic graph paper to illustrate that the same technique of transforming one axis of a graph to a logarithmic scale can be applied mathematically for trend line analysis and forecasting purposes, without graph paper. By transforming the data that describe a growth variable to logarithmic values, we achieve the same result: a curved growth relationship that appears linear wherever a constant rate of growth occurs. Such transformations, of which several exist, are called ***curvilinear relationships.*** They are relationships that, when plotted using ordinary arithmetic scales, appear curved, but, when transformed using logarithms or other transformations, show ordinary linear characteristics.

Consider first the semilogarithmic transformation. As an example, let's return to the situation faced by the machine tool manufacturer that seeks projections of gross domestic investment expenditures. Although trend line procedures were completed correctly from a mathematical point of view, the earlier results represent only a good first effort, at best. Certainly, the decision maker in this situation would have to ask the question, "How is it possible that investment expenditures projected to 1988 are estimated to be $285 billion when now, in 1981, the value is already $345 billion and growing?" The answer, of course, is that a straight-line trend grossly underestimates future values of a growth variable. Indeed, a straight-line trend quite simply is not a suitable model for forecasting growth. This fact is demonstrated quite clearly by Figure 17.4, which shows the inaccuracy and inappropriateness of the linear trend relationship applied to data that describe a curve. Mathematically, it is the best-fit line for the given data; analytically, and for forecasting purposes, it is a misfit indeed.

So let's try again to develop a model for the gross investment data that more adequately describes this curved relationship. The general case of a growth model is found in mathematics to be exponential growth, which has the following equation:

$$Y = ae^{bt} \tag{17.28}$$

We can take the log of both sides of this equation as follows:

$$\log Y = \log a + bt \log e \tag{17.29}$$

Indeed, if we use natural logarithms (denoted "ln" instead of "log"), which are logarithms with a base of $e = 2.7182$, then $\ln e = 1$ and:

$$\ln Y = \ln a + bt \tag{17.30}$$

Now observe the correspondence between this relationship and an ordinary straight line. If we transform the original data to the natural log of these data,

$$Y = \ln Y \tag{17.31}$$

and likewise transform the Y intercept to its natural log equivalent,

$$A = \ln a \tag{17.32}$$

then a linear result occurs. It is

$$Y = A + bt \tag{17.33}$$

This should really be designated a curvilinear result, because linearity is achieved only by means of a semilogarithmic transformation.

Note that (17.30) is entirely analogous to the purposes and results of semilogarithmic graphing of a growth variable. Now, however, having derived the curvilinear form of an exponential growth equation, we can apply ordinary regression techniques to obtain a curvilinear trend relationship. The same calculations must be performed as for an ordinary linear regression analysis, but now all Y values will be transformed to their natural log equivalents. Therefore, (17.26) and (17.27) become

$$b = \frac{\Sigma(t \ln Y) - \dfrac{\Sigma t \Sigma \ln Y}{n}}{\Sigma t^2 - \dfrac{(\Sigma t)^2}{n}} \tag{17.34}$$

and

$$a = \frac{1}{n}(\Sigma \ln Y - b\Sigma t) \tag{17.35}$$

Although dealing with natural logs is easiest with an electronic calculator that has this as an automatic function, tables of natural logs are available and can be used readily.

Next, we apply these two formulas as before to determine the best-fit regression relationship, but this time to determine a curvilinear trend. We need the sum of transformed Y values, the sum of cross-products (also based on transformed Y values), and the sums of t values and of t values squared. As before, we recode the time variable to an equivalent system of smaller numbers. These calculations are given in Table 17.10.

On the basis of the results we obtain from Table 17.10, we make the final computations

$$b = \frac{2747.4390 - \dfrac{561 \times 150.1719}{33}}{12{,}529 - \dfrac{(561)^2}{33}}$$

$$= 0.0650$$

$$a = \frac{1}{33}[150.1719 - (0.065 \times 561)]$$

$$= 3.4455$$

Therefore, according to (17.30), the curvilinear result is

$$\ln Y = 3.4455 + 0.065t \qquad (17.36)$$

Projection is accomplished, as before, by using the regression result calculated at some future value of t. For example, the curvilinear trend prediction of gross domestic-investment expenditures in 1985 (corresponding to $t = 40$) is

$$\ln Y_{1985} = 3.4455 + 0.065\,(40)$$

$$= 6.0455$$

This is the logarithm of the projected amount. The antilog of 6.0455 is 422.2. Therefore, on the basis of the semilogarithmic model, investment expenditures in 1985 are expected to be \$422.2 billion.

The curvilinear trend line has been superimposed on a graph of the actual data in Figure 17.5. We accomplish this by using (17.36) to determine a series of representative points along the curve and plotting and connecting them. Here, as in the foregoing projection calculation, we must determine antilog values in order to derive actual values of Y on the curvilinear trend. One can see that this yields a trend representation that is generally very close to the actual data.

Table 17.10 Worksheet for Computing a Semilogarithmic Trend

Year	Year Recoded t	Expenditures Y	Expenditures Transformed $\ln Y$	$t \times \ln Y$	t_2
1946	1	30.7	3.4243	3.4243	1
1947	2	34.0	3.5264	7.0527	4
1948	3	45.9	3.8265	11.4794	9
1949	4	35.3	3.5639	14.2555	16
1950	5	53.8	3.9853	19.9264	25
1951	6	59.2	4.0809	24.4855	36
1952	7	52.1	3.9532	27.6722	49
1953	8	53.3	3.9759	31.8075	64
1954	9	52.7	3.9646	35.6815	81
1955	10	68.4	4.2254	42.2537	100
1956	11	71.0	4.2627	46.8895	121
1957	12	69.2	4.2370	50.8440	144
1958	13	61.9	4.1255	53.6318	169
1959	14	77.6	4.3516	60.9219	196
1960	15	76.4	4.3360	65.0397	225
1961	16	74.3	4.3081	68.9298	256
1962	17	85.2	4.4450	75.5650	289
1963	18	90.2	4.5020	81.0365	324
1964	19	96.6	4.5706	86.8410	361
1965	20	112.0	4.7185	94.3700	400
1966	21	124.5	4.8243	101.3104	441
1967	22	120.8	4.7941	105.4710	484
1968	23	131.5	4.8790	112.2172	529
1969	24	146.2	4.9850	119.6394	576
1970	25	140.8	4.9473	123.6835	625
1971	26	160.0	5.0752	131.9545	676
1972	27	188.3	5.2380	141.4270	729
1973	28	220.0	5.3936	151.0216	784
1974	29	214.6	5.3688	155.6945	841
1975	30	190.9	5.2517	157.5525	900
1976	31	243.0	5.4931	170.2849	961
1977	32	297.8	5.6964	182.2855	1024
1978	33	344.5	5.8421	192.7891	1089
Totals:	561		150.1719	2747.4390	12529

Figure 17.5 Gross Domestic Investment Expenditures, 1946–1978, with a Semilogarithmic Trend

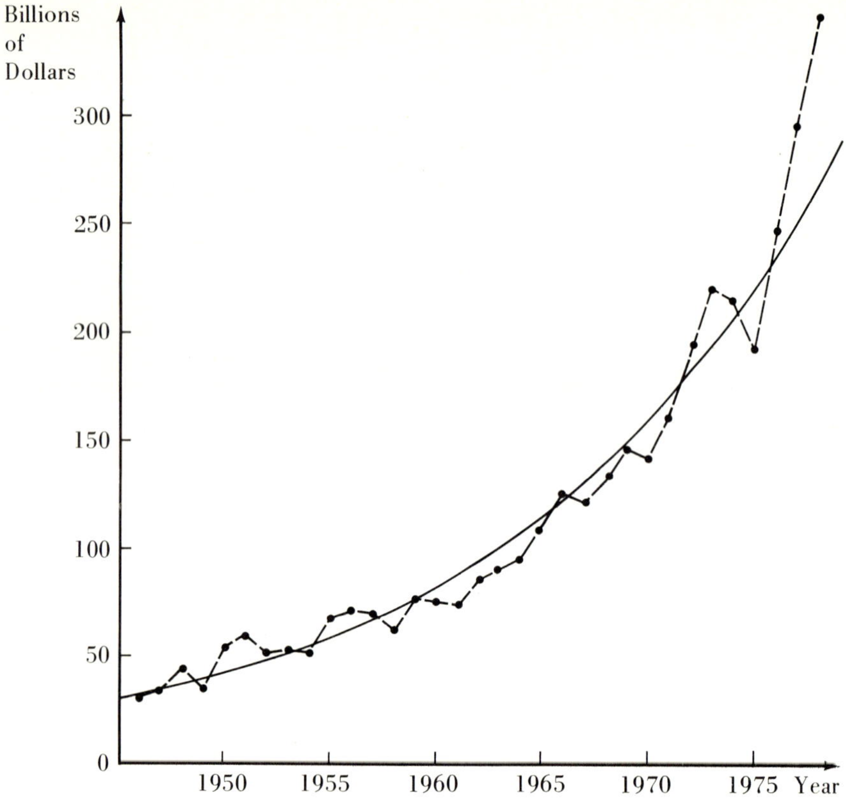

Various other curvilinear trend-analysis models can be constructed. Each is based on some transformation of the original data that describes a specific type of nonlinear relationship. For example, there are power curve, inverse, and quadratic regression models. Generally, however, the two models that are most widely applicable for trend analysis in business and economics are the ordinary linear and the semilogarithmic regression models. For further treatment of regression techniques and advanced forecasting methods, see specialized books in these areas.

17.4 Summary

Basic forecasting techniques generally employ either moving averages or trend analysis. No set rules tell us what type of approach is best in any given situation. One must experiment with alternative approaches until a satisfactory result is achieved.

Generally, moving averages are useful when irregular movement in a series of data dictates some degree of smoothing to make the underlying tendencies clear. Moving averages are well suited to situations that do not reveal any particular consistent trend, because they adapt to changes in a variable's direction of movement. If this adaptive ability is especially important and if the most recent movement is especially significant for accurate prediction of future values, then weighted moving averages should be used. An exponentially weighted moving average employs a weighting scheme that declines according to a geometric relationship, the characteristics of which are determined by a single smoothing constant. Depending on the given data, we can use moving averages for prediction purposes by applying them either directly to the time series or to differences between successive data values, whether absolute or proportionate. These choices determine the characteristics of the forecasting model that we must experiment with, evaluate, and revise, if necessary, until satisfactory results are achieved.

Trend analysis is performed primarily with regression techniques. Where trends exist, reasonably accurate projections are possible farther into the future than if no trend were evident. The more consistent the trend, the better the accuracy of projections based on the trend. Plotting the data graphically allows us to judge the linearity of the trend. Ordinary least-squares linear regression should be applied only in cases where linearity can be assumed in the trend of the data. Curvilinear models allow us to extend regression techniques to nonlinear situations, the most common of which is the fitting of a trend to a growth phenomenon using a semilogarithmic trend model. Trend analysis can be expanded to include correction factors for other components of time-series data, such as cyclical and seasonal characteristics. These complex models are generally used with extensive and detailed data and are usually managed by computer.

A forecaster must be intimately familiar with the characteristics of the data under consideration, must be innovative in fitting models with alternate characteristics to the data, must be critical in evaluating the predictive abilities of various models, and must interpret the degree of inaccuracy of predicted results and the assumptions on which they are based. Predicting the future is never a sure thing, but it is possible to forecast probable future outcomes by using the quantitative techniques described here. In many situations, forecasting can be very helpful for decision-making purposes.

Exercises

17.1 Distinguish between classical and econometric forecasting techniques.

17.2 Describe realistic uses to which forecasting results could be put. For example, what role might forecasting play:
a. In the automobile industry?
b. In the steel industry?
c. In the aerospace industry?
d. In hospital care?
e. In government planning?
f. In supermarket management?
g. In hotel and restaurant management?

17.3 Discuss the different purposes for which one may use forecasting results. Explain why the analyst's purposes influence his or her choice of forecasting techniques.

17.4 What are naive forecasting models? What is the reasoning on which such models are based?

17.5 Carefully examine the assumption of classical forecasting: that an underlying process will repeat itself. Is this assumption consistent with business cycle theories? There is an old saying that "The more things change, the more they stay the same." How is this idea related to classical forecasting? How far back in time should one look to find the patterns on which classical forecasting is based? In any particular situation, for specific data, should one judge the assumption of a predictable underlying process as part of a forecasting analysis? If so, how should one do it?

17.6 How does one determine predictive error when preparing forecasting results? Does the extent of predictive error change according to how far into the future one wants to predict?

17.7 Calculate the predictive error and evaluate the forecasting results for the following data.

Time Period	Predicted Result	Actual Result
1	135	107
2	279	346
3	303	350
4	420	400
5	490	446
6	618	659
7	763	791

Time Period	Predicted Result	Actual Result
8	813	774
9	910	878
10	906	942

17.8 Explain the difference between additive and multiplicative forecasting models. In practice, how should one choose between them?

17.9 For the following data, prepare forecasts of the series for periods 5 through 15 based, first, on the ordinary additive constant approach and, second, on an additive constant derived from the average of three prior differences. Calculate the predictive error for both sets of results. Interpret your findings.

Time Period	Observed Value
1	103
2	130
3	145
4	149
5	174
6	153
7	168
8	161
9	188
10	184
11	193
12	207
13	213
14	239
15	235

17.10 For the following data, prepare forecasts of the series for periods 5 through 15 based, first, on the ordinary multiplicative constant approach and, second, on a multiplicative constant derived from the average of four prior proportionate changes. Calculate the predictive error of both sets of results. Interpret your findings.

Time Period	Observed Value
1	502
2	516
3	529

Time Period	Observed Value
4	535
5	533
6	541
7	543
8	552
9	549
10	564
11	574
12	587
13	592
14	606
15	613

17.11 Refer to exercises 17.9 and 17.10. How do moving averages enter into the results, and what effect do the moving averages have on the forecasted results?

17.12 For the following data, compute four-term, eight-term, and twelve-term moving averages. Prepare three graphs, each with the actual data and one of the moving averages superimposed.

40, 38, 42, 46, 52, 48, 40, 34, 41, 54, 59,
49, 57, 53, 52, 45, 38, 35, 40, 31, 27, 26,
23, 24, 24, 27, 35, 37, 32, 33, 26, 35, 40

Discuss your results.

17.13 Explain the meaning of the term ***smoothing*** in relation to moving averages. How is the degree of smoothing controlled?

17.14 Discuss the various alternative methods of forecasting trend data and the advantages and disadvantages of each. Include ordinary moving averages, moving averages of differences, and regression techniques.

17.15 For the following data, prepare a five-term moving average. On the basis of the characteristics of the data, assess the results of the moving average in terms of their predictive ability. The data are 513, 536, 562, 583, 610, 630, 655, 677, 707, 729, 752, 772, and 797. What alternative methods of prediction might you consider using with these data? Why?

17.16 For the data given in exercise 17.15, prepare a four-term moving average of differences. Use this moving average to predict actual results one period in advance. Compute predictive error for this approach. Also compute the predictive error of the results you obtained using the ordinary moving average. Explain why these two approaches differ.

17.17 For the data given in exercise 17.15, prepare a regression trend line. What does the trend line predict for each period in the series of data shown? Compute the predictive error of this approach. Also compute predictions for one period, two periods, five periods, and ten periods into the future.

17.18 Business sales for the Smith Wire Company tend to be seasonal, as the following data show:

Year and Quarter	Sales (thousands)
1978	
I	$328
II	341
III	335
IV	315
1979	
I	326
II	352
III	347
IV	329
1980	
I	338
II	360
III	344
IV	341
1981	
I	357
II	373
III	362
IV	349

Prepare three-term and four-term moving averages for these data. Which provides the better smoothing characteristics? Why?

17.19 Prepare a three-term weighted moving average for the Smith Wire Company sales data given in exercise 17.18, using 0.3, 0.2, and 0.1 as weights. Describe the difference between these results and those obtained with the ordinary weighted average. Discuss the various reasons why an analyst might choose an ordinary weighted average rather than a weighted moving average for these data. Conversely, under what circumstances might the opposite choice be made? Explain your reasoning fully in each case.

17.20 Derive the formula for computing an exponentially weighted moving average.

17.21 Levin Manufacturing maintains an inventory of liquid solvent for its production needs. On the basis of weekly holdings of solvent (given in gallons in the following list), compute two exponentially weighted moving averages. Use a smoothing constant of 0.3. Explain the start-up process of your calculations. Plot the original data and the two moving averages. Interpret the differences in the results you obtained. The data are

8.7, 7.2, 7.6, 6.3, 8.3, 4.9, 3.3, 2.5, 1.1, 2.6, 4.4, 5.9, 5.8,
6.8, 6.0, 4.9, 5.7, 4.9, 5.6, 5.7, 6.4, 7.6, 8.2, 7.1, 7.4, 6.4

What is your forecast of the next week's inventory level of solvent? Explain fully your reasoning in making the forecast, any assumptions that you made, and the probable tolerance levels within which the prediction should fall.

17.22 Denver Copper Mining Corporation mines copper and sells copper wire primarily to the housing industry and the automobile industry. Monthly sales data are given in the following list. Prepare a weighted moving average ($a = 0.2$) of the percentage changes in the data. On the basis of this moving average, make a prediction for each of the following months.

a. March 1979
b. October 1978
c. June 1980
d. April 1978
e. September 1979
f. December 1979
g. January 1980
h. May 1978

What is your prediction for January 1981?

Year	Amount	Year	Amount	Year	Amount
1978		1979		1980	
Jan.	68.0	Jan.	70.0	Jan.	71.7
Feb.	67.8	Feb.	70.4	Feb.	71.9
Mar.	68.5	Mar.	70.3	Mar.	72.0
Apr.	68.3	Apr.	70.3	Apr.	71.8
May	68.0	May	70.4	May	71.6
Jun.	68.6	Jun.	70.7	Jun.	71.3

Year	Amount	Year	Amount	Year	Amount
1978		1979		1980	
Jul.	69.1	Jul.	71.0	Jul.	71.2
Aug.	69.3	Aug.	71.3	Aug.	71.4
Sep.	69.2	Sep.	71.3	Sep.	71.7
Oct.	69.4	Oct.	71.2	Oct.	71.9
Nov.	69.7	Nov.	71.4	Nov.	72.3
Dec.	70.0	Dec.	71.6	Dec.	72.5

17.23 Describe in detail the four components of time-series data that forecasters generally look for.

17.24 Plot each of the following straight lines. For each, indicate the slope and the Y intercept.

a. $Y = 5 + 3X$
b. $Y = 3X$
c. $Y = X - 1$
d. $3Y = 18 - 7X$
e. $2X + 3Y = 12$

17.25 The book value of shares in Atlanta Office Equipment Company has risen steadily over the last ten years. The management of the firm has asked you to forecast what the book value might be five years in the future. On the basis of the data for the past five years, what is your forecast? Describe fully all details of your technique, your assumptions, and the probable accuracy that should be included in your report to management. Book values for ten years up to the present were, in dollars, 34.3, 45.2, 50.2, 56.6, 60.0, 74.5, 70.8, 81.5, 96.2, and 90.8. Prepare a graph of the results of your analysis.

17.26 A major retail concern wants to analyze the growth in personal income since the end of World War II in order to make key planning decisions about the capacity requirements of future sales outlets. On the basis of the following data (obtained from the 1979 ***Economic Report of the President***), which are expressed in billions of dollars, prepare a five-year forecast of personal income in the United States. Analyze the data to determine whether straight-line or curvilinear analysis is more appropriate. Present all details of the analysis, your assumptions, your prediction, and the probable accuracy of your results in the form of a report to management.

1946	177.3	1957	349.3	1968	685.2
1947	189.8	1958	359.3	1969	745.8
1948	208.5	1959	382.1	1970	801.3

1949	205.6	1960	399.7	1971	859.1
1950	226.1	1961	415.0	1972	942.5
1951	253.7	1962	440.7	1973	1052.4
1952	270.4	1963	463.1	1974	1154.9
1953	286.1	1964	495.7	1975	1255.5
1954	288.2	1965	537.0	1976	1380.9
1955	308.8	1966	584.9	1977	1529.0
1956	330.9	1967	626.6	1978	1707.3

17.27 Determine an appropriate trend line (linear or curvilinear) for each of the following series of data. Graph the data and the trend together. Project each series five periods into the future.

Series 1	Series 2	Series 3
85	23	64
95	26	67
91	29	71
99	40	76
105	41	82
103	43	83
111	48	89
118	55	97
113	61	107
122	71	111
126	83	128
125	99	143

17.28 During the past six years, Patterson Realtors had the following sales:

Year	1975	1976	1977	1978	1979	1980
Number of Homes Sold	140	170	180	210	250	260

a. Graph the data and draw a straight line through the scatter of points.
b. Predict the number of home sales in 1985 by reading directly from the graph.
c. Determine the trend line by the least-squares method.
d. Give an economic interpretation of the slope of the trend line.
e. Using the least-squares result, forecast the number of home sales for 1985.
f. How does the least-squares analysis compare with your other pre-

diction? Give the theoretical reasons for employing the least-squares technique.

17.29 The following data on employment and revenue are provided by Lincoln Hospital:

Year	Employment (hundreds)	Revenue (millions of dollars)
1970	8	41
1971	7	34
1972	7	38
1973	10	67
1974	10	68
1975	11	84
1976	10	75
1977	10	72
1978	13	99
1979	9	67
1980	9	58

Use regression analysis to fit either a straight line or a curve (whichever best describes the relationship between the dependent variable, employment, and the independent variable, revenue). Show your analysis and computations, and explain your reasons for choosing either the linear or the curvilinear approach.

17.30 On the basis of the estimated equation you obtained in exercise 17.29, make a point forecast. For example, given a value of revenue (X) of 41, estimate the value of employment (Y). This estimated value of Y is compared with the observed value of $Y = 8$. Similarly, compare different levels of employment at different levels of revenue. Then compare the results with actual data by plotting them on a graph. How does this process help you judge whether the forecast is good or bad?

Suggested Readings

Bellman, R., and R. Roth. "Curve Fittings by Segmented Straight Lines." *Journal of the American Statistical Association*, 64, No. 327 (1969), 1079–1084.

Benton, William K. *Forecasting for Management*. Reading, Mass.: Addison-Wesley, 1972.

Box, G. E. P. *Time Series, Forecasting, and Control.* San Francisco, Calif.: Holden-Day, 1968.

Box, G. E. P., and G. M. Jenkins. *Time Series Analysis, Forecasting, and Control.* San Francisco, Calif.: Holden-Day, 1968.

Brennan, M. J. *Preface to Econometrics.* 2nd ed. Cincinnati, Ohio: South-Western Publishing Co., 1965.

Brown, R. G. *Statistical Forecasting for Inventory Control.* New York: McGraw-Hill, 1959.

Bry, Gerhard, and Charlotte Boschan. "Interpretation and Analysis of Time-Series Scatters." *American Statistician,* 25, No. 2 (April 1971).

Butler, W. F., R. A. Davesh, and R. B. Platt. *Methods and Techniques of Business Forecasting.* Englewood Cliffs, N.J.: Prentice-Hall, 1974.

Chisholm, Robert K., and Gilbert R. Whitaker. *Forecasting Methods.* Homewood, Ill.: Irwin, 1971.

Eby, Frank H., Jr., and William J. O'Neill. *The Management of Sales Forecasting.* Lexington, Mass.: Heath, 1977.

First National City Bank. "Has Mr. Phillips Thrown Policymakers a Curve?" *Monthly Economic Letter,* February 1971, 10–12.

Gibson, Weldon B. "Long-Range Forecasting as a Management Tool." *Business Economics,* 2, Spring 1967.

Johnston, J. *Econometric Methods.* New York: McGraw-Hill, 1963.

McNees, Stephen K. "An Evaluation of Economic Forecasts: Extension and Update." *New England Economic Review,* September/October 1976.

Montgomery, Douglas C., and Lynwood A. Johnson. *Forecasting and Time-Series Analysis.* New York: McGraw-Hill, 1976.

National Industrial Conference Board. *Forecasting in Industry.* Studies in Business Policy No. 77, 1956.

______. *Forecasting Sales.* Studies in Business Policy No. 106, 1963.

Neter, J., W. Wasserman, and G. A. Whitmore. *Fundamental Statistics for Business and Economics.* 4th ed. Boston: Allyn and Bacon, 1973.

18

Computer Applications of Operations Research Techniques

This text has emphasized methods of calculation for efficiently identifying optimal solutions or decision strategies, and the various examples and problems have admittedly been limited in size to ones that are manageable for hand calculation. While the various methods of analysis can often be extended routinely to much more difficult situations, larger problems may require a substantially greater computational effort. Indeed, there is a tendency for practical applications to grow in complexity as one attempts to allow for all the relevant conditions. If the techniques of operations research are to have practical value, it is especially important for us to be able to handle the computational burden of applied problems.

Electronic computers have greatly expanded the ability of operations research technicians to pursue complex analyses. The routine nature of computational algorithms has led to computer programs that supply the results of analysis quickly and accurately, thereby allowing the analyst to devote more attention to formulating problems and interpreting the results. This chapter demonstrates the use of computer routines in solving many of the problems we discussed in earlier chapters. A wide variety of computer programs are available at different computer centers; those used here are representative of, but not necessarily the same as, those you will find elsewhere. Generally, one must seek out the programs that are available at a nearby computer facility and follow the instructions for using them. These days, it is quite common to find ready-to-use programs for the standard operations research techniques.

18.1 Linear Programming Solutions by Interactive Computer Processing

In recent years, there has been widespread support of APL (**A** **P**rogramming **L**anguage) at academic computer facilities. Although an extensive treatment of this language would be inappropriate, we will mention three of its most basic characteristics. First, APL is oriented to "interactive" or ***time-sharing*** computer processing—that is, it uses a computer terminal for input and output and, in doing so, receives responses and queries from the computer programs or systems as processing proceeds. Thus the user "interacts" or communicates directly with the computer in a "session" during which data and results are exchanged. (This is in contrast to batch processing of computer tasks, in which the operator prepares 80-column punched cards containing all job-control, program, and data information and then submits them for processing: batch input and batch output.) A second feature of APL is its suitability to mathematical calculations and its powerful ability to specify processing operations very concisely. Third, APL supports "libraries" of computer programs that have been prepared and made generally available, complete with instructions and descriptions, for shared use. This last feature is a special convenience. Even with minimal knowledge of the programming aspects of APL, one can search the libraries of prepared programs, copy those that are appropriate, receive directions on their use, and perform the necessary calculations. The interactive feature of APL facilitates this process, because prompting helps direct the user through the steps required for the particular task at hand.

Here we will present computer solutions to linear programming problems using APL shared library routines. First, one supplies the nec-

Table 18.1 Initial Access to the APL Computer Systems

Terminal Command	Computer Response
LOGON	ENTER USERID
[user I.D., password, and accounting information]	READY
APL	SWITCH YOUR TERMINAL TO APL MODE. TYPE AN OVERBAR WHEN YOU HAVE DONE SO.
[overbar—upper-case 2]	VSAPL CLEAR WS

Table 18.2
The Selection and Directions for Use of Linear Programming Routines under APL

Terminal Command	Computer Response
) LOAD 612 STAT 9	SAVED 10:39:30 06/23/80 WSSIZE IS 77020
DESCRIBE	THIS WORKSPACE CONSISTS OF 4 GROUPS DESCRIPTIONS SIMPLEXIN SIMPLEXWORK PARAMETERS A) DESCRIPTIONS THIS CONTAINS THE DESCRIPTIONS FOR THE WORKSPACE AND THE OTHER GROUPS B) SIMPLEXIN THIS AND SIMPLEXWORK FORM THE SIMPLEXMETHOD. THE COMPUTATIONAL ROUTINE FOR OBTAINING THE OPTIMAL SOLUTION TO A LINEAR PROGRAMMING PROBLEM SIMPLEXIN CONTAINS THE INPUT ROUTINES AND THE FORMATION OF THE INITIAL TABLEAU C) SIMPLEXWORK THIS GROUP CONTAINS THE PROGRAMS THAT PERFORM THE ACTUAL ITERATIONS AND CHECK FOR EXCEPTION CONDITIONS, SUCH AS MULTIPLE SOLUTIONS DESCRIBESIMPLEX EXPLAINS THE DETAILS. D) PARAMETERS THIS GROUP CONTAINS PROGRAMS THAT PERFORM PARAMETRIC PROGRAMMING FOR CHANGES IN OBJECTIVE FUNCTION OR RIGHT HAND SIDES OF CONSTRAINTS 'DESCRIBEPARAM' DESCRIBES THE PROGRAMS IN THE GROUP IN ADDITION 'ILLUSTRATE' AND 'PROBLEM' SERVE AS AN ILLUSTRATIVE EXAMPLE

essary LOGON identification and password(s) to be recognized at a computer terminal by the main computer system. Then, one selects operation at the terminal under APL by entering "APL" (some computer systems use updated versions such as "APLSV" or "VSAPL"). Part of the initial set-up for APL processing includes switching to an APL-designated keyboard set that has many extra characters specific to the programming needs of APL. In general, however, one needs little knowledge of special characters to use APL program libraries. This initial interaction is demonstrated in abbreviated form in Table 18.1.

Different APL systems have different shared libraries or "workspaces" (WS). In this case, a search of the library revealed that workspace number 612 contains a shared library of programs called "STAT9" that handle linear programming problems. To access these, we give the "LOAD" command, which by APL conventions must be preceded by a right parenthesis. This interaction is summarized in Table 18.2.

The Potato–Tomato Problem

Now let us familiarize ourselves with these routines by finding solutions to problems that we have already performed by hand. The potato–tomato problem is a good starting point, and its solution comes from the series of interactions shown in Table 18.3. We recognize the values entered as the appropriate coefficients of the objective function and constraints

Table 18.3 The Potato–Tomato Problem Solved by Interactive Computer Routines

Terminal Command	Computer Response
SIMPLEXMETHOD	WHEN ENTERING CONSTRAINTS, BE SURE ONLY TO USE LESS-THAN-OR-EQUAL-TO INEQUALITIES, SEE 'DESCRIBESIMPLEX.'
	READ IN OBJECTIVE FUNCTION, MAXIMIZING ONLY:
40 50	READ IN NUMBER OF CONSTRAINTS:
3	READ IN CONSTRAINT NO. 1:
1 2 30	READ IN CONSTRAINT NO. 2:
3 2 60	READ IN CONSTRAINT NO. 3:
0 2 24	

BASIS	PRIMAL SOLUTION	DUAL BASIS	DUAL SOLUTION
1	15	1	17.5
5	9	2	7.5
2	7.5	3	0

OPTIMUM: 975

FINAL OBJECTIVE FUNCTION:

0 0 17.5 7.5 0 975

TERMS CORRESPONDING TO:
VARIABLES 0 0
SLACK VARIABLES 17.5 7.5 0
ARTIFICIAL VARIABLES

of the example we analyzed in Chapters 2 and 3. The computer solves this problem in much less time than one would normally spend creating the initial simplex tableau!

Specifically, how should one interpret this computer listing? The optimal value of the objective function is clearly identified as $975. The basis for the optimal solution (see Table 3.5) consists of variable X_1 at 15 units, variable X_2 at 7.5 units, and variable X_5 (the third slack variable, S_3) at 9 units. Thus the first two columns of numbers labeled "BASIS" and "PRIMAL SOLUTION" show the basic variables in the optimal solution and their corresponding RHS values. Next to these, the final "DUAL BASIS" variables, which correspond to resources, and their optimal values ("DUAL SOLUTION") are given (see Sections 4.1 and 4.2). Thus we know that an additional unit of one of the resources would increase the primal objective function by the value of the corresponding dual variable (for example, an additional unit of the first resource would increase the objective function by $17.50; see Section 4.3). Next, in row

Table 18.4 Demonstration of a Case of Multiple Optimal Solutions

Terminal Command	Computer Response
SIMPLEXMETHOD	WHEN ENTERING CONSTRAINTS, BE SURE ONLY TO USE LESS-THAN-OR-EQUAL-TO INEQUALITIES, SEE 'DESCRIBESIMPLEX.'
	READ IN OBJECTIVE FUNCTION, MAXIMIZING ONLY:
40 80	READ IN NUMBER OF CONSTRAINTS
[enter the same constraint sequence as in Table 18.3]	

BASIS	PRIMAL SOLUTION	DUAL BASIS	DUAL SOLUTION
1	6	1	40
4	18	2	0
2	12	3	0

OPTIMUM: 1,200

FINAL OBJECTIVE FUNCTION:

0 0 40 0 0 1,200

TERMS CORRESPONDING TO:
VARIABLES 0 0
SLACK VARIABLES 40 0 0
ARTIFICIAL VARIABLES

0, the "FINAL OBJECTIVE FUNCTION" values are listed for dual variables V_1, V_2, Y_1, Y_2, Y_3, and Z_y (compare these objective function values with row 0 of Table 4.1). And finally, in the last three lines of the computer listing, these are further identified according to the type of variable: "VARIABLES," "SLACK VARIABLES," and "ARTIFICIAL VARIABLES." Note that all row 0 coefficients associated with basic variables are zero.

Now consider the computer routine's handling of various special cases. For example, how is a multiple optimal solution indicated? The following case, presented in Table 18.4, is the potato–tomato problem with a revised objective function intentionally selected to fall parallel to the first constraint.

In this case, the row 0 coefficients associated with all basic variables are zero, but a nonbasic variable, X_5 (or the slack variable S_3), also has a zero coefficient in row 0 (see Table 3.7). Thus it is possible that another

Table 18.5 Demonstration of a Case of Degeneracy

Terminal Command	Computer Response
[enter "SIMPLEX-METHOD" objective function, number of constraints, and first-constraint coefficients the same as in Table 18.3]	
	READ IN CONSTRAINT NO. 2:
3 5 60	READ IN CONSTRAINT NO. 3:
0 2 24	

BASIS	PRIMAL SOLUTION	DUAL BASIS	DUAL SOLUTION
3	10	1	0
1	20	2	13.3
5	24	3	0

OPTIMUM: 800

FINAL OBJECTIVE FUNCTION:

0	16.7	0	13.3	0	800

TERMS CORRESPONDING TO:

VARIABLES	0	16.7	
SLACK VARIABLES	0	13.3	0
ARTIFICIAL VARIABLES			

Table 18.6 Demonstration of an Attempt to Offer an Unbounded Condition for Computer Processing

Terminal Command	Computer Response
SIMPLEXMETHOD	WHEN ENTERING CONSTRAINTS, BE SURE ONLY TO USE LESS-THAN-OR-EQUAL-TO INEQUALITIES, SEE 'DESCRIBESIMPLEX.'
	READ IN OBJECTIVE FUNCTION, MAXIMIZING ONLY:
0.05 0.2	READ IN NUMBER OF CONSTRAINTS:
2	READ IN CONSTRAINT NO. 1:
4 −1 100	READ IN CONSTRAINT NO. 2:
1.6 −1 10	THIS PROBLEM HAS NO SOLUTION; E.G., THE OPTIMUM IS UNBOUNDED.

corner point will offer a solution that is also optimal, and the computer lists this second solution as well. Of course, since these two optimal solutions correspond to two adjacent corner points of the feasible region, any point on the line segment between them is also optimal (see Section 3.3).

In the example given in Table 18.5 (taken from Section 3.3), the second constraint of the potato–tomato problem has been changed, causing degeneracy in the first iteration. This is no problem for the computer routine; the degeneracy is resolved internally by the built-in logic of the computer program. Even much more involved cases of degeneracy are handled in this way, as when we use the simplex method to solve assignment problems, which, you will recall, are inherently degenerate.

Now suppose (as we did in Section 3.3) that a linear programming problem is formulated incorrectly, in a way that results in an unbounded feasible region. Table 18.6 shows that the computer routine available under APL discerns the unbounded condition immediately and indicates the fault at the outset. The remedy, of course, lies in supplying the missing constraint (as we did in Section 3.3), whereupon a normal solution follows.

18.2 Various Minimization Routines

Each of the preceding applications of the APL library computer program SIMPLEXMETHOD begins with an indication that all inequalities must be less-than-or-equal-to constraints and that the objective function will be maximized. For a minimization problem, we must reverse any greater-than constraint by multiplying both sides of the inequality by −1. Likewise, the objective function must be changed by a factor of −1 (minimization occurs when we maximize the negative of a function). It is clear from the preceding examples that slack variables are added automatically as an internal computer process and that artificial variables are provided routinely without direct user specification.

The Presidential Election Problem

These basics are all we need to set up and solve any linear programming minimization problem. For example, in the presidential election problem we discussed in Chapters 2 and 3, changing the objective function from

$$C = X_1 + 0.5X_2$$

to

$$-C = -X_1 - 0.5X_2$$

caused minimization to occur. Similarly, to provide less-than-or-equal-to constraints to the program input, we alter the constraints by a factor of −1 (see Section 2.2):

$$-6X_1 - 2X_2 \leq -24$$
$$-3X_1 - 2X_2 \leq -18$$
$$-X_1 - 3X_2 \leq -12$$

As before, variables X_1 and X_2 must be greater than or equal to zero.

Remember that these requirements apply specifically to the APL library program that we are demonstrating. They are typical of, but not necessarily the same as, the requirements of other computer routines. Having constructed the problem in a form suitable for computer solution, we enter the coefficients and the results shown in Table 18.7 are supplied. The optimal solution is $X_1 = 2$, $X_2 = 6$, and X_5 (the slack variable S_3) $= 8$. All artificial variables are nonbasic in the optimal solution. RHS and row 0 coefficients are indicated as before (compare with Table 3.10). The optimal value of the objective function is $-C = -5$, or simply $C = 5$.

Transportation and Assignment Problems

The transportation problem is also a linear programming problem that requires minimization. The particular example used in Chapter 2 and at the beginning of Chapter 5 has both greater-than-or-equal-to and less-than-or-equal-to constraints (see equations 2.3b and 2.3c). Of

Table 18.7 Demonstrating Minimization: The Presidential Election Problem

Terminal Command	Computer Response
SIMPLEXMETHOD	WHEN ENTERING CONSTRAINTS, BE SURE ONLY TO USE LESS-THAN-OR-EQUAL-TO INEQUALITIES, SEE 'DESCRIBESIMPLEX.'
	READ IN OBJECTIVE FUNCTION, MAXIMIZING ONLY:
−1 −.05	READ IN NUMBER OF CONSTRAINTS:
3	READ IN CONSTRAINT NO. 1:
−6 −2 −24	READ IN CONSTRAINT NO. 2:
−3 −2 −18	READ IN CONSTRAINT NO. 3:
−1 −3 −12	

BASIS	PRIMAL SOLUTION	DUAL BASIS	DUAL SOLUTION
1	2	1	0.0833
5	8	2	0.167
2	6	3	0

OPTIMUM: −5

FINAL OBJECTIVE FUNCTION:
0 0 0.0833 0.167 0 1,000 1,000 1,000
−5

TERMS CORRESPONDING TO:
VARIABLES 0 0
SLACK VARIABLES 0.0833 0.167 0
ARTIFICIAL VARIABLES 1,000 1,000 1,000

course, this is typical of the LP formulation of transportation problems generally, since factory supplies cannot be exceeded and warehouse demands must not be shorted. Thus, in order to use the APL SIMPLEXMETHOD routine, we must reverse only those inequalities that were originally specified with greater-than-or-equal-to inequalities, which we do by multiplying both sides of the inequalities by -1. The less-than-or-equal-to inequalities, of course, are left as is. Similarly, minimization of the objective function is accomplished by multiplying all coefficients of the objective function by -1. In a more complex example such as this, we must take care to number all variables and position their coefficients properly.

Specialized algorithms for transportation and assignment problems can be computationally more efficient and more easily specified than is the case with the simplex method. We will demonstrate these specialized algorithms using a computer routine that is not one of the APL shared library programs but that conveniently prompts the user at a terminal in much the same way that the SIMPLEXMETHOD routine does. Let us start with the transportation problem that was presented in Chapter 5. After being called into action, this computer program prompts the user to enter a complete description of the cost matrix, including all supplies and demands (see Table 18.8).

Should the specifications of the problem not be "balanced" (should total supplies not equal total demands), the computer routine automatically adds a slack row or column, as necessary. This would occur, for example, in solving the transportation problem we discussed in Chapter 5 (see Table 5.6).

Table 18.8 Demonstration of an Interactive Computer Routine Used Specifically for Transportation and Assignment Problems

Terminal Command	Computer Response				
	ENTER NUMBER OF ROWS, COLUMNS IN COST MATRIX:				
2 3	ENTER 2 SUPPLIES:				
18 15	ENTER 3 DEMANDS:				
16 10 7	ENTER ROW 1 COST VALUES:				
6 5 1	ENTER ROW 2 COST VALUES:				
4 2 4					
	TRANSPORTATION PROBLEM				
	SUPPLIES				
	18 15				
	DEMANDS				
	16 10 7				
	UNIT COST MATRIX				
			. . .	TO	. . .
			1	2	3
	. .FROM. .	1	6	5	1
		2	4	2	4
	SOLUTION MATRIX				
			. . .	TO	. . .
			1	2	3
	. .FROM. .	1	11	0	7
		2	5	10	0
	TOTAL COST:			113.	

Table 18.9 Demonstration of Computer Solution of an Assignment Problem

Terminal Command	Computer Response				
	ENTER NUMBER OF ROWS, COLUMNS IN COST MATRIX:				
3 3	ENTER 3 SUPPLIES:				
1 1 1	ENTER 3 DEMANDS:				
1 1 1	ENTER ROW 1 COST VALUES:				
18 12 15	ENTER ROW 2 COST VALUES:				
23 20 14	ENTER ROW 3 COST VALUES:				
32 15 10					
	ASSIGNMENT PROBLEM				
	SUPPLIES				
		1	1	1	
	DEMANDS				
		1	1	1	
	UNIT COST MATRIX				
			...	TO	...
			1	2	3
	..FROM..	1	18	12	15
		2	23	20	14
		3	32	15	10
	SOLUTION MATRIX				
			...	TO	...
			1	2	3
	..FROM..	1	0	1	0
		2	1	0	0
		3	0	0	1
	TOTAL COST:		45.		

Finally, consider using this same computer routine for the assignment problem we discussed in Section 5.4. Because this is an assignment problem, a one-to-one match-up is required; that is, each available job or task is assigned to one and only one machine or worker. Thus the cost matrix must have the same number of rows as columns, and each individual supply or demand equals 1. The three-task, three-worker problem presented in Table 5.13 has been entered and processed by the same computer routine that was used for the transportation problem, as shown in Table 18.9. This input is automatically identified as corresponding to an assignment problem, the cost matrix is repeated for verification, and the matrix of optimal assignments, including minimal total cost, is given.

18.3 Batch Processing of Quantitative Decision Problems

Computer programs for a particular method of analysis may or may not be available in the interactive, time-sharing mode that we have described. Indeed, many analytical computer routines are available only in the more traditional mode of computer operating systems, batch processing. ***Batch processing*** involves following particular instructions that itemize the requirements for putting together all the details of a problem in one job, or ***batch,*** so that the computer program can operate within the parameters and according to the data that are supplied to it. This typically means preparing a deck of computer cards that are read, lead to the necessary processing, and yield a computer-printed output that displays the results of analysis. Prompting and interaction with the computer are not a part of batch processing. Errors, if they occur, must be corrected so that another, corrected, batch may be submitted and processed.

Simulation by Computer Using GPSS

The **G**eneral **P**urpose **S**imulation **S**ystem (GPSS), is a batch-processing system for performing computer-operated simulations. Because the simulation of real systems tends to be very cumbersome, with regard to both the number of calculations and the amount of repetition, it is especially advantageous to use computers for processing simulation problems. Without attempting to teach the use of GPSS, we will introduce the basic concepts that show how a computer simulation is performed when a simulation language such as GPSS is applied.

Any computer-simulation language is oriented toward identifiable and commonly used components of simulation processing. For example, the typical components of a queuing simulation are arrivals, a process by which arrivals are generated, a service facility with a measurable rate of delivery, the waiting-line discipline itself, and other elements of choice or action that depend on the nature of the situation and the participants involved. Starting without a simulation language would require setting up program steps to account for the operation of each of these elements, but with a simulation language, the basic characteristics of each element are specified and appropriate subroutines are called to perform the necessary operations. A set of many such subroutines allows the analyst to manipulate the elements of a system and the characteristics of those elements rather than requiring that the elements themselves be programmed in great detail.

GPSS identifies the elements of a system to be simulated in a way that directly parallels the elements that one would identify in a flow chart of the system. Thus, for example, a simple queuing system would first be organized in flow-chart form, after which the individual segments of the flow chart would be reinterpreted as particular elements of the GPSS simulation language. Consider Figure 18.1, which contains a straightforward example of a queuing system. GPSS has subroutines comparable to these blocks. For example, creating random arrivals is comparable to the "GENERATE" command of GPSS, and the queuing process is organized by GPSS using the "ADVANCE" command. A flow chart showing GPSS commands for this system is presented in Figure 18.2.

The characteristics of the various components of a working system must be specified as part of the GPSS language, of course. Thus, for example, because the arrival rate is related to the "GENERATE" operation, interarrival times must be added to the "GENERATE" statement as operands. Likewise, service rates are governed by operands

Figure 18.1 Standard Flow Chart for Simulation

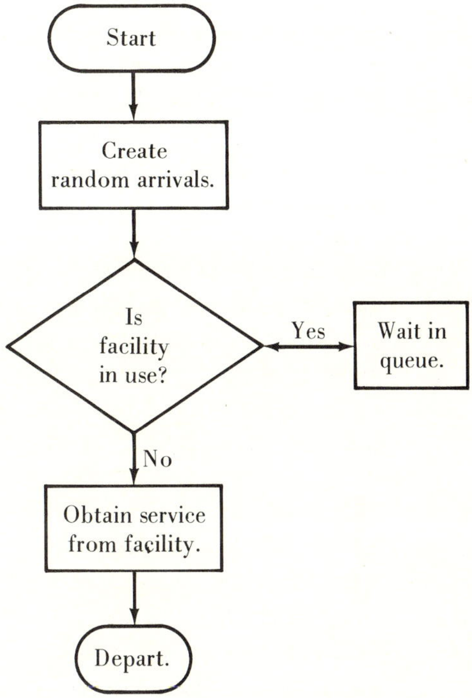

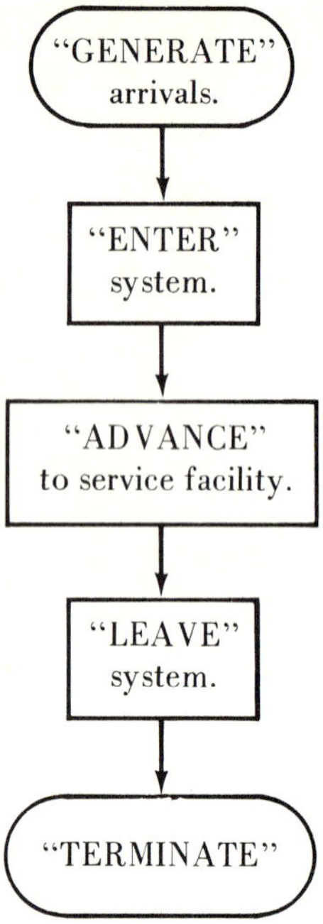

Figure 18.2 The GPSS Equivalent of a Standard Simulation Flow Chart

that must be specified with the "ADVANCE" operation. Branches in a flow chart can be performed by using a "TRANSFER" operation together with appropriate operands that will control the characteristics of this portion of the overall system.

Once a complete batch of GPSS specifications has been prepared, the computer interprets the blocks on which the system is based; sets up a real-time clock according to which the simulated system will function; and operates the system repetitively, keeping track of items in the system, their movements through the system, and statistics related to system performance. A completed GPSS run might therefore indicate, for the facility or facilities involved, such performance characteristics as average time spent waiting, average time in the system, percentage utilization of the service facilities, maximum line length, and so on. Equipped with these results, the analyst can draw conclusions about the performance of the real system being simulated.

PERT Analysis by Computer

The analytical nature of PERT also lends itself to computer processing. In fact, especially large and involved PERT networks would be very hard to analyze adequately without a computer (see, for example, the complex PERT diagram shown in Figure 10.1). PERT analysis by computer can be set up for either interactive or batch processing; the particular method of analysis used here is based on batch processing.

Figure 18.3
A Sample PERT Network to Demonstrate Computer Set-up and Solution

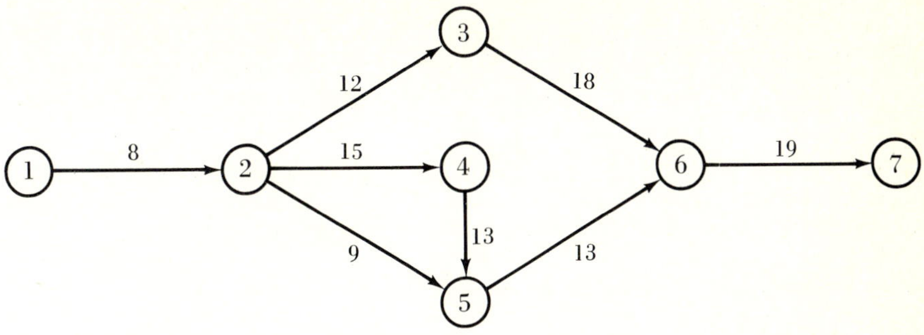

Consider the hypothetical PERT network presented in Figure 18.3. A quick visual analysis of the network reveals three possible paths through the network:

Path 1: 1 – 2 – 5 – 6 – 7
Path 2: 1 – 2 – 4 – 5 – 6 – 7
Path 3: 1 – 2 – 3 – 6 – 7

We know from the times given for each activity that the three paths require 49, 68, and 57 time units, respectively. Thus the critical path, which is the longest path through a network, must be path 2.

How do we specify this analysis for computer processing? We must somehow transfer the details of Figure 18.3 into a machine-readable format, which means showing the beginning and ending nodes of all activities and their respective activity times. This format is given in Table 18.10, which also contains a simplified account of the computer output.

Computer routines are capable of much more sophisticated analysis of PERT networks. In particular, many advanced PERT-analysis routines allow for most optimistic, most likely, and most pessimistic times for each activity and accumulate all of these to indicate expected completion times not only for the entire project but also for key segments of the project. Standard errors of time estimates can also be calculated to indicate the amount of tolerance that is associated with the completion estimates. Most computer routines compute and list slack times. Cost considerations relating to crash programs (programs designed to compress the critical path into a shorter period by applying more resources to the project) can be calculated and printed. Such indicators give the analyst a great deal of control in complex project-management situations.

Table 18.10 Batch Processing of a Hypothetical PERT Problem

Input Records				Explanation
7	8	1	7	According to input instructions, first: a. The number of events b. The number of activities c. The starting event number d. The ending event number
1	2	8		
2	3	12		
2	4	15		For each activity specify:
2	5	9		a. The starting node
4	5	13		b. The finishing node
3	6	18		c. The completion time
5	6	13		
6	7	19		

Computer Output

A. NODES ON CRITICAL PATH

1 – 2 – 4 – 5 – 6 – 7

B. TOTAL PROJECT COMPLETION TIME

68

18.4 Summary

The various demonstrations of computer use that have been presented in this chapter pertain to some of the most common algorithms of management science. Two observations should adequately summarize this experimentation with computer systems. First, the time spent doing calculations is virtually eliminated by an appropriate computer routine. Not only is the time spent calculating drastically reduced (fractions of a second by computer compared with hours by hand), but it is also unnecessary to follow the logic of a complex and repetitive computational procedure. Moreover, once it is verified for a known problem, the accuracy of computed results can largely be taken for granted (even though checking to see that the results are reasonable is always a good idea).

Second, many steps necessary to arrive at a solution can be shifted to the computer. Where, in this chapter, are the references to initial basic feasible solutions that were of such concern in other chapters of this text? For the simplex method, for transportation problems, and for the assignment method, the computer routines determine an IBFS automatically. Other contingency situations, such as degeneracy, multiple optimal solutions, and unbounded feasible regions, are also provided for in the internal workings of the computer programs.

Well-designed computer programs offer all of the conveniences that are technically possible; they require only bare essentials for input and present complete and intelligible results in the output. This reduction in manual operations allows the analyst to spend more time formulating problems; it dispels concern that the size of a problem will grow beyond one's ability to compute a solution by hand; and it allows for more emphasis to be placed on the complete interpretation of results.

Computer applications of other quantitative methods can be just as impressive. A computer system for inventory control may provide for the ***on-line*** recording (that is, recording via direct connection to computer processing and storage devices) of all routine transactions and the automatic determination of reorder needs, including the amount to be ordered. It may even initiate whatever paperwork is necessary to place the order. Depending on the underlying model, probability analysis and decision theory may be used. Once operable, the system can be used repeatedly and requires only routine updating, revision, and maintenance.

Some computer applications combine system needs with appropriate analytical techniques. They incorporate one or more basic quantitative methods to aid in the decision-making process and in the optimal allocation of resources. They are typically tailored to particular operations and circumstances and are best demonstrated in actual use.

Because computers are so useful, most analysts develop basic abilities in computer programming and the use of modern computer systems. But above all, it is important to be able to interpret the results of analysis thoroughly, whether these results are obtained by computer or by hand. Within a still broader framework, it is wise to have a sense of the interdependence of business operations that makes it possible to draw methods of analysis together in coordinated computer systems or models. Computer processing makes the application of highly sophisticated, complex analytical techniques realistic and practicable.

Exercises

18.1 Go to your local computer center and find computer routines to solve linear programming problems. Use them to solve the potato–tomato and presidential election problems, and check your results. Then use the same routines to solve the following problems.

18.2 A company produces four styles of television sets: standard, deluxe, super, and color sets. Each set must go through three production processes: subassembly, assembly, and testing. The labor-hour requirements for each productive process are listed in the following table.[1]

	Standard	Deluxe	Super	Color
Subassembly	12	15	15	25
Assembly	10	12	13	20
Testing	0.5	0.6	0.6	2.0
Profit per Set	$25	$30	$40	$100

According to a contractual agreement, the company has to produce at least ten standard and ten deluxe models daily. The net profit from the sale of each set is also presented in the table. Market analysis indicates that the company will be able to sell as much as it can produce for the given period. The goal of the company is to maximize profit for the company as a whole.

a. Formulate the problem as a linear programming problem.
b. Use computer routines to solve this problem.
c. Interpret the computer output.
d. Determine the dual solution from your computer output.
e. Give an economic interpretation of the dual solution.

18.3 Refer to exercise 18.2.

a. Does your linear programming computer solution provide ranges of variation for the objective function coefficients (the range of variation for each unit of profit contribution)? If so, how are these interpreted? If not, can you otherwise predict how far in each direction the unit profit contribution can vary without changing the current optimal solution?
b. "Due to personnel problems in the subassembly department and possibly to a relatively high rate of turnover, an average unfavorable labor efficiency variance of 10% is a distinct possibility."[2] How would this affect the current optimal solution? And by how much in terms of profit?

[1]This problem is based on Alfred Rappaport, "Sensitivity Analysis in Decision Making," *The Accounting Review*, July 1967, 441–456.
[2]Rappaport, p. 446.

c. How far can the availability of labor capacity be varied without affecting the current optimal solution?

18.4 Refer to exercise 18.2. Due to the recent surge in imports of black-and-white television sets, management imposes a new policy by restricting the production of the "super" model to a maximum of 20 sets. What is the new optimal production schedule? Calculate the change in profit that implementing this policy brings about.

18.5 Refer to exercise 18.2.

a. Using available computer routines, determine the impact of introducing another color model. Assume that the technological coefficients and net profit contributions of each unit are as follows:

Subassembly	30
Assembly	25
Testing	3

Profit contribution per unit: $110

b. What would be the impact of eliminating the deluxe model from production?

18.6 A poultry raiser wants to select the least-cost broiler diet that will meet certain nutritive requirements. Table E18.1[3] lists eight feed ingredients, the nutritive contents of each feed ingredient, nutritive requirements, and the price of 100 pounds of feed ingredients.

Note that the nutritive elements from different feeds are additive and that, because of mixing considerations, feed ingredients should be combined in units that weigh exactly 100 pounds. Each column in the table shows the minimal number of pounds of each required nutrient that must be present in 100 pounds of feed. For example, column 1 states that at least 20 pounds of crude protein are required in each 100 pounds of feed mixture. One can interpret the other columns similarly, except the column for fiber requirement. "For maximum broiler growth it is best not to have the fiber content exceed 4%. This is because fiber content itself makes no nutritive contribution, while at the same time it fills the broiler's limited appetite." Consequently, no more than 4 pounds of fiber should be present in 100 pounds of feed mixture.

a. Use computer routines to find the optimal feed mixture that meets or surpasses the given nutritive requirements at the least possible cost.

b. Show which requirements are surpassed and by how much.

[3]This problem is adopted from I. Katzman, "Solving Feed Problems Through Linear Programming," *Journal of Farm Economics*, 38, No. 2 (May 1956) with permission of the American Agricultural Economic Association.

Table E18.1 Nutritive Content of Feed Ingredients, Nutritive Requirements, and Wholesale Prices

Feed Ingredients	Nutritive Contents of Feed Ingredients[a]							Wholesale Price 1952[b]
	Crude Protein	Calcium	Phos-phorus	Argi-nine	Lysine	Trypto-phane	Fiber	
Wheat bran	16.40	0.14	1.30	0.95	0.54	0.24	9.00	3.13
Oats #3	12.00	0.00	0.43	0.60	0.40	0.12	11.00	2.88
Soybean oil meal (44%)	44.00	0.30	0.66	2.80	2.70	0.53	5.20	4.69
Fish meal (60%)	60.00	5.75	3.20	3.80	4.00	0.69	1.00	8.04
Meal and bone scrap (50%)	50.60	9.70	4.20	3.30	2.80	0.32	2.50	5.60
Steamed bone meal	10.00	29.30	15.10	0.53	1.12	0.16	1.00	4.99
Yellow corn #3	8.90	0.02	0.27	0.36	0.22	0.06	2.00	3.28
Wheat standard middlings	17.60	0.14	0.78	0.86	0.47	0.20	7.50	3.21
Nutritive requirements	20.00	1.00	0.60	1.00	0.90	0.25	4.00	

[a]Pounds of each element in 100 pounds of feed ingredient.
[b]Arithmetic averages of midmonthly quotations from January through December, (dollars per 100 pounds).

18.7 "Suppose a farmer has recently installed a loose housing and milking parlor dairy operation and is presently milking 100 cows. He now realizes that his hired labor and his milking facilities are not being used to capacity. He could add more cows, but his forage supply is limited. He produces his own forage, but cannot increase production beyond that needed for his 100 cows and 50 young stock. There are three possible alternatives [or three activities] under consideration. One [activity 1], he could buy additional hay. Two [activity 2], he could transfer forage from young stock to milking cows by buying replacement cows instead of raising them. Three [activity 3], he could have some combination of the first two alternatives [activities]."[4] The additional costs and returns per unit level of activity are shown in Table E18.2.

The total availability of resources and resource requirements at unit level of activity are shown in Table E18.3.

[4]This problem is adopted from Marvin W. Kottke, *Obtaining Identical Solutions Using Linear Programming and Partial Budgeting* (Storrs, Conn.: Storrs Agricultural Experiment Station, University of Connecticut), Bulletin 359, September 1960, p. 4. The authors are grateful to Marvin W. Kottke, University of Connecticut, for permission to use the problem in this exercise.

Table E18.2

	The Milking and Feeding Operation (per cow)	Activity 1: The Purchase of Additional Hay (per ton)	Activity 2: The Substitution of Purchased for Raised Replacements (per head of young stock)
Changes in Returns	+$540	$ 0	+$ 8
Changes in Costs	+ 242	+ 40	+ 85
Changes in Net Profit	+$298	−$40	−$77

Table E18.3

	The Milking and Feeding Operation (per cow)	Activity 1: The Purchase of Additional Hay (per ton)	Activity 2: The Substitution of Purchased for Raised Replacements (per head of young stock)	Total Availability
Capital (dollars)	300	0	−150	5,000
Labor (winter hours)	20	0	−10	300
Labor (summer hours)	10	0	−7	200
Forage (tons)	5	−1	−2	0
Young Stock (head)	0	0	1	50

Do you remember the economic interpretation of the signs of the coefficients (Section 3.3)? For example, the farm has zero forage, so the negative coefficients −1 and −2 mean that the forage can be supplied (not used up) by activities 1 and 2, if activities 1 and 2 come into the final solution. Note also that the total availability of young stock is limited to 50. "This means that the present farm has 50 head of young stock which may be replaced by purchased replacements. A maximum substitution of 50 head is assumed by the use of a coefficient of 1 for [activity 2]." The goal of the farm is to maximize net profit.

a. Formulate a linear programming model for the dairy farm.
b. Set up a simplex tableau and give an economic interpretation for each activity (column) and constraint (row). (***Hint:*** See Section 3.3.)
c. Solve the linear programming problem by using computer routines, and indicate what is (or are) the most profitable activity (or activities) for the farm.

18.8 Refer to the academic journals available in your library in the fields of accounting, marketing, management, economics, industrial engineering, and operations research. Find applications of operations research techniques and check the solutions using available computer routines.

18.9 Many production models in operations research involve several production or procurement sources for a single product in different time periods. Each source has a given capacity in each time period. The product may be stored from one period to the next at a known cost per unit. Each decision will have effects both presently and in subsequent periods. Consequently, the optimization problem is truly dynamic, because the economic trade-offs are not limited to activities within a single time period, but extend to activities in different time periods as well.

"Only inventory and procurement costs are relevant to the following four-period production planning problem:

	Period 1	Period 2	Period 3	Period 4
Regular time production capacity	100	100	60	100
Overtime production capacity	20	20	10	10
Subcontracting source capacity	40	40	40	40
Regular time unit cost	\$ 15	\$ 16	\$ 18	\$ 20
Overtime unit cost	17	19	21	24
Subcontracting unit cost	20	21	22	23
Demand requirement	90	110	100	115

The initial inventory is five units. No shortages are to be planned. The inventory carrying cost is \$1 per unit per period."[5]

Note that, in addition to the nonnegativity requirement within each period, there are two types of constraints to be observed. One is the

[5]This problem is adopted from Lynwood A. Johnson and Douglas C. Montgomery, *Operations Research in Production Planning, Scheduling, and Inventory Control* (New York: Wiley, 1974), p. 297. Used by permission.

capacity constraint. The other is the so-called material-balance equation, which means that:

Inventory level at the end of period t	=	Inventory at beginning period t	+	Planned production in period t	−	Demand in period t

The material-balance equations link consecutive time periods. These time-staged linkages are the basic characteristics of multiperiod production-planning models. To facilitate formulation of the model for this problem, the following set of decision variables are provided:

X_{it} = planned quantity to be obtained from source i in period t ($t = 1, 2, 3, 4$)

$i = 1$: regular time

$i = 2$: overtime

$i = 3$: subcontracting

D_t = units required in period t

P_{it} = capacity, in units of product, of source i in period t

I_t = inventory level at the end of period t, after satisfying the requirements in period t

C_{it} = variable production cost per unit from source i in period t

h_t = cost to store a unit (inventory) from period t to period $t + 1$

a. Formulate a multiperiod production-planning model for this problem by using the defined decision variable and LP technique.
b. Give an economic interpretation of the objective function.
c. Obtain a computer-generated solution for the minimal total cost and optimal quantity to be planned from each source in each period of production.
d. Formulate a generalized LP problem (for $i = 1, 2, \ldots, m$; $t = 1, 2, \ldots, T$) in symbolic terms by using the defined decision variables.

18.10 A library system consists of nine libraries, A through I.[6] Three of the libraries, B, F, and H, have audiovisual laboratories with the traditional equipment. There are 6, 11, and 10 projectors available in audiovisual

[6]This problem is adopted from Charles R. McClure, "Linear Programming and Library Delivery Systems," *Library Resources and Technical Services*, 21, No. 4 (Fall 1977). Used by permission.

laboratory B, F, and H, respectively. Because of budget restraints, it is impossible for other libraries to purchase more equipment, and the director of the system has decided to allocate the available projectors to other libraries on request. On one particular day, libraries A, B, C, D, E, F, G, H, and I request 2, 1, 8, 4, 1, 1, 6, 1, and 1 projector(s), respectively.

The number of projectors demanded and the supply, along with the cost of delivering equipment from the audiovisual (AV) laboratory of the supply library to the demand library, are presented in the following table.

From \ To	A	B	C	D	E	F	G	H	I	Supply
AV Laboratory 1 at Library B	15	1	8	14	12	7	4	9	19	6
AV Laboratory 2 at Library F	9	7	5	10	19	1	9	5	12	11
AV Laboratory 3 at Library H	16	9	7	9	14	5	7	1	15	10
Demand	2	1	8	4	1	1	6	1	1	

a. Formulate the computer inputs for this transportation problem.

b. Obtain a computer solution showing which AV laboratories should provide how many projectors to which libraries. What is the minimum total delivery cost?

18.11 The Tennis Wears Company is a manufacturer of women's tennis clothing. The items manufactured include a tennis dress, two styles of shorts, a one-piece shorts suit, three styles of shirts, a cotton sweater, and two styles of caps. The company purchases the raw materials (fabric, zippers, thread, buttons, elastic, and trim) on a wholesale basis. These purchases are made monthly, so that inventory during any given month is fixed.

The company handles the cutting, machine sewing, hand sewing, and pressing phases of production. Three full-time cutters are employed, which means that 120 hours of labor each week are devoted to cutting (based on a 40-hour week). Four sewing machines are used full-time, and there is one part-time employee who does only the hand sewing. All pressing is handled by one employee who works two hours a day five days a week. The company serves three retail outlets in a metropolitan area and has received orders in early February from these retailers. The goods will be delivered the following month.

Traditionally, March signals the onset of the tennis season, so retailers expect an increase in demand for tennis clothing this month. The combined orders of the three retailers are, at a minimum, 175 dresses, 200 one-piece suits, and 250 cotton sweaters. These three articles are the most popular items among consumers, but the retailers also request any

Figure E18.1

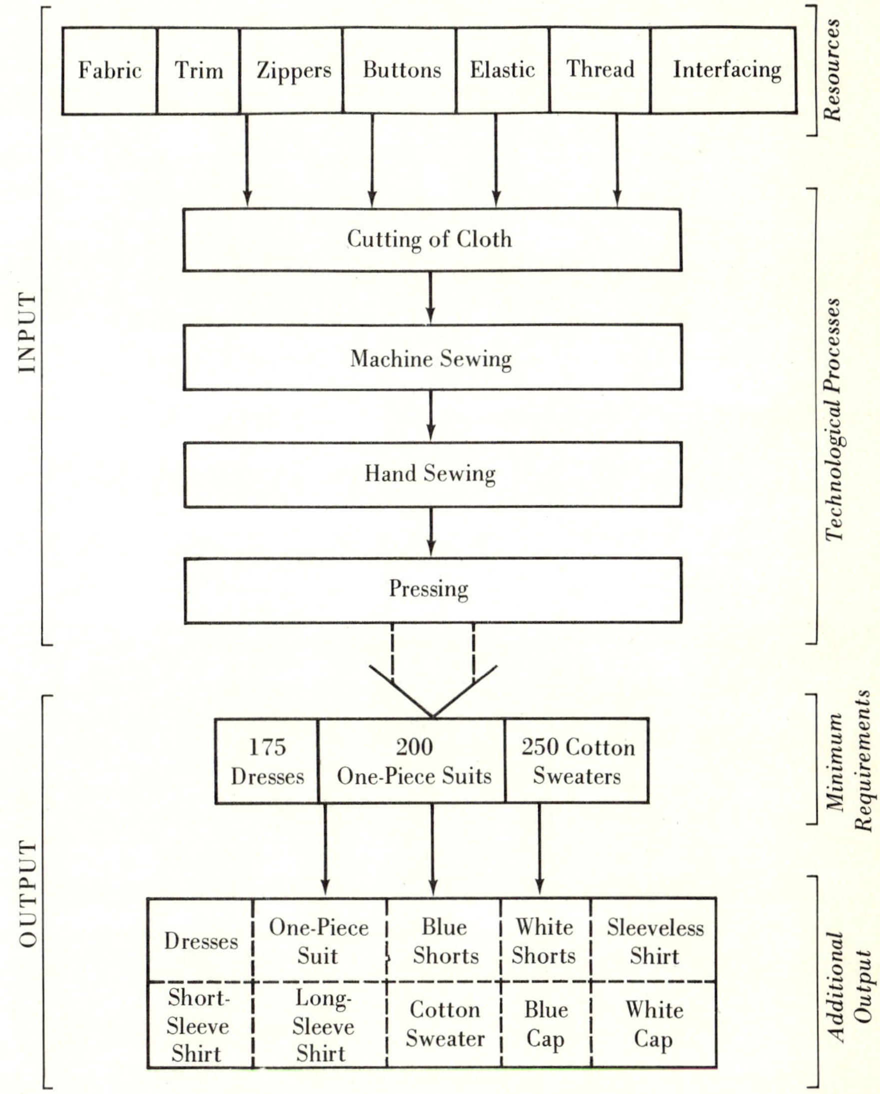

amount of the other articles that the manufacturer can deliver. Any articles not sold during March are to be used to build up inventory for the height of the tennis season expected during June and July.

The overall production procedure is described in the accompanying flow chart. Flow begins with the resources: the fabric, trim, zippers, buttons, elastic, thread, and interfacing shown in the diagram. These resources then pass through the cutting, machine sewing, hand sewing, and pressing processes that result in the final products: various articles of women's tennis clothing. This flow of resources through the technological processes that result in output occurs in a fixed relationship; that is, the technological coefficients giving the amounts of these resources necessary for the production of each unit of output are constant. The items produced, descriptions of all items, and their market prices are given in Table E18.4.

The technological coefficients, presented in the following table, are engineering data. For example, the production of each tennis sweater (column X_8) requires 1 yard of white cotton fabric, 1.75 yards of navy trim, 1.75 yards of red trim, 75 yards of thread, 6 buttons, 0.12 hours of cutting time, 0.25 hours of machine sewing time, and 0.03 hours of

Table E18.4

Item	(X_j)	Description	Price P_j
1. Tennis dress	(X_1)	White polyester, short pleat skirt, sleeveless V-neck top, blue–red trim	$18.95
2. Tennis suit	(X_2)	White polyester, one-piece shorts suit, sleeveless, crew neck top, blue–red trim	17.95
3. Tennis shorts	(X_3)	White cotton, cuffed shorts	7.95
4. Tennis shorts	(X_4)	Blue cotton, cuffed shorts	7.95
5. Tennis shirt	(X_5)	White polyester, V-neck sleeveless, pullover, blue–red trim	6.95
6. Tennis shirt	(X_6)	White polyester, short sleeves, crew neck, pullover	6.95
7. Tennis shirt	(X_7)	White cotton, long sleeve, crew neck, pullover	11.98
8. Tennis sweater	(X_8)	White cotton, cardigan, long sleeves, V-neck, blue–red trim	12.98
9. Sun cap	(X_9)	White cotton, elastic back	1.29
10. Sun cap	(X_{10})	Blue cotton, elastic back	1.29

pressing time. The technological coefficients associated with the production of the other items are interpreted similarly.

By reading the table of technological coefficients horizontally, one can also observe all the products that a particular resource is used to produce. For example, 0.25 hours of cutting time are needed to produce the tennis dress (X_1), 0.16 hours for the tennis suit (X_2), 0.11 hours each for the two shorts (X_3 and X_4), 0.08 hours for each of the two shirts (X_5 and X_6), 0.11 hours for the third shirt (X_7), 0.12 hours for the sweater (X_8), and 0.01 hours each for the two sun caps (X_9 and X_{10}). One can interpret the other resources similarly.

The resources necessary for the production process and the amounts available for the production period are shown in Table E18.6. The management of the company must now make a production decision.

a. With profit maximization as the goal, formulate a linear programming model for the company.
b. Prepare the simplex tableau.
c. What is the optimal production schedule?
d. What effect would a change in the market price of any particular garment have on this optimal decision?

Table E18.5 Table of Technological Coefficients

Resource	X_1	X_2	X_3	X_4	X_5	X_6	X_7	X_8	X_9	X_{10}
White polyester	1.75	1			.5	.75				
White cotton			.75				1	1	.25	
Navy cotton				.75					.25	
Navy trim	2	.5			1.5		1.75	1.75		
Red trim	2	.5			1.5		1.75	1.75		
Appliques	1	1		1	1					
Zipper white 6″		1								
Zipper white 12″	1	1								
Zipper navy 6″				1						
Interfacing	.25	.25							.12	.12
Thread	100	75	50	50	45	45	50	75	25	25
Elastic	1								.16	.16
Buttons			1	1				6		
Cutting board time	.25	.16	.11	.11	.08	.08	.11	.12	.01	.01
Machine sewing time	.3	.25	.16	.16	.06	.04	.06	.25	.04	.04
Hand sewing time		.16								
Pressing time	.04	.02	.02	.02	.02	.02	.03	.03		

Table E18.6

Resource	Amount of Resource Available for One-Month Production Period b_i
White polyester	1,100 yards
White cotton	450 yards
Navy cotton	100 yards
Navy trim	2,000 yards
Red trim	2,000 yards
Tennis appliques	600
White zipper, 6″	75
White zipper, 12″	625
Navy zipper, 6″	75
Interfacing	175 yards
Thread	300,000 yards
Elastic	250 yards
Buttons	2,000
Cutting board time	480 hours
Sewing machine time	640 hours
Hand sewing time	60 hours
Pressing time	40 hours

e. The firm has received a request to produce a new style of dress requiring 2 yards of white cotton, 1 yard of blue trim, 1 yard of red trim, a 12-inch zipper, 0.3 yards of interfacing, 125 yards of thread, 0.5 yards of elastic, and 0.25 hours of cutting time. The retailers have promised to purchase the output at a price of $21.98 per unit. At this price, is it justified for the firm to produce the new dress? If so, why? If not, indicate the minimal price level that ***would*** justify adding the new style of dress to the production line.

18.12 Which of the problems that you have completed in these exercises were done by interactive computer processing and which by batch processing? Describe briefly the differences between these two methods of computer use. Pick any one of the problems that you have completed, summarize the computer input requirements, and describe how this input procedure would be different if the other method were used—batch processing instead of interactive processing, or vice versa.

18.13 Either inquire or scan the manuals available at your computer center to find the simulation language or languages that are available for instructional and research use. Review the capabilities of these languages and then answer the following questions.

a. What is a simulation language?
b. Why is computer simulation particularly advantageous as a tool in the analysis of systems or facilities?
c. For general-purpose programming languages such as FORTRAN and PL/1, what subroutines are available for the specific needs of computer simulation?
d. Contrast your answer to part (c) with the subroutines that are available through the use of a higher-level computer-simulation language. For as many subroutines as you can identify, what are these subroutines called within the nomenclature of the simulation language, and what function does each subroutine serve?
e. What are the advantages of the higher-level simulation languages compared with, for example, FORTRAN? Are there any disadvantages in the use of higher-level simulation languages? If so, what are they, and what must an analyst do to assure, at the outset, that the simulation language chosen suits the simulation to be performed?

18.14 Obtain assistance in the use of a simulation language that is available at your computer center, and simulate the operation of elevators in a college dormitory during the following rush-hour conditions:

1. The dormitory has 7 floors above ground level, each housing 100 students.
2. Two elevators operate simultaneously at a single, central location in the building.
3. A stairway is adjacent to the elevators. Students always try to catch the elevator, but they use the stairway if the wait is too long. This "line balking" occurs more readily at the lower floors than at higher floors, as shown in the following table:

Floor	Time Students Are Willing to Wait before Selecting Stairway (minutes)
1	$\frac{1}{4}$
2	$\frac{1}{2}$
3	$\frac{3}{4}$
4	1
5	$1\frac{1}{4}$
6	$1\frac{1}{2}$
7	$1\frac{3}{4}$

4. An elevator travels at a rate of 3 seconds per floor. The pick-up of passengers requires an additional 9 seconds. Each elevator moves first to the highest floor registering a demand for service, and then

proceeds to the ground floor, picking up more students along the way if any are waiting.

5. In the morning, 80% of all students in the dormitory leave their rooms between 8 o'clock and 10 o'clock, at a fairly constant rate of flow. Assume, for simplicity, that all traffic is outward bound. On the basis of a computer simulation of this system, obtain a detailed listing of the characteristics of operation. Simulate many days to obtain data that are based on large numbers. How would this system work if one elevator were to break down and be inoperable during the entire morning rush period?

18.15 Obtain the necessary instructions for access to and use of locally available computer routines that have been set up for PERT project analysis. Use the computer to analyze the networks specified in exercises 10.4, 10.6, 10.7, and 10.9.

a. Compare your computer results with the PERT calculations that you completed by hand.
b. For each exercise, prepare a verbal interpretation of the results.
c. What special capabilities does the computer routine possess? That is, is a Gantt chart prepared automatically? How are slack times indicated? Are probability estimates given that relate to completion times? If so, how are these probabilities used in estimating project completion?
d. What further capabilities might one wish to see in the available PERT routine? Is the compressing or "crashing" of activities according to known cost increments a feature of the computer program? Are there other features that you might desire? If so, what are they?

Suggested Readings

Berry, William L., Charles J. Christenson, and John S. Hammond, III. *Management Decision Sciences: Cases and Readings.* Homewood, Ill.: Irwin, 1980.

Economos, A. M. "A Financial Simulation for Risk Analysis of a Proposed Subsidiary." *Management Science*, August 1968, B-675–682.

Kuehn, Alfred A., and Doyle L. Weiss. "Marketing Analysis Training Exercise." *Behavioral Sciences*, January 1965.

Mattessich, Richard. "Budgeting Models and System Simulation." *Accounting Review*, July 1961.

Naylor, T. H., E. T. Byrne, and J. M. Vernon. *Introduction to Linear Programming: Methods and Cases.* Belmont, Calif.: Wadsworth, 1971.

Perkins, William C., and Paul Paschke. "A Simulation Model of a Higher Education System of a State." *Decision Sciences,* 4, No. 2 (April 1973), pp. 194–215.

Vatler, Paul A., Stephen P. Bradley, Sherwood C. Frey, Jr., and Barbara Bund Jackson. *Quantitative Methods in Management: Text and Cases.* Part VI. Homewood, Ill.: Irwin, 1977.

19

Quantitative Techniques—A Final Perspective

Taken together, the topics of this text form a sort of "tool kit." That is to say, they are many of the recognized tools of analysts who must deal with complex situations in business in such a way as to increase the effectiveness of daily operations. The results are translatable into profits in dollars and cents. The process is one of implementing logically based analysis to render decision making more effective.

What are the contents of this took kit? And how are they used? It is evident from the preceding chapters that the characteristics of the situation to be analyzed dictate the methods of analysis. Insofar as some types of problems can be categorized, it is possible to apply set procedures. But tackling any problem requires a careful review of the assumptions of standard techniques to see whether they suit the particulars of the given situation. Just as a carpenter wouldn't try to build solid cabinets if there were no glue available for the joints, the operations analyst should not try to formulate results on the basis of an approach that relies on an important element that cannot be provided. The final results will be useful only to the extent that the techniques applied fit the given situation.

In practice, it is necessary to determine the fundamental characteristics of a working system that must be analyzed, the usefulness and applicability of established techniques, the need to alter or develop new techniques in unusual circumstances, and the validity of the results obtained. Various deterministic and probabilistic models have been presented in this text, and typical business problems have been analyzed using these models. Ingenuity led to the development of these techniques, and ingenuity is often required in their implementation. "Cook book" solutions, where they exist, can be delegated to computers or to support staff. New problems, which will continue to occur in endless variety, must be handled with an open mind, a willingness to adapt, and considerable persistence.

Users of these tools vary in their training, experience, and field of specialization. The industrious student who completes this text should be able to tackle reasonably complex problems that fall within well-defined areas of analysis. Study in greater depth of the individual topics provided here can lead to a high level of analytical expertise. Combined with appropriate practical experience, this background can be of great value to business organizations operating in dynamic and changing environments.

Efficiency is paramount in the success of a business organization that operates in a competitive environment. One fundamental characteristic arises so often in problems relating to the efficient allocation of resources that it deserves repeated emphasis here. The problems that require specialized analysis in pursuit of an optimal decision or decisions typically involve ***trade-offs.*** Advantages that can be gained through a particular decision or action are generally won at the expense of other considerations that are also important to the activities or operations of the organization. Consequently, the business analyst must be keenly aware of, and be able to identify, the conflicting results of any chosen course of action. The best solutions, if they exist, are found through appropriate analysis of the opportunity costs or marginal changes that will occur if those solutions are adopted. Always keep these basic economic concepts in mind when applying and interpreting the results of the techniques presented in this text.

19.1 Opportunities in the Field of Quantitative Business Analysis

Business enterprises have been quick to recognize and seek the benefits of scientific approaches to management. Staffs of analysts are not inexpensive, but in a dynamic business environment, the corporation with sizable assets can afford an operations planning or research group. Indeed, an effective "think tank" that supports the operations of a large organization should offset its own costs with the substantial business savings realized when the results of the group's analytical activities are implemented.

There are numerous reasons why analytical approaches to business management succeed. One is the sheer size of many business organizations in today's economy and the size of the market place in which they operate. The largest 500 industrial corporations in America generate more than half of the manufacturing and mining revenues of the nation. They produce and sell electronic equipment, consumer goods, raw materials, food, and machinery. They generate two-thirds to three-quarters of all profits in our economy and supply jobs for a substantial portion of the labor force. Improved efficiency in operations such as these can mean millions of dollars in savings.

Careful analysis of alternatives that arise in the decision-making process can contribute meaningfully toward an optimal allocation of available resources.

The sophistication and demonstrated utility of management-science techniques have contributed to the success of these techniques in business. Complex operations require sound analytical interpretation and scientific management in order to work effectively. Consider the scheduling of transportation (bus, rail, or air) covering many routes simultaneously, the organization of communications networks over great distances, the distribution of perishable food to numerous locations, and so many other business activities that we take for granted. As consumers of these goods and services we would be greatly dissatisfied if they were not efficiently organized. Careful analysis and planning have helped managers to deliver their products and services to the market place in an efficient and reliable fashion.

Certainly, too, the success of analytical methods in business owes much to technological developments in the past 30–40 years. Many techniques of business analysis rely heavily on long computational algorithms to derive accurate, representative, and reliable results. Linear programming is a clear example of this, as are simulation models and other approaches to optimal decision making that are computationally burdensome. The computational support of computer technology has made it practical to apply new techniques that could not otherwise have been widely used.

Perhaps the success of quantitative analysis in the business decision-making process can best be summarized in terms of "cost–benefit" reasoning. The investment required to effectively use decision-making techniques is generally returned in both improved operations and financial savings. The analytical approach to problem solving has become and will remain an important element of modern business management.

19.2 Management Science: The People and Their Approach

Who are today's business analysts, and how do they function in the decision-making process? Specialists in management science or operations research generally come from an academic background that emphasizes both general business management and quantitative techniques, including mathematics, statistics, and the many phases of business management. They generally cluster as small teams who work closely with top management on planning and operational problems. They may be a part of the business organization itself and deal exclusively with research and planning activities within that business, or they may be consultants who move from one business organization to another on a contractual basis.

The top nationwide accounting firms all have operations research staffs. Of the many firms that specialize solely in management consulting, the largest have outstanding reputations based on the talent of the individuals who do the consulting and the effectiveness of their results. In addition to their corporate clientele, some of these firms have prepared impressive studies for the U.S. government and for foreign governments.

The success of quantitative analysis in addressing business decision problems rests above all in the effectiveness of the results. Whether they are part of the organization or are brought in as consultants, specialists must work successfully in a number of important ways.

1. Specialists must work effectively with business managers, understanding and even anticipating the thinking of top management. Meetings must be well-organized and efficiently conducted.
2. There must be a clear understanding of the general goals and priorities of the organization and of the more immediate objectives of management.
3. The problem-solving process must be conducted expeditiously with a careful, appropriate, and realistic approach to the problem. The assumptions of quantitative analysis must be carefully scrutinized to be sure that they adequately reflect the situation at hand. If they do not, the approach must be reevaluated.
4. The specialist must be aware that quantitative solutions to problems are not necessarily absolute, and that nonquantitative parameters valued by top business management must be considered. The atti-

tude that "because it's scientific, it must be right" can lead to misunderstandings between analysts and management.

5. Any planning or research project should culminate in a well-written report that makes clear what the problem is, how it has been analyzed, the results of analysis, the implications of implementing the results, and the expected benefits.
6. Finally, whatever training or instruction is necessary to achieve the desired results must be organized or conducted so that the projected benefits are actually realized. One must avoid allowing good studies to be shelved or filed away simply because there is inadequate follow-through.

Achieving worthwhile and effective results is an integrated process, every step of which should be taken carefully and effectively.

19.3 Management Information Systems

Every business organization needs an informed management, and an important part of obtaining good information for decision-making purposes is the ability to conduct effective analyses of operating conditions. Today's decision that requires quantitative analysis will probably occur again in the future, perhaps repeatedly. If so, and if the techniques for achieving optimal results have been determined effectively, automatic systems should be implemented to handle the recurring problem.

For example, a manufacturing concern with several warehouses might set up systems on the basis of an initial transportation model to periodically assess the demand for manufactured output at the warehouses, its availability at production facilities, and the optimal routing of shipments. Key data are routinely collected, stored, analyzed, and interpreted to present management with systematic actions to take. The process of data acquisition, data entry, data processing (including quantitative analysis), and management reporting make up business operations called ***management information systems***, or MIS.

Implementing management information systems makes the special findings of business analysts routine. Typically, management information systems combine many disciplines and rely heavily on the effective use of computers. The process of data acquisition usually involves designing forms for collecting necessary data, managing forms over time—including their printing, distribution, and collection—and screening incoming data. Data entry is usually a ***key entry*** process, such as keypunching onto computer cards. More recently, keying directly to magnetic tape or to a computer disk pack has gained wide acceptance in computer applications. Any extensive system relies on effective organization of stored data in the form of a data base or data bases. These are effectively manipulated through ***data base management systems***, which facilitate efficient storage, access, and updating of data independent of the processing need. Programming a computer to process the data and to write easily understood management reports completes the process. Thus management information systems collect raw data, derive from these data the information that management needs, and (on the basis of appropriate analysis) supply decision information to the proper manager in a timely and useful fashion.

19.4 Summary

The business environment has made increasing use of quantitative methods to assist in effective decision making. At the same time, new analytical techniques have been developed, and rapidly advancing computer technology has made possible the successful application of methods that were unheard of only a half-century ago. It is reasonable to assume that the use of business analysts and analytical methods will continue to increase in the future. Expanding capabilities call for the skilled and informed application of sophisticated techniques. To lay the groundwork for understanding of these techniques has been the aim of this book.

Suggested Readings

Arnoff, E. Leonard. "Successful Models I Have Known." *Decision Sciences,* 2, No. 2 (April 1971), 141–148.

Gaither, Norman. "The Adoption of Operations Research Techniques by Manufacturing Organizations." *Decision Sciences,* 6, No. 4 (October 1975), 797–813.

Grayson, C. Jackson, Jr. "Management Science and Business Practice." *Harvard Business Review,* July/August 1973, 41–48.

Hertz, David B. "The Unity of Sciences and Management." *Management Science,* April 1965.

Newendorp, P. "Risk Evaluation Helps Make Better Decisions." *The Oil and Gas Journal* (October 18, 1976), 55–58.

Rader, Louis T. "Roadblocks to Progress in the Management Sciences and Operations Research." *Management Science*, February 1965.

Shycon, Harvey L. "Perspectives on MS Applications." *Interfaces*, 6, No. 1 (November 1975), 64–66.

APPENDIX

Selected Tables for Probability Analysis

Appendix A.1 Table of Random Numbers

8518	4422	0152	8263	3492	5642	0691	2436	4175	7469
0680	2759	9236	4248	2534	0136	0551	9847	4207	4647
1727	9288	7894	3654	9976	3428	4794	1956	5291	5346
9089	4019	6531	7314	1595	3164	8628	1192	9543	8400
8496	7168	4973	7609	5659	2010	0169	4253	1415	3904
0581	5666	4784	5886	0799	1892	7308	7788	1312	2383
6922	0536	3351	4580	0058	9206	5430	6007	7246	6319
2630	6408	3653	6369	2980	8858	0802	2813	8654	4974
1216	6111	9178	5042	6491	3034	3636	5050	5347	6626
9979	4249	6141	0584	6487	6131	4514	1996	9571	3314
1204	8188	4834	6236	3249	9141	1583	9880	3238	9464
6644	4905	2333	5130	3907	2547	7027	6386	4299	7267
7426	5579	3450	4148	1834	5237	0578	4845	3437	7257
5996	7569	1379	4052	7005	7032	4421	6545	7812	7880
3156	3690	9828	9592	8340	2376	2310	3216	8357	3695
4350	0448	5935	0428	3795	1449	6542	8434	1434	2437
1700	4784	4132	4122	8052	3560	0918	1225	0738	9490
2590	2128	5695	7223	3358	2304	0527	0888	0540	4583
1600	1199	0874	4681	7250	0747	4428	9319	3629	9801
2203	6220	0898	9085	1755	0284	5109	8882	7370	3587
7845	6911	7974	2214	5897	5837	4056	9990	3926	1080
5559	8114	7194	8755	9281	6563	2738	5964	2145	7014
4855	1983	2680	7480	0357	7698	9568	1772	1603	2741
4310	6168	7973	8607	5445	0112	3984	2606	9840	2876
3730	4108	7554	7274	7315	5202	3611	4875	4123	1659
1780	0459	6334	7456	3789	6921	4044	6706	8539	0169
9582	1124	4267	7870	7086	9199	0789	5922	2815	3703
6719	5250	6747	6426	8579	4449	7541	0383	1480	1245
0714	2201	9727	2088	1415	9265	4211	9075	3521	0245
3714	4642	3692	4072	0491	1036	9737	6715	1002	4213
5260	2817	0917	7618	0287	5208	8139	7369	9980	7856
6588	2913	7189	0720	7039	7195	2362	9733	6927	5686
9399	2189	5722	4612	5482	3471	0595	6164	1070	9489
3622	4552	9062	6630	4407	6047	1526	4281	7647	2725
9073	6307	9346	1018	1925	0277	6663	0963	3540	0942
8670	4600	2198	8185	8652	7760	0316	9811	1158	6905
3135	7943	0397	1978	7530	3592	6342	5591	6734	9535
2741	6785	3492	0700	4899	8215	1501	4106	6422	4151
2655	6583	4878	4944	3006	2640	2478	8145	9011	2673
1509	2962	0014	0498	4164	4907	9547	6025	2172	4403

Appendix A.2 Table of Values of the Binomial Distribution $P(n, r|p) = C_{n,r}\,[p^r\,(1 - p)^{n-r}]$

n	r	.01	.05	.10	.20	.30	.40	.50	.60	.70	.80	.90	.95	.99
1	0	.990	.950	.900	.800	.700	.600	.500	.400	.300	.200	.100	.050	.010
	1	.010	.050	.100	.200	.300	.400	.500	.600	.700	.800	.900	.950	.990
2	0	.980	.902	.810	.640	.490	.360	.250	.160	.090	.040	.010	.003	
	1	.020	.095	.180	.320	.420	.480	.500	.480	.420	.320	.180	.095	.020
	2		.003	.010	.040	.090	.160	.250	.360	.490	.640	.810	.902	.980
3	0	.970	.857	.729	.512	.343	.216	.125	.064	.027	.008	.001		
	1	.029	.135	.243	.384	.441	.432	.375	.288	.189	.096	.027	.007	
	2		.007	.027	.096	.189	.288	.375	.432	.441	.384	.243	.135	.029
	3			.001	.008	.027	.064	.125	.216	.343	.512	.729	.857	.970
4	0	.961	.815	.656	.410	.240	.130	.063	.026	.008	.002			
	1	.039	.171	.292	.410	.412	.346	.250	.154	.076	.026	.004		
	2	.001	.014	.049	.154	.265	.346	.375	.346	.265	.154	.049	.014	.001
	3			.004	.026	.076	.154	.250	.346	.412	.410	.292	.171	.039
	4				.002	.008	.026	.063	.130	.240	.410	.656	.815	.961
5	0	.951	.774	.590	.328	.168	.078	.031	.010	.002				
	1	.048	.204	.328	.410	.360	.259	.156	.077	.028	.006			
	2	.001	.021	.073	.205	.309	.346	.313	.230	.132	.051	.008	.001	
	3		.001	.008	.051	.132	.230	.313	.346	.309	.205	.073	.021	.001
	4				.006	.028	.077	.156	.259	.360	.410	.328	.204	.048
	5					.002	.010	.031	.078	.168	.328	.590	.774	.951

Table of Values of the Binomial Distribution (cont.)

n	r	.01	.05	.10	.20	.30	.40	.50	.60	.70	.80	.90	.95	.99
6	0	.941	.735	.531	.262	.118	.047	.016	.004	.001				
	1	.057	.232	.354	.393	.303	.187	.094	.037	.010	.002			
	2	.001	.031	.098	.246	.324	.311	.234	.138	.060	.015	.001		
	3		.002	.015	.082	.185	.276	.313	.276	.185	.082	.015	.002	
	4			.001	.015	.060	.138	.234	.311	.324	.246	.098	.031	.001
	5				.002	.010	.037	.094	.187	.303	.393	.354	.232	.057
	6					.001	.004	.016	.047	.118	.262	.531	.735	.941
7	0	.932	.698	.478	.210	.082	.028	.008	.002					
	1	.066	.257	.372	.367	.247	.131	.055	.017	.004				
	2	.002	.041	.124	.275	.318	.261	.164	.077	.025	.004			
	3		.004	.023	.115	.227	.290	.273	.194	.097	.029	.003		
	4			.003	.029	.097	.194	.273	.290	.227	.115	.023	.004	
	5				.004	.025	.077	.164	.261	.318	.275	.124	.041	.002
	6					.004	.017	.055	.131	.247	.367	.372	.257	.066
	7						.002	.008	.028	.082	.210	.478	.698	.932
8	0	.923	.663	.430	.168	.058	.017	.004	.001					
	1	.075	.279	.383	.336	.198	.090	.031	.008	.001				
	2	.003	.051	.149	.294	.296	.209	.109	.041	.010	.001			
	3		.005	.033	.147	.254	.279	.219	.124	.047	.009			
	4			.005	.046	.136	.232	.273	.232	.136	.046	.005		
	5				.009	.047	.124	.219	.279	.254	.147	.033	.005	
	6				.001	.010	.041	.109	.209	.296	.294	.149	.051	.003
	7					.001	.008	.031	.090	.198	.336	.383	.279	.075
	8						.001	.004	.017	.058	.168	.430	.663	.923

Table of Values of the Binomial Distribution (cont.)

n	r	.01	.05	.10	.20	.30	.40	.50	.60	.70	.80	.90	.95	.99
9	0	.914	.630	.387	.134	.040	.010	.002						
	1	.083	.299	.387	.302	.156	.060	.018	.004					
	2	.003	.063	.172	.302	.267	.161	.070	.021	.004				
	3		.008	.045	.176	.267	.251	.164	.074	.021	.003			
	4		.001	.007	.066	.172	.251	.246	.167	.074	.017	.001		
	5			.001	.017	.074	.167	.246	.251	.172	.066	.007	.001	
	6				.003	.021	.074	.164	.251	.267	.176	.045	.008	
	7					.004	.021	.070	.161	.267	.302	.172	.063	.003
	8						.004	.018	.060	.156	.302	.387	.299	.083
	9							.002	.010	.040	.134	.387	.630	.914
10	0	.904	.599	.349	.107	.028	.006	.001						
	1	.091	.315	.387	.268	.121	.040	.010	.002					
	2	.004	.075	.194	.302	.233	.121	.044	.011	.001				
	3		.010	.057	.201	.267	.215	.117	.042	.009	.001			
	4		.001	.011	.088	.200	.251	.205	.111	.037	.006			
	5			.001	.026	.103	.201	.246	.201	.103	.026	.001		
	6				.006	.037	.111	.205	.251	.200	.088	.011	.001	
	7				.001	.009	.042	.117	.215	.267	.201	.057	.010	
	8					.001	.011	.044	.121	.233	.302	.194	.075	.004
	9						.002	.010	.040	.121	.268	.387	.315	.091
	10							.001	.006	.028	.107	.349	.599	.904
11	0	.895	.569	.314	.086	.020	.004							
	1	.099	.329	.384	.236	.093	.027	.005	.001					
	2	.005	.087	.213	.295	.200	.089	.027	.005	.001				
	3		.014	.071	.221	.257	.177	.081	.023	.004				
	4		.001	.016	.111	.220	.236	.161	.070	.017	.002			
	5			.002	.039	.132	.221	.226	.147	.057	.010			
	6				.010	.057	.147	.226	.221	.132	.039	.002		
	7				.002	.017	.070	.161	.236	.220	.111	.016	.001	
	8					.004	.023	.081	.177	.257	.221	.071	.014	
	9					.001	.005	.027	.089	.200	.295	.213	.087	.005
	10						.001	.005	.027	.093	.236	.384	.329	.099
	11							.000	.004	.020	.086	.314	.569	.895

Table of Values of the Binomial Distribution (cont.)

n	r	.01	.05	.10	.20	.30	.40	.50	.60	.70	.80	.90	.95	.99
12	0	.886	.540	.282	.069	.014	.002							
	1	.107	.341	.377	.206	.071	.017	.003						
	2	.006	.099	.230	.283	.168	.064	.016	.002					
	3		.017	.085	.236	.240	.142	.054	.012	.001				
	4		.002	.021	.133	.231	.213	.121	.042	.008	.001			
	5			.004	.053	.158	.227	.193	.101	.029	.003			
	6				.016	.079	.177	.226	.177	.079	.016			
	7				.003	.029	.101	.193	.227	.158	.053	.004		
	8				.001	.008	.042	.121	.213	.231	.133	.021	.002	
	9					.001	.012	.054	.142	.240	.236	.085	.017	
	10						.002	.016	.064	.168	.283	.230	.099	.006
	11							.003	.017	.071	.206	.377	.341	.107
	12								.002	.014	.069	.282	.540	.886
13	0	.878	.513	.254	.055	.010	.001							
	1	.115	.351	.367	.179	.054	.011	.002						
	2	.007	.111	.245	.268	.139	.045	.010	.001					
	3		.021	.100	.246	.218	.111	.035	.006	.001				
	4		.003	.028	.154	.234	.184	.087	.024	.003				
	5			.006	.069	.180	.221	.157	.066	.014	.001			
	6			.001	.023	.103	.197	.209	.131	.044	.006			
	7				.066	.044	.131	.209	.197	.103	.023	.001		
	8				.001	.014	.066	.157	.221	.180	.069	.006		
	9					.003	.024	.087	.184	.234	.154	.028	.003	
	10					.001	.006	.035	.111	.218	.246	.100	.021	
	11						.001	.010	.045	.139	.268	.245	.111	.007
	12							.002	.011	.054	.179	.367	.351	.115
	13								.001	.010	.055	.254	.513	.878

Table of Values of the Binomial Distribution (cont.)

n	r	.01	.05	.10	.20	.30	.40	.50	.60	.70	.80	.90	.95	.99
14	0	.869	.488	.229	.044	.007	.001							
	1	.123	.359	.356	.154	.041	.007	.001						
	2	.008	.123	.257	.250	.113	.032	.006	.001					
	3		.026	.114	.250	.194	.085	.022	.003					
	4		.004	.035	.172	.229	.155	.061	.014	.001				
	5			.008	.086	.196	.207	.122	.041	.007				
	6			.001	.032	.126	.207	.183	.092	.023	.002			
	7				.009	.062	.157	.209	.157	.062	.009			
	8				.002	.023	.092	.183	.207	.126	.032	.001		
	9					.007	.041	.122	.207	.196	.086	.008		
	10					.001	.014	.061	.155	.229	.172	.035	.004	
	11						.003	.022	.085	.194	.250	.114	.026	
	12						.001	.006	.032	.113	.250	.257	.123	.008
	13							.001	.007	.041	.154	.356	.359	.123
	14								.001	.007	.044	.229	.488	.869
15	0	.860	.463	.206	.035	.005								
	1	.130	.366	.343	.132	.031	.005							
	2	.009	.135	.267	.231	.092	.022	.003						
	3		.031	.129	.250	.170	.063	.014	.002					
	4		.005	.043	.188	.219	.127	.042	.007	.001				
	5		.001	.010	.103	.206	.186	.092	.024	.003				
	6			.002	.043	.147	.207	.153	.061	.012	.001			
	7				.014	.081	.177	.196	.118	.035	.003			
	8				.003	.035	.118	.196	.177	.081	.014			
	9				.001	.012	.061	.153	.207	.147	.043	.002		
	10					.003	.024	.092	.186	.206	.103	.010	.001	
	11					.001	.007	.042	.127	.219	.188	.043	.005	
	12						.002	.014	.063	.170	.250	.129	.031	
	13							.003	.022	.092	.231	.267	.135	.009
	14								.005	.031	.132	.343	.366	.130
	15									.005	.035	.206	.463	.860

Table of Values of the Binomial Distribution (cont.)

n	r	.01	.05	.10	.20	.30	.40	.50	.60	.70	.80	.90	.95	.99
16	0	.851	.440	.185	.028	.003								
	1	.138	.371	.329	.113	.023	.003							
	2	.010	.146	.275	.211	.073	.015	.002						
	3		.036	.142	.246	.146	.047	.009	.001					
	4		.006	.051	.200	.204	.101	.028	.004					
	5		.001	.014	.120	.210	.162	.067	.014	.001				
	6			.003	.055	.165	.198	.122	.039	.006				
	7				.020	.101	.189	.175	.084	.019	.001			
	8				.006	.049	.142	.196	.142	.049	.006			
	9				.001	.019	.084	.175	.189	.101	.020			
	10					.006	.039	.122	.198	.165	.055	.003		
	11					.001	.014	.067	.162	.210	.120	.014	.001	
	12						.004	.028	.101	.204	.200	.051	.006	
	13						.001	.009	.047	.146	.246	.142	.036	
	14							.002	.015	.073	.211	.275	.146	.010
	15								.003	.023	.113	.329	.371	.138
	16									.003	.028	.185	.440	.851
17	0	.843	.418	.167	.023	.002								
	1	.145	.374	.315	.096	.017	.002							
	2	.012	.158	.280	.191	.058	.010	.001						
	3	.001	.041	.156	.239	.125	.034	.005						
	4		.008	.060	.209	.187	.080	.018	.002					
	5		.001	.017	.136	.208	.138	.047	.008	.001				
	6			.004	.068	.178	.184	.094	.024	.003				
	7			.001	.027	.120	.193	.148	.057	.009				
	8				.008	.064	.161	.185	.107	.028	.002			
	9				.002	.028	.107	.185	.161	.064	.008			
	10					.009	.057	.148	.193	.120	.027	.001		
	11					.003	.024	.094	.184	.178	.068	.004		
	12					.001	.008	.047	.138	.208	.136	.017	.001	
	13						.002	.018	.080	.187	.209	.060	.008	
	14							.005	.034	.125	.239	.156	.041	.001
	15							.001	.010	.058	.191	.280	.158	.012
	16								.002	.017	.096	.315	.374	.145
	17									.002	.023	.167	.418	.843

Table of Values of the Binomial Distribution (cont.)

n	r	.01	.05	.10	.20	.30	.40	.50	.60	.70	.80	.90	.95	.99
18	0	.835	.397	.150	.018	.002								
	1	.152	.376	.300	.081	.013	.001							
	2	.013	.168	.284	.172	.046	.007	.001						
	3	.001	.047	.168	.230	.105	.025	.003						
	4		.009	.070	.215	.168	.061	.012	.001					
	5		.001	.022	.151	.202	.115	.033	.004					
	6			.005	.082	.187	.166	.071	.015	.001				
	7			.001	.035	.138	.189	.121	.037	.005				
	8				.012	.081	.173	.167	.077	.015	.001			
	9				.003	.039	.128	.185	.128	.039	.003			
	10				.001	.015	.077	.167	.173	.081	.012			
	11					.005	.037	.121	.189	.138	.035	.001		
	12					.001	.015	.071	.166	.187	.082	.005		
	13						.004	.033	.115	.202	.151	.022	.001	
	14						.001	.012	.061	.168	.215	.070	.009	
	15							.003	.025	.105	.230	.168	.047	.001
	16							.001	.007	.046	.172	.284	.168	.013
	17								.001	.013	.081	.300	.376	.152
	18									.002	.018	.150	.397	.835

Table of Values of the Binomial Distribution (cont.)

n	r	.01	.05	.10	.20	.30	.40	.50	.60	.70	.80	.90	.95	.99
20	0	.818	.358	.122	.012	.011								
	1	.165	.377	.270	.058	.007								
	2	.016	.189	.285	.137	.028	.003							
	3	.001	.060	.190	.205	.072	.012	.001						
	4		.013	.090	.218	.130	.035	.005						
	5		.002	.032	.175	.179	.075	.015	.001					
	6			.009	.109	.192	.124	.037	.005					
	7			.002	.055	.164	.166	.074	.015	.001				
	8				.022	.114	.180	.120	.035	.004				
	9				.007	.065	.160	.160	.071	.012				
	10				.002	.031	.117	.176	.117	.031	.002			
	11					.012	.071	.160	.160	.065	.007			
	12					.004	.035	.120	.180	.114	.022			
	13					.001	.015	.074	.166	.164	.055	.002		
	14						.005	.037	.124	.192	.109	.009		
	15						.001	.015	.075	.179	.175	.032	.002	
	16							.005	.035	.130	.218	.090	.013	
	17							.001	.012	.072	.205	.190	.060	.001
	18								.003	.028	.137	.285	.189	.016
	19									.007	.058	.270	.377	.165
	20									.011	.012	.122	.358	.818

Table of Values of the Binomial Distribution (cont.)

n	r	.01	.05	.10	.20	.30	.40	.50	.60	.70	.80	.90	.95	.99
19	0	.826	.377	.135	.014	.001								
	1	.159	.377	.285	.068	.009	.001							
	2	.014	.179	.285	.154	.036	.005							
	3	.001	.053	.180	.218	.087	.017	.002						
	4		.011	.080	.218	.149	.047	.007	.001					
	5		.002	.027	.164	.192	.093	.022	.002					
	6			.007	.095	.192	.145	.052	.008	.001				
	7			.001	.044	.153	.180	.096	.024	.002				
	8				.017	.098	.180	.144	.053	.008				
	9				.005	.051	.146	.176	.098	.022	.001			
	10				.001	.022	.098	.176	.146	.051	.005			
	11					.008	.053	.144	.180	.098	.017			
	12					.002	.024	.096	.180	.153	.044	.001		
	13					.001	.008	.052	.145	.192	.095	.007		
	14						.002	.022	.093	.192	.164	.027	.002	
	15						.001	.007	.047	.149	.218	.080	.011	
	16							.002	.017	.087	.218	.180	.053	.001
	17								.005	.036	.154	.285	.179	.014
	18								.001	.009	.068	.285	.377	.159
	19									.001	.014	.135	.377	.826

Appendix A.3 A Table of Values of the Poisson Distribution, $\lambda = 0.1$ to 6.0 Number of Occurrences

λ	0	1	2	3	4	5	6	7	8	9	10	11	12	13	14	15
0.1	.905	.090	.005													
0.2	.819	.164	.016	.001												
0.3	.741	.222	.033	.003												
0.4	.670	.268	.054	.007	.001											
0.5	.607	.303	.076	.013	.002											
0.6	.549	.329	.099	.020	.003											
0.7	.497	.348	.122	.028	.005	.001										
0.8	.449	.359	.144	.038	.008	.001										
0.9	.407	.366	.165	.049	.011	.002										
1.0	.368	.368	.184	.061	.015	.003	.001									
1.1	.333	.366	.201	.074	.020	.004	.001									
1.2	.301	.361	.217	.087	.026	.006	.001									
1.3	.273	.354	.230	.100	.032	.008	.002									
1.4	.247	.345	.242	.113	.039	.011	.003	.001								
1.5	.223	.335	.251	.126	.047	.014	.004	.001								
1.6	.202	.323	.258	.138	.055	.018	.005	.001								
1.7	.183	.311	.264	.150	.064	.022	.006	.001								
1.8	.165	.298	.268	.161	.072	.026	.008	.002								
1.9	.150	.284	.270	.171	.081	.031	.010	.003	.001							
2.0	.135	.271	.271	.180	.090	.036	.012	.003	.001							
2.1	.122	.257	.270	.189	.099	.042	.015	.004	.001							
2.2	.111	.244	.268	.197	.108	.048	.017	.005	.002							
2.3	.100	.231	.265	.203	.117	.054	.021	.007	.002							
2.4	.091	.218	.261	.209	.125	.060	.024	.008	.002	.001						
2.5	.082	.205	.257	.214	.134	.067	.028	.010	.003	.001						
2.6	.074	.193	.251	.218	.141	.074	.032	.012	.004	.001						
2.7	.067	.181	.245	.220	.149	.080	.036	.014	.005	.001						
2.8	.061	.170	.238	.222	.156	.087	.041	.016	.006	.002						
2.9	.055	.160	.231	.224	.162	.094	.045	.019	.007	.002	.001					
3.0	.050	.149	.224	.224	.168	.101	.050	.022	.008	.003	.001					

A Table of Values of the Poisson Distribution (cont.)

3.1	.045	.140	.216	.224	.173	.107	.056	.025	.010	.003	.001					
3.2	.041	.130	.209	.223	.178	.114	.061	.028	.011	.004	.001					
3.3	.037	.122	.201	.221	.182	.120	.066	.031	.013	.005	.002					
3.4	.033	.113	.193	.219	.186	.126	.072	.035	.015	.006	.002	.001				
3.5	.030	.106	.185	.216	.189	.132	.077	.039	.017	.007	.002	.001				
3.6	.027	.098	.177	.212	.191	.138	.083	.042	.019	.008	.003	.001				
3.7	.025	.091	.169	.209	.193	.143	.088	.047	.022	.009	.003	.001				
3.8	.022	.085	.162	.205	.194	.148	.094	.051	.024	.010	.004	.001				
3.9	.020	.079	.154	.200	.195	.152	.099	.055	.027	.012	.005	.002	.001			
4.0	.018	.073	.147	.195	.195	.156	.104	.060	.030	.013	.005	.002	.001			
4.1	.017	.068	.139	.190	.195	.160	.109	.064	.033	.015	.006	.002	.001			
4.2	.015	.063	.132	.185	.194	.163	.114	.069	.036	.017	.007	.003	.001			
4.3	.014	.058	.125	.180	.193	.166	.119	.073	.039	.019	.008	.003	.001			
4.4	.012	.054	.119	.174	.192	.169	.124	.078	.043	.021	.009	.004	.001			
4.5	.011	.050	.112	.169	.190	.171	.128	.082	.046	.023	.010	.004	.002	.001		
4.6	.010	.046	.106	.163	.188	.173	.132	.087	.050	.026	.012	.005	.002	.001		
4.7	.009	.043	.100	.157	.185	.174	.136	.091	.054	.028	.013	.006	.002	.001		
4.8	.008	.040	.095	.152	.182	.175	.140	.096	.058	.031	.015	.006	.003	.001		
4.9	.007	.036	.089	.146	.179	.175	.143	.100	.061	.033	.016	.007	.003	.001		
5.0	.007	.034	.084	.140	.175	.175	.146	.104	.065	.036	.018	.008	.003	.001		
5.2	.006	.029	.075	.129	.168	.175	.151	.113	.073	.042	.022	.010	.005	.002	.001	
5.4	.005	.024	.066	.119	.160	.173	.156	.120	.081	.049	.026	.013	.006	.002	.001	
5.6	.004	.021	.058	.108	.152	.170	.158	.127	.089	.055	.031	.016	.007	.003	.001	
5.8	.003	.018	.051	.098	.143	.166	.160	.133	.096	.062	.036	.019	.009	.004	.002	.001
6.0	.002	.015	.045	.089	.134	.161	.161	.138	.103	.069	.041	.023	.011	.005	.002	.001

Appendix A.4 Areas Under the Standard Normal Distribution

Z	.00	.01	.02	.03	.04	.05	.06	.07	.08	.09
-2.9	.0019	.0018	.0018	.0017	.0016	.0016	.0015	.0015	.0014	.0014
-2.8	.0026	.0025	.0024	.0023	.0023	.0022	.0021	.0021	.0020	.0019
-2.7	.0035	.0034	.0033	.0032	.0031	.0030	.0029	.0028	.0027	.0026
-2.6	.0047	.0045	.0044	.0043	.0041	.0040	.0039	.0038	.0037	.0036
-2.5	.0062	.0060	.0059	.0057	.0055	.0054	.0052	.0051	.0049	.0048
-2.4	.0082	.0080	.0078	.0075	.0073	.0071	.0069	.0068	.0066	.0064
-2.3	.0107	.0104	.0102	.0099	.0096	.0094	.0091	.0089	.0087	.0084
-2.2	.0139	.0136	.0132	.0129	.0125	.0122	.0119	.0116	.0113	.0110
-2.1	.0179	.0174	.0170	.0166	.0162	.0158	.0154	.0150	.0146	.0143
-2.0	.0228	.0222	.0217	.0212	.0207	.0202	.0197	.0192	.0188	.0183
-1.9	.0287	.0281	.0274	.0268	.0262	.0256	.0250	.0244	.0239	.0233
-1.8	.0359	.0351	.0344	.0336	.0329	.0322	.0314	.0307	.0301	.0294
-1.7	.0446	.0436	.0427	.0418	.0409	.0401	.0392	.0384	.0375	.0367
-1.6	.0548	.0537	.0526	.0516	.0505	.0495	.0485	.0475	.0465	.0455
-1.5	.0668	.0655	.0643	.0630	.0618	.0606	.0594	.0582	.0571	.0559
-1.4	.0808	.0793	.0778	.0764	.0749	.0735	.0721	.0708	.0694	.0681
-1.3	.0968	.0951	.0934	.0918	.0901	.0885	.0869	.0853	.0838	.0823
-1.2	.1151	.1131	.1112	.1093	.1075	.1056	.1038	.1020	.1003	.0985
-1.1	.1357	.1335	.1314	.1292	.1271	.1251	.1230	.1210	.1190	.1170
-1.0	.1587	.1562	.1539	.1515	.1492	.1469	.1446	.1423	.1401	.1379
-0.9	.1841	.1814	.1788	.1762	.1736	.1711	.1685	.1660	.1635	.1611
-0.8	.2119	.2090	.2061	.2033	.2005	.1977	.1949	.1922	.1894	.1867
-0.7	.2420	.2389	.2358	.2327	.2296	.2266	.2236	.2206	.2177	.2148
-0.6	.2743	.2709	.2676	.2643	.2611	.2578	.2546	.2514	.2483	.2451
-0.5	.3085	.3050	.3015	.2981	.2946	.2912	.2877	.2843	.2810	.2776
-0.4	.3446	.3409	.3372	.3336	.3300	.3264	.3228	.3192	.3156	.3121
-0.3	.3821	.3783	.3745	.3707	.3669	.3632	.3594	.3557	.3520	.3483
-0.2	.4207	.4168	.4129	.4090	.4052	.4013	.3974	.3936	.3897	.3859
-0.1	.4602	.4562	.4522	.4483	.4443	.4404	.4364	.4325	.4286	.4247
-0.0	.5000	.4960	.4920	.4880	.4840	.4801	.4761	.4721	.4681	.4641

Areas Under the Standard Normal Distribution (cont.)

0.0	.5000	.5040	.5080	.5120	.5160	.5199	.5239	.5279	.5319	.5359
0.1	.5398	.5438	.5478	.5517	.5557	.5596	.5636	.5675	.5714	.5753
0.2	.5793	.5832	.5871	.5910	.5948	.5987	.6026	.6064	.6103	.6141
0.3	.6179	.6217	.6255	.6293	.6331	.6368	.6406	.6443	.6480	.6517
0.4	.6554	.6591	.6628	.6664	.6700	.6736	.6772	.6808	.6844	.6879
0.5	.6915	.6950	.6985	.7019	.7054	.7088	.7123	.7157	.7190	.7224
0.6	.7257	.7291	.7324	.7357	.7389	.7422	.7454	.7486	.7517	.7549
0.7	.7580	.7611	.7642	.7673	.7704	.7734	.7764	.7794	.7823	.7852
0.8	.7881	.7910	.7939	.7967	.7995	.8023	.8051	.8078	.8106	.8133
0.9	.8159	.8186	.8212	.8238	.8264	.8289	.8315	.8340	.8365	.8389
1.0	.8413	.8438	.8461	.8485	.8508	.8531	.8554	.8577	.8599	.8621
1.1	.8643	.8665	.8686	.8708	.8729	.8749	.8770	.8790	.8810	.8830
1.2	.8849	.8869	.8888	.8907	.8925	.8944	.8962	.8980	.8997	.9015
1.3	.9032	.9049	.9066	.9082	.9099	.9115	.9131	.9147	.9162	.9177
1.4	.9192	.9207	.9222	.9236	.9251	.9265	.9279	.9292	.9306	.9319
1.5	.9332	.9345	.9357	.9370	.9382	.9394	.9406	.9418	.9429	.9441
1.6	.9452	.9463	.9474	.9484	.9495	.9505	.9515	.9525	.9535	.9545
1.7	.9554	.9564	.9573	.9582	.9591	.9599	.9608	.9616	.9625	.9633
1.8	.9641	.9649	.9656	.9664	.9671	.9678	.9686	.9693	.9699	.9706
1.9	.9713	.9719	.9726	.9732	.9738	.9744	.9750	.9756	.9761	.9767
2.0	.9772	.9778	.9783	.9788	.9793	.9798	.9803	.9808	.9812	.9817
2.1	.9821	.9826	.9830	.9834	.9838	.9842	.9846	.9850	.9854	.9857
2.2	.9861	.9864	.9868	.9871	.9875	.9878	.9881	.9884	.9887	.9890
2.3	.9893	.9896	.9898	.9901	.9904	.9906	.9909	.9911	.9913	.9916
2.4	.9918	.9920	.9922	.9925	.9927	.9929	.9931	.9932	.9934	.9936
2.5	.9938	.9940	.9941	.9943	.9945	.9946	.9948	.9949	.9951	.9952
2.6	.9953	.9955	.9956	.9957	.9959	.9960	.9961	.9962	.9963	.9964
2.7	.9965	.9966	.9967	.9968	.9969	.9970	.9971	.9972	.9973	.9974
2.8	.9974	.9975	.9976	.9977	.9977	.9978	.9979	.9979	.9980	.9981
2.9	.9981	.9982	.9982	.9983	.9984	.9984	.9985	.9985	.9986	.9986

INDEX

ABCDEFGHIJ-H-898765432